HOTELS, HOSPITALS, AND JAILS

A MEMOIR

ANTHONY SWOFFORD

TWELVE

LARGE PRINT

Twelve

Hachette Book Group

237 Park Avenue

New York, NY 10017

www.HachetteBookGroup.com

Printed in the United States of America

RRD-C

First Edition: June 2012

Twelve is an imprint of Grand Central Publishing.
The Twelve name and logo are trademarks of Hachette Book Group, Inc.

The Hachette Speakers Bureau provides a wide range of authors for speaking events. To find out more, go to www.hachettespeakersbureau.com or call (866) 376-6591.

The publisher is not responsible for websites (or their content) that are not owned by the publisher.

10 9 8 7 6 5 4 3 2 1

Library of Congress Cataloging-in-Publication Data
Swofford, Anthony.
  Hotels, hospitals, and jails : a memoir / Anthony Swofford. — 1st ed.
    p. cm.
  ISBN 978-1-4555-0673-6 (regular) — ISBN 978-1-4555-1351-2 (large print)   1. Swofford, Anthony.   2. Swofford, Anthony—Relations with women.   3. Swofford, Anthony—Family.   4. Swofford, Anthony—Drug use.   5. Authors, American—Biography.   6. Persian Gulf War, 1991—Veterans—United States—Biography.   7. Veterans—Mental health—United States.   8. Veterans—Family relationships—United States.   9. Veterans—Drug use—United States.   10. Fathers and sons—United States—Biography.   I. Title.
  PS3619.W64A3 2012
  818'.603—dc23
  [B]
                          2012003936

This book is for my father,
John Howard Swofford
&
my love is for
Christa

HOTELS, HOSPITALS, AND JAILS

WAR IS THE POETRY OF MEN, BY WHICH
THEY SEEK TO GAIN ATTENTION AND RELIEF
THROUGHOUT THEIR LIVES.

—THOMAS BERNHARD
GATHERING EVIDENCE

Prologue

There are days I still fantasize about combat, long nights when I wish I had rejoined the Marines as an infantry officer after September 11 and gone back over and got some war to score that kill I'd missed the first time. Most people don't understand that desire, but I was born a war baby: my father impregnated my mother while in Honolulu on R & R from Vietnam. And I believed that there existed no grander test for a man than combat. Every other pursuit was pure, unimportant leisure when compared to a firefight. I didn't know if another war would make me a better man, but it might. It certainly would have changed me. Or it might have killed me.

What did I do instead of heading back to war? My first book, *Jarhead*, was turned into a movie, and I wrote and published a novel. I divorced one woman, and I spent many years falling in love with various versions of the wrong woman and walking away from the right woman once. I bought two engagement rings. I bought a beautiful apartment on West Nineteenth Street in Manhattan. I taught at a few different colleges. I ate at some of the best restaurants in the world (in Paris, Madrid, Tokyo, Istanbul) and at some of the worst (in Ho Chi Minh City and Australia's Pilbara region). I spent an unconscionable amount of money on Burgundy wine and I drank most of it. I bought and used the occasional batch of recreational drugs. I nearly killed myself in a sixty-thousand-dollar sports car. I watched my father get sicker and sicker from a heinous disease that was possibly partially the result of his twenty-three years in the military and his exposure to Agent Orange. I thought about killing myself for months on end. A few times I fantasized about killing my father.

I flew women to London and Tokyo and Oakland and Seattle and other cities I've forgotten.

Once I slept in a hotel room in Shinjuku, Tokyo, with my girlfriend Ava. Staying in a room ten floors below us was a woman named Anya whom I had flown to Tokyo from Munich. A few Metro stops away in Roppongi was a Japanese girl I'd just spent a week with before my girlfriend Ava and my ex-girlfriend Anya arrived, a few hours apart. Somehow, I had sex with all of these women throughout the week and I did not get caught. This is to say, I took risks. And the meaning of the word *girlfriend* had a lot of elasticity. I thought I'd created a new language of lust, but really I spoke artifice and despair.

I told so many lies about my whereabouts late at night or early in the morning I'm certain I set a record for the audacity of my libido.

I believe that having been a marine and having gone to war helped me become a great liar. Growing up with a Vietnam War veteran for a father helped me become a liar, too. I learned this from my father: If the lie will not get you blown up, the lie is worth whatever the cost. My father excelled at deceit. He deceived his wife and children about what kind of husband and father he was, but mostly he deceived himself about how that little war in Southeast Asia had changed him.

Like many combat veterans I know, my father and I lived with the wickedly exciting and doggedly exhausting knowledge that we had once, for a short period of time, flirted with death, and won. This knowledge is like a drug, the purest cocaine or eighty-year-old Highland single malt scotch: once you have had some it alters your understanding of the world and of other people and of consequences.

If I lied to a lover about what neighborhood or city or country I'd slept in the night before, it didn't really matter: the relationship might sour but she would never *kill me*. Lying about sex became fun. It became a hobby. Manhattan bored me, drinking bored me, drugs bored me, but lying about sex never bored me.

Eventually I had wasted such a massive amount of money on women, wine, drugs, cars, and booze that my dissipation and deceit blew up in my face. I looked up one day and could no longer afford the mortgage on my apartment. I had to sell and became, in a way, homeless.

I would have liked to ask my father for advice but at the time our relationship was in complete disrepair.

But for some time my father had owned a Winnebago and a dream: that we two traverse the country and come to an understanding and discover a friendship. One trip wasn't enough. Neither was two. It took three.

I

Goodbye to All That

In February 2004, on the first night in the apartment I had bought on West Nineteenth Street in Manhattan, Ava and I slept downstairs. The mattress had been delivered that afternoon and I told the delivery guys to leave it in the living room. I liked the idea of the bare apartment, the walls freshly painted gallery white, nothing in the apartment but a new mattress, a bottle of champagne in the refrigerator. We brought in food from the Indian deli on Ninth Avenue. We drank the champagne and we made love.

My last night in the apartment, in May 2010, I dragged the mattress downstairs and splayed it on the bare living room floor. It was the last piece of furniture I needed to rid myself of.

Ava and I had been broken up for nearly three years but we habitually slept together every few months, whether or not one or both of us had a partner. Sometimes these evenings went well. Sometimes they did not.

I'd called her earlier in the week and asked if she wanted to say goodbye to the Mountain Lodge. The apartment invoked a Tahoe ski condo, with a two-story brick fireplace and a brick sitting window and dark wood spiral staircase.

Ava had been with me when I first saw the apartment and had somehow convinced me that I should make an offer on the most expensive property I'd looked at during my two-month, seventy-three-apartment search. That was the morning after the first night I had done cocaine with her, and only the second or third time in my life I had taken the drug.

(*Note to reader:* when purchasing an apartment, do not do so after a night of cocaine.)

Now we sat on the terrace and looked at the Empire State Building. We champagne-toasted the apartment. Six years earlier, at the age of twenty-eight, she had been beautiful. Now she was just pretty. I was six years older than she but her face held numerous and deeper lines. She'd spent her college years and her early thirties running around Manhattan doing cocaine and sleeping with many men, and smoking packs of cigarettes, and those men and that cocaine and those cigarettes had begun to take a toll.

She asked, "How many times do you think we had sex here?"

"Thousands."

We went inside. I had thrown a plain white sheet over the mattress.

Knowingly, playfully, she asked, "And why is this still here?"

"I thought you might want to say goodbye to the mattress."

"I thought that for once you might want to do this the right way," she said.

"What is the right way?"

"Marriage. Babies."

"We have never known the right way," I said.

We undressed ourselves and made love slowly and deliberately, as though defusing a bomb.

Afterward we walked around the corner to a new hip restaurant. We sat at the bar and drank gin martinis, hers dirty, mine with a twist.

After I paid the bill she said, "Once more."

We returned to the apartment. I felt as though we were entering a crime scene and the crime had been my life in New York City. We went straight to the mattress.

An hour later she dressed and we kissed at the door. She said, "Goodbye, Mountain Lodge. I'll miss you."

She did not say that she would miss me nor did I say I would miss her. I never saw her again.

I sat down on the mattress. I looked around the apartment. It had been the center of my life for many years: work, lovers, cooking. Writing. Sex. Eating.

I dragged the mattress three stories down and out of the building and threw it on the sidewalk. An old man I knew from the neighborhood passed by. He stopped and stared at the mattress, stared at me, pointed at the mattress with his cane.

He said, "You gettin' rid of that? It's a perfectly good mattress!"

I said, "That mattress should burn."

I hailed a cab to my girlfriend's house.

The next morning I moved alone to a cabin in Mount Tremper, in the Catskills.

MY NEW HOME sat on ten acres on the side of the mountain. From my former life in Manhattan I had brought with me two pieces of art, an abstract figurative painting and a drawing. The caption beneath the drawing—a dehumanized fool's version of tic-tac-toe—read: WHAT ARE YOU TRYING TO SAY TO ME? I DO NOT UNDERSTAND.

I'd bought the drawing five or six years earlier but the relevance of the artist's quotation to my life had in the prior six months reached its zenith. I understood no one. Others had difficulty understanding me.

I needed the solace of a cabin on the side of a mountain in order to redirect my life. But the cabin I found had thick beams and the forest around me was comprised of very tall old-growth pine trees, and thick beams and tall trees were an invitation to a self-hanging.

In addition to the artwork, I dragged to the mountain a few suitcases of clothes; a desk I'd had custom-made in Manhattan by a Japanese woodworker whose family had been creating beam-and-trestle furniture for five hundred years; a pair of handmade cowboy boots I'd had fashioned in Austin; ten cases of Burgundy, whites and reds; one hundred books from my library; two Turkish rugs I'd bought in Istanbul; a collection of family photographs; a wooden airplane that my paternal grandfather had constructed as a boy during the Depression; my maternal grandfather's baseball glove from the same poor period in American life; two jump ropes, one leather and one plastic; one Le Creuset Dutch oven, yellow; a large and perfectly seasoned cast-iron skillet; a memory foam pillow.

I decided that over this summer I would rid myself of the waste from a number of troubled romantic relationships. Recently there was the Bad Writer; the charming but sexually incapacitated ER Physician; the beautiful, dynamic, and sweet but troubled Dancer I almost married; the Rich Girl/Boho Artist I almost married; the Canadian Writer I should have married; another Canadian Writer I might have married.

But the grand master of my romantic ruin was Ava, the woman I'd moved to New York for in 2004.

I remember the temptation, the first kiss, and the moment when passion overrode and crushed common sense.

We met at a party in Topanga Canyon on the deck of a house with a Pacific Ocean view. We were both in town for the *Los Angeles Times* Festival of Books. She was twenty-eight and Cuban American. Her hair was black and long and straight. She had a wide girlish smile and a deep throaty laugh. She sold advertising for a New York art magazine and wanted to be a psychologist.

She said, "I have a live-in boyfriend in Brooklyn. He's lousy in bed and has a crap job in television. And he won't marry me. My father says 'Why buy the cow when the milk is free?'"

I knew that when preparing to cheat certain women malign the husband or boyfriend and invoke the folksy wisdom of the father.

I said, "I have a girlfriend who lives in SoHo and Victoria, BC. She's a wonder in bed and a great writer."

She stroked my beard and said, "I like your beard. My father has a beard."

She read aloud the time from my Rolex dive watch and said her father also wore one and that like all the old Cuban guys in Miami her father pretended to run a scuba diving company but was really still trying to assassinate Castro. She said her father was a friend of Luis Posada and had been in Caracas in September 1976 and after reading his journals she thought he might have been involved in the downing of Cuban Airlines Flight 455. I assumed that all the Cuban American girls from Miami made this boast. All of this is to say she was beautiful, dark-skinned, and possibly dangerous.

She looked at my watch again and said, "Let's get out of here."

I had no license but I drove her rental car down from Topanga to the beach at Malibu because we determined that I was less drunk. We walked toward the water and kicked our shoes off.

She said, "I want you to kiss me."

And I did.

Her shoes, stylish red Italian flats, were sucked out to sea in the wash and I broke the kiss and waded into the water to retrieve them. They were her favorite shoes and I had saved them and we returned to kissing. I don't know how long the kiss lasted, a few minutes, twenty, an hour, a month. I forgot about my girlfriend who was meeting me in Seattle the next day, I forgot about any woman I'd ever loved or kissed. We kissed more and I held her wet, red shoes in my hand.

We returned to the car and continued to kiss.

And then the Malibu cops rolled up and asked us both to get out of the car. The cop who interrogated me was Japanese American, about my age, compact and ripped, and fast-talking. I'd grown up with kids like him. My best friend from childhood was a cop in Sacramento. This guy in front of me, I knew exactly where he was coming from: he wanted to bust bad guys but didn't care too much what you did if you weren't an absolute menace.

He asked me for my license and I told him I didn't have one, that me and my girl were just sitting in the car, and that we were about to switch places so she could drive back to the hotel because I would never break the law and drive without a license.

He stared at me, as if to say *Are you kidding me, you expect me to believe that?* But he broke a half smile and said, "Quick thinking, smart-ass. Are you drunk or on drugs?"

And I said, "No." False.

He said, "If you don't have a license, who drove here?"

I said, "Her." False.

He said, "Why were you in the driver's seat?"

I said, "I wanted her to have more legroom." False.

He looked at me, either disgusted or impressed with my commitment to the lie. He walked over to her and asked, "Is your boyfriend on cocaine?"

She said, "No." True.

He asked, "Are you on cocaine?"

She said, "No." True.

He said, "There's a ten o'clock beach curfew in Malibu. If you move your car about twenty-five feet south, you can hang out on that beach or in your car and do whatever it is you need to do. I don't care. But get out of Malibu."

I don't know why the cop didn't press the issue. Maybe his shift was ending or maybe he didn't care what we were on as long as it wasn't cocaine.

Years later I would wish the cop had pushed the issue—after all, I had been sitting in the driver's seat, and any fool would have known that I'd intended to drive without a license. So what if the cop had pressed things, what if he'd checked my sobriety, what if he'd pulled me in for the night?

Ava and I wouldn't have gone back to my hotel room and been unfaithful to our partners. And I wouldn't have changed the course of my life for the next many years.

Ava studied for her PhD in psychology during our three years together. I paid for everything except her rent. I overheard her tell a friend that she was on the Swofford Stipend. Once I caught her stealing fifties from my wallet but I didn't confront her: if I had she might have left me. She introduced me to the regular recreational use of cocaine. I cheated and lied; she cheated and lied. We turned each other into animals.

I TOLD MYSELF that the side of the mountain would save me. Down the block from my cabin sat a Buddhist monastery, and while I didn't plan on attending meditation, I read my Shunryu Suzuki and felt that if I was close enough, it just might count as meditation. The mountains, they say, have magnetic forces, and the mountain magnetism would pull some of the good forces across the side of the mountain from those bald monks and into my cabin oasis. When it comes to spiritual health, propinquity is everything, right?

But the two six-by-sixteen-inch beams in my cabin were close, too, as well as that multitude of old-growth trees and a fittingly thick length of rope I'd been carrying around for a few years. I once wrote that the suicide is brave, which would make the rest of us cowards. I felt a coward. It would have been easy enough for me to drive down to Kingston and buy a shotgun and a single shell at Wal-Mart. I made the excuse that I didn't want to make a mess for my new landlords, a kindly hippie-ish string-instrument-playing couple in their mid-fifties with two liberally educated daughters and a happy plot of land with a very fine old mountain dog, and what a complete *dick* I'd be to blow my brains out all over their carefully constructed and manicured and maintained mountain ideal. Also, what would happen to all my stuff? My life was currently in storage on five pallets in East Williamsburg, Brooklyn. All my papers, and most of my books, and a few pieces of furniture, the few I hadn't given away while I prepared to leave Manhattan.

During the day I stayed on the mountain and I wrote. At nights I might drive to Phoenicia and drink beer and watch sports with construction workers. I walked to the top of Mount Tremper, three miles up and back, once a week.

On weekends a twenty-five-year-old hedge-funder from Manhattan would take the bus up after she got off work on Friday afternoons. We would drink and have sex, and sometimes do drugs, and watch sports until Monday morning, when she took the bus back to Manhattan. We did stupid things like buy scratcher lottery tickets, and drive forty-five miles for bad Mexican food and to get drunk with the locals. We'd flip a coin to see who got to drive home at two or three a.m.

But one weekend I'd had enough and I told her not to come up because I had a lot of work to do, and I never saw her again. She was a very pleasant girl and I am sorry that things ended abruptly. She sent me a few text messages accusing me of ruining her life, but I told her this was impossible, and that she was young and smart and pretty and by most measurements had a full and good life waiting in front of her.

I THOUGHT ABOUT suicide. I read Suzuki's *Zen Mind, Beginner's Mind* again and again.

I rewrote, thousands of times, this quote:

A good father is not a good father.

2

John Howard Swofford

My father sat in a chair in the corner of his hospital room, upper body hunched over a brand-new government-issued aluminum walker. This was December 1999. The last time I'd seen him, in August, he'd helped load my U-Haul for my move from Sacramento to Iowa City. He'd lifted boxes and furniture, and he'd bought the beers and pizza, and later he'd treated my friends to a strip club, lap dances for everyone. Now he could barely lift his head to greet me.

"Hey, Bubba," he said, deploying my least favorite of the multitude of nicknames he had for me: Tone. Old Tone. T-Bone. Pussy Hunter. Jarhead.

"Hey, Dad," I said. "What's the word? When can we wheel you out of this fleabag joint?"

"You ain't wheeling me nowheres. The doc says walk. I'm gonna walk."

"So let's hit it." I clapped my hands twice. I had

a date that evening in San Francisco with my old college girlfriend.

A few days earlier I'd received a phone call from my sister Kim telling me that the Old Man had bit it hard in his living room—he'd collapsed, grasping for life, gasping for air. And whom did he call? Nine-one-one? No, he called a guy who performed menial labor for him. And the guy drove over in his pickup truck and heaped my father into the front seat, and here at the hospital his doctor told him to stop smoking or he would die soon.

When? he asked.

Now.

He'd smoked for forty-five years. He'd also spent twenty-two years in the Air Force, thirteen months in Vietnam, many of those months within the Agent Orange–tainted jungles and many other years breathing the fumes from the narcotics of war that drive the workings and skeletons of every military base.

Here we were on a military base, the same place I'd been born, Travis Air Force Base. In the late 1960s, while her husband fought in Vietnam, hippies spit at my mother's car as she entered the base to take her children to the hospital or to buy groceries.

My father pointed out the window. "You see that building, that short building over there? That's where you were born."

"You tell me that every time we're on base."

"Well, Bubba, maybe it's important to me."

It would be many years before I could understand the importance of such a building to a man.

Right now all I wanted was to wheel the Old Man out of here. Hell, I'd fireman's-carry him, if need be. I had a seven p.m. drinks date in San Francisco, forty-five miles away, and nothing would stop me from making it. I hadn't been laid since moving to Iowa City. My father was alive and breathing. I needed to get him home and I needed to hit the road.

"Have some patience with me, Son. I'll be slow a few days and pretty soon here I'll be back up to speed."

We stopped by the pharmacy and picked up a twelve-pack of meds. It took the pharmacist half an hour to explain the proper usage and the possible negative reactions and interactions. Other than to treat a bad batch of migraines in the 1970s, when he'd returned from Vietnam, my father had never been medicated.

He asked the pharmacist, "How the hell do you guys expect me to remember all of that?"

"We don't," he said. He handed my father a card with the pharmacy number on it. "Give us a call anytime."

I carried my father's meds and the overnight

bag my sister had packed for him. My father slowly scooted along the corridors of the hospital—a working military hospital that also served the large retiree population in the area. Creaking GIs lurked everywhere. Many wore baseball caps from whatever unit they were most proud of serving with.

It took half an hour to get to the car.

He said, "Now, Tone, how about you take me grocery shopping? And I want to rent some movies. I think I'll be bed-resting for a week."

Within the confines of the hospital my father had not seemed out of place. Hobbling around were other addled men; whether it was from disease or old age or drink or smokes or government-sanctioned pesticide campaigns, the sick men belonged there in the massive sick bay of Travis Air Force Base. With a glance around I could easily find some guy worse off than my father: the blind, the amputee, the insane.

But in the parking lot of the strip mall near his house I registered just how incredibly sick he was. I knew this would only worsen. I removed his walker from the trunk and opened it at the passenger door. He needed help up. Hanging from the walker was a toy figurine of some cartoon character I vaguely recognized.

"What is this?" I asked my dad.

"The candy stripper gave me that, Tone."

"Candy striper. Not stripper. But they don't even use that term anymore."

"Oh, right. That was one of them, what do you educated people call it? Freudian trips?"

"Slips."

"Right. Freudian strip. Candy stripers. Well, they'd get more business if they hired some candy strippers, don't you think?"

"I suppose the dirty old GIs would like that."

"Who you calling dirty and old?"

"Who do you think?"

With his stripers and strippers and Freudian trippers, I could not tell if my father was playing with me. Probably so. But I did not have the patience for this. The time was now four forty-five p.m. and I had less than three hours before I needed to be seated at a bar with a girl, a girl who would definitely have sex with me.

"Dad, just tell me what groceries you need and what movies you want. I can do this in twenty minutes. We'll be out of here."

It was nearly the shortest day of the year and already getting dark.

Dad said, "Give me some patience, Tone. I want to be outside. I got stuck in that room a week."

And so we took our time. I walked slowly

alongside my father. The severity of his disease began to register for me. I noticed how people looked at my father: the Man Lugging an Oxygen Tank. I knew the first thought that came to my mind when I saw a person using oxygen: poor white riverboat gamblers in the Midwest or South chain-smoking the Social Security Administration and Medicare into oblivion.

I wanted to say to the people who stared: *No, you've got it all wrong. He's a veteran. He was in Vietnam. It might have been Agent Orange.* But of course I knew it wasn't Agent Orange: it was forty-five years of Marlboros.

This was not my first experience with feeling humiliation because of someone else's dire medical condition: in 1997 and 1998 my brother, Jeff, slowly died of a cancer and I was always ashamed of his illness whenever we were in public.

Is this a moral weakness in me?

Perhaps, I thought, as a little girl stared at the cartoon toy hanging from my father's walker and then looked in horror at the oxygen tube shoved up his nostrils. With a shriek the girl recoiled into her mother's pants leg.

We bought groceries for one of my father's favorite one-pot meals, something he called goulash but that was really just a mash of over-boiled vegetables and meat in canned tomatoes, massively dosed with paprika.

We rented a stack of Clint Eastwood and Arnold Schwarzenegger movies.

Back in the car Dad said, "You know, I'd like to have dinner with Clint Eastwood someday. Jeff met him down in Carmel, didn't he say?"

"Jeff claimed a lot of things," I replied.

"Maybe when I'm catting around again I'll go down to Carmel and look old Clint up."

"You should do that."

"Other than Johnny Cash, Clint is my guy. When I was your age they used to say I looked like Johnny Cash. That's what old Margarita in Texas used to say. 'Johnny, you look just like Señor Cash.' Damn that tickled me. Old Margarita. I'll have to visit her, too."

My father either did not grasp the immensity of the medical event he'd just survived, or he refused to recognize the totality of change it would bring to his life. This stubbornness or ignorance probably kept him alive for so many years while other patients might have just given up and died. His diagnosis was COPD, chronic obstructive pulmonary disorder. Others might call it emphysema. COPD sounds, I don't know, snappier? Less trashy? Emphysema connotes poor white riverboat gamblers in the Midwest or South chain-smoking the Social Security Administration and Medicare into oblivion. COPD? It's just an acronym. But the end result is the same: your lungs will quit working someday and you will die. The elasticity of the oxygen sacs in your lungs will eventually fail, the sacs will dry up and calcify, and eventually you will want to inhale but there will be no room. All around you, everywhere, there will be oxygen, but you will be allowed none of it.

When I thought of my father's lungs I thought of an old hunk of white coral that I'd had as a kid. I knew that it was bad to have a piece of coral. I knew that the coral reefs of the world were diminishing, but I liked having this strange piece of the ocean. The coral sat on my desk next to the piece of lava from Mount Fuji.

Brazenly, my father wanted to stop by one of his drinking holes just to say hello to the guys. It was now six-thirty. My date in San Francisco would never happen. I called the ex-girlfriend and she agreed to meet me in Fairfield later that night. I took my father to his bar.

I never understood it then, because he never articulated it, but I guess my father was proud of me. I was his son who had gone off and joined the Marines and served in a sniper platoon and gone to war and kicked Saddam's ass, and returned home and gone to college, and paid his way through it working in a warehouse and with a little help from the GI Bill. And now I was in graduate school in Iowa City.

He introduced me to the bartender, a woman in her fifties wearing ten pounds of makeup and thirty years of rough road. She looked as though she'd been drinking since the previous night's shift ended. "This is my son Tony. He's gonna be a famous writer someday. He's studying it in Iowa. The Writers' Warehouse, right, Tone?" He winked at the bartender.

"Something like that. Can I have a double shot of bourbon?" I asked the bartender.

"That all they teach you in writing college, how to drink?" he asked.

"That's one of the rumors about the place."

Writers' Warehouse. Freudian strip. If I had paid more attention, it was a funny skit my father performed: the father playing redneck to his smarty collegiate son. But the animosity that ran through his commentary was so obvious, or obvious to me. Anyone else would just see a charming older Southern gentleman who liked flirting with the ladies. Now he was not only old, but sick, too. His virility and vanity had taken a mortal blow. The handsome dark devil, the Johnny Cash look-alike, the wild man, the ravishing lover, his lungs had

failed him and he was down for the count. Everyone knows the dick needs oxygen in order to perform. He did not want to admit it, but this was
a major loss. This was *the* major loss. My father
lived for good times and he also lived for the ladies.
My father took the ladies out dancing and drinking and he took them home. Good-Time Johnny.
Good-Time Johnny might have to take a final bow.

I drank my bourbon in silence while my father
talked with his bar friends. They were happy to
have him back in the crowd. Everyone always loved
my father and his Southern charm. He was a good
fella, that John Howard Swofford.

I stepped out to make a call to the girl in San
Francisco. Hell, why not meet here at this divey
little bar? I gave her directions.

My father asked me what all the commotion
was on my phone. "What are you planning? You
got that look in your eye. I know that look. That's
the Pussy Hunter. Swofford libido. A blessing and
a curse. Who is it this time?"

Did I like this? Did I like my father calling me
Pussy Hunter? Yes.

"Marin County," I said. When I'd dated this
girl in college my father could never remember
her name, only that she had grown up in Marin
County, and so that is what he called her.

"Goddamn, Tone. Pulling out the reserves? Marin County. Nice girl."

"I was supposed to meet her in San Francisco. But she's coming here."

"Right here? To the bar? Hell, Tone. Don't do that. Take her out somewhere nice. Take her to dinner. Take her out dancing."

Lessons from a pro.

He continued, "This must be a generational thing. You can just meet a girl out for a few drinks and call it a night? Just like that?"

"It depends on the girl and the night. We have known each other awhile."

"I might know a woman awhile but still take her out on a Friday night. There's a good steak house downtown. Take her there, for Christ's sake."

"She's a vegetarian."

"Jesus, Tone. Jesus. My own son. Meeting a girl at a shitty bar and gonna try to get in her pants. You gonna get a hotel room?"

"Nope. I'm going to fuck her in your Cadillac."

"Goddamn, Son. You can't do that. You'll get you both arrested. And I'm not gonna bail your silly ass out. Fucking in a car. Jesus Christ."

Marin County never showed.

I helped my father settle into his home, into this new lifestyle of sickness.

I arranged his meds by day and dose. I plugged in the oxygen system that had been delivered to the front stoop that afternoon and cut a hundred-foot length of medical tube. I cut up the veggies and the meat and threw it all in a large pot with a few quarts of water, four chicken bouillon cubes, canned tomatoes, and a cup of paprika. We watched *Hang 'Em High* and my father fell asleep next to me on the couch. His oxygen tube hung from his nostrils like a clear snake and the oxygen machine howled.

The next afternoon a guy from the company that would service his oxygen came by. He was a big burly dude with a goatee. He said that his own father had succumbed to this disease.

"My old man," he said, "he did what most people do when they get the diagnosis. He sat on his ass and got fat and stayed lazy and he was dead in two years, right there in the chair he sat in when he got home from the hospital. I couldn't tell you if he ever moved once."

"I plan to stay active. I plan to keep my job. This thing won't take me down. Not soon, anyway," my father said.

"Sir, I can't say it's a pleasure to meet you. It's never a happy occasion when I meet a new customer. But I do hope we'll have your business for a very long time."

I couldn't help but think that someday this big

burly dude with a goatee would show up to deliver my father his oxygen and instead find him dead.

I SPENT THE rest of my winter break from grad school kicking around Northern California, crashing on friends' couches or floors or in the bed of some former girlfriend or another. Every few days I'd drop in on my father and run errands for him or complete chores around his house.

One night Marin County met me at my dad's house.

"Good to see you, darling," my dad said, extending a hand and making a slight bow. "It seems like it's been years."

"Only months, Mr. Swofford. I saw you in August when we helped Tony load his truck for Iowa."

"Right, right."

I had not reminded my father of her name and I saw his brain working hard to retrieve it from his cloudy memory bank. And I knew he would not. Throughout my boyhood he never remembered my friends' names. He referred to them by the names of the streets they lived on: Boyd, Marconi, Walnut, Lillian Lane.

"Your folks still live over in Marin County?" he asked.

"They do. And my younger brother."

"Right. Right. Your father has a younger wife, and a son?"

My father could not remember this woman's name but he recalled that her father, a man his own age, had a wife in her late thirties and a young son.

"So, Dad. How about I make dinner?" I offered.

"There's goulash in the fridge!"

"I'm not feeling the goulash. I picked up steaks. I'll throw them on the grill."

My father looked lewdly at Marin County off and on throughout the evening. She was seven years younger than I and possessed a freshness and innocence not yet fractured by the bigger world. She worked as an intern with a radical publishing company and her father paid her rent in the Mission. She made bad art with crushed eggshells, and she wanted to change the world. And she was gloriously open in bed, or wherever we had sex.

For a few months while we dated in college she had lived at home and I would drive to Marin from Sacramento. We'd head into San Francisco for a date and then later return to Marin. We'd drive to the top of Mount Tamalpais and have sex in my truck, and then I'd drive her home. I'd park my truck around the corner from her dad's house and sleep in the cab, and in the morning we'd reconvene. Sometimes I'd do this for three days straight without a shower.

I cleaned the dinner dishes while they watched a Clint Eastwood movie.

"Hey, Pops," I said, interrupting a gunfight. "We're going to head out for a drink. You mind if I take your car?"

"No problemo. Just don't drive her drunk."

"We'll only have a few. Back at your local."

"Tell them you are Alabama John's son."

We didn't make it to the bar. We didn't leave my dad's driveway. We jumped in the backseat of his car and turned it into our own little sex dungeon.

During a break, Marin County said, "I like your dad. He's a sweet guy. I like his accent. Is he going to be OK?"

"I don't think that being on oxygen is OK. But he plans to stay active, and he seems to have a pretty good attitude right now. He's not overly depressed and he's not giving up; he's not talking about where he wants us to bury him, so maybe he'll hang on awhile."

"Will you tell him we screwed in his car?"

"He'll figure it out."

"You are so bad."

Later when I entered my dad's house he was asleep on the couch. I awoke him and helped him back to his room.

He said, "Goddamn, Tone. As soon as you

walked out the door I remembered her name. And now I've forgotten it. You have a good time?"

"We didn't leave the driveway."

"Dang. Something wrong with the car?"

"Nothing wrong with the car. We sat and talked."

He looked at me with a sidelong glance.

"You're bullshitting me, Bubba. You had sex with that girl in my goddamn car! Jesus. You better pay to get that interior detailed tomorrow. God knows what you did in my goddamn brand-new car. Thank god it's leather seats."

Was it cruel of me to invite a young, beautiful woman into my father's house and parade her sexuality and her youth in front of the dying beast and then have sex with her in his car? Probably. But maybe it got him off.

The next day I mowed his lawn and made a few more pots of goulash before heading back to Iowa City. He stood in his driveway as my taxi backed away. He leaned on his walker. He hadn't dressed. He wore the uniform of old sick men: white T-shirt and briefs. His legs were pale as rice and his forearms deeply sun-stained by decades of outdoor labor. The oxygen tube snaked down his body, a river, a story, a life. I waved to my father, not knowing when I'd see him again, or how long he might live.

3

Fairfield to Billings, the Joker Is Out of Breath, April 2009

One afternoon in April 2009, nearly a decade after his first collapse, I arrived at my father's house and he greeted me in his driveway wearing white briefs with a T-shirt tucked in so that the look approximated that of a onesie. These days he wore dentures, but he hadn't had a chance to put them in. He grinned at me, all gums, like a baby.

In the age-old tradition of crotchety and stubborn men, my father fought his diagnosis of COPD with abandon and verve. He held on to his job running a strip mall maintenance crew, even though a medical retirement coupled with his military retirement would have provided enough financial security for him to thrive and even head to Mexico for the winters.

I want to live, he screamed every morning as he cleared his lungs of muck and prepared for work.

Friends of his had gotten sick and died dozens of different ways, and the Old Man was still kicking. I'd been married and divorced, and the Old Man was still kicking. I'd lived in Iowa City, Portland, Oakland, and now Manhattan; I'd traveled around the world twice; I'd written and published two books; and the Old Man was still kicking. I'd been engaged and unengaged to two different women, and the Old Man was still kicking.

He did not say hello, he said, "Goddamn, Tone, we got a lot of work to do to get this rig road-ready!"

The next morning I'd enclose myself with my father in his forty-four-foot Winnebago to drive from Fairfield, California, to Billings, Montana, in order to attend my niece's college graduation. Over twenty-five hours, twenty-three minutes, and 53.7 seconds we'd carve our way through 1,100 miles of the western United States. The physical sensation of driving a Winnebago at high speeds approximates that of sitting in a Manhattan studio apartment while a 5.5-magnitude earthquake revs unabated within your four thin walls.

My father had prepared a twenty-five-point pre-trip checklist.

During my middle school and high school years

my father dictated my daily routine with a check-list he prepared every Sunday evening for the following week:

Brush teeth. (Daily. AM, at school after lunch, PM)

Floss teeth. (Daily, PM)

Eat three pieces of fruit. (3x daily: breakfast, afternoon snack, dinner)

Feed and water dogs. (2x daily)

Shower. (Daily)

Wash cars with Dad. (Saturday or Sunday)

Pick up dog poop. (Saturday, regardless of weather)

Mow lawn. (Saturday, weather permitting, check with Dad)

Perform pool maintenance. (Chemicals, vacuum, maintain flower planters)

Dust, straighten, and vacuum bedroom. (Saturday)

(All of these chores must be performed in order to receive the full allowance. Deductions will be made for failures. It is possible to receive Zero Allowance and to attain a Negative Balance. Further punishment is also possible: groundings from: TV privileges, phone use, and friend visitations.)

The allowance of a few dollars fluctuated. I think I topped out at $5.50 a week in 1986.

The reward for completing the Winnebago checklist remained elusive. And how might my father punish me for failure?

In his kitchen I made a pot of goulash for the road. We'd shopped earlier at the commissary on Travis Air Force Base. As we passed the old hospital where I was born, now an administrative building, he'd pointed to it and said, once again, "Hey, Bubba. That building there is where you were born."

I loaded the RV cabinets with bags of chips and crackers and cookies. The goulash-filled Tupperware went in the refrigerator. On the RV I checked the oil and transmission fluid and wiper fluid levels. I checked the water level on the batteries. I checked the oil level on the generator. I made sure the hydraulics worked. I made sure that the slide-out bedroom and living room worked. I popped a bag of popcorn in the microwave. I made certain the refrigerator and freezer refrigerated and froze. I flushed the toilet. I ran the shower and the sinks. I turned on the TV. I checked the slide-out stairs. I tied down ten cylinders of my father's oxygen. I climbed on the roof and had a peek around, and everything looked attached. I stood tall on the roof. I looked up and down my father's suburban street. I spread my arms wide. The sun beat down on me heavy and bright. I wanted to ride all the way to Montana on the roof.

BEFORE LEAVING NEW YORK for this trip I'd had a drink with my friend Oren, and he asked me, "What the hell are you going to talk to your father about for one thousand miles?"

I said, "He'll piss me off by spewing a bunch of garbage about Mexicans and Arabs and Asians, and I'll tell him he's a stupid old racist fuck. And then we'll drive for a few hundred miles in total silence. And simply to piss me off he'll spew more racist shit he doesn't even believe. And I'll call him a racist fuck. And he'll tell me that I'm young and stupid. And he'll tell a story about his best friend when he was a young boy, the black kid whose mom worked for his grandparents, and how he was banned from playing with this best buddy of his in the front yard, and he never understood why, and it hurt his feelings that he couldn't play with his best buddy in the front yard, so one day he just did it, he walked to the front yard with his best buddy, this black kid, and they played with their toys in the front yard, and it lasted a few minutes, until the black boy's mother came running around the corner and snatched the boy up by his arm and dragged him to the backyard. And then the lady grabbed John Howard by the arm and dragged him into the house through the front door, where he was yelled at by an old blind aunt, and he never saw the black boy again. And he will say that that is the reason he left the South when he was seventeen and never wanted to return. And somehow this will stand as his defense against the politically incorrect shit he says. He'll say that I know nothing about the South and nothing about race because I was raised in color-blind California, and that he went out of his way to raise me in an integrated and open community and that I had many black friends growing up and I should thank him for that. And I'll say, 'You are fucking crazy.'"

"Will you talk about your brother?" Oren asked.

"Only if I bring him up," I said.

"That's going to be a long one thousand miles."

WE CRESTED WELLS, Nevada, the Winnebago whined, and I pushed us east on Highway 50. Above my head a cupboard jutted open and a dozen CDs crashed to the floor and scattered like playing cards.

We were on our sixth time through Merle Haggard's *Greatest Hits* and our third stretch of total silence after a fight over some racist and politically incorrect garbage that had come out of his mouth.

But my father wanted to talk. He said, "This is just between you and me. You take everything so serious. So I say something about Koreans eating dogs, and your little sister is Korean? What does that mean? It's a joke from Vietnam."

"Vietnam? A joke? Kim is not a joke. She is your daughter, my sister, our family. You don't get it, man? It is not cool to say racist shit about Koreans eating dogs. Not. Fucking. Cool."

"You know the Vietnamese eat dog. You told me you ate dog sausage in Vietnam. So what's the difference?"

"It's not a joke. It's not funny. You sound totally ridiculous. Do you not understand that they are totally different countries?"

"We fought 'em both. It's all Orientals to me."

I deliberately swerved toward the right and hit the deep gashes in the pavement, which made a sound like a torso being beaten with a hose, and my father said, "Ho, Tone, keep her steady."

As we entered Wells my father said, "Wells, Nevada, home of the famous Cottontail Ranch. Wanna get some tail?"

My father is a self-proclaimed joker. I've used the word *antagonist* to describe him more than once. He likes to, as he puts it, "get under your skin." He likes to "stir the pot" and "keep it interesting." But maybe he's serious this time? And for a minute I thought about it. I thought about those stories of French fathers taking their sons to visit a prostitute when they turn sixteen or twelve or whenever it is that Frenchmen start frequenting brothels. We could swing in, just have a beer, and take a look-see at some girls. I thought, I admit, that it would make a good story, and I could write an essay about drinking beer in a Nevada whorehouse with my father, sell it to a slick magazine, pay for a trip somewhere.

But I said, "No, thanks."

At age eighteen while a marine in the Philippines it was one thing to walk into a bar and let a girl sit on your lap while listening to Duran Duran or New Order. But at age thirty-eight, outside the depressed town of Wells, Nevada, traveling at sixty-five miles per hour in a metal earthquake with my oxygen-depleted father, hanging out with prostitutes was an entirely different concept.

"Obscene," I said to my father. "That would be obscene."

He yelled, "It's legal!" And he laughed. "Hell, Tone, you've turned into a little pansy. Ain't you a marine? Don't marines live off beer and whores? I never met a marine didn't live off beer and whores."

If life were so simple as beer and whores we'd all be drunk and laid.

Silence.

Twenty miles later he said, "I guess that's what happens when you go big-time. Now you gotta be a gentleman."

I ignored him. It was midnight and I'd been driving for about eight hours. I'd stopped for gas and a candy bar in Winnemucca and otherwise I'd been at the wheel trying to keep this traveling earthquake between the lines.

I'd never been a headache man but my head throbbed; it felt as though power drills had split my temples open, the pain bled down into my jaw, into my teeth, so bad my tongue hurt and the roof of my mouth stung. I thought about calling the physician I was dating in New York and asking her to call in a prescription to a pharmacy in some shit town in the middle of nowhere in Nevada or Idaho, in the middle of the night, for something big, something strong to knock me out—an antipsychotic, that's what I needed. A buffalo tranquilizer. I needed to get so high that my father would have to drive the rest of the way and I could sit in the seat next to him, drooling, pain-free.

I THOUGHT OF how easy it would be to end this trip: first yank the oxygen tube out of his nose, then just keep driving. He'll wallow a bit in pain, he might grasp for me but I'll easily swat him away: if I must, I'll beat him away, I'll beat him with my closed fist; he's a small man now and I weigh two hundred pounds, my forearms are as muscled as his legs and I will crush him, I will watch him slowly expire. I'll drive all night in splendid silence and pull into a gas station, say in Whitehall, Montana, I think I have enough gas to get there, and I'll walk in and ask the nice lady behind the counter with feathered and unevenly bleached hair if she'll call the police because I think my father has died in his sleep in the passenger seat of his RV.

I'll walk outside and sit on the curb with my head in my hands, wait for the sheriff to arrive; the sheriff will be a real cowboy. He'll wear a sheepskin-lined denim vest with his badge pinned near his heart, he'll wear cowboy boots caked with horse shit and hay, he'll wear on his hip the biggest pistol east of Butte. And I'll tell the sheriff the story of how my father and I went to the Cottontail Ranch in Wells, Nevada, and how my father watched me fuck a prostitute and just after that said to me one of the last things I heard him say: *Tone, that sure was fun, we'll have to do it again someday.* And then he fell asleep and I kept driving and he seems to be out of breath.

"He's expired," the sheriff will confirm after a brief investigation. And he'll console me the way cowboy sheriffs do: squeeze my shoulder, say he's sorry for my loss, and tell me to keep on truckin'.

And when he realizes I don't understand, he'll say, "We don't got a morgue here, son. Whyn'cha take 'er on down the road."

And this is how I will come to drive around with my dead father next to me in his RV.

BACK IN THE RV, in the middle of the night, my father said, "Can't I joke a little? You sure are high-strung."

This is the most ironic statement in the history of spoken language. My father calling me high-strung. The man was so tense and angry when I was a kid that I cowered at the mere mention of his name.

"Just guy talk, Son. Don't be so goddamn serious. Locker-room talk." He said this as though I'd hurt his feelings. He stared out the window. Silence. The Joker was hurt.

AT A PARTY back in New York I told a friend the story about my father asking me to become a paying customer at the Cottontail Ranch. The friend was disappointed when I told him that I said no. He thought I'd ruined a perfectly good story.

I said, "Can't the story be *not* going?"

"That's no story," he said. "Writer doesn't go to whorehouse with father. That's no story!"

With a few keyboard strokes I discovered that the Cottontail Ranch had been closed since 2004. It was on the market. I found Web images of the old ranch. It looked like a bleak place where dark men did bad things to women. Though some women probably put themselves through college working weekends at the ranch, and some girl probably bought her daddy a gold Cadillac, and some girls probably raised a family and paid a mortgage, and some girls probably made a party out of loving.

AT TWIN FALLS we stopped to change drivers, not a simple matter of switching seats. Each time my father exerted himself he was challenged to fill his lungs with oxygen. The man wanted to breathe easily; he simply couldn't. The man wanted to live, he worked hard at it, but he didn't have long: eventually his lungs would simply quit. In the ten years since he'd collapsed his lung capacity had slowly diminished and the number of meds he was on had increased.

At the side of the road in Nevada he had to dope himself up. I realized that he'd been lying subtly to me for a few years. He'd always told me that there was a schedule for the inhalers, and that made sense to me and I paid no attention to his timing and it made me think that he was somewhat healthy, or healthy enough to be medicated on a schedule, but alongside the desert in Nevada I realized that he took the inhaler whenever he exerted himself and that at this point moving meant exertion.

He stood at the RV's kitchen sink and administered an inhaler. At some point in his treatment he'd discovered a system for the inhalers; a respiratory therapist had told him that he shouldn't immediately stack the meds but rather take a break between the two inhaled medicines in order to increase their efficacy, ten minutes—and so he took one and then he stood at the kitchen sink of his RV, and he breathed heavy for ten minutes, bent at the waist.

He set a kitchen timer shaped like an egg. He hadn't unwrapped the timer, it was still in its packaging just as it had been when he'd bought it, likely on a military base: in the store you'd give it a spin and see if the sound of the alarm agreed with you. Apparently it satisfied my father.

I walked outside. I pissed. I thought I saw the eyes of a coyote in the brush. The moon hung thin in the sky like a silver splinter in the universe's thumb. The desert smelled like my piss and dirt.

Back in the RV, on his second inhaler, my father gargled water and spit it out. I found this disgusting. I'd spent my childhood listening to my father, each morning, coughing the smoker's phlegm up from his lungs. I'd sit eating Wheat Chex and drinking Sunny Delight with my siblings, and down the hall he'd gag on the by-products of his own body. Gargling, spitting.

But now that he was sick the gargling and spitting were part of his treatment: the sick person must wash his mouth of the medicine after it has been inhaled—the remains of the medicine, for some reason my father can't articulate, must not stay in the mouth. And so he gargled and spit: and again my father disgusted me.

He took the wheel.

I USED TO say that my father was a builder. In reality he was a handyman. He fixed a fence, he threw up some Sheetrock, he fixed your plumbing, replaced your toilet, rewired your electricity, added a new living room, converted your garage into a place where your drug addict nephew could crash for a few months. If he needed to, he'd hire a guy or two for the serious labor, ripping up the earth or tearing down a wall, mixing and pouring concrete, hauling broken appliances out of a kitchen or mudroom.

But I never told anyone this. I wanted my father to be a master of the universe. This is the wish of every boy. But what I really wanted was for him to master love: I wanted my father to love and protect me forever, until the day I died: an impossibility.

*   *   *

THIS IS A story about my father almost getting his
ass kicked in a dive bar in Fairfield, California,
three days before Christmas in 1996. The next day
I'd go hiking on the Lost Coast with my roommate, so I visited my father in Fairfield for an early
Christmas. Since I'd returned from the Marine
Corps four years earlier my father had insisted on
being buddies. He called me "Bubba." He called
me "Old Tone." He thought we should hang out
and drink and talk about women. He liked talking
about cars but he loved talking about women even
more. He might be halfway through a story about
the 1956 Thunderbird that he and my mother
drove from Washington State to Georgia, and then
he'd pause, thinking of all the women he might
have had along the way had he only been single.

"That car," he'd say, "was a pussy magnet. I'd
loan that to single guys on the weekends and they'd
get so much tail."

The bar where we drank was just outside Travis Air Force Base. When I was born it was called
Cats. It was a strip club back then. I imagine that
just prior to and shortly after my birth my father
probably put in some quality time on tip row at
Cats. Strip bars across the world are filled with
men whose wives are heading to the delivery room.

I'm quite certain that this Christmas visit was the first time that my father told me about Margarita, his "Mexicana lover," as he referred to her. He'd once told me about going to a whorehouse in Juárez, and at first I thought he was conflating the stories, that the sad prostitute from Juárez was a stand-in for all the Mexican women he'd wanted to or had slept with. My father's storytelling is maddeningly circular and often devoid of proper pronouns and temporal markers, and back when he drank, this confusion-laced narrative style was even more pronounced. After half an hour of hearing about Margarita I realized that she was a real woman and that when they'd met she'd been married to another Air Force guy and had lived outside an Air Force base somewhere in Texas and that at this time I was seven years old.

I said, "So you cheated on Mom with a married woman?"

"Her old man was an asshole. He never fucked her. And what your mom never knew never hurt her."

I thought of my young mother: a woman who gave up college for life as a military wife. I see her drying dishes at the sink, apron tied in a bow at her waist. My father's poison, his lies and marital misdeeds, piles up in her bloodstream as she goes about the house. There she is: a happy wife and

a generous and loving mother, there she is changing my diapers, tending my brother's bloody knees,
dressing my older sister.

A photo: we are on the lawn of the Vacaville house,
my mother, brother, sister, and me. My younger sister has not yet been adopted. It's Easter 1973, I'm
two and a half years old. My mother is dying and the
only person who knows this is my father, the man
taking the picture, the man poisoning her blood and
the blood of our family with his lies and misdeeds.

So we were at the bar that used to be a strip
club, one of my father's locals, and the bartenders
and other regulars knew him. They called him
Alabama John. They talked about so-and-so,
the Fuckup, and so-and-so, the Wife Beater, and
so-and-so, the Drunk. I sensed that they envisioned themselves in a television show: as famous
as all the famous drunks in television shows about
bars, because in the television shows no one pukes
in the bathroom and no one bangs up the family station wagon on the way home; in television
shows the drunks are pretty and handsome and
witty and well-read and never too obviously drunk
in public, the place where most drunks spend a lot
of time drinking and embarrassing themselves.

The actual bar was shaped in a circle, with the
liquor shrine in the middle. The liquors on offer were

low- to middle-shelf. Beer came in the can. My father alternated between blended scotch and soda and beer. I guessed this was some old trick for getting less drunk. I'd always thought that the trick was alternating water with drinks or not drinking alcohol at all.

"Look at that hot Mexican girl over there," he said. "Damn I love the Mexican girls. I bet her name is Margarita. She's with a fucking convict. Look at that piece of shit covered in tattoos."

Now I followed him: drunk in a bar sees a pretty Mexican woman, thinks of the Mexican woman he cheated on his wife with, tells his son the story of his infidelity so his son knows that he was once a virile man who could have any woman he wanted.

"Hey, Pops, maybe it's time to roll. I can drive."

"It's early. Let's have another."

I had a girlfriend at home in my bed in Sacramento. What was I doing out on a Friday night with my father in a shitty dive bar in Fairfield?

He got up to take a piss. He needed to navigate through the area with two pool tables in order to make it to and from the bathroom. On the way back from the bathroom he nudged the pool cue of the young ripped Latino guy who was with the pretty Mexican girl.

My father was fifty-six and still holding on to his good looks and dark hair. Despite decades of smoking, his skin was taut, and because of working outside he had a suntan that announced vitality. He had a bit of a beer belly because he'd never exercised. But he was a laborer from a long line of laborers. In the past two hundred years there had been a few businessmen, a lawyer or two, one professor, but otherwise the Swoffords had been farmers or laborers. His arms and shoulders were strong, the strength gained by humping ninety-pound bags of concrete and stacks of four-by-four studs, hanging Sheetrock, laying roofs, digging ditches.

He considered himself a pretty bad motherfucker, the kind of crazy bastard only a fool would mess with, the kind of crazy bastard who would challenge an ex-con on a Friday night in a seedy bar in Fairfield.

My father had his finger in the guy's face, the way he used to shove his finger in my face. I started across the bar. By the time I got there the ex-con had my father shoved against the wall with his pool cue crushing my dad's chest.

"Hey, brother," I said. "That's my pops. He's an old man. He's just drunk and talking shit. Let's walk it off, man. No one needs this. It's Friday night, no way to start the weekend."

"Your pops needs to watch where he's walking. He's been bumping into my cue all night, and looking at my girl like he's gonna try to fuck her. She don't fuck old men."

"You never know what she does when you're in jail," my father said.

"You're lucky I'm on parole. I'd break your face."

I peeled the cue out of his hand and pushed him a few feet back.

To my father, I said, "Go back to your seat," as though chastising a kindergartner.

The ex-con stared at me. He was a beast. He'd crush me.

I said, "Sorry, bro. He's being stupid. Holidays. Bad time of year."

We settled back into our seats. One of his drinking pals took a couple digs at my dad. He didn't appreciate it.

"This place is full of assholes," he said.

But we stayed for another.

It took him a few minutes to cool down.

"So, Bubba," he said. "Tell me about this little hiking trip you're doing with Mike."

My father rarely asked questions about my life. Mostly he talked, about cars and women and how the government was screwing him, the post office, the DMV, the IRS.

His question surprised and excited me. My father, interested in my life!

"It's going to be great," I said. "The Lost Coast. It's one of the most remote hiking areas on the West Coast. We're getting dropped off at the north trailhead and picked up three days later twenty-five miles south. We probably won't see more than two or three other people for the whole trip."

"Twenty-five miles?" he asked. "That's it? That's a little Boy Scout hike. I can hike that trail better than you young bucks. You think you're tough? You think you're hot shit? Why don't you do fifty, down and back?"

"I don't think I'm tough shit. That's the way people do the hike. It will be difficult in parts. We have to know the tides to navigate beaches. There might be intense weather. It's no Iron Man but it's not a Boy Scout hike either."

"Well, when you ladies want to do some serious hiking, when you want an old pro to teach you how to hike, like we did back in the jungle, give me a call."

I could only laugh. I laughed in his face, and said, "Dad, you couldn't hike two miles without having to stop and catch your breath. In my entire life I've never seen you exercise a day."

He got snarly. I remembered this nastiness from when I was a kid, a brand of anger and bravado and quick temper that constantly threatened to explode: a bucket of dynamite with a short fuse.

"OK, Tone. You think you can take your old man? You think you can hike farther than me? You think you're stronger than me? You want to take it outside, is that what you want?"

At this point in my life I was of out of shape. I'd rarely worked out since leaving the Marine Corps, but was still fairly solid; I hadn't lost much muscle, and I worked in a warehouse five nights a week, palletizing about a ton of groceries every night. I'd crush him.

"No, Dad. I don't think that's a good idea. Why don't we have another drink?"

At the time my father was living with a woman in a house they'd bought together, but for some reason he'd wanted to stay with me in a hotel, so we'd booked a room at a budget chain. After drinking a while longer we returned to the hotel and ate at the chain restaurant nearby, the kind of place where you can get pancakes, eggs, three kinds of sausage, and hash browns for five bucks.

I slept fitfully. I wanted to be back in Sacramento in my own bed with my girlfriend. But here I was in a roadside hotel with my drunken father. In the middle of the night he got up and puked all over the bathroom. I left at six a.m., without a shower, without saying goodbye.

I sat in my beat-up pickup truck in the parking lot for a while. It was a chilly Sacramento Delta morning, some drifting dense fog rolling in through my windows, the wetness of outside gathering on me and the interior of the vehicle. I thought I could sit there forever in my junker truck in the fog.

IN TWIN BRIDGES, Montana, I sat in the passenger seat of the RV in a massive truck stop parking lot. We'd pulled in at five a.m. when it was still dark outside but now it was beginning to be light. A heavy fog had descended on the mountains to the north and west. The truck stop overflowed with big trucks and cowboy pickups. I watched the cowboys and the truckers get out of their rigs and head toward the restaurant that promised "Eggs as Easy as You Want 'Em, All Day."

At the kitchen sink my father administered his inhalants, and he coughed and gagged, bent over barrel-chested at the waist.

"Breakfast, Pops?"

"Not for me, Tone. Not sure I can make it."

The restaurant was seventy-five feet away. He was in really bad shape.

I ate alone at the counter. The chatter behind me was about hay, and horses, and barns. I liked Montanans. Good people. I'd spent some time here over the years. My older sister had lived in Montana for more than a decade. And my ex-wife's parents had retired to a spread in Whitehall, thirty miles up the road. Sarah Freeman and I had divorced before I saw the finished place. I had not seen her parents in six years. They were two of the finest people I had ever met and I missed them immensely. It was difficult for me to think of Susan and Les without weeping. I recalled a mentor once telling me that it took a man ten years to get over a divorce.

AT THIS POINT I was pushing six years, a long recovery considering Sarah and I got married six weeks after we met.

After our first night of sex, over omelets at a crappy Iowa City diner, Sarah said, "Let's get married."

And I replied, "Yes. Let's."

It was March 27, 2000. We decided to marry on Friday, April 21. Sarah had her poetry workshop on Mondays and I had my fiction workshop on Tuesdays, so Friday would work. We were broke, so we couldn't do Vegas or Mexico, and her parents lived in Chicago, so we had to go west: destination Omaha. We swore silence; that we'd tell no one. At the Iowa Writers' Workshop, a fishbowl devoid of privacy, we would pull off a privacy coup.

On the drive to Omaha from Iowa City we stopped at a restaurant called The Machine Shed. I remember eating a massive breakfast. I had some second thoughts about marrying Sarah. There was plenty of reason for pause. We had only known each other for six weeks. We were both in graduate school. I'd met her parents but she'd not met mine. I ate my massive breakfast—three eggs, bacon, sausage, biscuits, and pancakes. Sarah ate a single poached egg. And neither of us brought up any of the reasonable objections to getting married so soon.

At that point in my life she was the most beautiful woman I had ever known and I still don't understand why she wanted to marry me. She came from a Hyde Park academic family. I came from a military family. She'd gone to Reed College out of high school; I'd joined the Marine Corps and then hit the Sacramento community college circuit, eventually transferring to a state university. When I talked to her about having been in the Marines I might as well have been telling her about the few years I worked in the carnival or the time I traveled in a flying saucer.

Judge Samuel V. Cooper married us. We paid his two clerks twenty bucks each to be our witnesses. I wore black loafers, gray slacks I'd bought at Nordstrom a few years before, and a blue long-sleeved shirt. She wore patent leather high heels that looked as if they might have cost a few hundred dollars but that she'd found at a discount store for seven bucks. She wore a black pencil skirt and a black blouse and her grandmother's pearl earrings.

Judge Samuel V. Cooper told us that he could give us the traditional municipal court vows but that he liked to personalize the affair, based on his Native American heritage. We agreed to follow his lead. He said something about the couple and the village and the village building shelter for the couple. He said some things about rain and lightning. It all seemed to make sense to us. We traded plain gold rings.

We walked outside, to a bright sunny Omaha day. An old couple nearby offered to take our picture in front of the courthouse. I felt certain that Sarah Freeman and I would remain married forever.

BACK IN THE RV my father and his lungs were up and running and he wanted to hit the road. The radio said we might hit snow on the other side of Bozeman. We needed to make it to Billings tonight, and a storm would stop us in our tracks.

We pushed along I-90 at a good pace. I was exhausted. I wanted to deliver my father to his RV park and check into my hotel. My girlfriend would already be there from Manhattan. She practiced emergency room medicine, and I knew she'd come prepared with pills for all that ailed us both: pain, anxiety, insomnia, malaise, and roadway ennui.

But for now the hills and farmland of central Montana ensorcelled me.

My father sat next to me in his tighty-whities. His handsomely silver Einsteinian hair looked as though it were going through a chain reaction. I wore a pair of yellow boxer shorts with black dachshunds on them, cowboy boots, and a green T-shirt that declared GETTIN' LUCKY IN KENTUCKY. Quite a sartorial sensation this morning, the Swofford men.

My father reached across the cab and grabbed my forearm, and said, "Tone, I think we need to get some things out in the open and clear the air. I think you need to get some venom out."

So this was the reason my father had asked me to fly to Fairfield and drive a thousand miles with him in his RV. It was a reconciliation ploy. I drove a few miles in silence. I popped my ears, stretched my neck, cleared my throat. I banged my left foot against the door. I felt a rage like none other come over my body. The rage burst at the top of my head and oozed down my body like lava. But the rage was good. I wanted the rage like I wanted those pills stowed in my girlfriend's carry-on. The pills were legal, prescribed by a doctor. The rage was legal, too.

"What makes you think I have venom?" I asked calmly.

"Look at you, Son. The steam is coming out of your body. I can feel your rage."

"Why do you think I have rage?"

"I don't know. Only you know what enrages you. But I can tell you it's not good for you. It'll kill you. And if I die before you get it out, it'll kill you even faster."

I drove a few more miles. Yes, I had rage. Yes, I had homicidal rage. Yes, I had fantasies about killing this man. Don't all sons fantasize about killing their fathers? But I suppose most sons get over it by their early twenties. Maybe I'm just a slow learner. After all, it had taken me six years to get a bachelor's degree.

I focused on the beautiful landscape. I stared at massive free-range cows.

"Do you really want to know what enrages me? Because I will tell you. But I don't think these are things that you are prepared to hear. They are not pretty things. They are not the kinds of things that families like to talk about at this point in the life of the family. By now everyone is supposed to be over their shit, they are supposed to have their own families, and they are supposed to move on and shut up so the older generation can look in the mirror and lie to themselves about what kind of parents they were. By parents, I mean you, Father.

Mom is not a part of this conversation. Mom was a saint. All she did was try to protect us from you and your bullying ways."

"I don't need to talk about your mother."

"I don't care what you need to talk about. I spent my entire childhood being spoken to and being told what to do by you. You never asked me questions. You told, you directed. You would have been a wonderful tyrannical film director. I remember that you liked to talk about Generalissimo Franco from your time in Spain. You admired the guy. You considered him a benevolent dictator. Do you know how many people he killed?"

"What does Franco have to do with this?"

"A man is the sum of the men he admires."

"Jesus, Tone. What kind of crazy talk is that? What is burning you up, Son?"

I liked the sound of the rush of the road beneath the RV. It was a humming, a mad march. I could take us over the cliff like a herd of bison. My father did not want to hear what I had to say. He considered the case closed on most of my grievances, the statute of limitations expired. I knew this much from a letter he had written me a few years earlier. He wanted me to tell him that I was over all those bad times from my childhood and now we could be friends. But my father failed to recognize that what

I wanted and needed was a father, not a friend, not some old dude who would tell me stories about banging prostitutes in Juárez. I had plenty of lunatic friends who told better prostitute stories than he. What I needed was a father who would ask me questions about my life, ask me what I strived for, ask me how I'd failed, ask me why my marriage hadn't worked, tell me to give it another try with another woman, tell me that having a family was worth sleeping with only one woman for the rest of your life. Even if he didn't believe it.

I said, "Please never tell me another story about cheating on my mother. It doesn't make you cool. It simply makes you look like a jerk. Do you think I'm impressed? I'm not. I know about having a lot of women. I have done all of my screwing while unmarried. For every sex story you have, I have twenty. It's no big deal. Some men fuck a lot of women. Others don't."

"I'm not bragging, Tone. I thought I could talk to you like a man, I thought."

I interrupted him, "Do not tell me that when I was seven years old in Vacaville that you did not shove my face toward a pile of dog shit in the backyard. You did not put my face *in* the dog shit, I will concede that. But you dragged me across the yard by the back of my neck and you shoved my face within inches of the pile of dog shit that I had missed while performing my weekly chore. While doing so you yelled at me at the top of your lungs and accused me of being a liar. Tell me how you would feel right now if I grabbed you by the back of your neck and dragged you out of the RV and shoved your face in a pile of bison shit while yelling at you. I was seven years old. You were a thirty-six-year-old man. You had absolute physical power over me and you abused me. I will never forget that. On the day I die, in five or so decades, I will think of the day my father dragged me across the backyard to shove my face toward a pile of dog shit."

"We have different memories of that event," he said, obviously shaken. "You were a young boy and you needed to be taught how to properly perform your chores. I will admit that I did things then that today people would consider abusive. It was the way I was raised, it's what I knew."

"That's bullshit, and you know it. You had a wife who told you that was not the way to raise a family. Didn't you admire her parents? Did you not see that the way she was raised was superior to the backwoods Georgia way you were raised? I know you loved her father. Albert was the first grown man you admired and loved. You knew that he never abused his children. Why did you not use his model?"

"Things might have been different if Albert was still around when you kids came along. I loved him."

My father looked away from me and out at the prairie. He quietly cried.

After a few miles he cleared his throat and blew his nose into a handkerchief.

He said, "Albert Warner was a very fine man. It crushed your mother to lose her father at such a young age. Hell, it crushed me."

Road sign for a Vista Point Ahead. I needed to pull over and get some fresh air. Luckily there were no other vehicles stopped. I walked out in my cowboy boots and boxers. Snow had begun to fall. I felt the cold in my dick. I walked to the edge of the parking lot and pissed in the grass. I looked out across the prairie. I saw bison and a perfect red barn, a white farmhouse in the distance. I wondered who lived there and how dark their lives had ever become. I knew that my childhood could have been darker than it was. I thought of something good from my childhood. I couldn't keep beating my father up. I thought of the time we stopped in Yosemite and drank fresh water from a waterfall. I thought of spending summers driving through national parks. But then I thought of the time in the Grand Tetons when my father had reached through the doughnut hole that opened up the cab of the truck to the camper and grabbed me by the neck and bashed my head against the edge of the camper because I had asked a stupid question, probably about what time we were eating breakfast. It was on a cold morning just like this. I had to get that out of my head. I needed something good. I needed a happy memory. I loved my father, I knew this. And he must have known it, too. But there was so much dark shit. I was tired and strung out. I needed to settle down. I needed to exercise. I went into the RV and exchanged my cowboy boots and boxers for running shoes and a pair of sweats.

My father said, "What the hell is going on? We need to get to Billings. This thing ain't snow-safe. We'll skid off the road and kill ourselves or the highway patrol will turn us around, one or the other."

"Give me ten minutes. I need to clear my head."

"OK. I'll do an inhaler."

While my father administered his meds to his dying lungs I ran circles around the parking lot on the side of the prairie. I loved the man. I hated the man. I knew that he must love and hate me. I looked just like him. I wondered if that made it harder for the parent to separate from the child. It was impossible for him to look at me and not see his younger self. And for my father youth meant virility, Johnny Cash, the ladies. I was stealing his virility. Consumed by disease, he bequeathed to me all the power that had once been his. But he could not respect me because I had not yet fathered a child. He could not pass anything on to me because I had not yet had a child, but he *had* to pass it on to me because he had lost all his power and my older brother was dead. I ran for fifteen minutes and came down from my rage.

Back in the captain's chair I steered the beast toward the road.

My father said, "It's good for you to get this venom out. I don't know how I can help you. But I'll do whatever I can. I admire you, Son. I'd like to have a grown-up, adult relationship with you. I had problems with my own father. But in my twenties I realized the problems weren't going to be solved and it was time to be an adult and recognize that he'd done the best he could given the circumstances, and to hold on to my anger would do more harm than good."

"I don't understand what you mean by an 'adult relationship.' "

"Spend time together. Talk about life."

"Why suddenly do you want to talk about life? Why were you unable to talk to me about life when I was a boy? This inclination of yours would have come in handy for me when I was an awkward and lonely boy. I don't remember one incident during my teen years when you asked me how I was doing, or what I wanted, or needed."

"Damn, Son. Give me a break. I wasn't a great father. I should have been around more. I should have been more present in your life and asked you more questions."

"But you were too busy fucking your secretary, right?"

"I can't do this. Nothing will appease you. If you hate me, then you hate me. Why do you hate me?"

"I don't hate you for my childhood. I don't hate you for having a zipper problem. You are a pretty cool guy. People love your company, and I see why. You tell good stories. You've got a good and hearty laugh. I hate you because eleven years ago my brother died and you didn't go to his funeral. That is why I hate you. I hate you for that and for that alone. And I will never forgive you."

We drove in silence for about a hundred miles. They were good smooth road miles. The snow had stopped dropping and blew across the asphalt in psychedelic curlicues and paisleys of white. An SUV with Oregon plates, loaded down with ski gear, buzzed by and I was sure it was my friend Tom from Portland, but I called him on his cell and he said no, he wasn't in Montana, as far as he could tell he was doing bong hits in his basement.

Around Big Timber, my father said, in the quietest voice I'd ever heard from him, "I do not expect you to ever know what I felt when Jeff died. I hope you never experience anything like it. To lose my firstborn son was the most heart-wrenching thing that could ever happen to me. There is no other pain in the world that could ever compare. And I can't promise you that if you die tomorrow I will have the strength to make it to your funeral. I have no idea how I would react. No one ever does. Please do not hold that against me until the day I myself die."

"I can't promise you that."

AT BILLINGS I set my father up at the RV park and caught a cab to my hotel. My girlfriend was there, in bed, totally passed out at four p.m. after munching down three or four sleeping pills. We had a dinner for my niece that night, so I stayed away from the doctor's collection of pills. For the moment.

The dinner went well. It was the first time in five or six years that all five of us—me, my two sisters, and both parents—had been together. I largely ignored my father and mostly talked to my niece's dorky boyfriend. Dez is a tall girl and this short little guy came up to her armpits, at best. It was obvious that he did not like this height situation by the way he talked about the fast cars that his father owned.

I said, "Dude, someday you're gonna have to buy your own fast car."

The doctor passed me a pill under the table and I took it. A few minutes later everything began to float and I said I needed to get back to the room, that the drive from California had exhausted me.

But the doctor and I went to a bar downtown filled with a bunch of hard mothertruckers. I was completely doped out of my mind on whatever muscle relaxant she'd given me. While we sat drinking Budweiser for two hours there were at least five fistfights in the bar, two of them involving massive Native American lesbians.

Eventually we returned to our hotel room. The doctor and I had Ambien sex. I never loved her but I used those words when she did. Before I dated the doctor I had been engaged to a dancer who once threw away books from my bookshelves by female writers she suspected I might have slept with. I had in fact slept with only two of the ten accused. In contrast, the doctor, despite her pill use and urge to share, was a sea of total calm, the classic rebound after the chaos-producing dancer. The dancer had world-class beauty and a dancer's body; the doctor had plain looks and the body of an overworked ER physician who ate a lot of takeout from Staten Island Italian joints. The doctor ended our relationship after she had worked three straight overnighters and broke into my phone and read e-mails about me having sex in the women's bathroom at the Brooklyn Inn with a twenty-five-year-old hedge-funder while she saved lives in a crappy ER in Staten Island. There was also the e-mail about the one-night stand with the Australian academic.

But here now in Billings the Ambien sex satisfied me in the way that Ambien sex always satisfies: you are having sex while on Ambien so what can possibly be wrong with the sex? Nothing. And you wake up in the morning as though it never happened.

I was supposed to retrieve my father from his RV park at eleven in the morning in order to make certain that he made it to the graduation event, but he called me a few minutes before I planned to leave the hotel to tell me that there was no way he was going to make it, his lungs just weren't up to it.

I said, "Are you serious? I flew to Northern California from New York to drive you a thousand miles in order to attend Dez's graduation and you can't make the ceremony?"

"I'll try to make it to the party," he said. I hung up. The doctor gave me a few pills.

We made it to the massive sports complex for the graduation. I was sitting in the stands with my family when I realized that no one had any flowers for Dez.

I asked my sisters, "Do you have flowers somewhere? Dez needs flowers. Look around, everyone has flowers to give their kids!"

I panicked. A woman can't graduate from college without a bunch of flowers. What on Earth were we thinking?

I said to my mother and sisters and the doctor, "I'm going downtown to get some flowers. I'll be back before it's over."

In my pill-addled state I had trouble finding a florist. Eventually I did, after driving recklessly around Billings for half an hour or so. I made it back to the complex just as the show broke up. I'd procured two massive bouquets of flowers. I gave one to my sister and one to my mother in order that they could hand them to Dez. The photo session went off without a hitch. I'd saved the day!

My niece threw a party for a few dozen friends. We got some great family photos. I did not speak much with my father. The doctor chain-smoked cigarettes with my sister Tami's drug addict parolee girlfriend, and at some point the girlfriend took me to a country-and-western store and I bought a massive belt buckle with a steer on it. It never occurred to me how wrong it was that during my niece's graduation party I drove around town with her mother's parolee girlfriend, a stash of pills in my pocket. Eventually the girlfriend would rob my sister blind, steal a church van, and pawn all of Tami's jewelry in Spokane. We Swoffords have trouble finding the right women.

I went out dancing that night with my niece and her short boyfriend and their friends. The doctor slept. We went to the most cutting-edge club in Billings. It was way out in the industrial part of town. On one side was a good old cowboy honky-tonk bar, and on the other side something approximating a massive Chelsea dance club in miniature. Bottle service here meant a six-pack of Buds.

The doctor had loaded me up on pills and I was totally twitched out of my mind. But I could not betray this to my niece. Somehow I kept it together. I danced all night with her friends, all very nice young people. At some point, while on the honky-tonk side of the bar, and away from my niece and her friends, I kissed a cowgirl. Later I tangled limbs with the cowgirl in the cab of her boyfriend's pickup truck.

The next thing I knew I was back in Manhattan.

I talked to my father a few weeks later and we agreed that the RV trip had been a success and that we should hit the road again together soon.

4

Brother, to Thy Sad Graveside Am I Come

X-POP3-Rcpt: swoff@pop3
To: ahswofford@ucdavis.edu
Subject: Talk to me
X-Mailer: Juno 1.38
From: jswofford@juno.com (Jeff Swofford)
Date: Fri, 23 Jan 1998 13:54:47 EST

Dear Tony,I left a message on your telephone today at about 12:30 to call me ASAP.
I'm planning a big party the end of next week and want you to be here.
You can get discounted tickets to visit relatives who are facing impending death. I can tell you on the phone how to show proof, if required. I can help with the money. I know you just started

school and I'm sorry to die at such an inconvenient time, but I really need you here little brother. There won't be any gloom out here, just guitars, singing and lots of partying. Call me soon.

Love,
Your Big Brother

Impending death. Upending death. How do you show proof to the airline that your brother is dying? Photographic evidence?

See here, Mr. Airline Representative, this is a photo of my brother a year ago, the picture of health, a thirty-four-year-old father of two: notice the shine and elasticity of his skin, the sheen and splendor of his red hair; notice the bulky forearms, the wide strong chest; notice the two radiant children, notice the smiling pretty wife.

Now, Mr. Airline Representative, here is a photo of my brother from last week: notice the sallow and hollow cheeks; notice the grayish pall of his skin; notice the hairless head; notice the thin weak body. Notice the children at the back of the frame, watching their father as death watches him, and notice the wife, turned away from the camera, eyes on the distance unknown.

May I have a discounted rate? Sacramento to Atlanta?

I don't recall if I received a discount or not. I wouldn't have asked of my own accord. There are those people you've just met who will give you their entire medical history along with the histories of their parents and lover and siblings: leukemia, heart murmur, childhood diabetes, heart failure, intubation, constipation, hernia, dementia, delirium tremens. I do not share such information with total strangers.

MY YOUNGER SISTER Kim picked me up at the airport. At the time she lived in Atlanta and during the past few years, when she and my brother both lived in the city, they had become very close. Twelve years separated them so Kim barely remembered Jeff from her childhood.

Over the last year while my brother was ill Kim had been a regular caretaker for the children and for my brother's family in general—staying with the kids when my brother was at chemo with his wife, driving them to school, doing the shopping, performing all manner of errands.

I jumped in the passenger seat and gave Kim a kiss on the cheek.

"How is he?" I asked.

"Dying," she said morbidly. "They're increasing the morphine. The hospice nurse is at the house now, with Mom and Melody. The kids are a mess."

She took us out to Camp Creek Parkway and drove the long, sloping road southwest toward Douglasville. As a kid I'd taken this route many times, always on happy occasions: a family reunion, my grandparents' wedding anniversary, a summer vacation trip to Six Flags.

We passed Six Flags, shuttered for the winter.

Kim said, "Iris wants to see you again."

Iris was her friend and whenever I was in town we flirted and drove around the rolling hills of West Georgia in her beat-up car listening to the Velvet Underground and talking about living someday in New York City.

We passed the chain stores and restaurants that signaled I was in another country: Piggly Wiggly, Chick-fil-A, Winn-Dixie.

MY BROTHER WAS the only true athlete in our family. When it came to sports, I was a dilettante: a few years of unimpressive football play; four years of wrestling in high school where I was known more for guts and conditioning than moves, with one strong season my junior year; two seasons of rugby during which I scored one tri, received a concussion, and split my face open twice—causing my mother to faint at least once.

Jeff ferociously played defensive back for the same school where later I'd founder. He received a small scholarship from Sacramento State College. He joined the Army, I'm still unsure why, halfway through his junior year of college.

In the Army he stayed ripped by spending hours at the gym. In Munich, in the mid-1980s, he competed in bodybuilding competitions. The photos of him from that era show a man with a deeply chiseled body and a confidence that could have been bottled, copyrighted, and sold.

In early 1997, at the age of thirty-four, Jeff still committed himself to tenacious workouts. Despite being married with two kids and attempting to start a new career after thirteen years in the Army, he always made time for exercise. Such was his dedication to the gym that I wondered if he might have a slight mental imbalance that manifested in manic fitness pursuits. Or, equally likely, he was simply vain.

I'd taken a trip to Atlanta during my winter break from college.

On this trip I'd mostly hung around with my brother and his family and Kim, visiting the outlying aunts and uncles occasionally or seeing them when they dropped by my brother's house.

Jeff relished being older and in better shape.

"Hey, kid, want to race three miles? I can still kill it in seventeen minutes, twenty seconds," he'd say with a big grin, or "Hey, kid, want to see how much you can deadlift? Bench-press? Squat?"

One afternoon I agreed to a session at the gym. He said his body had been aching, that he'd been going to a chiropractor. He chalked it up to "old age" and the rigors and stresses of raising children and starting a new career.

I expected that Jeff would kill me at the gym, beat me by a hundred pounds on squats and fifty or even seventy-five at bench.

We warmed up on bench with two plates, 135 pounds, merely feathers. I knocked out fifteen repetitions. I knew I'd hurt badly the next day, but I didn't want to look like a total wimp in front of my brother. We jacked it up to 185, then 205, then 225. I held my own with Jeff. We were both surprised. He complained about pain in his back. He stretched. He said the sauna would cure all that ailed him.

We set up the squat rack. Two hundred and twenty-five pounds. Three sets of fifteen repetitions was our plan. Jumped rope for two minutes to warm up. I was sweating. I liked this, I felt good and strong and able. Jeff blew out his first set without a problem, going way deep into the squat, his ass just inches from the ground. I knew that if I tried to go that deep I'd rip something—my shorts, my quadriceps, or my brain stem.

I barely completed a full squat and my brother heckled me. But I finished my reps.

"Dude," I said, "I haven't done squats in four years. I won't be able to walk for a week if I go as deep as you."

"You're weak, kid."

He slapped me on the ass, lovingly.

He blasted out another set. I watched my brother, a fine physical specimen, and I thought of the man inside the body—the mind, the heart— the father, husband, son, brother. I was a son and a brother but not yet a husband or a father. These two other, further dimensions made him seem, in some ways, deeply ancient and removed from the petty rush and tumble of my life: books, beer, girls, and moody rock music.

I wanted to know the man inside the body. I'd seen him with his children, patient and loving. He spoke to them in a calm and reassuring voice. I'd seen him discipline them occasionally, for minor childhood infractions: running inside, screaming at the top of their lungs, an innocent food fight at the table—flying orzo and broccoli.

These same kinds of crimes when we were

children would have warranted major censure from our father: no television for the night; no phone for a week; occasionally, a spanking or the belt.

Jeff didn't have the best marriage. He and Melody mostly disagreed on child rearing: she approached the children as friends, colleagues, seeking their advice; Jeff thought that this was destructive to family cohesion and consistency and that being friends with your children was something best attempted when they were out of college or later.

They'd both had affairs a few years earlier, he first, then she. I never got the complete story, but he'd told me once about making love to a woman in the Arizona desert and that he'd paid dearly for the misdeed, a misdeed returned in kind. He'd deserved it, he said. Now back to the work of the marriage.

He was trying to start a new gig, as a physician headhunter for hospitals. He lacked eighteen credits for his bachelor's degree. He had plans to pull together his education and career and marriage.

I grunted out my next set. Jeff began limping around the squat rack.

He said, "I think that's it for me, little brother. My back is wrecked. I need to ice it tonight and see my chiropractor ASAP. I hate getting old."

To his chagrin I threw on another fifty pounds and pounded out a last set.

"Thirty-four is old," I said.

THAT NIGHT JEFF and I went out alone to dinner. We grabbed BBQ at a down-home place off the interstate.

"Look at these disgusting people," he said, gesturing around the restaurant. "You and I worked out today. We're in shape." He paused. "Well, I'm in shape and you're coming back. We can afford some ribs and a few beers. These people eat like this every day, go home and sit on their asses, and drink more beer and wake up tomorrow morning and do it again. I gotta get out of the South. I miss California. People are in shape, they care about what they eat, they exercise."

"Not everyone out there is in shape, bro. There are fat people everywhere."

I knew he harshly judged overweight people, a bias he'd inherited from our maternal grandmother, but tonight he was particularly critical. There were, in fact, a number of people in our own extended family who could stand to lose twenty pounds or more, and I didn't feel like condemning them.

"Not like this fat. This is pure obesity. This is gluttony." He spit the word *gluttony* out, condemning the entire South to heart disease, diabetes, sepsis, and a well-deserved early grave.

He went into his story about lifting weights one weekend at Venice Beach, way back in the eighties. I'd heard it dozens of times and I tuned him out, gazing at the mountains of discarded pork ribs and the empty sweet tea glasses and beer bottles that littered the tables. Gluttony, indeed, a very fine portrait of.

I thought I knew the source of his agitation. During my shower I'd heard him and Melody fighting, in the closed-lip, low-boil way that couples practice when other adults are in the house—or at a nearby table if they're dining out. I chose not to bring it up. Really, I didn't care why they had been fighting. I was enjoying my ribs and my beer.

And my little sister had set me up on a date later that night with one of her friends and I looked forward to meeting the girl.

"Listen, bro," he said, pulling me out of my fantasy about Iris.

He paused and his face hardened; he worked his jaw, and his deep blue eyes darkened and his mood went from sun-bright baby oil muscle beach revelry to deep South thunderstorm: hail, flooding.

"I might need to come out and live with you for a while. We're talking about splitting up. For a trial. Melody will take Kelley back to her mom's in Minnesota. And I'll take Christian with me. I want to come back to Sacramento. I'll bang out three quarters at UC–Davis, finish my degree, and start grad school. I'm thinking physician's assistant."

I had no idea how to respond. Did my older brother just say he wanted to come live with me, his five-year-old son in tow? How could he possibly have just said that?

"Of course," I said. "Whatever you need. I've got a roommate right now, but I think he's moving out soon. If you need it, I'll keep the room free."

"I could give Christian that room, and you and I could share your room. I want him to feel like he has his own space. It's going to be tough on him. But I think this is the right move."

Share your room? Where will I have sex with girls? The last time I shared a room with my brother I was five and he was thirteen.

"Let's just see how it works out," I said, my eyes ablaze with worry. "I'm sure Christian will want to sleep with you for a while. It'll be new and scary for the little guy. And it's a big room. It's the master. There's room for two beds."

But if my brother needed a place to stay I would

share a room with him, or sleep on the couch, on the floor, wherever.

"It's just not working out. I thought getting out of the Army would save our marriage. No more moving around, no more nights and weeks and months alone. Home every night with the wife and kids. I just don't know if that is what she wants. Sometimes I think she wants me gone. And sometimes I want to disappear."

We drove back to his house in total silence. I'd never been married but it didn't seem to me as if splitting up and taking your kids to near-opposite ends of the country could do any good for a couple and their family. But I couldn't say that to my brother.

We entered the house and the kids came running and Jeff and Melody kissed and embraced and I wondered what kind of nutty drama these people were living.

LATER I HAD my date with Iris, a skinny little Georgia punk goth with dyed black hair and combat boots and a foul mouth. She drove me around the rolling West Georgia hills to nearby cemeteries, many of which held dead Swoffords, and we listened to the Velvet Underground and some bands I'd never heard of. She smoked clove cigarettes and we kissed in church parking lots, at the edges of graveyards.

*　　*　　*

A FEW WEEKS later, back in California, I answered my home phone one afternoon. It was Jeff. He sounded small and far away.

He said, "Brother, I've got cancer. It's bad. And I'm dying."

OVER THE NEXT several months I visited Jeff whenever I could. His prognosis was never great, but he always put a positive spin on his illness: he was going to beat the thing, he was young and otherwise healthy and there was no reason he wouldn't survive—no reason other than that he had stage four non-Hodgkin's lymphoma and that the cancer had appeared on his spine, in his left lung, in his stomach.

The reason his back hurt so much when we were lifting weights that day was that the tumor on his spine was about the size of a grapefruit—a grapefruit on his spine, blueberries on his lymph nodes, peach on his lung, plum in his stomach.

Why when describing tumors do we invariably use fruit comparisons? Is this to soften the blow of the horrible news? Throw fruit, not cinder blocks.

So with my brother it started with a grapefruit. The word was on everyone's tongue, as if to say *grapefruit* was to not say *cancer*. You say grapefruit, I say live.

*　　*　　*

WHILE MY BROTHER died I lived in Sacramento, putting the finishing touches on my five-and-a-half-year bachelor's degree. I worked three or four nights a week at a unionized grocery warehouse, the swing shift, five p.m. to one-thirty a.m.

If it looked like overtime, we'd send a guy to the Texaco truck stop down in the shadows of the Highway 80 overpass to buy five or six cases of beer before the two a.m. cutoff.

I drank beer behind the truck stop two or three nights a week for five years. The beds of our pickup trucks and the hoods of our cars were our local bar, and we were the bartenders—tellers of bad jokes, keepers of dark secrets. Many of the older guys had fought in Vietnam. Most of the talk was about the shit work we did and the shit union that took so much of our pay and the shit bosses who constantly broke up our poker games because they regularly ran an hour or longer past lunch. Shop talk.

Most of the older men had been divorced once or twice. There was Dave who made ninety grand a year with overtime and still somehow managed to live from his car. There was Evan, who broke his ankle in a snake hole his first night in Vietnam and spent six months recuperating and screwing Navy nurses on Okinawa, clearly one of the luckiest men

on the planet. For decades he'd played blues gui-
tar downtown at the Torch Club. He told stories of
playing with the legendary Johnny Hartman back
in the day.

There was the other Dave, my age, smart as hell,
but he loved the work of a forklift jockey. He'd
start a semester at some college or another every
year and drop out two or three weeks in.

"Just in time to get a refund. What a bunch of
dummies," he said one day, after dropping out.

"The kids at college?" I asked, feeling implicated and hurt.

"No, man," he said, with a grand gesture toward
the warehouse floor. "Douche bags like me who are
gonna drive a forklift for the next forty years and
break their backs three times humping hundred-
pound bags of dog food."

But Dave would leave. His parents owned a
massive dairy farm south of Sacramento, and the
Valley construction crawl would soon take over the
farm, to the likely tune of tens of millions of dollars. He knew that. Everyone knew that.

There was my best friend, Douglas Ahim, a former Ugandan child soldier who somehow in hell
ended up in Sacramento after running with Jamaican gangs in London throughout his early twenties.
I was one of only about three guys in the warehouse

who could understand his Swahili/British English/ Jamaican English/American English mash-up.

Supervisors were constantly yelling for me: "Swofford, what the hell did Ahim just say?"

I learned years later that his incomprehensible accent was a ploy when he said to me, "If they don't know what you're saying, they can't bust you."

Somehow he got a job as a plant mechanic and spent the next few years sleeping on the roof of the warehouse while making thirty dollars an hour, laughing at the rest of us as we sweated and cursed and loaded hundred-pound bags of dog food onto pallets.

They were all good men, solid working-class guys, but they called me college boy or college fuck, good-naturedly of course, but some didn't like me because they knew I'd get out.

But there were nights behind the Texaco, while my brother died, and I drank beer until five a.m. with this motley band of laborers, when I felt closer to them than I had to other men, closer than I'd felt to my marine comrades, closer than I felt to my father or brother or the boys I'd grown up with: they all knew my brother was dying in Georgia, but here in West Sacramento, behind the Texaco, no one mentioned it, and this not mentioning it showed they cared.

We sat in the shadow of one of the greatest highways in the Western world. I could jump in my truck, gas up, head straight east, and five days later I'd arrive in Manhattan.

While we drank and talked shit to one another dozens of big rigs idled behind us, truckers pissed next to their trucks, truck stop prostitutes worked their turf, dogfights and human fights broke out, drug deals went down, and we smelled the stench of commerce; the brilliant shine of vice assaulted us in the burning fluorescent lights of the truck stop; on the other side of a massive dirt berm rolled the Yolo Causeway, nectar feeder to the Sacramento Valley, feeder of the world.

And none of the men I drank beers with talked about my dying brother. This is the brute civility and humility of the working-class man, the man from Springsteen songs and Carver short stories. For many months this brute emotion held me up when otherwise I might simply have crashed to the pavement under the weight of my grief and the weight of the deadly flesh rotting in my brother's body.

A BIZARRE BEHAVIOR I acquired during the year Jeff was sick: The first time this happened, I had ordered through the intercom at a fast-food drive-through lane. Tacos. But as soon as I'd ordered I knew I did not want to eat those tacos. Tacos were all wrong. There was no way that tacos would satisfy me. And if I ate tacos my brother would die. But I'd already pulled forward, and someone else was behind me, so I couldn't back out. At the window I paid for the tacos, but before they had a chance to hand me the food I sped out of there. I drove around for a few hours trying to find the right restaurant. I sat in my car in dozens of restaurant parking lots: Italian, Mongolian BBQ, Chinese, French, New American, steak houses, burger joints, chain family-styles, fast food.

At the Mongolian BBQ restaurant I sat down, and then I realized that if I filled that bowl with meat and noodles and had the guy behind the grill cook it, my brother would die. I sat at the table and drank iced tea for a while, glass after glass of iced tea. I hated iced tea. The nice waitress asked me every few minutes if I was OK and didn't I want to fill my bowl, didn't I know how it worked at the Mongolian BBQ , that you filled your bowl with vegetables and noodles and meat, and selected any number of tasty sauces, and then gave it to the man behind the massive grill; it was a grill, not really a BBQ , but the man behind the grill sautéed your bowl of food at high heat and then you ate it at your table, and you could return as many times as you pleased, up to three trips, before incurring a three-dollar surcharge for more visits? Did I understand?

I performed this extreme act of indecision a few times a week for many months until my brother died.

One night I did this with my girlfriend. We sat down and ordered food that I refused to eat at two or three different restaurants. Finally she said, "Why don't we drink some whiskey?"

JEFF CONTINUED ROUNDS of rigorous treatment throughout the spring and early summer. He'd lost his hair months before and had dropped about thirty pounds, but the athletic vitality that had always defined him remained noticeable in his graceful movements and his carriage.

I'd arrived for the July 4 holiday weekend and was told there would be hiking and a picnic during the day, followed by fireworks at night. A friend of Jeff's had made a big run to an Alabama fireworks mecca and once dusk settled we were going to light up the neighborhood.

Jeff had been in some pain in the morning and we had made a slower start than intended. I could tell he didn't like Melody's driving. As we pulled out from their subdivision he sharply criticized her for not using her turn signal. My sister Kim and I, in the very rear seats, rolled our eyes at each other. There were times when Jeff reminded us of our father, and that scared us: Kim because of the memories of the stern authoritarianism of Dad, and me because of the fear that the father/son cycle was unbreakable and that regardless of will at some point every man becomes his father.

But I also considered that it might just be that the man was dying and that not using a turn signal seemed like a flagrant dismissal of the safety mechanisms he required for every aspect of his life, as though while he censured his wife he meant to say, *Honey, I might beat this goddamn thing, so please do not kill us in this car.*

Sweetwater Park teemed with families in full Fourth of July regalia: flag-printed shorts and caps and socks and shoes and blankets and coolers, shirts and backpacks and blankets. I couldn't scan farther than three feet without being assaulted by some form of Old Glory.

Jeff said, "Jesus, we don't even have a flag to wave. We must look like communists. Why didn't we think of this?"

I couldn't tell if he was joking or not. I assumed no. Jeff still defined himself by Country and God. I'd mostly given that up after the Gulf War. And then I realized that it must have just dawned on him that this might be his last Fourth of July with his family, and why not go all out and show your pride in your country.

Kelley and Christian wanted to play, so Melody and my sister took them to the swing sets and the jungle gym. Jeff and I decided to go for a walk on one of the trails. He wanted to do a three-mile loop.

I said, pointing at the map, "Maybe we should start with one of these little milers, just to see how you're feeling."

"I'm not an invalid yet, little brother. I can handle this. Last year this time I was jumping out of airplanes!"

I wanted to say: *Last year this time you didn't have a constellation of tumors attacking your body.*

We stepped off at a brisk pace. Since the night in January when Jeff had told me he and Melody were splitting up, we had not talked about their marriage. My mother had told me that they had renewed their vows at a ceremony at a new church they'd joined, but Jeff had said nothing about this to me. It was as though our conversation about the demise of their marriage and his probable move to Sacramento had never occurred.

I said, "So what's going on with you and Melody?"

"Things are great. We renewed our vows. The kids are getting along. We're going to beat this cancer, and we're going to remain a family."

"It would be tough to be sick and alone. I can't imagine that. I wonder what my girlfriend would do if I got sick."

"Every man always wonders that," he said. "What will this woman do if I lose my legs, get cancer, get my dick blown off at war? I always knew Melody would stand by me no matter what. All that trouble back there, it was a testing period. And then I got sick. Another aspect of the test. If we make it now, nothing will stop us. We've been together twelve years. That's huge."

"Do you think you'll be together forever?"

"I want to grow old with her."

We walked for a while in silence. The blur of red, white, and blue mingled with the oaks and the warmth of the sun. Jeff was holding up, a bit of perspiration gathering on his forehead. I hadn't noticed, but somewhere along the way he'd acquired a walking stick. I wanted him to say, *I'll grow old with you, too, little brother. Someday we'll be frail men walking in the woods with sticks, our children behind us, thick as thieves.*

Jeff said, "Don't rush into marriage, Tone. I did. It's been tough."

"I'm twenty-seven next month," I said. "I'm not rushing anything. You were twenty-two when you got married? I've already got five years of bachelor-hood on you."

This struck a nerve with my brother.

"I guess." He paused. "That means you've probably slept with more women than I have. Than I ever will. Damn. That seems strange. You were such a little thin-lipped dork."

At this he jabbed me in the ribs, and we play-grappled there in the middle of the trail, other walkers looking at us as though we were two crazies come out from the woods.

I said, "What did Dad tell you when you turned sixteen?"

"To never drive drunk. And he gave me a box of condoms and said that Swofford men were blessed and cursed with a high-powered libido. And then he went back to tuning his Jaguar. What did he tell you?"

"The same thing. How old were you when you lost your virginity?"

"Seventeen. In the backseat of my Phoenician Yellow Mustang. No condom. Fifteen seconds, max. You?"

"Seventeen. Cab of my pickup, a Datsun. I used a condom. I think I might have gone for thirty. I dropped the girl off and I rushed home and jumped in the shower and washed my dick with Ajax and Lysol. I got some crazy rash, obviously from the chemicals. I was sure I'd caught AIDS."

"You were one dumb kid."

We laughed.

I said, "Why did you get a tricked-out Mustang for your sixteenth birthday and I got a jalopy pickup truck?"

"I guess Dad liked me more."

"I guess so."

More silence as we walked.

Since Jeff had been diagnosed in February, our father had not visited him. I didn't know what kind of pain, if any, this caused my brother. I considered my father's willful absence completely unconscionable. But I couldn't say so to my brother, for fear that that might cause him further anguish. He had cancer to worry about so why add a dose of absentee father to the wicked emotional cocktail he ingested each day?

"I loved that Mustang," I said. "You picked me up at school in it one day. I felt so cool."

"There is no other smell like the interior of a '66 Mustang. It's a drug."

We finished the hike and returned to the van. Jeff had been correct—he'd had no problem with the three miles. But by the time we made it home, after feeding the kids and gassing the car, he felt exhausted and needed a nap.

The night was a festival of burgers and hot dogs and brats, firecrackers and bottle rockets and shrieking children. I flew home the next day. I wouldn't see Jeff again until November.

AS THE DREAD gray winter chill knocked leaves from their trees and the industrial pall of Nashville thickened, Johnny Cash lay in Baptist Hospital due to heart trouble. Nearby, at the Veterans Hospital attached to Vanderbilt University, Jeff lay dying. He'd recently suffered a number of grand mal seizures that led to the discovery of an apricot-size tumor on his brain.

I thought of the apricot tree in the backyard of the California house where we'd lived as children, and I thought of the sun glowing behind its branches heavy with soft golden fruit, and I thought of my brother running through sprinklers with neighborhood girls, but nothing lifted my gloom.

I'd flown in to be with Jeff and Melody and my sister Kim while Jeff's doctors decided what to do. Eventually they chose to operate.

The night before his surgery I went out to see some jazz at a club downtown: Joshua Redman performing with his band, including the legendary drummer Brian Blade. (Because of his talent he seemed to me decades my senior, but years later I'd discover he's just three weeks older than I am.)

I took a seat alone at the bar, drank a bottle of wine, and enjoyed my first live jazz show. I don't remember a lot about Redman's sax playing because I was so mesmerized by the drumming of Blade. He sounded to me like a maniac, a man totally in love with yet divorced from the sound and rhythms he made. Blade controlled the band and he controlled everyone else in the room too—the bartender took his cues from the drummer, as did the waitresses and every member of the audience. We didn't drink until Blade said drink, we didn't eat until Blade said eat, we didn't shift in our seats until Blade told us to shift in our seats, and we didn't clap like madmen in love with a daring religion until he told us to. It's still one of the best live music shows I've ever seen. After the show I went to the bathroom and found Blade standing at the urinal next to mine. It felt strange to compliment a musician while pissing, but why not?

I said, "Great show, Mr. Blade."

He said, "Thanks." And he nodded and flushed and left.

I made my way out of the club and into the musical chaos of downtown Nashville. In one bar I listened to a teenage girl do religious songs, way off-key and out of pitch. I could see she had the hunger, but hunger is never enough. I heard bad rockabilly and bad country and more bad country.

Outside one bar I asked if there was a Waffle House nearby, and someone pointed me up the road. I made my way up a dimly lit lane, and from the shadows a man called me over.

He said, "Hey, Rockefeller, can't you help a broke feller?"

I was drunk or dumb enough to not be afraid.

I looked at him. I said nothing. I thought about going for my wallet before he did.

"Come on, brother," he said. "I got two girls in my car. Take your pick or take them both."

He put his hand on my arm and squeezed. His fingers were scrawny and scratchy and cold. This guy was as hungry for something as the girl onstage singing Bible songs.

"How about some crack? You smoke cocaine?"

"I don't smoke anything. I'm going to the Waffle House. I'll buy you and your girls some breakfast." Once I spoke, it sounded like an absurd and naïve proposition.

He looked at me, suspicious. He seemed as if he was used to white men lying to him and to paying the price for the white man's lies.

"Seriously, man. I don't want crack or your girls but I'll buy you breakfast."

After he sussed me further he agreed to the meal and said he'd meet me up the hill in five minutes.

The Waffle House is a Southern staple. The food is generally awful and always bad for you. I can't imagine it's possible to escape a Waffle House without ingesting 1,500 calories and a million grams of trans fats. If a food is vaguely Southern and at least partially deep-fried you'll find it on the menu. They might as well serve a shot of deep-fryer oil with your meal the way Russians do vodka. All of this said, I've never not been satisfied after leaving a Waffle House at three or four in the morning.

I settled into a booth and told the waitress that I had a few friends on their way. The restaurant brimmed with the youthful well-heeled of Nashville. I imagined a few lawyers in the bunch, some IT guys, and they were with their girlfriends, professionals as well, lawyers and human resource VPs, and they all put off the slight odor of Greek brotherhood and sisterhood from their college days at Duke or Vanderbilt or Southern Miss.

I'd been out of the Marine Corps for almost five years. The next semester I'd transfer to a respectable university after a four-and-a-half-year slog through community college. These handsome folks, a few of them younger than I, reminded me of the complete and utter failure my life had been. I was twenty-seven, lived with a roommate in a four-hundred-dollar-a-month apartment in downtown Sacramento, and worked the swing shift at a grocery warehouse.

The crack dealer/pimp barged into the Waffle House with his ladies. The harsh fluorescent light did none of the trio any favors. Their clothes were dirty and I could smell them from where I sat. The odors were of the body: sweat, urine, and vaguely, shit. The ladies and gentlemen of the white Southern upwardly mobile were shocked and appalled.

The waitress stepped forward to stop my new friends from advancing farther but I called out, "They're with me."

The waitress, an African American woman in her late thirties who probably held two other jobs and supported a large extended family, was too exhausted to argue with me, but the look on her face was one of complete puzzlement, as if to ponder, *What in the hell is this stupid white boy doing with this crackhead and his hos?*

I don't remember their names but I remember their vacant eyes and the desperation of their breathing and the pure insanity of their minds. I didn't know what crack did to a person's psyche.

Did they know, I wondered, how completely gone they looked, how much like ghosts?

The Southern ladies and gents whispered just below audible levels but I knew they were joking about me and my companions. I stared at a blond girl, the VP of something, and mouthed obscenities. She turned away and mumbled at her date.

The dealer said to me, "Don't mind. Ain' nothing new."

One of his girls—she wore tight jeans and a blue-and-gold plaid shirt tied up like a bikini, braless—threw her menu down and said, "I don't know what I want but I want it smothered and covered!" That meant with cheese food and onions. She let out a cackle, and her friend, in a dirty black Snoop T-shirt, snorted loudly.

Only then did I realize our somewhat awkward seating arrangement: it was a small booth, and the three of them sat mashed together on one side with me on the other. I wondered if they were afraid of me or simply wanted to keep their distance and if at some level I wasn't, because of my whiteness, just like those fucking crackers in all the other booths. I offered to scoot over and have one of the women sit next to me but the dealer, sitting between them, leaned back and put his arms around them both and said, "My girls stick close."

At the time I didn't realize, or didn't want to realize, that I wasn't simply buying breakfast for a trio of down-and-out drug addicts: this man was a pimp and his girls were strung out on drugs; in fact he'd probably strung them out himself, and they had sex with men in order to get more drugs, the drugs that allowed them to blow their minds away and not think about the fact that they were having sex with men for drugs.

SACRAMENTO IS THE capital of West Coast homelessness due to its climate and the numerous public and private relief agencies, and the downtown air is always aflutter with the sound of shopping carts flailing through alleys. Being generous to homeless people seemed like part of the culture. I shared food on my porch with homeless guys, and more than once I gave my couch for the night to a homeless guy we knew as Mr. Incense because he sold incense, and another guy named James Brown because he did spot-on renditions of James Brown songs for all the young, drunk hip kids stumbling from the three bars worth drinking at.

Some nights James Brown made hundreds as kids flush with student loan money threw tens and twenties at his feet while he thrashed through a rendition of "Papa's Got a Brand New Bag." Before

Brian Blade he might have been the only musical genius I'd seen in person.

BUT MAYBE I was just a fucked-up cracker and I thought it was cool and enlightened of me to buy a crew of drug-addled and sex-selling African Americans waffles and fried food at three in the morning in this yuppie town. Does it even matter? We all ate, and we ate well, and we laughed at the yuppies in their blue oxford shirts and khakis and penny loafers. Maybe that's all that mattered: as my brother lay dying a few miles away, his stomach empty for pre-op, his lips chapped and dried and yearning for an ice chip while he waited to be kicked behind the curtain of consciousness by a friendly anesthesiologist, I sat around a trashy, fluorescent-lit, and orange-laminated restaurant and ate like an animal with a few other people, in the middle of the night in Nashville in Tennessee.

We ate waffles and eggs and biscuits and bacon and sausage and fried chicken fingers and fried catfish and French fries and hash browns and fried whatever and most of it arrived smothered and covered with gravy, and we were happy, or I was, and I assumed they were, too, because they laughed with me and we high-fived and we laughed some more at the yuppies.

And then the show closed, a glaze came down over their eyeballs, the night darkened, and they needed to get high now and they needed money now and they needed to exit.

The man said to me, "Sure you don' want a girl?"

Both of the girls stared through me. Did they picture me in the backseat of the Olds, as they'd seen so many other men, sweaty dirty men on top of and inside them, whimpering because they couldn't get it up? Or just stupid, stupid men sleeping with prostitutes in the backseat of a broken-down car, ruining further these already broken-down lives?

"Nah, man," I said.

To pull the girls from their daze he squeezed them on the shoulders. They all three dragged themselves from the booth. It seemed as though they weighed a thousand pounds each, such was their effort to move their bodies.

The girls walked on ahead and out of the restaurant without saying goodbye. Some of the yuppies stared but most didn't care anymore. They were drunk and smothered and covered and that's exactly why they'd come downtown tonight.

The man looked at me and said, "Can you help me out?"

I pulled sixty dollars from my wallet and put it in his dry, scratchy palm.

He said, "Thanks. And for breakfast. I ain't eat that much in a long time."

He shuffled out. I sat for a while in the booth, looking at the detritus of our feast, looking at the glare and shame of the restaurant, the beckon to eat cheaply and to eat a lot and to not care about what goes in your body. I thought about the crackhead and his prostitutes and what they'd soon be putting in their bodies, what they'd been putting in their bodies for years.

I looked at my watch. It was four in the morning. In an hour my brother would be awakened by a nurse and wheeled from his room toward the operating room. He might die in there: they were opening his skull and extracting a ruined piece of brain.

I wandered around the city and attempted to grab a cab but there were none. It wasn't so far to my hotel and the hospital, so I walked. Along the way a man approached me from a side street. It took me a moment to recognize the same man I'd just fed.

His eyes as glassy and pocked as the full moon, he said to me, "Hey, Rockefeller, can't you help a broke feller?"

MY BROTHER FELL in love with Melody in the way that all Swofford men fall in love with beautiful women: madly and passionately, screaming down the street at three thousand miles an hour with their jockstraps on fire.

They met at a talent night on Fort Ord Army Base in Monterey, California. She'd arrived with a date and she left with my brother. Jeff sang a song— let's say it was "More Than a Feeling" by Boston. Because the event occurred on base no booze was served, but the GIs knew how to get around this, filling their soda cups from the mess with whiskey.

He had been with only two women in his life. He was a twenty-one-year-old enlisted dental hygienist. He'd dropped out of college a year before, after losing his football scholarship. His hair was as red as the core of the Earth and he'd ripped his physique down to 3 percent body fat. The freckles all over his white skin looked like small suns.

Melody cut a vaguely Mediterranean figure through the piney hills around Monterey. She, too, spent many hours a week in the gym and had the dark tan skin of a bodybuilder, though it came naturally. Later the two of them would laugh, in bed, when comparing their skins.

But this first night they went off base to a bar in town and had a few beers. The bar fancied itself a roadhouse or honky-tonk of sorts, a stopping place for wayward urban cowboys posing as GIs.

Jeff ordered cheap beers and cheap shots and

they sat in a booth while all around them beer signs and country music and drunken GIs rioted.

"So where are you from?" Jeff asked.

"I was born on Long Island, where my parents ran an antiques shop. During the gas crisis they went bust. And we moved to Lanesboro and opened up another shop. We pulled into town, a caravan of crazy. Two vans, six children, seven dogs, fourteen cats, and two monkeys. That little town had never seen anything like it."

"Monkeys," Jeff said. "Where is Lanesboro?"

"Oh, right." She laughed and ran her hands through her hair. "It's in Minnesota. Bed-and-breakfast capital of Minnesota, they call it. I'm not sure why."

"Lots of bed-and-breakfasts?" Jeff asked with a smirk.

"No more than any other town. Where are you from?"

"All over. Military brat. Washington State. Seville, Spain. Tokyo. Vacaville. Sacramento. I guess Sacramento is kind of a home. My family lives there. I dropped out of college after two years."

"Why did you do that?"

"Boredom, I guess. I lived in a football house off campus. I got a few tryouts with pro teams. I went hiking in Nepal. Did journalistic work in South

America. There was talk of me doing some speech-writing for Reagan."

"But you hadn't even graduated college."

"Neither did Andrew Jackson."

"Oh, geez," she said, and he heard the Midwesterner in her and he liked it. "What kind of lies will you tell me on our next date?"

"I'll pick you up at your barracks tomorrow at six. Clint Eastwood is loaning me his Ferrari."

AT JEFF'S FUNERAL the elephant in the room was his lies. He had never been a drunk, so no one could talk about his drinking. A few times during his chemo he smoked pot to keep the nausea at bay, but I doubt he took drugs at any other time in his life. He wasn't a womanizer. He didn't beat his wife or children.

But he lied. He didn't tell small lies, he told monster lies, the kind of lies that the listener was incapable of refuting. The listener might be able to say, "Ah, man, you're full of it." Jeff would laugh right along, and blow some more heat into the lie.

Thus, when he talked about having a walk-on tryout with the San Francisco 49ers football team, the first lie was a small one, a jest over a few beers one Sunday football afternoon, drinking with the guys from the church. Throw it out and see if anyone bites.

"I once caught a few passes from Joe Montana," Jeff says.

"Yeah, right. Me, too," his listener replies.

"It was 1984. I was trying to figure out what to do with myself. I screwed up academically and lost my scholarship at Sacramento State. But I knew I was a receiver. I was a born receiver."

And here Jeff would force his hands into the listener's face: he did have big hands, big strong football-catching hands. The listener would compare them to his own small hands and think, *Well, shit yeah, this guy could catch some footballs with those hands.*

And Jeff says, "The Niners' summer camp was up in Rocklin, you know, just twenty miles up the road from downtown Sacto. So one day I'm on my couch, trying to figure out my future, and I think, 'Why don't I try out for the Niners? What's to stop me from walking on and catching some passes and showing them I've got juice? I run a 4.2 forty.'"

And the listener whistles and says, "That's fast for a white boy."

The fact is very few people on the face of the Earth can run a 4.2 forty-yard dash. This must dawn on the listener. Jeff moves toward the listener. He thinks he's losing him.

Jeff's muscular legs are as hard as an oak. He stands. He flexes his legs, his quads and hamstrings taut, and he takes the listener's hand and puts it on his leg and says, "Squeeze. All of that is muscle. That is how I run a 4.2 forty. Yes, I am fast for a white boy."

And the listener nods.

Jeff says, "So I'm in Rocklin, and I just walk up to the fence. I've got my gear on. Little kids press their faces to the wire, fathers are reliving their glory days, there is Jerry Rice, there is Montana, there are footballs flying everywhere, whistles blowing, grown men yelling, other grown men crying, doubled over in pain. I see a guy in coach shorts, a whistle around his neck. I say, 'Hey, Coach. I'm a receiver. Give me a chance.'"

The listener says, "Just like that, you tell a coach to give you a chance? You're just a chump who walks up from the parking lot."

"But the coach," Jeff says, "the coach is trained to spot desire and talent. And he sees both in me, he sees fire."

And at Jeff's funeral, in the church foyer before the service begins, the listener walks up to me, the dead man's brother; the listener is now the dead man's mouthpiece, the carrier of the dead man's lie.

The listener says to me, "Man, your brother lived a crazy life. A full life. I just been in this little Georgia town my whole life. I admit I used to live a little through his stories. Can you imagine catching a touchdown pass from Joe Montana? I know it was just an exhibition game. But still. It was against the Raiders. Your brother caught a winning touchdown pass from Joe Montana against the hated Raiders. How many men can say that?"

"Not many," I say. "Not with a straight face, at least. Yeah, I guess I'd forgotten about that."

"How the heck could you forget that? I loved hearing him tell that story. A seventy-yard touchdown bomb from Joe Montana, fighting Mike Haynes off his back. Life don't get better."

Lies don't get better either. I look through the foyer to the front of the church, through the old ladies shuffling sideways across the aisles, through my uncles and aunts and cousins finding their seats, to Jeff's closed coffin.

The man dies. His deeds remain. And so, too, his lies.

My younger sister Kim corners me, mortified. "Oh, Jesus Christ," she says. "Some guy just told me about Jeff working with the CIA in Berlin. What the hell else will we hear?"

We will hear about the time he sang with the Mormon Tabernacle Choir.

We will hear about the time in Tokyo as a teenager when he practiced kung fu with Bruce

Lee even though Bruce Lee died a year before we moved to Tokyo.

We will hear about the time Clint Eastwood loaned him a Ferrari for a date with a married woman. We will hear that the married woman's husband showed up at the hotel room carrying a shotgun and demanded that his wife leave the room; and somehow Clint Eastwood appeared, looking for his Ferrari, it would seem, and Clint Eastwood defused the situation, sent the married man home without his wife.

We will hear about the time he danced in Michael Jackson's "P.Y.T. (Pretty Young Thing)" video.

Jeff's son is at my side. He's a cute little five-year-old boy and he looks just like my brother. He has no idea that all these people are here to say goodbye to his father forever. He has no idea what forever means. He knows that for some reason his father is in the metal box at the front of this room. He knows that the tie around his neck is constricting and that the suit pants are scratchy and that he had to take a bath early this morning. He knows that his mother and his grandmothers and his aunts and uncles and all the adults in his life are crying.

Because my father has refused to attend Jeff's funeral I am the only adult Swofford male in our line. I lead the death procession, little Christian's hand in mine. We sit in the first pew, far right. Christian sits on my lap. He hugs my neck, and he cries, and he asks me, "Why is Daddy in the box?"

I can't answer him. I don't know how to say, "Daddy is dead." The three words, they are too cruel for his ears.

I kiss the boy on the cheek, and I smooth his pretty red hair.

The preacher talks about the things that Christian preachers talk about: salvation, the spirit; the afterlife, God's Army: this is garbage to me, smoke and mirrors.

A man is dead. The man is my older brother. His five-year-old son sits crying in my lap. That is all. That is the everything and the nothing of this day.

There was a military honor guard. They fired rifle blanks and I flinched at each report; they folded a flag and handed it to Melody. The corpse-laden hearse drove off to the funeral home, where later a worker whose name I'll never know would incinerate my brother's body.

The February Atlanta day was crisp but not bitterly cold. Back at the house, in the yard, I threw a football with Christian. We did not speak of his father. We threw the football. We played catch with a baseball. We shot hoops in the driveway. I wondered if Jeff also had some pro basketball and baseball lies that he bandied about. I hadn't heard them, but I wouldn't put it past him.

In the house my mother and sisters and Melody and a few of my aunts and uncles told stories about Jeff. Some of these stories would probably qualify as lies, or aberrations, but can you really lie about a dead man? The dead man is not present: he can neither confirm nor deny the reports. Death is the ultimate Fifth Amendment.

I remember that we drank some wine that day. No one called my father and he didn't call us.

I wanted to call and shame him for not being there, but I did not possess the courage. I knew that while nearly a hundred members of his nuclear and extended family buried his son in Douglasville, Georgia, my father sat in a shitty dive bar in Fairfield, California, getting drunk with other sad men. I knew the bar. I knew the pungent smell of the place, the combination of booze and vomit and industrial-strength cleaning supplies. I know what it is like to waste months or years of one's life drinking in one of these bars. Mine is on West Nineteenth Street in Manhattan.

I called my girlfriend in Sacramento. I felt bad for not having invited her to the funeral. I'd boxed her out. We both cried on the phone. She said she loved me, and she did, but I was unable to believe her. Within months we'd break up.

Later that night when enough wine had been consumed that we were all a little drunk, Melody asked me to follow her into the garage.

"I want you to have Jeff's pistol," she said as she pulled the plastic case from behind a toolbox.

She opened the case. It was a beautiful Czech handgun, a CZUB semiautomatic .45 caliber.

She said, "I want you to hold on to this until Christian is old enough to own it. And then I want you to teach him how to shoot."

"I don't want a gun around," I said. "When I get back to California, I'll figure out a way to have it shipped to me. And I'll store it in a safe-deposit box. I don't—"

I stopped. The nearer truth was: I didn't trust myself with a gun in the house. I might blow my brains out.

"OK, fine. There's something else."

She fumbled through the toolbox and retrieved an envelope and handed it to me.

"Jeff would want you to have this," she said. "It's a thousand dollars."

"Why would Jeff want me to have this? I don't need it. I have a job. What were you saving it for? And why was it stuffed in a toolbox?"

"It was an emergency fund. That's all. Or vacation. I don't know. Just take it. Buy yourself something nice."

I felt like I was being bought off, but I didn't know what for.

I shoved the envelope in my suit pocket and returned with Melody to the dining room table, where my now-drunk mother cried uncontrollably, her head buried in her hands. I sat down next to her and rubbed her back.

Somewhere in the house Christian screamed for his mother. We found him curled up in Jeff's hospice bed, the green flannel Jeff wore when he died wrapped around his body.

This was the same room where Jeff had, a few nights before, asked me to take Jesus into my heart and life. It would have been easy for me to tell Jeff that I'd do this for him. He was in and out of a morphine cloud. I'd been reading to him the Christian inspirational verses he'd requested.

"Brother," he said, "I want you to live a good life. I want you to have a family. You need God for a family. For cohesion."

I said, "You know I'm an atheist. I have been since I went to war. I respect your beliefs. I just don't believe them."

"Pray with me," he said.

"I can't, Jeff. It wouldn't be right. It would make a joke of us both. I love you. I love your family. I love your children. I will do anything for your family. What do you need from me?"

"Let's pray for you."

"No prayers, Brother. Let's talk. What will your family need?"

"Mel has it covered. She knows. You're just a kid. Make your own family. Someday you'll find God."

I wanted, more than anything, to tell my brother that he was right, and that one day I would find God, but none of that would have been true.

I did say, "I will have a family someday. And I will be a good husband and father. And I will tell my children about you and how much I loved you. I can promise you that."

I read some more from the verses, poorly written inspirational Christian drivel. Jeff stopped me. He needed to piss.

He couldn't walk on his own. He asked me to carry him to the bathroom across the hall. I cradled his body and I carried him down the hall. His skeleton pressed against my body. Where once there had been so much muscle there was now only bone and skin. His chin rested on my shoulder and I felt his faint breath against my ear.

He wore the green flannel and gray sweats. I steadied him in front of the bowl and helped him shimmy the elastic-waistband sweats down his bony hips.

"I am happy to piss on my own," he said. "I need to keep pissing on my own. When I can no longer piss standing up I want this to end."

I looked at my brother's dick. It was shaped like mine, a natural bend toward the right. It was about the same size. He had no pubic hair. His piss was dark yellow with a faint trace of blood: the water in the toilet bowl looked as though a teaspoon of saffron had been dropped in.

"I haven't fucked in so long," he said. "I don't even know what sex is. Or what it means. I wish I could fuck my wife once more. No. I wish I could live and keep fucking her for the rest of my life."

I helped him back to bed. My mother and Melody came into his room. They administered another morphine patch and Jeff floated away.

I called Iris and met her at the Waffle House by the interstate. We ate the usual greasy mess of food. I didn't want to eat, though. I wanted to fuck. I wanted to fuck for my brother.

We jumped in her car and drove around for a while, our usual trip, the Velvet Underground our musical guides, from old church to old church, from cemetery to cemetery. It was late now, past midnight. I asked her to drive to my brother's house. We'd had sex here before, in the spare room, on the ground floor where Jeff now slept in his hospice bed. We entered the dark and quiet house through the downstairs patio.

I held Iris's hand and I walked her into Jeff's room. A reading light at the side of his bed lit his wan face. She stared at him for a moment and then she followed me down to the floor.

I heard my brother's soft breathing.

Iris giggled. "What are you doing?"

I took her shirt off. And her bra.

"Jesus," she said.

Yes, Jesus, I thought. I kissed her and took her breasts in my mouth.

"Jesus," she said.

She slid down my body and took me out of my pants. I looked at my brother. I thought his eyes were open but I couldn't tell. I thought I saw a smile, but I couldn't tell. I wanted him to watch.

I pulled her on top of me. I had never had sex in front of someone else before and here I was inside a woman in front of my dying brother. I was usually a fairly attentive lover but this time I was not. I was hard and I was deep inside Iris and I pulled her hips roughly against mine and all I thought of was my dying brother: his gap-toothed smile as a carrot-topped little boy; his high school football number, twenty-two; I thought of his Phoenician Yellow '66 Mustang; about playing catch with him in the yard, the way he taught me to use the laces on the football; I thought of his once-powerful body and I thought of women riding him, I thought of my brother fucking Iris; I closed my eyes and I saw him under the sexy young Iris and I saw myself dying in his hospice bed.

THE NEXT DAY occurred the party Jeff had summoned me for. And for the first time since Jeff had become ill, my father traveled from California to visit his dying son. I know that Jeff and Dad spent some time alone. I don't know what was said.

I do know that while a number of my aunts and uncles and cousins hung out in Jeff's living room and played guitars and sang songs, just as Jeff had wanted for his Dying Party, my father had cajoled me into joining him in a search for a bar that served his brand of scotch. I knew nothing about scotch at this point. Later I would know that other than a sexy ad campaign, this particular scotch had little going for it. But it was my dad's drink and in these dry and half-dry and downright parched counties of the South, a man sometimes had to work hard to find a bar with his particular brand of scotch.

"Goddamn," my father said as we left yet another sports bar, out of luck. "I know when I was back here in '92 those guys had my Chivas. You can get a pot of black-eyed peas on every corner but they're damn near to kill you looking for your scotch. I got another idea."

I wanted to say, *I have an idea. Why don't we go back to Jeff's house and hang out with him and the rest of the family, since he's going to die in a matter of days, and the reason we are here is to spend time with him before he dies, not in shitty roadside bars all over Douglas County looking for your scotch?*

To my great shame I did not say this. I spent the afternoon and into the evening driving around the hills and towns of West Georgia while my father looked for a bar that poured his scotch. We'd pop into a place and have a beer, or a lesser scotch, and then head back out on the road. I suppose that if I worked hard I could turn this search of my father's into something symbolic, epic even. But it was neither symbolic nor epic. The search was sad and pathetic, my father's sick and deranged attempt to stay away from his dying son and his family. But wait, I could make this day about me and my father, my father's choice to bond with me, the living and thriving son: the father choosing to hunker down in the cave with the young, healthy son while out in the wilderness animals devoured the older son.

No, that doesn't work either. The only thing that works is this: my father was a coward. And so was I.

By the time we returned to Jeff's house the party had ended and the place was quiet and smelled of the dying: that humid, earthy smell of failing flesh. I went downstairs to apologize to Jeff for missing the party, but he was already so high on morphine he had no idea I was even there.

A FEW DAYS after Jeff's funeral Melody called and asked me if I could convince my mother to watch the kids for the night while the two of us went out for dinner. I was leaving the next day and she wanted to talk before I left.

I dropped my mom off at the house for her babysitting duties. An animated movie of the Disney variety played on the TV. Melody always kept an extremely clean and tidy house, and the death of her husband had not changed this.

We drove to a strip mall nearby and went to a chain restaurant. Melody ordered a massive drink, a quart of blue liquor, the glass festooned with fruit and umbrellas. Bad pop music blared from scratchy speakers. The server looked at us intently while reading the specials, though there was nothing special about the specials. I'm certain that I ordered enchiladas. I drank one beer. Melody ordered another blue drink, and a playful and mischievous drunkenness descended upon her. I saw why my brother had fallen in love with her.

She told me stories about the years they lived in Munich. She talked about how sexy they had both been. They were gym rats, and everyone on base envied their bodies. Even after children, she said, they still had a sex life.

"Even when we fought," she said, "even then, we made sure to keep up a sex life. It's important."

I didn't want to hear my brother's widow talk about their sex life. I changed the subject to the children, or the weather. But she kept coming back to sex.

"God, he was a great lover. If it's there, you think it will always be there. And then he got sick. And it was gone. Like that, in a day, gone. At first we tried some things. Alternate things. At one meeting for cancer spouses they even had a pamphlet for it. Cancer sex. Can you believe it?"

She slapped the table hard enough to tilt and

spill her drink a bit, the blue liquor cresting the levee of the glass.

"But that didn't work. I won't lie. I thought about other men. But I never did anything. A few men from the church made advances, but I pushed them away."

This got my attention: some dirtbag hit on my dying brother's wife? Where was he? I'd kill the bastard.

"Once." She paused. "I shouldn't say this. But once I thought of you. It seemed—it seemed normal. My dying husband's little brother. Isn't that how they used to do things?"

I didn't know if I had heard her correctly. Had she just said that she had thought of sex with me and that it had seemed normal? That was not normal. My brother's ashes weren't even in the ground. None of this was normal.

The waiter approached and she motioned for another round of drinks.

"Melody," I said. "You've had two huge drinks. That's probably enough. Let's get the check."

"I don't want the check. I want another drink! My husband is dead and I want another drink!"

Some heads turned and looked our way.

"OK," I said. "Have another. I just. I don't know what to say. I really don't."

"You're such a child," she said. "You will always be the baby. Your brother is dead but you are still the baby boy. As long as your father is alive you are the baby boy."

She told me that for many years she had thought the demons visited upon my brother by my father would never dissipate, but that they finally had when Christian was born.

"One child," she said, "was not enough for your brother to get out from under the sway of your father. But Christian did it. Christian was the magic bullet. Suddenly your father no longer haunted him. They became friends. I couldn't believe it."

She pulled a box from her purse.

"Here, it's Jeff's watch. It's a cheap thing. But take it. Keep it. And I still want you to take the pistol. Give it to Christian when he's eighteen. Will you do that?"

"I'll do whatever you ask." I'd do anything to get out of the booth, out of the restaurant, out of this time zone.

"Tell me about when you had sex with that girl in Jeff's room."

Melody had once chased Iris out of the house. It was the first night we'd slept together, the first time I'd come out to visit Jeff after his diagnosis. We'd parked her jalopy in the driveway and it leaked oil all over Jeff's pristine concrete. He'd been pissed. Melody had kicked at the locked bedroom door and told me to get the girl out of the house. We'd sneaked out the back and later in the day I'd spent hours washing the oil stain from the driveway.

"I saw you come home late with her that night last week. I saw you sneak around the back."

"Yes. I snuck her in. I had sex with her on the floor of Jeff's room."

She slapped the table again, harder. "I told your mother. I'll tell everyone in the family. They'll think you're sick."

"Maybe I am."

I'd been caught. But I didn't believe that she had told my mother or that she would tell anyone else. It wasn't her style. Melody liked owning secrets.

"Did he watch?" she asked.

"I don't want to talk about this. That was between Jeff and me. Maybe it was wrong. I don't know."

"Yes. It was wrong."

She finished her drink and I paid the bill.

I drove toward their subdivision.

"Let's get another drink somewhere," she said.

"I need to grab my mother and get back to Granny's and sleep. I have an early flight and I have to work at the warehouse tomorrow night. I'm already two over my grief days."

"How much do they pay you for a grief day?"

"It's normal pay," I said.

I realized she was toying with me.

"Use your grief pay to buy me another drink. I need a grief drink. I need to feel normal!" she screamed.

I continued toward their subdivision. As I pulled into the settlement Melody put her hand on my thigh and said, "Take me into the woods. Like your brother would have."

I slowed the car down. I felt a hollow sickness in my stomach, the vomitous stirring of my insides. I started to sweat and my field of vision sank down to a tunnel, straight ahead.

She said, "You can't. You're not a man like your brother. You are still a boy. But you want to. I saw the way you used to look at me when I first married Jeff. I caught you once, playing in our laundry at your parents' house, looking at my underwear."

This could very well have been true but I didn't remember it.

I said, "I was fourteen years old. I looked at any pretty woman that way. It's called puberty."

"Your brother would laugh at you, just laugh. He said you'd never get laid, what a sad case. Your mommy still cut your hair. You were such a dorky kid. We had a bet. He thought you'd be a virgin until you turned thirty. You're a boy. Still a baby boy."

I pulled into the driveway and turned off the car.

I said, "Mel, I'm going to go upstairs and sit with my mom and your children. I'm going to sit there for as long as you need. You stay here in the car. You think about Jeff. You think about your children. Think about yourself. We'll be up there playing games and laughing. You just sit here, and think about what you need from life. And I'll be upstairs with my mother and the kids. And when you want to join us, come on up."

Half an hour later she walked in the door.

Christian asked, "Mommy, where were you?"

"I just went for a walk, honey. I needed a walk. Did you have fun with Grandma and Uncle Tony?"

ON MY WAY to the airport I swung by the cemetery. There were already two Swofford men buried here, my grandfather and my uncle. I didn't know when they were going to inter Jeff. The Swofford plot was at the top of the hill, at the deep right curve of the horseshoe drive. I knew its position well. When I was a boy, every time we visited Georgia my father took us to look at his brother's headstone. I could find my way there in the dark.

As I banked toward the plots I saw two cemetery workers in the Swofford grounds. One man leaned against a shovel and another man sat atop a small backhoe, working the blade into the earth, working out the dirt, making way for my brother's ashes.

YEARS LATER, WHEN I begin to try to write about my brother I sort through boxes of notes, years of notes and photographs. I find an official Army portrait of my brother when he must have been going for a promotion. He's thirty or so and handsome in his rugged tough-guy-soldier way.

I find my DD-214, the military discharge, and also the DD-214s of my brother and father. And I find a note in my mother's perfect cursive script. The word *Jeff.* The words *Nurses Station.* And a phone number. I call the number. It is the VA hospital in Nashville. They instruct the caller to call the VA's 888 suicide hotline number if it is an emergency.

Well, is it?

5

Letter from My Father

On October 10, 2006, my father mailed to me a nine-page handwritten letter postmarked Sacramento, CA. The missives are dated July 06; August 06; August 10-06; Sun, August 13, 2006 (a day after my thirty-sixth birthday); Oct 4, 2006; Oct 8, 2006. All the entries but the last are written on one side of college-lined white paper with one-inch margins and three-ring holes. The last entry is written on the back of the eighth page: at two and a half lines it is the shortest of the lot, a haiku of the epistolary fistfight:

> *I have sat on this for much too long. The more I sit the longer it grows. It is well past time to shred or mail. So mail here it comes.*
> *With Love,*
> *Your Father*

With sickening clarity I remember removing this letter from my mailbox. It must have been the thirteenth or fourteenth of October. I'd had dinner at the apartment of my best friend, more a brother than a friend. Let's say we'd eaten delivery of some pan-Asian sort, the kind readily available in Midtown. Once their two kids had gone to bed after fighting the sleep demons for a while, Oren and Yael and I would have stayed up for an hour or so talking and drinking more wine, listening to music, getting drunk but not wasted, just drunk enough for a weekend night when the next day everyone had work to do.

Yael would have retired first, probably to sleep for a while with one of the restless children.

I would have sought Oren's counsel on the matter of my deteriorating relationship with Ava. We'd recently taken a number of breaks, meaning we'd cheated extensively on each other. From early on Oren had told me to leave her and he would have done the same thing again tonight. "Nothing good can come of this" is a typical Oren comment about my relationship with Ava. "Don't you want a family and real love?" Yes, I wanted a family and real love; yes, I needed to leave Ava in order to have a family and real love.

I walked home that night, twenty-seven blocks

south and nine avenues west, a short city walk. At a bar or two along the way I beat the temptations of drink and women and kept on toward home. I called Ava and she didn't pick up. I guessed she was in a dank bar in the East Village, snorting cocaine in the bathroom with a man she'd just met. I knew the bar and the bathroom, but not the man.

I entered my building and checked my mail for the first time that week. I sifted through the various generic mailers and the other waste, tossed it in the recycling bin, and found among the remaining envelopes a thickish cream-colored one adorned with my father's recognizable steep script.

I thought, *This is the letter you've been waiting for.*

My father wrote a curse letter to my brother when Jeff was twenty-three. When Jeff died twelve years later my younger sister found it among his effects, in a binder, in protective wrapping. She and I read the letter together and wept.

We wept for our brother, our father, the death of our family, and the calamity in script we were experiencing, the father killing his son, the father backing his son against the stone firing wall.

In his memoirs Elias Canetti writes that the most awful thing a father can do is curse his son. Cursing a son is an invitation to the destruction of the family. Canetti's grandfather cursed his father and shortly after his father, a young and prosperous businessman, fell dead at the table.

SO WHEN I held the envelope in my hand, kind of drunk, rather heartbroken over a beautiful and fucked-up woman, thirty-six and alone in New York City, I knew these pages contained a curse from my father. I put the letter, unopened, in my top desk drawer.

AND ONE NIGHT a few weeks later I opened it.

Dear Tony,

July 06 [2006]

I write this because your schedule makes it impossible to have a sit down conversation or a meaningful telephone conversation. There are a couple of reasons why I am reluctant to do this. First it is the type of thing I think should be discussed in person rather than one-way communication. Secondly if you decide to save it—years from now someone may find and read it—assume it is something; it is not. Just as you assumed my letter to Jeff was my reply to his attorney letter. I have never seen that letter. I gave you a pass on that. The divorce was between your mom and me. I tried to keep you kids out of it. Some way you and Jeff got involved but not by my doing. Had you wanted to know—? Why the letter—? Why not ask?

My father is correct that at this point in my life my schedule made it tough for me to have a sit-down conversation. I lived in New York and he lived in California and I traveled often. And I was loath to have an important conversation about our relationship and my childhood over the phone. A friend of mine had recently been in therapy with her father in California, and I had for many months considered offering this option to my father: I'd fly out to California twice a month and we could sit with a psychotherapist to try to figure it out. But I spent enough time with my own therapist talking about my father that to add two more sessions a month might well have killed me. And my father is not exactly the therapy type.

The "attorney letter" he speaks of is a letter that my brother wrote to my mother's attorney that was put forth for the record in their divorce, wherein my brother outlined the various ways in which my father was verbally and occasionally physically abusive to his children, mostly my older brother and sister. I can't imagine that my father never saw this letter, and in fact in the letter he wrote to Jeff he referenced it. In return for this letter my father sent my older brother a scathing letter attacking his character and his manhood and challenging him to a physical fight.

The Cub/Boy scout thing was the first week or the first and second week. To that time you had only had overnight and weekend visits with buddies, a week would be your longest time away from home. This being your first summer camp I was sure you would be ready to leave after the first week. I explained it would be better to plan for two weeks the following year, which did not make it into your book. But you the big tough guy insisted on two weeks. I would have been an asshole to keep you from going two weeks. Turns out I was an asshole after all, trying to teach my young son that mature people keep their word or if not take responsibility for the convenience it cost others.

This camp episode is addressed in my first book. I wanked out of Boy Scout camp a week early and my father insisted I repay him for the second week that I missed. I hated camp. I couldn't tie knots,

I was horrible at fishing, I had no friends, and I couldn't, for the life of me, get my hands around that greased-down watermelon as it floated atop the pristine High Sierra lake.

I missed my mother. Of course I came home early. So he was right. And maybe, years later, I was being a little punk to complain in writing about having had to repay him. But should twelve-year-olds be taught about maturity? Shouldn't they just be welcomed home and given another chance the next year, no questions asked? Perhaps a father should offer a model of maturity rather than a lecture on maturity? If life is all lessons, when the hell is a kid supposed to have fun?

But you the big tough guy. My father wastes no time getting straight to the gut shots and questions of manhood, even mocking the twelve-year-old me.

So, he seems to be saying, *you thought you were so tough when you were twelve, and how about now? I've got this pen in my hand, writer boy, and I'm going to kick your ass with it.*

In fact I hadn't thought I was tough: I had thought I was a weak, cowardly little boy and my father was more than happy to support me in this conclusion.

He doesn't even suggest that a reason he may have wanted me to go for just one week was that he would have missed me. But maybe he wouldn't have missed me at all.

My friend Oren is a wreck when his kids are at camp. He can't sleep. He calls it abnormal. He says, "You have children so they sleep under your roof, not to send them away to camp." If my father had similar feelings, he might have just told me.

There are other things you wrote that did not happen and others much different than the way you remember. Friends and family have inquired and said I must have been a real bastard. Which put me in the awkward position of explaining various parts of your book. Some of which I failed to recall, requiring a return read of the subject, which at times made me think you intentionally portrayed me as a "real bastard." You get a pass on that.

Truthfully the man *was* a real bastard. I spent most of my childhood in fear of my father. Rarely did I do the right thing. Rarely was he pleased. I understand that he might have different memories of events, but it is not my fault his son became a writer.

No one else will write about my father so I am his writer. And in the act of writing I hope to become again his loving son.

Everyone must understand: when someone writes a memoir people get scorched.

A couple of friends asked for autographed copies of JARHEAD. *Since I had to buy my own, I knew you would not furnish them one. It would have been an embarrassment to me having to tell them that my bestselling author son is such a cheap ass. I had to buy my own— so you'll have to buy yours. I purchased copies for them which you so graciously autographed. Kim offered to buy me the book on CD but I told her you had half-assed said you would send me one. Maybe it will happen some time when I am still on the green side of the turf. She did buy me the music from the movie. I just purchased the movie for myself so cancel that request. Your continued failure to send Art* [an old Air Force buddy of my father's] *a book and his continued asking embarrassed your mother so much that she sent him one. But she would never admit to this as being irresponsible on your part. Life is better if some things are never said. Just as my thoughts here may be, as I believe some should not be in your book, I took as first-timer's gloating. After the movie release the maliciousness continued.*

What is causing the unexplained behavior?
Maybe you await a certain reaction. If so this
may be it.

I sent my father one copy of the galley and three of the hardcover of *Jarhead*. For some reason he doesn't recall receiving them. And I explained to him that my publisher gave me only forty copies of my book and that there were a number of people I needed to send books to—former teachers, old friends, friends of the family. I also explained to him that if I went out and bought a book for everyone who asked me for one I'd be making about negative twenty dollars per hardcover, which seems like a foolish way to make a living—writing already being a foolish enough plan for making money. I know that my father wanted me to provide books to all of his bar and military cronies and some of the men who worked for him; I simply didn't think it was my responsibility.

And here is where I get angry for the first time, when he calls me a cheap-ass. He doesn't know the money I've provided to my niece for rent and some help with college tuition. He doesn't know the number of times I've bailed my older sister out of debt. He doesn't know that I'm paying my younger sister's university tuition and textbook costs. He

doesn't know that I'm paying for a medical procedure my aunt in Pakistan must undergo. He doesn't
know I paid my brother's widow's mortgage for
six months. He doesn't know any of this because
I would never tell him. I am not a cheap-ass. I just
thought that if my father was so proud of his son
he wouldn't mind going down to the bookstore
and buying a few copies of the book for his buddies. Or, rather, tell them, "Go buy copies yourself,
how do you think the little shit makes money?"

*The purpose of this is an attempt to discover
why you keep adding distance between us—do
I contribute? A reply is not expected but perhaps
I will find the answer, as I continue.*

This is the first place in the letter where my
father posits that he might be responsible for some
of the distance between us. In typical John Howard fashion he asks the question and then tells me
that I need not reply. By writing on, he'll figure
the answer out himself. But does he even want to
know if he contributes?

*I would like to know more about your
activities but I ask little, as you seem to feel it
is an intrusion. I have asked you to do only a*

*few things, but repeated requests have brought
no results. I had hoped they could at least
have been put in the form of a present—trip
present—Christmas present—return from
Europe present—Father's day present—
Birthday present. Fake hope. Several months
ago I repeated my request. You said that your
novel was completed and you were going to
spend the next couple weeks catching up on
things. I had been unable to shame you into
granting my requests but hoped that would be
included in "catching up." Now after many
months I see they are of no importance and I
not much more.*

I know a bit about shame. My father built a roof
of shame for his family to live under. You do not
shame your father with your poor manners. You
do not shame your father with stupidity in public. You do not shame your father by asking foolish
questions. You do not shame your father by talking
to adults, by speaking unless you have been spoken to. This shame turned me into a treacherous
little kid: I was sneaky, I was a liar, I trained my
hearing so whenever I heard my name, anywhere
in the house, I'd pick up on the fluctuations and
intonations of the voices so that even if I couldn't

hear all the words, I knew the intentions of the conversation: Tony will be grounded for not doing his chores. Tony will not go to Scott Seltzer's house for a sleepover. Tony's allowance will be reduced for eight weeks.

The thing my father didn't understand about shame was that once the son is in his early twenties the father can't shame him. In fact, the attempts of the father to shame the son look, to the son, like little more than feeble attempts to regain a control lost many years ago. So my father's attempts at shaming me backfired.

And I wondered why, suddenly, when I'd had some success, he chose to become so involved in my life. He'd never been involved in my life when I was a boy, an adolescent, a teenager, or a young man. The other Little League parents thought that my mother was a single mother because over my six years of playing ball my father never came to watch one game or pick me up from a single practice.

Once when I was in college he gave me two hundred dollars for books. When I loaded my rental truck to move for grad school he showed up and bought my buddies pizza and later took us out to a strip club. When at grad school in Iowa I eloped, he sent me and my bride a card and fifty bucks and he failed to show up for the marriage party at my mother's house, an hour's drive away from his. He didn't even bother to call.

You make trips to the area but no time to stop, not even time for a fuck-you phone call.

He's correct: there were times I traveled to Sacramento or the Bay Area and didn't spend time with him. There were other times when I went out of my way to make sure I saw my father and that we shared a meal or a few drinks.

And there is this, which he fails to recall or mention: during the spring of 2006 he'd been feeling rather fatigued each afternoon, and this, coupled with some low-level anxiety, had led the doctors to assume that there might be something amiss with his heart. All his other tests came back normal— his blood work was fine, they didn't find a bleed on his brain, there were no signs of a stroke, so they decided to go into his heart, take a look around, and most likely they'd insert a stent.

We talked on the phone about the procedure and I could tell that my father was quite nervous. I told him I'd come out. It was a Sunday afternoon, and his procedure was Tuesday. I booked an early flight out of JFK for Tuesday, which would put me in the Bay Area right around the time they'd be rolling him out of surgery.

I felt like a good son, like I was doing the right thing by my father and my family. After my brother's death we'd all been rather hospital-averse, so I thought being there with my younger sister, for my father, was the only right thing to do.

I took a flight at a hideously early hour and landed in San Francisco at around ten a.m. As soon as we touched down I frantically called my sister for some news, any news. I called my mother in Sacramento and my sister in Montana; no one picked up. I started to panic.

I picked up my rental and sped toward Fairfield and the big Air Force base where my father was being treated, the same base where I'd been born. My younger sister called and I picked up while ripping through the 880 exchange near Oakland.

"How is he?"

"Oh." She laughed. "He's fine. They took a look and his arteries looked great and that was it. They didn't do anything. We're on our way to Outback. Wanna meet us?"

I almost rear-ended a semi-truck.

"Sure. I mean. That's great. Amazing. Outback? Like, the steak house?"

"Yeah. In the mall near Dad's."

"I'm almost at Berkeley. I can probably be there in forty-five minutes."

"See you then."

I dropped the phone onto the passenger seat. My father's heart was fine. No stent. No worries, mate. Now, on to Outback. I'd flown all the way across the US to eat subpar steak at a chain restaurant.

I dropped my speed. I liked driving through the Bay Area. In the hills and waterways many fond memories of my early twenties lurked—epic drinking nights, making love in an almond orchard, houseboat parties on the Delta, making love in the Oakland Hills, circumambulating Mount Tam and making love at midnight in Muir Woods.

I drove toward Vacaville and, without thinking much about it, more on impulse than from thought, I got off the freeway and tried to find the house from my childhood. I found it. A simple shingled ranch, oak tree in the front yard, bay windows, flower garden.

I sat for a few moments and drove on to the nearby Outback.

My father and sister were in a great mood, already settled into a booth. An enormous appetizer platter of fried food-like items landed just as I joined them.

"So what's the doc say?"

"The ticker is fine, Tone. He thinks I'm suffering anxiety. Gave me some pills. Gonna check in in three months and see what he sees. Let's eat some steak."

The irony seemed lost on my sister and father: a few hours after my father had left the hospital for potential heart trouble, here we sat at a steak house, ingesting heart bombs.

My father didn't thank me for flying out for his non-procedure. After the lunch I drove to Sacramento and spent a few days visiting friends and my mother before returning home.

June has come and long gone with no greetings from you. No passes there.

When I was a youth June loomed large as school ended and ceded to shirtless bicycle days and sunburns and poolside daydreams of girls I'd never kiss—and three family celebrations took place that month: my father's birthday, my parents' anniversary, and Father's Day.

June-time Sacramento sun warmed the pool and in it on those festive days we kids would splash and play, bark like dogs, while my father grilled burgers and brats and my mother made potato salad in the kitchen, occasionally yelling for assistance from my sister or me—we need more soda in the cooler! More napkins on the table! Gambler (our beloved Boston terrier) is chasing the neighbor's cat!

One particular Father's Day I remember well, if for no other reason than that the gift I gave my father resides with me now. I must have been eleven or twelve. A few days before the big day I rode my bike the mile or so to the nearest supermarket with a friend of mine and we perused the aisles for presents for our fathers. My friend didn't find anything that suited his father, but I thought I had.

I remember my mother helping me wrap the cumbersome object and tape it up, place a bow on top. I was excited because this was no run-of-the-mill Father's Day present, not socks, not a tie, not a new alarm clock or coffee cup or T-shirt. I gave my father a beer stein—which I now use to store spare change.

My younger sister and I had been swimming for hours and our hands were puckered like an old lady's. Picnic debris littered the table and the dogs ran circles around the pool, chasing the cat, chasing the rabbit, chasing their shadows as the sun dropped west. Country music drifted outdoors from my father's massive reel-to-reel setup in the family room. Johnny Paycheck. Johnny Cash. One of the Johnnys.

My father poured his Löwenbräu into the mug, and he drank from it, and I thought I was a pretty fine little son.

Our most recent face to face was a dinner at Arden Fair. [Arden Fair is a large mall in Sacramento, but actually the dinner was at a great Thai restaurant called Pardees in a swank little mall in Carmichael called Town and Country. My mother and younger sister were in attendance along with my friend Douglas and his wife Sachiyo.] *Which was well after your two weeks of "catching up." You were finishing your taxes and had gifts. You gave me "Sorry about that Dad." (No importance) I wasn't sure how to respond, so I didn't. What a snub! The likes of which no one deserves. Maybe payback for something in the past? No pass here.*

I recall giving my mother and sister textiles from a trip I'd taken to Vietnam. Before traveling there with Ava I asked my father if he wanted to join us, and he said no. I also asked him if he wanted pictures of any place, or any particular thing—a market in Saigon, a building, a street, a rice paddy, a particular stretch of jungle or river. And he said no to this as well. He told me he'd gotten out of Vietnam with his life and that that was the only thing he'd ever wanted out of the godforsaken country. I asked him if I should look around Saigon for any half siblings and he smiled and said, "Why not?"

Giving my sister and mother gifts in front of him while offering him nothing was extremely rude. I feel horrible about it now. But I don't know what I would have brought him. Maybe one of those red T-shirts with Che splashed across the yellow Communist Party star? I plead guilty to the charge of showing up empty-handed.

He's correct: I may have been trying to get back at him for something, or for everything.

Last Christmas I sent you a check rather than a gift, which is what I normally do. I know it wasn't much compared to what you are now accustomed to, but you cashed it. I wonder why I didn't get a thank you, it would take very little of your precious time. Is thanks of no importance to you anymore? Or for such a small gift? Should a pass be given? Or should

I chalk it up to an absent minded ~~professor~~
writer? Maybe even the thought behind the gift
is of no importance to you? Should that excuse
your ill-mannered conduct?

I distinctly remember calling my father when I received the check and thanking him for it. I told him I'd used it to buy a great bottle of wine that Ava and I would share around the holidays. This is the first sign that he's fixated on the sums of money he thinks I now make. The striking of the word *professor* indicates that he considers me a fool for walking away from a tenure-track teaching position to move to New York for a woman and to write full-time, as well his hierarchy of the two titles, professor and writer. A professor is, well, a professional. A writer is a bum. Any man with a pen can say he's a writer. What man can say he's a professor and a writer? My father's maternal grandfather could; he taught music at Auburn and wrote church hymns. But I do not write church hymns.

Maybe this stems from the time you
borrowed my GMC. You stated you only
needed it for a short period of time, until you
purchased one of your own. Several times in
the past you used my red S-10; only once do I

remember you replacing the fuel. Failing to get an estimated return date [on the GMC SUV] other than "as soon as I have time to buy one of my own"—you offered to make monthly vehicle and insurance payments until it was returned. Since you were no longer a struggling student—it seemed reasonable to me. I have never had such a good deal and this arrangement would keep you from being rushed buying one of your own and cost you substantially less than renting one. You got distracted several times and kept it longer than most folks would consider reasonable and made no payments during that time. Maybe you felt for the first time you were in control of something in my life and were going to take full advantage. When you finally returned it, giving me a check which included reimbursement for one of your parking tickets; there was an air of arrogance as if you felt I should not accept your money. Which was confirmed later, when you accused me of gouging you—my own flesh and blood by taking money for the use of a vehicle. When it was time to renew the registration surprise— there were two more unpaid tickets plus late charges. Which had to be paid right there before DMV would validate the renewal.

You had told me you were paying these tickets.
What a lie! You never offered to pay for the
oversight, which indicates you never intended
to pay in the first place. I suppose you justified
not keeping your word because I screwed you by
having the audacity to expect and take payment
from my own "flesh and blood" for the use of a
vehicle. To this day I cannot understand why
you would expect me to furnish the vehicle "fee
gratis," then stiff me for your tickets. Especially
since you were financially able.

In memory my father and motor vehicles are intertwined. Even the genesis of my parents' relationship involves combustion engines and speed: As a young airman in Moses Lake, Washington, my father ripped around town in a sleek 1957 Chevy. A high school senior with a bright red coiffure worked at the drive-in where my father and his military friends hung out on weekends. It was late in her senior year, she'd just turned eighteen, and she was supposed to start at Washington State in the fall.

My dad was a madly handsome Air Force kid of twenty, and he wanted to take her out. He spoke in a deep amber Southern drawl and words fell from his mouth like sex. But the redhead said no, and again no, and no again. This dark-haired handsome kid returned each weekend in his tricked-out hot rod and the redhead always said no and sometimes added *Go away.*

And then one night, near the end of her shift, a guy drove off with the tray and dishes my mother had delivered to his car. My father knew that the waitresses were charged for any loss of dishes and utensils, and he gave chase. As my father told it, the guy pulled over a mile down the road and handed over the tray, with all the dishes intact. My father returned the goods to my mother and finally she said yes. I now wonder if my father hadn't put one of his buddies up to the stunt, or if he had handed a stranger a few dollars to enlist him in the charade. What does it matter? The redhead said yes and the Swofford motor vehicle legacy began.

I use the word *vehicle* just like my father. Often when I employ it casually, say walking down the street with a friend and spying a Ferrari, I'll say, "That's a nice vehicle." And the friend will laugh at my use of the word.

"Why not just say *car?*"

Car seems so casual. *Vehicle* has a formality and manliness to it, the assumption that the person behind the vehicle knows the power and perils of said vehicle, knows how to fix it with his own tools if need be, understands the meaning of torque, the piss-your-pants sensation of blasting through the desert in a high-horsepower sports vehicle, taking hairpin turns up the mountain at fifty miles per hour, feeling death's breath on your neck as you dance at perilous heights and speeds along California 1.

On a bookshelf in my office is a simple wooden car my father and I made when I was three years old and we lived in Ohio. Making the car with my father is one of my first memories; the other is of a fierce lightning storm that took out the big oak tree in our front yard the same summer. I'm unsure which came first, the car or the lightning.

The car is made of simple scrap wood, two one-by-fours nailed together; one is one-third the length of the other and represents the roof of the vehicle. The wheels are made from one-and-a-half- and two-inch dowels, the two-inchers in the rear so that the car has an aggressive stance, as though it's always revving RPMs at the start line, ready for the go.

My father and I sat in the backyard and we used my red wagon as a workspace. My father put my fist on the handle of the saw and covered my fist with his own, and together we sawed the one-by-four, two cuts against the soft pine grain. It would have been the first time I took a tool in my hand. I can feel now the reverberation of energy along the spine of the saw, up through the handle, into my tiny fist. From an early age my father taught me to respect tools, to respect their power and to know the consequences of abusing the power of the tool. Using the wrong tool was, for my father, tantamount to praying to the wrong god, or not praying at all.

My father cut the wheels from the dowels and he spray-painted the body pieces red and the wheels black.

While the paint dried he would have gone back to whatever father chore monopolized his time that day—building a fence, fixing a basement door, mowing the lawn. I involved myself in the intricacies of my mini swing set and the balance required to careen on my belly down the slide.

He called me back when the paint dried and I watched as he hammered the roof to the body with three nails. He handed me the car, my first and only homemade toy.

As a boy I logged hundreds, if not thousands, of hours playing with that car in my room or outside on the sidewalk or in the dirt, making car noises, running the vehicle through its paces—sprints, jumps, laps, smash-up derby. Six cheap simple pieces of painted wood made a boy so happy.

I occasionally take the car down from the shelf

and place it in front of me on my desk. And as I roll it back and forth on my desk the feeling is the same—power, movement, escape.

I flip the car upside down. At some point, with a nail, I scratched axles, a drivetrain, and a transmission into the wooden undercarriage.

I doubt my father remembers this cheap toy. Sometimes I wonder why I have held on to it for so long. So many times I might have tossed it in the garbage like any other piece of the past, another junked vehicle.

THE CONTROVERSY OVER my extended use of my father's car might never die. We disagree on every element of the exchange. You've heard his story, here is mine:

In August 2003 I moved to Oakland, from Portland, in order to start a tenure-track teaching job at a Bay Area college. Back in Portland I never drove, the city being a bastion of public transportation, walking, and biking. I needed a vehicle for my commute from Oakland to Moraga. I told my father that I planned to do car shopping over a few weeks but that in the interim my friend Douglas had agreed to let me borrow one of his cars. My father told me that that was ridiculous, that he had four cars in his driveway and there was no reason for me not to drive one of them. He rarely drove the SUV and so offered it to me.

My father is very particular about his vehicles and his tools. They are always in perfect condition and any time a person tarnishes a vehicle or a tool he knows instantly. He knows if the mirror is a centimeter out of place, if the driver's seat or steering wheel has been shifted and not returned to its original position, if the head of the hammer has been chipped. I knew this about my father, and I knew that I should decline his offer, even lie—tell him that Douglas was on his way down from Sacramento as we spoke, delivering a car to me.

But I accepted his offer. The car wasn't really my style—it screamed soccer dad—but it would do the trick for a few weeks while I found my own car. He gave me the keys and we agreed that I'd return the car by the fifteenth of September, a little less than a month away. There was no discussion of money, car payments, or insurance.

My first day of teaching I rushed out of my apartment, running late as usual, and jumped in the SUV. I turned the key. Nothing, nothing but a cosmic joke. My first full-time teaching job, the first day of classes, which commenced in ninety minutes, and the car my father loaned me is a lemon. Speeding through the Oakland hills one can make it to campus in thirty-two minutes. I call a taxi driver I know, Singh, and luckily he's free. He's in Alameda but can be to me in ten minutes, he says. Singh is the only cab driver in the history of civilization, from donkey cart jockeys in the desert to Hummer limo cruisers in the city, to arrive in ten minutes when he says ten minutes.

After a few flights in and out of Oakland, Singh and I have built up a bit of a professional friendship. I know his kids' names; I know his wife wants to open a restaurant in Alameda; I know his brother is also a cabbie and that they grew up in Mumbai. He knows I'm a writer and that this is my first day of class at a new job.

He pulls up, the screech of his tires announcing his arrival to the neighborhood.

"Brother!" he yells at me. "Let's go. You gonna be late."

I'm sitting on my stoop. It's about eighty degrees outside and I'm wearing a wool suit and tie. Books and papers are splayed at my feet. I have the feeling that moving to Oakland and taking this job was a big mistake, and that my father's lemon car is only the first indication.

I jump in the back of Singh's cab.

He says, "Brother, your first class is at noon, right? Shit, we better move."

"Forty dollars on top if we make it in time."

"You da man," Singh screams, and he guns it down Fairbanks Avenue and into the Oakland hills.

I made it on time and my classes went well. A colleague gave me a ride home. I called my father and told him about the trial of my day and we shared a laugh about it and decided it meant nothing. He gave me his AAA card number so that I could get the vehicle towed and inspected.

I hung up and called Marin County, who lived now in Berkeley. She arrived a few minutes later and we ordered in and had sex a few times and I felt better. She asked me if I'd missed her body and I said yes, because I had. She asked me to do things to her she'd never asked for before, and I did. I hadn't slept with her in four years and I wondered what else she'd learned in the interim. In college we'd usually had sex in my truck, parked in front of her father's house in San Rafael, or in the bathroom in the house she shared with nine people in Davis. Everything about the sex felt new, though it also felt old and stultifying and I wondered again why I continually returned to old lovers. Comfort? Ease? Dread over the future?

The chill Oakland night sneaked into the room and we slept comfortably. In the morning I made eggs and bacon and we spent most of the morning in bed reading and fucking and talking about nothing of importance.

When she left I thought about my ex-wife, and I tried to remember why I'd left her. And then I remembered the dead car and I called AAA.

I'LL ADMIT THAT I am terrible at paying parking tickets and other fines. This is part laziness, part the scofflaw in me. Like my father, I seek adversity. Adversity gives me a story, a narrative to write against. So I didn't pay a few parking tickets. But I swear I never told my dad I would pay his car payments and insurance.

Our setup seemed pretty good to me as well— my father, who owned a surfeit of cars, would allow me to borrow one of them until I bought my own. If he'd asked me to pay for the use of the vehicle I would have asked my friend Douglas for the use of one of his, which would have been free of charge. And it didn't seem far-fetched that a father would allow his only living son to borrow a car for a month, maybe six weeks at the outside, free of charge. Isn't that what fathers do for their children?

I'll admit that I took a bit longer than I originally intended to buy my own car. In the end I settled on a seven-year-old Mercedes 320, an old man's car if ever there was one: silver on silver, four doors, straight six with a bit of torque but nothing for the long run. I didn't want speeding tickets. I wanted transportation that wouldn't break down, with a low insurance premium.

Before I could get my father's car back to him, I had to run out of town for a weekend reading in the Midwest. I called my dad from Chicago O'Hare and told him that I was traveling again but that I'd have his car back to him Monday—I'd already enlisted a friend to help me in the handoff, and I'd be to his place by noon; he could check out my new ride and we'd run over to Suisun City for those great carnitas at Puerto Vallarta.

I heard the sigh, the Swofford Sigh, as I've come to call it. It's not always an indication of anger; sometimes it's mild irritation, or bemusement, but in this instance, listening from concourse whatever at O'Hare, I knew the Swofford Sigh meant anger.

"You promised me the vehicle back sooner than this, Tone."

"I'm sorry, Dad. I've had a hectic schedule, teaching, traveling every weekend. It took me longer to buy a car than I thought it would. I found one in Sacramento with help from Douglas and Cliff. They saved me from buying a clunker."

"You don't know how to shop for your own car?"

"It was more fun playing around with the salesmen with Cliff and Douglas. They know about buying cars."

"I know about cars. I could have found you a car in a weekend. What did you boys do? Play grab-ass, chase girls, drink beer when you were supposed to be looking for cars?"

"It took a few weeks. Isn't that normal?"

"Normal is sticking to your word. What did you buy?"

"A seven-year-old Mercedes. A sedan. An old man's car."

"Getting fancy, Tone."

"It's not fancy. It's German. It won't break down. It cost less than any one of your cars did brand-new."

"That might be. But listen. You're returning my vehicle so late I'm gonna have to charge you something."

"What? You wouldn't have even used it."

"But it belongs to me and you betrayed my trust. I'm gonna need the cost of the payment, and insurance, and wear and tear at industry standard, which is about twenty-two cents a mile, if I recall."

"Industry standard? What are you talking about?"

"That's what a company pays an employee for wear and tear on a private vehicle."

"My flight is boarding. I've got to go."

"See you Monday, Tone."

My flight wasn't scheduled to depart for two hours. I went to the Bennigan's and ordered a double vodka.

MY FATHER LEFT town for a few days and informed me that I should leave the vehicle in his driveway, locked, with the keys in the glove compartment. He told me that he'd put an invoice in the mail.

I FORGOT ABOUT the invoice. The semester had bogged me down, teaching full-time filled up my schedule. I was trying to get in shape, riding my mountain bike through the Oakland hills every day I could. The casual, regular sex with Marin County was a bonus that I hadn't counted on when I moved to Oakland, and the sex kept me sane. I had no time to waste on dating.

And everything I did—cook, write, eat, teach, read, screw—was an attempt to banish my ex-wife from the currents of my daily life.

Then one day the handwritten invoice arrived. All totaled, my father wanted about seven hundred dollars. I fumed. I couldn't believe the old bastard had actually gone through with it. My own father wanted to charge me for the use of his vehicle. I went for a bike ride. I shot some hoops alone in my driveway. I called a friend. He agreed my father was a jerk. I called another friend. He agreed my father was a jerk. I called another friend. He told me that my father and I were both jerks. I told him he was a jerk and that that was the last time I'd ever ask for his opinion.

A few days later my father called and told me he was going to be near Oakland, and that he hoped to swing by my place to pick up the check I owed him because he didn't know whether or not a guy like me even used the post office.

He stopped by late, around ten, when Marin County was already in my bed. She wanted to say hello to my father, but I asked her to stay in my room.

I let my father in and he glanced around my apartment.

"Nice place, Tone," he said.

"Thanks."

"Where do you write those masterpieces?"

"The large bedroom in back is my office. I sleep in the smaller room."

My father, an amorous man, always in tune to the presence of a woman, glanced at the couch and

Marin County's purse and sweater, draped over an arm. He smiled.

"Girl in the back?"

"Marin County."

"Oh, sure. Pretty girl. You're never gonna give that one up, are you? She's too shy to say hi to your old man?"

"She's asleep."

"I gotta hit the road, Tone. You got that check?"

I handed it to him and he put on his glasses in order to read. "Looks about right," he said. "All righty, then. I'd say let's get a drink but I bet you got business to 'tend to. Catch you on down the road."

He clipped my shoulder with his open palm, an attempt to bring me in for a hug, but I stood as still as a flagpole.

"Give your old man a hug," he said with obvious glee.

He knew the matter of the check was burning me up inside, that I considered him a complete bastard for charging me to use his vehicle, and that I would say nothing about it because I was a coward and I never challenged my father.

We hugged and he departed.

I returned to bed and the only thing that might offer solace.

*We have never discussed the voicemail you
left shortly after events mentioned in the last
paragraph. I felt we should have discussed it,
but you said you were ok—which I took to
mean you weren't interested in talking about
it. The preposterous accusation that I stuck
your face in dog shit; is untrue and makes me
wonder what other atrocious memories of me
you hold. I turned your head down toward the
ground for you to see but never stuck your face
in shit. How did this not make it into your
book? It may seem real to you and you may go
to your grave believing I did but it simply did
not happen.*

This episode has never appeared in any of my
writing, but I can't let it go. I had tried to write the
scene into my first book but it was more painful
than any of the wartime scenes I wrote. I gave up.
I'm not sure if my father believes it appeared in the
book and I misrepresented the event or if he is asking me why I *didn't* put the scene in the book.

Either way, one Saturday in 1977, in Vacaville,
California, I woke up at the usual kid hour and
watched cartoons from the prone position, a few
feet back from the television, my porcelain-white
chin resting in my hands, bowl-cut ink-black hair

hanging in my eyes, diaphanous curtains. Let's say Bugs Bunny, Donald Duck, Speedy Gonzales, Elmer Fudd. I wore pajamas, a superhero of some sort emblazoned on the front. Aquaman.

The Saturdays of my boyhood were as regimented as the process for docking a nuclear sub: watch cartoons and do not disturb late-sleeping parents; eat the breakfast mother prepares; dress in yard clothes; perform yard duties; stand by for father's inspection; if inspection is passed, go play with friends until dinner; if inspection is failed, redo yard chores until perfection is achieved.

My sisters followed a similar routine, though they helped my mother with the indoor chores. My older brother had some leeway. He'd leave the house early and ride his bike with his buddies, shoot hoops down at the school, cause chaos in the neighborhood—later in the afternoon he'd help my father tune up and wash and wax the cars, or assist in major reconstruction works: mending a fence, patching the roof, planting or tending our mother's flower or vegetable garden.

As a child, I never understood why my parents refused to wake up with me and join in my world, but obviously they were catching up on sleep and romance.

When my cartoons finished, my mother emerged

from the back of the house and made pancakes and eggs for my sisters and me. My older sister, Tami, helped my mother with the boxed batter, beating hard with a wooden spoon in order to remove the lumps. My younger sister, Kim, and I sat and talked about the things a seven- and four-year-old talk about—our bikes, her dolls, school, coloring books. We shared the Saturday newspaper comics.

The big breakfast—eggs, bacon, pancakes, orange juice—sated us all.

I went to my room and changed into my yard clothes—a worn pair of plaid Toughskins, a faded Tokyo Giants T-shirt that read TOKYO GUTS on the back, and a football jersey from my time as a linebacker with the Tachikawa Steelers, way back in '75.

I gathered the week's newspapers from their haphazard pile in the garage and placed them in a paper shopping bag and placed the bag in the backseat of my mother's car. Later, when she and my sisters shopped for groceries on base, they'd drop the papers off at a recycling bin.

At the time we owned two dogs, French poodles, a mother/daughter super-duo of black curly hypoallergenicness. I loved the two dogs, Gini and Fifi, but they were not a boy's dogs.

G & F did not play catch like my friend's lab; G

& F did not run the grassy amber hills behind our house with me and the neighborhood kids, the way another boy's German shepherd did; G & F had assumed a snooty French pose and for the most part looked at us as the French look at most Americans—as uncivilized brutes. They never rushed to the door upon our return; their tails knew not the excited wag of canine recognition for dear owner. Never once did either dog lick my face ecstatically, bestowing on me the slobbery dog kisses called love.

Someday boy-appropriate dogs would enter the family.

The worst dog chore in the family fell to me: every Saturday morning I skulked around the backyard, a double-thick paper shopping bag in one hand, a pooper-scooper in the other.

In a singular stroke of parenting genius my mother and father allowed me to choose my own pooper-scooper every few months—they were way ahead of the curve on the concept of "ownership." Whenever the wear and tear of G & F's intestinal tracts had put the damage to the tool of my trade my father took me down to Lumberjack, the lumber and hardware store of choice in Northern California, and allowed me my pick of the litter, so to speak.

Back in the mid-seventies pooper-scoopers were rather rudimentary compared with today's options— Four Paws, Yard Pup, Little Stinker. The tool I used looked like a fish spatula. Design and decoration variation occurred only at the handle: with my handle choice I expressed both my character and my aesthetic principles. I admit I favored flower prints.

On this October day the grass shone a brilliant green and among the blades a riot of dew softened my step. I was a sojourner, a Native American tracker in search of scat. My life depended on it. The backyard became my jungle, my Laos, my lost country. There—evidence of G & F: I bent and scooped. My father had taught me a system of poop appropriation that many years later in the Marines I would recognize as "policing." You walk a grid: you leave no swath of ground uncovered by the eyes. If it doesn't grow, it goes, the saying went: cigarette butts, bullet casings, ration packaging, and bandoliers. But here in southeast Vacaville I looked only for the evacuations of our stuck-up poodles, the ladies, as my mother called them. Here: bend and scoop. There: bend and scoop. Everywhere: bend and scoop.

I held my little nose. I breathed into the bend of my elbow. I dragged the increasingly heavy bag along the damp grass, toward the garage. My chore done! Another weekend in the trenches and I had survived. I heaped the bag into the open garbage container—the weight of nations no longer taxing my shoulders.

On Saturdays my father woke up late, or left the bedroom late. He's neither a reader of books nor much of a television watcher, so I'm not sure what he would have been doing in the bedroom a few hours past my mother other than sleeping or daydreaming. He was famous for his stash of candy, and he always had a bit of a belly, so he might have been feeding himself candies and relaxing in bed and dreading coexistence with his family. For most of his life work allowed him an escape. The man must leave for work.

But not on Saturdays—on Saturdays the father cannot escape the brood, and the wife, and the building we call a home. Some men escape with golf, or race cars, or the local bar, but my father never had a hobby that I know of.

I reread the comics at the kitchen table while around me my mother and sisters created a portrait of efficiency and cleanliness: laundering, dusting, vacuuming, poofing pillows, shining furniture, making early preparations for dinner.

When my mother passed me she'd muss my hair

and kiss my forehead and I was then and would always remain her baby boy.

My father exited the marital chamber and told me to get ready for the yard inspection. With a start I ran to the backyard and stood on the patio. Nerves rattled my knees; my heart raced: I generally missed a spot, but lately I'd been on a roll, say five or six weeks straight without a penalty. I wanted an undefeated fall season.

"What is this?" my father called from about twenty feet away.

"I don't know," I said. Knowing exactly what this was. My undefeated season had been crushed.

"Well, why don't you come take a look?"

"I don't know."

"I don't care if you don't know. Come here, Son."

I sidled up next to my father. Usually he lectured sternly about the finer points of policing the area, of paying attention to my surroundings, of the responsibility we each had in making the family ship run properly. I suppose this is what most fathers spend their time doing: making minor corrections in the navigation.

But this time my father grabbed me by the back of my neck and he forced my face down toward the pile of dog shit; I fell to my knees, my nose now inches away from the pile. So close I could smell and taste it, the wet meaty aroma of dog shit. My stomach heaved.

"What is that?"

I cried. I gagged. I failed to speak when spoken to.

"What is that, Son?"

"Dog. Poop," I said through tears.

He held my face an inch or two above the dog shit for a few more seconds. And then snatched me away as though he'd saved me from something.

"Now go get your scooper and clean that up."

I did as told while my father watched me from a chair on the patio. When I finished he called me over. He sat me in his lap.

He said, "I don't want to do that. I don't want to have to look after you all of the time. You're a big boy. You know what your job is. If you don't do your job right then no one else can do the right job. And then nothing works around here. If you don't do your job I can't mow the lawn, and then you can't hose down the patio and the driveway. You see?"

I sniffled. I nodded.

"I can't be mowing over the dog poop. That just causes more of a mess. We gotta be on top of this stuff, Tone. OK?"

I sniffled. I nodded. I went about my Saturday.

*   *   *

AFTER PAYING THE car invoice from my father I left him a phone message asking if he remembered that backyard event. I asked him if he remembered shoving his son's face in a pile of dog shit. It is true my face never touched the dog shit, but this seems to me a matter of semantics. I could have used the word *toward*, or *near*, but neither seems specific enough, or close enough to the experience of a seven-year-old boy.

I don't know what the car invoice and the dog shit event have in common. I remembered the dog shit event after ranting to a friend about the car invoice: we sat in a bar in Oakland, King's Lounge, and we drank cheap drinks and looked at girls and I told him what a prick my father had been about the car, and in the middle of telling him the story I saw myself and my father in grainy sixteen-millimeter memory film, in that backyard in Vacaville, a father and son already locked in emotional combat.

For the use of his vehicle my father received from me more than a check. I handed back to him this awful memory.

It appears that most fond childhood
memories are shared with your mother.
Imagine life without them. Mine are imagined,

based on my grandmother's love, which I share
at my mother's grave.

Here is my father's best writing yet. He acknowl-
edges that my childhood was smoother and sweeter
under my mother's watch and invokes the fear of
every person who walks the Earth: life without
Mother. What is life without Mother? Nothingness. He finalizes the paragraph with an image of
himself at the foot of his mother's grave. *Whatever*
you might think of me, he says, *don't forget this fact.*

My father's mother died a month after he was
born.

I DECIDE I need to move the TV from the foot of
my bed into the closet. I don't have cable and rarely
watch DVDs and the TV is an eyesore.

My closet is full of five or six boxes of books and
miscellaneous papers from the office in Brooklyn I
moved out of a year ago.

In the boxes of books I discover a few gems I
haven't seen in a while: *The Oxford Companion*
to Italian Food; the Leonard Michaels novel *Syl-*
via; *The Letters of Sigmund Freud*; Gary Snyder's
Mountains and Rivers Without End.

I find three pairs of earphones, scotch tape, rub-
ber bands, tax documents, a Japanese foot mas-

sager, and a stapler. And a manila envelope with my aunt Janna's familiar script: *Forms to Keep*. I have no idea what this could be. I pull out the forms and the top form is a photocopy of the obituary page of the *Opelika Daily News* from Monday, July 21, 1941:

Mrs. Annie Swofford, Auburn Route 1, Dies at Opelika Infirmary

Mrs. Annie Laurie Swofford, age 20, of Auburn Route 1, died at the Opelika Infirmary Sunday, at 2:45 p.m., following four weeks illness and funeral service is to be held at 4:00 p.m. daylight saving time today, from the Baptist church in Auburn, internment in Auburn cemetery. Short Funeral Home is in charge of arrangements.

Deceased was born Annie Laurie Howard, on Auburn Route 1, residing there all her life. She was married August 29, 1937 to J. C. Swofford, who survives. Other survivors are: baby son, John Howard Swofford, mother Mrs. S. L. Howard, twin brother, Hodge Howard, now at Camp Blanding, Fla, David Howard, brother, of Auburn Route 1; sister Mrs. J. H. Crawford, Opelika, sister, Mrs. H. S. Strickland, Selma, ALA; brothers,

Robert Howard, Auburn and Lafayette Howard, Perry, Fla.

Dr. J. R. Edwards is to conduct services and the following are to act as pallbearers: Earl Wood, Carson Cooper, Cecil Waller and Wilton Thorp.

Mrs. Swofford's father, Samuel Lafayette Howard died in October, 1940.

Baby son, John Howard Swofford

My father was just a month old when his mother died.

She came from a well-to-do family in Auburn, Alabama. Her father taught music at Auburn University. Her mother was a homemaker. My grandfather was a young guy trying to put together a chain of gas stations and sundries stores, but he never pulled it together. His young wife died, he took his son home to Georgia, a few months later he went to the war and his parents raised his son until he came home in 1945.

I have always heard, money changes people.
I met people who were down to earth folks,
with class and integrity and sound moral
and ethical strength and did not wear their
money on their sleeve. It took a while for me

to see they had money and I could not imagine it changed them. I hoped that if I ever got money (too late for that now) I would have the fortitude to keep it from changing my character. Other money people show it right away, they act like their money makes them better than others and entitles them to royal treatment, usually believing they are not subject to normal social behavior. I would like to see how they are treated on their way back down, by the ones they treated with arrogant indifference as they passed on their way up.

You had as much choice in choosing me as father as I you son. Do memories justify rude and irresponsible behavior—? Did you blind me—or have you changed that much in the last few years? Maybe a combination, whatever my contribution—it is unintended.

Another brilliant rhetorical turn on his part—after reminding me of the tragic death of his mother and softening me, he goes back on the attack.

I remembered the last line of that first paragraph as "See you on your way down." Here my father is trying to be sly and anecdotal, trying to impart folksy Southern wisdom.

He believes money has changed me. Yes, for a few years I made very good money, banker money, but my father doesn't understand that the writer's life is feast or famine.

My father can't imagine that the rift in our relationship has anything to do with *our relationship*. He's looking for someone or something to blame, and money and I are to blame. *Money, money changes everything.* For my father, it's as simple as that. Also, he'd like the past erased.

And more than anything, perhaps, he is hurting inside: still smarting eight years after my brother's death, as is everyone else in the family. But he needs to lash out. A part of him, I'm certain, hates me for being alive while Jeff is dead. Just as if I'd died and Jeff had lived, he'd hate Jeff for the same reason. He had been waiting for a reason to hate me, and suddenly he had it: my first book, wherein he thinks I treated him unfairly, when in fact I treated him with kid gloves; what he deems my wild financial success; and the fact that I have failed to put a few things in the mail, which is a behavior common to me since I was a little boy: I'm a daydreamer; I don't always follow through on the directions I've been given. This angers him, too. He can no longer boss me around, he has no control over me, and he doesn't like that at all.

My father has cursed me: *See you on your way down*, he says.

> *This turned out to be rather lengthy. I am*
> *proud of you and your accomplishments, more*
> *than you will ever know. You have many*
> *more to come. Stop and smell the flowers once*
> *in a while. Don't forget your roots. I fear*
> *that money is bringing unfavorable change.*
> *Keep that from happening! As I said before I*
> *can't expect an acknowledgement and at this*
> *moment, am not sure this will be sent.*
> *Love, Dad*

My father, whatever else, has chutzpah. I believe he knows he will send the letter. But this is a great narrative and emotional punch: I get to the end of his six-page-long assault and I read that he might not have sent it. What would have happened if he hadn't? We'll never know.

Sometime in August he picks his pen up again:

> *August 06*
> *Granny told me you didn't call her to let her*
> *know that you were not interested in receiving*
> *the cross of military service. You simply did not*
> *send a copy of your DD-214. What a way to*

let her know——. Even though many would like to rewrite history it cannot be changed. Your Swofford roots go back through the Southern Confederacy. Your great-great-great-grandfather was a Confederate soldier. If he had been killed and not made it back to Dog River neither of us would be here. You can be proud or ashamed but you can't change it. Your Warner roots [my mother's] *could go through a Union Soldier. How many people know where their great-great-great-grandparents are buried?*

Granny is Anice Swofford, my father's step-mother. She's a sweet old lady, my sweet old granny, with a gleam in her blue eyes and she likes the acronym GRITS: girls raised in the South. She makes the best sausage biscuits in the world and she's a member of United Daughters of the Confederacy.

The Cross of Military Service is a medal the UDC gives to combat veterans who are direct descendants of Confederate soldiers, and as my father outlined above, I seem to be one of those.

It's my understanding that when Granny accumulates citations and awards for her family she gains esteem from her colleagues. And I don't begrudge Granny her hobby. But I couldn't accept a medal from an organization that associates loosely with neo-Confederate groups that would gladly wipe half my friends off the face of the Earth.

Sure, I could've called Granny and told her that, but it seemed easier to simply ignore her request for my military discharge papers. She's a smart lady. She knows I'm a progressive. She'd get the hint. No need to smack down Granny over the phone, was my thinking.

Of our Southern ancestry my father writes, *You can be proud or ashamed but you can't change it.* This is true. And I like the South, and as a kid I loved visiting all the family down there, and still do, but I can choose to not accept an award from an organization that fights to keep the rebel flag flying.

Aug 10-06
Now that we have had this pissy phone call
I will probably be sending this and still no
response is expected. Helping Tami is not the
issue. You will know this will not be the last
time she hits bottom and needs financial aid. I
am glad that you are willing and able to help.
I no longer have the resources, mainly because
of being on a fixed income, which is much less
than when I was working. You having the
money to pay me back is not the issue. The
issue was the question you would not answer.

There you were being evasive, not answering the question, but asking others that had nothing to do with a re-payment date. Why do you think I was pressing for a re-payment date?

My father was visiting my older sister in Billings and she had gotten into some financial trouble. She needed some cash, not a large sum of money, as I recall, around a thousand dollars. I was cheating on Ava in Vancouver at the time and didn't have a checkbook on me so I asked my father if he wouldn't mind writing Tami a check and then as soon as I was back in New York, in a few weeks, I'd drop one to him in the mail.

For whatever reason this threw him into a rage. I remember well the argument. He wanted an exact date that I would put the check in the mail and I refused to give him an exact date because I hadn't bought my return ticket. I was sitting on the terrace of an apartment in Vancouver BC. Inside the apartment was a woman I had just made love to. I drank coffee and took in a view of the sea, and I let my father scream at me and I refused to respond.

I ended up wiring Tami the money. Cut out the middleman.

*Since you have made it "Big Time," I am
no longer dazed at your treatment of family.
You should be embarrassed at not calling
Granny and ashamed about James's books.* [I
was delayed in returning signed copies of
Jarhead to a cousin of mine.] *Your mother
will take exception, as usual. You seem to
gloat at being an arrogant, self-centered person
exhibiting the lowest level of responsibility.
Why would your time be more valuable than
theirs?*

Love, Dad

Perhaps I should have called my grandmother and said, "Thanks, Granny, but I'd rather not receive an award from your neo-Confederate organization."

Sometimes silence speaks wonders, even to your sweet, sweet-tea-drinking granny.

I should've returned those books to my cousin James sooner, but I didn't. I'm unorganized. I lose stuff. I don't write things down. I miss appointments. I piss people off. It has nothing to do with any success, or any sums of money. It's just who I am. When I was a dirt-poor college student subsisting on ramen and PBR I behaved exactly the same.

None of this makes me arrogant or self-centered.

But if your father thinks you are arrogant and self-centered, you are.

> *Sun Aug 13, 2006*
> *It was good to hear your voice, know that*
> *you had a good birthday. You may not open*
> *this for three or four months or for that matter*
> *ever; since you said you have no reason to open*
> *mail as you have no bills. How fortunate*
> *for you. If it were a publisher or Hollywood*
> *type, would it sit that long? Now that I see*
> *most family matters are of little importance*
> *to you—should I call James and tell him he*
> *will be lucky to ever get his books back? Is*
> *it unreasonable that we expect responsible*
> *behavior from you?*

My father the pit bull: *It was good to hear your voice, know that you had a good birthday*—now let me reiterate the myriad ways in which you are a failed son and a failed person and rip your throat out.

Guilty, guilty, guilty: I suck at paperwork. I don't open mail for months. In my mother's study in Sacramento is a box of my unopened mail from the Portland years, 2001 to 2003.

Are these *character* flaws? And who is *we*? Above, he writes that he knows my mother will take exception to the notion that I am flawed, so he can't be including her in his *we*. This is the global We, the world knows I am a failure, that I let my family down, that I don't follow through, I am a bad citizen and a worse son and my father is here to teach me a lesson.

I've just turned *thirty-six* years old. Who the fuck does he think he's talking to?

He addresses my financial situation in a rather snide way, but shouldn't a father be pleased that his son is unencumbered by debt?

I like the part about *publisher or Hollywood type*. Another fine rhetorical flourish—I have somehow come to represent the world of wealth and fame, the world that debases family in the name of self.

I don't know my cousin James well; in fact, I've met him only two or three times. He's a nice fellow, with a pretty wife and a cute scrappy young son whose face is all freckles and smile and teeth. And he seems like a pretty understanding dude who wasn't stressing over the fact that it took me a while to get the books back to him.

August 13 is the day after my birthday. My father and I have a habit of missing each other's birthdays—sometimes by weeks, or days, or even months, but for some reason my father nailed it in 2006.

He's been stalking me for months, he's on top of me, he knows my birthday, he'll nail the date this time, show me that he cares even though he knows—he knows he's about to light the fuse of his epistolary cannon. If during one of our phone conversations I'd said the right thing, apologized for my indecent and selfish behavior, he might have folded the letter away in a drawer, or burned it—he's giving me the chance to avoid this attack without telling me. *If you turn around and apologize I won't punch you in the back of your head.* He knows I won't say the right thing, he knows I'll be the self-centered prick he's come to consider me, and then he'll have to light the cannon and wait, and wait, and wait for the sound of the explosion. He wants fury and he will get fury.

Oct 4, 2006
I enjoyed our conversation last night. Best
visit we've had in a few years. Do you see us
as having so little in common? You seemed in
good spirits, more relaxed and upbeat than the
last couple of years. I hope it is a sign that you
are happier and more comfortable with life.
But you're still reluctant to share life experience
and that underlying bitterness remains.

I don't recall this conversation at all. But in fact my father and I have very little in common. We share no hobbies or recreational pursuits. He doesn't read, he rarely sees movies, and he doesn't cook. I have no idea what my father does with his time other than sit around his house and think about what a shit son he had the great misfortune of bringing into this world.

When he mentions my mood, *relaxed and upbeat,* I recognize that he cannot conceive of me in the world without his view of me in the world. He doesn't understand that with friends and lovers I have been *relaxed and upbeat* for years, that in fact with my mother and sisters and the rest of my family I have been *relaxed and upbeat* for most of my life. My father thinks he still owns me.

> *Oct 8, 2006*
>
> *I have sat on this much too long. The more*
> *I sit the longer it grows. It is well past time to*
> *shred or mail. So mail here it comes.*
> *With Love,*
> *Your Father*

I didn't call my father after reading the letter. I didn't respond with a letter of my own. I didn't know what to do, really. My father had shipped a letter bomb and it blew up in my face, the particles of sharp ink marred my face and hands, disrupted my spirit, unhinged me.

I called friends who had trouble with their fathers and they all confirmed for me that my father was a complete asshole, and that he hated me for some reasons I might never comprehend. Some went Oedipal, others went *Great Santini*; others took his side and said that when I became a father all of this would change (of course, they were fathers).

My therapist told me to write my father off, that we couldn't choose our birth parents but that we could find other parents in the world. I'd already turned a few teachers and older friends into father stand-ins. And my therapist's willingness to write my father off so casually caused me to take my father's side, something I did fairly often when discussing the man with other people who might not take such a generous view of his verbal and sometimes physical abuse, his womanizing, his combat-deranged mind.

In late December 2006 I found an opportunity for a peace offering to my father: my publisher had sent me forty hardcover copies of my forthcoming novel. My father had complained so bitterly about how few copies I'd given him of *Jarhead* that I decided I'd make amends here: I'd send him ten copies; he could hand them out to his work and bar cronies. This time around I'd be the good son, the dutiful son. I'd not make my father look like a chump in front of his buddies.

I was in upstate New York at my winter rental, in Germantown. I drove to the post office and boxed up ten books, having signed a few of them, and having dedicated one to my father: DEAR FATHER, THANK YOU FOR YOUR SUPPORT, YOUR LOVING SON.

I didn't know what support he'd given me, but it felt like the right thing to write, the kind of sentiment that would resonate. When it came time to address the box, I realized that I didn't have my dad's PO box information memorized. I knew his home address but he didn't like receiving mail there. For some reason he felt that the government had more access to his private life if he received mail at home. More than once I'd forgotten his injunction about using his home address and gotten an earful. So I decided to call for his address. It would be the first time we'd spoken since I'd received his letter. I thought it best to not even mention it.

"Hey, Tone," he shouted on his end of the line.

My father is one of those people who have decided that the louder you talk into a cell phone the better your reception.

"Hey, Dad," I said. "I've got some copies here of my new book and wanted to send some out to you. I'll send ten, so you can hand some off to your buddies. I need your PO box number."

"Ah, hell, Tone. You don't gotta do that. I already read that, um, that, what do you call it? The gallery? I got it from your mother."

"Galley. Yeah, I know, but you got upset with me last time over how many books I sent out, so this time around I thought I'd send you some stock."

"That's all right," he said. "I'm not really sure any of those guys would be interested. And I don't need to read it again."

I'd set myself up for this: the contrite son returns to the father for approval, possibly even for a joyous embrace, but receives instead a beating.

"OK then. Goodbye," I said.

I hung my phone up without hearing his response. I stood in the small Germantown post office, burning with rage. It was a familiar feeling, my father denying me: this time praise, acceptance—he didn't say that he liked or hated the book, simply that he'd read it and didn't need any more copies hanging around, littering up his place. I wanted to burn the box of books. I wanted to burn the post office down. I wanted to burn all of Germantown, all of Columbia County—to scorch the entire United States, east to west, and my father there in Fairfield, California, on Meadowlark Lane.

It was a week before Christmas and I was alone upstate.

I sat in my BMW M3, the engine idling mean. I was a cliché: an angry man in a sick-fast car—zero to sixty in 4.3 seconds. My shifts weren't expert enough for me to have hit a track time like that, but my shifts weren't bad, and no matter what I did, I *felt* fast driving that car, and the speedometer said so, too.

For sex, which might have calmed my rage at my father, I had a few options: both of them were in the city and neither of them was my girlfriend, she who was in Miami quite probably engaging in sex with someone other than me, her boyfriend.

I could drive to the city and be out at dinner with a beautiful one of those options by nine o'clock, or I could invite one of them up to the country, Amtrak to Rhinecliff—I'd done it before.

Or I could drive country roads like a madman and sleep alone.

I headed up 9G North, toward Hudson. I didn't speed along this stretch, but occasionally I downshifted and jacked the rpms toward the red line, feeling the torque, feeling the tires chew into the road. The desolate months had begun to settle on upstate New York: frozen ground, brittle tree branches signaling the death of another autumn, the occasional pine straining green through the gray muck of it all. Darkness fell early these nights. I had only an hour or so to drive wild without headlights.

I booked across the Rip Van Winkle Bridge and ambled through Catskill, driving like everyone else, the parents on their way to retrieve a child from some practice or another, or a rehearsal, or detention. But my car was faster than most on the road.

Out of Catskill I turned onto 9W South and began to rip through the gears. From the left an asphalt truck abruptly pulled out in front of me and I gunned it around the guy, not looking for oncoming traffic, nor caring. The speed limit was forty-five and I was going ninety. The week before I'd hit 120 on this road, and I wanted at least that much again. I wanted more. The governor on the car would stop me at 133. What value did the car have if I didn't run it out like that? None. Who wants to say *I once owned this incredibly fast German sports car, and one time I went eighty-five in it?* Only a fool.

The road ahead thinned to one lane, beneath a railroad overpass. I slowed down for the red. Between the stop line and the tight underpass lay about thirty yards of road. We went green. I gunned it, I ripped through the gears, and I shot through the short tunnel at forty-five, the traction holding deep on the slight right bend. In front of me was about two miles of mostly straight road, and I killed it, I chewed it up, the speedo climbed to ninety, and then 105, and then 120, and then 130, and then it hovered and ticked at 133; the world flew by, seasons changed, my heart hung at the edge of the world. I could die, I could kill myself with a flick of my wrist and it would look like a mistake, a daredevil young writer, war veteran, pushing all the limits at once and doing a header into a tree with his sixty-five-thousand-dollar car. But I took her down, slow, descending, 115, 105; let's hold on here at a hundred for a moment, it feels good, it feels fine, brakes now, eighty, sixty-five, fifty; there we are at forty-five, the speed limit, the boredom experienced by every other man and woman behind the wheel of a minivan.

The quiet. I hated the quiet.

I drove back across the river to Tivoli. I'd decided that in fact I wanted to have sex with someone this night, a stranger. I thought, Bard grad student! Perfect. Smart, possibly a bit crunchy and certainly young.

I ate at the bar at the Mexican joint in town. Bad chicken something, so-so margaritas, at least a few, possibly many. Nothing happened in the girl department there, a stringy blonde tried to chat with me but stringy blondes are not my style.

A fake English pub down the street drew my attention. I parked behind the bar. I started with whiskey. I remember the bartender being a friendly young guy. At some point he stopped charging me. I talked to a few locals, and a few male undergrads killing time before their flights home for winter break. Word on the street was all the girls were gone. Tivoli: Land of the Hand.

I can't tell you that I was wasted but neither can I tell you that I was sober. Certainly I'd had too much to operate my car completely safely. One of those families from the minivans? I might have taken them out: band instruments and soccer clothes tweaked in the jumble of metal and flesh. But I didn't.

I drove faster than I should have on the country

road leading to my place. I pulled into the gravel driveway, safe, but decided I needed a late-night snack. Some popcorn, perhaps.

I headed the three or so miles back to town. At the Stewart's I bought chips and salsa and a pint of ice cream. I started for home. I had the sunroof open, the bitter cold air ripped through the car. I'd driven this road hundreds of times. I remembered the exhilaration of my late afternoon speed fest, and I kicked the speed up. Yes, a stupid move. The road, I knew this road, and about a mile before my house it made a kinky tight S, posted speed limit fifteen mph. I'd hit it at forty a few times without a problem, but also without a few margaritas and whiskeys coursing through my bloodstream. But this time I pushed fifty, and fifty was no good, the S in the road became an M and then a Z and then a Q.

The sound was deafening and people from three or four houses along the road emerged to witness the results of tonight's match. Man and BMW versus Three Trees and a Telephone Pole.

Man and BMW lost.

I'd concussed myself against the now-shattered driver's-side window. I smelled gasoline, and all I saw from the windshield was hood, the beautiful crumpled racing silver hood. I heard the noise of the onlookers, cheering me out of my car, the loser. The shattered window was still intact, but I broke it away with my upper arm and climbed from the car. Dizzy, I sat along the side of the road and waited for paramedics or police. The onlookers inquired about my condition and I told them that I was fine and that I could just walk the half mile home and have my car towed in the morning. It seemed like a good plan.

The paramedics arrived first. They checked me out and said I was free to go.

The cops were young and polite, early thirties. They asked me to blow into a Breathalyzer and I refused. The few lawyer friends I had said to always refuse, if you've had more than two drinks, refuse the Breathalyzer. In order to avoid paperwork the cops tried to convince me that blowing was a good idea.

"If you just blow, no matter what the reading, we'll drop you off at home. Otherwise, we gotta pull you in front of a judge tonight, and the judge will not be happy, I assure you. And you will spend the night in jail."

"I still refuse," I said.

"OK, sir, have it your way."

Somewhere along the Taconic State Parkway on the way to State Police Troop K headquarters, one of the cops said, "Hey, wait a minute. Swofford? Didn't you write that book *Jarhead*?"

I felt like a fool. "Yes," I said, "I did."

"I got a marine buddy. He hated that movie. I thought it was pretty good. My wife read the book. Nice to meet you."

At the station a bit of hell had broken loose. A local kid had gotten drunk and somehow made it into his neighbor's house, where he'd decided he'd eat some leftover pizza and watch a movie. The captain knew both families and was trying to decide how to proceed. Most people were of the mind to give the kid a break, bust him on some bullshit misdemeanor trespassing charge, but scare the shit out of him and teach him a lesson. I thought how I might like to get a bullshit misdemeanor charge and be taught a lesson. But it didn't seem as if that was going to work out tonight.

The station had just taken shipment of an electronic fingerprinting device and my boys were having a bit of trouble operating the touch pad. While somebody got on the horn with IT, one cop said, "So how did you like the movie? I mean, that must have been weird, some pretty Hollywood kid playing you, your name and everything."

Over the years since my first book had been turned into a film I'd had this question thousands of times. But never from a cop while waiting to be fingerprinted. But I didn't flinch, and I gave my standard reply: "He's a good actor. I think he nailed it. But my abs are tighter."

The cop laughed, like he was supposed to, as thousands of other people had over the years.

And he was right. The judge did not appreciate being dragged from whatever she'd been dragged from in order to send me to jail for the night. The charge was driving under the influence, but they had no evidence, other than the observations of the police, who told the judge that I'd been polite and cooperative throughout our evening together.

The orange jumpsuit fit snugly and the deputy taking my mug shot said, "So you're the *Jarhead* guy? Nice to meet you. Who you gonna call, Mrs. Jarhead?"

I called Ava and asked her to post bail, which her father did the next morning around ten or so. The night in jail had been uneventful. No lunatics, no murderers, nothing exciting, just the same old jailhouse Bible and rubbery chow I used to be served in the Marines.

As the sheriff handed me my clothes and a check for the cash that had been in my wallet he said, "Goodbye, Jarhead. Hope to never see you again. Good luck."

I took a cab to the wrecking yard where my car had been towed. I pulled my warm winter jacket and the box of books from the trunk. The car was totaled, crumpled down to economy size from sport coupe. I noticed my chips and salsa in the backseat, so I grabbed those, too, and headed home.

MY BROTHER TOLD me this story about our father. It happened in 1974, when my brother was twelve and I was four.

My father's squadron had given him a going-away party before our family shipped off to Japan. He had a long drive home, from Sacramento to Vacaville, about fifty miles. He was drunk, and somewhere along the way the highway patrol red-lighted him, but my father didn't pull over. He was driving a fast Jaguar XK-E, and he didn't feel like stopping, so why stop?

My brother claimed to have been in the garage, working on his bike, when my father ripped around the corner followed closely by three CHP cruisers. My father slid the XK-E perfectly into the driveway and made a dash for the front door, at his heels the three cops, but my father slammed the door in their faces.

In my brother's version, my mother talked to

the police and told them that she would take care of her husband, and the police left.

Both of my parents deny the veracity of this story. I've queried my father about it numerous times and he always says, "Never happened."

This story might be one of the first lies my brother told me. But it might also be true.

Maybe most important was the fact that my older brother believed he had a father who took such extreme risks with his own life and the safety of his family. The police chase might have happened only in my brother's twelve-year-old head. The father he knew was a veteran of the Vietnam War and a pretty tense and keyed-up thirty-three-year-old man. My father loved and owned fast cars. My brother must have felt that he was a passenger in one of those cars, always moving at unsafe speeds.

6

Bethesda

Somewhere between Elizabeth and Princeton I looked at my speedometer and realized that I was going 120 miles per hour. In my mind I'd been back in the desert driving a Humvee. We were spraying fire everywhere, me driving with my left hand, my M16 in my right, the barrel out the window and me letting loose on burst. I didn't care who or what I hit.

Now I let the engine drop speed slowly. On the shoulder ahead of me a guy changed a tire on his beater truck. My first thought was VBED, vehicle-borne explosive device. Then I saw the wife and child holding hands at the rear of the vehicle. They waved. The man wore dirty ConEd overalls. In black and white it could have been a scene out of Dorothea Lange or in a novel it would have been Steinbeck.

People driving shitty cars in art and books: someone should write a dissertation.

My right hand gripped the gearshift as though it were the pistol grip on my rifle. No, as though it were the pistol grip on my life. But I had no ammunition here on the road to Bethesda, and the targets remained unclear. I poured water over my head and blasted the radio. I took the speedometer back up to ninety. I thought of the young kids missing limbs at Bethesda. What would I say?

I ARRIVED AT the Naval Hospital at three in the afternoon. The lobby was enormous and tile-floored, dotted with large planters housing massive, boring plants: the echoes from boot heels driven hard into the ground moved through the space in the timbre of death. Like most other military buildings it was well signed, but all the signage bore acronyms, so that if you didn't know what CFSSB stood for, even if you were looking for someone inside that particular labyrinth, you were totally lost.

As on any military installation people in uniform, mostly fit and youthful, hurried from one destination to another as though the world were on fire. And of course, it was. From the uniforms each wore you could tell very little other than rank. One colonel might be a bean counter in the motor pool, and another might be a Special Forces genius who'd been killing for America since the age of twenty-two, but you'd have trouble telling them apart. Only the eyes gave a clear portrait: the bean counter witnessed the world with bemused detachment, aware of how lucky he was to have worn the uniform for so long and to have missed combat; the genius killer watched the world with a weary gaze, constantly tuned to the threat wave, looking for danger real or imagined. Men and women in unfortunate naval khaki uniforms entered and exited the building, as well a few marines in short-sleeved dress blue uniforms. It was one of the easiest uniforms in the world to get laid in. It still made me proud.

AND UNFORTUNATELY FOR me hospital acronyms were some of both the most complicated and the least-known in the Marine Corps. No marine planned ever to enter a hospital. I noticed across the lobby an office with maroon-and-gold signage, which lead me to the correct assumption that this was the liaison office for injured marines and their families.

A staff sergeant greeted me, "Can I help you, boss?"

He wore a shrapnel-enhanced smirk and in his eyes swam the deep constant pain of having killed and watched others die.

"I'm here to meet up with the DAV," I said.

"Swofford?"

"Yes." It had been years since I'd spoken to a marine staff sergeant in uniform. I hadn't done anything wrong, but still he made me nervous. This guy had been jacked up overseas, he was probably ten years younger than I, but he looked hard and he looked mean, and I knew he had lived some years. When I was a corporal in the Corps I looked up to staff sergeants as if they were gods.

"Fucking Jarhead," he said. He half smiled. But I wasn't sure if he wanted to shake my hand or punch me in the face.

I was wearing a suit. I must have looked like a real civilian piece of shit to him.

"Yo, PFC Colon, weren't you with 2/7?" the sergeant yelled over his shoulder.

"Hells yes," a young voice called. "Who wants to know?"

"Jarhead is here," he said.

In the Corps I had gotten used to being called fuckface and retard and shit-for-brains. But for many years now people had called me Tony or Anthony, or Swofford, or Swoff. I had not yet acclimated to being called by the title of my first book.

"You can call me Swofford," I said. We finally shook hands.

Colon came from behind the cubicle. He had the youthful gleam and game on his face of a Dominican from New York, a kid who had probably seen as much crazy shit in the neighborhood as he ever had in the Corps, other than the IEDs and car bombs. He was in a wheelchair.

"Swofford," Colon said. "Fucking Jarhead. We all read that fucking book. Man, and the movie. That is some lucky shit. Me, not so lucky. Fucking sniper, spinal cord. Paraplegic. Can't even jack off. But fuck it, I coulda been killed dead."

"When did you get hit?" I asked.

"August oh-five. I think it was a Chechen. The fucker shot me like no Koran-drunk hajji ever could."

"That rash of sniper casualties. And then they stopped," I said.

"We either killed the fucker or he went back to Chechnya when his visa expired!" Colon laughed.

That was the thing that always blew my mind about injured marines. Here was Colon, a fiercely handsome young man of nineteen or twenty who would never get laid again—to fuck is the only thing any nineteen-year-old marine thinks about—and his attitude was so overwhelmingly positive and so filled with humor and delight at the madness of it all. I'd seen the same attitude while hanging around Camp Pendleton a few years earlier, and it was hard for me not to break down in front of this overwhelmingly positive outlook. Didn't he want to know why, didn't he want to rage against the world? Someday he would, when the Corps's goodwill ran out and it canceled his sweet desk job, or when he showed up at the VA one bright day with a broken wheelchair and they handed him a wrench to fix it himself. It would happen. But for now let Colon have his humor and his youth, I thought.

"Hey, Swofford," the staff sergeant said. "Have you heard of these Warrior dinners the big shots in DC throw every Friday night for outpatients? It's like, they got a band and some minor celebs. I saw Bob Dole a few weeks ago. And Chelsea Clinton one weekend. And TV types from New York, and they put on this big dinner for guys in long-term care, take about a hundred of them a week out for a night on the town, steak and shrimp and a shit-ton of beer. And their families can come. You want to attend tonight? We got an extra slot for a non-injured. No shit."

"I'd love to go, Staff Sergeant."

I'd heard of these dinners. A local restaurant had been putting them on since the first injured had begun to arrive in a slow stream, and now that they arrived from overseas in a river of carnage, the popularity of the dinners had soared.

"So you want to go see some injured marines?" the sergeant asked.

Colon said, "There is some fucked-up mother-fuckers up there, Swofford. This ain't no hundred-day war. This ain't no friendly fire. This ain't no boo-hoo-I-didn't-get-to-shoot-back-at-the-bad-guys bullshit."

He popped wheelies in his chair and he looked right through me. I knew he was challenging me and my easy little war, and I'd let him have it because he was right. My war was not shit and his was. I wrote a fucking book out of my little war and from his big war he got his dick blown off. You do the motherfucking math.

"This is the real fucking deal, I mean, double amps, faces blown off, brains splattered to the Funky Cold Medina and back. You think I got it bad? I ain't got shit bad on some of those fucked-up motherfuckers. You want to see some fucked-up jarheads, go on and see the show."

I'd forgotten how much marines curse. *Mother-fucker* was the equivalent of *oh really* or *no kidding*, or you could use the word to talk about the cosmos and life and death. Two guys could sit on watch for four hours in the middle of the night and the only word that would pass between them would be *motherfucker*, but that word meant: Here come some suspicious bastards; I don't think she's fucking around on me; I go home in three days; Do you think the *Rig Veda* is correct when it says, "Breath of the gods, embryo of the universe, this god wanders wherever he pleases"?

"What is the mood up there?" I asked.

Colon was popping wheelies and doing 360s in his wheelchair, and he said, "Most of the guys got a pretty good attitude. If a guy didn't lose his dick, you know, that's good. When a guy wakes up, you know this, Swofford, the first thing he does is reach down to see if he's still got a cock on him, and then he looks at the doctor or the nurse and says, 'Is it gonna work?' Or if he no longer has hands, he just looks, cranes his neck to see the bulge."

I did know this: that at one level the carnage breaks down to the dudes who lost their dicks and the dudes who didn't.

"Penis, big fucking erect penis, Mom," as Tom Cruise playing Ron Kovic said.

I'd need a year on the ward to figure out all the other layers of love and hatred and confusion and ecstasy.

"How long will most of the guys be here?" I asked.

"Of course, that's up to the docs. A month for some, six for others. And then some guys they'll send over to that fucking hellhole Walter Reed and fit with a bionic arm or leg. A guy might not even want pussy after jacking off with a bionic hand for a few months. Bionic hand won't tell you to take out the garbage, bionic hand won't tell you it's got a headache."

Colon sad this loudly and it elicited howls from all corners of the office. I'm sure they'd heard it before. And I had no doubt it would remain funny for many years.

"And you see with me, Swofford, I got some new territory to explore with the ladies. 'Cause, like, I never went down before; we just don't do that that shit where I'm from. But if I want a woman now I got to rethink my strategy. You ever see that movie *Coming Home*? So the crippled Vietnam vet Jon Voight goes down on Jane Fonda like crazy. I think it's the best movie orgasm of the 1970s. Honestly, I don't think Hanoi Jane could've faked that."

The sergeant said, "Colon Googled 'cunnilingus in films' and got back about five thousand hits. He's renting all of those movies and learning technique."

Colon continued to pop wheelies. "What I'ma do is write this manual, right? It's gonna be called

The Finer Points of Going Down. Maybe the Naval Academy will publish it for me and it will become a textbook."

More laughs from behind the cubicles.

I'd heard differing opinions about the quality of the health care the injured were receiving. Without any medical training and without talking to the troops, there wasn't a lot I'd learn, but I thought I could hang back and observe; to observe and deduct had been most of my job in the Corps, and it was now, too, so I'd do it here and see what I could come up with. Word was that Bethesda was running a cleaner operation than Walter Reed, but I didn't know if that was bullshit marine pride getting in the way of an honest appraisal of the treatment.

A NAVAL OFFICER from the Bethesda media team arrived to escort me to the injured marine floor. I made plans with the marines to meet up with them later at the dinner in DC.

As we walked onto the ward my first impulse was to bolt. I hadn't been to a hospital since my brother died. I knew the smells and the sounds, the antiseptics and the low whirl of machines that give and take life—I knew the collective heartbeat of a hospital floor holding so many lives in fine balance. I did not belong here. I would wreck the balance.

I wanted to be back in Manhattan in my clean little life, in my Chelsea apartment with clean white museum walls and art pieces hanging from those walls; I wanted to drink Burgundy wine from my cellar; I wanted to cook in my professional kitchen; I wanted to eat at my eight-thousand-dollar table while wearing my two-thousand-dollar cowboy boots; I wanted to take a woman other than my girlfriend out to a five-hundred-dollar dinner and take her home, and upstairs while staring at the Empire State Building I wanted to fuck her and forget that a place called Bethesda Naval Hospital existed exactly 230 miles away from that clean Manhattan life.

But that was not the plan of the day. The naval officer showed me into a room where a mother bent over her young marine son. He'd arrived two days before. They were not sure the kid would live. A week earlier he'd taken a sniper round to the forehead. The swelling was down. He blinked when his mother spoke to him. But he could blink for only a few hours a day. I remember that the family was from Ohio. Someone from the naval media team asked me to sign a copy of *Jarhead* for the kid. I wrote it out to Tommy or Timmy or whatever his name was, knowing he'd never read it. His mother took the book from me and smiled and said she'd read it to him.

I thought, *Jesus, please read the kid something with a little bit of hope, not my bleak book.*

What are you going to give a mother from Ohio to read over the deathbed of her nineteen-year-old son?

I walked out of the room with my minders. My brain hurt. I was short of breath and thirsty. The minders got called away for a moment and they asked me to stand by.

Ahead of me in the hall I saw a man in his fifties leaning against the wall just outside a patient room. He wore a red T-shirt emblazoned with MARINE DAD. The guy was big, he'd once been an ox of a football player, somewhere in the Middle West, I guessed. I approached him.

"Excuse me, sir, can I ask you a few questions?"

"Who are you, son?" I read former marine officer right away, Vietnam, '68 to '70. I saw it in his eyes.

"I'm a former marine and a writer. I wrote a book about the first Gulf War. I'm here to listen to some stories, find out about the quality of the treatment. Who are you here visiting?"

"My boy," he said, and he pointed at his sweatshirt and looked at me as though I were stupid.

He continued, "He's in surgery right now. Below the knee on one leg, above the knee on the other, once it all shakes out. Goddamn it, son, I was in 'Nam, I saw a lot of men die, but I've just spent three weeks up here, and I never saw men injured so heinously. The boys are ripped to shreds. Go room to room and you'll see. And look at all the mothers. I'm one of the only fathers up here because the fathers are back at home earning money or they've never been around. I'm lucky, after my time in the Corps I was an executive at a bank. I retired a year ago. I've got two pensions. I can afford to cool my heels here and look after my son. I can do this for the rest of my life. But look at the mothers. Some of them are married, but you know the story, many of these boys come from broken homes, poor homes, single mothers. These women, they thought they were going to refashion themselves after fifty, live new and dazzling adventures. But they're going to be feeding and bathing their sons for the rest of their lives."

He placed his hand on my shoulder and asked me to look after any marine I could. A woman approached. She was clutching copies of a newspaper article to her chest.

"This is the article they ran on Sam yesterday in the paper. It's so touching. They captured him. He couldn't speak but he blinked his eyes and they captured his soul."

The woman began to cry and the Marine Dad comforted her.

"May I give you one of these about my son?" she asked me.

"Yes, ma'am," I said. I glanced at the article, a front-page story with color photo from Wednesday's paper, this woman at her son's bedside, the son immobile, neck brace, oxygen mask, legs in traction, the boy barely visible beneath his bouquet of medical matériel.

"Who are you with?" she asked.

Just then my minders arrived and introduced me to the woman. She asked for a signed book and I gave her one. She told me that a week or so before Wolfowitz had been on the ward but she was much more excited to meet me.

The woman told me that the care her son received was top-notch and that the support staff had been wonderful. I glanced at the photo of her son on the cover of the newspaper.

"He's a sweet boy," she said.

The Marine Dad walked away.

The woman looked at me and said, "I'm happy for him his son has a small wound."

When losing most of both of your legs was a small wound I would never be able to truly understand the depth of the despair these marines and their families were suffering. During my war I'd spent a short time at the entry point of this calamity, at the end where the bombs blew and rifles and RPGs shattered bodies, where Warthogs sometimes fired on friendly troops, and I had totally forgotten about this end, the sick end, the destroyed end of it, the utter ruin of families.

"May I hug you?" the woman asked.

"Yes, of course." I felt awkward but I couldn't say no, could I?

And she hugged me tight: she gripped me for life, for a memory of who her son had been: young, clean-shaven, strong. She would never again hug her son while he stood upright. She wept into my shoulder. The lioness had lost her family. The moon darkened. Ice caps melted. How could we go on?

She locked on to my eyes in a mildly wild and erotic way, her face full of tears. She was attractive in that high school librarian way, orderly and considered. Handsome, that's what she was, and sturdy, and she possessed the orderly smell of all good mothers. Her son would be fine. He would never walk and he might not talk, but he would have his mother and somehow they would both know this and be well.

This could not have been true but it is what I told myself then and it is the same lie that other

Americans have been telling themselves for a decade, and we believe this because we have to.

Nurses and orderlies swam around us in a school of green and blue scrubs. From every room came the nauseating white sounds of resuscitation, prolongation, the beginnings of altered lives.

One of the minders grabbed me at the elbow and ushered me on to another room.

In the two visitor's chairs of the room sat an extremely old woman and a girl who could not have been older than ten. They wore colorful indigenous clothing that to my untrained eye shouted Bolivia. The old woman chewed at her leathery lower lip and the young girl beamed a smile that was as incongruous as their dress.

My minders introduced me to the marine. He was an infantry staff sergeant and had been blown up in a convoy. Both of his legs were in traction.

He said, "I'm gonna walk, man. I'm gonna walk again."

His face bore the burns from human shrapnel.

He said, "My guys got blown up. I lived, you know? I lived. I got blown up, and I woke up right here in this bed, how many days later I don't know. I was having this dream of the Philippines, like a little island and there were women and I was with my platoon and we were partying with the women. But I open my eyes and look at the end of the bed and there is sitting my grandmother and my niece, and I haven't seen anyone from Bolivia in fourteen years, since I left, and I think, 'Well, goddamn, I died in Baghdad and here I am in heaven with my grandma and my niece. Isn't that nice.' But then I think, 'Wait, they aren't dead, how can they be dead?' And they walk up to my side and say, 'You are alive.'"

The grandma eyed me suspiciously and the little girl continued her intense and beautiful smile.

"I love the Corps. Can you believe I got blown up in Baghdad and before I wake up here in the US they bring in my grandma and my niece?"

I had to admit that I was totally impressed.

"All I want to do is go back over and fight again. Fight for my dead brothers."

I could see he was slightly doped up and it looked as if he got shot up again through his IV because he faded away into a deep mind wander. Where did the drugs take his brain? Back to the desert or that Philippine island stalked by willing women, the West's Shangri-la, not unlike the Moslem's promised land overflowing with virgins for every martyr?

My minders showed me out of the hospital.

*　　*　　*

I HAD NEVER driven in DC and had only the slightest idea where I was going. I wanted to visit the Marine Corps War Memorial, which abutted Arlington, prior to heading somewhere near Capitol Hill for the dinner, which started at seven. I found the memorial. It was a replica of the famous flag-raising at Iwo Jima, the second one, of course. Everyone knew the story about the poor bastards who'd done it the first time, stupidly, without a photographer in tow. Never go to combat without a camera (or a blog).

Around the massive base of the memorial were stenciled the names of every campaign, large and small, that the Marine Corps had ever participated in. The crowd was one of those truly American collections of people: white, Latino, black, Asian, Middle Eastern, and recent Eastern European immigrants. Some of the men were Vietnam vets, others the sons and daughters of vets. A man being pushed in a wheelchair had to be from the Island Hopping Campaign; he wore a cap emblazoned with the badge of Guadalcanal and the 1st Marine Division, the division created specifically to jump the islands all the way north into the heart of mainland Japan.

I wanted to feel deeply patriotic. I smelled burned sand and scorched asphalt. That was all.

I walked toward the edge of Arlington. There were two funerals under way, each held beneath a blue plastic tarp. One coffin had already been dropped, the family and friends staring into earth; at the other a priest hovered above the box in mid-prayer, offering absolution. I wondered who rested in the coffins, young men from the current wars or old men passed on from emphysema or colon cancer, mad in the head from Alzheimer's, or a peaceful sleepy end, just one last breath, a snore.

Arlington's austerity chilled me, a tapestry of green-and-white silence. The tapestry did not hide the fact that most of those men and women had died horrible deaths in combat.

TWO TOUR BUSES unloaded their passengers in front of the appointed restaurant, a few blocks from the Hart Senate Office Building. These were the men and women, soldiers, sailors, and marines, undergoing outpatient care, on their way to recovery. They used crutches and walkers and wheelchairs, and some of them walked on their own: he with a prosthetic leg, I could tell by the slight flag-like snap of the pants leg, or she missing an arm and choosing thus far to go without the prosthetic, the left shirt sleeve delicately folded and pinned to the front of the shirt, the single phantom hand in a gesture half of prayer and half of defiance.

And here now more mothers. Of the many legacies this war would produce the one not yet considered by most observers was this, which the Marine Dad had pointed out to me in the hospital corridor: mothers—a few as young as forty, women a man my age might date—looked at the horizon and saw themselves escorting their sons to VA hospitals for the next forty years. The greatest burden of a war always falls on the mothers. The men on both sides kill; the men have their mortal fun, they blow each other up and post the deeds on YouTube, and the mothers carry the casualties to the Rasa River, wash and dress the wounds, count casualties. The mothers bathed the wounded at Hiroshima. They have done so on the Seine, the Thames, the Missouri, the Danube, the Oostanaula. Name a river. It has received our wounded from the backs of mothers.

I heard someone calling my name. I watched the staff sergeant push Colon up the hill. Both men were wearing dress blues and Colon surreptitiously took a nip from a bottle of whiskey. It was a prelude to a horror film or a Dada fantasy, and I couldn't decide which.

Colon said, "We got big plans tonight, brother. After this proper sit-down meal we are going to show you how to get it on in DC. The girls are wild, man. There's like forty thousand college girls within the city limits. How can that be bad?"

"That sounds perfect, my friend."

"It's a circus. Didn't you come up here and party when you were in Jacksonville?"

"Not really. I had a girlfriend in California. I spent most of my time running up a long-distance phone bill with her."

"A girlfriend," Colon said. "I got one of those, but she's in the DR, left me for the motherfucking pizza delivery man, I shit you not."

I could see this conversation turning south in no time. We were under the awning in front of the restaurant and the other injured servicemen and -women walked between and around us. Infidelity was a hot-button issue in the military that no one wanted to touch. Other than beer and sports and hamburgers, it was the main thing enlisted men talked about. Infidelity, the fear of it—real and more often imagined—haunted the ranks; it ranked just behind the fear of dying.

I motioned to the two marines that we should head in. There was a serious queue at the elevator, we were expected in a ballroom on the second floor, and most of these men and women weren't exactly prepared to climb the stairs. The guys told me to take the stairs and that they'd meet me up there. I offered Colon a piggyback ride but he said he didn't trust my scrawny civilian legs.

The reception looked like a middling version of the New York parties I'd casually attended for a few years. The food spread was not as ambitious as at a Hollywood party and about on par with something for a party a poetry magazine might throw. In ranking New York parties in terms of sex appeal and food and booze I'd give hedge funds the number-one spot, then the art world, television, magazines, books, and in an ugly and distant last, the NGOs.

The bar here consisted of one guy behind a folding table, two kinds of bad wine, red or white, and a number of sixty-gallon coolers full of ice and beer and soda. But it didn't matter. The arriving troops were pumped. They weren't eating hospital food tonight, but rubbing elbows and wheelchair wheels and prosthetic limbs with the affluent and influential.

I saw the secretary of the Army and an admiral whose face I recognized from some congressional hearing or another. I saw Bob Dole. I saw half a dozen congressmen and a few senators whose faces I knew from the papers but whose names I couldn't recall. Most if not all of these politicians were Republicans. Of course, this party didn't hold priority this evening for these kings of social DC. They were the power wave in this room, the surge, and in this city, as in every other city in the world, when you are the power and the money you can spend only so much time around the masses before an uncomfortable silence falls over the room.

The troops and their families will not be able to hold conversations with you about holidays in Europe, about that new sailboat, the new nanny, the summer home remodel.

This gathering is supposed to be a casual social hour but eventually the masses will want to talk about health care and prescription drugs and a living wage. And how many times can you ask the kid with a metal plate in his head, the kid with no legs, the bomb-blinded kid, where he grew up and where in Iraq or Afghanistan did this horrible unfortunate awful thing happen and how he was progressing and if he missed the men in his unit; how many times could you ask these questions without the guilt and horror blinding *you*?

I sensed that these princes of the ocean would debark from our listing cocktail lounge within twenty minutes and jump in a schooner and sail to a party where none of the tough questions had to be asked: calm seas, no visible injuries, good martinis, Beltway bottle blondes. And I was right. Twenty minutes later someone on a microphone asked us all to be seated and the power left through the back door having done their good deed for the week.

I sat at a table with Colon and the staff sergeant, two injured army personnel, two female volunteers for a nonprofit veterans advocacy group, and two members of a lobbying firm who seemed to be a couple. I gathered that the guy from the lobbying couple ran a celebrity gossip blog on the side. He had a digital recorder in front of him and he was talking about Britney Spears. I wanted to tell him that his marks had just escaped through the emergency exit, that the famous among us had left. As the salad arrived I began to talk to the woman at my right, his date.

She introduced herself in a Texas accent that sounded like summer and smelled of the color yellow and tasted of watermelon and pit BBQ.

"I'm Amy. I work for a lobbying firm. Health care, mostly. But in my spare time I shoot short docs."

"You kill vertically challenged physicians?"

She didn't like my joke.

"I direct and produce short documentary films, films with a social conscience. Films about America. What is your name?"

She stabbed a tomato on her plate and kept her fork in it and with the tomato acting as a broom head she pushed her salad in circles around her plate.

"My name is Anthony. I sit in a chair. I punch small square keys on a keyboard and try to find meaning."

"Does it pay?" she asked.

"It depends on the weather."

I could tell by the way his left leg was shaking and the number of times he'd taken a drink of nothing from his empty water glass that the gossip blogger next to her was getting a little antsy. This Amy was a truly lovely piece of Texas, the main bed partner, I assumed, for the freelance gossip blogger. Twenty-eight years old, probably a year out of grad school. By the length of her upper torso and the bit of leg I could see that wasn't hidden under the table I guessed she was five feet ten. Her natural blond hair was full, with a flip and bounce on the ends. She had those Texas blue eyes that make one think of hunting and roasting wild boar on the back forty, feeding the family, and then fucking for the next ten hours of one's life.

"Sweetheart," the gossip blogger said, "you really

need to eat. You know what happens when you don't eat and you have a few drinks."

"I become a total irredeemable bitch?"

"I didn't say that."

"But last night you used that phrase."

I extracted myself from earshot of the quarrel and said hello to the young woman at my left. Young girl, I thought. She looked about sixteen, strawberry-blond hair, wide sweet smile, blue jeans and a flower-print blouse. I wondered if her father was one of the injured men among us. I looked for him.

She said to me, "I served as a private in the 82nd Airborne Military Police." She lifted her right leg and with her knuckles pounded on it. The sound was of titanium. "Guess how they got me? You don't have to guess. IED."

It was the first time that day that I'd found myself speechless. This girl, this woman, who looked as though this very morning her mother had made her scrambled eggs and rushed her off to homeroom, was living the pain of war right here next to me while at the same table a pair of ill-fit lovers quarreled stupidly about nothing.

I thought I'd been handling the carnage fairly well: the ruined mother holding the clippings from her son's newspaper story, the Bolivian sergeant with his grandma and niece, Colon with his lessons in cunnilingus. None of it had been pretty but it had all been tolerable. In advance of this trip I'd prepared psychic shelves for these brands of trauma.

The injured young female private had drilled this war too deep.

Our salad plates were replaced with entrées, steak.

"Hello, Private," I said. "I was in the Marine Corps during the first Gulf War. But I'm out now. How is your treatment?"

"Mostly good, sir. It's a long process, you know. The barracks are kind of cruddy, worst I've ever had. Food tastes like shit; that's why I come to these as often as possible. That, and I got an autograph from Tiger Woods for my dad a couple months ago. And I get to see Fernando." She motioned to her left. A young kid sat up straight in his chair, chewing steak, Army cap with sergeant stripes pulled down tough over his forehead, black silk Army jacket, alert eyes. Fernando nodded slowly at me, every move tentative with pain.

"The Army doesn't want us together because he's a sergeant and all, but we're both getting out; he broke his back when his Bradley flipped, so we're getting out. But they can't stop us here. They can't keep us from these dinners."

On my other side, from Amy and her man, I heard the low-voiced, choking hatred of two people who are no longer in love. They'd traveled shockingly far from the early romantic terrain where you buy each other used copies of your favorite books and spend whole weekends fucking and drinking Bloody Marys or margaritas, depending on the weather, and nothing on Earth strikes you as more romantic or fulfilling than the relationship that is a slowly closing noose around your neck.

I had no appetite. I nodded at the private and her illicit sergeant boyfriend and excused myself to the terrace. Here, mostly male soldiers and marines stood or leaned and smoked. I'd never smoked, I'd never had a cigarette in my life, but I asked a young marine with a high and tight haircut if he could spare one.

"Sure thing, dude," he said. He'd flared *dude* into a sharp and shrill California beach cliché. His buddies loved it.

My hair wasn't long, but it was longer than any military guy's. I tried to fake the carriage of a US Marine, especially around this crowd, but my hair read Slimy Civilian and so did those extra pounds and my suit. I noticed myself looking at the men, grading their appearance and behavior for military bearing and discipline. How absurd. The marine lit my cigarette for me and I inhaled deeply and coughed. The smoke was bitter and burned. I threw the thing into a planter that was being used as an ashtray. This drew a chorus of laughs.

"Damn, where'd you learn to smoke?" the kid who'd given me the cigarette asked. "You owe me like a dollar, man."

"I'll smoke it." And someone else picked up my waste and lit it.

"That was my first one ever. And my last," I said.

"If that's the case," the kid said, "could you go on a beer run?"

"What are you guys drinking?"

"Beer." The huddle of smokers laughed.

I counted eight of them. "Eight beers."

"Make it sixteen," one of them chortled.

"I'll see what I can do."

Inside, waiters set dessert in front of diners and at the stage a country band made ready for its show. I asked the bartender for sixteen beers. He didn't want to give them to me.

He said, "We can't get these kids too wasted. Some bad shit has gone down in the past. Who knows what meds they're on."

I pulled a fifty out of my wallet and handed it to him, and he put sixteen beers in a wine box.

On the terrace I put the beer at the feet of the smokers and they all exclaimed and whistled and clapped their hands, as though I'd handed them the spigot from the fountain of life.

"Those bastards will never give us more than one beer per person. They think we're going to get drunk and get in a fight back at the barracks, a bunch of gimps beating the shit out of each other with crutches and canes."

"No, they're worried that we'll skip out on the bus and go to a bar and beat the shit out of some civilians."

"All I want to do is get drunk. I don't give no fuck about the senator's son and I don't give no fuck about you gimps."

"It's *a* fuck. I don't give *a* fuck, not *no* fuck."

"He learned to cuss in the Air Force. They use proper grammar when telling you to go fuck your mother."

"How'd you get sixteen beers out of that guy?"

"I pulled rank," I said.

Back at my table the staff sergeant and Colon seemed to be making exemplary progress with the two ladies from the nonprofits. Maybe for these girls tonight there would be true profit in veteran advocacy.

Amy and her man were still engaged in

clenched-mouth carpet-bombing of each other's
character. The private and the sergeant had disappeared, likely to a broom closet or toilet stall, I
assumed. I tried to figure out how a guy with a broken back and a woman with a prosthetic leg would
fuck in a toilet stall. There had to be a joke in there
somewhere, but I could not locate it.

I ate my spongy mousse cake in peace and
solitude.

Amy put her hand on my leg and said, "We
have something else to get to, a bar birthday for
one of his friends. But here's my card. And I'd love
to get your information in case I'm—in case we're
in New York sometime we can all get together."

The gossip man and I exchanged nothing, not a
look or a handshake or a business card.

They left.

I read her card. I flipped it over and on the back
she'd written the name of a bar and cross streets and
the joyous greeting: SEE YOU IN AN HOUR OR SO.

The country music band was turning the volume way up, which meant it was time for me to
go. I thought I'd leave the business card on the
table and let someone else meet her in an hour
or so. Blondes in the lobbying game weren't my
ambition. I thought about it long and hard, and I
decided it had been at least ten years since I'd slept

with a blonde. It wasn't yet ten o'clock. I could push it hard and be home by two in the morning. I could call Ava and she would be in my bed when I got to Manhattan. After a day like this I needed a body in bed and I needed to fuck. I couldn't sleep alone tonight. But the question was whether or not I wanted to drive four hours or a few miles to not sleep alone tonight.

I decided to save the gas.

I wished everyone at the table a good night and told Colon and the staff sergeant that I planned to see them the next time I came to town.

I DROVE TO Georgetown and found the bar, somewhere off of Wisconsin. I assumed that I'd show up to the gossip blogger's friend's party and that it might take me hours to peel the lobbyist away from her crowd, or that I had completely misread her intentions or that she was playing a game with me. All of these possibilities swirled in my head. There are only three things a man enjoys more than sleeping with a woman within hours of meeting her. And at this moment I couldn't remember what those things might be.

Dance music thumped, people spilled and drank drinks, bartenders poured more, a pushing match broke out between two heavily muscled kids in polo shirts, and I spotted Amy in the back of the bar. She sat alone.

"Where is the rest of our party?" I asked.

"I'm a party of one," she said.

I retrieved whiskeys from the bar.

"So what are you doing, research for another book?"

"Book?"

"Those marines told me you're a writer. They think you're spying on them. They think you're trying to do an exposé on Bethesda."

"If I'd seen poor care or dirty conditions I would write about it. But that place runs pretty tight, as far as I can tell. I was only on the ward for ninety minutes, but I sensed that the care is expert. A naval hospital is different from an Army hospital, in that there are no members of the Army running the show."

"Of course. Even the old marine loves the Navy. All this services pride is such bullshit."

"Maybe so. Maybe not. They found rat shit all over Walter Reed, right? My Polish cleaning lady would have been impressed with the spit shine on that ward. As they say, Joseph's baby mama could've eaten off of that floor."

"So tell me, who the fuck are you?" she said.

"I'm just a guy drinking whiskey with a stranger

in a strange town. I should've driven home hours ago."

"Girlfriend?"

There was no need to lie. "Depending on the week and which lies we are telling one another. I believe that for most of this week I had a girlfriend. But I can never tell. Where is your boyfriend?"

"That guy? He was a one-night stand that turned into something it should never have. A wasted year. Still some nights he comes around. Did you sleep with this woman the first night you met her?"

"Two days later. She had a live-in boyfriend in Brooklyn. I lived in Oakland and had a girlfriend in Manhattan. It was messy. It still is."

"Aren't you too old for that?"

"Someday I hope to be too old for it. But right now I am not."

"Neither am I," she said.

The bar had filled with more young drunk people. I wondered where they had all come from. They were so goddamn happy and carefree. I thought about the marines I'd scored the beer for earlier that night, sleeping on bunks now, listening to the nightmare confusion of one another, fighting their way through the long war.

I smelled burned sand and scorched asphalt.

Someone spilled a drink on Amy's leg. I wiped her leg with napkins. She asked me to kiss her and I did and then she asked me back to her apartment.

The sex from a one-night stand is never spectacular, it rarely breaks land speed records, but with Amy it was great. She was under thirty but she knew her body and was proud of it. She wanted me to want her and I did. We continued to drink whiskey, a not-very-good Canadian whiskey, as I recall, and we were still awake and talking when the sun came up.

"So if you weren't there to report about Bethesda, why were you there?"

"I am often asked about the wars. And I say that the wars are a waste of human life on both sides and a deep strategic blunder. But I had never sat in a room with a wounded marine. And I needed to do that. But I am no clearer on what the wars mean."

"Do they have to mean anything? Can't they just be a show of American force and power in a region full of Islamists and enemies of freedom?"

"Wars mean something whether the wagers of the war want them to or not. Vietnam is still being fought here in DC. Kerry lost in 2004 because of the swiftboaters; Bush won in 2004 because he was a crafty and ardent draft dodger and thirty-plus years later he stuck to his story: 'Oh, yeah, I forgot I was supposed to be flying planes in the National Guard. Sorry guys.'"

"I just fucked a liberal," she said. "My father will kill me. Aren't you a marine? Like, don't marines want to go to war and kill? Jesus. I haven't fucked a liberal since freshman year."

"You are the first conservative I have ever fucked. We might as well do it again."

WE WERE UP front about never needing to contact each other again unless one of us was in the other's town and wanted sex.

I HURRIED BACK to Manhattan. Ava and I were throwing a dinner party that night at my apartment. I still needed to shop. I'd make roasted leg of lamb, pierced with anchovy and slivers of garlic and sprigs of rosemary.

I drove I-95 back to the city. I took it slower than I had on my way down. Mostly I went the speed limit. I listened to NPR. I smelled burned sand and scorched asphalt.

7

Welcome to Fabulous Las Vegas

Before heading to Iraq again my friend Sammy threw himself a going-away party in Vegas. I'd had a strict twelve-hour rule for Vegas: land at six p.m., fly out by six a.m. the next day. Any more time in that town is completely ruinous to one's cash flow and sanity. But Sammy talked me into a long weekend, Friday morning through Sunday night, and I hadn't seen him for a while, and Ava and I had just broken up for the twentieth time and she was in the UK fucking some puffer with bad teeth and I needed to get out of Manhattan.

Sammy knew some guy who knew some guy who had gotten us into a club with five-hundred-dollar bottle service, but before that we were eating the subpar food at the attached restaurant, a Manhattan import that had done ten cycles of anabolic steroids before being dropped down on the Strip. A couple of Sammy's marines were along with us, senior enlisted guys who'd seen the same shit as Sammy in western Iraq. In this town, this club, this bar with all these dolls and all these straight guys wearing corset T-shirts and waxed eyebrows and Botoxed faces, the marines' hostility was apparent: their hair was short and so were their tempers. They looked around the room as though choosing targets for an easy hundred-yard shoot. Their targets: anyone who might get in the way of their mission, and the mission, clearly, was women.

I remember dancing and doing watermelon shots with a gaggle of Filipina girls from San Diego. It crossed my mind that a thirty-six-year-old man might spend his time in more sober or age-appropriate pursuits: say, whiskey and bull-riding. But it is hard to argue against the beauty of a twenty-five-year-old Filipina doing watermelon shots on a dance floor. I couldn't decide if I looked like a pervert or like a cohort or simply lost.

A few bottles later, it was late, and the attrition rate for our evening was high: Sammy and I were the only ones left. While barely five-four and not much over 120 pounds, Sammy had been drinking like a pro all night, downing shots, beers, cocktails, whatever made its way in front of him. He had a war to get to but first he needed to drink.

I would have been drinking the same way had I been on my way to or from Iraq. The first time he'd gotten back he'd been a little jumpy and had been smart enough to go to the base doc for some help. But all the pills did was keep him from getting hard and he couldn't have that so he flushed them down the toilet. He downplayed what he'd done and seen but I knew whatever it had been, it had been enough. No one ever wants more war. But Sammy was going back. He didn't have to go back. After twelve years in the Marine Corps he'd resigned his commission and matriculated in a graduate writing program. We'd talked about it and it seemed like the right thing to do. Certainly his mother agreed.

And then one day he called me: the commandant of the Marine Corps had signed his resignation, but Sammy couldn't say goodbye to the Corps. That afternoon, observing the marines he'd been training for six months, it hit him like a roadside bomb—he knew he couldn't send them back over alone. He'd rescinded his resignation, and that is why we were wasted in Vegas.

I looked up from our booth and a meaningless conversation with someone and saw that three bouncers, three huge bouncers, had cornered Sammy by an elevator bank. Together they probably weighed ten times as much as he did.

He was smiling, that big huge dumb marine smile, the smile that says, "Come on, fellas, let's have a dance."

I rushed over.

One of the bouncers said, "Is he your boy? You better get him the fuck outta here if he's your boy."

I said, "He's cool, man. He's a crazy-ass marine, and he's going over to Iraq again. Give him some leash."

"He's wasted, you gotta get him out of here or we'll send him down the trash chute."

I talked Sammy into the elevator and, stumbling, we made it back to our room. I delivered him to the shower, where he stripped and cold-showered himself.

It was late, but it wasn't yet daylight, which meant I still had time. I'd gotten a local girl's number back at the club. Wanda. She had drugs and she came to my room. In the suite, sunk down into the couch, with this girl I'd just met, I did drugs until noon. She had a story, and that's why I sat doing drugs with her. She was completely gone, but she had a story.

Earlier that night she'd stolen her boyfriend's Yukon and driven in from the suburbs and she wanted to party. She'd left her kid at her mom's house and she was going to party all weekend, because she'd found out her boyfriend was sleeping with one of her friends, because that is how you teach a man who is treacherous with your heart: you steal his SUV and drugs and you go off and play with strangers.

I don't know why I loved her story so much, the bleakness of it, the raw fact of people fucking each other over, the totally ballsy act of this petite woman stealing her thuggish boyfriend's car (and his drugs) on a Saturday night and going into the city for a party, so clearly a death wish that it must have resounded with me. I knew all about the pleasures of the death wish. Here I sat in the middle of my own, blowing my brains out with cheap drugs.

Of course, this was neither the first nor the last time I'd done drugs with a stranger in a hotel room.

I JEOPARDIZED SAMMY that night. If the girl's boyfriend had somehow found us, if hotel security had gotten a tip that two people were doing blow in a large suite on the thirty-fifth floor, who knows what could have happened, and Sammy would have been implicated despite being passed out in the shower, and I would have ruined his career. I hadn't given Sammy enough thought, and in retrospect I'm ashamed. A marine always looks out for his platoon. How had I forgotten?

And I was too wasted for sex. I'd wanted nothing

more than to get a screw on with a sexy black girl from the Las Vegas suburbs, but we just sat there all morning talking about what a crazy place Vegas was and how you had to be an animal to live there.

SAMMY HAD ANOTHER friend who knew a guy who knew a guy, and we got some choice real estate at a pool party. The scene at the pool party replicated the scene from the night before except everyone wore fewer clothes. I was neither tan nor in very good shape, and so I stood in a corner of the pool drinking beer and not chatting with anyone.

Sammy attracted an unending parade of girls, and I talked to some of them, and they all seemed the same: attractive, in very good shape, possibly fake breasts; mostly they lived in LA or New York and they worked in film or real estate. We talked a lot about TV shows I'd never seen but had heard of, a particular show from that series, the amazing second season of that series.

We met a couple, Claire and Tony, from Long Island. They were on vacation with their parents. She was a nurse and he ran an auto body shop. They were great people, the kind of people I had grown up with and never met in New York City. He talked vaguely about being a criminal as a kid, and she laughed and rolled her eyes. And we drank.

I had a flight out at two but I changed it to three, and then to four, and then to five. I was supposed to fly to LA to see a woman I'd met on the East Coast a few weeks earlier. I didn't want to see her: making the plan had merely been a function of boredom.

I've wasted tens of thousands of dollars on flights booked late at night, out of boredom: meet me in London, meet me in Baden-Baden, meet me in Seattle, meet me in Rome; I'll fly you to Tokyo, I'll fly you to Paris; I'll fly you anywhere but here.

I finally stopped calling the airline to change the flight and instead I started calling around town for a new room. I wasn't sure how many days, at least three or four, I told reception at every place I called. I finally found a room at the Wynn, in the tower suites, for five hundred dollars a night.

THE ROOM WAS twice as big as my apartment; the bath could hold three people. I settled in for a bath. I was sunburned now, and kind of drunk. I'd been ignoring my phone, ignoring the thought of Ava in London, or wherever she was, fucking someone else. I dialed her and hung up. I sat in the bath, reading *In Cold Blood*.

I stayed in the suite a week.

8
Freddy Business

Freddy drove a different car every time and he'd meet me anywhere in Manhattan. He didn't go to Brooklyn, only punks dumb enough to drive miles for a single deal did that, and the drivers in Brooklyn were shit crazy out of their minds, worse than Chinatown. Freddy said he'd be there in twenty minutes but then he took an hour. It was a smart tactic for a drug dealer, always keep them guessing, always keep those dumb rich white motherfuckers wanting more, sitting around in their dumb rich white bars paying ten dollars for a beer. And the next time he told me an hour he was there in five minutes, texting, "WTF? There are f'ing cops all up in this place."

It was Manhattan, so of course there were cops everywhere. But it was below Ninety-Sixth Street and above Canal so the cops didn't do much but try to get laid.

Sometimes it didn't matter how long Freddy Business took because I was already high, because someone had copped so much the night before that, despite our having been awake until noon, there were still a few bags going around, and it seemed like the party would never end and that the cops were after me no matter what I did so why not do a shit-ton of drugs?

Freddy pulled up in his car in front of the Swan on Twentieth Street. One of my friends was doing yoga on the sidewalk and another was talking to an NYU coed who was reading *Sophie's Choice* at the dim light of the bar. But I was buying tonight so I jumped in Freddy's car. Freddy never drove; big enormous black guy who would either break your neck or shoot you if you did some stupid shit always drove and he never said a word, but he looked at me and nodded and I thought, *He must think I am one stupid white boy.*

Freddy didn't like this block so his driver drove east and then south on Park, west on Sixteenth to Sixth Avenue, and then up to Twenty-Sixth and east again. Pulled up in front of 15 West Twenty-Sixth Street, where I'd once had an office. What did I do there? Nothing. What did this mean? It meant nothing, it was simply a place to pull over, but it made me nervous. It made no sense, it made no sense at all, but why would a twelve-hundred-dollar drug deal make any sense wherever the dealer parked? Across the street people were paying astronomical prices for Texas BBQ and beer. Who would spend so much money on BBQ? Some nights I would, but not tonight, tonight I'll eat nothing, I'll barely eat anything for three days.

I was buying for three and for the weekend so I told Freddy I'd go big, and I pulled the cash out of my pockets; I hadn't even counted, eight hundred of it was mine, four hundred cobbled together by friends, and Freddy counted it and said it was a thousand, but maybe I didn't give a fuck because it was Thursday night and Freddy had the drugs packed like jewels in his glove compartment.

My father once told me: always carry hundreds and fifties. It is proof you go face-to-face with a banker. If you walk around with a bunch of twenties in your wallet you look just like all the other assholes who use the ATM, so I handed Freddy hundreds.

Freddy was jumpy tonight, and he kept counting the money again and again, coming up with different numbers, saying now it was seven hundred, telling his guy to drive around the block again, down Broadway now, past Madison Square Park.

"Dumbass white motherfuckers in line for two hours for a ten-fucking-dollar cheeseburger," Freddy says. "Let's call it a thousand," Freddy says.

Now I'm nervous, now I want out of the car, I want my money back and never want to do drugs again: *Go back in the Swan and flush the drugs you have down the toilet*, I think. *Tell those assholes you're doing drugs with to fuck off.*

"Naw," Freddy says. "It's nine hundred. I'll give you a shitload for nine hundred."

Can I argue with a lying drug dealer named Freddy Business who has all the drugs and all the money and all the guns? Not really.

But I do.

"Freddy Business," I say. "There is more than a thousand there, man. There's twelve hundred. I know there is twelve hundred. I fucking counted it."

The driver looks over his shoulder at me. A threat?

"Maybe it's twelve. Yeah, it's twelve. I can give you four large and four small, a little extra for your trouble and continued patronage."

Yes it's a sign of trouble when the drug dealer gives you a deal. But who ever sees the signs until it is too late?

I never do.

Freddy drops me off in front of Pete's Tavern

on Irving and I call my friends and tell them to meet me there, and they will because I just spent all their money on drugs. My pockets are literally bulging with drugs.

This allows me time to consider how I got to this place, how I got to Sixteenth and Irving in Manhattan with twelve hundred dollars' worth of cocaine in my pockets, enough drugs to send me to prison for a fair stretch of time; even though it's not crack and I'm white, I could still spend a lot of time in jail for the drugs in my pocket. I couldn't just explain it away.

"I pulled on someone else's jeans this morning, Officer."

But I don't have the answer to how I got here. I don't even know where I am. Once I was married, once I lived in a beautiful house in Iowa City and I was married to a beautiful woman and then we lived together in a beautiful house in Portland, and then I fucked that all up, destroyed it, and I hate myself, and rather than think about that I go downstairs at Pete's Tavern, the Place O. Henry Made Famous (how did he do that, by doing blow in the bathroom?), and I do some more drugs because it's easier, so much easier to do drugs than to think about my old life, that old good life I ruined.

But I think about it. No matter how hard I try

to blow my brains out, I think about it. I think about the various good lives I have lived, how long these periods usually last, and I wonder why, now, in the richest city in the world, in the loveliest city in the world with the most beautiful women in the world and the best food and some of the best architecture and the best art and the best parks, and the most money that I have ever had in my bank account and a piece of real estate in this rich city and five hundred bottles of wine in my cellar, why, of all the cities on Earth, I am here now fucked up on drugs and deeply depressed in this great shining city on the island?

I come back from the bathroom and some blue shirts have taken my place at the bar, so I leave. I tell my friends to return to the Swan but they never left, so I walk there.

One friend is still doing yoga on the sidewalk. The other friend is mumbling into his own hands at the bar. And I talk to the girl reading *Sophie's Choice*, and she tells me her name is Sophie but I assume this is a lie.

The drugs are passed around and Sophie joins. She says she never does this stuff, just maybe sometimes on weekends and holidays or when her mother is in town.

Much later Sophie comes home with me. I do

drugs with her all night and read Styron aloud, and I'm in bed with her and during sex breaks I read more Styron. We spend the morning taking turns reading the entirety of *Darkness Visible* aloud, and I wonder if Styron would get a kick out of this, a writer in bed with a twenty-year-old, high on cocaine, reading aloud Styron's book about the crippling effects of his depression and his years of self-medicating.

9

Genesis: an Imagining

For a not-wealthy man of twenty he wears a fine new suit. It is not borrowed. The suit is black, and a thin gray tie parts the white sea of his shirt. The young man is handsome, and if he were smiling the smile would be large and welcoming, a bit crooked to the left, and his teeth would be in perfect shape, a gap between the front two. His white skin is lightly tanned; this is not a laborer's tan but neither is it a banker's. His nose is thin at the bridge and widens considerably at the nostrils. His blue eyes look like jewels. Beneath the hat his hair is thick, dark, and wavy. Sweat has begun to darken his collar. He stands with other similarly attired and sweating men. The women wear black dresses and cool themselves with silk fans but the women do not sweat.

His wife died a few days earlier. And here we join him at her graveside. The graveyard is the Old

Auburn Graveyard in Auburn, Alabama, for whites only. It is July 24, 1941.

The man's thoughts are a swirl of hatred for God, forgiveness for God, guilt and shame, and love for his newborn son. He does not hear a word the Southern Baptist preacher says, but later at the reception at his in-laws' home the guests will tell him it was a spirited sermon and that for certain her soul left her body at the end of it, rising to the great heavens above.

The man shovels dirt onto his young wife's casket. The sound is hollow, a fist of knuckles against pine. He buries the spade in the pile of dirt and balances himself with the handle. He looks at the gathered crowd: his wife's mother, her sisters and brothers, a smattering of nieces and nephews, a few of her dead father's colleagues from the university. The man is poor and these people are not. He suspects they have designs on his baby son. He has sent word back to west Georgia that a cousin should come fetch him sometime in the next week so that he can return to Georgia with the baby boy.

He thinks, "Lord, God, our eternal savior, take from us now the soul of Annie Swofford. She is yours. Her body belongs now to the earth. She died with the love of Christ in her heart. She will be renewed in your Kingdom of Heaven. Amen."

John Columbus Swofford walks through the streets of Auburn in the procession mourning his wife, Annie Swofford. The sweat on his body feels like devil spit. He wants a shower. He wants to put on a pair of work trousers and boots and a white cotton undershirt, and he wants to go out to the woods and chop down an acre of pine. But he must go home and take care of his month-old son.

JOHN COLUMBUS SWOFFORD first met Annie Howard when she stopped by the little gas and sundries station he owned and ran out by Ridge Grove. To say he owned it gave him pride but it wasn't exactly true. He'd worked there a year for Mr. Shanker, and then Mr. Shanker died and his widow told John Columbus to take it over and give her 10 percent of the monthly. And so he did. But he felt like an owner, kept the books, ordered the gasoline and the Coca-Cola and the ice cream and the hard and soft candy and work gloves, fan belts, and motor oil and tires.

Mr. Shanker had had a side business of moonshine, doing his part to whet and supply appetites in this dry county, but after taking over the station John Columbus lined those thirty liquor bottles up at the edge of the wood behind the store and plinked them one by one with his .22 rifle. He'd left one standing and named it Temptation but in a year he'd never given in.

When a man asked for moonshine John Columbus said, "Plumb out, fella."

And when Adolphus Rickman came by each month with a new supply John Columbus said, "Mr. Rickman, with all respect, we don't traffic 'shine no more."

John Columbus considered affixing a name to the station, J. C. Swofford's, something of the like, but the store had never had a name, it had always simply been "the station at Ridge Grove," and the old-timers might not think it right if a name were attached.

One afternoon John Columbus sat in his stoop chair, shading himself from the sun, thinking about the future, thinking about a chain of J. C. Swofford's stores, and a trucking company, because he had the sensation that the roadways were gonna be big. He had plans.

A Ford coupe pulled up and out jumped a girl of about seventeen. The car pulled off and left the girl in a cloud of dust. All the girls he'd ever seen around there were in Opelika or Auburn. Other than stocky old Miss Shanker he'd never seen a woman at Ridge Grove, except maybe in the back-seat of her daddy's car. He'd never seen a girl in a pretty white dress *standing* in the middle of his gravel driveway.

"Sir," she said.

He stared, dumb.

"Sir?"

He stood. His deep baritone boomed, "Yes, ma'am?"

"I got me a flat tire driving my car back to town. I was coming in from Slaughters, where my cousins live. Ain't this a gasoline station? Ain't you a mechanic?"

He said without really thinking about it, "I'm the owner, not a mechanic, but I know a thing or two about changing a wheel."

He pointed to his dilapidated flatbed Ford. He opened the passenger door for her. Inside the cab of the Ford it looked as if two raccoons had gotten into a fistfight. Only the faintest rumor of upholstery remained on the seats, and the floorboards were even less of a rumor.

"Hold yourself a moment," he said, and ran inside the store and grabbed a package of clean white shop towels.

He covered the passenger seat with the towels and ushered the frightened girl in.

"There ain't hardly no floor," she said. "Where do I put my feet?"

"On the edges," he said. Rust-chewed floorboards accessorized every vehicle he'd ever driven and he knew that this girl had never seen such a thing.

His tires tore the gravel as he pulled onto the hardtop.

"May I ask why that gentleman in the Ford didn't help you?"

"He was a salesman of some sort, Bibles, maybe, brushes, I don't know. But he said he was already late to Opelika by an hour but he'd drop me to your station. The car ain't but around the turn up here. It's a, what they call it? A Cadillac."

"Your daddy's?" he asked, with hope.

"It is."

"He let you drive that big car all the way to Slaughters and back?"

"Ain't that far. But he don't know I'm gone. He's with the university choir on a competition down Montgomery. And my mama never notice nothing."

"Your daddy sing in the university choir?"

She laughed. "No. 'Course not. He's a professor of musicology. He lead 'em. He writes hymns and they sing 'em."

"You sing in the choir?"

"Not in the university. At the church. Opelika First Baptist."

John Columbus had been to First Baptist to hear

the preacher a few times. He'd left unimpressed. After two years in town he was still preacher-shopping. He'd never paid much attention to any choir. But now he would.

Off to the opposite side of the road was a black 1938 Cadillac.

He pointed at the Cadillac. "That your daddy's?"

"Yes it is."

He drove past it and then flipped a U-turn and pulled up behind the gleaming Caddy. He knew this car. He loved this car. It was a 1938 Sixty-Special. That first year it had outsold every other Cadillac on the market. John Columbus thought the car a bit daring for a university man, but quiet men often took dares with their automobiles.

He'd pumped gas into a Sixty-Special before, but no man driving a Caddy would let a redneck grease monkey play around with his car at backward Ridge Grove—*A rich man more likely to push his fancy car all the way to a proper mechanic in Auburn than allow me to fool around it*, John Columbus thought.

Once he'd nicked an owner's manual from the glove compartment of a Sixty-Special while the man used the toilet.

John Columbus sat up at night reading that manual, memorizing it and hoping the man would come back someday so he could return the manual, but that had never happened. And last night, after reading the Bible for an hour, he'd glanced through the manual and had in fact been studying the whereabouts and the functionality of the jack, and the location of the spare tire. It was as though a divine intervention had occurred and here was the result: a pretty girl in a white dress with a flat tire on her daddy's Cadillac and no one in ten miles to fix the flat but him.

She didn't know his name because he hadn't offered it nor had he inquired of hers. She stood near the right front wheel of his falling-apart hauling truck, her arms crossed, and she watched the man work. He removed his checked button-up and set the shirt on the backseat of her daddy's car. His brown cotton work pants were clean and the white undershirt fit his body tight. She wondered if he had a woman, a mother or sister, who took care of him, or if he was a wanderer, a Southern vagabond of the type her father had told her to stay away from.

"Beware the man with a big smile and a box of tools and no home address," her father had once said.

This man beneath her daddy's car seemed unschooled but overtly and severely polite.

He jacked up her daddy's car. The muscles in his forearms rippled with each heavy turn of the crank, and the monstrous car slowly lifted from the earth. She smelled the dirt and the pine from the woods and she thought she might smell her own body. On the ride from Slaughters she'd sweat a thunderstorm; the sun had beat from the west into the back window, the car had become an oven. Or maybe she'd already been burning up for this blue-eyed man before meeting him. She stared at him and enjoyed the effect, a rugged handsome face: long nose thin at the bridge but widening at the nostrils, wide strong forehead, sharp chin, sly smile of white teeth. His body lengthy and fit.

He stopped cranking the jack and looked at her, pleased with his work, shot her that smile, and stood.

"Well, miss." He stopped. "I do believe I've failed to properly introduce myself. I'm John Columbus Swofford. And you are?"

He stepped forward, offered a slight, awkward bow. No man had ever bowed to her. She didn't know how to respond. She curtseyed, and flirted with her eyes.

"Mr. Swofford, my name is Annie Laurie Howard, of Auburn, Alabama. I'm pleased to meet you."

"The pleasure is mine, Miss Annie Laurie. If you've got ten more minutes to spare I'll have you on the road back to Auburn and let's hope you beat your daddy home from that singin' competition in Montgomery."

"Well, sir, the car don't look a bit movable right now, so I'll give you ten minutes or twenty if you need 'em. But I do must beat my daddy home, if you can be of any help."

He moved quickly, assured of every action, not stopping to chat nor waiting for comment from her. He lowered the car back to the turf, stowed the jack in the trunk. He leaned against the open trunk, his right arm wide and high above her, holding the flat in the other hand.

"Miss Annie Laurie," he said, "you've got a predicament. Now if I place this ruined tire back in that side panel, one day your daddy is gone be driving and get a flat, and go for his spare, and find his spare is also flat. Not just flat, but looks to me like you run on it a few miles at least, it's got teeth marks of a hyena all over it. Every man I know stay attuned to the whys and hows of his vehicle, and your father would, I'm guessing, find this mangled spare a queer event, not to mention a major inconvenience."

"What do I do?"

He knew. He'd been thinking it with every crank of the jack. But he paused; he knew not to seem too eager. He looked to the woods. He looked to the ground. He played his chin with his fingers.

"I think I got it. Figuring two days from now is Sunday, and you'll be at Opelika First Baptist with your family, what I could do is drive down tomorrow, get a proper Caddy tire on this wheel, and while you are in church with your family on Sunday, I'll return it."

"That seems like a perfect idea, Mr. Swofford. You'd do that for me? But I'm a stranger. Oh, my daddy would be on fire, as much fire as he ever get, if he knew I'd took his car out to Slaughters. You'd save me an awful lot of trouble."

"Consider it done. How early your family gets to church?"

"Bible study starts at ten and the service at eleven. We try to get there by nine forty-five."

"Well then, I think you're ready to get on home."

"How will I know you've replaced the tire?"

"If you see me in the pews, listenin' to you singin' to the Lord, you'll know."

He slammed the trunk shut and leaned the wheel against his truck. He grabbed his shirt from the back-seat of the Sixty-Special, and opening the front door waved Miss Annie Laurie toward the driver's seat.

She sat down with a flourish, a bit of pomp, and he closed the door.

Through the open window he watched her start the car, and heard the beautiful purring of the V-8.

"You drive safe now," he said.

"What I owe you?" she asked.

"Nothing just yet."

She smiled and headed home.

JOHN COLUMBUS SLEPT in the tiny storeroom at the back of the station. His sole belongings: a camp cot and linens, a lantern, a Bible, ten undershirts, ten button-ups, three pairs of work trousers, a pair of dress trousers and almost-matching sport coat, two ties, one pair of black wing tips that he kept in a paper sack, and the owner's manual to a 1938 Cadillac Sixty-Special. He did not have to live this way but chose to. Back in Lafayette, Georgia, his parents lived in a big country house. They were not wealthy people but they were "of means," as would be said.

John Columbus felt he should strike out on his own when he reached eighteen. He sent small amounts of money home when he could. He'd wanted to design airplanes but didn't have the schooling and didn't have the patience to get the schooling.

He'd spent a year doing highway work for Georgia, and then at the state line he took over work for Alabama, and the road crews pushed their way west, eventually to settle on the outskirts of Auburn, near the train tracks, waiting for work.

After a month he grew tired of the tent city where the road authority housed him, grew tired of the drinking and whoring and gambling that most of his cohorts took to as a profession, and he left the camp, and after a few days of wandering around, sleeping in let rooms, and asking questions of anyone who might listen, he ended up spending the night in the let room of a Mr. Shanker. Didn't take long for the men to hammer out the details of his new employment.

And now here he was.

Tonight he'd give the Lord a rest. Every page of his Bible marginalia and eraser smudges evinced a man working hard for the Lord. John Columbus never proselytized but he knew his Bible better than most men. But tonight he'd spend more time with the Sixty-Special.

SATURDAY AFTERNOON HE pulled up to the Cadillac dealership in Auburn. The manager's face broadcast his horror: what redneck in his shit-jalopy Ford truck just pulled into my lot?

John Columbus wore his church clothes.

"Hey, partner," he said to the manager. "Blew this tire out on my Sixty-Special. What it take to get me a new one?"

The salesman looked at John Columbus, and to

his truck and back, and said, "I know every man who bought a Sixty-Special over the last three years within a hundred miles of here, and I know you ain't one of 'em."

"That's 'cause I bought mine up in Atlanta, sir. And good to meet you, too, my name is John Columbus Swofford."

The salesman uneasily shook his hand.

"Well, sorry about that, on account of your truck and them 'Bama plates I assumed you was from around here."

"Can't a man buy a car in one state and drive it to another? I know the answer to that. So what's it gonna set me back?"

The salesman inspected the wheel and tire.

"You just sit in the waiting room. I'll get the mechanic to take a look. And, pardon, but do you mind wheeling that truck behind the building? Don't look quite right up against all my Caddies. I'm trying to sell cars here."

"You just find me when it's all done."

Before pulling around back he walked among the half-dozen Cadillacs, sat down in one or two, smelled the new-car drug.

He was napping when the salesman rapped on the hood of his truck.

"Hey, buddy," the man said. "I got you road-ready. That'll be six dollars."

John Columbus had planned on paying two dollars but he couldn't really argue with the man now. He pulled the cash from his pocket and paid. For the next few days he'd be eating canned food out of the store—chili, franks, green beans. No bacon breakfasts at Mama's Roadside and no chicken-fried steak dinners down at Earl's. These were lean times until the end of the month.

SUNDAY MORNING HE drove slowly through the gravel parking lot of Opelika First Baptist, keeping his eyes out for the Sixty-Special. He felt like a thief when in fact he was the opposite of a thief, but he imagined it could go either way if someone saw him with the side panel of Mr. Howard's car swung open and a wrench in his hand.

There sat a black Sixty-Special, but he'd remembered the plate number, 488-531 D, and this wasn't it. In a lane opposite he spotted the car, parked between a Packard and an older-model Cadillac, the style he didn't know offhand, but it paled next to the Series Sixty. He parked a few spots away. It was fifteen past ten and the Sunday schoolers were deep in their Bibles by now, and he had plenty of time before the rest of the congregation arrived for the service. The coast looked clear.

He used a shop towel to carry the wheel and the tire iron he'd use to screw the wheel back in place. He wanted Miss Annie Howard to appreciate this gesture, to recognize him as a gentleman, and to say yes when he asked her out for a walk downtown after the service, maybe a Coca-Cola at the fountain. He hadn't been on a date with a girl since leaving home almost two years before. That foolish bow he'd offered her the other day still haunted him. What kind of imbecile *bows* to a woman? Next time politely shake her hand.

He slithered up to the passenger side of Mr. Howard's car. He easily unlatched the spare compartment, a revolutionary design a few years earlier. He swung open the panel, and to his surprise there was a spare already affixed. He looked around, confused. He squeezed the tire, it had air. He checked the plates and confirmed that this was the right car. He started to sweat. Had he been set up? If so, for what? Set up to do a good deed? He had no choice but to get the heck out of there.

He'd wasted a week's salary on a Cadillac tire for no one, for nothing. There would be no date with Annie Laurie. He couldn't walk into that church and sit through a service. He didn't like the preacher's way with the Bible. What a way to spend a Sunday morning. He felt the pressures of class, he felt money laughing at him; he knew his jacket did not perfectly match his trousers, that anyone could see that.

He started to latch the spare compartment when he heard the crunch of shoes against gravel.

"Hey there, son," he heard a man shout. "What exactly do you think you're doing with my Cadillac?"

He turned to see two men in their fifties approaching quickly. They both wore fine linen suits and straw hats. He'd seen clothes like these in the windows of the finest men's shops in Atlanta.

He noticed one of the men, the manager from the car dealership the day before.

"You must be John Columbus Swofford," the man on the left said. "I'm Mr. Howard, father of Annie Laurie. This here is my good friend Tad Williams, who sold me my car a few years back."

John Columbus nodded. "I am J. C. Swofford, and I'm acquainted with Mr. Williams."

Williams gave him a wicked smile.

Howard said, "Well, son, I hear my daughter Annie Laurie got into a little bit of trouble and roped you into it. It sure was kind of you to replace my tire. A seventeen-year-old girl does generally find herself in a mess of trouble once she starts fooling with her daddy's car."

"Yes, sir," John Columbus said.

"And sometimes a twenty-year-old boy finds himself in a mess of trouble when he starts doing favors for a seventeen-year-old girl."

"Yes, sir," John Columbus said.

"We got a preacher in there can *preach*. Why don't you join us?"

AFTER THE SERVICE John took Annie for that walk he had been planning on. He got on well with the family. His lack of learning was evident to a painful degree to everyone, but his Bible knowledge could not be challenged by anyone at any table, not even Mr. Howard, who taught choral singing and hymn-writing at Auburn. In fact, more than once the professor had pulled the mechanic aside and asked for a critique of a hymn or some advice on biblical fact.

John and Annie were married in the summer and a few years later she was pregnant before Halloween, or possibly on Halloween. For a while the couple called the unborn baby Jack-o'-Lantern. Eventually they settled on John Howard.

Annie gave birth to my father and a month later she died.

10

Atlanta to Austin, Dead Swoffords, August 2010

I didn't socialize much while living in Mount Tremper. One night I landed at a birthday party at a bar in Kingston and later that evening ended up in bed with a woman, but I forget her name and never saw her again.

Occasionally I traveled down to the city for sex.

There was the Budding Comedian: mostly she had a serious pill problem, which worked well for me given my state of mind. We chomped a lot of pills and snorted cocaine and ended each night in her bed, fucking and watching reruns of *Celebrity Rehab*. To watch *Celebrity Rehab* while totally high as a kite on pills and cocaine is one of life's finer pleasures.

One Monday July afternoon I stumbled out of the Comedian's apartment and on to the Bowery. I found the nearby International Bar and fortified myself with bourbon. I was not yet ready to return to my cabin in Mount Tremper, so I contacted a former fiancée of mine, the Boho Artist, and luckily she was free for dinner. I dumped my bag off at a friend's house, and the former fiancée and I had a great dinner at one of our old romantic spots on the Lower East Side and then we went to her apartment and had sex and watched *Charlie Rose*.

The next morning, after she confessed to being involved with someone else, I returned to Mount Tremper. That night I sat on the couch for eight hours thinking about killing myself. I had the rope and the sturdy beam, or any one of thousands of trees to choose from. But I chose to live.

LATER THAT SAME week the Boho Artist was visiting friends in Kingston one afternoon and I picked her up. She had recently become a devotee of the teachings of Gurdjieff. I assumed that the man she was involved with was also a devotee or even a Gurdjieff Guru. Gurus get tons of ass.

I am not opposed to anyone's spiritual development but I did some reading on this Gurdjieff and he seemed to me a positively masterful con artist. I'd been reading a biography of the young Joseph Stalin, and Gurdjieff might easily have traded places with him. Perhaps in two thousand years

Gurdjieff would be the new Buddha, but it seemed unlikely.

The Boho Artist and I talked about our past and the possibility of starting anew. We had once been engaged and then that hadn't worked out, and the resultant mess still caused a bit of anxiety and animosity between us. It hadn't worked out because I'd called it off. But still during the following two years we had had a lot of sex and had seen each other regularly. I thought we might work things out but I did have a serious problem with the fact that she had a boyfriend.

We had sex. I grilled steaks. We drank a 1999 Volnay. We had sex again, and again in the morning, and I took her to the bus station. At the bus station we talked about her boyfriend, how she had broken up with him for the week and he was waiting to hear from her a verdict. She asked me to come down and see her later in the week.

I had been down this road before, sexual relations with a boyfriended woman, and I did not like the feeling one bit. In the past there had been jerks who fucked my girlfriend, and I had been a jerk and fucked people's girlfriends, and generally I frowned on the act. It was, as they say in the South, a messy affair.

Later in the week I did visit her. We ordered

in, at her apartment on the Lower East Side. We had sex before and after dinner. She told me that she was still in contact with the Gurdjieffian but that she had not been able to come to a conclusion about the affairs, or which affair to end and which to continue. I finished my wine and left and never saw her again. She occasionally sent me nasty text messages but I never responded.

IT WAS LATE July 2010 and I was officially out of women to have hassle-free sex with in New York State. A novel I was working on had stalled. I'd grown tired of the beauty of the Catskills. I planned another RV trip with my father. This time I agreed to meet him in Atlanta and travel west with him as far as I could handle. Also, this time I would figure him out; I would crack the code on John Howard Swofford and thus crack the code on myself.

WE DROVE FROM one small west Georgia town to another and wandered around the cemeteries looking for Swofford headstones. Or, rather, I wandered around the cemeteries looking for dead Swoffords because my dad's lungs were in such bad shape that he couldn't get out of the RV. My dad knew these towns from his youth and he knew that people we were related to were buried all over these cemeteries, and for a reason I could not extract from him he wanted photos of their headstones. He'd pull the RV into a town, find the cemetery, and send me out.

"Who are these people, Dad?"

"I don't know for certain. I musta known some of 'em. My old blind aunt. Um. You know, hell, Tone. They are your kin, Swoffords! Just go on now, take me some pictures."

And that is what I did, in Villa Rica, Temple, Mount Zion, Bremen, Carrollton and Whitesburg, and other towns, at the little church cemeteries.

I remembered the Whitesburg cemetery from drives with Iris when my brother was dying.

It was one of those hot Georgia August days when you look into the sky and expect to see birds stuck in mid-flight, so muggy and thick is the air.

We relaxed in the RV and looked through photos on the camera.

"Yep." He pointed at the screen. "That there, in Bremen. That is cousins of my aunt. So what does that make them to you?"

"Dead cousins of your dead aunt?"

"This is family history."

I didn't see it as family history. I saw it as my father bringing to life the dead Swoffords whom he knew he would be joining very soon. It didn't really matter what their names were or how they were related or even if they were related. He wanted to jam his digital camera with as many Swofford headstones as possible. If here, now, decades after these forgotten people had died, an old man wandered around their old tired towns and cemeteries and instructed his son to take photos of their headstones, they were not forgotten, and thus he must believe that someday decades from now another man might do the same. In 2070 a man might drive his son around west Georgia and instruct him to take photos of Swofford headstones, and one of those dead Swoffords would be a John Howard Swofford. And the living men would not have known him but they would have taken the photo of his headstone and thus brought him back to life in 2070.

The next afternoon we pulled into Auburn, Alabama. The university town's streets were tight and narrow. When oxygen-depleted, my father was unable sometimes to remember the names of his own brothers and sisters, unable to recall what year he'd lived in Seville or Tokyo, but with ease he glided his massive RV to the old whites-only cemetery in Auburn. I had been here many times as a boy and the place had always scared me. It was out of a movie set, an old white Southern graveyard, the stench of history so heavy about the place.

"This here is my mama's grave," my dad said.

"I know that."

"Just so you know the importance. This ain't like those anonymous Swoffords yesterday."

"I understand. Do you want to give it a shot? Want to try to make it to her graveside?"

"Don't think I can make it, Tone."

"Do you know where it is?"

He hopped down to the curb and pointed toward a massive oak. "Right around there. Right near that big oak. One way or the other from it. Probably this way from it."

I grabbed his camera from his hand and headed toward the oak. I walked with my head down. I was not here to read the names of other dead Southerners. I was here only to make it to my paternal grandmother's grave and snap a picture. Once my father died, there would be no reason for me to truck around the South. I'd probably never be back. I knelt at the grave, a very simple stone marked with her name and the dates 1921–1941. I realized that if she had lived I would probably not exist. What did this mean? Nothing. The life of the animals. But I grieved for my father. I grieved for that cute little chubby boy who never knew his mother. He sat one hundred yards away from me in his RV and the wounds from July 1941 burned still today.

Back at the RV my father stared at the digital photo of his mother's grave marker.

"Same as I remember it," he said. "I'm gonna be buried here, Tone. There's still a few spots in the plot, you probably seen. My cousin is looking into it. Looks like I probably got rights to it."

"It's probably the place for you," I said, without knowing whether I believed this or not.

THE NEXT DAY we drove along the Gulf Coast. When my grandfather returned from World War II the family moved to Biloxi. I knew that my father's years in Biloxi had been the happiest of his boyhood. We drove up and down the coastal strip in Biloxi for hours and my father looked for the ghost of the little boy John Howard. We also drove by the VA old soldiers' home. It was one of my dad's favorite cracks, to say he wanted to retire to an old soldiers' home. We pulled up to the gates but they wouldn't let us in. The compound had been destroyed by Katrina.

"You OK with me setting up in an old soldier's home, Tone?"

I knew that what he wanted me to say was "No, I'm not OK with that. Come live with me."

"I'll visit you here in Biloxi," I said. "I like the weather and the oyster po' boys."

*   *   *

NEAR HOUSTON WE saw a fuel tanker catch fire on the roadside. The flames shot a hundred feet in the air. We pulled into a roadside hotel and my father slept in his rig and I got a room for the night.

In the morning while my father took his medications I went for a long run. It was a hundred degrees and I was out of shape, and about three miles out, down a long flat road, I was pretty certain that I'd initiated a cataclysmic cardiac event. I thought: *Jesus Christ, my sick old dad is in his RV sucking meds for his failing lungs and I'm going to have a fucking heart attack on the side of the road and die a week before I turn forty, in the middle of nowhere, in Texas, with an unfinished novel languishing on my laptop.* There along the deserted road in Texas I swore off drugs of all kinds.

An old lady in a powder-blue Cadillac stopped and asked me if I needed a ride and I took her up on it: I swear she looked something like Jesus. The air-conditioning in her car was the best I'd ever experienced in my life.

Over a lunch of canned soup, my father said, "Can you help me out with something I been trying to figure out?"

"I'll give it a shot."

"I don't understand why you rented out that

fancy New York City apartment and moved up to the woods to live in a shack."

I'd been lying to my father. I'd told him that I was renting my Chelsea apartment to a friend and that I'd decided to move to the woods to escape the city for a while.

"I mean," he said, "I seen photos of that Manhattan apartment, and I seen photos of that shack, and I don't see why any young single man would choose to move to the woods when he got that bachelor pad in the city. Ain't all the women in the city?"

"I can confirm that most of the women are in the city. But I'm not young. I'll be forty next week."

"It's a private writer's retreat, or something like that? I just don't get it, Tone. Don't make a lick of sense to me."

I could not keep the lie going any longer.

I said, "In that letter you sent me a few years back you said that someday you would see me on my way down. Well, here I am, Pops. I'm on my way down. You got what you wanted. I'm in total and complete financial ruin. I had to sell my apartment to scratch up some cash to live on. I live in a shack in the Catskills because it's all I can afford right now."

"I never wanted you to fail," he said. "I just

wanted to point out to you that sometimes people make money and it changes them. And then they turn around, and they have nothing. Not money. Not family. Money don't mean shit. You always got family if you don't alienate them."

I left the RV and went to the hotel pool. By now it must have been over 110 degrees out. There were no vehicles other than my father's RV in the parking lot, and I assumed no employees would leave the air-conditioned comfort of the hotel. I took off my clothes and stepped into the pool. I floated belly-up for as long as I could take the sun burning my body.

I thought, *So that's it? I have assumed for all these years that my father wanted me to fail, but in fact he did not want me to fail? And so now I have failed, in order to give him what he wanted, but it is not what he wanted?*

From the pool I watched my father moving around in his RV. He lived alone in Fairfield and he mostly traveled alone in the RV. I knew that this solitary life he had created for himself fit in well with his fantasies of being a Clint Eastwood character from a western—the epic wanderer, the stoic, the man who lives on canned beans and shoe leather and the hard-bought realities of the road. But wouldn't my father have been happier if he were in love with a woman and living in a clean and tidy house? I loved my father, and I understood the allure of this iconic western fantasy, but the possibility that I might end up like my father—old, alone, and dying—scared the shit out of me as I floated naked on my back in the hotel pool west of Houston.

It frightened me so intensely that back in the RV I told my father that I needed to return to New York ASAP to take care of some things. We made it to Lockhart that afternoon and ate BBQ at Kreuz Market. We made it into Austin and drank a few beers at a bar and my father glared with passion at the college girls who served us. So did I. In the morning I flew home.

II

The Girl from Tarawa Terrace II

I don't remember much of August. Friends in the city threw a party for my fortieth birthday.

And then it was September. I counted my money. I thought of moving to Los Angeles, where a friend was shooting a movie, or to Phnom Penh, where from god knew I'd never return.

I DIDN'T WANT to go to the reading in Rhinecliff. I wanted to spend my Sunday afternoon watching NFL football in Phoenicia with construction workers and bikers. But a good friend of mine was reading from some anthology or another, and my landlords, old-time country musicians, happened to be the band for the occasion, and I lived upstate and I had no social life other than driving down to Phoenicia and watching NFL football with construction workers and bikers and eating a burger

283

and drinking a few beers. In other words, I needed to get out.

I drove across the river to Rhinecliff from Mount Tremper. I stopped somewhere along the way and checked the score. The Jets were up. I arrived early for the reading.

I drank a few glasses of cheap white wine and ran into Betsy, an acquaintance from the city. She was cute, and used to work for a nonprofit but had recently moved upstate to find meaning or find a project, or find a man, who knew.

She answered me the same way I answered people who asked me why I'd moved upstate, evasively and with a bit of cunning: I needed a change; it's just for the summer; I love the Catskills, it was either the Hudson or the Amazon.

For me this would have been the only true answer: After seven years of a completely deviant and ridiculously expensive life in Manhattan I ran out of money and nerves, at about the same moment. I didn't have the balls to move to Cambodia or Ecuador so I took the baby step up the Hudson, incubator for lost city souls. When I figure out what I want to do with my life, I will move somewhere else. The only thing I really want to do with my life is write books and fall in love with a talented and beautiful woman, but how realistic is that? And I want to hold on to her, and make a life with her, have a family. This is no midlife crisis: I have already plowed through women and wrecked a sports car. This is the reverse midlife crisis: I want a wife and a family and a station wagon.

When Betsy asked me why I had moved up from the city, I said: I needed a change; it's just for the summer; I love the Catskills, it was either the Hudson or the Mekong; I feel a strong magnetic pull from these mountains.

She didn't believe any of it and that was the point.

After the reading we exchanged numbers and said goodbye and I assumed I'd never see her again, or I'd see her in another five years at a horrible party in the city.

And then a week later she called and said, "You should meet my friend and me for dinner tonight. She's up from Brooklyn. I think you will like her."

We met at the cheap Mexican place in Tivoli. I hadn't been since my unfortunate evening involving the police nearly four years earlier. Just as then, the chicken something I ordered was so-so and the margarita was weak, but when I first met Christa I knew that she would be in my life for a long time, perhaps forever.

She wore a short skirt and a flirty, blowsy top and cowboy boots. Here at the end of summer she was dark but I could tell that in winter her skin would turn a luxurious white. She said funny, unflattering things about hippies and monks and yoga masters, and every time she had a chance she showed off her legs or her brilliant smile. Occasionally she played with her dark hair.

She'd gone to Bard in the late nineties and one semester she'd worked at this Mexican restaurant. When she said this I must have stared at her both stupidly and longingly: after a decade of dating and once marrying and twice engaging and unengaging myself to women who were doctors or lawyers or the daughters of doctors or lawyers or academics or wealthy bankers I'd decided earlier in the summer that the next woman I was with would need to have been a waitress at some point in her life, not for "fun and experience" but in order to make the rent, or if she hadn't been a waitress her mother needed to have been one in order to feed and clothe her children.

Not only had Christa been a waitress at this Mexican restaurant, her mother had once been a waitress at the Officers' Club on Marine Corps Base Camp Lejeune. And as a child she'd lived on Camp Lejeune, in base housing in a development called Tarawa Terrace II. Tarawa was the bloodiest battle of World War II. Upon my joining the

Marine Corps twenty-two years earlier this fact had been drilled into my head. Some nights I still had nightmares wherein a drill instructor yelled to a room of recruits, *Tarawa!* And the recruits, me included, standing and straining in some stress position or another involving a rifle and a heavy rucksack, replied, *Sir! Tarawa, bloodiest battle of World War Two, sir!*

This smart and engaging and beautiful woman had heard of Tarawa, a small and now inconsequential island in the Pacific that in my mind was still soaked with the sanctified blood of marines. Most beautiful women from New York City would have guessed that Tarawa was a kind of chutney or a new method for removing pubic hair.

She'd been student council president at her school in Tarawa Terrace II in Camp Lejeune, and each morning she and the secretary were responsible for running the US and Marine Corps flags up the flagpole and then announcing over the PA system the names of the children bound for detention that afternoon.

She hinted at an adult darkness: a car wreck or two, some off-prescription dabbling in psychotropics, a failed early marriage that had infidelity written all over it, a recently terminated volatile relationship with a Viagra-popping old man.

But she'd spent this summer alone in the woods writing a book and taking pictures and meditating at a Zen monastery that happened to be on my road in Mount Tremper: the days of wild-haired glory and abandon were over, it was time for her to settle down, or so she said.

She asked me why all my most important belongings, my library and my kitchen, were in storage in Brooklyn, and why I lived alone in a cabin in the woods. I answered stoically, I looked away, I said I'd had work to do, that Manhattan and its people had begun to bore and depress me: the bubble city had become difficult to breathe in.

She knew that what I meant was: *That place nearly killed me; it was a children's zoo and play park and I had had many a turn on all the rides, and there was no longer any joy in standing in line with a bunch of morons waiting to spend many hundreds of dollars on dinner and oblivion every night of the week.* What I was saying was: *I need to build a nest and I need a lover who won't drive me crazy.*

Betsy sat at the table with us but she wasn't really there, or rather, Christa and I paid her no mind: she was the fairy dust that had brought us together but otherwise totally irrelevant.

We talked about Christa's photography and the novel I was working on, and we talked about the weather, and the best swimming holes in the Catskills, and the best pancakes, and we talked about traveling to foreign countries, and slow-cooking short ribs in red wine and braising leeks and preparing salmon poached in champagne, but really, what we were asking each other was: *Are you possibly the one or is this all another hoax?*

Betsy ended the dinner abruptly and awkwardly with an urgent outburst about needing to feed her cat. I wanted to ask Christa if she would travel across the river and have a drink with me and then stay awhile. But of course I didn't. We hugged and said goodbye.

There are many moments that I could point to in our quick courtship and say, *That is when I knew she was good.* But the first moment occurred when we said goodbye that night on the sidewalk in Tivoli: she nearly jumped as she hugged me, and she wrapped her arms all the way around my neck and she hung from me for the briefest moment; she hung from me and we floated together in space; with her body she said, *I already trust you, please do not injure my heart*, and she squeezed me deep and hard with her thin little bird arms and I knew she was good.

On my drive home I realized that I hadn't even asked for her last name.

*   *   *

IT HAPPENS A few times in a man's life that as soon as he meets a woman and shakes her hand an electric current rushes through his body that sends the signal: someday soon, possibly even within hours, you will sleep with this woman. If I were to be honest I would say that that electrical current had coursed through my body about a dozen times in my life, but it had always settled in my crotch and stayed there. It is, indeed, an enjoyable sensation, full of the promise and potential of one's manhood and the easy procurement of sex with attractive women. I have never ingested a drug that produced anything nearly as satisfying.

But with Christa the sensation bounced around my head for a few hours, and then a few days: I saw her visiting me in my cabin; I saw us on the rocks at the Big Blue swimming hole; I saw us eating a meal I'd prepared, perhaps those slow-cooked short ribs with a Volnay to wash it all down. Yes, I saw sex, I saw us giving each other our bodies without remorse or keeping score.

This was a crazy, sexy, perhaps irresponsible waking dream: I began to see her next to me in our family car, and the blurry outline of a child in the backseat and then another. And I saw sports games and badly performed children's plays and hiking in the woods, and family dinners, holidays, the wonder.

We did not waste any time falling in love. We had one date in the city and one in the country, and then we were never apart. We walked into each other so completely it was as if we'd known each other for decades. And really, we had. I knew that if I was ever going to be in a relationship that lasted it would have to be with a woman who didn't care about my past, who wouldn't ask me how many women I'd slept with, and who didn't care because she was so totally confident in herself and the love she was capable of giving and receiving.

The woman would also have to be otherworldly talented. I'd tried dating a few bad artists and dilettantes and it was worse than being with a woman who was bad in bed.

By November we were engaged and living between her Fort Greene apartment and Mount Tremper.

I guess word spread. The Rich Girl/BoHo Artist texted me: *I hear you are engaged! You move fast!* I never responded.

The Hedge-Funder texted me: *You ruined my life!* I never responded.

The Physician e-mailed me: *Anthony, please can we have dinner?* I responded: *I'm getting married.* I never heard back.

We decided to get married at City Hall when my friend Oren and her friend Amanda were both in New York. We chose the twenty-seventh of December.

A few days before Christmas I was wandering around the East Village after taking a steam at the Turkish and Russian Baths on Tenth Street. I bought Christa a Christmas present at a dressmaker on Seventh Street near Cooper Square. I popped in next door at McSorley's for a burger and a beer.

It took me a while to realize that I had trouble in mind.

I had lived in Chelsea for years but a majority of my debauchery had gone down in the East Village and the Lower East Side. I knew three drug dealers within a five-minute walk of where I stood. There were a dozen women I'd slept with a hop, a skip, and a buzzer away. The sun had set.

Christa was out with friends and didn't expect me back in Brooklyn for many hours, midnight or later, whenever. I felt the old twinge, the cheater's twinge and the casual drug user's twinge. Christa would not tolerate cheating or drug use. But those phone calls are so easy to make.

I walked to First Avenue and stepped into Tile Bar. I knew she'd be there: the Comedian. On a stool. She jumped up and gave me a hug. She was high as a kite. And she looked good.

She said, "You shopping for me?"

"Of course," I said. I hugged her close and I thought I could smell the drugs sweating out of her body.

"I heard you were, like, getting married?"

"Maybe." I smiled and sat down and ordered a double bourbon.

She rubbed my leg. "Oh, Tony. You're back! I'm so happy!"

She handed me a few pills in the sly practiced way of someone who passes and receives illicit drugs all day. And I took them with the same sly expertise.

She said, "Let's buy some coke. My guy can be here in twenty minutes. Let's go back to my apartment and get high and fuck and watch *Celebrity Rehab*!"

She turned to her friend at the bar, some wasted chick she must have been passing pills to all day, or all week. I drank my bourbon. I thought about the dozens, no, the hundreds of times I'd cheated on women with this exact protocol. I knew how to do it without getting caught. I was so fucking *good* at it. Who on Earth could fly two women to the same hotel in Tokyo, from two different continents, and have sex with them both for an entire week without getting caught? I could! I had done that! Who could go out at midnight in Madrid while his girlfriend was asleep in their hotel room and meet a British girl in a bar and take her back to the same hotel and get blown in a broom closet? I could! I was a Zen master of infidelity. I was untouchable. I spoke a language no one else had ever even heard of.

I drank my bourbon. I was about to get married, but I wasn't married yet. The pills were beginning to melt in my hand. I needed to swallow them and get this thing rolling. The Comedian's friend was pretty and thin. I could have them both. Isn't that the way to go out just before getting married? I'd have my own private bachelor party with two women and pills and blow, and Christa would never know.

I thought of Christa. I thought of the family we talked about raising one day. I thought about my children respecting their father.

I ordered an ice water.

I dropped the pills on the floor and crushed them with my boot. I crushed them and crushed with them everything I hated about my past and myself.

I said to the Comedian, "I'll be back in fifteen. Gotta run an errand."

CHRISTA'S FRIENDS HAD canceled on her and she was home. We talked about our marriage plans. We trimmed our Christmas tree and talked about the rest of our lives together.

A MASSIVE SNOWSTORM hit the night of the twenty-sixth and shut much of the city down. But Mayor Bloomberg knew that marriage was good revenue for the city and the show at the Marriage Bureau went on on the morning of the twenty-seventh.

I wore a black pin-striped suit, a white shirt, and a pink tie. Christa wore a cream dress and she looked like a fierce pale bird. When I said yes, I knew that I would be married to this woman forever. We were married. We had a wedding lunch at Lupa with friends and family. We walked around the West Village together in the snow. We bought champagne on Seventh Avenue and walked around the city, drinking champagne from the bottle, married.

It is that simple.

FOUR DAYS LATER, on New Year's Eve, up in the cabin in Mount Tremper, I made short ribs for dinner. A little before midnight I stepped out to grab some firewood and to pull in a bottle of champagne that I'd buried in the snow. When I reentered the cabin, Christa was sitting on the couch. She had a surprised and delighted and terrified look on her face. She stood up and walked toward me, holding what looked like a thermometer in one hand.

She said, "Sweetheart, I think I'm pregnant."

I said, no; I screamed, "Amazing!"

She began to cry sweetly and she fell into my arms and she said, "Oh my god, baby, we are going to be parents. We're going to have a beautiful baby."

My body shook, my entire body shook, and I held Christa close, and I said, "You will be a beautiful mommy. You will be the best mommy in the world. That will be our lucky baby."

THE NEXT DAY we went to see a movie. We were still in shock, but after having tried three more tests the night before, we were pretty certain that she was pregnant. But just in case, Christa took another one in the bathroom at the theater. It, too, was positive. We watched *The Fighter*.

12

Fairfield to Aspen, Getting the Venom Out, March 2011

My father's home is a mess, not in terms of clutter or food waste, or dust, for he has a cleaning lady he employs occasionally to bring the place up to an acceptable level of cleanliness and even neatness. The home is a structural mess. It is a ranch home from the 1960s, and he bought it for less than one hundred thousand dollars in the nineties, and at the zenith of the 2000s housing bubble bankers and appraisers told him that it was worth many times what he paid for it, and he borrowed their money on that lie, and he kept borrowing, the way many people did back then. But what made my father a special case was that he was convinced he would never live to pay the money back. He considered these offers free money, and really, that's exactly what they should have been to a man in his mid-sixties with chronic lung failure who could not walk more than ten feet without using an oxygen tank. If the banks had been paying attention to the people they were loaning money to they would have looked at my father and said, "Wait, this man will never live to pay us back." But the beauty and stupidity of that money meant they did not look at dying men prior to loaning them large unrecoverable sums.

I'm certain my father intended to perform repairs on his house with the proceeds from those loans. One night over Mexican food he drew on his napkin plans for attaching a second story, a penthouse of sorts that he planned to rent to businessmen. I'd grown up hearing my father's remodeling and adding-on fantasies, and sometimes they came true: on Vale Drive in Carmichael he added fifteen hundred square feet to the house one year—two bedrooms, a bathroom, and a family room. My mother dubbed our home in Tachikawa, Japan, the Winchester Mystery House: every few months my father would knock down a wall and build out another room or hallway. But usually his large-format plans remained mere fantasy.

Here in Fairfield he had replaced a toilet in the spare bathroom, and he ripped up the bathroom floor and he paid some day laborers to install a new bath and shower stall and a vanity.

A few moments after I arrived for this visit I made the mistake of stepping into the second bathroom to take a leak and I almost fell through the framing to the earth below. I looked at the disused bathroom, the manufacturer's labels still attached to the toilet and the vanity and the shower kit. My father had told me about this remodel months before. It's the kind of project that, when I was a kid, he would have banged out over a weekend.

On a Friday night he said to my mother, "Hey, Momma, how about we redo the kids' bathroom?" After *Dallas* he retreated to his office and drew plans. I helped out with some measurements. He awoke me early in the morning and I joined him on the materials run to Lumberjack.

The wet, woodsy, and thick smell of lumber and the pungent metallic bouquet of a box of nails will always bring forth for me the image of my father with a hammer in his hand, ready to build.

We bought everything he needed to redo the entire bathroom: toilet, vanity, shower kit, tile and grout, mirror, and medicine chest. We ripped the bathroom apart with hammers and crowbars and then began the rebirth. By noon on Sunday my father was on his hands and knees, installing the tile. It was beautiful tile, Moorish in design. He skipped dinner. By the time Andy Rooney wrapped up *60 Minutes* my father had completed the bathroom redo. He was a master craftsman. That bathroom is where a few years later I would hide the major volumes of my pornography stash and do most of the masturbating of my teen years. I can never look at Moorish tile and not think of that bathroom and the thousands of hours I spent on my back on that cold tile floor masturbating to Ginger Lynn and cheerleaders and other girls I'd never have.

And here in Fairfield his bathroom had no floor. That my master-craftsman father had neither the strength nor the desire to finish the job distressed me. In fact it shamed me. Shouldn't I complete the work for him? I am the son that the master craftsman raised—shouldn't I have the skills to pick up my father's tools and finish the job? I am nearly the same age he was the weekend he refinished my boyhood bathroom. If I were a complete man, I'd pick up my father's tools and finish the job for him. But I am not a complete man. Once I sanded and painted a café tabletop two feet in diameter for the small terrace of my Manhattan apartment. That is the extent of my building experience in the past few decades.

I say to my father, "Dad, do you need a hand finishing up that bathroom? We have a few days before we leave for Aspen. If you've got the energy, you can supervise and I'll do the work."

He looks at me and laughs. "Ah, Tone, you used to be my best helper when you were a boy. But you got those soft writer hands now. I'll pick up some guys at the Home Depot and have them finish the job."

I wanted nothing more than to help my father finish his bathroom remodel. But I didn't push the issue.

My father had no energy for dinner out so I left him alone at his kitchen table and he listened to KGO on the radio.

There was not much to do in Fairfield. I went to a coffee shop and got online and tracked down a high school buddy who had been living nearby in Alameda for a few years. I finagled an invitation for tacos with his family that night.

I knew the East Bay freeways like the back of my hand. When I'd lived in Oakland for a lonely year after my divorce I spent many nights driving the 580 and the 880. There were two women I regularly slept with, Marin County and the counter girl from my optician, freeway-close the both of them. The Mercedes 320 had been an old man's car but still sleek and fast enough as I raced my libido around the East Bay trying to forget Sarah.

I PULLED UP to Danny's house in Alameda. Christa was home in New York, fourteen weeks pregnant, and Danny, a kid I had looked up to and admired all through high school, greeted me at the door, his wife and two daughters behind him, smiling.

Their condominium was piled high with the matériel of raising children: plastic jungle gym and play kitchen and bouncy chairs, dolls and books and dolls and toys that made noise. Danny opened his arms and took me in for a big hug—he was a heavyweight wrestler in high school, I wrestled 154s. He might have crushed a few of my ribs, but that was fine.

I had last seen him a few years before in LA. He'd drunk ginger ale and taken me around to music venues and later for chicken and waffles at Roscoe's. I'd met his wife briefly, but never his two daughters.

Danny prepared the taco meat and I drained a few beers while his daughters worked on homework at the dining table. I was forty years old and most of my cohorts had been at this parenthood game for a number of years, but my new wife was pregnant with our first child. This life Danny lived seemed like a television show I'd seen dozens of times, reels from a lifestyle I might never attain: *Lifestyles of the Happy and Stable.*

As Danny cut and then cooked steak he fielded his daughters' questions on California history and math. He interrogated them. A teacher himself, he wasn't about to feed the answers to the kids, no matter how sweetly they asked. A few important homework matters were settled, and we sat for dinner.

I remember that his girls were polite at the table, and that there was much laughter, and a light-heartedness that my childhood family table rarely achieved. Mother and father kidding with the children, the children kidding back. None of this was a show for me, the stranger. I ate too many tacos. I didn't want the fun to end. The girls were sent off to ready themselves for bed, and Danny and I headed out for a drink.

For Danny and his family I'd joined them for Tuesday Taco Night, no big deal, tacos, homework, and baths, but to me their routine resonated: *This happy life is possible.*

At the bar in town Danny had a ginger ale and I took a Manhattan. He was excited about the imminent birth of my daughter.

I said, "You have a beautiful family."

He said, "Growing up my family life was kind of a mess. I thought happy families happened elsewhere. But they happen wherever people want them to happen. My wife and I, we want a happy family, so we will have it, at all costs."

"It can't be that simple," I said.

"Dude. Christa will have your baby and then you will have the knowledge. Capital *K*. You will see that baby girl and you will understand. Capital *U*. And you will know it is that simple. You know how men fuck up their families? With their dicks! You've had your fun, motherfucker! Where'd it get you? Last summer you were living alone in a cabin in the Catskills!"

"That was my choice," I said.

"Don't tell me you wanted to be there."

"I needed to live there. I nearly killed myself in the city."

"You spent nearly an entire decade living the life!"

"You flatter me. You don't want to know how many nights I spent alone, and how many mornings I awoke, staring at the Empire State Building from my bed, thinking about what an awesome height that would be from which to jump."

"But you didn't jump! You wanted a wife to love and a baby. And you found the right woman. Just in time. She will have your baby daughter and you will have the knowledge. Someday you'll tell me I was right about how simple it all became."

I dropped Danny at home and headed back toward my father's house in Fairfield. I got lost trying to find my way out of Alameda, and before finding the freeway I drove around the island for twenty minutes, at the posted speed limit of twenty-five. I inspected the neighborhoods. Many of the homes were grand, and if they were not grand they were modest in an orderly and respectable way. A man raising his family here in Alameda would feel safe and responsible. Simply driving the roads made me feel like a respected member of society.

IN THE MORNING I awoke on my father's couch with an aching back and the unshakable need to hold my wife. She'd flown home from our LA vacation four days earlier. Since our third date we'd never spent more than a few nights apart. I felt like a schoolboy separated from his summer camp love. In every other relationship I'd ever been in, other than my first marriage, this kind of distance and time away from the lover would have meant that I would be waking up with some other woman and telling the girlfriend lies about where I was and where I was going, what that noise in the background was, and even which continent I'd called from.

What a pleasure to wake up at seven a.m., sober, and to call my wife in New York and tell her *Hello*, and *Good morning*, and *I love you*, and to tell her that my back hurt from sleeping on my dad's shitty couch. We checked in about our day, the POD, we called it, military jargon, the Plan of the Day. I told her that today finally my father and I planned to depart. He'd put our departure date off a few times, but the day before, his fresh oxygen supply had arrived and he had no more excuses. And if we didn't leave sometime today I'd have to cancel the driving portion of the trip altogether and fly to Aspen alone in order to attend the disabled veterans' sports clinic.

We talked about the baby in her womb. We'd been calling her the Baby Animal. The Baby Animal is hungry. The Baby Animal wants to disco. The Baby Animal wants to hear her favorite Wallace Stevens poems before she goes to bed.

I said, "I love you, sweetheart, and I love the Baby Animal. I'll call you from the road. Goodbye."

THE OTHER BIG RV trips had ended with me seriously considering patricide. Why on Earth would this trip be any different? The elevation? Why another trip at all? It was true I needed to be in Aspen to teach a writing class to injured veterans, but I could've flown. None of the other RV trips had accomplished what they were supposed to: the Reconciliation—an unbreakable bond between father and son, bygones becoming bygones. The stakes were higher than during last year's trip because with my father the stakes increased every day his lung capacity decreased.

He always played his medical cards close to his chest, but with enough reading about his disease, and the right laser-accurate questions, I surmised that his lungs were at 20 to 25 percent capacity, meaning that while most healthy breathers inspired and expired 150 milliliters of air per breath, what is called tidal volume, my father subsisted on about thirty milliliters. If my father challenged an Olympic sprinter to a fifty-yard dash it would be like a drag race between a 1970 riding lawn mower and a 2011 Ferrari.

My father sat at his dining room table and tuned up his lungs: the terrible coughing, the inhaled medicines, the gurgling and spitting, the very prolonged and agonizing sound of his lungs opening for partial business.

I loaded the RV with my suitcase and his clothing, and some of the prepared foods he subsists on:

microwavable food-like items such as shells and cheese, and chili, and dry items like crackers with peanut butter paste and sweet buns. What exactly are sweet buns? I wondered. After reading the ingredients I decided it's better not to know.

As befits a former Southern Baptist turned lapsed Catholic, my father liked his rituals. He also respected machines and the process of prepping the machine. This machine, this massive Winnebago, needed a lot of mojo, and oil and fuel, and as far as I could tell from the trips I'd taken with him, an infusion of good luck.

My father would not allow his Winnebago to budge an inch without preventive maintenance.

I knew that it drove my father crazy that I was not as attuned as he to the finer mechanical details of the vehicle. He thought of the Winnebago as his castle. After logging in my two thousand plus miles I considered it a dilapidated blue tarp on the fringe of a homeless encampment. It's true that the beast had cost nearly two hundred thousand dollars. But to me the RV trips seemed like very expensive camping excursions. I'd done the math and we'd have been financially better off in a Prius, stopping every night at a roadside budget motel for a shower and some actual sleep. We could have bunked in the occasional Four Seasons or Ritz and still maintained a tighter budget. But RVs and boats share this: only the owner of the vessel can truly understand its beauty and perfection. And RVs, just like boats, are always breaking down.

But I needed this trip. I wanted something: I wanted that Reconciliation.

I began to think of the RV as a truth machine, a narrative machine, like a photo booth but better— a story booth. The story of my father. And I realized that he, too, must feel this way: story equals truth and truth equals forgiveness. Driving along America's roads on each trip we talked, and our mouths were spades, digging toward truth. He wanted me to forgive him and he wanted to go back to the beginning of time. It was naïve of me not to have recognized that part of my father's RV dream, his desire for constant motion, was the wish to slow life down inside that machine, to stop time, to stop the decline of his health, to stop his aging, even to stop his own death and the death of his family.

"Drive faster, drive farther, and you will cure all that ails you," I can hear him telling himself. And "You might even bring Jeff back to life."

He handed me the maintenance list:

Install and secure oxygen tanks.
Check engine oil.

Check coolant level.
Check transmission fluid level.
Check water level on house batteries.
Check house water (shower and toilet).
Check generator oil (vehicle must be level).
Install and secure oxygen tanks.

My father didn't notice that he'd listed the oxygen tanks twice. If I had needed those things in order to breathe I'd have listed them three times.

I performed the duties mostly as directed and a few hours later we hit the road. We decided to take the southern route because a storm was heading straight toward the Sierras.

There is much American romance made of the Road. And I have driven much of that romanticized American Road and I'd say that if you are not on coastal Highway 1 in California, or certain blank desert stretches of Utah, or a length of coast along Biloxi, or certain mountain roads in Colorado and Montana, most of what greets you on American roads is intended to bore you with mind-crushing familiarity.

Other than about twenty miles of the Tehachapi Pass, where the southern Sierras and the Tehachapi Mountains meet, the distance of road on the southern route between Fairfield, California, and Las

Vegas, Nevada, is so boring you must bang your head against your steering wheel in order to remain awake.

We left Fairfield so late that we arrived at the Tehachapi Pass in darkness. I knew that beyond the windows existed a rather awesome landscape that I'd miss on this trip.

I was tired, and I said to my father, "I need some jalapeños."

"Some what?"

"If you want me to keep driving I'm going to need some jalapeños to stay awake."

"That's just plain crazy, Tone. Whatever happened to a cup of coffee?"

"Coffee won't do it. And I'm nostalgic. It's how I used to stay awake when heading back to base late at night on a Sunday from a long weekend in Los Angeles."

"Well, let's load up on fuel and jalapeños," he said.

We did just that and pushed toward Vegas.

MANY HOURS LATER as we drove through town and saw the city throwing its garish light against the sky, my dad said, "Vegas. That's a place where a man can find some trouble."

I nodded while doing my best to keep our

massive metal coffin on the road. I thought of my week in the hotel suite and the various kinds of trouble and destruction I had invited along for the party. I shuddered.

I said, "I came very close to killing myself there once or twice."

"How's that, Tone?" he asked, and sat up in his seat. My father was always game for a good self-destruction story, especially if the self was mine.

"You don't need to know. In the same way that I never needed to know about your sexual exploits in Vietnam and Taiwan, you don't need to know about my adventures in Vegas."

"Goddamn, Tone, you brought it up. My son says he almost killed himself somewhere I want to know the story. Ain't that fair?"

"I have no idea what is fair and what is not. I don't care about fair. Fair means nothing."

"Hell, what's the wrong with me trying to live vicariously through my own son? I don't got the plumbing anymore. You do. You can screw all the gals you want."

"No I can't. Nor do I want to. I'm married."

"You got a nice wife, Tone. But you can at least tell your papa some of your old carousing stories. Someday you'll want to relive them."

"You're wrong. That's the difference between the two of us."

"You like to talk about our differences, don't you?" he said.

From the tone of his voice I knew I'd hurt him, and a part of me enjoyed it. I couldn't beat the old man with my fists but I could rough him up with words.

He said, "Look in the mirror, Son. There are very few differences between us."

"Sometimes all I see is differences. It's hard not to."

"You were a dirty dog, Tone. I was a dirty dog. You got it from me. I'm not ashamed to say it."

I thought of what Danny had said in Alameda the night before.

"Let me tell you one difference between us. You got married young and you were unfaithful to your wife and thus your young children and the life of your family. I did all of my fucking around in my thirties, without a wife or child. It wasn't even fucking around. I was living the life of a man in a large city inhabited by many beautiful women. The numbers were in my favor. But I'm married now. In six months my wife is having our first baby. I'm a different man than you. I'll respect my wife and the life and sanctity of my family. I'm not so stupid as to fuck it all up with my zipper."

At this point my rage and derision for my father were so heightened that I thought I just might run us off the road. But I couldn't think of what this kind of death would be called. Death by misadventure? That's how dear old drunk Malcolm Lowry went. But no, on the contrary, this would be pure adventure. I supposed they'd have to call it a homicide/suicide by Winnebago. Right here in Vegas, a Winnebago homicide/suicide. They might talk about that one for a while, at least until an escort went missing in the desert.

"I can't talk to you when you're like this," my father said. "You're totally unreasonable."

He had a point. I was, after all, considering ending his life and mine by running our tin can off the road. It didn't matter that while growing up he was the most unreasonable person I knew and I'd been forced to live with him for nearly two decades. Why was I still unable to get over events like him shoving my face in dog shit? Or, in his version, *toward* dog shit? What is the difference, in terms of the psychic wound, in shoving a small boy's face *toward* rather than *in* dog shit? I'd say the difference is nil.

I ran atop some of the road Braille and it made the staccato sound of gunfire.

He said, "Please drive safely."

From the freeway I noticed the signage for a famous strip club.

I pointed and said, "One night I spent five thousand dollars at that strip club."

"That's more money than most folks make in a month. We all know where that got you, smart guy."

Any time I mentioned my profligate spending he turned quiet with rage. I wanted him to shut up for the next thousand miles or so and this might do the trick.

Moab was about five hundred miles away and I knew that the sooner we made it there the sooner we'd make it to Aspen and I could escape this RV and check in to my hotel, and shower, and drink some bourbon with my veteran friends and relax.

I was aware that I'd started the journey with my father only about eight hours ago, and that the journey is supposed to be the point, and that I had things I wanted to extract from my father during this trip—I wanted him to apologize for not attending my brother's funeral, but at this point I couldn't stand the man. The hatred I felt for my father at this moment rivaled the hatred I'd felt for Ava at the worst of our relationship, when she called me from a hotel in Miami, high on cocaine, to tell me she was about to sleep with a man she'd just met.

Maybe it sounds strange to compare a father to a lover, but it isn't, really. All family love is also a romance, and every romance suffers. And my romance with my father had been suffering greatly since approximately the day my brother had been buried thirteen years earlier and my father had decided not to show up. Goddamn, I hated the man for that. That is a long time to hate your father. To stomach this hate any longer just might kill me, I knew. But parts of me loved the hate.

I needed to calm down. I felt the stress coursing through my neck and across my shoulders and down my spine. It felt as if my spine were in a vise, and with each mile we traveled the vise tightened.

I said, "How far do you want to make it tonight?"

"As far as you can go, Tone."

"Why don't I try to make it all the way to Moab? We can check out the Arches first thing in the morning."

"Damn, Tone. That's near eight more hours down the road. You can make that? Don't kill us."

"I'll see what I can do."

"Maybe you need some more of them jalapeños?"

I did not need jalapeños. The adrenaline that

my rage at my father produced might keep me awake for days.

He said, "I think I'll try for some shut-eye if you don't mind."

"Not a bit, Dad. I'll see you in the morning."

He stood and steadied himself. The RV shook and rattled. My father's oxygen cord hung and swung in unison with my rhythm on the road. The noise the oxygen tank produced always haunted me, the mechanical breath it forced down into my father's lungs sounded like a tire slowly deflating. He retired to the back cabin.

I drove on through the desert. Occasionally I passed a big rig. I blasted through the desert like a massive comet rumbling toward the Earth. My father never allowed me to take the RV up over sixty-five without a stern admonition about safety and gas mileage. But now he was asleep in the back and the road and the desert and the RV were all mine. I felt like a teenager. I thought of the night I took out his 1970 Impala, a monster of a car with a sickeningly fast engine for its time. I picked up two friends and we drag-raced all over the suburban sprawl where we lived. I beat a Mustang and a Camaro and I lost to a Corvette. When I pulled into the driveway at five a.m. I ran over our mailbox. That one had been difficult to explain.

But here in the desert my father was in the back cabin and there was no one to explain anything to. I hadn't driven over one hundred miles per hour since I'd busted up my BMW in Germantown. The beastly RV was no one's idea of a race car, but one hundred miles per hour felt the same in your stomach whether you did it on a motorcycle, in a BMW, or from the command post of an RV. Any slight wrong move and it was all over. I saw visions of the RV busting into thousands of pieces all over the desert. They'd need the NTSB to figure out what the hell had happened.

I slammed the accelerator to the floor. The V-12 engine screamed and whined, and our massive tin shell hurtled across the desert. The turtle and his son are on the move.

Everything in the rig shook and rattled: I thought the TV above my head was going to fall out of its carousel. This was the earthquake I wanted. I heard my father's metal oxygen canisters rubbing up against one another, a shrill, nervous sound. The refrigerator door slammed open and food spilled all over the floor. I knew that in the back of the cabin my father was being thrown all over the bed like a cowboy riding the fiercest bull at the county fair. I was the fiercest bull. I made it to ninety-five miles per hour. The big beast disappointed me and refused to be pushed faster. I kept it at ninety-five for twenty miles.

I blew by big rigs and minivans and a yellow Porsche. The Porsche driver must have felt emasculated because a few minutes later he tore past me like a rocket; he must have hit 130. How I wished I were driving that Porsche.

I PULLED INTO Moab at about seven in the morning and my father continued to sleep. I parked at a gas station. The cabin of the RV was a total mess: tools and boxes of food and oxygen tanks were strewn all over the floor. I'd clean it later.

I stepped out. My road exhaustion heightened all my senses. The smell of a desert town early in the morning is unlike any other—damp smoky earth and history and the mountains on fire from the sun. I'm rarely up this early. It made me feel that I was a part of society.

I stepped across the street to support the local economy by purchasing a cup of coffee and a breakfast burrito at a café. The clientele were a mix of tough construction workers wearing Carhartt, tar, and mud, and young carefree outdoorsy people in neon fleece and hemp products. I wore flip-flops, food-stained jeans, and a red-and-blue plaid flannel shirt I'd bought for three dollars at a truck stop a few hours before. A handful of swishy elderly British men sporting brand-new walking shoes and smart sweaters snickered and judged us all for our sartorial calamities.

I entered the RV and my father was bent over the sink, taking one of his inhalers, doing the morning routine of tuning up the lungs. He looked at me as though I were an intruder. He was in white briefs and a white T-shirt, his Uniform of the Day. He'd worn this ensemble every morning of his adult life. His white hair looked Einsteinian. His blue eyes shone wild. He could not speak during the administration of this medicine. He wanted so badly to speak. He held up a finger in the air, telling me to wait. I knew this gesture from my childhood. It meant "Stand by for your punishment."

He gestured around the room at the mess that my racing had caused, and shrugged his shoulders and frowned. I liked this game. I shrugged back and moved to the front of the cab and sat down to call Christa.

We talked about the Baby Animal. Christa had never been to Utah. I described to her the beautiful landscape and the sensation that one was not only in another state but also on another planet. I promised to take photos at the park.

My father said, "What the hell kind of mess is this, Tone? It looks like we got robbed."

"I hit some rough road last night, Pops."

"That wasn't just rough road. Utah's got good road. How the hell fast were you going? You damn near knocked me out of bed."

"I got her up to seventy-five," I said.

"I think you're lying to me, Son. How goddamn fast did you go? Jesus, my oxygen canisters all came loose. You coulda blown us sky-high."

"Eighty, Pops. That's all she'd go."

"Can you clean it up? I thought you said seventy-five?"

It took me about half an hour to tighten and tidy the place. I went back across the street and bought my dad a burrito. And finally we headed to Arches National Park.

I admired how much a fan of national parks my father was. He aimed to see as many of them as possible before he died. When I was a kid our road trips always included a national park or two. I'd always thought it was because my dad was too cheap to pay for other family entertainment— sporting events, a deep-sea fishing trip, a house on the beach for a week. And money might have been a part of his motivation. But later I realized what a fine education in the natural riches of the country we'd received on trips to the parks. It was also for my father a point of patriotism: *Look at what belongs to our country.* At a visceral level, as a veteran of a foreign war, he felt a bit of personal ownership of these parks: *I fought for this, I saw men die for this.*

I dropped my dad in front of the visitor center and parked the RV out by the big rigs. Moab was at four thousand feet and I noticed the elevation already affecting him. Once we got to Aspen we'd be near eight thousand.

The desert sun beat down hard on my face as I walked through the parking lot. My dad had not made it far, only about fifteen feet toward the door. He leaned against a bronze sculpture of a bighorn sheep.

"Goddamn, Tone," he said, shaking his head. "Lord, what I'd do for a new set of lungs."

Seeing my father incapacitated out in the world was a totally different experience from seeing him stuck in his RV. In his RV he ran the show—all his meds, his oxygen, his timers, his potions, his magic, were available, and the disease seemed manageable. But under the intense winter desert sun, in front of the visitor center, he looked weak and small. I wanted my father the mountain cat to take down that bighorn sheep, but all he could do was lean against the bronze sculpture and pray to the Lord for a different set of lungs.

My rage at my father melted.

Strangers stared at my father and his oxygen contraption. I hated the strangers for staring. And I'll admit I was ashamed of his disease, the stupidest disease a man could possibly come down with, COPD. It could have been the flight line chemicals he spent decades around, but most likely he did it to himself by smoking for forty-five years. What a stupid goddamn disease and what a stupid man. My father was sixty-nine years old, and other than his failing lungs, the man was an ox. With healthy lungs he would have lived to be a hundred.

We drove north through the park, up Park Avenue, and frightened other road warriors with our bulk. At every viewing point we pulled the beast over and I got out of the rig and hiked as near as I could to a rock formation and took pictures. I snapped the Organ and the Three Gossips and the Tower of Babel. Snapped the Petrified Dunes and Ham Rock and Balanced Rock and the Garden of Eden.

At the Windows Section I had to take a proper hike to make it to the sights. It was hot enough that I took a bottle of water with me.

"Be safe, Tone," my father said.

I walked out into the desert because my father could not. I looked at the groups of friends and families on their way back to their vehicles, laughing and carrying on as friends and families do. I felt robbed. In my twenties, before my brother died and while my father and I still enjoyed a loving relationship, I had dreamed someday of family vacations like this—a healthy group of Swoffords heading to a splendid sight in Yosemite or Yellowstone, my father hiking with my family and me.

But at the Arches I walked alone. Christa sat at home in Brooklyn writing her own book about her own dysfunctional family, and my father sat in his RV, a half mile away from me, taking his meds and asking the Lord for a new set of lungs.

The Windows are an impressive rock formation. I took some snaps. I walked as far from the crowd as I could and looked out on the desert. In the end, the Windows and the Tower of Babel and all the rest of them are just rocks. Someday gravity and erosion will do their work and these massive formations, too, will be dust. But the desert will remain a large expanse of nothingness and everything.

I took my time walking back to the RV. My father's illness had transformed him from a man of constant action and movement into a man who might die from too much action and movement.

"How's it look?" he asked.

"Looks like a rock with massive holes. Good stuff."

To our west was another formation, and I decided that we must have at least a few photos with my father and me present. I stood my father up against an old ranch fence and took his picture with a beautiful expanse of desert and towering massive red rocks in the background. I ordered him to smile, and he did offer a big smile. His oxygen tube was wrapped around his face, and his Einstein hair blew wildly in the wind and he looked happy. My old sick father leaning against the wooden ranch fence with towering massive red rocks in the background looked handsome and even beautiful. I switched spots with him and he snapped my picture. I suppose I could have used the timer and taken a shot with us both in it but it didn't cross my mind. I'm sure that someday I'll regret that.

We made our way out of the park to grab lunch in Moab. By the time we hit the road it was almost six. I knew a storm would hit Aspen overnight and I wanted to arrive by midnight so I could get the keys to my room. My friend Dan, who had my keys, would be crashed out if I arrived any later. I hadn't showered since we left Fairfield. I wanted a shower and a fire in a fireplace and a few shots of bourbon. And none of those things were available in the RV.

AN HOUR OR so out of Moab my father said, "We need to empty the septic. If we get on up that mountain and all that shit freezes it'll be a god-damn nightmare. You want your old man to shit in an icebox?"

"Shit freezes?" I asked. "When was the last time you emptied that thing?" I'd been careful to take toilet breaks on land.

"Hell, Tone. I don't know the last time I emptied it. Three or four months ago? Not since your mom and I went to Mexico. We gotta empty it. It'll ramp up our gas mileage heading up the mountain."

Outside Grand Junction my dad saw a sign denoting a septic dump at the next rest stop.

We pulled into the stop. Some weekend ATVers were dumping from their small camper trailer. It was a man and his young son. The kid must have been ten or twelve and the guy was my age. I watched as the man instructed the son on how to pull the septic tube from the rear bumper of the trailer and then do the dump.

They pulled away and I pulled our rig into the spot.

My father said, "I think I need to get out for this, Tone."

"Are you serious? Dad, I'm mildly educated. I can figure out how to dump the shit out of your RV. It can't be rocket science."

"I have my system. If you don't follow my system this time then next time the system will be totally fucked."

"The system is called gravity. Your septic system is above the dump. I attach the tube and open the lever and God or whatever you want to call it does the rest. If a twelve-year-old kid can do it, so can I."

"That was a very rudimentary system they were running on that rig. You see that thing? That was from the eighties at the earliest."

"Gravity barely changed from the eighties to today."

"I've got my system, Tone. I'd appreciate it if you follow it."

This displeased me greatly. It would take my father twenty minutes just to walk around to the other side of the RV, and then if I was dumping the shit at his slow and meticulous pace, this could take us hours. The storm was coming and the last thing I wanted to do was spend another night in this RV, or even at a Motel 6 in Glenwood Springs at the bottom of the mountain.

It turned out that my father's septic system was slightly more complex than what the ATVers before us had sported. There was a red tube for evacuating the system, a black tube for washing the system out, and a white tube for refilling the entire system with new water. My father directed me throughout. I had flashbacks to my boyhood and receiving instruction from my father on how to change the oil on a car or how to roof a house or how to run a hot wire from a breaker box. I suppose these are skills that a boy should learn from his father, but ultimately my father's lesson plans included a major dose of his anger and my humiliation when I didn't complete a task exactly as he'd detailed.

In order to stay sane while following my father's directions for flushing the septic system, I fantasized Jack Rebney of *Winnebago Man* fame. Rebney became known for the profanity-laden outtakes from a 1980s Winnebago instructional video he'd recorded. I turned my father's directions into Rebneyesque insanity:

> What you've got here, you fucking fuck, is your basic septic fucking system that moves your sick shit from your asshole down into the toilet on this piece-of-shit fucking Winnebago. See those goddamn flies? The

flies are here because you are a lazy fucking prick and you waited four months to empty your fucking feces from the goddamn Winnebago. The issue here is not the fucking Winnebago but you, the asshole who drives the Winnebago and thinks he can shit in it endlessly, as though this is a goddamn toilet at Yankee fucking Stadium. Your fucking Winnebago, I see you got the thirty-four-footer because you didn't have the fucking balls to buy a forty-footer, so your fucking thirty-four-footer won't carry as much of your putrid shit so now you must ask me, Jack Rebney, the Winnebago Man, how to empty your shit store, right? Well, what the fuck do you want from me? Do you want me to get down on my fucking hands and knees here in Grand fucking Junction, Colorado, and empty your shit for you? I guess you do, you lazy fucking prick. So here we go: the 2008 Winnebago has a holding tank that holds what we call the fucking gray water, which comes from your kitchen, where you wash your dishes, and from your sinks and shower, when by some fucking chance you wash your rotten fucking ass. There is also the black water, which, no shit, is the water in which your shit and piss are held. It is important to never cross-contaminate the hoses. If you do this you are a stupid fuck and you deserve dysentery or whatever fucked-up third-world disease you get because you are fucking stupid. So now you have emptied the gray and the black water and you, fucking numbnuts, have managed to spill some shit and piss on the sleeve of your flannel, and how does that feel to have your parents' shit and piss spilled on your flannel fucking shirt? That's payback for all the times you shot shit and piss out of your goddamn diaper and all over your loving parents when your numbnuts were the size of fucking raisins. Now you attach the fucking white hose to the tank and fill it up with non-potable water. *Non-potable* means you cannot fucking drink it, so don't be a dumbass and drink from the fucking sink in your fucking thirty-four-foot Winnebago. Don't even use that water to brush your fucking crooked and rotten teeth. So now that this bullshit took you almost an hour, you better hurry the fuck up or that storm is going to catch your stupid ass and you'll be sitting at the bottom of the mountain sleeping in this fucking piece-of-shit recreational vehicle while all your friends relax in their very nice ski condominiums. So don't be an asshole. Get the fuck out of my face.

WE PULLED INTO the village at Snowmass, above Aspen, around two in the morning. My friend Dan was incommunicado, so that meant I'd be spending one more night in the RV with my father.

We found a good parking spot in the rodeo grounds parking lot. I made a few bags of microwave popcorn and my father and I sat at the kitchenette table and drank beer.

Snow began to fall in big clumps. At eight thousand feet my father had serious trouble breathing. He could speak only a few dozen or so words before needing to catch his breath.

He asked me, "I gotta know, Tone. How long is it gonna be before you get this venom out? This is our third trip. That's a lot of goddamn gas. And you still seem pissed off at me. I don't know what you want."

"I want to know what happened in Vietnam. I want to know why you cheated on my mother. I want to know why you didn't go to Jeff's funeral."

"My answers are never good enough for you, Tone."

"How many times did you cheat on my mother?"

"I don't know."

"Ten?"

"I have no idea."

"Twenty?"

"I have no idea."

"Thirty?"

My father shook his head. He pounded his arm, karate-chop style, against the table. "You sound like a fucking lawyer. 'Would it be between five and ten, or ten and fifteen?' Does Vietnam count?"

"Vietnam doesn't count," I said.

"Vietnam don't count." He chopped at the table. "Does Taiwan count?"

"No."

"Taiwan don't count. Does Texas count?"

"Texas counts," I said.

He frowned. "Texas counts. Does Spain count?"

"Spain counts."

"Spain counts. Does Germany count?"

"Germany counts."

"Does Copenhagen count?"

"No."

"Copenhagen doesn't count." This pleased my father.

He twirled his oxygen line and thought about Copenhagen. With the backs of his fingers he scratched the beard on his neck in an upward sweeping motion exactly the way I do. He must have appreciated the freebie I'd given him. His marine brother was dying in a hospital in Copenhagen when he visited. That means while his brother died in a nearby hospital and his wife and two infant children were alone in Seville my father was in his hotel room banging some girl he met in a Copenhagen bar.

"Does Japan count?" he asked, somewhat hopefully, I could tell.

"Yes."

"Japan counts." He exhaled heavily, defeated. I could see him in some dim Shinjuku sex parlor. Who knows, he might have taken me with him and had the mama-san watch over me while he took care of business in the back. I wouldn't put it past him.

He asked, "Does Guam count?"

"No."

"Does Okinawa count?"

"No."

"I don't understand your logic, Tone. No on Copenhagen but yes on Tokyo?"

"Combat deployments don't count and cities where your brother is dying don't count. I assume you went through Guam and Okinawa on your way to Vietnam."

"That's correct. Does Hawaii count?"

This was a tough one. My father took leave from Vietnam in Hawaii and my mother met him there. I was conceived on this trip.

"Yes, Hawaii counts."

"OK. I don't remember anything."

"That's good work, Dad. I think it qualifies you as a pussy hound."

He paused. He let my compliment soak in. He glanced at me and looked away. Now he wasn't certain whether it was a compliment or not. He took the barrel-chest pose, hands on his knees, attempting to open up his chest as wide as possible. Physiologically this did nothing, but it must have helped psychologically: *If I open my chest as wide as possible to the world, the world will offer more oxygen.*

He said, "When I was stationed there in Moses Lake, Washington, we'd head to Spokane on weekends." He chopped at the table a few times. "That university there, Gonzales?"

"Gonzaga."

"Gonzaga. It was a good pussy town, Spokane was. We'd go down to the lakes. That's where the girls hung out. This was before I married your mother. We met a lot of girls. Back on base one Monday morning, I worked for two German civilians on a roofing crew. I pulled into the warehouse where we worked. One of the old Germans pointed at me and then pointed at my car and he said, 'You are *Scheidenjäger.*' And I said, 'What?' And he pointed at my car. 'There are panties hanging from your bumper. *Scheidenjäger.* You are pussy hunter.' From then on I was known as the Pussy Hunter."

That was my father's explanation for decades of infidelity: *I am pussy hunter.*

I won't lie. A part of me liked this characterization. Virility is intoxicating, and virility in one's father means the gene has been passed down. My father was a very handsome young man, and I like to think of him scoring women all over the world, why not? But he was also a married man and my mother's husband, and a cheating bastard.

I looked out the window. Over a foot of snow had fallen and I couldn't see five feet beyond the RV. On the radio they said we might get eight feet overnight.

"I don't know what to say, Dad. You lived an amorous life that some would envy and others would despise. It's hard to listen to one's pussy-hunter father detail his worldwide pussy-hunting exploits. I don't know what to do with it."

"I always loved your mother. This was never about you kids or your mother. The world was different back then. Men were different. What qualified as acceptable behavior was different."

"Maybe I've wanted to know too much."

"Then it's my turn, there are some things I want to know, too. Like why all you want to do is talk about our differences. Makes me think you are afraid of our likenesses. Look in the mirror. Look at your nose and your chin. Your eyes. Look at your hairline. You are Swofford. You got Swofford blood, boy. You can't change that. You ran all around the world and fucked all the girls you wanted, just like your old man."

"I wasn't married."

"OK. Next question. Why did you ignore your Granny when she wanted to give you a medal from the Daughters of the Confederacy?"

"This again? Give it up."

"You got your questions, I got mine. Now answer me. I'm genuinely interested to know."

"I didn't want a medal from a neo-racist organization. Fuck the Daughters of the Confederacy. I did not grow up in the South. I don't care about the DOC. It's a bunch of old racist white ladies holding on to bullshit ideas about why the South got their asses kicked in the war."

"Now you not only disrespect your Southern heritage but you disrespect your blood."

"I have no emotional link to the old dead

Swofford Confederates whose gravestones Granny shines."

"You're pushing me, Son. You got Swofford blood. My great-great-grandfather Solomon Willis Swofford fought for the Confederacy. You got linkage whether you like it or not."

I thought, *You want me to push you, old man?*

I said, "You care more about those Swofford Confederate gravestones than you do about Jeff's. You didn't attend your own son's funeral. You disgraced yourself and your entire family."

My father and I have been having this fight off and on since shortly after Jeff died. I'm like a pack of hyenas at a felled buffalo. And when I'm done with that I want another. And now give me another.

I say, "What happens if I die tomorrow? Will you show up? Or will you stay home and get drunk alone and cry in the corner rather than show your face? Is that how you'll show your love?"

When my father is extremely angry, at his angriest, he gets very quiet, deathly quiet, and his face looks ghost-white, and the anger sparks off his face like micro-explosions. I know that if he were capable he would try to beat me physically right now. I know that he would like to beat me down into the ground with the same force and remorselessness with which I would like to ruin him.

He cleared his throat. "You will never understand what it was like for me to lose my firstborn son. There are no words. You will never understand. I couldn't handle it. And I won't apologize for how I behaved. It was all I could do. Goddamn, Son, how many times I have to tell you? Wait until Christa has your baby. Then ask me that question again."

"All you could do after your thirty-five-year-old son died was drive around to the same shitty GI bars in Fairfield where you'd been drinking for thirty years? Did those people offer you solace? Where are they now that you can barely breathe or walk? You think they care about you? What did they offer you then? A couple of free rounds because your son died? Your family was there in Georgia, in your hometown, grieving for your son. I was there. Kim and Tami were there. We grieved for our brother. All of your brothers and sisters were there grieving for their nephew. Mom was there. Mom. The woman who gave birth to him. You want to pull some hierarchy of grieving bullshit? OK. The woman who gave birth to Jeff sat in the room with him the night he died. She read his Bible to him and she listened to him expel his last breath. And she attended his funeral. You lose."

I knocked the bowl of popcorn and the two empty beer cans off the table.

"You cheated on your wife, you mentally and occasionally physically abused your children. One of your sons died and you didn't go to his funeral. You can't guarantee that you'd go to my funeral. I know your mother died when you were a month old, and I know that fucking sucked, Dad, I can't think of a sadder way to grow up than carrying that horrible knowledge with you. And I know your half brother died. And I know you watched people die heinous deaths in Vietnam. And I know that Jeff died. That is one shitstorm after another, but it gave you no excuse to treat your children the way you did."

My father was scared. I knew it. And I liked it. He looked anxious and he could barely breathe, the elevation had nearly knocked him out.

He said, "I need a Xanax, Tone. Can you hand me my meds?"

I handed him his meds backpack overflowing with medications. He shook while he looked through the bag for the right bottle. He shook one out and took it down with a gulp of water.

"The elevation. I didn't think about the elevation.

I can barely breathe. Goddamn, Tone. I need those new lungs."

"I need an apology."

"I won't apologize no more, Tone. I'm done. I apologized a couple years ago about my behavior. I'm done. I don't know what else to tell you. I want to help you get the venom out. It'll kill you, Son."

"You never really apologized. You said that you understand that the way you treated us kids then would today be considered child abuse. That is not an apology. That is a finely crafted disavowal of responsibility."

I stood over my father now. He could barely breathe.

He said, "Get the venom out. Do you want to beat me? Do you want to kick my ass the way I once kicked your ass? Will that help? You can do it, if that'll help."

I ignored my father and walked to the back of the cabin. Yes, I did want to beat him; I wanted to grab him by his neck and shove his face in a pile of dog shit and tell him he was stupid and tell him he would never amount to shit, and I wanted to beat his face in, and bloody it, and I wanted to make him weep and cower the way he had once made me weep and cower. I felt sick to my stomach. I lay back on the bed and closed my eyes. I thought of

Christa and the Baby Animal. I thought about the life we would live and the loving home we would build for the Baby Animal, without rancor, without violence, without hatred. But still I wanted to go to the front of the rig and beat my father.

And then the rig started to move. I looked out the window, and yes, we were on the move. My father had started to drive. The snow was up at about five feet now, it was deep, and it was four in the morning. I walked to the front of the cab.

I said to my father, "Where are you going?"

"I can't handle you anymore. I'm dropping you off. There is a bus stop down the road. You're such a big man. You can take your suitcase and get out of my rig. I can't be treated like this anymore. I can't help you. You can take your venom with you."

My father drove wildly through the massive and empty parking lot. He didn't know where he was going; he could barely see and he certainly couldn't see his way out.

"Goddamn it, Tone, how do I get out of here? Where is the exit?"

I stood above him, he in the captain's chair, speeding in circles around the huge snowy parking lot. The lot was the width of two football fields and he drove it like a madman, looking for an exit, but the lot hadn't been plowed and there was no way out. Cabinets banged open and food and tools flew about the back of the cabin in a reprisal of my show from the night before.

"Tell me how to get out. I want you out of my rig."

"You're going to kick me out of your RV at four in the morning in the middle of a blizzard? You do this and you might never see me again and you'll never see my daughter."

"You're a big man, Tone. You don't need your pop. You don't even like me."

He gunned it on a straightaway. Our tracks in the parking lot made it look as if we had our own little ice car race going on. When my father said that I didn't like him it was one of the worst things anyone had ever said to me. Because I did like him. Sometimes I didn't love him, and sometimes I hated him, but he was an immensely likable fellow, with a charming Southern accent and whiskey barrels full of engrossing and engaging stories, some of them far too bawdy for him to have told his son, but still, he had the stories and he had the charm and everyone loved my father. And I loved him and I even liked him. I didn't want to be him. I didn't want to be the kind of father that he had been. I hated him for not being a good role model. I hated him for not giving me a happy family history to tell. If I want to tell a story of longevity, and commitment, and happiness, I will have to make it my own. As he sped around the parking lot trying to find a way to evict me during the snowstorm, I loved my father more than I ever had before. I loved him for standing up to me and telling me to get rid of my venom. I loved him for showing me what kind of father not to be.

"Stop," I said. "Just stop the RV. You can't get out of the parking lot. If you want me out of here I'll walk up the hill. It's a mile to the lodge. I know where I am."

My father stopped the vehicle and slumped over the wheel.

"Goddamn, Son," he said. "I was not a perfect father. I am not a perfect man. But cut me some slack. I love you. I love your company. I love your fellowship. You are my son and I love you."

I dropped to my knees at my father's side and I put my hand on his back. I rubbed his back. I looked out the massive RV windshield and saw nothing but a thick white snowfall, a blanket of white. A purity and newness I'd never seen before.

"I'm not a perfect son. I love you, Dad. And I like your company, too. Let's get some sleep. Let's get over this."

*   *   *

WE SLEPT TOGETHER in the back of his RV in the queen-size bed. I hadn't slept in the same bed with my father since I was three or four years old. It took me a while to fall asleep. I was exhausted from fighting with my father and driving twelve hundred miles in a day and a half.

My father slept next to me in a deep quiet. The only sound in the world was his oxygen machine feeding him what he needed in order to live. The workings of the machine sounded like the distant whine of an airplane engine.

I thought of one of the few Vietnam stories my father ever told me. His unit was assigned to go deep in the bush and build landing strips for C-130 cargo planes. The planes were to land empty and leave full of evacuated villagers and the few belongings they could carry in their bare hands. It was a classic and totally absurd Vietnam tactic: if you bomb the entire infiltrated village to high heavens then there will no longer be a village for the Viet Cong to control. On one of these missions the timing was super tight. They had twenty minutes to evacuate the village and take off before the bombers arrived overhead to drop their loads.

They hustled the civilians onto the plane. The GIs were tense. There were probably VC among

the villagers, there might be a guy with a gre-
nade buried in his armpit, and the bombers might
arrive early and blow them up, too. My father was
at the rear of the plane, helping the last few villagers embark as the plane began to pull away.
He got them all on and he hopped on the tongue.
The sound of the engines was loud and violent.
An old lady holding a scrawny chicken under each
arm, everything in the world that she now owned,
lurched as though she wanted to run back for
something else. A photo of a child or a husband?
It didn't matter; she couldn't go back. My father
grabbed her around the waist and held her tight as
the plane picked up speed, bouncing over the landing strip he'd built the day before. She screamed
an animal scream and dug her old lady elbows into
my father's ribs and her chickens made a racket
and my father held tight as the plane gained alti-
tude and the bombers began to drop their loads.
My father and the woman watched as her village
and her home were destroyed.

13

Oh Josephine

Christa and I wanted to bring our baby home to a stress-free environment. The stretch of Washington Avenue where we lived in Brooklyn did not qualify as such. I called it Little Kandahar. Most nights there were fistfights on the street; the occasional gunfight erupted nearby; once a car careened into the building; from the apartment window I'd witnessed a hit-and-run; and there were at least two men who patrolled the block in wheelchairs and aggressively panhandled and cursed and threatened physical violence against anyone who didn't hand over money.

A block away one might eat at one of the better Italian restaurants in the city and pay twenty-five dollars for a plate of pasta. This neighborhood was wildly popular with art students and kids just out of college working their first shitty jobs before they had to depart the city for Montgomery or wherever they'd come from. Also there were a lot of white creative types in their thirties and forties who had for a number of years reportedly been civilizing the place with their wit and vigor and children. I saw no indication of this.

I admitted that my years in Chelsea had blinded me to the harsher realities of the outer boroughs and the inanities of the white creative class.

In early summer we moved full-time to Woodstock.

We spent the summer nesting. I painted the baby's room Persian Violet and we acquired all of the matériel required for the first six months of her life. We hiked and hung out at swimming holes that only locals knew. We made fun of the hipsters who visited the Catskills on the weekends.

In early September Christa's due date passed and we began to panic. She'd had a healthy pregnancy. Nothing indicated a problem birth, but her doctor talked about inducing her if she made it to a week past. Christa wanted a natural birth but she'd grown tired of pregnancy.

She said to her doctor, "Please get this baby out of me."

The doctor said, "We'll talk next week."

We continued to nest: now we painted the large main room of the house. I went to the gym twice a day. I cleaned out the gutters on the house. I swept the chimney. We walked the three-mile route along Upper Byrdcliffe Road where we lived. The baby sat on Christa's bladder like a queen on a throne, and our walks aggravated the situation. Christa learned how to squat at the side of the road and pretend to admire flowers when actually she was taking a pee.

We considered driving fifteen hundred miles to Tennessee so she'd be certain to have the baby naturally at The Farm, the birthplace of contemporary American midwifery. But we realized we'd have to drive home that same fifteen hundred miles with a newborn and that seemed cruel to everyone involved.

There had been talk of castor oil to induce a natural labor, an old trick of the midwives. All tricks have believers and naysayers: the believers said, *Go for it*, while the naysayers said, *Enjoy sitting on your toilet for a day or two*.

We'd heard of a restaurant in Georgia where they guaranteed that at your due date or beyond you'd go into labor within twenty-four hours of eating their eggplant Parmesan. Christa wanted a dozen servings delivered express.

One afternoon I stopped by the butcher and decided that for dinner we must eat a massive three-pound porterhouse.

At home I dropped it on the kitchen table and dubbed it the Labor Steak.

Christa said, "God, I'll do anything to get this baby out of me."

And I knew she meant it.

"The Labor Steak will do it, sweetheart. A steak must work better than eggplant Parmesan."

In the early evening I returned again from the gym and found Christa reclining on the couch, a glass of syrupy pink liquid in front of her.

She said, "God, this tastes awful."

"What is it?"

"Fruit juice and castor oil."

"Where did you get castor oil?"

She laughed. "I bought it weeks ago."

"How much did you take?"

"A teaspoon."

"That's child's play. You need at least two table-spoons or it won't work," I said with the certainty borne of a Google search. I fixed Christa a higher dose.

It was the chilliest night since we'd moved to Woodstock, and we decided to have our first fire-place fire. Castor oil. Labor Steak. Romantic fire. We couldn't go wrong.

Christa loved eating a steak so nearly raw you'd think it still had a pulse. Like a good husband I'd refused to allow her a rare steak throughout her pregnancy, but at nearly a week past her due date I decided she'd earned a steak at whatever temperature she desired. Outside on the deck I prepared the charcoal.

Inside, the fireplace spat out flames and Christa set the table. I stared at her through the window. She was my extremely beautiful and massively pregnant and petite wife and I knew that very soon, possibly within hours, our lives would change forever.

Like every other night we ate late. It was almost ten when I threw the meat on the grill. The woods that surrounded our home were dark and quiet.

The beastly three-pound porterhouse crawled off the grill and onto a serving platter after a few minutes of cooking.

We sat down for dinner, and the shadows from the fire licked our freshly painted walls and we ate our steak there in our charmingly rustic family home. All we were missing was that darn baby.

We'd each had a few bites of the steak. I wanted to ask about the castor oil but also I didn't want to ask about the castor oil. I knew that during her pregnancy she'd spared me the details of a number of the bodily mortifications she'd suffered.

I assumed that if the castor oil experiment failed she'd keep the results to herself. I didn't mind this.

Christa looked at me and her large doe eyes grew wider and she said, "Oh. Jesus. I think I need to spend a lot of time alone on the toilet." She looked bashfully at the floor and pushed her plate away.

I said, "I'm sorry. This isn't going to be fun, is it?"

"I'm sorry to ruin our dinner," she said.

"Don't be silly."

Her eyes grew wider and she said, "Wait. I think my water broke?"

"How do you know?" I stupidly asked.

She reached down between her legs and said, "I know."

She grabbed her phone and called the hospital.

I used the fireplace tongs to throw the burning logs into a large copper cauldron and dragged the cauldron outside and onto the deck. If my wife hadn't needed to rush to the hospital I would have paused to admire the awesome sight of flames shooting five feet high into the dark night. But I doused the logs with a hose, and by the time I made it back inside Christa was already out front waiting in the car. The birthing center in Rhinebeck was forty minutes away.

She said, "Speed, speed, speed. I'm going to have this baby in the car!"

I have never regularly obeyed speed limits and the slightest encouragement from a passenger will always cause me to slam down the gas pedal. But this night, with the most important life at risk, I refused to speed.

"It will take longer if I get pulled over," I said.

"You speed on this road every fucking day, like three times a fucking day. Are you kidding me?"

"I'm not kidding. Delivery is a long way off."

I'd read the books for expectant fathers. They were all very clear that the father shouldn't speed toward the hospital. They also advised that when your partner no longer thinks your jokes are funny she is definitely in labor. We drove by the bar in Woodstock where my old landlord from Mount Tremper played bluegrass every Thursday night.

I motioned toward the Wok 'n Roll and said, "Want to hear some live music?"

She did not laugh.

"Let me drive," she said. "I'll speed."

I refused to relinquish the wheel. We arrived in Rhinebeck without birthing the baby in the car.

We settled in the room. Christa had hired the help of a doula, a woman named Mary. Mary had about her the old mountain wisdom and also, I'd thought, a whiff of the hippie grifter.

My main job was to play the *Josephine Birth Mix* from my laptop. Over the summer Mary had urged us to forgo the usual birthing classes, and when Christa asked about breathing techniques Mary said, "You are alive. You already know how to breathe. You were born for this. When the time comes just relax and have your baby. She'll tell you when she's ready."

Which is what happened.

I won't say that I did nothing. I'd like to think that I was a calm and supportive presence for my wife during one of the most intense physical and psychological moments of her life. This might be true. I played the Black Crowes' song "Oh Josephine" on repeat for about an hour around three-thirty in the morning. At about five I played "Into the Mystic" on repeat. I held the oxygen to Christa's mouth when Mary told me to.

I repeated, "You are an amazing woman and you are giving birth to our beautiful baby and we will both love you forever."

But mostly I watched four women—Christa, Mary the doula, the nurse, and the midwife—take part in the craziest thing I'd ever seen in my life. I'd been shot at during war and I'd seen what American-made five-hundred-pound bombs do to the human body, but nothing I'd witnessed compared to the intensity and immensity of my wife giving birth.

I watched these women take part in the natural birth of Josephine and I realized men could never accomplish this: four men trying to bring life into the world? Two would be engaged in a fistfight, one would be doing whiskey shots in the corner, and the other would be on the floor in a fetal position, weeping.

Josephine did tell us when she was ready for the world, at exactly 5:22 a.m. I caught her, as they say. She was a small bundle of loose limbs and of vernix, crying a beautiful cry. Her head looked like a collapsed hothouse tomato. I wondered if it would ever regain human shape, but I didn't betray my alarm to Christa.

I moved Josephine to her mother's chest, and I said, "Oh, Josephine, welcome to the family. We've been waiting so long to meet you."

She latched on to Christa's breast and we both held her little body. We were a family.

At first Josephine looked like every other baby, and then she began to fill out. There were days when I glanced at her and she looked like a complete stranger. And other days she looked just like Jeff. She usually looked like Jeff in the mornings, for some reason. I could see him in her brow and eyes and dear sweet smile. Around this time one of my aunts happened to send me a package with dozens of photos, many of them from the years when my parents lived in Spain and Jeff was an infant. And these photos confirmed for me Josephine's resemblance to her uncle Jeff.

ON THE LAST weekend of October we're warned to prepare for the biggest and earliest snow in New York State in decades. In a matter of hours the mountain we live on in Woodstock has turned from leaf-peeping ideal to deep winter landscape. The tourists who booked up the hotels months ago for the last look at red and yellow leaves descending from oak and poplar must change their plans. The leaves and trails are now frozen, which means no rigorous hikes up Overlook Mountain this weekend. Perhaps they might drive down to Kingston and purchase a sled at a sporting goods store and sled-race down the hills, or buy bourbon at a liquor store and submit to the baser instincts during a storm: get drunk and stay warm.

The tourists will be smart to learn from the twenty-two-year-old hiker Ryan Owens, who managed to get lost hiking near Moon Haw Road in the Slide Mountain Wilderness on Friday afternoon. He and his friend's dog Maggie spent the evening in a cave, and in the morning, as the big snow began to drop, they covered seven miles through rugged mountain terrain before finding civilization. Ryan had with him only Maggie and a bottle of water and he wore a long-sleeved thermal T-shirt.

Just over a year ago, had I been this Mr. Owens, I would have welcomed the snow and the fury of this freak early storm, and I might have stayed in the cave to die.

Tonight Josephine has been fussy, something new for us. My mother is visiting from California but she offers no baby-calming advice, and we appreciate this. After all, I am the last infant she took care of, forty-one years ago. The techniques have changed and this she must be aware of. And if my mother offers advice, I can counter with the knowledge that she smoked while pregnant with me and continued to smoke in my presence until the day I left home for the Marines. I often joke with her and claim that her in utero and second-hand smoke caused both my bad eyesight and my slow times in the forty-yard dash, and that if not for her smoking I might have been a fighter pilot or a football star or both.

Some truth and rage course through the nuances of my joke. I still blame my mother for some of the hurt and fear I suffered throughout my childhood: *Why did you not protect me from your secondhand carcinogenic smoke, and why did you not protect me from my father? You must have known that both were toxic.*

The snow falls steadily and Christa worries that we will lose power. We lost power for a week during Hurricane Irene and were lucky to retreat to a friend's vacation cottage in Maine during that time. A lengthy power outage with the baby in the house might be enough to scare us off the mountain and back to New York City.

Christa says, "If we lose power again, I'll tell Byrdcliffe we just can't take these risks with the baby. I'll kick the renters out of the Washington Avenue apartment and we'll be home in Brooklyn for Christmas."

Here in Woodstock we rent an idyllic converted barn from the Byrdcliffe Artists Colony. It is a wonderful place to have brought the baby home but we are ready for a return to city living. The mountains are too slow. The power outage flirts with our city dreams, and the lights flutter off and on throughout the evening, but the power remains on. We both want the power to fail and to have to head to the Thruway and get a few rooms at the Holiday Inn and use this as the ammo for breaking our lease. Dragging your baby to a Holiday Inn so she doesn't freeze to death is reason enough to break a lease, right?

This evening my mother cooked dinner. She made the enchiladas I grew up eating. I've been talking up these enchiladas to Christa since our first date. I remember from my boyhood only a few good feelings as constant and certain as the news that my mother planned enchiladas for dinner.

Tonight the enchiladas disappoint with a surprising blandness, and my mother knows it and I know it and Christa knows it, but we tell my mother that the enchiladas are great and we both take seconds because this is what you tell your sixty-eight-year-old mother. Growing up I loved my mother's cooking, but now I am a rather accomplished self-taught home cook, and I can cook smoke rings around my mother, but no one needs to say it. And it doesn't matter.

Yesterday I took my mother to the grocery store and she bought the same canned enchilada sauce she has used for decades. I wanted to tell her that she could make her own sauce from scratch, that it would be very easy in fact to make from scratch a flavorful and robust red enchilada sauce, and that in our pantry we had everything she would need for this tasty sauce, but I bit my tongue. Sometimes food is not about the flavor but the gesture. My mother made dinner for me and my wife and my newborn baby daughter. That is more important than the flavor of the meal, isn't it? Someday when my mother has passed I will remember the night in Woodstock when I left my foodie pretensions in the canned food aisle of the supermarket and my mother cooked the enchiladas of my childhood for my wife and daughter. I will not remember that the enchiladas tasted bland. I will cherish the fact that as a winter storm streaked the Catskills with flashes of freezing snow, my mother labored in my kitchen and after the meal we were all full and we were happy. And by that time I will even forget that as a boy my mother failed to protect me from my bully father and that she smoked Pall Malls and ruined my speed in the forty-yard dash. Won't I? Mothers are immensely forgivable creatures.

For the fussy baby, Christa and I have tried all the tricks we know as new parents: slings and swings and lullabies and Van Morrison and college football. Neither of us says so, but we are both thinking the same thing: *Some ingredient from the canned enchilada sauce has entered into Christa's breast milk and turned our baby into a monster!*

I watch a close football game and bounce the baby on my knee while Christa scans a number of child-rearing books trying to locate the exact cause of our daughter's sleeplessness and distress. We count the diapers Josephine soiled today, we count the feedings, and we count her farts. We add the values and divide by our anxiety squared. Baby sleep is a science and we are both humanists, total failures at science.

I say to my mother, feeling guilty about something, "JoJo never does this. It's midnight. She's usually asleep by nine."

And my mother says, "Sometimes babies don't sleep."

This is the wisdom from a mother of four children. It is basic and it is true tonight just as it was forty-one years ago: sometimes babies don't sleep.

You need not blame yourself or your mother's canned enchilada sauce.

Christa is tired and I have work to do, and I say to her, as though I am now an expert, "Sweetheart, sometimes babies don't sleep. Go to bed; I'll work with her on my chest."

A friend who had a baby a few weeks before we did sent me an e-mail one night that said only: "Skin-to-skin solves everything."

I took off my shirt and unclothed the baby and

I slung her tight to my chest. I walked around the warm main room of our house and I sang her Van Morrison tunes, and I looked outside at the thick white blanket of snow on the ground and the tree branches weighted with snow.

At first the weathermen said the storm might drop eighteen inches, and then they revised that down to twelve, but it looks to me as if so far we took on eight inches at the top end, if the snow on my picnic table is any fair measure. But eight inches is a good snow for late October, a real snow.

It is only one in the morning, and we might still lose power. That is the measure of a proper storm. Some people must die: there must be danger. A storm also measures the man: will you protect your family when the storm shows? In the life of a family many storms threaten and some arrive full force. I'll pass this first test. I will pass them all, I tell myself.

Josephine sleeps against my chest. Some of her slobber has dripped down into my chest hair. I find this charming and beautiful. I find everything about my daughter charming and beautiful. Someday this will probably change. For instance, she will steal money from my wallet for beer and cigarettes. Hell, I will find this charming, too.

I will make enchilada sauce from scratch but

my baby will not care; all she will want and need from me is guidance. She will need my sure and steady voice. During storms and during calm, she will long for my sure and steady voice, she will say, "That is my father, that is his sure and steady voice." And I will calm her.

I walk the house and I think about Mr. Owens spending the night in the cave last night. I wonder how or if his parents slept knowing their son was lost in the wilderness with his friend's dog. I can't imagine sleeping in such a situation. Sometimes I can't imagine sleeping ever if I do not know exactly where my baby daughter is sleeping.

I think of my father out in California, in his house, his cave, the place where he rests each night, oxygen mask tied to his face, knowing that if somehow he loses that oxygen overnight his life will end. For my father a power outage really could be a matter of life and death. I think of my mother sleeping upstairs in my home. I haven't slept under the same roof with my mother in at least twenty years. I like having her here. I wish my father were here, too. I know that he is alone in bed in Fairfield struggling to breathe. I hope that tonight he thinks of me, his son, holding his newest granddaughter to my chest.

I join Christa in bed. The baby makes some of

her snorting noises and then settles back to sleep. The spotlight in the back of the house is on and I can see snow falling and I can hear the calm nothingness of the night, the quiet eternity of an evening with my family.

The baby warms my chest, and we sweat on each other. I feel JoJo's life against my chest, an inferno. I hear next to me my wife snoring. I hear the snowfall. I hear the baby breathing and I feel the baby's life burning against my chest and I am on fire and I am in love with my wife and my daughter. I am a husband and I am a father. This is my life now and this is how I live.

Postscript

My father's death clock had been ticking for over a decade, but since Josephine's birth the thrum and thunder of the clock had increased so much so that when my father and I spoke on the phone I could barely hear our conversation—I heard only one recurring thought: *He is dying, he is dying; bring your daughter to meet him.*

It was warm in Fairfield when we arrived. It is a town where people wear the warmth with pride the same way old soldiers wear their worthless and tattered ribbons.

My father greeted us standing in his driveway. Usually he wore a white T-shirt and briefs but now he sported a western suit and shirt with a bolo tie we had sent him for Christmas. He wore his black leather zip-up boots I had admired as a teenager because they looked like something Johnny Cash might wear.

I carried Josephine toward him. He also wore

his oxygen tube stuck into his nostrils. She wore a pretty pink dress I had picked out.

He held her close to his chest and said, "Hello, Miss Josephine. I am your grandpa John."

She cooed when he kissed her cheek.

He seemed to strain under the weight of my fifteen-pound daughter. He stared at her. She had his blue eyes and his forehead and his ears. He must have noticed the glimmers of Jeff. I watched my father staring at my daughter and I finally understood the life-shattering loss that he'd suffered when Jeff died. I would never again challenge him on his behavior surrounding Jeff's death.

He said, "Take her back, Tone. I don't want to drop the beauty. I'm weak."

Christa greeted and kissed my father and we all entered his home.

We sat in his living room and he presented to us some things of his mother's that he wanted us to give to Josephine when she got older—her wedding and engagement rings, her watch still in the case, and her cedar keepsake chest.

Christa fed Josephine.

My father asked me to do him a favor by installing a motion-activated spotlight over his driveway.

"Thieves," he said. "They are everywhere. Gotta scare 'em off."

As his sickness worsened my father's paranoia increased. It was as though he waited every evening for an ambush. I did not point out to him that not many thieves would want to make off with his 1970s-era reel-to-reel stereo system unless they were throwback hi-fi aficionados.

It had been years since I had used my father's tools but I knew where to find everything. I needed a ladder and a drill and bits and the fixture itself. The sun shined bright and hot on me while I worked, and sweat stung my eyes.

I'd been at the work for a few minutes when my father appeared at the side of the house. He'd crept up silently enough that I hadn't seen him until he was ten feet away. He was bent at the waist.

"Hey, Dad, need a hand?" I said.

He pointed an index finger skyward, the John Howard Swofford sign that he was catching his breath.

I assumed that he'd appeared in order to micromanage my work on the spotlight. My father would never change. I readied myself for a tense scene like when I'd emptied the septic system on the RV. I thought, *Jesus, Old Man, give it a break.*

He propped himself up against the ladder I was standing on and took a few deep breaths.

He said, "You know, I've been talking about

being buried in Opelika next to my mother for so long. I checked it all out, and it's a done deal if that's what I want."

I said, "I always liked the idea of you being buried next to her."

"The thing is, I ain't Southern, Tone. I left the South when I was seventeen. Ain't nothing but ghosts there. I'm a Californian. I love this state. I want to be buried over there at Dixon at the national cemetery next to all them other dead GIs."

"Whatever you want."

"Will you visit me there?"

"Of course."

He shuffled slowly back into the house and I returned to my work on the fixture.

I thought about my father and Christa and Josephine inside and of the spotlight I was installing and how it might scare off a thief but I hoped that what it would do was help my father to *see*.

I wanted him to see that whatever kind of father he had been to me I would become a very different father to Josephine. I knew that he must want that, too. For many years I had considered combat the only test of a man's greatness, but I'd begun to understand that for me fatherhood would be the real measure.

I wanted my father to look at his only surviving

son and say to himself, *That is a man I admire, that is a father I admire; I wish I had been more like him, everything in this life can be new.*

When we left, he kissed Josephine goodbye and she cooed some more. We made plans to see him the following day.

As we pulled away from his home it was just becoming dusk. The spotlight shined upon my father and he waved.

Acknowledgments

I must first thank my agent Sloan Harris for his unyielding support and generous spirit, on the page and beyond the page. Sloan, thanks for kicking me in the teeth when I needed it and talking me back from a number of ledges.

Thank you, Cary Goldstein, at Twelve. You wielded the book and deduced where I'd been hiding and the corridors I'd yet to search. Your comradeship proved invaluable throughout. Brian McLendon: thank you for your hard work. It is a treat to have one's book in passionate hands. Libby Burton: thanks for your assistance in moving the manuscript along. Mari Okuda and S. B. Kleinman: thank you for tending to the copyediting and pointing out the corrections I'd missed. Catherine Casalino: you nailed the cover.

Kristyn Keene at ICM is a rock star and I thank

her for all she does. And my thanks to Shira Schindel at ICM.

Thanks to C.H. for his friendship and discussing and dissecting my father over burgers and beers in dive bars throughout the city. To my numerous other male friends for the talks we had about those unyielding beasts, our fathers, thank you. You know who you are. I'll never tell your fathers what you said about them.

Dan Clare and Rob Lewis are true heroes for the work they do at Disabled American Veterans. I appreciate their bringing me into the fold and introducing me to dozens of remarkable young injured men and women, veterans of the wars in Iraq and Afghanistan.

The Movermans: you are my family. Father: thank you for all your flaws and your beauty and your tragedy.

I should note that I borrow my book title from the first line of a James Tate poem called "The Private Intrigue of Melancholy."

My wife Christa is a brilliant writer and artist and a loving mother and the most amazing partner a lumpfish like me could possibly hope for. Every day with her is a splendid gift. She read this manuscript more times than is healthy for a spouse and she made me make it better when I was lazy or dumb or wanted only to walk in the woods with her and our beautiful daughter. Thank you, sweetheart, and our dear daughter, Josephine Clementine, joy of our lives.

DAVID FINLEY

Quiet Force for America's Arts

DAVID FINLEY

Quiet Force for America's Arts

DAVID A. DOHENY

National Trust for Historic Preservation

WASHINGTON, D.C.

This book was made possible by a grant from the Estate of Paul Mellon.

Published by the National Trust for Historic Preservation in the United States with the assistance of the National Gallery of Art, Washington, D.C.

Distributed by the University of Virginia Press

Frontispiece: David E. Finley, oil portrait by Gardner Cox, 1956. U.S. Commission of Fine Arts, Washington, D.C.
Page viii: 1785 Massachusetts Avenue, N.W., Washington, D.C., where Andrew Mellon had an elegant apartment and David Finley helped him complete his art collection between 1927 and 1937. Now the headquarters of the National Trust for Historic Preservation and site of the David E. Finley Rotunda
Page 5: East Garden Court of the National Gallery of Art, which David Finley convinced the architect to include in designing what is now called the West Building
Page 362: The Old Patent Office Building, which David Finley saved for the National Portrait Gallery

Library of Congress Cataloging-in-Publication Data
Doheny, David A.
     David Finley : quiet force for America's arts / David A. Doheny.
        p. cm.
     Includes bibliographical references and index.
     ISBN 0-89133-398-3 (hardcover : alk. paper)
     1. Finley, David E. (David Edward). 2. Arts administrators—
United States—Biography. I. Title.
NS768.F56D63 2006
709.2—dc22   2005025582

Editor: Tam Curry Bryfogle
Designer: Andrea Thomas
Copyeditor: Paula Brisco
Proofreader: Laura Iwasaki
Research Associate: Mary L. Pixley
Research Assistant: Jonathan Powell
Typeset in Fournier by Marissa Meyer
Printed on 120 gsm Naturalis Matt
Color separations by iocolor, Seattle
Produced by Marquand Books, Inc., Seattle
   www.marquand.com
Printed and bound by CS Graphics Pte., Ltd., Singapore

Contents

To C. T. D., with love

For J. B. W., with thanks

Foreword

IN 1963 DAVID FINLEY wrote a history of the National Trust for Historic Preservation, where he had just completed twelve years of service as chairman of the board. In that book he characteristically downplayed the significance of his own role in the creation of the Trust—but all of us who are heirs to Finley's legacy of leadership know that his role was anything but modest. We realize that his vision largely defined the need for a nationwide preservation organization in the United States, just as his energy and dedication guided it through its formative years. We know, in short, that today's National Trust—a vigorous organization encompassing a loyal membership of 270,000 people, a staff of 300, a unique collection of 26 historic sites, a nationwide network of regional offices, and an expansive range of programs and services befitting its role as the private-sector leader of the American preservation movement—is built on the foundation laid by David Finley more than a half-century ago.

The leaders of ancient Athens took an oath "to transmit this city not less, but greater and more beautiful than it was transmitted to us." It is abundantly clear that David Finley had a strong commitment to that goal, and he expressed it through the many institutions—including the National Gallery of Art, the National Portrait Gallery, and the White House Historical Association as well as the National Trust—that he founded or shaped.

I am enormously proud of the National Trust's work in helping Americans understand the importance of preserving the richly diverse heritage that unites and defines us as a nation. Much of our success is due to the fact that we stand on the shoulders of giants, and this perceptive biography offers new reasons to honor David Finley as one of the noblest of those giants.

Richard Moe
President
National Trust for Historic Preservation

Prologue
David Edward Finley, Statesman of the Arts

FOR MORE THAN TEN YEARS during the mid-1980s to the mid-1990s, I walked several times each workday through the handsome oval foyer of the National Trust Building at 1785 Massachusetts Avenue in Washington, D.C. Above a short flight of stairs leading to the first-floor reception area is embossed the inscription:

THE DAVID E. FINLEY ROTUNDA

For the first half of my tenure as general counsel to the National Trust for Historic Preservation, I knew that David Finley had been the first chairman of the board of the Trust but nothing else about him. He had died in 1977, eight years before I joined the National Trust, and there were very few people still around who had known him. A somewhat stiff and tight-lipped portrait of him in the boardroom did not encourage greater familiarity. So for several years David Finley was just a name to me.

Then in 1991 the National Gallery of Art mounted an exhibition marking its fiftieth anniversary, with photographs, documents, and information explaining how and why the museum had been born in the 1930s. And there, sitting at the elbow of its founder Andrew W. Mellon in a photograph from around 1930, was his earnest young assistant, David E. Finley (see fig. 29). There I learned that Finley had been Andrew Mellon's right-hand man at the Treasury Department and had continued to work for him to help complete his art collection and lay the plans for the great National Gallery of Art that was Mellon's gift to the nation. After his mentor's death in 1937, Finley had gone on to become the first director of the National Gallery, serving from 1938 to 1956, and had put it on the road to greatness.

During Andrew Mellon's years in Washington as secretary of the treasury, he had lived on the top floor of what was then known as the McCormick Building, 1785 Massachusetts Avenue, the same building that since 1979 has been the headquarters of the National Trust. It was there that Mellon, with the tireless assistance of David Finley, had assembled most of his famed art collection, which still forms the nucleus of the National Gallery's collections. This was not just an interesting coincidence but in fact the link between those two great national institutions, the National Gallery and the National Trust, that owe so much to David Finley.

I soon learned that in addition to the National Gallery of Art and the National Trust, Finley had had a hand in many other public causes in Washington. But when I looked for more on his life, I found that very little had been written about him, other than a fine chapter in Philip Kopper's 1991 book about the National Gallery.* Fortunately, there were still a few people around Washington who had known and worked with him. As I met and talked with them, the idea of writing a brief biography of David Finley began to take shape. Here was a man who had made remarkable contributions to the cultural life of his nation over the course of some fifty years, and he had almost entirely vanished from the public view less than twenty years after his death.

When the National Trust moved into its restored beaux-arts building in 1979, two years after David Finley's death, and named its foyer

---

* Philip Kopper, *America's National Gallery of Art: A Gift to the Nation* (New York, 1991).

for him, his place in the cultural life of Washington was already a memory. And memories are short in this information age. Thus thirty years later many visitors to the National Trust and indeed the National Gallery may now ask, "Who was David E. Finley?" This book attempts to tell the story of this prodigiously talented yet unassuming man—what he did as well as how and why. More broadly, it may serve to illuminate the way for new generations of Americans who care about their country's cultural heritage and seek ways to protect and further it.

David Finley had an extraordinary career as both the first director of the National Gallery and the founding chairman of the board of the National Trust. Simultaneously, he served as chairman of the U.S. Commission of Fine Arts as it considered such important projects as the Kennedy Center for the Performing Arts, the Watergate complex, and an early proposal for a memorial to Franklin D. Roosevelt. He was also the principal force behind the founding of the National Portrait Gallery and at the same time preserved the landmark Old Patent Office Building in which the museum is housed. He was on the building committee for the Washington National Cathedral. And he was a key player in saving the historic character of Lafayette Square from destruction, forming a close collaboration and friendship with Jacqueline Kennedy in the process. She and he together established the White House Historical Association.

Of David Finley's eighty-six years, he spent some sixty-five in Washington. He saw it grow from a quaint Southern town with a lively social scene but little culture into the world's most powerful city with cultural attractions of the first rank, and he was a prime mover in developing the latter. He knew every president from William Howard Taft to Richard M. Nixon and worked closely with five of them: Herbert Hoover, Franklin D. Roosevelt, Harry S. Truman, Dwight D. Eisenhower, and John F. Kennedy. A fervent Wilsonian Democrat in his youth, he rose to prominence under a rock-ribbed Republican, Andrew Mellon, and ultimately mastered the art of mustering bipartisan support for his many missions.

Finley's father was a U.S. congressman from South Carolina who served in Washington from the time the son was eight years old until he was twenty-six. The young Finley worked in two of the three branches of government—as a clerk with two congressional committees (1910–1915) and in the Departments of War (1918–1919) and the Treasury (1921–1932)—with brief interludes as a lawyer in private practice in Philadelphia (1915–1918) and Washington, D.C. (1920–1921 and 1933–1937).

Finley moved with sure-footed grace through Washington society both before and after the First World War. In 1922 he met Margaret Morton Eustis, whom he married in 1931 and whose family was second to none in Washington's social hierarchy. They had beautiful homes in Georgetown and next to her family's country estate of Oatlands in Loudoun County, Virginia. Their close friends included such prominent and influential personages as Justice Felix Frankfurter, columnist Joseph Alsop, Ambassador David Bruce, and Lord Kenneth Clark.

Small in stature, modest in manner, but with superb social graces, legendary charm, and a dry wit, David Finley had a core of iron. He also had the rare gift of being comfortable with presidents, congressmen, wealthy art collectors, and eminent art scholars as well as with ordinary working people. He was the consummate insider, not only in Washington but in New York and Europe, and he traveled in the highest intellectual and social circles. David Finley set very high standards. He was satisfied with nothing but the best, for himself and for the benefit of all Americans, and he left an indelible mark on the rich cultural and historical life of this great nation.

D. A. D.

1. Congressman David E. Finley Sr., c. 1914

2. Elizabeth Lewis "Bessie" Gist Finley, c. 1911

I

Son of the Old South

1890—1915

THE YORK COUNTY HISTORICAL CENTER, South Carolina, has as its motto: "Where the Past Is Always Present." Or as William Faulkner, the great writer of the South, wrote, "The past is never dead. It's not even past."[1] David Edward Finley Jr. was born into that South on 13 September 1890 in the small up-country town of York, South Carolina, thirty miles southwest of Charlotte, North Carolina. He was the eldest of eight children born to David Edward Finley Sr. and Elizabeth "Bessie" Lewis Gist. On both parents' sides his Southern roots ran deep, not just to the Civil War but back to the American Revolution and colonial times (see pp. 8–9). His mother came from an illustrious line that, like many others in South Carolina, had experienced severe losses in the Civil War.[2] His father, of humbler origins but high ambitions, was a young lawyer about to embark on a long and distinguished political career. Family ties had lasting reverberations in the Old South. As Finley noted in his journal at the age of twenty-four, "To most of us, South Carolina is a personality rather than a geographical expression, and we feel about her in a way people from the North and West could never understand."[3]

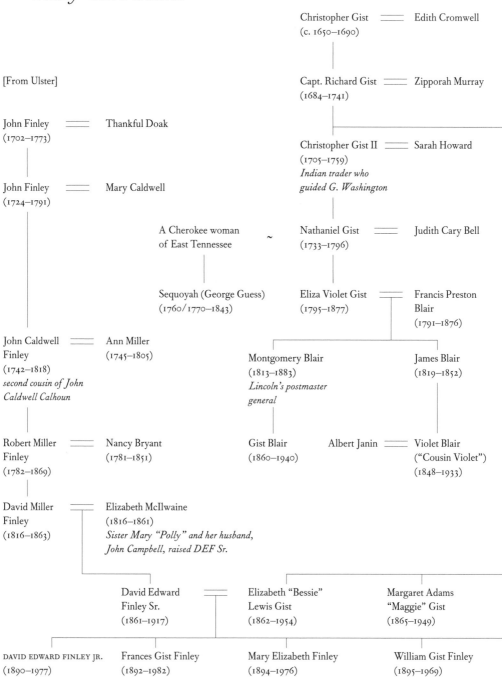

Finley-Gist Families

[From England]

Christopher Gist ═══ Edith Cromwell
(c. 1650–1690)

[From Ulster]

Capt. Richard Gist ═══ Zipporah Murray
(1684–1741)

John Finley ═══ Thankful Doak
(1702–1773)

Christopher Gist II ═══ Sarah Howard
(1705–1759)
*Indian trader who
guided G. Washington*

John Finley ═══ Mary Caldwell
(1724–1791)

A Cherokee woman   ~   Nathaniel Gist ═══ Judith Cary Bell
of East Tennessee   (1733–1796)

Sequoyah (George Guess)   Eliza Violet Gist ═══ Francis Preston
(1760/1770–1843)   (1795–1877)   Blair
                                                           (1791–1876)

John Caldwell ═══ Ann Miller   Montgomery Blair   James Blair
Finley   (1745–1805)   (1813–1883)   (1819–1852)
(1742–1818)   *Lincoln's postmaster
second cousin of John   general
Caldwell Calhoun*

Robert Miller ═══ Nancy Bryant   Gist Blair   Albert Janin ═══ Violet Blair
Finley   (1781–1851)   (1860–1940)   ("Cousin Violet")
(1782–1869)   (1848–1933)

David Miller ═══ Elizabeth McIlwaine
Finley   (1816–1861)
(1816–1863)   *Sister Mary "Polly" and her husband,
                 John Campbell, raised DEF Sr.*

                 David Edward ═══ Elizabeth "Bessie"   Margaret Adams
                 Finley Sr.   Lewis Gist   "Maggie" Gist
                 (1861–1917)   (1862–1954)   (1865–1949)

DAVID EDWARD FINLEY JR.   Frances Gist Finley   Mary Elizabeth Finley   William Gist Finley
(1890–1977)   (1892–1982)   (1894–1976)   (1895–1969)

m. Margaret Morton   m. Joseph Dexter Brown   m. Walter Bedford Moore Jr. m. Gilbert Cary Jeter
Eustis

Principal Sources

Finley Papers, National Gallery of Art, Gallery Archives;
and Wilson Gee, *The Gist Family of South Carolina and
Its Maryland Antecedants* (Charlottesville, VA, 1934)

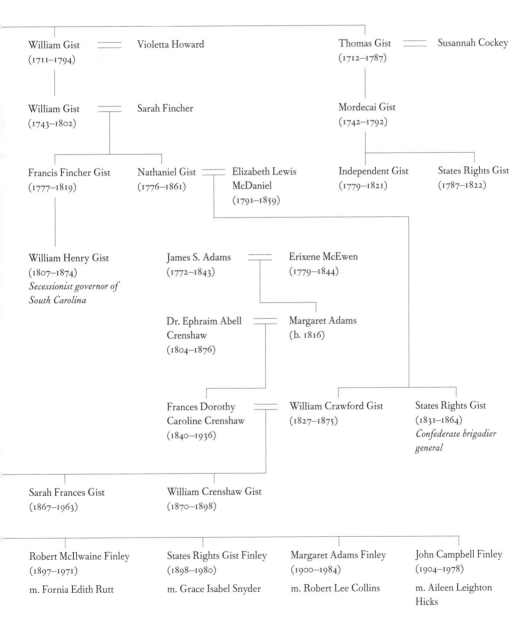

William Gist
(1711–1794) ═══ Violetta Howard

Thomas Gist
(1712–1787) ═══ Susannah Cockey

William Gist
(1743–1802) ═══ Sarah Fincher

Mordecai Gist
(1742–1792)

Francis Fincher Gist
(1777–1819)

Nathaniel Gist
(1776–1861) ═══ Elizabeth Lewis
McDaniel
(1791–1859)

Independent Gist
(1779–1821)

States Rights Gist
(1787–1822)

William Henry Gist
(1807–1874)
*Secessionist governor of
South Carolina*

James S. Adams
(1772–1843) ═══ Erixene McEwen
(1779–1844)

Dr. Ephraim Abell
Crenshaw
(1804–1876) ═══ Margaret Adams
(b. 1816)

Frances Dorothy
Caroline Crenshaw
(1840–1936) ═══ William Crawford Gist
(1827–1875)

States Rights Gist
(1831–1864)
*Confederate brigadier
general*

Sarah Frances Gist
(1867–1963)

William Crenshaw Gist
(1870–1898)

Robert McIlwaine Finley
(1897–1971)

m. Fornia Edith Rutt

States Rights Gist Finley
(1898–1980)

m. Grace Isabel Snyder

Margaret Adams Finley
(1900–1984)

m. Robert Lee Collins

John Campbell Finley
(1904–1978)

m. Aileen Leighton
Hicks

The Finley Family

Finley (or Finlay) is a common surname in Scotland, and David Finley's ancestors went to Ulster as part of the Protestant plantations in the seventeenth century. A chart written in David Finley's hand traces his lineage back to Scotland, where a John Finley "was rented a twelfth part of the abbey lands of Cupar Angers Cistercian Abbey at Pentecost in 1457."[4] After the first wave of English immigration to America had settled the Atlantic seaboard in the 1600s, hardy Scots-Irish moved to the inland frontier in the 1700s.[5] The Finleys came to colonial America from Ulster in about 1720 and settled first on the Pennsylvania frontier in western Chester County (now Lancaster County), then in Augusta County in the Shenandoah Valley of Virginia. In the eighteenth century a John Finley worked as an Indian trader, helped found the Tinkling Springs Presbyterian Church in Fisherville, and served in the French and Indian War. He married Mary Caldwell, of the Scots-Irish family that also produced John Caldwell Calhoun, the vigorous American defender of states' rights and slavery. Their son John Caldwell Finley, who was David Finley's great-great-grandfather, moved to the up-country Carolinas before the Revolution and settled land along the headwaters of Catawba Creek in what is now Gaston County, North Carolina. He fought on the Patriot side in the Battle of Kings Mountain in October 1780, an action that led to the British retreat and the final showdown at Yorktown.

Despite their ancient lineage and kinship to John C. Calhoun, the Finleys remained small farmers with few if any slaves.[6] They belonged to Bethel Presbyterian Church near Clover, South Carolina—in northwest York County, four miles from the North Carolina border. This was one of the historic backcountry churches that furnished many of the Patriots of the Revolution and filled the ranks of both sides in the Civil War. David Finley's great-grandfather, Robert Miller Finley, had lived his entire life on the family farm in Gaston County, North Carolina. His son, David Miller Finley, married Elizabeth McIlwaine at Bethel Church in 1841 and later emigrated from that area to Trenton, Arkansas, where their youngest child, David Edward Finley, was born in 1861.

Tragedy struck early in the Civil War years in the form of an epidemic, wiping out the entire family except for David Edward and leaving him an orphan at age two. Word somehow reached his aunt Mary "Polly" McIlwaine and her husband, John Campbell, back in York County, and they dispatched a black servant to Arkansas to bring their young nephew by horseback to the Campbell farm near Rock Hill, where they raised him. Life was not easy in postbellum South Carolina, but David Edward Finley received many kindnesses from his foster parents, for whom he later expressed warm affection (he named several of his children after the McIlwaine and Campbell families). A bright and hardworking lad, he managed to get an education at the local public schools in addition to handling his farm chores, then went to South Carolina College in Columbia, graduating with a law degree in 1885. Looking back in 1914 (fig. 1), he recounted: "I lost my parents during the War when I was an infant. My brothers and sisters are all dead. I have no nieces and nephews, and, as a matter of fact, do not remember my parents. The War swept away what little property I would have received from my father and my mother. I never had a dollar until I was able to work and make it. I am a graduate of no literary college, but I did graduate from a law school and have taken an extensive course in the school of poverty, adversity and experience."[7] After earning his degree, he returned to York County to hang out his shingle near the courthouse in York and established an active law practice.

The Gist Family

David Finley's maternal ancestors, the Gists (pronounced with a hard G, as in "gift"), who came from England, had settled in Baltimore County, Maryland, by 1682 and soon rose to prominence.[8] Captain Richard Gist had a large family, which produced several notable descendants. His eldest son, the well-known frontiersman and Indian trader Christopher Gist, guided the twenty-one-year-old Major George Washington on his trek to the Ohio country on the eve of the French and Indian War in the winter of 1753–1754.[9] Christopher's son Nathaniel, also an Indian trader, fathered a son by a Cherokee woman. That son, George Gist, or Guess, but better known by his Cherokee name, Sequoyah, invented an alphabet for his people in a futile effort to help them resist the advance of white settlers. Nathaniel also had a daughter Eliza, who married Francis Preston Blair, an influential journalist and politician in Washington, D.C.

In 1838 the Blairs bought a fine Federal-style house on Pennsylvania Avenue across from the White House, just west of Lafayette Square. Still known as Blair House, it was acquired by the federal government in 1942 as a guesthouse for visiting dignitaries.[10]

Another grandson of Richard Gist, William Gist (or Guist), was the great-grandfather of David Finley's mother, Bessie Gist (fig. 2), and ancestor of most of the Gists from South Carolina who achieved renown before and during the Civil War.[11] William Gist moved to the area before the Revolution and acquired large landholdings in what became Union County, just west of York County. A Loyalist during the Revolution, he was imprisoned in Charleston but released. Joining the Loyalist forces, he saw hot action against the Patriots around Ninety Six, South Carolina, and at the Battle of Kings Mountain. At the close of the war he fled to England, forfeiting a thousand acres of land, while his wife, Sarah Fincher, and their five children moved in with her parents. His wife regained half of his confiscated acreage in 1785 and established a business selling goods that he shipped from England. In 1789 Gist returned to Charleston, where his family joined him, and he ultimately recouped much of his fortune.

Bessie Gist's grandfather, Colonel Nathaniel Gist, who ranked among the wealthiest men in the state of South Carolina, was a large landholder who owned more than a hundred slaves and grew cotton at his plantation, Wyoming, in Union County. His son States Rights Gist was a lawyer who rose to leadership of the South Carolina Militia in 1860.[12] It was States Rights Gist, fittingly enough, whom Governor William Henry Gist, his first cousin, entrusted with the mission of personally delivering letters to the governors of the Southern states in November of 1860, asking for their support as South Carolina considered seceding from the Union; Governor Gist signed the Ordinance of Secession adopted on 20 December 1860. States Rights Gist served throughout the war he had helped set in motion and at the age of thirty-three was among six Confederate generals killed at the Battle of Franklin in Tennessee, on 30 November 1864 (fig. 3).[13] One of David Finley's brothers carried the name of this collateral ancestor into a future generation.

Bessie Gist's father, William Crawford Gist, graduated from South Carolina College in 1847, but being "lame from birth," he stayed at home during the war. He took over the family plantation when his father died in 1861 and in that same year married Frances Dorothy Caroline Crenshaw, a belle from York and the daughter of a local physician, Dr. Ephraim A. Crenshaw, and his wife, Margaret Adams. The war and its aftermath took a heavy toll on the Gist family, particularly when Sherman's army cut a swath marching north through South Carolina in the winter of 1865.[14] Bessie's father died in 1875, while still in his forties, and Bessie's mother moved with their four young children back to her family home in York, where she lived until her death in 1936 at the age of ninety-five.[15] Bessie attended local schools and finished her education at the Female Institute in Gordonsville, Virginia. Hers was a strict Presbyterian upbringing, her maternal grandmother having been raised in the Bethel Church near present-day Clover in York County. Bessie was engaged to another man when the up-and-coming lawyer David Edward Finley wooed her and won her hand. They were married on 9 October 1889 at the Associate Reformed Presbyterian Church in York.

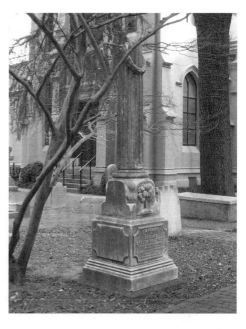

3. Grave monument of Brigadier General States Rights Gist, C.S.A., Trinity Episcopal Church, Columbia, South Carolina

The Finley-Gist Family

Now allied with the Gist family, among the most distinguished in the district, David Edward Finley built a prospering law practice, and he and Bessie began a family of their own, starting in 1890 with David Edward Jr., called "Edward" by members of the family (fig. 4). But the senior Finley had higher ambitions than the local courthouse, and he soon went into politics. Elected to the South Carolina legislature in 1892 and the state senate in 1894, he ran for the U.S. Congress in 1896 and lost. Two years later he ran again, this time winning a seat as a representative of the Fifth Congressional District of South Carolina. He won reelection biennially and was about to start his tenth consecutive term as a congressman at the time of his death.

Congressman Finley was a conservative Southern Democrat whose political views can perhaps be gauged by the name of his fourth son, christened States Rights Gist Finley after his wife's uncle but always known to the family as "States." The fact that States Rights was born in August 1898 during his father's winning run for Congress may not be wholly coincidental. York County was one of the most conservative counties in one of the most conservative states after the Civil War. It had a high proportion of blacks among its population and was a hotbed of the Ku Klux Klan during and after Reconstruction.[16]

4. David "Edward" Finley Jr. at age four, c. 1894, Columbia, South Carolina

Congressman Finley set out to provide a system of free rural mail delivery throughout the country, perhaps reflecting his experience as a boy on a farm in York County, where he had to walk several miles to the nearest post office to pick up the family's mail. He was able to achieve this legislative goal as he gained seniority on the House Committee on Post Offices and Roads, which he eventually led as either chairman or ranking minority member. In 1913 he sponsored a bill to authorize the transportation of mail by "aeroplanes," as was already being done in France.[17] He also served as chairman of the Committee

5. David E. Finley birthplace, York, South Carolina

on Printing. Known for his political courage and independence, he took a public stand on the contentious issue of Panama Canal tolls for coastwise shipping, speaking against the position urged by President Woodrow Wilson and many voters in his state.[18]

In the meantime his family was growing. Following David Edward came Frances Gist; Mary Elizabeth, called "Elizabeth"; William Gist, known as "Gist"; Robert McIlwaine, called "Bob"; States Rights Gist, or "States"; Margaret Adams; and John Campbell. David Edward had been born in a neat one-story house at 200 North Congress Street in York, a tree-lined avenue just north of the business district (fig. 5),[19] and the family lived in two other rented houses before buying a substantial redbrick dwelling on North Congress Street in about 1905, with a white portico and two-story columns that bespoke the gracious lifestyle of the antebellum South. Mrs. Finley and the older children paid occasional visits to Washington, where the congressman maintained a suite in a residential hotel and later leased an apartment at the Rochambeau and then a private residence. But she and the family continued to live near her mother and two sisters in York.

At the Finley home the Sabbath was taken very seriously. The Gists were uncompromising Presbyterians, and on Bessie's maternal grandmother Margaret Adams's side they were proud to count no fewer than thirty Presbyterian ministers.[20] As young David Finley recalled:

I always thought Sunday in York quiet enough. Having been raised myself in the era just preceding the advent of automobiles, the utmost laxity allowed us was a walk in the country or to spend the afternoon at Grandmother's [Dorothy Crenshaw Gist]. For reading we were allowed books from the Sunday School library, of a rather inane sort mostly, but because of their Sunday School origin supposed to contain the necessary amount of diluted virtue. We never saw the Sunday papers until Monday, whereas the funny papers and the sporting sheet now form an important part of John Campbell's day.[21]

David Edward Finley Sr. died in January 1917 at age fifty-six in a North Carolina sanitorium after a lengthy illness. The stress of politics doubtless had taken its toll, and he had battled an alcohol problem for some time. He was eulogized on the House floor by his colleague Representative James Byrnes of Charleston and other members as well as on the floor of the Senate.[23] In the mid-1920s David Edward Finley Jr. somehow arranged for the placement of a bronze bust of his father in the rotunda of the State Capitol in Columbia, South Carolina. On the other side of the door an identical niche contains a bust of Robert E. Lee. The congressman would be proud of the company he keeps.[24]

Youth and Education

Not much is known of David Finley's boyhood, but there is some suggestion that it was not altogether happy. In an enigmatic journal entry in 1920 he wrote: "Childhood is frequently quite tragic. I think I know my own was & I suffered torture from shyness & morbid terrors of death, etc."[25] Despite these insecurities, he was a precocious youth, and Bessie's sister Margaret (fig. 6) had a profound influence on him. A teacher at the local high school and well versed in literature and the fine arts, she also had a passion for history—local, state, and national. She was a prime mover in achieving recognition for the Revolutionary War battlefield of Kings Mountain as a National Historic Site in 1909 and worked with a New York sculptor and the governor of South Carolina to erect a monument to John C. Calhoun in the state capitol in 1907. An ardent Presbyterian, she authored an impressive volume on the history of women in the Presbyterian Church of South Carolina. She did extensive primary research on the Gist family history and was active in local chapters of the Daughters of the American Revolution and the United Daughters of the Confederacy. Young Finley learned a great deal from his aunt.

After attending the public schools in York and spending a year at the University School in Washington, D.C.,[26] Finley entered the University of South Carolina at Columbia in 1906 at the age of sixteen. "Carolina" was just emerging from the trauma of the Civil War and Reconstruction. It had been chartered in 1801 as South Carolina

6. Margaret Adams Gist, Finley's aunt and early mentor, portrait painted c. 1940

College and had closed from 1862 to 1865, when virtually the entire student body had gone off to the war. During the next twenty-five years the institution became embroiled in the social and political upheaval of postbellum South Carolina. Reconstruction brought a large number of black students, and when this period ended in 1877, Governor Wade Hampton closed the university for three years before reopening it as an all-white agricultural college. In 1887, rechartered as the University of South Carolina, it assiduously pursued academic respectability, although blacks were not admitted again until 1963.[27]

According to family tradition, young Finley had received a scholarship to Yale, which he wanted to accept; but his father, whose last election had been close, argued, "Edward, if you go to Yale, it will cost me the election." So Finley enrolled at South Carolina, where he studied history, economics, Greek, and Latin. He was the editor in chief of *Gamecock*, the college magazine. He joined the Sigma Alpha

7. David E. Finley, University of South Carolina, c. 1910

Epsilon fraternity, and he served as president of the York County Club. Described in the yearbook as "Flippant, Flitty, Flirty Finley," he was elected vice president of the Lady Bird Club, a group claiming "to allow the ladies a little pleasure"; he fell short of winning the presidency of the club by one vote, although some of the girls thought he should have had the higher office. He was also elected by his classmates in his senior year as "Most Cultured Man." Finley graduated from the University of South Carolina in June 1910 at the age of nineteen with a bachelor of arts degree (fig. 7). He apparently attained high academic standing, as his biographies in *Who's Who in America* list his membership in Phi Beta Kappa.[28] South Carolina was not Yale, but Finley got a solid education and distinguished himself among his peers. And a dozen years later it was said to be one of his Carolina friends who led him to the Treasury Department and thus to his close association with Andrew W. Mellon.

Finley returned to Washington in 1910 and, as his father wished, entered George Washington University Law School. From 1911 until 1913 he worked from 11:00 a.m. until 6:00 p.m. as a clerk for the congressional Committee on Printing, one of his father's official assignments.[29] Considerable light is shed on this period by the journal Finley kept during most of 1913. It touches briefly on his job with the committee, which was an important one, because he assumed much responsibility during his father's frequent absences due to the illness that was to take his life four years later. Finley showed an early grasp of the realities of political power and the ways of Washington. He also managed to pass all of his law school classes, but his journal did not dwell on his studies, other than to reveal that he had mastered the art of cramming for his exams at the last minute, in time-honored student tradition.

What is remarkable from these jottings is the very busy social life Finley led at the same time, both in South Carolina and in Washington, and the interest he maintained in a wide range of current and political events. According to his journal, he ushered in 1913 by escorting his sisters Frances and Elizabeth to a New Year's Eve dance in Rock Hill, near York, then caught a train to Charleston to attend the traditional St. Cecilia's Ball at Hibernian Hall on New Year's Night. Finley was small and slight in build, with fine features and courtly manners.[30] He was an avid dancer and enjoyed the supper dance with "Miss May Heyward." He noted the dignity and decorum of the St. Cecilia's Ball, which he compared favorably to dances in Washington, where "they howl down the Blue Danube for a turkey trot piece." The following day he paid several calls to homes on the Charleston Battery, including a visit with "Miss May at Gen. & Mrs. Heyward's," then had lunch with his brother Gist, a student at the Citadel in Charleston at the time; the two brothers paid their respects at the grave of their great-great-grandfather William Gist in St. Michael's churchyard.

Returning to Washington, he was immersed in congressional business as well as a constant round of social calls. Hostesses had regular calling days, and he went to many dinners and dances, large and small, either at clubs or in private homes. On one Sunday he paid no fewer than twelve calls. When his sister Frances arrived for a visit in January 1913 and they opened up the family apartment at the Rochambeau, the two went to call on their cousin Violet Blair Janin and her friend, Countess Pioli-Caselli. A distant cousin on their mother's side, Violet Blair was born in 1848, the niece of Montgomery Blair, Lincoln's postmaster general: "She was a very beautiful and attractive woman. She had every advantage wealth and high social position could bestow. Splendidly educated and very cultured, reading and speaking several languages, she was greatly admired and much sought after, especially in the diplomatic circles of Washington."[31] By the time David Finley met her, just before the First World War, she was in her late sixties, lived on

Lafayette Square, and was still very active socially. Of her many friends in the diplomatic corps, she was especially close to the Italians, and Finley received his introduction to polite society in Washington largely through her.

In Washington young Finley sometimes attended St. John's Episcopal Church on Lafayette Square with Cousin Violet, and he enjoyed it more than the small Presbyterian Church on Twenty-second Street that he sometimes attended with his mother. In early February 1913 he wrote, "I started church going again this morning for the first time since Christmas. It had seemed impossible to go all last month, though I suppose it was not. Nevertheless I enjoyed getting back. That is one of the habits, so strongly ingrained in my early youth, that even Washington has not made me feel any more comfortable when I do not go."[22]

On 10 January 1913 he had a cold but went to a dance for Cousin Violet's good friend Mrs. Grover Cleveland and her daughter Esther, with whom he had a "very nice dance," adding: "Miss Cleveland is quite attractive but labors under the disadvantage of being the daughter of a celebrated mother."[32] A couple of weeks later he was disappointed to have to decline an invitation to a dance at the Chevy Chase Country Club because of his law school exams: "I would have enjoyed that greatly for not being a member of Chevy Chase & having no prospect (the initiation fee is $200). I always enjoy a chance to go out there, particularly on Saturday nights, when lots of parties are out there."[33] That same January Finley's father, mother, and youngest brother, John Campbell (age eight), arrived in Washington and settled into the Rochambeau. His mother regretted leaving Bob, States, and Margaret in York, apparently in the care of her sister Maggie (Margaret Adams Gist), but thought they were "much better off" there. Although Finley clearly respected his father, he felt closer to his mother, remarking when she returned home, "Mother is so awfully unselfish & hard working that when she goes we all feel lost."[34]

Finley was always at ease with people of varied backgrounds and interests. The night before his last midyear exam he went to a large tea at the Washington Club, where he met Mary Custis Lee, the daughter of General Robert E. Lee, who was then in her late seventies. Finley brought her a second cup of punch, despite the admonition of the hostess presiding at the punch bowl that "Miss Lee was enjoying herself entirely too much."[35] At a Phi Delta Phi fraternity meeting at the Press Club around the same time, he met the famous Norwegian explorer Roald Amundsen, who had discovered the South Pole. Shortly after this, when the news reached Washington of the deaths of Captain Robert Scott and his companions on another Antarctic expedition, Finley clipped and saved a lengthy article from the *Evening Star* and recorded his emotions over Scott's fate in his journal.[36]

Finley's interest in current events and his facility with different types of people continued in the political arena as well, and on 15 January 1913 an old Carolina friend, Fitzwilliam "Brother" Woodrow, arrived from Princeton, New Jersey. A nephew of President-elect Woodrow Wilson, he had cast New Jersey's electoral vote for Wilson, and when his photograph appeared in the *Washington Times,* Finley noted that "Washington is much interested in everything pertaining to the Wilsons, for it is the incoming administration that is of importance here."[37] Then in February, when the Taft administration held its last reception at the Army and Navy Club, Finley observed, "people are worried for fear it may be the last of the White House receptions. Wilson's attitude in doing away with the Inaugural Ball has dampened the ardor of a great many people."[38]

On 4 March 1913 David Finley attended Wilson's inauguration with his family, and three weeks later his father took him to the White House, where he met the President in person. Wilson was the first of at least nine incumbents he came to know personally over the next six decades, several of them quite well: "Had a short but very nice talk with Mr. Wilson. He is much better looking than his pictures indicated & has a very agreeable manner. I liked him very much & think he will make a wonderful President."[39] A few days later he took his father home to York to recuperate from an illness. While there, he savored the Southern spring, enjoyed his family, and slept twelve hours a day, exhausted from having maintained such a hectic schedule. Returning to Washington after he had missed a week of classes, he attended Wilson's address to Congress, the first personally delivered by a President since John Adams in 1800, and noted, "I grow more enthusiastic over Wilson every day."[40]

Finley became a fervent admirer of Woodrow Wilson, the first Democratic President he had ever known, following sixteen years of Republican administrations under William McKinley, Theodore Roosevelt, and William Howard Taft. Wilson was a Southerner by birth, upbringing, and education, and he retained, as Finley did throughout his life, the social graces of the Old South, even after many decades in the North. Wilson was a strict Unionist, who "deemed a Decoration Day for the Union dead a means of sustaining national bitterness" and who "ultimately came to view the loss of the war as an actual benefit to the South, ridding it of slavery and keeping it in God's union."[41] It is likely that Wilson had much to do with Finley's feelings of American patriotism starting in 1915.

Finley was also keenly aware of the President's three comely daughters, Margaret, Jessie, and Eleanor, who naturally made quite a splash in Washington society. He met them first with Brother Woodrow when the latter was returning to Princeton after the inauguration, and he commented that they "had extremely nice looking faces & very pleasant manners."[42] He met them again at the White House when he took a relative there to call on Mrs. Wilson, as arranged by his mother. And he found Mrs. Wilson "most pleasant." In April he went to a dance given for the three Wilson daughters and "rescued" Jessie from the unwanted attentions of a Latin American diplomat: "I went up & had a very nice talk with her. We went in very soon and danced—a waltz at her request—& she told me about the supper. Said just as she was starting off to dance with Mercer Vernon, up rushed the Dago, saying he had been commanded to take her out to supper. She demurred, but he insisted that he was the Minister from Guatemala & she must, which she said she did very meekly. She is awfully nice & I like her."[43] On 9 May 1913 he went to a garden party at the White House and chatted with Eleanor Wilson, whom he found "very good fun" and who recognized the Carolina seal on his ring. Later he spoke with Margaret Wilson and "also had a very nice talk with Miss Jessie, who looked beautiful in a gray & lavender dress with a lavender hat."[44]

Another theme touched on in his journals concerns race relations. As an indication of where Finley started, he summed up his early views in 1915, writing: "Slavery was good for the negroes; they were better off then than they are now, from a material & physical standpoint; but it was very bad for the white people. It was a canker that lay at the bottom of all Southern civilization; & while I probably would not have thought so in 1860, I am very glad now that slavery is done with forever."[45] Sometime between 1915 and 1920 Finley recalled a story told by a guest at Cousin Violet's of an uncle who had left Virginia to fight with the Northern Army and afterward returned to visit some old friends, seeking out "Uncle James," the coachman, who had stayed with the family through all the vicissitudes of war. Finley recalled the conversation: "'Tell me, Uncle James,' he said, 'You are a person of sense & judgment. Are the negroes better off now than they were in slavery, when they were at least well taken care of?' The old man looked at him. 'How can you ask that question, Marse Henry? Then we were only *things*. Now we are *men*.'"[46] Thus while the young Finley partly accepted the commonly held justification among many white Southerners of the material benefits of slavery for the blacks, he tempered it with a flat condemnation of the inherent evil of that institution. And in recounting the dignity and feelings of the freed slave, he shows sensitivity and an enlightened perspective—at least for that time and place.

Despite the gay social life of Washington, young Finley often lamented the official side of life there. Reflecting on his father's lingering illness, he noted "as long as his Father is in town, he will continue going to the Capitol, which means being harassed by a lot of people all wanting something. The more I see of politics, the less happiness I see to be found in it. Like the old man, 'the more I see of some men, the more I like my dog.'"[47] But he was sufficiently under the sway of his powerful father that after graduating from law school on 11 June 1913 and being admitted to the bar in the District of Columbia, he remained on Capitol Hill for two more years, working on the staff of the clerk of the House of Representatives, at a salary of $1,680 per year, while taking some additional courses at the law school.[48]

In August 1915, with Congressman Finley back in South Carolina pursuing yet another primary campaign against a challenger named Stevenson, David Finley tended to business on Capitol Hill. On 15 August he wrote his father a four-page letter on the official stationery of the Committee on Printing, enclosing a campaign message he had drafted. The letter explains in detail why he had highlighted certain issues in the political appeal, from the Panama Canal tolls to separate railway coaches for the races. It reflects young Finley's firm grasp of both policy issues and the nuts and bolts of campaigning on the stump. It also shows both his respect for his father's political judgment and his own courage in advising him frankly on matters of strategy and tactics. And it speaks volumes to the father's confidence in his eldest son.[49]

During the long summer recesses he returned to York, which he continued to consider home until the summer of 1915. Just before leaving that home for good, he observed:

> I, myself, am disillusioned of politics. To be governor or congressman or senator is something of an honor and very pleasant; but I don't believe it pays. No one gets out of it all they must put in it; at least they don't get happiness or contentment; and the fruits of long-continued success are usually selfishness & cynicism. At least that is my judgment after five years of Washington. Two things are capable of changing such a result: the possession of sufficient money to take away from a man the fear that by losing his job he is also losing his living; and the ability to let whisky alone. That is what destroys most careers, but it is more generally true in Washington than anywhere else. The late and irregular hours, hard mental strain & worry are all conducive to drinking; and one employee in the House Office Building told me that never a week went by without the taking to a Washington hospital of one and sometimes two congressmen in a state bordering on DTs.[50]

Thus, in September 1915, the young Finley said good-bye to politics, and to South Carolina, for the very different life of a Philadelphia lawyer.

NOTES

1. William Faulkner, *Requiem for a Nun* (New York, 1952), act 1, scene 3. York County was established in 1785, and the village that grew up around the county seat was called Yorkville from 1841 to 1915, when its name was formally changed to York. For the sake of clarity, this book will refer to both town and county as "York," even for events that took place before 1915.

2. That war started in South Carolina and lingered there well into Finley's lifetime. At least one member of Finley's family continued to stand up for the "Cause" for a half century after Appomattox. His "Aunt" Clara McLean, who had been in Charleston during the attack on Fort Moultrie, was unrepentant when she told Finley in 1913 how she had traveled to Washington, D.C., during the Grant administration and had met with Mrs. Grant but tried to avoid meeting President Ulysses S. Grant: "but it was impossible to escape an introduction. Just then, she remembered that Gen. Lee had shaken hands with Grant, so when he put out his hand, she took it. 'I am a rebel, Mr. President,' she told him, and she said he answered smiling, that 'he was just as glad to meet her & he hoped she would soon be reconstructed.' 'Never,' she answered, & her son Stuart says she never has been until Woodrow Wilson became President, and on that day she became an American again." Finley journal, 20 June 1913. Finley Papers, National Gallery of Art, Gallery Archives (hereafter NGA Archives).

3. Finley journal, 30 August 1914.

4. Finley genealogical chart in David Finley's hand. Finley Papers, NGA Archives. There is no citation of the source for this information.

5. See, generally, Rory Fitzgerald, *God's Frontiersmen: The Scots-Irish in Colonial America* (London, 1989). See also our genealogical chart for the Finley and Gist families (pp. 8–9). From at least the late 1920s David Finley and other members of his family took considerable interest in their ancestry and went to some pains to trace the family roots to colonial America, and thence back to Ulster and to Scotland.

6. Robert Miller Finley (1782–1869), great-grandfather of David Edward Finley Jr., appears in the census returns for Lincoln County, North Carolina, in 1820 and 1840, when the number of slaves in a household was recorded (the southern part of Lincoln County became Gaston County in 1845). In 1820 there were none. In 1840 there was either none or one (the original handwritten return is unclear). A John Finley in 1800 and a Robert Finley in 1790 were recorded as owning no slaves.

7. Letter to Allen H. McQueen, Cheraw, South Carolina, 28 September 1914. David Edward Finley [Sr.] Papers, South Caroliniana Library, Columbia, fol. 10. A biographical sketch on Congressman Finley's letterhead in 1910 adds: "He was brought up accustomed to perform all the duties and labors incident to farm life, and labored on the farm from the time he was 10 years of age until he was 20. He received a limited education in the schools at or near Rock Hill and Ebenezer, in York County, by attending schools two or three months during the year, when not engaged in farm work. After the death of his aunt and foster mother Mary [McIlwaine] Campbell, in 1883, he entered the South Carolina College Law School in 1884 and graduated with the degree of LL.B. in 1886.

He then located in York, South Carolina, and commenced the practice of law and has had an extensive and successful practice."

8. This section owes much to the research of David Finley's aunt, Margaret Adams Gist. A dedicated genealogist, she traced the lineage of the Gist family in England, Maryland, and South Carolina from original wills and other documents. The Margaret Adams Gist Papers at the South Caroliniana Library at the University of South Carolina at Columbia contain hundreds of pages of notes in her hand, with genealogies, copies of wills, correspondence, and other materials pertaining to the Gist and allied families, which Margaret Gist had compiled over a period of several decades. Young Finley must have absorbed at an early age the stirring history of his ancestors.

A Christopher Gist settled near Baltimore by 1682. One of David Finley's genealogical charts identifies this Christopher Gist's mother as "Anne Washington, daughter of Sir Lawrence Washington, d. June 4, 1642, buried at church at Garsden Manor, England." No source is cited. George Washington was also descended from a Lawrence Washington in England, but Finley apparently never claimed kinship.

9. Douglas Southall Freeman, *George Washington* (1948), abridgment by Richard Harwell (New York, 1995), 36–47. Christopher Gist saved the young Washington's life at least once. He later served with Washington at Fort Necessity in 1754 and in General William Braddock's ill-fated expedition to the Monongahela in 1755.

10. David Finley came to know one Blair cousin, Violet Blair Janin, well during his early years in Washington. She was a first cousin of Gist Blair, the last member of the family to live at Blair House, remaining there until his death in 1940. Gist Blair was a grandson of Francis Preston Blair and Eliza Violet Blair and the youngest son of Montgomery Blair, an ardent antislavery advocate, appointed by Lincoln to his War Cabinet as postmaster general. James M. McPherson, *Battle Cry of Freedom* (New York, 1988), 268, 505, and 557, describes several courageous stands taken by Montgomery Blair: after Lincoln's inauguration in 1861, as the crisis over Fort Sumter loomed, only Blair counseled the President to resupply the fort in Charleston harbor. He also advised Lincoln not to issue the Emancipation Proclamation on the grounds that it would alienate the Border States.

11. Bessie's great-grandfather, William Gist, was the son of one of Captain Gist's middle sons, William. The younger William Gist had several sons, including Nathaniel Gist, who was Bessie's grandfather, and Francis Fincher Gist, whose son William Henry Gist was the governor of South Carolina when it seceded from the Union. It was William Henry Gist who signed the Ordinance of Secession adopted on 20 December 1860, setting the stage for the Civil War. See the Finley-Gist genealogical chart, pp. 8–9.

Another grandson of Richard Gist—through a younger son, Thomas—Mordecai Gist served with distinction during the American Revolution as an officer in the Maryland Line and rose to the rank of brigadier general in the Continental forces. He fought throughout the war, from Long Island to Yorktown, and afterward settled in South Carolina. Mordecai was the father of two sons, named Independent and States Rights.

12. Brigadier General States Rights Gist (1831–1864) was one of ten Gist men listed in the records of South Carolina College (later the University of South Carolina) as having attended the college before the war. He went on to attend Harvard Law School for a year.

13. Walter Brian Cisco, *States Rights Gist: A South Carolina General of the Civil War* (Shippensburg, PA, 1991).

14. McPherson, *Battle Cry of Freedom*, 827. Not as famous as Sherman's March to the Sea in Georgia in late 1864, his march north through South Carolina was even more destructive and "ten times more difficult" as a military feat, for it required bridging countless rivers, streams, and swamps in the wettest winter in twenty years. On 17–18 February 1865 Columbia was burned, as Atlanta had been. The war had come full circle in South Carolina.

15. Two of her daughters, Margaret Adams Gist, known as "Maggie," and Sarah Frances Gist, called "Daisy," remained unmarried and lived with her at the family home, where they died in 1949 and 1963, respectively.

16. Allen W. Trelease, *White Terror: The Ku Klux Klan Conspiracy and Southern Reconstruction* (Baton Rouge, LA, 1971), 362 et seq.

17. Study to accompany House Report 3933, *Transportation of Mail by Aeroplanes*, 63rd Cong., 2nd sess., 10 December 1913.

18. In doing so, Congressman Finley expressed his "admiration for the man described in the last clause of the fourth verse of the fifteenth Psalm": "He that sweareth to his own hurt, and changeth not." See *Memorial Addresses on the Death of David Edward Finley*, 64th Cong., 2nd sess., 25 February 1917. Library of Congress.

19. The house now bears an historical marker, dedicated by the Yorkville Historical Society, 27 May 2000. The inscription on the front reads: "DAVID E. FINLEY BIRTHPLACE David Edward Finley, Jr. (1890–1977), first director of the National Gallery of Art, was born in this house. Finley moved to Washington, D.C., as a child when his father was elected to Congress and was educated at the University of S.C. and George Washington University Law School. He practiced law, served in World War I, then worked for Secretary of the Treasury Andrew W. Mellon." The text continues on the back: "Finley and Andrew W. Mellon worked for years to establish a national art gallery with Mellon's collection as its nucleus, but Mellon died in 1937 just as the project began. Finley directed the construction of the National Gallery and was its director 1938–1956, building it into 'a treasure trove of art.' He was also chairman of the National Trust for Historic Preservation 1950–1962."

20. In addition, Margaret Adams's family included thirty-three wives of Presbyterian ministers. See Finley journal, 1 August 1915. The Adamses were stalwarts of Bethel Church near Clover, in York County, the same Presbyterian church attended by David Finley's paternal ancestors.

21. Finley journal, 1 August 1915.

22. Finley journal, 2 February 1913.

23. James F. Byrnes was first a congressman, then a senator, a justice of the U.S. Supreme Court, the head of the Office of War Mobilization, a secretary of state under President Truman, and finally governor of South Carolina.

24. Until very recently the Confederate battle flag flew atop the capitol dome, and it now stands beside the Confederate monument in front of the capitol. The inner sanctum of the capitol rotunda is dominated by the heroic statue of John C. Calhoun, facing the busts of David E. Finley Sr. (sculpted by Bryant Baker) and Robert E. Lee.

25. Finley journal, 15 August 1920. Despite his fears of death, he was destined to live into his eighty-seventh year. And he soon overcame his shyness.

26. Application for employment with the Department of Commerce, 13 September 1921. NGA Archives, RG 28, box 27-7.

27. *Life and Times at the South Carolina College: 1805–1905*, exh. cat., McKissick Museum, University of South Carolina (Columbia, SC, 2003).

28. The South Carolina chapter of Phi Beta Kappa was not established until 1926, but as the executive director of that organization explained in a telephone interview in December 2001, Finley could have been elected an honorary member. This is the most likely explanation, for it would have been out of character of Finley to have embellished his résumé.

29. Personal data, David E. Finley, 29 January 1943. NGA Archives, RG 28.

30. On an application for government employment in 1921, Finley gave his weight as 125 pounds and his height as "66 inches." Finley Papers, NGA Archives, RG 28, box 24-7.

31. Wilson Gee, *The Gist Family of South Carolina and Its Maryland Antecedents* (Charlottesville, VA, 1934), 10. Violet Blair married Albert Janin of New Orleans, was active in the Daughters of the American Revolution, and was the head of the Society of Colonial Dames in the District of Columbia from 1914 until her death in 1933. She was well versed in family history and was the source of much of Finley's aunt Margaret Adams Gist's dossier on the Gist family.

32. Finley journal, 10 January 1913.

33. Finley journal, 26 January 1913. Later in life David Finley was an active member of the Chevy Chase Country Club for many years.

34. Finley journal, 8 March 1913.

35. Finley journal, 30 January 1913. Finley noted that Mary Custis Lee had lived for many years in Rome, where everyone knew she was the daughter of a great American general, and where she once received an official invitation addressed to "Miss Grant."

36. Finley journal, 11 February 1913. Inserted in Finley's journal there is a press clipping on Scott's death from the *Evening Star,* 10 February 1913.

37. Finley journal, 15 January 1913.

38. Finley journal, 4 February 1913.

39. Finley journal, 25 March 1913.

40. Finley journal, 8 April 1913.

41. Louis Auchincloss, *Woodrow Wilson* (New York, 2000), 6.

42. Finley journal, 9 March 1913.

43. Finley journal, 25 April 1913.

44. Finley journal, 9 May 1913. Jessie Wilson married Francis B. Sayre in a White House ceremony in November 1913. Their son Francis B. Sayre Jr. became dean of the Washington National Cathedral and a good friend of David Finley's.

45. Finley journal, 2 June 1915.

46. On a loose sheet, inserted into his journal for the year 1915.

47. Finley journal, 20 May 1913.

48. Personal data, David E. Finley. NGA Archives.

49. David Edward Finley Jr. to his father, 15 August 1914. David Edward Finley [Sr.] Papers, South Caroliniana Library, Columbia, RG 8373.

50. Finley journal, 2 September 1915.

8. Lieutenant D. E. Finley, U.S. Army, Aviation Service, 1918

2

The Law as a Bridge

1915–1924

DAVID FINLEY WAS FAR TOO MODEST to write the story of his own life, but in his account of the founding of the National Gallery of Art, he permitted himself a few personal asides. In one he looked back on his early career: "I had read art history and always preferred art to law, which I studied at my father's suggestion, during the years we lived in Washington when he served as a Congressman from South Carolina. I shall only add that I never regretted my legal training, which was to prove of great value to me in later years, and was the bridge which led me to the Treasury."[1]

A Philadelphia Lawyer

In the spring of 1915 Finley was spending time at his parents' home in York, when his friend Bedford Moore heard that a prominent lawyer in Philadelphia, Joseph Hill Brinton, was looking for an ambitious young lawyer to share his busy practice, with a view to eventual partnership. Moore, who had just settled in York, recommended David Finley.[2] As Finley's prospects in South Carolina did not seem promising just then, he went to Philadelphia in June and met with Brinton. Finley liked what he saw, and when he was offered a starting salary of $1,000 per year until he passed the Pennsylvania bar, he accepted the position.[3]

On 15 September 1915 Finley reported for work at Brinton's law office in the Commonwealth Trust Building in downtown Philadelphia. Initially he stayed at the Montgomery Inn in Bryn Mawr, which cost $10 a week for room and board; he had a twenty-three-minute commute by train to the Broad Street Station, which cost 20 cents, round-trip. Later he moved to 1104 Spruce Street in what is now the historic district, where he had a room in a Federal-style townhouse owned by Ellen and May McMurtrie, two unmarried sisters with decidedly radical political views, and he attended the historic Christ Church Episcopal.

Finley enjoyed life in Philadelphia and compared the city favorably with Washington.[4] His journal entries indicate that he considered himself "very fortunate" to be associated with Brinton, whom he liked personally and respected professionally: "He has the highest sort of standing at the Bar and a very considerable practice." Brinton immediately gave him two or three cases, and Finley recorded candidly: "I am relieved to find that I am going to enjoy Law. It is a very practical profession, & here it is remunerative, which is also a consideration. Everything is done in a businesslike manner, and that is most satisfying. I would never have enjoyed the desultory manner in which law is practiced down home. Certainly, there is no danger of my not becoming a *practical* man, so Father's fears should be dispelled on that score."[5]

Yet Finley's early hopes of practicing law with Brinton met with disappointment, and his salary only reached $1,500—less than he had earned as a congressional clerk.[6] He made no further comments in his journals concerning his career in Philadelphia until after the First World War, when he attended Brinton's funeral in January 1920 and reflected:

> Poor man, he got less happiness from life than anyone I know. He had a very brilliant mind, an attractive personality, and a very warm, friendly nature. But he was also very selfish and managed not to have many friends. . . . He brought me to Philadelphia on the expectation of certain definite things & failed absolutely to make good. I understand him well enough not to

let it embitter me & I have managed also to preserve my friendship for him, and in the end he made it impossible, just as he did with everyone else. His life is the greatest tragedy I have come in close contact with. He missed practically everything, in spite of his great gifts. And it was due to the fact that his nature was marked by the smug, hard Quaker respectability of Westchester, and by marrying & continuing to live in Media, a place whose standards he despised but to which he was forced to conform.[7]

Despite his frustration with Brinton, Finley looked back fondly on his years in Philadelphia, and he returned for visits with friends or for social events such as a ball given by Mrs. Wilmer Biddle in February 1923. In his journal he wrote with nostalgia of the "restful and friendly atmosphere of a place, which next to Washington and York seems most like home to me. I wish I could go back there to live. It has the vilest climate in the world, and it is ugly and dirty, but there is a stability in both people and places that is lacking in New York."[8]

The First World War

Finley's stay in Philadelphia ended during the First World War, when he enlisted in the army in February 1918. He had closely followed developments in the war from its beginning in August 1914,[9] quickly taking the Allies' side and deploring the German destruction of Louvain in Belgium and Rheims Cathedral in France. Then as the German threat to Paris settled into the grim stalemate of trench warfare from the Alps to the English Channel, his focus shifted to the ruinous impact of the war on his home state of South Carolina, where the one-crop cotton farmers could no longer send their products to market across the Atlantic. On 8 June 1915 when Finley went to the White House with his father, a U.S. congressman, they met briefly with President Wilson: "Father told Mr. Wilson that we all hoped he would be able to avoid trouble with Germany. The President said he was doing all in his power, but that he had to be firm. He looked quite determined as he said it, and I think it would be well if Germany could understand first rather than last that not only is the President firm in his determination not to be run over by Germany, but that the country is firm behind him."[10]

In late 1916 Woodrow Wilson won a second term as President on the strength of his claim to have kept the country out of the war, and Finley approved of Wilson's skill in maintaining America's neutrality.[11] But Wilson, soon provoked by acts of belligerence toward the United States, went to Congress on 2 April 1917 and asked for a declaration of war against Germany, which was passed four days later.[12] General John J. Pershing, the commander of the American Expeditionary Force, landed in France with a token staff force in early June 1917, and though the first few U.S. casualties came in November 1917, Pershing refused to be rushed into action. But when two million fresh American troops finally joined their allies at the front in May 1918, they turned the tide. Within six months Germany had collapsed and signed the Armistice of 11 November 1918, which ended the war.

It seems surprising, in view of his support for the Allied cause, that Finley did not enter the armed services early in the conflict. Because his journal lapsed from late 1917 until April 1919, the reasons for his delay will never be known, but it probably related to his father's death on 26 January 1917 at the age of fifty-five. As the oldest son and a lawyer, Finley naturally assumed responsibility for his mother and younger siblings, having functioned for years as his father's aide on congressional campaigns and committee assignments. He sold the imposing family home in York, no longer needed to support his father's congressional status, and he arranged for farmlands near Rock Hill and other investments to provide his mother a modest income. He had to juggle these filial duties with a busy law practice in Philadelphia, eight hundred miles to the north.

Once he had settled his father's estate, Finley enlisted as a private in the U.S. Army on 7 February 1918 and received a commission as second lieutenant in the Army Air Service of the Signal Corps on 13 August (see fig. 8), serving out the war in Washington, D.C.[13] He was honorably discharged on 15 February 1919. His three brothers of military age also served during the war: Gist and Bob as army lieutenants, and eighteen-year-old States as a private in the Marine Corps. None saw battlefield action, though Gist was aboard a troopship crossing to France when the Armistice was declared.

Finley's year of military service was not a high point of his life. But it did lead him to one of his early mentors. Early in 1919, following his discharge, Finley joined the staff of Colonel Arthur Woods, a well-connected New Yorker who had made his reputation as a crusading New York City police commissioner before joining the Wilson administration in 1917, then being commissioned in the Army Air Service.[14] After the war Woodrow Wilson appointed Woods as assistant to the secretary of war for reemployment of demobilized soldiers. Because construction of all public works unrelated to the military effort had been suspended during the war, it was Woods's strategy to persuade state and local governments to resume such projects immediately to provide jobs for the returning doughboys.

Woods delegated Finley, as a field representative earning a salary of $3,600 per year, to meet with governors, mayors, and other officials around the country to promote jobs for returning soldiers. Finley first traveled by train to New England, and after concluding his duties at the statehouses or city halls, he would take time to visit local points of interest and meet people in parts of the nation he had not seen before. He visited Boston for the first time in May 1919 and stayed at the Parker House for two weeks. After one meeting at the statehouse on Beacon Hill, he walked across Beacon Street to the Robert Gould Shaw Memorial, the classic bas-relief by Augustus Saint-Gaudens of Colonel Shaw leading his black troops of the 54th Massachusetts Infantry into battle during the Civil War (fig. 9). Finley frankly recorded his impressions in his journal: "The faces of the Negroes are particularly well done. The monument stands on the spot where Gov. Andrews commissioned Col. Shaw to undertake the difficult & doubtful task of leading a Negro regiment against the South. Col. Shaw was later killed in the assault on Ft. Wagner, South Carolina, and his action in leading Negroes against them aroused the bitterest resentment in the South. While I do not approve of what he did, I can understand now the motives which actuated him."[15] Finley's innate taste contended with the racial views of his Southern youth.

While in Boston, Finley sought every opportunity to broaden his cultural horizons, visiting historic sites at Cambridge, Lexington,

9. Augustus Saint Gaudens, Shaw Memorial, 1900, Boston Common, which drew
Finley's attention in 1919

Concord, Marblehead, Salem, and New Bedford, Massachusetts; Newport and Providence, Rhode Island; and Conway, New Hampshire. He
found Daniel Chester French's statue of the minuteman in Lexington
"very fine" and the village of Concord "absolutely unspoiled": "The
square white houses in which Emerson & Thoreau lived are there just
as they were 70 years ago."[16] His impressions of Salem, which he visited "for the express purpose of seeing the old houses," show not only
a reverence for America's past but conflicting emotions over changes
the country was undergoing. He admired the fine historic houses on
Washington Square and Chestnut Street, built during the era of Salem's
shipping prosperity:

> The House of Seven Gables stands at the foot of Turner Street
> & its well-kept garden goes down to the harbor. The house
> itself is in a good state of preservation and is used as a part-
> time community settlement house where activities are badly
> needed in support of the hordes of . . . foreigners . . . [in] the

old houses bordering on the waterfront. . . . It depressed me to see the dilapidation of the old houses. I wanted to take to Salem Mary Antin and some of the other self-satisfied apostles of the new immigration, and show them the slum which the new Americans have made of one of the most beautiful & historic settlements in New England.

Nothing has so impressed upon me the difference between our God-fearing and soap-loving colonist ancestors and these latter-day immigrants who came to America because it offers the easiest chance to get [ahead]. I am glad to have them come. They fought well in the present War, and they add something worthwhile to America's greatness & prosperity.

I no longer want to keep the country a little community of English, Scotch, and Irish, for America, by a blending of all the nations, has made a great democracy, which at least offers to the greatest number of people the greatest opportunities for life, liberty & happiness. But I do not want to see the fundamental civilization which the English, Scotch & Irish have made overrun by people of alien races who seek to impose their will upon our institutions. . . .[17]

These private thoughts of a twenty-eight-year-old, never intended for publication, show Finley's maturing views on the way America was changing. Although he applauded the progress of the new Americans, he feared the erosion of the old values that had made the country great.

Woods sent Finley from New England west to Denver, Salt Lake City, Los Angeles, San Francisco, Portland, and Seattle for more than two months on War Department business. Finley was delighted to have the chance to see the West (and at government expense). Stopping in Chicago en route, he was impressed with Michigan Avenue, Lake Shore Drive, and Lincoln Park but thought the Potter Palmer mansion "a terrible mid-Victorian castle, with turrets." He spent three "very strenuous" days in Denver and met with thirty officials, including the mayor, the superintendent of public instruction, and Governor Oliver Shoup, "a nice old fellow who, as usual with governors, wanted to talk all the time." The superintendent proved very helpful, writing her colleagues in all Colorado school districts and "urging them to push the building of schools to give employment for soldiers now and to make a report to her immediately." Finley noted at the time, "She wanted to write me up, but I prevented any mention even of my name, for we are not supposed to give out interviews. We have to be very diplomatic and not offend by seeming too pushing & interfering. The hardest thing I have to do is get publicity for the work & yet be sufficiently cautious and restrained."[18] Finley learned well the value of keeping a low profile while advancing the public good, and he put this into practice for the rest of his life.

After stopping in Colorado Springs and admiring the view of snow-clad Pikes Peak—too early in the season to visit it—Finley described in his journal the awe he felt on seeing the mountains and gorges from the train through the Rockies en route to Utah. In Salt Lake City he stayed at the Hotel Utah across from the Mormon Temple and went to see Temple Square and the Mormon Tabernacle. He expressed profound admiration for the perseverance and industry of the people but was emphatic in dismissing the dogma of their religion.[19]

From Salt Lake City Finley went on to Los Angeles (population 600,000), where he visited the San Gabriel Mission, built by the Franciscans in 1771, then spent a Sunday on Catalina Island, where he took a tour in a glass-bottomed boat and marveled at the clarity of the water, with visibility to a depth of eighty-five feet. He had almost completed making his rounds in Los Angeles when he received a telegram ordering him to Sacramento to meet with Governor William D. Stephens. He admired the rich farming country around San Jose, planted mostly in fruit trees as well as wheat and barley: "The living on the ranches here is much more pleasant than in our mud-baked farms in the South. If I were a farmer, I would come to California, just as I would go to Washington if I were a Negro. Why risk an uncertain hereafter when one can be certain of a near heaven on earth?"[20]

From Sacramento Finley proceeded to San Francisco, where friends of his cousin Violet Blair Janin welcomed him warmly. Like generations of visitors, before and since, he was captivated by the Bay Area. From there he went on to Portland, Oregon, which he called the "prettiest city on the West Coast," and to the state capital at Salem, where the profusion of roses amazed him. Continuing on to Seattle and then

Olympia, the capital of Washington State, he met with the lieutenant governor, the governor having just died.[21] After stopping to see Tacoma, Mount Rainier, and Spokane, he proceeded to Helena and Butte, Montana, where he looked after government business and toured the Anaconda copper mine. He took a side trip to Yellowstone National Park for a weekend on his own, staying at the Mammoth Hot Springs Hotel and the Grand Canyon Inn, with a visit to Old Faithful. At this point he returned to Salt Lake City and was pleased that the state of Utah had entered many contracts since his meetings there the month before. He next stopped in Cheyenne, Wyoming, where he found the granite state capitol building with its gilded dome "not particularly good architecture, even as State Capitols go,"[22] and had a long talk with Governor Robert Davis Carey.

Returning to Denver, he found that Colorado's state highway commission had developed a promising plan for large road-building projects, intended to put many returning servicemen to work. In Albuquerque, New Mexico (population 20,000), he became fascinated by the history and the Mexican and Indian influences. He made a pilgrimage to Isleta Pueblo but did not risk eating at the only available Indian restaurant, sampling the apricots being sold by colorfully dressed Indian women, or even drinking a glass of water until he got back to Albuquerque at the end of the day. He then doubled back to Los Angeles, with an intermediate detour to the Grand Canyon—"a most heavenly spectacle and I shall never forget it"—and Fresno, where he discovered considerable prejudice against the Armenians, who had settled "the richest and best raisin land in the valley," arousing the resentment of "the 'white people,' as the citizens of Fresno call themselves in contradistinction to the Armenians."[23]

From Los Angeles he took the "motor stage" to Santa Barbara, "the most beautiful spot in Southern California," where he particularly wanted to see the Santa Barbara Mission, founded in 1786. He stopped at Yosemite on the way back to San Francisco, where he visited friends from Washington and Philadelphia. He continued up the coast once again to Portland, Tacoma, and Seattle. Spending a day at Mount Rainier National Park, "the most beautiful of all the places I have seen,"[24] he climbed on the glaciers with a guided party and rode on horseback

10. David Finley at Mount Rainier, touring the West for the War Department in 1919

to the higher elevations with another party, enjoying dazzling views above the clouds (fig. 10). Before returning to San Francisco, he took a boat from Tacoma to Victoria on Vancouver Island in Canada, which he found enchanting. This was the first of many visits outside the United States.

Back in San Francisco for the third time, he spoke at a Rotary Club luncheon at the Palace Hotel and followed that up the next morning with a personal letter to each of the three hundred members. In Chinatown a fortune-teller told him that he "would marry a rich wife and do easy work—by which he meant head work."[25] After several more pleasant days in San Francisco, from which he visited Carmel, Monterey, and Pebble Beach, he was summoned back to Washington by a telegram from Colonel Woods. He hated leaving "this delightful fog" and San Francisco, which he said he had gotten to know almost as well as Philadelphia. Yet he reflected on the great majority in California society "who are very materialistic, never go to church, and secure divorces whenever it is convenient."[26] Returning by train, a journey of four days and five nights, he had time to think about his experiences in the West. He read *The Education of Henry Adams*, lent to him by a lady friend, and mused, "I enjoy my friends more than any other possession—more even than books."[27]

From Washington to New York and Back

When Arthur Woods left the War Department at the end of 1919, he returned to New York, where he was appointed chairman of the National Americanism Commission of the American Legion. And Finley, despite his misgivings about living in New York, joined the commission on 1 January 1920 as personal assistant to the chairman at an annual salary of $3,600. Woods was both a mentor and a friend, and Finley also admired his wife, Helen Hamilton Woods, whom he described as "very handsome and a good dancer." Her father was a great-grandson of Alexander Hamilton, and her mother was the daughter of J. P. Morgan. Despite Finley's friendship with Colonel and Mrs. Woods, through whom he met many notable New Yorkers, he did not feel comfortable with the American Legion's political philosophy, so sharply at odds with his support for Woodrow Wilson, and he disliked living at a hotel in midtown Manhattan. Later biographical accounts never mention this work in New York.[28] A long and loving letter from his mother in Washington, addressed to him in New York in May 1920, reveals their continuing closeness.

Late in 1920, though reluctant to part company with Colonel and Mrs. Woods, with whom he remained good friends, Finley returned to Washington. Arthur Woods himself soon left the American Legion to work for John D. Rockefeller Jr. As president of the Metropolitan Square Corporation in the late 1920s (fig. 11), Woods signed the lease for the land and helped select and oversee the team of architects for Rockefeller Center. He became the first president of Rockefeller Center, Inc., but illness forced him to resign.[29] Along the way, he also became the first president of Colonial Williamsburg, a favorite philanthropy of Rockefeller's. Woods returned to government service from January 1931 to August 1932 when President Hoover tapped him as the first chairman of the President's Organization for Unemployment Relief, but health problems again compelled him to resign.[30]

11. Colonel Arthur Woods, an early Finley mentor at the War Department and in New York

Finley, for his part, returned to private law practice, taking a job as counsel with Roper, Hurrey, and Parks, a small firm of tax lobbyists. This move allowed him to keep an eye on some of his younger brothers and to rejoin Washington's busy social scene. But he found tax law a terrible bore, later remarking that he did not like to read his own tax return, much less anyone else's. His principal clients seem to have been Colonel and Mrs. Woods, who owned property in Washington, but he was expected to bring in new business, which he evidently did not do well. Soon he began to look for a new position. He filled out an application for a job with the Commerce Department in September 1921 but did not turn it in. Then two months later, in November 1921, another opportunity arose. Raymond Mason, a friend of Finley's in New York, had recommended him for a position with the War Finance Corporation, and Finley was invited to come in for an interview. Things moved fast in Washington back then. He was offered a job that very day as assistant counsel at an annual salary of $5,000, accepted it the next day, and began work at the War Finance Corporation the following Monday.[31] This independent federal agency had offices in the Treasury Building under the auspices of the secretary of the treasury and the secretary of agriculture, with Eugene Meyer as managing director.[32]

About this time Finley and some of his Washington friends formed a "study club," which met regularly at the homes of the various members to discuss historical, political, economic, and cultural topics.[33] This was no light social conclave, as indicated by the meeting of 21 April 1922 that Finley described:

> The subjects listed will be under discussion, led by the persons indicated, and may be controverted by anyone present.
> The Development of Scholarship in Italy—Mr. Ceccato
> Path and Incidents of the Revival of Learning in Western Europe—Mrs. Mason
> Effect of the Renaissance on the Reformation—Commander Todd
> The Purification of the Roman Catholic Church and the Decay of the Protestant Reformation—Major Hall

Another study club meeting that year focused on the "Greek Period, 490 to 146 B.C.," and Finley's topic was "Homer and the Epic—Iliad and Odyssey." Following the presentation of eleven such papers, the program closed with a debate on the proposition that "Greek was greater than American civilization, taking into consideration literature, the arts, inventions, education, intelligence, comfort, beauty, human happiness."[34] Clearly Finley was exploring a growing interest in things cultural at this stage in his life.

The bridge to the Treasury Department led first to the War Finance Corporation, where Finley spent ten relatively uneventful months. Then in September 1922 S. Parker Gilbert Jr. (fig. 12), undersecretary of the treasury, hired him as one of five lawyers on the war loan staff, matching his then-comfortable salary of $5,000 a year. Gilbert was already recognized as one of the brightest and best minds of his generation. Two years younger than Finley, he had graduated from Rutgers University at the top of his class and from Harvard Law School cum laude. He joined a prominent Wall Street law firm, then came to Washington in 1918 to serve as counsel to the war loan staff. When Andrew W. Mellon arrived in 1921 as secretary of the treasury, he persuaded Gilbert to stay on rather than leave for a lucrative job on Wall Street by doubling his salary to $10,000 and making him undersecretary and second in command of the nation's finances at the age of twenty-nine.[35]

Finley described Gilbert as "our own Alexander Hamilton," who served as acting secretary of the treasury while Mellon traveled in Europe during the summer of 1923:

> Gilbert is almost essential to the Treasury. No one is completely so, but certainly there will never be anyone else in the Dept. who combines Gilbert's genius for getting to the bottom of things, his clear & felicitous statements, his tireless energy, originality & extraordinary judgment.
>
> . . . He was a shy fellow when he came here, but "all brains," as Mr. Leffingwell remarked, and he knows the Treasury from beginning to end. . . . Of course, he is a made man. He goes back to N.Y. at the top of the heap—all as a result of 5 years in Washington. That is certainly a quick way to the top. I hope the Treasury may prove an equal vantage point for the rest of us.[36]

A bachelor at the time, Gilbert amazed colleagues with his habit of returning to his office after dinner, often staying into the wee hours, yet coming to work again the next morning at the usual time. Finley emulated that practice during his Treasury years and doubtless learned much from Gilbert during the two years he worked under him. Gilbert

To David Edward Finley
With sincere appreciation and regard
January 24, 1929.   S. Parker Gilbert

12. S. Parker Gilbert, undersecretary of the Treasury, who hired Finley in
1922, leading him to Andrew Mellon

finally left the Treasury for Wall Street in late 1923, after accomplishing
a $3 billion reduction in the national debt under Secretary Mellon.[37]

Finley first worked strictly on legal issues under Gilbert but soon
branched out into policy matters as well, and his writing skills led to
assignments drafting reports and speeches for Secretary Mellon himself.
After Gilbert departed, Finley continued drafting materials for Mellon
under Gilbert's successor, Garrard Winston, who was impressed with
Finley's abilities—and agreed to let him publish a book under Mellon's
name to promote the secretary's tax policy. In early 1924 Finley put in
long hours at the Treasury writing a text based on Mellon's firmly held
views that reducing the level of taxation would stimulate the economy,

an idea that has resonance to this day. Once Winston and Mellon had approved the manuscript, Finley worked with Macmillan, the New York publisher, on every detail of the book's production. And when *Taxation: The People's Business* appeared in print during tax season in April 1924, it had the desired effect: indeed, not only did it convey Mellon's tax message to the public in clear and readable prose but it also had considerable popular success. Mellon was very pleased. Although Finley's name appears nowhere in the small volume, his efforts brought him squarely to Mellon's attention, and he vaulted into the role of writing most of the secretary's speeches, policy papers, and official correspondence. David Finley thus crossed the bridge to the Treasury, but more important, he had found his destiny at the right hand of Andrew Mellon.

NOTES

1. David Edward Finley, *A Standard of Excellence: Andrew W. Mellon Founds the National Gallery of Art at Washington* (Washington, D.C., 1973), 19.

2. Walter Bedford Moore Jr. had grown up in York County, attended Harvard Law School, and was a member of the South Carolina bar. He married Finley's second sister, Elizabeth, in 1916, and they lived in York and Columbia, where they raised four children and were pillars of their communities.

3. Finley journal, 13 June and 24 July 1915. Finley Papers, NGA Archives.

4. In contrast to his comments on the people he met casually in Washington, he noted, "I have never seen such uniformly nice-looking people than ride back on forth on the Main Line District." Finley journal, 26 September 1915.

5. Finley journal, 26 September 1915.

6. Application for employment to the Department of Commerce, 13 September 1921, NGA Archives, RG 28, box 24-7.

7. Finley journal, 15 January 1920.

8. Finley journal, 23 February 1920.

9. Finley journal, 2 August 1914.

10. Finley journal, 16 June 1915.

11. "Wilson, with passionate sincerity, was trying to keep the nation neutral, and aiding the Allies only to the extent that neutrality was not threatened" (Auchincloss, *Woodrow Wilson*, 65).

12. In January 1917 the Germans resumed their unrestricted submarine attacks in the Atlantic, which had already cost more than a thousand American lives. What tipped the scales was the infamous Zimmermann telegram of January 1917, from the German foreign secretary to his ambassador in Mexico, proposing that Mexico enter into an alliance with the United States, with "an understanding on our part that Mexico is to reconquer her lost territory in Texas, New Mexico, and Arizona." This clumsy proposal, decoded by British intelligence and released by Wilson just before his second inauguration, struck a sensitive nerve with Americans after the border clashes with Mexico in 1916. These two events finally brought Wilson and America into the war.

13. His last journal entry before the war, written on 26 November 1917, clearly places him in Philadelphia. Although no official records have been found, Finley's dates of service appear on a typed sheet of personal data from 29 January 1943. Finley Papers, NGA Archives, RG 28.

14. Arthur Woods (1870–1942) had come from Boston, was educated at Harvard University and in Germany, and served for ten years as a master at Groton School in Massachusetts before moving to New York.

15. Finley journal, 5 May 1919. A plaster cast of the Shaw Memorial now occupies a place of honor at the National Gallery of Art in Washington.

16. Finley journal, 5 May 1919.

17. Finley journal, 5 May 1919.

18. Finley journal, 18 May 1919.

19. Finley journal, 23 May 1919: "It is a preposterous mass of fabrication, and how so many intelligent persons can believe it is more than I can understand."

20. Finley journal, 27 May 1919.

21. Finley journal, 16 June 1919: "However, he [the lieutenant governor] will be sufficient for my purposes."

22. Finley journal, 26 June 1919.

23. In a journal entry on 9 July 1919, Finley recorded that the chairman of the city board of education assured him that "they felt in Fresno towards the Armenians as the people of the South do toward the negro."

24. Finley journal, 2 August 1919.

25. Finley journal, 16 August 1919.

26. Finley journal, 27 August 1919.

27. Finley journal, 31 August 1919.

28. Such as the lengthy biography in *The National Cyclopedia of American Biography*, vol. 1 (New York, 1953–1959), and briefer biographies in *Who's Who in America* over the years.

29. See Daniel Okrent, *Great Fortune: The Epic of Rockefeller Center* (New York, 2003), 53, 131, 193, 331.

30. See Herbert Hoover, *The Great Depression* (New York, 1952), 53, 150.

31. Finley journal, 18 November 1921.

32. Eugene Meyer (1876–1959) had been a successful Wall Street banker who joined the Wilson administration during the First World War as managing director of the War Finance Corporation and stayed on to serve three succeeding Republican Presidents. In 1930 he was appointed governor of the Federal Reserve Board and in 1932 became the first chairman of the Reconstruction Finance Corporation. In 1933 he bought the struggling *Washington Post* at a bankruptcy sale. Serving as publisher and editor, he made the newspaper a financial and journalistic success, further enhanced by the efforts of his daughter, Katharine Meyer Graham.

33. Dr. G. B. Ceccato was a founder of the study club, which Finley sometimes called the "Ceccato Study Club." He was economic counselor at the Italian Embassy, and apparently Finley met him through his cousin Violet Blair Janin. Finley kept in touch with Ceccato when he was transferred to London about 1924. Ceccato returned to Italy in 1940 and sat out the war in Venice on sick leave. After the war he became head of the Italian Restitution Mission in Germany. He apparently retired there and died in the late 1950s. See Finley Papers, NGA Archives, box 4-3, Ceccato correspondence 1946–1958.

34. Undated insert in Finley journal, 1921.

35. Gilbert's obituary in the *New York Times*, 24 February 1938, called him "the most extraordinary man of his years in the field of public finance since Alexander Hamilton." Library of Congress, "Pro-Quest Historical Newspapers in the *New York Times* (1851–2001)."

36. Finley journal, 25 June 1923.

37. Then in 1924 Gilbert became agent general for German reparations payments and spent five and a half years in Berlin and Paris, where he displayed rare political instincts, earning the respect of both the Germans and the Allied leaders and restoring pre-Hitler Germany to some semblance of economic stability. He returned to New York in 1930 as a partner at J. P. Morgan, where he was a noted authority on European as well as American banking and was said to have the "financial map of Europe in his head." Edgar Ansel Mowrer, "An International Bombshell: 'Germany Can Pay,'" *The Literary Digest* (19 January 1929). Andrew Mellon asked Gilbert to serve on the first board of trustees for the National Gallery of Art in June 1937, but Gilbert died less than a year later at age forty-five, cutting short a brilliant career in law, government, and finance.

13. *Andrew W. Mellon*, portrait by Oswald Birley, 1933. National Gallery of Art

3

Mr. Mellon's Finley

1924–1931

ACCORDING TO FAMILY TRADITION, David Finley first met Andrew W. Mellon when walking down a corridor at the Department of the Treasury just as Secretary Mellon appeared outside his office looking for his assistant. Finley asked if there was anything he could do for Mellon, and the rest is history. Although this may indeed reflect their first meeting, it was more likely Finley's usefulness to Mellon's principal lieutenants—first Parker Gilbert, then Garrard Winston—that brought him to Mellon's notice. By 1924 Finley not only had written *Taxation: The People's Business* for Mellon but had visited the Wallace Collection with him while both were in London that August. From then on, Mellon came to rely increasingly on Finley, first in his work at the Treasury and later in efforts to create the National Gallery of Art. By 1927 Finley had become Mellon's right-hand man. After Mellon's death in 1937, Finley spent the next nineteen years fulfilling his mentor's plans for the National Gallery. In the 1950s and 1960s he spent a great deal of time helping to establish the National Portrait Gallery, another of Mellon's dreams. And in 1974 he published *A Standard of Excellence*, a detailed and moving eyewitness account of Mellon's founding of the National Gallery. Other than his own family, by far the biggest influence in Finley's life was Andrew Mellon (fig. 13).

Andrew W. Mellon

In March 1921 Andrew Mellon, the Pittsburgh financier and industrialist, had accepted an appointment as secretary of the treasury in the cabinet of Warren G. Harding. At the age of sixty-six and as one of the three richest men in the United States alongside John D. Rockefeller and Henry Ford, Mellon at this point was almost unknown to the American people. That was about to change.

The Mellons, like the Finleys a century earlier, had come to Pennsylvania from Ulster. Their history in Ireland, unlike that of the Finleys, is well known, thanks to Andrew Mellon's father, Thomas, whose lively memoirs tell a fascinating story that includes his migration with his family from County Tyrone to western Pennsylvania as a boy of five, which he recalled with amazing clarity.[1] Thomas Mellon personified the American dream, rising through hard work and a close-knit Scots-Irish farm family to become a lawyer and judge before starting a bank in Pittsburgh with his sons in 1870.[2] A financial panic in 1873 nearly wiped out the Mellon Bank, but the business so prospered under Andrew's quiet, diligent care that by 1881 Thomas decided to turn over the bank's management entirely to this gifted son.

Andrew Mellon had a genius for recognizing promising young men who needed financial backing, and he would negotiate for an equity share in their fledgling businesses. His fortunes thus soared through his ground-floor positions in blue-chip Pittsburgh industries such as Alcoa, Gulf Oil, and U.S. Steel. Andrew remained a bachelor, living with his parents until age forty-five. Then in June 1898, when crossing the Atlantic with his friends Henry Clay Frick and his wife, he met a nineteen-year-old English girl, Nora McMullen. Despite the twenty-four-year difference in their ages, Andrew Mellon was smitten and visited the McMullens twice that summer. The next summer he returned and proposed marriage to Nora, who first rejected his suit but accepted a year later. Following a splendid wedding at Hertford Castle in September 1900, he brought his bride back to Pittsburgh.

Although the couple had two children—Ailsa, born in 1901, and Paul in 1907—the marriage faced daunting odds from the start. Not only did sooty, industrial Pittsburgh lack the allure of the green English countryside, but Andrew, consumed with his business interests, failed to give his young wife anything like the attention she had enjoyed as the only sister of eight older brothers. Visiting England whenever she could, Nora eventually fell under the sway of a charming English scoundrel named Alfred Curphy. The upshot was that in 1909 Nora asked for a divorce, and Andrew's countersuit finally resulted in a settlement granted in July 1912, but not before Pittsburgh newspapers had splashed the ugly battle across the headlines. The contestants and their children were scarred for life.[3]

14. President Calvin Coolidge, Treasury Secretary Andrew W. Mellon, and President Herbert Hoover, 1920s

Politics and Art

After the divorce Andrew Mellon became involved in Republican politics and focused intense energy on building his art collection. As a Pennsylvania delegate to the Republican convention in 1920, he helped raise funds for Warren Harding's presidential election. After serving Harding as secretary of the treasury, he continued in that capacity under Presidents Calvin Coolidge and Herbert Hoover (fig. 14). Considering Mellon's immense wealth and patrician bearing, one United States senator commented wryly that "three Presidents had served under Secretary Mellon."[4] Although perhaps more poetry than fact, it is true that Andrew Mellon, more than any other one man, set the tone for the three Republican administrations during the Roaring Twenties, and all three Presidents showed him great deference.[5]

15. Etching of Herbert Hoover, c. 1928, inscribed to David Finley "with Kind Regards"

Beginning in 1924, David Finley came to know two of these Presidents well through Andrew Mellon. He understood that Mellon had no use for Harding, who committed the unforgivable sin of wasting his time, but that he respected Coolidge.[6] Mellon's relationship with Hoover was more complex. Almost twenty years his senior, Mellon had overshadowed Hoover in the cabinets of Harding and Coolidge. His support for Hoover at the 1928 Republican convention, however, proved decisive, and he did consent to stay at the helm of the Treasury.[7] Finley quotes Mellon after the first Hoover Cabinet meeting that morning as saying, "It went off very well & I was agreeably impressed with the new Cabinet. Hoover does not waste time. Neither did Coolidge, but he was more brusque in manner than Hoover." Mellon also told Finley after going to the White House for tea and a musicale the day following the inauguration: "I don't see why Cabinet officers must do that sort of thing. Anyhow, I had luck. I spoke a few minutes with Mrs. Hoover, then had a cup of tea . . . and talked to whoever was around [Finley notes here that Mellon 'likes his tea']. They all went into the East Room, so I hung back around the tea table, drinking my tea, & when they were all gone, I slipped out and came back to work."[8]

David Finley himself was an unregenerate Wilsonian until the early 1920s and privately recorded a scathing dismissal of Harding, whom he saw at a charity ball in early 1922.[9] About the same time, Finley described Vice President Coolidge as "bleak and New England," but by 1927 a signed photograph of President Coolidge was a prized possession. Finley also became friends with Hoover during his presidency, and the two men retained a mutual regard ever after (fig. 15).[10] But Hoover and Mellon did not always agree with one another, and the onset of the financial crash and Great Depression strained the relationship, prompting Mellon's resignation in March 1932.

Mellon was a serious man who had no interest in sporting activities or showy houses and gardens. His sole indulgence was buying fine Dutch, British, and American paintings. He had begun this avocation on a European tour with his Pittsburgh friend Henry Clay Frick in 1881, visiting Ireland, Scotland, England, and the Continent in a leisurely fashion. They stopped to see the Wallace Collection in London, which made a deep impression on both men, and in Paris each bought a modest painting, the seeds of what were to become two of the finest private art collections in the New World.[11] By the 1890s Mellon was crossing the Atlantic on vacation almost every summer and making regular purchases of paintings from Knoedler & Co., the New York art dealers who were also Frick's primary source of paintings. By the time he became secretary of the treasury in 1921, he had assembled an impressive private collection of mostly Dutch and English masterpieces along with some early American portraits. These works filled both his Pittsburgh home and his grand apartment in Washington, D.C., which occupied the entire 11,000-square-foot fifth floor of the beaux-arts McCormick Building at 1785 Massachusetts Avenue. David Finley was to spend many hours at this address working with Secretary Mellon.[12]

Enter Duveen

About this time a colorful new player entered the stage: Joseph Duveen (fig. 16) of the British firm Duveen Brothers, with galleries in London, New York, and Paris.[13] A larger-than-life figure in the world of art, Duveen established a transatlantic presence of notable controversy, not only during his lifetime but to this day. With no higher education or formal study of art, he "noticed that Europe had plenty of art and America had plenty of money, and his entire astonishing career was the product of that simple observation."[14] As the greatest entrepreneur in a great age of art collectors, he specialized in the sale of British and European paintings to wealthy American collectors, such as Frick, William Randolph

16. Saul Steinberg, *Joseph Duveen*, 1951, ink on paper, originally published in *The New Yorker*, 29 September 1951

Hearst, H. E. Huntington, J. P. Morgan, John D. Rockefeller, Peter A. B. and Joseph Widener, Andrew Mellon, and later Samuel H. Kress. He relentlessly pursued the best art available, paid the highest prices for it, and got even higher prices in return, mostly from the Americans.

Duveen also adopted devious tactics to advance his interests. He kept a long-standing secret contract with Bernard Berenson that assigned the revered scholar a hefty sales commission for providing attributions to Italian Renaissance masters.[15] He maintained a network of paid informants that included the butlers and valets of his clients. Having met Mellon through Frick in 1913, at a time when Frick was Duveen's principal client and Mellon's collection was relatively modest,[16] he turned his attentions to Mellon after Frick's death in 1919. And he put Mellon's man Flore on his own payroll, giving him a mole in the heart of Mellon's household beginning in at least 1925. Regular reports forwarded immediately to Duveen wherever he might be—often using coded telegrams—covered everything from Mellon's travel plans and social schedule to the visits of Duveen's competitors from Knoedler & Co. (and all purchases from them) and where various pictures were hung in Mellon's home.[17] Flore even revealed Ailsa Mellon's disappointment just before her wedding in May 1926 that she had not received a wedding gift from Duveen. In fact, Duveen's extravagant gift was already en route.

For all his guile, Duveen's most potent weapons were his high-voltage energy and relentless, single-minded personal charm, which seemed to intoxicate otherwise sober magnates, cloud their judgment, and loosen their purse strings. The director of London's National

Gallery, Kenneth Clark, said, "His bravura and impudence were infectious, and when he was present everyone behaved as if he had had a couple of drinks."[18] Berenson's wife enthused that Duveen was "like champagne"; her husband glumly replied, "more like gin."[19] Knighted in the 1920s and made a peer of the British realm in the 1930s by King George V for his generosity to the National Gallery in London among other British institutions, this formidable self-promoter finally became Lord Duveen of Milbank. This is the man with whom Mellon and Finley negotiated for some of the most important paintings to fill the planned National Gallery of Art. He would meet his match in Andrew Mellon and David Finley.

The Stars Align

Mellon's gift for spotting up-and-coming talent, which had served him so well in business, also characterized his eleven years at the Treasury, where he surrounded himself with an unusually gifted group of lieutenants, including S. Parker Gilbert, Odgen Mills, Eugene Meyer, Garrard Winston, and Donald D. Shepard as well as David Finley.[20] Finley, the diligent, outgoing young tax lawyer, soon became Mellon's indispensable man (fig. 17). Secretary Mellon placed growing trust not only in Finley's professional abilities but in his character and judgment as well. And Finley came to display an almost selfless devotion to his mentor, putting his writing talents, his social skills, and his interest in art, history, and culture completely at Mellon's disposal.

Mellon had never done much public speaking until 1921, but as one of the most prominent figures in Washington during the 1920s, he was frequently called upon to give speeches of an official or semiofficial nature. Fortunately, Finley could have been a professional speechwriter, having learned his craft by writing his father's campaign materials a decade earlier. Knowing that Mellon wanted to "say something" meaningful rather than simply mouth popular platitudes, Finley would first prepare a draft of a speech and sit down with Mellon to go over the text. Then he would incorporate Mellon's ideas into subsequent revisions until the secretary was satisfied. Finally he would underline and highlight the approved version and go over it with Mellon once again to be sure the secretary was as comfortable with it as possible. Although

17. David E. Finley during his early years at the Treasury, c. 1924

never entirely at ease as a public speaker, Mellon managed to get by, with Finley's help.

In the financial boom of the 1920s, several of Mellon's assistants, including Parker Gilbert and Garrard Winston, moved to New York to take high-paying jobs. In March 1927 Floyd Blair, a Treasury lawyer and close friend of Finley's, went to a Wall Street bank and was urging Finley to do likewise.[21] When Finley received an offer from a bank in New York sometime in 1927, he asked Mellon's advice:

> He [Mellon] said, "With your tastes, I am sure you would
> not be as happy in New York as you would be here, especially
> in some work I have in mind for you." Then he went on to say
> that he was leaving his collection as a nucleus for a National
> Gallery and would like to have me with him to work it out.
> I told him that under those circumstances I would much rather
> stay on here, and that nothing in New York would interest
> me as much as that. After that, I never thought of leaving
> the Treasury, and Mr. Mellon and I talked constantly about
> building up his collection with a view to the future National
> Gallery.[22]

Finley's journals up to 1924 disclose a discriminating mind and an educated taste in architecture, history, and literature but make little mention of painting. Yet the entries from his first trip to Europe in 1924, when he was dazzled by the riches of the Louvre in Paris, the Uffizi and Pitti in Florence, and the Gallerie dell'Accademia in Venice, reveal a considerable knowledge of art history.

When Mellon received a constant stream of letters throughout his years at the Treasury offering to sell him works of art, Finley took responsibility for many of Mellon's responses. One inquiry came from Helen Hamilton Woods, the wife of Colonel Arthur Woods, Finley's old mentor and boss at the War Department and in New York. Mrs. Woods wrote to Mellon in January 1923 about a Gainsborough portrait that her mother wished to sell. In this case Mellon responded personally: "I am so much occupied in Washington . . . that it is difficult for me to turn my attention to something like art," adding that he was "very well supplied with pictures . . . for the time being."[23] By the mid-1920s Finley answered most such letters to the effect that Secretary Mellon was too busy with official duties and was not then buying paintings. Depending on the situation, Finley would draft a letter for Mellon's signature, write on Mellon's behalf, or simply draft a note to be signed by Mellon's secretary.[24]

The year 1927 marks the true beginning of the Mellon-Finley partnership. Mellon established a new position for Finley as special assistant, which allowed him unfettered access. Finley became a combination chief of staff and chargé d'affaires—writing Mellon's policy papers, correspondence, and speeches and traveling with him on official business, on private business, and even on vacation to Europe in 1928. This collaboration deepened their already close ties. Indeed, Mellon greatly enjoyed the company of Finley, who became a friend as well as a great professional asset, providing invaluable support not only at the Treasury but in building his art collection. Mellon's divorce and the resulting scandal in Pittsburgh had made the intensely private man even more reserved. But after his daughter Ailsa married David K. E. Bruce and moved to New York, while his son Paul was away at Choate and then Yale and Cambridge Universities, David Finley would often have lunch with Mellon at 1785 Massachusetts Avenue, where they would talk about art, and he sometimes joined the secretary and his guests for dinner.

Finley seemed to have an inexhaustible source of energy and an infinite capacity for challenging and complex projects. Self-effacing to a fault, he made sure his mentor, whom he invariably called "Mr. Mellon," received all the credit for his achievements. He was the ideal courtier: talented, modest, cultured, courteous, and absolutely loyal. Later in life he shared a number of admiring and affectionate recollections and insights:

> Mr. Mellon has been described by people who did not know him as a shy, silent man, not given to speech if he could avoid it. He was a reticent man but not shy, and he was a very forceful character. If he had nothing he wanted to say, he kept silent; and while he did not suffer fools gladly, he gave his full attention to anyone with whom he happened to be talking.

Actually he liked talking with anyone whom he knew well and trusted. Once he and I were going to Pittsburgh for a meeting. I asked some questions about the beginning of the Aluminum Company. He told me with great detail and went on to talk about other companies in which he was interested or had founded and from which he had resigned as chairman or director when he became Secretary of the Treasury. Suddenly, after several hours of conversation, largely by Mr. Mellon, I saw we were coming into the Pittsburgh station and we hastily decamped.

Mr. Mellon had a dry but delightful sense of humor and a very infectious laugh. He disliked garrulity or serious talk that made no sense. He had a disconcerting way of saying "Why?" when someone had been making statements or proposing something to which not too much thought had been given. "It sounds well," he would say, "but it won't work." And he had long years of experience to back up his judgment.[25]

Finley also gave this example of Mellon's humor: at a dinner during the stock market boom in the spring of 1929, "some woman asked the Secretary when the present speculating wave would subside, to which his answer was 'When Gentlemen Prefer Bonds.'"[26]

Mellon's 1928 diary indicates an increasing reliance on David Finley. More than forty references mention Finley—taking Mellon's son Paul to a dance, working with Mellon on speeches or articles, coming to tea or dinner and discussing art acquisitions. Mellon took his brother, nephew, and Finley to the Republican convention in June 1928, traveling in a private Pullman car to Kansas City, where Mellon skillfully engineered the presidential nomination of his fellow cabinet member Herbert Hoover. Finley recalled that Senator Charles Curtis of Kansas had asked Mellon to endorse him for President and that when Mellon declined but offered to support him for vice president Curtis walked out. According to Finley, "Mr. Mellon, who was an excellent poker player, said to me with a smile, 'He will take it just the same.'"[27] Hoover and Curtis were duly nominated and elected.

In the summer of 1928 Mellon invited Finley to join him and several family members on a six-week holiday in France and England. Delighted, Finley explained, "I enjoyed Mr. Mellon's company and he treated me and his other younger friends as though we were all the same age."[28] Sailing from New York with Mellon's nephew Larimer and his family aboard the *Majestic*, they disembarked at Cherbourg, and spent three weeks in Brittany after a stop at Mont-Saint-Michel. Joined by Paul Mellon and two friends from Yale, they drove to La Rochelle, where they visited a Mellon manufacturing plant that made steel sleeping cars for Wagons-Lits. They continued on to Lormont near Bordeaux, where they met a French wine merchant named Paul Mellon, whose father, by a curious coincidence, had been André Mellon.[29] After a few days in England "we went back to Washington, having had, from my point of view, a very restful summer, and from Mr. Mellon's, a very exciting one."[30]

Changing the Face of the Capital

In 1928 Mellon gave Finley a very visible role in one of the most ambitious projects undertaken by the government in the 1920s: the creation of the "Federal Triangle" in Washington. The federal government had long since outgrown its assortment of office buildings, scattered around downtown Washington among stores, hotels, and markets north of the Mall. Unworthy of the capital of an international power, several of these accommodations consisted of flimsy temporary buildings thrown up during the war—some actually squatting on the Mall itself. Although they were inefficient and ugly, the notoriously tight-fisted President Coolidge was finally persuaded to do something about this only because it cost more to rent the buildings than it would to own them.

Coolidge had signed the Public Buildings Act of 1926, which provided $275 million to the Treasury Department to erect new buildings "as needed," including $75 million for Washington alone. This gave the Treasury virtually carte blanche, rather than allowing Congress to dole out the money as part of pork-barrel projects. In the hands of a less honorable man it could have been an enormous boondoggle, but Mellon took a far-sighted interest in the project and hired an able assistant secretary with responsibility for nothing but public buildings.

Mellon's initial conception focused on the triangle between Fourteenth Street and Constitution and Pennsylvania Avenues (which converge at Sixth Street). He favored classical architecture, and his architects designed a series of stately white, beaux-arts–inspired buildings to house the Commerce Department, the Internal Revenue Service, the Justice Department, the National Archives, and the Federal Trade Commission. Additional plans would provide for a new Supreme Court building, a new House office building, and removal of the jerry-built structures on the Mall and on parkland between the Capitol and Union Station.

As preparations for the Federal Triangle neared completion, David Finley suggested producing a motion picture to explain the capital building program to the public and to Congress. Secretary Mellon liked the idea but did not want to spend Treasury funds on it. He "offered to foot the bill" personally, but Finley, "after many tries in different directions," finally persuaded General Electric to fund the film and to supply the professional and technical help to produce it.[31] Finley devoted so much time to the film in the early months of 1929, basically writing the script and supervising the production, that his colleagues at the Treasury began to call him "D. W. Griffith."

With this film—screened for the newly elected President Hoover as well as his cabinet and members of Congress at the annual meeting of the American Institute of Architects on 25 April 1929—Finley had essentially produced an architectural history of Washington, beginning with the L'Enfant Plan of 1791, continuing through the McMillan Plan of 1901, and ending with what he called the Mellon Plan of 1928. The screening functioned as both a political and a public relations event, and Finley wrote not only Secretary Mellon's speech but also those for President Hoover, for Senator Reed Smoot, chairman of the Senate Appropriations Committee, and for Congressman Richard Nash Elliot, chairman of the House Committee on Public Buildings and Grounds. One night he went to dinner at Mrs. Woodrow Wilson's, then returned to the Treasury and worked until after midnight on the President's and Secretary Mellon's speeches.[32] Finley also oversaw every detail of the ceremonies, from preparation of a model of the buildings to arrangements for the Marine Band to play and fifteen Coast Guardsmen to serve as ushers. The following night the film received a public screening at Fox's Theater in Washington, inspiring warm applause; then it traveled to the Roxy Theater in New York for a one-week showing.

The film garnered the desired publicity. *Time* magazine gave the story extensive coverage, including a prominent photograph with the caption "Mr. Mellon's Finley" (fig. 18) and the text: "At the forefront of the capital planning has been Secretary Mellon himself, ably, painstakingly assisted by his self-effacing alter ego, Special Assistant David Edward Finley. The latter, a little South Carolina thoroughbred, lawyer by profession, connoisseur and cosmopolite by taste, engineers most of Mr. Mellon's personal, non-political doings. He it was, who between arduous hours of writing speeches, receiving news gatherers, answering correspondence, gathered the material, wrote the scenario and produced the historico-architectural cinema viewed by the President last week."[33] Mellon proclaimed himself "immensely pleased" and handed Finley a personal check for $3,500, which the latter used to pay miscellaneous expenses of the film.[34] Three weeks later Secretary Mellon laid the cornerstone for the Internal Revenue Building, the first building in the Federal Triangle complex.

The Legacy Emerges

At about the same time, Andrew Mellon's plans to create the National Gallery of Art started to come together. From his many years of European travel, he had gained an acute awareness of the lack of a true national art gallery in his own nation's capital, and he had been embarrassed when foreign leaders visiting Washington asked to be taken to the American national gallery. As Finley recalled, "Mr. Mellon would reply that there was no such National Gallery of old masters, but that he had a few paintings in his apartment which he would be glad to show his visitors."[35] Secretary Mellon also received numerous requests to view his private art collection.[36] He granted many of them, often sending Finley as a guide. Indeed, when Finley showed the collection to Leonello Venturi, professor of art history from the University of Turin, in early 1929, he took the opportunity to ask the scholar's opinions on several items under consideration for purchase and wrote a detailed memorandum to Mellon with a summary of Venturi's comments, both positive and negative.[37] Finley added a postscript that apparently did not go to Mellon but was intended as an aide-mémoire for his own future reference, suggesting his increasing confidence in his own judgments about important paintings.

In 1927 David Finley, of course, had heard firsthand of Mellon's intention to establish a national gallery of art, and as early as 9 November 1927 the *Washington Times* reported the rumor that a site had been selected on the Mall: "Speculation as to the donor of this munificent gift to the people mentions the name of Andrew W. Mellon, Secretary of the Treasury."[38] Despite public remarks to the contrary, Mellon had continued to buy art throughout his time as secretary of the treasury, almost exclusively through Knoedler & Co. or Duveen. And Finley continued to advise him, almost always behind the scenes. By 1928 the competition between the two firms for Mellon's business bristled with intensity. His diary shows almost weekly lunches at his apartment either with Carlton Messmore of Knoedler's or with Joseph Duveen.[39] Mellon noted the result of one significant meeting in a spidery hand at the back of his 1928 pocket diary:

Bought from Duveen Apr 25 1928

Gancart [?]	400
Holbein	480
Romney	285
Either Rembrandt	
or Gains	350
	1510
Less 17½ %	264.25
	1245.75
Less return Vandyke	225
	1020.75

In these laconic banker's figures the secretary of the treasury casually records the purchase of more than a million dollars' worth of art over lunch.

Finley played a critical role in a number of transactions. For instance, Messmore wanted Mellon's authority in April 1928 to bid on what he referred to as the "Panshanger Rafael," then owned by an

TIME

Vol. XIII, No. 18   *The Weekly Newsmagazine*   May 6, 1929

NATIONAL AFFAIRS

THE PRESIDENCY
International Week

Never monotonous are the weeks of a U. S. President. Last fortnight President Hoover was preoccupied with domestic matters—Law Enforcement, the Press, Farm Relief. Last week his focus shifted to world affairs.

Elder Statesman Elihu Root arrived at the White House, just back from Geneva where, with other famed jurists, he had been revising World Court statutes. President Hoover kept him for luncheon. They talked of Mr. Root's new formula for getting the U. S. into the Court over the Senate's reservation against advisory opinions. Secretary of State Stimson was present, a statesman with an ear quick and open to Elder Statesman Root, who gave him his first law job and later took him in as a junior partner.

Then Idaho's Borah, in his capacity as chairman of the Senate Foreign Relations Committee, called upon the President. He had many a thing to say about the World Court, about reparations, about naval armaments.

Then, most exciting of all, Hugh Gibson, U. S. Ambassador to Belgium, chairman of the U. S. Delegation to the League of Nations preparatory Arms Conference at Geneva, delivered at Geneva the Hoover formula for *reduction* (not limitation) of naval armaments. How would the Powers take to his plan? Carefully, secretly President Hoover had planted his armament reduction idea in Chief Delegate Gibson's mind during quiet White House evenings a month ago, when the Powers despaired of success at the forthcoming conference.

Last week, as in upon the White House rolled a worldwide rumble of praise for the U. S. President who had suddenly freshened a stale subject, that U. S. President looked pleased.

❡ Forty famed engineers gathered at the White House luncheon table. After the meal they awarded to their host, President Hoover, the John Fritz gold medal, highest honor of the American Engineering Societies—civil, mining & metallurgical, mechanical, electrical.

❡ President Hoover appointed Lawrence M. Judd, rancher and county supervisor of Honolulu, to be Governor of Hawaii, succeeding Wallace Rider Farrington, eight-year incumbent. Another appointment: William D. L. Starbuck, New York mechanical engineer, patent attorney, Democrat, to the Federal Radio Commission. As President Coolidge had unsuccessfully done before him, President Hoover sent to the Senate for confirmation the name of Irvine Luther Lenroot, onetime (1918–27) Senator from Wiscon-

© *Keystone*

MR. MELLON'S FINLEY
The President went to his cinema.

(See p. 10)

sin, to be Judge on the U. S. Court of Customs & Patents Appeals.

❡ President Hoover takes joy in slipping away from his newsgathering shadows. Last week he succeeded in motoring without them to Catoctin Furnace, Md., to fish peacefully in Hunting Creek with Detective-Secretary Lawrence Richey. All that the newsgatherers learned was that the President caught a pound-and-a-half trout, inspected a site for a ten-room log cabin, ate a picnic supper under the trees with Mrs. Hoover. After dusk he drove back to Washington. His shadows politely rebuked him.

CONTENTS

THE CABINET
"Federal City"

(See map, pages 10 & 11.)

Into the brown-paneled Council Chamber of the U. S. Chamber of Commerce in Washington, last week, went President Hoover, Secretary of the Treasury Mellon, Chief Justice Taft, Senator Reed, Smoot, and many a member of the American Institute of Architects. They were gathered to talk of Washington's development as a beautiful city, to pledge allegiance to a capital building program now well under way. Speeches were made. Models of new Government buildings were admiringly examined. A cinema of the capital's rude start, its ragged growth, its sudden bursts of classic beauty, its future nobility, was shown. This story was told:

Site. A political trade planted Washington on the Potomac mudflats. Thomas Jefferson gave Southern support to Alexander Hamilton's campaign to have the U. S. assume the full cost of the Revolution. In return, in 1790, Hamilton helped Jefferson pass legislation locating the new capital in the South on the Potomac River. President Washington picked the site—100 sq. mi. ceded by Maryland and Virginia to the U. S. at the head of tide water. He called the new Capital "The Federal City." Jefferson, Madison and the three commissioners chosen to lay out the city, referred to it from the start as "Washington."

L'Enfant Plan. Major Pierre Charles L'Enfant, a French engineer and Revolutionary War officer, was engaged as chief city-planner. Engineer L'Enfant placed the Capitol on a low eminence ever since called "The Hill." About a mile west and north he set the President's House, connecting them with a broad avenue (Pennsylvania). From the Capitol and from the President's House (later the White House) were to radiate other avenues cutting the city's network of smaller streets. A parkway or Mall was to sweep westward from the Capitol to the Potomac. Stately public buildings were to fill the triangle between Pennsylvania Avenue and the Mall. President Washington's watchful eye saw the President's House begun (1792), the Capitol cornerstone laid (1793). But George Washington was dead before the Government took possession of its new city (1800).

"Wilderness City." Carved out of the wild, the city's growth was feeble at first. After being burned by the British in 1814, it made a fresh start, sprawled out of the bounds of the L'Enfant plan. Impatient at delays, President Jackson thrust his cane into the ground and said: "Here,

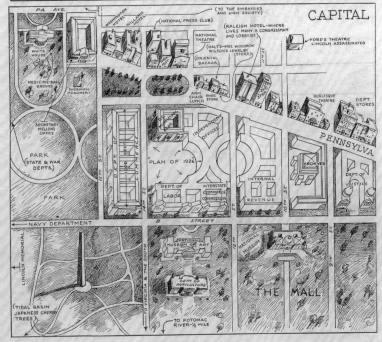

CAPITAL

right here let the corner stone of the Treasury Building be laid!"

Classic in design, the building rose there, squarely blocking the view between the White House and the Capitol along Pennsylvania Avenue.

Fifty haphazard years of jerrybuilding followed. The Civil War focused national attention upon the capital and its miserable estate. Arose Alexander R. Sheppard, great public spirit, great builder, to pave and light streets, lay sewers, plant trees, pauperize himself. Washington grew out of its youthful squalor, but recklessly, without unity or good taste. Architecture went on a gingerbread spree—viz. the State, War & Navy Building, the Post Office Department Building. The L'Enfant plan was forgotten.

Plan of 1901. For all its growth, Washington had little to be proud of on its hundredth birthday. A commission of architects and artists was formed to plan improvements. This, the McMillan Commission, brought forth the Plan of 1901, reviving the L'Enfant plan. Never officially adopted, the Plan of 1901 did cause the removal of railroad tracks and station from the Mall at 6th Street, the construction of the new Union Station as a worthy

city gateway, the location of the Lincoln Memorial in Potomac Park on a line with the Capitol and the Washington Monument.

War. City plans for Washington were temporarily ruined by the War. Shacks of plaster and board to house workers sprang up in the Mall, in parks, around the Capitol. To flat stucco buildings on B Street were transferred the expanded activities of the War Department and the entire Navy Department. The U. S. rented office buildings at random about the city for Departments like Labor and Commerce, for independent bureaus and commissions.

Plan of 1926. President Coolidge found that for economy's sake it would be cheaper in the end to build Federal offices in the capital than to rent them. He had the strong support of Secretary Mellon, whose Department has charge of public buildings, and of Senator Smoot of Utah, potent on the Senate's Appropriations Committee and chairman of the U. S. Public Buildings Commission. A new program, known as the Plan of 1926, bringing the L'Enfant plan to life once more, was formulated. Congress voted 75 million dollars for new Federal buildings

in the capital. An Assistant Secretary of the Treasury was assigned to handle nothing but public buildings.

Chosen for this Treasury post was Carl Schuneman, St. Paul lawyer and department store manager. Rebuilding the capital is only part of a comprehensive program, first of its kind since 1913, for housing expanded Federal agencies throughout the land. For this program as a whole, the Public Buildings Act of 1926 authorized 275 million dollars—a bill unique in that it gave the Treasury *carte blanche* to erect buildings "where needed," instead of specifying the desires of adroit log-rollers.

At the forefront of the capital planning has been Secretary Mellon himself, ably, painstakingly assisted by his self-effacing *alter ego*, Special Assistant David Edward Finley. The latter, a little South Carolina thoroughbred, lawyer by profession, connoisseur and cosmopolite by taste, engineers most of Mr. Mellon's personal, non-political doings. He it was who, between arduous hours of writing speeches, receiving newsgatherers, answering correspondence, gathered material, wrote the scenario and produced the historico-architectural cinema viewed by the President last week.

English family;[40] but Mellon noted on 9 May, "Messmore to lunch. They had offered 750,000 for Panshanger Rafael but Duveen got it." Then, significantly, on 20 October 1928 in New York: "David Finley arrives. Breakfast at Biltmore. See Duveen about pictures and see Panshanger Raphael." On 2 November: "Duveen at lunch. Price of Rafael $775,000. Entirely satisfactory to give it up. Has other customers & if not will keep it & never sell. Keep for own house—or I can buy and return any time." On 5 December: "Duveen to luncheon. Agree to take the Panshanger Rafael."

Duveen clearly beat Messmore on this deal, but Mellon purchased the painting, now known as the *Niccolini-Cowper Madonna* (plate 1), only after seeing it with David Finley. As Finley later explained, "Mr. Mellon had an unerring eye for quality in paintings and impeccable taste. He made his decisions after careful thought; but he liked to talk things over with someone whom he trusted and who could approach the matter with only Mr. Mellon's interests in mind. It was here that my usefulness to Mr. Mellon arose, insofar as art was concerned."[41] Finley was particularly useful to Mellon in considering Italian paintings. As discriminating as Mellon's tastes were with respect to British, Dutch, and American paintings, until the mid-1920s they had not extended to the masters of the Italian Renaissance. Yet once Mellon decided to create the National Gallery of Art, he knew he had to expand his collection, and he came to depend heavily on the counsel of David Finley, who loved Italy in all its dimensions. Duveen's inside track with the Italian school gave him a competitive edge at this point. But Duveen had been trying to interest Mellon in buying Italian paintings for years. Only after Finley began advising him did Mellon respond in a big way.[42]

Soon, however, Mellon's dealings with Duveen were eclipsed by a stupendous purchase from the Hermitage in 1930 and 1931. Finley later recalled Mellon's decisiveness in acting on this unique opportunity.[43] Represented by Knoedler & Co., which collaborated with two other dealers—Colnaghi's in London and Mathiessen in Berlin—in a complicated series of transactions with the famously inscrutable Soviets, Andrew Mellon managed to acquire twenty-one masterpieces, mostly Flemish and Italian, from the Hermitage Museum in Leningrad (now St. Petersburg) for $6,654,000.[44] These works, collected by Catherine

🎗 PLATE I   Raphael, *Niccolini-Cowper Madonna*, 1508.
National Gallery of Art, Andrew W. Mellon Collection, 1937.1.25

PLATE 2   Jan van Eyck, *The Annunciation*, c. 1434/1436.
National Gallery of Art, Andrew W. Mellon Collection
1937.1.39

❧ PLATE 3   Sandro Botticelli, *Adoration of the Magi*, early 1480s.
National Gallery of Art, Andrew W. Mellon Collection, 1937.1.22

PLATE 4   Raphael, *Saint George and the Dragon*, c. 1506.
National Gallery of Art, Andrew W. Mellon Collection,
1937.1.26

the Great and the Russian czars of the eighteenth and nineteenth centuries, ranged from Van Eyck's *Annunciation* (plate 2) to Botticelli's *Adoration of the Magi* (plate 3), Raphael's *Saint George and the Dragon* (plate 4) and *Alba Madonna*, and Titian's *Venus with a Mirror* as well as five Rembrandts, including *Joseph Accused by Potiphar's Wife*, four Van Dycks, including *Isabella Brant* and *Susan Fourment and Her Daughter*, a Perugino, and a Veronese.[45]

The intrigue over the Hermitage sales had an international cast worthy of an Alfred Hitchcock thriller. In addition to Mellon and his trilateral agents, both Calouste Gulbenkian and Armand Hammer also bought some of the Hermitage treasures, while numerous supporting characters from half a dozen countries became involved, including Joseph Duveen. The Duveen Archives sheds light on some of the schemes this ambitious salesman pursued in trying to seize control of this historic exchange of large sums of hard currency for essentially priceless works of art. His spy network had uncovered Mellon's negotiations with the Soviets through his archrival, Knoedler's, and in September 1930 Duveen went to extraordinary lengths to try to cut Knoedler's out of the deal.[46] He even traveled to Leningrad himself, but in the end he failed to secure any serious part of the action.[47]

In the words of John Walker, a later director of the National Gallery, "Mr. Mellon's acquisitions from the Soviet Union will always rank among the greatest transactions in the history of collecting."[48] The coup was a crucial step toward Mellon's founding of the National Gallery of Art.[49] But before that came to pass, the masterpieces found a temporary home in an unused room at the Corcoran Gallery of Art, where Mellon and Finley went to see the paintings once a month. These visits were private, and Mellon did not announce the acquisitions, intending the public's first viewing to take place in the National Gallery he was planning to build.

Mellon did miss a number of opportunities. In 1928 a famous painting by Johannes Vermeer, *The Artist in His Studio*, came to his attention, and he asked David Finley to negotiate with the art dealer in Vienna who represented the owners, the Counts Czernin.[50] For several months a succession of cables and letters crossed the Atlantic, as noted

PLATE 5   Francisco de Goya, *The Marquesa de Pontejos*, c. 1786.
National Gallery of Art, Andrew W. Mellon Collection,
1937.1.85

in Mellon's diary entries about what he called the "Vienna Vameer." Ultimately, however, the dealer proved unreliable, and the owners held out for more money than Mellon was willing to pay. The painting fell into Hitler's own hands after the Nazi seizure of Austria, and since 1946 it has been the sole Vermeer in the collection of the Vienna Kunsthistorisches Museum.[51]

Reflecting on Andrew Mellon's successes as an art collector, David Finley observed: "To many people the making of a great collection represents only a combination of money and luck. These elements are usually necessary, but there is far more to it than that. To make a really great collection, the collector must have taste, the ability to recognize quality, and perseverance in getting the best works of art obtainable in his field or period. . . . Mr. Mellon had some lucky breaks, but he also had the determination to take advantage of opportunities as they arose."[52] As an example he cited Mellon's purchase of Goya's full-length portrait *The Marquesa de Pontejos* (plate 5) in 1931—which also illustrates Finley's growing influence. The wife of a diplomat at the American embassy in Madrid contacted Finley concerning Mellon's possible interest in a major painting by Goya. She telephoned him from Spain to say that the canvas was available at a certain price. Finley went to the Library of Congress for an illustrated book on Goya's work, which he showed to Mellon, "who was delighted with the Marquesa." But the family that owned the painting was about to leave Madrid for Paris because of the unsettled political situation in Spain. Finley placed a long-distance call from Mellon's office to the diplomat's wife, saying that Mellon wanted the work if could be had for his price.[53] The deal was done, and David Finley said that Andrew Mellon was always greatly amused at having bought an important painting over the telephone.[54]

* * *

In May 1929 Mellon returned to Washington from New Haven, where he had been visiting his son, Paul, who had his heart set on attending Cambridge University after graduating from Yale (fig. 19). Andrew Mellon told Finley that he wanted his son to return to Pittsburgh and go into the family businesses but that Paul's persistence reminded him of the time when his own parents had taken him Christmas shopping when he was

19. Paul and Andrew Mellon aboard a ship crossing the Atlantic, 1927. Paul Mellon and David Finley shared a lifelong commitment to both the National Gallery of Art and the National Trust for Historic Preservation.

four or five years old and he had wanted a drum; his parents tried to direct him to less noisy things but, he confided to Finley, "I said yes, I liked them, but I wanted that drum, and I got it!"[55] And in the end, Paul Mellon got Cambridge instead of Pittsburgh.

When Finley asked Mellon why he had never sat for John Singer Sargent, the premier portraitist of his day, Mellon replied with what seemed to Finley "a really tragic story" about having had an appointment for a sitting with Sargent in London about 1904, when he was in the prime of life, which he had to break for some reason. When he returned to London the following year, he had tried to arrange another sitting, but Sargent adamantly refused, saying he would "go to jail first." Then in 1921 or 1922, when he had just become secretary of the treasury, Mellon met Sargent on the North Shore of Long Island. Sargent agreed to paint Mellon then, "to make amends," but died before the sitting could be arranged.[56]

In the spring of 1929 Andrew Mellon sat several times for a portrait by the English artist Douglas Chandos, who had come to Washington to paint the members of Hoover's cabinet for *Time* magazine. Finley helped entertain Chandos and find him suitable lodgings and a studio in Washington. But Mellon was disappointed with the portrait, and Finley thought that the artist had tried too hard to please the sitter rather than follow his own conception: "But frankly, I do not believe Chandos would ever have caught that queer, half wistful, half calculating expression that comes & goes & makes Mr. M. such a complicated person to understand on short acquaintance."[57]

NOTES

1. Thomas Mellon, *Thomas Mellon and His Times*, 2nd ed. (Pittsburgh, 1885). With major support from the Mellon family in America, the old Mellon homestead near Omagh, County Tyrone, has been restored as part of the Ulster-American Folk Park, which vividly portrays the Scots-Irish story on both sides of the Atlantic.

2. Thomas Mellon (1813–1908) encouraged his sons to start their own businesses, and the family enterprises soon included real estate, lumber, coal, and railroads. "A. W.," as Andrew Mellon was known to his family, did well at Western University (now the University of Pittsburgh) but left shortly before graduation in 1873 to work full-time.

3. Paul Mellon candidly detailed this painful story in his memoirs, *Reflections in a Silver Spoon* (New York, 1992).

4. S. N. Behrman, *Duveen* (New York, 1952), 274.

5. In the words of Coolidge's best-known biographer, "so completely did Andrew Mellon dominate the White House in the days when the Coolidge Administration was at its zenith that it would be fair to call the administration the reign of Coolidge and Mellon." See William Allen White, *A Puritan in Babylon* (New York, 1938), 251.

6. Mellon even offered Coolidge the presidency of one of the Mellon businesses after Coolidge left the White House, but the former President was not interested and retired to Northampton, Massachusetts, where he wrote his 1929 autobiography and occasional articles on public issues.

7. See Andrew W. Mellon diary, 8 January, 21 February, 6 March, and 12 November 1929; and Finley journal, 9 March 1929. NGA Archives.

8. Finley journal, 10 March 1929.

9. Finley journal, 30 January 1922: "Harding beamed continuously his foolish, meaningless smile & when the band, by request, played Mrs. Harding's favorite 'The End of a Perfect Day,' the First Lady stood with her white-gloved hand resting on the President's & smiled domestically into the Presidential eyes. Main Street has certainly come to the White House!"

10. In the 1950s Hoover agreed to serve on Finley's board of trustees for the National Trust for Historic Preservation.

11. Henry Clay Frick (1849–1919) was six years Mellon's senior and a wealthy client of the Mellon Bank. As Finley recalled: "Either then or on a later trip, [Mellon] brought home a painting for which he had paid a thousand dollars. He never identified the painting to me, but I understood it had disappeared from the Mellon Collection long before its owner came to Washington. Mr. Mellon told me his father's friends were rather horrified that he, Andrew Mellon, a young man of sense and judgment, should have paid so much money for a painting." Finley, *Standard of Excellence*, 9.

12. Not only did Finley work with Mellon at 1785 Massachusetts Avenue on his ambitious plans to establish the National Gallery of Art, but he later served as founding chairman of the National Trust for Historic Preservation, which purchased the building from the Brookings Institution in 1977, undertook extensive restorations, and opened

it as the Trust's national headquarters in 1979. The building had provided office space for the British government and others during the Second World War, then subsequently for the Brookings Institution.

13. Joseph Duveen (1869–1939) was born in England into a family of Dutch Jewish émigrés who made a fortune in selling paintings, china, furniture, and antiques to wealthy patrons in England, Europe, and America.

14. Behrman, *Duveen*, 3.

15. Bernard Berenson (1865–1959), the American connoisseur who lived in Italy for most of his life, was the foremost authority on Italian Renaissance paintings.

16. John Walker, *Self-Portrait with Donors* (Boston, 1974), 103, says Frick introduced Mellon and Duveen in 1919. Colin Simpson, *Artful Partners: Bernard Berenson and Joseph Duveen* (New York, 1986), 226, places the meeting in 1913. Simpson also says that Duveen had redecorated Mellon's Pittsburgh home in 1918 and that Mellon and Duveen went to California together in 1919 and toured the Huntington Collection. Duveen's records confirm that Mellon had bought from Duveen in 1918. Behrman's story of how Duveen cunningly stalked Mellon until he cornered him in an elevator at Claridge's in London in 1921 is good theater but dubious history. See Behrman, *Duveen*, 253; and Meryle Secrest, *Duveen: A Life in Art* (New York, 2004), 299–300.

17. Mellon liked to invite comments on his paintings from friends and visitors; overheard by Flore and duly relayed to Duveen, these drew particular interest, for Mellon could and often did return to Duveen a painting worth half a million dollars within his option period. Copies of these reports abound in the Mellon account files in the Duveen Records at the Getty Research Institute in Los Angeles and on microfilm at the Metropolitan Museum of Art in New York.

18. Kenneth Clark, *Another Part of the Wood: A Self-Portrait* (London, 1974), 227.

19. Walker, *Self-Portrait with Donors*, 99.

20. Andrew Mellon had three undersecretaries at the Treasury between 1921 and 1932. The first was S. Parker Gilbert (1892–1938), whose career is noted in Chapter 2. He was succeeded by Garrard B. Winston (1882–1955), a Chicago lawyer who served from 1923 to 1927 before leaving to join the Wall Street law firm of Shearman & Sterling. Winston was succeeded by Ogden Mills (1884–1937), a wealthy New York politician who had been defeated for governor by Al Smith in 1926. Mills was heir to a fortune established by his grandfather, a forty-niner who struck it rich and invested his winnings in San Francisco real estate, cattle ranching, oil, and mines. When Mellon resigned in March 1932, Mills succeeded him as secretary of the treasury. Donald D. Shepard later became David Finley's law partner, with Andrew Mellon as their primary client; Shepard was one of the first trustees of the National Gallery, resigning in 1939 but continuing as secretary-treasurer and general counsel until 1943; as chief advisor to Ailsa Mellon Bruce's Avalon Foundation, Shepard played a role in Finley's efforts to found the National Trust for Historic Preservation.

21. Blair and Finley correspondence, 1927–1931, Finley Papers, NGA Archives, box 2-10. Floyd G. Blair was a New York lawyer and banker who worked at the Trea-

sury Department from 1924 to 1927, after which he returned to New York as an officer of National City Bank. He was an usher at David Finley's wedding in 1931 and later became a director and president of the New York Philharmonic.

22. "Conversation between Mr. Burton Hendrick and Mr. David E. Finley," week of 12 October 1942, transcript. Finley Papers, NGA Archives, box 28-1. Burton J. Hendrick (1870–1949) wrote more than thirty books on history and biography, including the lives of Andrew Carnegie, Jefferson Davis, and the Lees of Virginia. In 1940 Paul Mellon, with David Finley's help, hired Hendrick to write a biography of Andrew Mellon. Hendrick completed the manuscript by the end of the Second World War, but it was never published.

23. Andrew W. Mellon to Helen Hamilton Woods, 18 January 1923. Finley Papers, Library of Congress. In 1936 Mellon did buy George Romney's *Mrs. Thomas Scott Jackson* from Mrs. Woods's mother, Juliette Morgan (Mrs. William) Hamilton.

24. Mellon correspondence, 1921–1932. Finley Papers, Library of Congress, box 16.

25. See Finley, *Standard of Excellence*, 8–9; and Behrman, *Duveen*, 254–260. Finley's remarks about Mellon's alleged shyness may have been meant to correct Behrman's account. Behrman, a successful playwright, portrayed Mellon as the "Apostle of Silence," who conversed with Calvin Coolidge "almost entirely in pauses." But Behrman never knew Mellon and never interviewed Finley, who was still director of the National Gallery when Behrman was writing. Unfortunately, later authors have tended to follow Behrman, the dramatist, rather than Finley, the colleague and eyewitness (e.g., Secrest, *Duveen*).

26. Finley journal, 21 April 1929.

27. Finley, *Standard of Excellence*, 13–14.

28. Finley, *Standard of Excellence*, 14.

29. The French Mellons may have been distant relations, for a number of Irish, Scots, and English families settled in Bordeaux and entered the wine trade in the eighteenth century.

30. Finley, *Standard of Excellence*, 14.

31. Finley journal, 13 March 1929. In stark contrast to today's corporate practices, General Electric refused to take any public credit for the film on the grounds that its sponsorship might be misinterpreted.

32. Finley journal, 9 April 1929.

33. *Time* (6 May 1929), 9–10.

34. Finley journal, 26 April and 1 May 1929. Although GE had funded the entire production of the film, there had been additional expenses for promotion, special screenings, and the like.

35. Finley, *Standard of Excellence*, 12.

36. W. R. Valentine (director of the Detroit Institute of Arts) to Andrew W. Mellon, 2 March 1926, with a referral from Joseph Duveen. Finley Papers, Library of Congress, box 16.

37. David Finley to Andrew Mellon, 12 February 1929. Finley Papers, Library of Congress, box 16. Venturi thought that the *Virgin and Child* by Filippo Lippi was beautiful and decorative but more likely by the School of Filippo Lippi. It had been considerably restored—the Virgin's left eye and chin had been repainted, as had the Child's mouth, as evidenced by the different quality of pigment used.

38. *Washington Times,* 9 November 1927.

39. For example, Messmore came to lunch on 19 March 1928, and they discussed the "Petworth Rembrandt" as well as paintings by Holbein, Fragonard, and Gainsborough. Duveen came to lunch the next day. Then on 12 April, in New York, Mellon conferred—separately, of course—with both Messmore and Duveen. Andrew W. Mellon diary, 19 and 20 March 1928.

40. Painted by Raphael in 1508 and owned by descendants of the Earl Cowper of Panshanger. See NGA Web site, www.nga.gov; and John Walker, *National Gallery of Art, Washington,* rev. ed. (New York, 1984), 176. Mellon's diary makes several references to this painting in April 1928.

41. Finley, *Standard of Excellence,* 19.

42. In 1926 Mellon purchased Raphael's portrait of Giuliano de' Medici from Duveen, but he returned it a year later. In 1927 he bought a Titian but also returned it the next year. (Mellon's standing arrangement with Duveen allowed him to return a painting for full credit, for any reason, within certain periods of time, usually two years.) In April 1928 Mellon finally acquired the first Italian painting from Duveen that he kept: Bernardino Luini's *Portrait of a Lady.* Purchased 25 April 1928 for $290,000. List, Duveen Brothers to Price Waterhouse, 16 November 1937, Duveen Records, reel 344, folder 4.

43. Finley, *Standard of Excellence,* 22–23.

44. Walker, *Self-Portrait with Donors,* 119.

45. Walker, *Self-Portrait with Donors,* 115, 119. Walker details many facets of the Hermitage story, but the following incident gives a sense of the awkwardness: when Charles Henschel of Knoedler's went to Leningrad and offered a cigarette to one of the Hermitage officials, it was refused unless Henschel was prepared to give a cigarette to every employee at the museum, including guards and laborers.

46. Duveen sent his henchman Bertram Boggis to Washington; Mellon's man Flore (also in Duveen's employ) admitted him to Mellon's apartment, where he "had a look around"; Boggis pumped Mellon's secretary at the Treasury Department for information (after finding him somewhat inebriated), and he managed to convey a message to Secretary Mellon that Duveen was also bidding on the Hermitage paintings. Boggis to Duveen, 17 September 1930, Duveen Brothers Records, Mellon files.

47. Simpson, *Artful Partners,* 225, says that Duveen backed away from the Hermitage deal because he did not want it to become known that he was dealing with the Bolsheviks, but he had a secret agreement with Knoedler's for a percentage of the price "which is preserved in the Metropolitan archives." Duveen's most recent biographer, Meryle Secrest, makes no mention of this agreement.

48. Walker, *National Gallery of Art*, 30.

49. Another step had been the creation in 1930 of the A. W. Mellon Educational and Charitable Trust—following the advice of his lawyer Donald D. Shepard, another former member of his Treasury staff—to which he systematically began to donate his paintings in 1931. Mellon ultimately took charitable deductions from his income tax for the value of these gifts, as permitted by law. These deductions became the center of a legal storm that broke over Mellon three years later.

50. More than a dozen Mellon diary entries between August 1928 and February 1929 indicate that Mellon had delegated to Finley the responsibility for negotiations on the Vermeer, conducted in Finley's own name. Finley worked through a Mrs. Creelman and a Mrs. Klugler in New York, and the latter went to Vienna to negotiate with the owners.

51. See James S. Plaut, "Hitler's Capital," *Atlantic Monthly* (October 1946). See also Lynn H. Nicholas, *The Rape of Europa* (New York, 1994), 47–49.

52. Finley, *Standard of Excellence*, 21.

53. Mellon purchased the painting in July 1931 for $212,700. See H. W. Johnson of the A. W. Mellon Educational and Charitable Trust, Pittsburgh, to David E. Finley, 13 June 1939. Finley Papers, Library of Congress, correspondence.

54. Finley, *Standard of Excellence*, 22.

55. Finley journal, 13 May 1929.

56. Finley journal, 25 June 1929.

57. Finley journal, 11 June 1929.

20. *Margaret Eustis Finley*, portrait by Philip Alexius de Laszlo, 1932,
hanging in her family home, Oatlands House, Virginia

4

Marriage to Margaret Eustis

1931

AS BUSY AS ANDREW MELLON KEPT HIM, David Finley found time for an active personal life, enjoying a whirlwind of social engagements detailed in his journals. At the Treasury Department, he earned an annual salary of $5,000, which was sufficient in those years to rent a nice house with a full-time cook/housekeeper so that he could entertain as well as provide a home base for visiting family members. Finley described "a most fascinating little 2½ story red brick house at 1911 I Street. It is almost 75 years old, with black marble mantels, open fires, 2 baths, hot air heat, 2 drawing rooms, dining room on the first floor and fine bedrooms on the second floor." All for $75 a month.[1] At the same time, he was swept up in the round of formal and informal entertaining that revolved around the diplomatic corps and a number of well-to-do families. He made new friends easily among both sexes and all ages. Life in Washington then, for those who had the access, energy, and means—and Finley now had all three—brought an endless round of luncheons, teas, dinners, parties, and dances.

He also went back to Philadelphia to see old friends and attend formal dances at the Academy of Music. He returned to New York, where he visited Arthur and Helen Woods as well as Helen's mother, Juliette Morgan Hamilton. He even befriended Helen's grandmother, Mrs. J. P. Morgan, whom he found delightful. He was a guest of Mrs. Hamilton's both in Manhattan and at her country place in Sterlington, New York, where he admired a fine Romney portrait that hung in her dining room. The painting, *Mrs. Thomas Scott Jackson*, had come from her father, J. P. Morgan, and she confided to Finley that its insurance required the presence of a watchman at all times.[2]

Finley's official life and social life occasionally came together, as in January 1923 when a British delegation to negotiate its nation's war debt arrived in Washington to meet with Secretary Mellon. Finley went to a reception at the British embassy for the Right Honorable Stanley Baldwin, chancellor of the exchequer, and Montague C. Norman, governor of the Bank of England. Finley and several friends were invited to escort Baldwin's daughter Betty to a dance at the Willard Hotel. When one of the friends, Walter Boyd, told her he planned to visit England that summer, she said he must come and see her, and when he asked where, she replied, "O! 11 Downing Street."[3]

Three weeks later, in February 1923, Finley went to New York for a grand dinner and dance at the Cornelius Vanderbilt mansion at 640 Fifth Avenue—"a marvelous house in perfect taste." A large contingent from Washington took the train up for the event, including General John J. Pershing, Parker Gilbert (then Finley's boss at the Treasury), Ailsa Mellon, and a number of foreign diplomats. Seating for dinner in the picture gallery, the state dining room, and the family dining room accommodated 280 guests, and another 200 joined the party for dancing afterward in the ballroom. Even though he was not feeling well, Finley chatted with the Vanderbilts, danced with all the Washington ladies and many from New York, and stayed until 3:30 a.m.[4]

In April 1924 he attended another Vanderbilt event: the wedding of Cornelia Stuyvesant Vanderbilt of Washington to the Honorable John Francis Amherst Cecil of the British embassy at her family's baronial estate, Biltmore, near Asheville, North Carolina. This union followed the tradition of wedding American wealth with British nobility, as

Cornelia was a granddaughter of Commodore Vanderbilt and would inherit the Biltmore estate, while Cecil was the son of Lord William Cecil and Baroness Amherst, and the grandson of the marquis of Exeter.[5] The *New York Times* breathlessly published details of the wedding, emphasizing the prominence of the couple. A Washington newspaper reported: "Winant Johnson, John Purdy, Foxhall Daingerfield, and David Edward Finley left Washington last evening for Biltmore, N.C., to attend the marriage tomorrow of Miss Cornelia Vanderbilt to the Hon. J. F. A. Cecil."

Later in 1924 Finley made his first trip to Europe, sailing from New York for Liverpool on 2 August aboard the RMS *Adriatic* and returning in early September on the *Olympic*. Accompanied by his friend Walter Boyd and Boyd's father from Boston, he traveled in the grand manner, reading in deck chairs during the day, dressing in "dinner coats" for the evening meal, and playing bridge after dinner. In London he stayed with his friend G. B. Ceccato in fashionable Mayfair and paid a call on Andrew W. Mellon, his "chief," who was staying at Claridge's: "Mr. Mellon seemed pleased to see me & we talked about London & art & various things. He said that a number of people had spoken to him about the book [*Taxation: The People's Business*]. Mr. MacDonald had told him of several references to it made in the course of debates on taxation in the House of Commons. Mr. Mellon is very pleased about that book."[6]

Finley made the time-honored rounds of the principal monuments and took particular interest in fine old buildings such as a little Norman church beside the Tower of London, St. Paul's Cathedral, Westminster Abbey, Eton College, Christ Church at Oxford, and Canterbury Cathedral, whose towers he thought "the most beautiful thing I have seen in England." Before he left London, he saw Andrew Mellon again: "that old gentleman from the Treasury had come up from the country to see me & very amiably wandered around with me. He begged that I do not miss the Wallace Collection so we went and spent an hour at Hertford House & I was very glad, for it contains a marvelous array of pictures, gold clocks, china, miniatures, etc."[7]

After just one night and day in Paris, where he was shown the major sights on a motor tour by the author Richard Eaton and attended a

Russian Orthodox church service, he took the Orient Express to Venice. As soon as his train emerged from the Simplon Tunnel, he was dazzled by the sun-drenched Italian countryside. He became enthralled not only by the scenery but by the people, the food, the wine, the buildings, and especially the art. After two days in Venice he went to Florence. He had obviously read up on what he wanted to see, and he visited churches, galleries, and historic palazzos voraciously.

> [At the Uffizi Palace] where I spent 2 bewildering hours, the paintings are marvelous—especially the early Italian ones by Cimabue & Giotto with their gorgeous coloring of red and gold. It is in color, rather than line, that Florentine art is most distinguished, it seems to me. I saw the Madonnas of Andrea del Sarto, Correggio, Raphael (of the Gold-finch, my favorite), Lippi & Ghirlandaio's Adoration of the Shepherds & also the same subject by Gherardo delle Notti.
>
> Next day at the Pitti I saw in one room those two incomparable Madonnas by Raphael—the Seanduca [?] & the Madonna of the Chair; Murillo's Madonna; del Sarto's John the Baptist; Sodoma's San Sebastian (the beautiful martyred youth seems to rival David as a favorite subject for paintings); Perugino's Adoration of the Bambino; & del Sarto's Annunciation. There are also a bewildering array of Greek statues, the Medici Venus, the Augustus, Canova's Venus, etc. & tapestries everywhere I went thru the Pitti. . . . it was too much to combine with the Uffizi.[8]

Having discovered the joys of European travel, Finley crossed the Atlantic almost every summer for the next dozen years. In late August 1925 he took the British liner *Arabic* to Cherbourg, visiting Mont-Saint-Michel and Normandy en route to Paris. He stayed again at the Hotel Lotti, spent three hours at the Louvre, and paid a visit to Notre Dame Cathedral, which impressed him deeply. While in Paris, he conferred with Theodore Rousseau of the Guaranty Bank about Ailsa Mellon's car.

Another wedding of greater note to Finley than the Vanderbilt-Cecil union took place in May 1926, when Andrew Mellon's daughter

Ailsa married David Kirkpatrick Este Bruce, son of a United States senator from Maryland. Finley organized the seating for the ceremony in the Bethlehem Chapel of the Washington National Cathedral, which was attended by President and Mrs. Coolidge and the justices of the Supreme Court and was followed by a reception for two thousand guests at the Pan American Union Building. David Bruce, who grew very close to his father-in-law, also became a lifelong colleague of David Finley's. Bruce pursued a career in law and business, then served in important positions at the National Gallery of Art and as a colonel in the Office of Strategic Services (OSS) in London during the Second World War. He went on to a brilliant diplomatic career as an ambassador to France, West Germany, Great Britain, and NATO.[9]

The Finley-Eustis Marriage

Although Finley's journals mention many young women, he did not single anyone out for real attention until Margaret Morton Eustis. He first mentioned her in December 1922: "I had an engagement to go to a tea Miss Eustis, daughter of Mrs. Wm. Corcoran Eustis, was giving in that large house on Rhode Island Ave. built by Mrs. Eustis' father, Mr. Levi P. Morton. They sold their beautiful old W. W. Corcoran House on H Street which has now been demolished to make way for a Grecian temple, which will house the U.S. Chamber of Commerce. The onward rush of progress is sometimes rather devastating."[10] After the tea he went to dinner with Margaret Eustis and his friend Foxhall Daingerfield at the home of President Wilson's physician, Rear Admiral Cary Grayson, and his wife: "After dinner we saw the marvelous collection of autographed photographs in Admiral Grayson's library. He has pictures of the Wilsons with the British and Belgian royalties, etc. & a little book containing the photographs & autographs of every member of the Versailles Peace Conference. It was lying on the library table & I told him I would leave my liquor out & put that book in the vault."[11] Finley's journals mention Margaret Eustis numerous times, but only in a casual way among other friends and acquaintances in his busy social life. Then in February 1923 he described seeing her at a party: "I had a long talk with Margie Eustis, whom I like best of any girl I have met here. She has a wonderful high bred face & a real intelligence & is very attractive besides."[12] The two shared a strong interest in art and architecture; indeed, Margaret was an accomplished amateur sculptor.

Margaret Morton Eustis (see fig. 20) belonged to one of Washington's oldest and most distinguished families. She grew up in the old Corcoran mansion on Lafayette Square and at the historic Oatlands estate south of Leesburg, Virginia. After studying at Foxcroft School and traveling in Europe, she had returned to Washington and was studying art when Finley met her. Though not a conventional beauty, she was tall and elegant, and in temperament she and David complemented one another perfectly. But Margaret Eustis had just turned nineteen, while David was thirty-two, and neither seemed in any hurry to wed. Over the next few years Finley mentions seeing "Margie" on many occasions, both in the Washington area and in New York, as well as once in 1925 at the Savoy Hotel in London for tea, but they waited until 1931 to marry.

Finley's expansive journal entries stop in late 1929, and no letters between Margaret and David have been found from that period, so their courtship cannot be traced in any detail. But their wedding, which took place at Oatlands on 10 June 1931, made news in Washington and New York (fig. 21). One chronicle described it as:

> the social event [that] seemed to tie together the Cave Dwellers and the Mellonites of the Hoover administration, and both Washington and Aiken—possibly Democrats and Republicans. . . . Finley got on the same public service escalator on which [Eugene] Meyer had risen. He, at forty, was almost as fragile and wispy looking as Secretary Mellon and became closer to him than Meyer. . . . Briefly, he was a subordinate of Meyer's in the War Finance Corporation under Harding. By 1927, however, he had become special assistant to Mellon. Also (Meyer still was not), he was listed in the *Social Register.* Nothing indicated his social place better than his marriage to a Eustis.[13]

The wedding was relatively simple, given the prominence of the bride's family. It was celebrated in the octagonal drawing room of the Oatlands mansion by an Episcopal priest in the presence of the bride's and groom's families and a few close friends. Margaret wore a traditional white chiffon gown with a veil of old lace that her mother had worn at

21. Announcement of Margaret
Eustis's engagement to David
Finley, *New York Times*, 2 June
1931

New York Times – Tuesday, June 2, 1931

from D. P. Coulter

SOCIAL NEWS   THE NEW YORK TIMES,

**MARGARET EUSTIS
TO WED D. E. FINLEY**

Her Troth Announced by Her
Mother, Mrs. William Corcoran
Eustis of Washington.

A MEMBER OF COLONY CLUB

She Is Granddaughter of Late Levi
P. Morton—Her Fiance Is Assistant to Secretary Mellon.

Mrs. William Corcoran Eustis of
Washington, D. C., has announced to
her relatives and friends here the
engagement of her daughter, Miss
Margaret Morton Eustis, to David
Edward Finley of York, S. C., and
Washington, D. C., special assistant
to Secretary of the Treasury Andrew
W. Mellon. The engagement is of
wide interest here, for Miss Eustis
has many relatives in New York.
She is a granddaughter of the late
Levi P. Morton, Vice President in
the administration of President Benjamin Harrison and Governor of New
York in 1894, and the late Mrs. Morton, who was Miss Anna Street. She
also is a granddaughter of the late
George Eustis, member of Congress
from Louisiana before the Civil War,
and a great-granddaughter of the
late W. W. Corcoran, philanthropist
of Washington, D. C., who built and
endowed the Corcoran Gallery of Art
in the national capital. She is a niece
of Mrs. Thomas Hitchcock of West-
bury, L. I., and Aiken, S. C. Her
father, William Corcoran Eustis, died
several years ago. Miss Eustis was
graduated from Foxcroft School and
is a member of the Junior League
and the Colony Club of New York.
Mr. Finley is the son of Mrs. David E. Finley of York, and the
late Mr. Finley, who for many years
was a member of Congress. His
mother is a member of the Gist family of South Carolina and Maryland
that has been prominent in those
States since Colonial days. He attended the University of South Carolina and the George Washington
University Law School. He practiced
law in Philadelphia and now is at
the Treasury Department as special
assistant of Mr. Mellon. He is a
member of the Metropolitan Club of
Washington, D. C.
The marriage will take place shortly at Oatlands House, Oatlands, Va.

Photo by Harris & Ewing.
MISS MARGARET MORTON EUSTIS.

her own wedding. Margaret's youngest sister, Anne, just sixteen, was
her only attendant, and her brother Morton "gave away" the bride.
David's best man was his brother Gist, and the eight ushers included his
brother States and friends from Washington and New York, including a
British and a Belgian diplomat, all wearing formal cutaways. The afternoon reception was held on the lawn at Oatlands, with a string orchestra
and family retainers passing champagne and canapés.[14] Two days later
the newlyweds sailed for Europe for a two-month tour of England and
the Continent.

Their honeymoon was interrupted by a telegram from Andrew
Mellon, summoning Finley to join him in Paris and London with secretary of state Henry Stimson in early July for a week of consultations
with the British foreign office on a German financial crisis: "I remember
one of the German delegates saying in an impassioned voice that if we

22. David Finley at Ragusa (now Dubrovnik), photograph taken
by Margaret Finley, August 1931, during their wedding trip

didn't help Germany, the German people would turn to Hitler. . . . A moratorium on reparations was approved, and Germany was given time to get her finances in order so that reparations and debt payments might be resumed. But it was all to no purpose, and we finally got Hitler and the chaos that followed World War II."[15] With the crisis abated for a time, Mr. and Mrs. Finley resumed their wedding trip, continuing on to Italy, the Dalmatian Coast (fig. 22), and the classical sites of Greece before returning home.

The Eustis Family

David Finley married into a formidable family. A lesser man might have been daunted, but not he. Margaret Eustis's family stood at the top of old Washington society at a time when "society" was paramount. By comparison, the Mellons were almost nouveaux riches. The Eustis roots in Washington went back to the beginning of the nineteenth century (see page 92), when William Eustis of Boston served as secretary of war under both Presidents Thomas Jefferson and James Madison before and during the War of 1812.[16] William's nephew George Eustis settled in New Orleans, where he became chief justice of Louisiana. George Eustis Jr. graduated from Harvard Law School and won election to Congress from Louisiana in 1855. In 1858 the younger George Eustis married Louise Morris Corcoran (figs. 23, 24), the only child of William Wilson Corcoran and Louise Amory Morris. Corcoran, who was a banker, philanthropist, and the richest man in Washington, was Margaret Eustis's great-grandfather.

Margaret's grandfather, George Eustis Jr., joined the Confederate cause when the Civil War broke out. He was sent to Paris as part of a delegation seeking recognition from France,[17] while former senator James M. Mason of Virginia headed to London on a similar mission. They managed to reach Havana and boarded the British steamer *Trent*, but on 9 November 1861 a Union warship stopped the *Trent* on the high seas, arrested the Confederate diplomats, and imprisoned them at Fort Warren near Boston. Outraged over the violation of its neutrality, Great Britain threatened war, and President Lincoln, deciding that "one war at a time is enough," ordered the Southerners released in January 1862.[18] Eustis proceeded to Paris and Mason to London, but they

Eustis Family

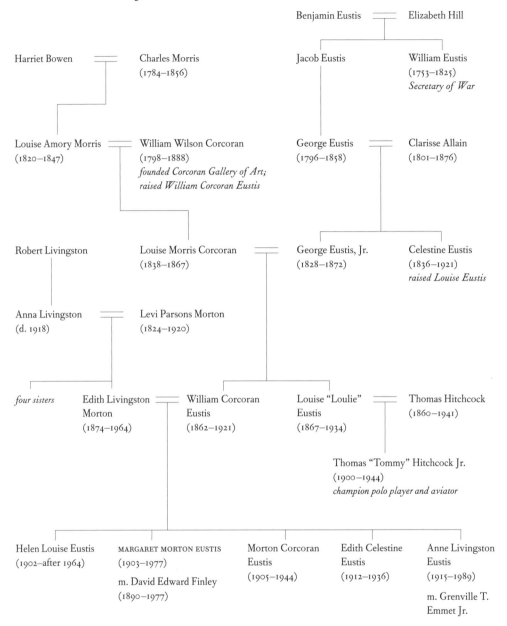

Principal Source
Warner Eustis, "The Eustis Families in the United States
from 1657 to 1968," Newton, MA, 1968, updated 1970.

23 and 24. Margaret Eustis's grandparents, Louise Corcoran Eustis and George Eustis Jr., portraits by Aldobrando Capetti, 1860. Oatlands House

failed to win recognition for the Confederacy. Eustis chose to remain in France, where his wife joined him, along with her father, William Corcoran, an outspoken Southern sympathizer. They all lived together at Villa Louisiana near Cannes.

Margaret's father, William Corcoran Eustis (fig. 25), was born in Paris in July 1862 and lived in France until his parents both died—his mother in 1867, and his father in 1872. He then moved to Washington and lived at Corcoran House on Lafayette Square with his grand-father, William Wilson Corcoran, who had returned home after the war with his Confederate fallacies forgiven and his fortune largely intact. Corcoran lived into his ninetieth year as one of the city's most beloved citizens, noted for his many charitable works, including the founding of the Corcoran Gallery of Art.[19] At Corcoran House, built in 1819, William Eustis had very distinguished neighbors, with Decatur House diagonally across the corner to the southwest and the John Hay and Henry Adams houses to the east—Hay being Abraham Lincoln's

25. Margaret's father, William Corcoran Eustis, portrait by Bradford Johnson, c. 1918. Oatlands House

wartime secretary and subsequent biographer, who later became secretary of state; and Adams being an author, historian, and both grandson and great-grandson of American Presidents. St. John's Episcopal Church stood along Lafayette Square just to the east of the Corcoran, Hay, and Adams houses (see fig. 61).

William Eustis graduated from the University of Virginia and Harvard Law School, but he did not practice law for long. When his grandfather died in 1888, he inherited a fortune as well as Corcoran House, where he lived for the next thirty years. Apart from a brief stint as secretary of the American Legation in London in 1901–1902, he was content to live the life of a gentleman of means. His younger sister, Louise, or "Loulie"—who had been raised by their aunt Celestine Eustis of New Orleans and Aiken, South Carolina—married Thomas Hitchcock, a Long Island banker and polo player, whom she had met in Aiken. Thomas Hitchcock had captained the first American international polo team in 1886. In the 1890s he and William Eustis were teammates on a championship team in Aiken.[20] Loulie was also a famous horsewoman and founded a school that produced many champion polo players, including their son, Thomas, better known as "Tommy."[21] Both father and son served in the First World War—as "the youngest and oldest aviators in the service of any country"—and between the wars Tommy Hitchcock "became perhaps the leading polo player in the world."[22] Tommy married Margaret Mellon, the daughter of Andrew

Mellon's nephew, William Mellon of Pittsburgh.

In 1900 William Eustis married Edith Livingston Morton (fig. 26), who came from a similarly illustrious lineage. Her father, Levi P. Morton, had risen to a successful banking career on Wall Street from modest origins as the son of a New England parson, while her mother, Anna Livingston, was a descendant of the great colonial landowner Robert Livingston of Rhinebeck, New York.[23] Edith had enjoyed a privileged youth, growing up with her four handsome and spirited sisters in the family townhouse at 681 Fifth Avenue in Manhattan, which had its own ballroom;[24] at their country estate Ellersie on the Hudson, near Rhinebeck; and in Paris, where her father served as minister from 1881 to 1885. Levi Morton entered Republican politics and won a seat in Congress, then

26. Margaret's mother, Edith Livingston Morton Eustis, portrait by Charles A. E. "Carolus" Duran, c. 1898. Oatlands House

served as vice president of the United States under President Benjamin Harrison from 1889 to 1893 and as governor of New York from 1895 to 1897. When he came to Washington as vice president, he purchased a townhouse on Rhode Island Avenue near Scott Circle. Edith had been a New York debutante in the golden age of such events and had been a bridesmaid for Consuelo Vanderbilt at her marriage in 1895 to the ninth duke of Marlborough.

Edith Morton's wedding to William Eustis took place on 30 April 1900 at Grace Church, New York, with an Episcopal bishop officiating. A "breakfast" at the Morton residence followed, with such guests as former President and Mrs. Benjamin Harrison, John Jacob Astor,

Mr. and Mrs. James Roosevelt (Franklin Roosevelt's parents), and Mr. and Mrs. Stanford White. As Edith settled into the social life of Washington at Corcoran House, she shared amusements with her neighbor Henry Adams: "She told him about her aging father who with others of his wealth and class regarded Theodore Roosevelt as a dangerous radical. The only way to wake him from his lengthening dozes, she told Adams, was to say 'Roosevelt!' to him. Whereupon he would arouse crying, 'To think that a daughter of mine.'"[25]

Perhaps under Adams's influence, Edith Eustis wrote and published two novels, one of which received favorable, though not enthusiastic, critical reviews.[26] But literary aspirations for women were frowned on in her social circle, and Edith soon turned to the more conventional pursuits of raising a family and being a Washington hostess. The Eustises had five children: Helen Louise in 1902, Margaret Morton in 1903, Morton Corcoran in 1905, Edith Celestine in 1912, and Anne Livingston in 1915. They bought the historic Oatlands estate south of Leesburg in Loudoun County, Virginia (fig. 27), in 1901. The mansion at Oatlands, constructed in 1803 in the Greek revival style, had presided over a three-thousand-acre working plantation until the Civil War but had fallen on hard times. The grounds, barns, and stables afforded William ample scope for his horses, foxhunting, and sheep dogs, while Edith restored its beautiful gardens. These gardens comprise some two acres of stone-walled terraces descending a hillside from the front lawn. Footpaths, steps, fountains, benches, and brick walls gracefully frame boxwood hedges, overhanging trees, and extensive beds of annual and perennial flowers. Full-time gardeners were required simply to maintain the gardens, not to mention the major restoration and expansion overseen by Edith Eustis. Under her care the gardens at Oatlands could hold their own with those of many fine country houses in England or Italy. In addition to Corcoran House and Oatlands, the Eustises owned an estate in Ireland's horse country west of Dublin, where William won the County Meath Hunt Cup three times.

When the United States joined the First World War, Margaret's father, then in his mid-fifties and without previous military experience, was commissioned a captain on the staff of General John J. Pershing and sailed for France with the first American contingent in June 1917.

27. Oatlands House, gardens and grounds, Loudoun County, Virginia, the Eustis family's country estate, where Margaret and David Finley were married in 1931. Margaret Eustis Finley and her sister Anne Eustis Emmet gave Oatlands to the National Trust for Historic Preservation in 1965.

He spoke fluent French, and this, combined with his wealth and social connections, qualified him for this prestigious posting. Pershing's mess at Chaumont was said to serve the best cuisine in the U.S. Army. In 1918 assistant secretary of the navy Franklin Delano Roosevelt met Eustis in Paris and reported to the family that he was "in fine form and doing really useful work."[27]

Returning to Washington after the war, William Eustis caused consternation among his neighbors on Lafayette Square when he sold Corcoran House. The U.S. Chamber of Commerce bought the property in 1919, then demolished the historic mansion, as lamented by Finley in 1922, and replaced it with an ornate headquarters building, which still stands on the site. This marked the end of an era, for the neighboring houses of Henry Adams and John Hay soon fell to the wrecker's ball, to be replaced by the Hay-Adams Hotel.[28]

William Eustis died of pneumonia in 1921, but Edith Eustis lived until 1964, reigning among the grandest of Washington's grandes dames in the first half of the twentieth century. Indeed, Edith Eustis was a force to be reckoned with. Her social circle included the highest ranks of Washington's power elite. During the First World War, for instance, she was one of several friends of Franklin Roosevelt's to facilitate his relationship with his wife's secretary, Lucy Mercer, which Roosevelt ended after Eleanor discovered it.[29] Two years later, with Edith's blessing, Lucy married Winthrop Rutherford, the recently widowed husband of Edith's sister Alice. Edith remained close to them both, but after Winthrop suffered a debilitating stroke some years later, her friendships with Lucy Rutherford and Franklin Roosevelt would play a role in their renewed liaison during the Second World War.[30]

David Finley always got along well with women of a certain age, especially those of intelligence and refined taste, like Mrs. Eustis—as he invariably called her, even after thirty years of marriage to her daughter. Edith Eustis liked David Finley and may in fact have been the one who first encouraged Margaret's romance with the small but charming Southerner.[31] Finley always treated Mrs. Eustis with the greatest deference, and they remained close over many years.

*　*　*

David and Margaret Finley had a happy marriage and made their home in an 1870s Georgetown townhouse at 3318 O Street, N.W. They spent weekends and holidays at Little Oatlands (fig. 28), an old farmhouse atop a broad knoll on the Oatlands plantation with splendid views of the Virginia countryside, which Edith Eustis had presented them as a wedding gift. They traveled regularly to Europe on vacation, on government business, and in pursuit of Renaissance art for Andrew Mellon. Although many suffered severe privations in the midst of the Great Depression, the Finley and Eustis families seemed exempt, continuing to live very much in the grand manner of an earlier age.

The Finleys had no children, but in 1935 they assumed guardianship of Renée and Joan Beauregard, ages nine and eight, whose father, P. G. T. Beauregard—a grandson of the famous Confederate general as well as a friend and legal colleague of David Finley's—died of

28. Little Oatlands, the hilltop estate next to Oatlands House and country home of David and Margaret Finley for more than forty years

tuberculosis in 1931, followed by his wife in 1935. The Finleys did not legally adopt the girls, thinking it important that they retain their own distinguished Beauregard name. But they took these two of the four young Beauregard children into their home and raised them as their own.

NOTES

1. Finley journal, 11 February 1923.

2. Finley journal, 25 October 1921. In 1936 Juliette Morgan Hamilton sold this Romney portrait to Andrew Mellon for his National Gallery collection.

3. Finley journal, 10 January 1923. Stanley Baldwin (1867–1947) became prime minister in 1923 and served two later terms in that office. Able on domestic issues, he would be blamed for Britain's late response to a rearmed Germany in the 1930s.

4. Finley journal, 11 February 1923.

5. In 1895 Consuelo Vanderbilt, a cousin of Cornelia's, had married the ninth duke of Marlborough, of Blenheim Palace. The duke's cousin Winston Spencer Churchill was himself born of such a union, the marriage of Brooklyn heiress Jennie Jerome to Lord Randolph Churchill in 1873.

6. Finley journal, 15 August 1924. He is referring to Ramsay MacDonald (1866–1937), who in 1924 had become the first Labour prime minister of Great Britain.

7. Finley journal, 15 August 1924.

8. Finley journal, 22 August 1924.

9. See Nelson D. Lankford, *The Last American Aristocrat: The Biography of Ambassador David K. E. Bruce* (Boston, 1996). David Bruce and Ailsa were divorced in 1945, but both continued to work closely with David Finley at the National Gallery and at the National Trust for Historic Preservation.

10. Corcoran House stood on the northeast corner of H Street and Connecticut Avenue, diagonally across from Decatur House.

11. Finley journal, 7 December 1922.

12. Finley journal, 11 February 1923.

13. Jonathan Daniels, *Washington Quadrille: The Dance beside the Documents* (New York, 1968), 238–239.

14. "Smart Wedding Makes Bride of Miss Eustis: Select Company Witness Rites of Union with D. E. Finley," *Washington Post*, 11 June 1931; see also a home movie of the wedding in the Finley Papers, NGA Archives.

15. Finley, *Standard of Excellence*, 16–17.

16. William Eustis, of the Harvard class of 1772, Revolutionary War surgeon, was a Jeffersonian congressman from Boston who was defeated by John Quincy Adams. Madison appointed him minister to Holland in 1814, and he later returned to Congress before serving as governor of Massachusetts from 1823 until his death.

17. George Eustis served as secretary to John Slidell of New Orleans in this mission.

18. McPherson, *Battle Cry of Freedom*, 389–391.

19. The original Corcoran Gallery of Art, at the northeast corner of Pennsylvania Avenue and Seventeenth Street, is now the Renwick Gallery.

20. Aiken Polo Club Web site, www.aikenpolo.net, consulted on 10 March 2005.

21. Loulie Eustis Hitchcock died from a fall in her late sixties while foxhunting with the Aiken Hounds, of which she was the master.

22. Daniels, *Washington Quadrille*, 168, 317.

23. Robert Livingston, a Scottish immigrant, acquired 160,000 acres of land along the Hudson River and founded a family that was prominent in the Revolution and in the early years of the republic.

24. Edith Wharton, *A Backward Glance* (New York, 1934), 77–78.

25. *Letters of Henry Adams 1892–1918*, ed. Worthington Chauncy Ford (Boston, 1930), 489; cited in Daniels, *Washington Quadrille*, 169.

26. *Marian Manning* was "a story of politics, love and infidelity on the Washington scene," in the Edith Wharton genre. See Daniels, *Washington Quadrille*, 170.

27. *F. D. R.: His Personal Letters, 1905–1928*, ed. Elliott Roosevelt (New York, 1947), 412; cited in Daniels, *Washington Quadrille*, 172.

28. William Wilson Corcoran's papers, donated to the Library of Congress by his grandson, provide a rare record of financial, social, and political affairs in nineteenth-century Washington. Among the Corcoran Papers is a series of stiff letters exchanged in 1835 between William Wilson Corcoran and Commodore Charles Morris concerning the elopement of the sixteen-year-old Louise Amory Morris with thirty-seven-year-old Corcoran, whom Morris evidently regarded as a fortune hunter at best. Morris was a naval hero from the era of Stephen Decatur and became one of the builders of the U.S. Navy. The Morrises lived in an elegant Federal-style townhouse on N Street in Georgetown, which was left to the National Trust for Historic Preservation in the 1970s by Colonel and Mrs. William Macy. The Trust continues to hold an easement on this historic property, assuring its preservation.

29. Geoffrey C. Ward, *A First-Class Temperament: The Emergence of Franklin Roosevelt* (New York, 1989), 366: "Edith was fond of both Franklin and Lucy and dependably closed-mouthed."

30. Daniels, *Washington Quadrille*, 297–298: "Edith Eustis on occasions called the President to say, 'There is someone here you want to see.' He understood whom she meant."

31. A common impression among the Washington "cave dwellers" during the 1950s. Interview with Richard Howland, conducted by the author, December 2004.

29. David Finley with Ambassador Andrew W. Mellon and Ray Atherton at the
U.S. embassy in London, 1932

5

Realizing Mr. Mellon's Dream

1932–1937

IN MARCH 1932, at the age of seventy-seven, Andrew Mellon resigned his position as President Herbert Hoover's secretary of the treasury and accepted an appointment as American ambassador to the Court of St. James's. Mellon arranged for David Finley's assignment as counselor to the embassy (fig. 29), at the nominal government salary of a dollar per year, which allowed him to continue in federal service while Ambassador Mellon personally paid his actual compensation of $20,000 per year.[1] That was a handsome income indeed in the depths of the Depression.

Margaret and David Finley accompanied the new ambassador to London in April 1932. In keeping with his princely style, Mellon had some of his best paintings crated and shipped to the embassy residence, which, Finley observed, had "never looked the same before or since." Someone in Washington had warned Mellon "that the English might be embarrassed to find their ancestors on the walls of the American embassy, as painted by Gainsborough, Romney, Raeburn, and Lawrence." But at Mellon's suggestion, Finley consulted a friend, Sir Ronald Lindsay, then British ambassador to the United States, "who laughed heartily and said: 'The only embarrassment Mr. Mellon will suffer will be in refusing to buy more paintings of British ancestors!'"[2]

In fact, Mellon had determined not to buy any paintings while he was ambassador, believing that he would not have sufficient time to study potential acquisitions. This doubtless came as a disappointment to Joseph Duveen, who had courted Mellon since the First World War and had begun to rival Knoedler's for his favor. But Mellon would not be rushed. In the purchase of art, as in all financial decisions, he considered every aspect of a proposed transaction before making a move. He knew very well that Duveen badly wanted his patronage, and he knew from prior dealings that both the quality of Duveen's paintings and the prices he asked for them were second to none. The time would come when Mellon would make a major purchase from Duveen. But not yet.

In the meantime Duveen had begun to turn his potent charm on David Finley as well. The shrewd and charismatic businessman could see that Mellon's outgoing young associate carried real influence with his mentor. Thus in July 1931, while the Finleys were in London on their honeymoon, Duveen offered to introduce David Finley to the legendary Bernard Berenson later that summer: "if you let me know a few days before you are going to be in Florence, I might arrange for him to be there to show you his Library and Collection. Drop me a card or telegram as soon as possible at the Grand Hôtel, Vittel. Hoping the dear Lady is well. How beautiful she looked last Friday morning! Give her my kind regards."[3] This obvious flattery accompanied a savvy professional courtesy, and Finley later told a Mellon biographer, "I liked Lord Duveen. He was always extremely polite to me. I didn't socialize with anybody who wasn't polite to me."[4]

Finley knew that Duveen had a peerless inventory of paintings and sculpture, particularly of the Italian Renaissance, but he probably gained a somewhat different perspective on Duveen while in London than that accepted in the States. Duveen awed his clients in New York with the splendor of his regal headquarters at Fifth Avenue and Fifty-sixth Street and lavish entertainment at his palatial townhouse. With his urbanity and wit, he had refined his technique of making clients feel that he was conferring rare gifts of beneficence upon them, not just selling them art. Duveen met a cooler reception in England. While his manner captivated many Americans, it did not play as well with English aristocrats.

A perceptive critic was Kenneth Clark, director of the venerable National Gallery on Trafalgar Square from 1934 to 1945. Unlike Duveen—or Finley for that matter—Clark had impeccable credentials in art history. A graduate of Winchester School and Trinity College, Oxford, he spent two years as a disciple of Berenson's in Italy before becoming curator of art at the Ashmolean Museum in Oxford. He rose to the leadership of London's National Gallery at age thirty and remained at the forefront of British cultural life for the next half-century.[5] Duveen had secured a position on the National Gallery's board of trustees before Clark became director.[6]

A revealing incident occurred early in Clark's directorship, when he convinced his trustees to make an offer for a series of superb fifteenth-century Sienese paintings of the life of Saint Francis by Sassetta. The American owner, Clarence Mackay, had purchased them from Duveen but had suffered financial losses because of the Depression and might, it was thought, be willing to sell them. Letters and telegrams to Mackay brought no response, however, before Duveen casually admitted at a trustees meeting that Mackay had never seen the offer because his butler was on the Duveen payroll. It turned out that Mackay had never actually paid for the Sassettas. Thus the National Gallery bought them from Duveen at a substantially higher price than it had offered Mackay. Clark finally rectified the blatant conflict of interest in having an art dealer as a trustee when he persuaded Prime Minister Neville Chamberlain not to reappoint Duveen. The National Gallery of Art in Washington has been careful to avoid this mistake.

During Mellon's embassy in London, both Ailsa Mellon Bruce (fig. 30) and Margaret Eustis Finley (see fig. 20) were presented at court to King George V and Queen Mary, while Ambassador Mellon and Counselor Finley had almost a full year to study the British National Gallery—not only its collections but its architectural design and the interior decor of its galleries. Yet the ambassador held fast to his promise to himself not to buy any paintings. Finley did make one purchase on Mellon's behalf during this time. When David Bruce, Mellon's son-in-law, learned that a portrait of Pocahontas was available, painted after an

30. Ailsa Mellon Bruce, early 1920s. Ailsa served as her father's official hostess during his embassy in London. She was close to David Finley and supported not only the National Gallery but also the National Trust for Historic Preservation.

engraving of her done in 1616 during her visit to London and owned by an expatriate American, Francis Burton Harrison, Finley proposed a solution: "I haven't made any promises of any kind. I know Mr. Harrison. If you will put enough money in the bank in my name to pay Mr. Harrison's price, I will go and talk with him."[7] Mellon agreed, with some amusement, and Finley stepped in to purchase the painting, which now hangs in the National Portrait Gallery in Washington (see plate 32, p. 325).

Mellon on Trial

In November 1932 President Hoover lost the presidential race to Franklin Delano Roosevelt of New York. When Hoover left office in March 1933, Ambassador Mellon and the Finleys returned to America. Mellon went back to Pittsburgh but maintained his Washington apartment at 1785 Massachusetts Avenue. David Finley went into law practice in Washington in partnership with Donald D. Shepard, Mellon's principal lawyer. As Finley put it, "Don devoted himself, as before, to Mr. Mellon's legal interests in Washington, and I was concerned mostly with Mr. Mellon's plans for a National Gallery."[8]

But those plans were interrupted on 11 March 1934, when the Roosevelt administration announced its intention to seek a criminal indictment of the former secretary of the treasury for income tax evasion, alleging improper deductions for securities transactions in 1931. The government's case hinged on Mellon's 1931 sale of a block of stock at a loss to the Union Trust Company of Pittsburgh, which sold the stock a few months later to a corporation owned by Ailsa Mellon Bruce and Paul Mellon. The government claimed that the deductions taken for the loss were fraudulent. For much of the next three years, the frail and aging Andrew Mellon had to devote time and energy to defending himself against charges of tax fraud, both criminal and civil, while his work with David Finley to establish the National Gallery of Art was largely put on hold.

Franklin Roosevelt is generally regarded as one of America's greatest Presidents. Born to wealth and privilege, of blue-blooded descent from the Dutch patrons of the Hudson River Valley, he was elected governor of New York in 1928 and trounced Herbert Hoover for the U.S. presidency in 1932 at the depths of the most severe depression in American history. His drastic social, political, and economic policies, and his defiance of the nation's ills, jauntily voiced in upbeat tones over the radio—"We have nothing to fear but fear itself"—started a badly shaken nation on the long road to recovery, which was not fully achieved until the Second World War. When that conflict erupted, he skillfully nudged Congress, which reflected the largely isolationist American public opinion, into providing critical aid for Great Britain. And after Pearl Harbor, he brilliantly teamed with Winston Churchill to lead the Allied cause in finally crushing both Hitler's Germany—with a huge assist from Joseph Stalin's Soviet Russia—and the military fanatics of Japan.

Roosevelt was elected President four times, and at his death just before the end of the war he was seen as a hero throughout the free world. But as many of his biographers have pointed out, he had his share of human flaws. And notable among the low points of his administration is its prosecution of Andrew Mellon for tax fraud. A *New York Times* reporter put it plainly: "Probably the single most brazen display of the Roosevelt administration's willingness to use the tax agency for political purposes was its attack on Andrew Mellon, the millionaire capitalist who served as the Republican secretary of the treasury from 1921 to 1932."[9]

FDR and his advisors blamed the dark economic and social malaise of the Great Depression on the greed of the moneyed class, of which Mellon was then perceived as the most visible symbol. After the

Roosevelt administration took power in 1933, treasury secretary Henry Morgenthau personally ordered the Bureau of Internal Revenue to pursue a criminal investigation into Mellon's 1931 federal income tax return.[10] Morgenthau believed that Mellon had taken unfair advantage of his position as secretary of the treasury to reduce taxes on those with great wealth. He recruited Robert H. Jackson and admonished him: "You can't be too tough in this trial to suit me." Morgenthau went on to explain: "I consider that Mr. Mellon is not on trial but Democracy and the privileged rich, and I want to see who will win."[11]

Certainly Mellon had taken advantage of every lawful device to minimize his taxes, in a complex series of corporate and family transactions. He had even asked for and received a memorandum from a senior staff member at the Treasury Department detailing the various lawful means by which a taxpayer could reduce his tax burden. But the critical issue was whether he had committed fraud, which required proof of intent to break the law.

Elmer L. Irey, the head of the Treasury's intelligence unit, was a veteran of criminal probes in tax cases going back to the Wilson administration. A tough, seasoned, and very skillful investigator, he had made the case that sent Al Capone to Alcatraz when all others had failed. In his memoirs Irey said:

> The Roosevelt administration made me go after Andy Mellon. I liked Mr. Mellon and they knew it, so the F.B.I. took the first crack and got tossed out of the Grand Jury room.
>
> Bob Jackson was made chief counsel of the Internal Revenue Department, and he said to me: "I need help on that Mellon thing. The F.B.I. investigation was no good. You run one on him."
>
> [I] said to Jackson, "If I wasn't to be trusted before, why now?" Jackson's answer was "I don't know anything about that. You are qualified and I need help. I'll have to see the Secretary."
>
> In a short time [I] got a call from Henry Morgenthau Jr., Secretary of the Treasury. The Secretary said, "Irey, you can't be 99 2/3 on that job. Investigate Mellon. I order it."[12]

As ordered, Irey assigned the case to his best investigator, who worked with Jackson for months preparing for trial. The government concluded that Mellon's deductions for charitable contributions to the A. W. Mellon Educational and Charitable Trust, which Mellon had created to fund the proposed National Gallery of Art, were fictitious, partly because they had not been claimed when the original return was filed.

Roosevelt's Justice Department under Attorney General Homer S. Cummings[13] and the Treasury Department under Morgenthau decided on the surprising strategy of seeking a criminal indictment against Andrew Mellon for tax fraud. The man who spearheaded the government's case was Robert H. Jackson, a self-described "country lawyer" from the small town of Jamestown in western New York and an activist in Democratic politics in New York, where he had known Roosevelt for more than twenty years. Jackson arrived in Washington at FDR's behest in February 1934 to become general counsel to the Bureau of Internal Revenue. He immediately inherited the Mellon tax matter, which had been under investigation from the previous year.[14]

After a federal grand jury in Pittsburgh refused to indict Mellon criminally and returned a verdict of "no true bill" in May 1934, the Justice Department brought a civil action against him before the Board of Tax Appeals, seeking over $3 million dollars in additional taxes and penalties based on fraud. Jackson was not a tax lawyer and had never before tried a tax case. But he was an experienced trial lawyer and saw at once the difficulty of proving a charge of fraud against an elderly man who had led an exemplary life. Jackson recommended that the government drop the fraud count, but he was overruled by the attorney general and even the President himself. A recently published account of Jackson's private views of FDR makes this clear.[15]

> I recommended that fraud not be charged and no fraud penalty be assessed. I later learned that, had this course been followed, the taxes would have been paid. I recommended this not because I was convinced on the merits of the matter, but as a matter of trial strategy. Under the statutes, if fraud was charged, the burden was on the government to prove it, while if we only charged a tax to be due, the burden was on the

31. Andrew Mellon on trial before the Board of Tax Appeals, 1935, is cross-examined by the government prosecutor, Robert H. Jackson (far right), as defense counsel Frank Hogan stands poised to intervene.

taxpayer to show it was not. This may seem like a technical point, but it is a very important matter of trial strategy.

The Department of Justice was opposed to my recommendation and the matter was taken to the President. I was not present when it was discussed and my memorandum was not read to him. He never reached the question of strategy. When Attorney General Cummings told him of some of the details of the Mellon transactions, the President closed the discussion, I was told, by holding his nose and saying we must proceed with the fraud charges.[16]

Homer Cummings's diary entry on a conference with the President the day before Justice announced the indictment confirms FDR's personal involvement:

I discussed tax matters with him, and obtained his approval of a proposed release which I expected to give out to the newspapers that afternoon. This release in substance states that Attorney General Cummings had authorized the United States Attorneys in New York, Cleveland, and Pittsburgh to present to Federal Grand Juries for tax violations cases of Thomas S. Lamont, James J. Walker, Thomas L. Sidle, and Andrew W. Mellon. I talked to the President quite awhile about these matters, and he concurred with me that unless we made an attempt to secure indictments in these cases we might as well give up the whole tax program.[17]

On the key issue of the validity of deductions for the value of the paintings donated to the A. W. Mellon Educational and Charitable Trust, Mellon's lawyers, Finley and Shepard, responded that in the original return Mellon had already exceeded the allowable amount of charitable deductions, so the contributions intended for the Gallery could not be used. But on the substance of the issue Mellon was effectively required to convince the court that he had intended to use the trust to create a national gallery of art. As Jackson makes clear, Mellon would have agreed to settle the tax claims except for the fraud charges, but he flatly denied fraudulent intent and retained Frank Hogan to defend him. Hogan was Washington's leading trial lawyer at the time and had defended many high-profile cases brought by the government, both civil and criminal, with spectacular success (fig. 31).[18]

With two seasoned trial lawyers, a famous defendant, and millions of dollars at stake, the trial attracted wide publicity across the country.[19] Its climax was the testimony of Joseph Duveen, called as a witness by Hogan on the question of Mellon's intention to create a national gallery of art. A highly theatrical man by nature, Duveen basked in the limelight as the key witness for his patron. As Behrman set the scene:

Duveen entered with the assurance of a popular comedian who knows he is irresistible and knows he is funny. He addressed opposing counsel—headed by Robert H. Jackson, attorney for the Bureau of Internal Revenue—with the condescension of an Olympian talking down to worthy, but fumbling and misinformed, groundlings. Duveen must have quickly sized up Jackson . . . and set about educating him. . . . "The ex-Secretary's collection," he said concisely, "is the finest in the universe." . . .

When the issue was really joined and Jackson tried to prove that Mellon had formed his foundation to escape taxes and had never intended to let the public enjoy his art collection, Duveen testified that as early as 1928 he had discussed with Mellon the project of a national gallery to house the art treasures he was helping get together for him. . . . Hogan asked a question about the site. Jackson didn't want to hear any more about it, but Duveen saw that he heard more. "Oh, yes, there was a site," Duveen said. "By the obelisk near the pond." . . . The spectators howled with laughter, and attendants had to shout for order.[20]

Duveen's testimony, though self-promoting and histrionic, turned the tide in Mellon's favor.

Independent evidence confirms that Mellon had decided by at least 1928 to create a national gallery of art. In his pocket diary for that year, Mellon made two references: on 26 February he wrote that his daughter Ailsa asked if he had "given Art Gallery to Govt."; and on 3 September he jotted, "Go over to 'Triangle'—view work on location of Commerce & Int Rev Bldgs. Also view site for Nat Gallery." And David Finley, who knew Mellon's mind on this subject as well as anybody, wrote in his memoir on the founding of the Gallery: "Mr. Mellon was making his own plans to erect a handsome building and to give his collection of works of art for a National Gallery of Art which he hoped to establish. . . . I do not know how early he came to a definite decision, but he told me about his plans in 1927, and said that he hoped that I would stay on at the Treasury and help him organize the new gallery."[21]

A hallmark of Frank Hogan's trial work was his brilliant closing arguments, which he could deliver for hours with total mastery of the facts of his case without ever consulting a note.[22] He also made liberal use of emotion to sway a jury. Before the tax board on the Mellon case, even though no jury was present, Hogan delivered one of his most memorable lines: "God doesn't place in the hearts and minds of men such diverse and opposite traits as these; it is impossible to conceive a man planning such benefactions as these and at the same time plotting and scheming to defraud the government."[23]

The tax board was persuaded, and its decision, in Finley's words, "was considered a complete vindication of Mr. Mellon"—and, of course, of his lawyers as well. Though based on a thicket of complex accounting and legal theories, at heart the unanimous verdict was a confirmation that Andrew Mellon had indeed planned to donate his art collection to the nation and that his transactions with the A. W. Mellon Educational and Charitable Trust in 1931 constituted a means to that end.[24] With the trial completed and final briefs submitted to the court in June 1936, it took over a year before Mellon's formal and final exoneration on fraud charges and the imposition of relatively minor adjustments to his tax bill. By that time Mellon was dead, but his gift of the National Gallery of Art would live on.

Perhaps the last word on the tax case should go to Herbert Hoover:

> While Mr. Mellon was in my Cabinet the question of a certain site for a public building came up. After the Cabinet meeting he came to me and asked that the particular site be kept vacant. He disclosed to me his purpose to build a great national art gallery in Washington, to present to it his own collection which was to include a large number of old masters which he was then purchasing from the Soviet government. He said he would amply endow it and thought it might altogether amount to $75,000,000. I urged that he announce it at once, and have the pleasure of seeing it built in his lifetime. He was a shy and modest man. The only reason he told me at all was that he wanted the site reserved. He asked me to keep it in confidence. Had he made this magnificent benefaction public at that time, public opinion would have protected him from the scandalous persecution under the New Deal. He was accused of having evaded income taxes. I knew that in the years he was supposed to be robbing the government he was spending several times the amount charged against him in support of public institutions and upon the unemployed in his state.

While every agency acquitted him, he felt the wound to a lifetime of integrity and many years of single-minded service. The whole was an ugly blot on the decencies of democracy.[25]

Grace and Vindication

Returning good for ill, Andrew Mellon went ahead with his plans for the National Gallery of Art. In January 1935, while still immersed in his tax case, Mellon had bought his first piece of sculpture, an important late fifteenth-century marble bas-relief, *Madonna and Child* (plate 6). Finley was an advocate of sculpture, and later noted that this purchase was "a happy augury of more to follow."[26] Then, with the fate of the tax case in the hands of the Board of Tax Appeals, Mellon and David Finley traveled to London in the summer of 1936, visited a number of museums, then called on Joseph Duveen. Finley recalled: "Lord Duveen was overjoyed to hear that Mr. Mellon felt that he was at last in a position to make his great gift of a National Gallery to the nation. 'I have many masterpieces in New York which have been hidden in storage during the Depression,' Duveen told Mr. Mellon. 'You must see them when you get back to America. They will help you round out your collection before you give it to the country.' Mr. Mellon said, yes, he would come."[27]

In October 1936, however, the time of Mellon's scheduled meeting with Duveen, Mellon called Finley from Pittsburgh and said, "I don't feel well enough to go to New York and see Duveen and all those paintings. Will you go and bring back everything you think is good enough for the National Gallery. Then I will come to Washington and decide what I want to buy. I have telephoned Duveen and he will have everything in readiness for you to see." Finley consented at once and asked if he could also bring back sculpture from the Dreyfus Collection for Mellon's consideration. Mellon agreed, and Finley proceeded to New York to see what Duveen had in store.[28]

John Walker later observed that "the influence of Joseph Duveen on Andrew Mellon . . . has come to be greatly overstated."[29] This stemmed largely from a serial profile in the *New Yorker* written by humorist and playwright S. N. Behrman and published in book form in 1952 as *Duveen*.[30] Duveen's posture as a titled Englishman may have impressed many of his American clients, but it did not cut much ice with

PLATE 6   Style of Agostino di Duccio, *Madonna and Child*, 1460s or later.
National Gallery of Art, Andrew W. Mellon Collection, 1937.1.116

Byzantine thirteenth century, *Madonna and Child on a Curved Throne*.
National Gallery of Art, Andrew W. Mellon Collection, 1937.1.1

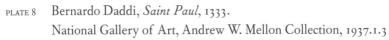

PLATE 8   Bernardo Daddi, *Saint Paul*, 1333.
National Gallery of Art, Andrew W. Mellon Collection, 1937.1.3

PLATE 9   Desiderio da Settignano, *Bust of a Little Boy*, 1455/1460.
National Gallery of Art, Andrew W. Mellon Collection,
1937.1.113

PLATE 10 Duccio di Buoninsegna, *The Nativity with the Prophets Isaiah and Ezekiel*, 1308/1311. National Gallery of Art, Andrew W. Mellon Collection, 1937.1.8

Andrew Mellon or David Finley, both of whom had spent much time in England.[31] Mellon, even in his eighties, was more than a match for Duveen, and Finley doubtless knew Duveen's reputation and Mellon's mind in such matters. Ever the soul of discretion, Finley never went so far as to say that Mellon actually distrusted Duveen, but he did say that Mellon liked to consult "someone whom he trusted" in considering a purchase.[32] Thus when Finley went to see Duveen in October 1936 to make the preliminary selection for Mellon's National Gallery of Art, he was well prepared:

> I took the midnight train and next morning was with Lord Duveen at 720 Fifth Avenue. We were there for the greater part of three days. Lord Duveen had his people bring into the velvet hung room one painting and sculpture after another.
>
> I had been told to bring back "everything I thought good enough for the National Gallery." So after much agonizing on my part, I settled on thirty paintings and twenty-one pieces of sculpture. The paintings were not only fine examples of the work of great artists, but were needed to fill the gaps in the Mellon Collection, so that it would give some idea of the achievements in Western painting from the thirteenth to the nineteenth century.
>
> The earliest of the paintings was that of the *Enthroned Madonna and Child,* painted, according to Bernard Berenson, in Constantinople around the year 1200 [plate 7]; there was a fine painting attributed to Cimabue, and still another was the large figure painting of *St. Paul,* which hangs in the National Gallery and is attributed to a follower of Giotto. Lord Duveen showed me the painting with a flourish, announcing it as by Giotto. I said: "I know the painting. Mr. Berenson says it is by 'A Follower of Giotto.'" Lord Duveen insisted, "I say it is by Giotto and it will be by Giotto." I said, "It is a fine painting and I think you might send it to Washington for Mr. Mellon to see. But, if he buys it, it will be as 'A Follower of Giotto.'" When I went back to Washington, I told Mr. Mellon the story. He smiled and said, "I will remember." And later when Mr. Mellon and Lord Duveen met in Washington to settle

about the pictures, Mr. Mellon said firmly, "I will buy the St. Paul painting as 'A Follower of Giotto' and at a suitable price, not the price of a Giotto, and it will so hang in the National Gallery," as it does today, with an attribution to Giotto's follower, Bernardo Daddi [plate 8].[33]

In fact, the plot was even thicker than Finley's tactful account would suggest. He and Duveen had been in correspondence on the attribution of the painting for over a year. In a letter dated 16 May 1935, Finley asked Duveen point-blank for Berenson's opinion on *Saint Paul*.[34] Duveen knew perfectly well that Berenson had attributed the painting to "a contemporary and close follower of Giotto" and that, despite strenuous efforts to get him to change his mind, Berenson had recently reaffirmed his long-held opinion that *Saint Paul* was by a follower and firmly rejected an attribution to Giotto, sending a letter that Duveen received just days before meeting with David Finley in New York.[35] How much of this Finley knew at the time may never be documented. But he sensed Duveen was bluffing and called his bluff.

Once Finley's selections were made, Duveen asked him, "How am I going to show all these things in Washington?" Finley suggested leasing space in Mellon's apartment building, and when Mellon returned from Pittsburgh, Duveen had installed the works on the second floor at 1785 Massachusetts Avenue. Mellon spent hours on end walking around the rooms with Finley, contemplating and commenting on the art. Mellon never did anything in a hurry. He considered every possible aspect of every potential investment and acted only when sure he was ready. Following a favorite maxim he was fond of quoting—"There is luck in leisure"—he took several weeks to study the objects and consulted with Duncan Phillips and other trusted advisors before he made his choices.[36] He finally decided to buy twenty-four of the paintings and eighteen of the sculptures "and fixed in his mind a definite amount he was willing to pay for them" (see plates 7–10).

Finley then telephoned Duveen to invite him to lunch with Mellon:

I was the only other person present, to watch these two keen minds at work and both enjoying the contest immensely. Lord Duveen asked astronomical prices. Mr. Mellon countered with lower ones. At one point Mr. Mellon said: "Well, Lord Duveen, I think you will have to take all these things back to New York," and Lord Duveen replied: "Mr. Mellon, I would give these things to you for the National Gallery rather than take them away." Finally it was all settled; Mr. Mellon had everything he wanted, and both he and Lord Duveen were very happy at the outcome of the great transaction.[37]

Duveen had good reason to be happy. The purchase price totaled $8 million—a truly staggering sum in those Depression years, when the monumental Gallery building itself came to just $15 million.

Correcting the Record

Various accounts have perpetuated a mistake concerning the amount Mellon paid for his great purchase from Duveen. Behrman in 1952 claimed: "This was the largest transaction ever consummated in the world of art. Duveen had easily outdone the Soviets. There were twenty-one items in the Soviet deal, forty-two in Duveen's. Mellon paid the Soviets seven million dollars; he paid Duveen twenty-one million."[38] The records of Duveen Brothers and of the National Gallery of Art, however, are clear evidence to the contrary. Duveen's invoice to the A. W. Mellon Educational and Charitable Trust, dated 15 December 1936—twenty-nine pages describing each painting and sculpture in detail—specifies the price for each work and adds up to $3,025,000 for the eighteen sculptures and $4,975,000 for the twenty-four paintings—totaling exactly $8 million.[39] Behrman said that the deal enabled Duveen to liquidate a $6 million credit at his London bank and create trust funds for his wife and daughter.[40] And the timing was perfect. Andrew Mellon died eight months later, and Duveen died in May 1939.

Mellon's Christmas Gift

With Finley's help, Andrew Mellon now had in place a collection of paintings and sculptures to form the nucleus of a national gallery of art, and he devoted the remaining months of his life to creating it, even though the government's tax case against him was still pending. A lesser man might have changed his mind about entrusting his treasures to an administration that had treated him so harshly. But as Finley recalled, Mellon never wavered: "I am not going to be deterred from building the National Gallery in Washington. Eventually the people now in power in Washington will be dead and I will be dead, but the National Gallery, I hope, will be there and that is something the country needs."[41]

Mellon must have known his time was short. The week after his purchase from Duveen was settled, he wrote a letter to President Roosevelt (no doubt drafted by David Finley and Donald Shepard), dated 22 December 1936. In it he offered to give his art collection to the United States and to construct a proper building for the National Gallery of Art, along with a $10 million endowment, contingent on the federal government's providing a suitable site between Constitution Avenue and the Mall and adopting legislation to accept the gift as well as agree to maintain the building and the collection in perpetuity. The Gallery building alone cost $15 million, and the total gift has been estimated at $80 million—"what may well be the largest single gift ever given to a government by a private citizen."[42] Mellon stipulated that the National Gallery not bear his name, because he believed that that would discourage other collectors from donating their collections.[43]

Just before Christmas, appropriately enough, Andrew Mellon's offer was hand delivered to Franklin Roosevelt by Frederick Delano, the President's uncle and an old friend of Mellon's. On 26 December the President responded warmly in a letter that began: "My dear Mr. Mellon: When my uncle handed me your letter of December 22 I was not only completely taken by surprise but was delighted by your very wonderful offer to the people of the United States."[44] He invited Mellon to the White House to discuss the matter. The two met for tea in the late afternoon of 31 December 1936, accompanied only by David Finley and Attorney General Homer Cummings. The President treated his guest to his legendary charm and quickly agreed to the terms proposed by Mellon, with the concurrence of his attorney general.[45] Naturally, no one mentioned the awkward fact of the multimillion-dollar tax case and fraud charges brought by Roosevelt and Cummings against Mellon, still pending before the Board of Tax Appeals.

Legislation sailed through Congress, accepting the gift on Mellon's terms—with the museum belonging to the Smithsonian Institution but having an independent board of trustees headed by the chief justice of the Supreme Court—and the President signed it in March 1937. This gave the eighty-two-year-old Mellon enough time to confer with his architect, John Russell Pope, and approve the basic exterior design of the monumental neoclassical structure before he left Washington in July for David and Ailsa Mellon Bruce's home in Southampton, Long Island. As he rode up Pennsylvania Avenue to Union Station, he had the satisfaction of seeing the excavation for his National Gallery under way at last. But Mellon's health had been failing for many months, and he died within two months, on 26 August 1937, in Southampton. Within twenty-four hours John Russell Pope also died, leaving many exterior details and most of the interior design of the National Gallery building for his associates and David Finley to finish.

* * *

Finley's papers include a one-page note, unfortunately undated, with the heading "Philosophy," which records a poignant exchange:

> One night during the tax case just before his [Andrew Mellon's] birthday, my wife, Mr. Mellon, and I were sitting in his library before the fire. Suddenly, without any preliminary remark, he quoted Matthew Arnold:
>
>> The wind lifts curtains behind,
>> The wind lifts curtains before.
>
> It seemed to impress him that man had only a little crust of the earth in which he could live—50 miles deep and it was molten fire—"even an oil well, 2 miles deep gets pretty hot—and 10 miles up, the atmosphere which we can breathe, ends. Think of all those worlds with their own suns, exploding energy, like ours, of which we are for such a little time such a little part. We are not really important, any of us." "Man goeth to his long home."[46]

NOTES

1. David E. Finley, "Memorandum for Mr. Banks, Internal Revenue Agent at Pittsburgh," 5 October 1937. Finley Papers, NGA Archives, box 28-4.

2. Finley, *Standard of Excellence*, 31.

3. Joseph Duveen to David Finley, 28 July 1931. Finley Papers, NGA Archives, box 6-25.

4. Burton Hersh, *The Mellon Family* (New York, 1978), 342.

5. Kenneth Clark (1903–1983), Lord Clark of Saltwood, became familiar to many Americans as the creator and narrator of the television series *Civilization*, which became popular in this country in the 1970s.

6. Clark, *Another Part of the Wood*, 226, indicates that Joseph Duveen had been made a trustee through the influence of two senior trustees, "from both of whom he had bought pictures at inflated prices."

7. Finley, *Standard of Excellence*, 31–32.

8. Finley, *Standard of Excellence*, 35.

9. David Burnham, *A Law Unto Itself: Power, Politics, and the IRS* (New York, 1989), 229.

10. Henry Morgenthau Jr. (1891–1967) was a neighbor of FDR's in Dutchess County, New York, who became his close friend and political ally during his years as governor. He served as Roosevelt's secretary of the treasury from 1933 to 1945.

11. John Morton Blum, *From the Morgenthau Diaries* (Boston, 1959), 324–325.

12. Elmer L. Irey, *The Tax Dodgers* (New York, 1948), xii.

13. Homer S. Cummings (1870–1956), a graduate of Yale and its law school, was a former chairman of the Democratic National Committee and worked for Roosevelt's nomination in 1932. He served as FDR's attorney general from 1933 to 1939 and was a key figure in FDR's unsuccessful 1937 plan to pack the Supreme Court with up to six additional justices in an effort to overcome the resistance of older, conservative justices to New Deal legislation.

14. Jackson's handling of the Mellon tax case marked the beginning of a stellar career in Washington, which led him to the highest reaches of the legal firmament: solicitor general, attorney general, chief U.S. prosecutor at the Nazi war crimes trials at Nuremberg, and more than twelve years as a highly regarded justice of the Supreme Court.

15. While a Supreme Court justice in the early 1950s, Robert Jackson (1892–1954) wrote a manuscript based on his long personal knowledge of FDR, but he died before it was finished. The manuscript lay in his son's closet for almost fifty years until it was discovered, edited, and published by John Q. Barrett, a Jackson scholar. See Robert H. Jackson, *That Man: An Insider's Portrait of Franklin D. Roosevelt* (New York, 2003). It provides unique and sharp insights on both the subject and the author.

16. Jackson, *That Man*, 125.

17. Homer Cummings diary, 10 March 1934. Homer Stillé Cummings Papers, Alderman Library, University of Virginia, Charlottesville, box 234.

18. Francis Joseph (Frank) Hogan (1877–1944) founded the firm of Hogan & Hartson, one of the city's premier law firms to this day. Hogan's own caliber may be judged by his opponents, three of whom—Owen J. Roberts in the Teapot Dome cases, Robert H. Jackson in the Mellon tax case, and Senator Hugo L. Black in Senate contempt matters—were later appointed to the U.S. Supreme Court. See Lester Cohen, *Frank Hogan Remembered* (Washington, D.C., 1985), 41–49, 82–88, 89–94.

19. *Time* magazine used the case as a centerpiece of a cover story on Hogan's career as a lawyer. See Cohen, *Frank Hogan Remembered*, 87.

20. Behrman, *Duveen*, 266–270.

21. Finley, *Standard of Excellence*, 12.

22. In his celebrated defense of a California oilman in a Teapot Dome case in 1930, Hogan gave a summation that lasted six hours and extended over two days, without referring to any notes. The jury returned a verdict of "not guilty" in an hour. See Cohen, *Frank Hogan Remembered*, 47.

23. Cohen, *Frank Hogan Remembered*, 87; quoted in Behrman, *Duveen*, 265.

24. Finley, *Standard of Excellence*, 36. See *A. W. Mellon, Petitioner, v. Commissioner of Internal Revenue, Respondent*, 36 B.T.A. 977–1101, 7 December 1937.

25. Herbert Hoover, *Memoirs: The Cabinet and the Presidency, 1920–1933* (New York, 1952), 59–60.

26. Finley, *Standard of Excellence*, 38.

27. Finley, *Standard of Excellence*, 38. In a 1942 interview Finley quoted Duveen as also saying, "I am going to retire from business, and you are getting ready to give your collection for a National Gallery. This is a combination of circumstances that could never come again." See "Conversation between Mr. Burton Hendrick and Mr. David E. Finley," week of 12 October 1942, transcript. Finley Papers, NGA Archives, box 28-1.

28. Finley, *Standard of Excellence*, 38. The Dreyfus Collection of Renaissance Sculpture, assembled by Gustave Dreyfus, was later purchased by Joseph Duveen.

29. Walker, *Self-Portrait with Donors*, 129. Duveen no doubt encouraged Mellon's concept of an American national gallery, for it presented an unparalleled opportunity to sell the trove of Italian masterworks he had accumulated over the years. But the idea was Mellon's, not Duveen's, as some have suggested.

30. Behrman's *Duveen*, while highly entertaining, provides no references to support his claims.

31. Finley had come to know Kenneth Clark, whose candid opinion of Duveen reflected extensive experience. Clark, *Another Part of the Wood*, 245–246, describes a lavish dinner at Duveen's "large and pretentious" New York townhouse in 1936, attended by his rich clients in white tie and "creaking" shirts, their wives weighed down with jewelry: "We dined on a blue and gold Sèvres service made for the Empress Catherine of Russia. Since my boyhood I have had a mania for ceramics, and I expressed my delight to Lady Duveen. She replied 'Yes; it is nice. And we don't get it out every day I can tell you. The

last time we used it was for Mr. Ramsay MacDonald' [the former prime minister]. After dinner, I said to my host (whom one had to address in his own language) 'Marvellous that Sèvres service. Privilege to eat off it.' 'Sèvres service,' said Lord Duveen, 'Sèvres service? Nothing. Eat off it everyday.' In London he might be a clown; in New York he was a king."

32. "It was here that my usefulness to Mr. Mellon arose, insofar as art was concerned." See Finley, *Standard of Excellence*, 19.

33. Finley, *Standard of Excellence*, 40–42.

34. Finley Papers, NGA Archives, RG 28, box 6-25.

35. See letter to Edward Fowles of Duveen's Paris office from J. H. Allen of Duveen's New York office, 9 July 1935, and "Paris Letter to New York re B.B.," 16 October 1936. Duveen Records, Mellon files, microfilm, Metropolitan Museum of Art, New York. See also Berenson to Duveen, 20 October 1935. Finley Papers, NGA Archives, RG 28, box 2-7.

36. "Conversation" between Hendrick and Finley, 11, 16; Finley, *Standard of Excellence*, 30. Duncan Phillips (1886–1966) created the Phillips Collection at his family's mansion in Washington, D.C., concentrating on nineteenth-century French paintings. Originally from Pittsburgh, the grandson of a founder of Jones & Laughlin Steel Co., Phillips was well known to Mellon.

37. Finley, *Standard of Excellence*, 42.

38. Behrman, *Duveen*, 273. Philip Kopper's *Gift to the Nation* (1991), David Koskoff and Burton Hersh in their books on the Mellon family (1978), and Meryle Secrest's *Duveen* (2004) all cited Behrman but made no independent confirmation. David Finley and John Walker gave no values.

39. Duveen Records, box 152, reel 54. The curatorial records of the National Gallery of Art confirm the $8 million figure; letter from Earl A. Powell III, director, to the author, 15 June 2005.

40. Behrman, *Duveen*, 273.

41. Finley, *Standard of Excellence*, 36–37.

42. President George H. W. Bush, foreword to Kopper, *Gift to the Nation*, vii.

43. Finley, *Standard of Excellence*, 47–48.

44. Quoted in Finley, *Standard of Excellence*, 49.

45. Finley, *Standard of Excellence*, 50.

46. Finley Papers, NGA Archives, RG 28, box 28-1.

32. Rotunda of the National Gallery of Art, West Building, which Finley
helped design

6

Mr. Finley's National Gallery of Art
1938–1956

DAVID FINLEY RETURNED TO WASHINGTON from the funerals of Andrew Mellon and John Russell Pope, which he and Margaret attended in Pittsburgh and Newport at the end of August 1937, "with a devastating sense of loss."[1] Lord Duveen wrote him on 1 September 1937:

> It seems impossible to realize that that great man is no longer with us. I well know what he meant to you, and you to him, and you have my deepest sympathy at being parted from the great personality to whom you were so closely attached. I need not praise him to you, but I have often said of the many eminent men in all walks of life that I have met both here and abroad, none has ever made such an impression on me as Mr. Mellon, and I shall always cherish the many and varied memories I have of him. . . . There is an old saying somewhere to the effect that God buries the workers but carries on the work, and that was very true in his case.[2]

Finley responded to Duveen two weeks later:

I have wanted to write you before, but I have felt dazed, as I know you have been, by the loss of two such friends as we have both sustained. I find it hard to adjust myself to a world without Mr. Mellon. He has been such a vital factor for so many years and my affection for him was such that I find myself missing him more and more each day.

Then the death of Mr. Pope less than 24 hours later was a great blow for me. I had been with him at Newport (my wife and I were at Woods Hole on Cape Cod with her mother and went for a short visit with the Popes) and left him only the day before he was taken to the hospital. He was on a diet but not really ill and had no thought of anything serious until after they went to New York for the examination. He was so gay and happy when we were with him. The design had been approved *in toto*—dome and all—and the matter of the Tennessee marble was settled. We spent several hours in his studio in the garden going over interior designs, and I am glad to say that the garden courts and all the most important things were settled to his complete satisfaction.

It is all the more incumbent on us to see that the Gallery is built and arranged as he and Mr. Mellon wished—and that we shall do, as of course you know. But much of the joy we would have had in working with Mr. Mellon and Mr. Pope has gone and that can never come back.[3]

Mellon's death was not unexpected, as he had weakened steadily since returning from England at the end of the summer of 1936. Finley believed he had never really recovered from the strain of the tax trial, and its verdict still had not come down from the Board of Tax Appeals. But Mellon had accomplished much in the last months of his life, including the major acquisitions from Duveen, the formal offer of the National Gallery of Art to President Roosevelt, its acceptance on his terms by both the President and the Congress, and the basic structure of the Gallery building established with Pope. Now both Mellon and Pope were gone, with the interior design of the National Gallery building still a work in progress. Finley had little time to mourn, considering the enormous task ahead. There were three pressing issues—completing the building, assembling a museum staff, and, vitally important, securing other art collections for the Gallery.

Mellon and Pope had conceived of a grand classical domed building to house the Gallery but had settled only on its overall size and shape and its exterior marble walls. Much of its cavernous interior had not taken shape or form, and the architects on Pope's staff not only lacked his exceptional talent but proved somewhat difficult. Dozens of issues remained unresolved: the size, shape, and decor of the galleries; the types of materials to be used in the Rotunda and throughout the building; whether to include statues and other embellishments on the facades. And who should make those decisions—the architects, the trustees, or the museum's director, who had not even been formally named?

The First Board of Trustees

In June of 1937 the board of regents of the Smithsonian Institution had elected the original trustees of the National Gallery, whom Andrew Mellon approved, in accordance with the authorizing legislation. In addition to four ex-officio trustees (the chief justice of the United States, the secretary of state, the secretary of the treasury, and the secretary of the Smithsonian), the five general trustees were Andrew W. Mellon, David K. E. Bruce, S. Parker Gilbert, Duncan Phillips, and Donald D. Shepard.[4] But it took time before the group coalesced sufficiently to make its most important decisions.

At Andrew Mellon's death, his thirty-year-old son Paul took his place on the board, but the young man had had very little influence in putting together the Mellon collection or in planning the National Gallery. Andrew Mellon loved and admired his only son, as his diaries and letters make clear, but he had not given him any significant say in the Mellon business or philanthropic interests. Paul and Ailsa felt very hurt when they learned that without consulting either of them their father had transferred his entire art collection to the A. W. Mellon Educational and Charitable Trust in 1934 as a vehicle for forming the National Gallery—including beloved paintings, almost members of the family, like Joshua Reynolds's *Lady Caroline Howard,* which had hung in Ailsa's bedroom for years.[5]

Finley, who had befriended Paul when he was a student at Yale and saw that he was invited to dances and dinners at embassies and private homes on his visits to Washington, did ask the young Mellon in 1936 to show preliminary designs for the National Gallery to Kenneth Clark, director of the National Gallery in London: "I thought it was encouraging of Finley to involve me, even if it was largely a courteous gesture."[6] But in 1937 it was too late for Paul Mellon to fill his father's shoes and too soon to assume his own leadership of the National Gallery. He and his wife, Mary, spent a lot of time in Europe between 1938 and 1940, including a winter studying with the famous psychiatrist Carl Jung in Zurich.[7] Paul Mellon resigned as a trustee in May 1939 and did not take a major role in Gallery affairs until well after the Second World War.

A second trustee was Andrew Mellon's son-in-law David Bruce, who had been closer to him in some ways than his own son. In 1937, at age thirty-nine, Bruce had already shown some of the qualities that blossomed into a distinguished diplomatic career following the Second World War. He had accompanied his wife Ailsa to London when she served as her father's hostess during his year as the U.S. ambassador to the Court of St. James's. He is the one who discovered the painting of Pocahontas that Finley bought on Mellon's behalf. But Mellon had never really consulted Bruce about any matter of importance having to do with the Gallery.[8] And in the late 1930s Bruce had other distractions. His marriage to Ailsa Mellon had become strained, and he began spending more time on his own, moving from the Long Island estate Andrew Mellon had bought for them to an old family estate in Virginia that he started to restore.[9] Although he backed Finley on architectural design issues, one of his few substantive suggestions was for the paneling in the Founders' Room off the Rotunda. With Paul Mellon's resignation as a trustee, Bruce was elected president of the board and was reelected to that position in early 1941. His entry into the Office of Strategic Services (OSS) later that year, however, limited his active service at the Gallery.[10]

A third trustee was Parker Gilbert. Both Mellon and Finley had kept in close touch with Gilbert after he left the Treasury Department in

1924, both professionally and socially. He had an extraordinary career in public and private finance but died of a heart ailment at age forty-five in February 1938, less than a year after accepting a place on the Gallery's board of trustees (Ferdinand Lammot Belin took his place). Parker Gilbert was remembered in a long obituary in the *New York Times* and in a laudatory notice on the editorial page that closed, "Having with brilliant success performed one of the major tasks of the world, he may be counted as having been old in hours and as having done a full lifetime's work in his few years."[11]

A fourth trustee, Duncan Phillips, was another scion of Pittsburgh wealth who had created the small but fine Phillips Collection in Washington. His connoisseurship of art and his practical experience in museum management were invaluable to Finley as well as to his fellow trustees in the early years of the National Gallery.[12]

The final trustee was Donald Shepard, Andrew Mellon's tax lawyer and David Finley's former law partner. Tough, crusty, and a zealous guardian of the funds that Andrew Mellon had entrusted for the Gallery, he had neither the interest nor the expertise to make decisions concerning the Gallery's art collections or the design of its building. He resigned as a trustee in May 1939 but served as secretary-treasurer and general counsel to the Gallery until 1943.

The choice of a director for the National Gallery was foremost among the decisions faced by the first trustees. Paul Mellon recalled his father's saying in November 1936 "that really in the end good management was the only thing that mattered."[13] By good fortune, he, David Bruce, and Donald Shepard had observed David Finley's close working relationship with Andrew Mellon for more than a decade, particularly with respect to plans for the National Gallery. Had Andrew Mellon lived longer, he would surely have named Finley as director of the new National Gallery. Yet he had left no formal instructions in that regard, and the final decision fell to the trustees. Finley appeared the logical choice, for no one knew Mellon's wishes and Mellon's art collection better than he. But he had had no formal training in art history and no experience in the management of an art museum or any other large organization. Could he pull it all together? Or should the trustees seek an experienced museum director from New York, Philadelphia, or

Chicago for so large an undertaking? This weighty question may well explain why the trustees waited over six months after Andrew Mellon's death to announce a formal appointment.

On 9 March 1938 the trustees named David Finley to the position of director of the National Gallery of Art. Finley was very pleased and sent a telegram to his mother with the news.[14] The trustees knew Mellon's gift for finding the right person for a job, they recognized Finley as Mellon's intellectual heir in matters concerning the Gallery, and they let him exercise the good judgment and managerial skills that Mellon himself had trusted. Finley never forgot that he was ultimately responsible to the trustees, and he took care not to get too far in front of them. But he also had a quiet confidence in his own abilities and pursued his mentor's vision for the National Gallery with single-minded devotion. At first he had an office at 716 Jackson Place, on the west side of Lafayette Square, courtesy of the A. W. Mellon Educational and Charitable Trust. Another three years passed before the Gallery itself could house offices.

Completing the Building

The immediate concern was to complete the plans for the monumental National Gallery building. Andrew Mellon had wanted a structure large enough to house his own collection and also attract other collections over the next twenty-five to fifty years. Using the National Gallery in London as a model, Mellon had asked Pope to design a building that could display 1,300 paintings, plus appropriate storage space and ancillary features such as garden courts, a cafeteria for both visitors and staff, a lecture hall, a library, and administrative offices.[15]

David Finley had been intimately involved with the design of the Gallery building even before the deaths of Mellon and Pope:

> Mr. Pope's design was inspired by the old Court House building in Washington, designed by George Hadfield and built about 1820 in Judiciary Square. Mr. Pope and I sat in front of it for hours. He explained how he intended to design a building in the form of a double-H, surmounted by a low dome, with columns and pediments on each end as well as on the two sides. Mr. Mellon was not happy with the multitude of columns. I

suggested that we talk to Mr. Pope about it. "Mr. Pope is a very high-powered man," said Mr. Mellon, "I would not want to hurt his feelings." "I know Mr. Pope very well," I said. "Let me talk with him." "Go ahead," said Mr. Mellon, "and see what you can do."

Mr. Pope was always amenable to suggestions, if he thought they had merit. I explained that, in Mr. Mellon's and my opinion as laymen, it was enough to have a pediment and columns in the center of the north and south sides of the building but that a pediment and columns on the east and west ends would distract the eye from the central motif and make for restlessness. Mr. Pope said he thought that might well be the case and he would study the designs and come back to us. He did so, with the beautiful blank walls and the large doors on the east and west sides of the building, and the setbacks on the roof which hide the glass skylights that otherwise would have glittered in the sun. He was delighted with the change and so was Mr. Mellon.[16]

On 26 October 1937 Finley, before he was formally named director, met with Paul Mellon and with Pope's successor, Otto Eggers, in New York.[17] Eggers wanted to continue the classical motif of the Gallery building with colonnades, pediments, niches, urns, and statuary. Both Finley and the younger Mellon expressed discomfort with these embellishments and urged simplicity. Finley credited Paul Mellon with the suggestion for a sloping floor in the auditorium to improve sight lines and with ideas for a reception room to the right of the Mall entrance, which eventually became the Founders' Room.

Eggers had designed at least one other art museum—the Walters Art Museum in Baltimore, which was of much smaller scale—but Finley later took John Walker to see it and was anxious to avoid some of the problems they saw there.[18] In December 1937 an officer of the Association of Art Museum Directors contacted Finley to recommend James Francis McCabe, superintendent of the Art Institute of Chicago, a man with a solid understanding of the systems and operations of an art museum. Finley had studied the aesthetic design of the National Gallery in London and other great art museums of Europe but realized that he lacked experience in the inner workings of the buildings. He hired McCabe as a consultant to the construction engineer, and McCabe produced an extremely useful review of the mechanical and practical aspects of the design.

Eggers proposed two sets of green marble columns for the Rotunda, with two slightly different colors of stone. Finley liked the spatial concept, but he and Paul Mellon preferred uniformity and using the darker green marble. Pope and Andrew Mellon had agreed on the dome, but Eggers and Finley finished the design of the interior spaces. Finley loved fountains, having seen many during his travels in Europe, and he had encouraged Andrew Mellon to include eighteen pieces of sculpture in his last major purchase from Duveen, including the small *Mercury* that stands at the apex of the fountain Eggers designed for the center of the Rotunda (which now serves virtually as a logo for the National Gallery).[19] John Walker, soon to be appointed chief curator, suggested the coffered ceiling, borrowed from the Pantheon in Rome.

The green marble for the Rotunda's columns was quarried near Lucca, Italy, cut into enormous drums and shipped to Vermont in the summer of 1939 for final polishing, then trucked to the Gallery's building site and hoisted through an opening in the floor for assembly in the Rotunda, five drums for each column: "Finally Mr. Eggers told me that all the columns were in place, and that the wooden sheaths had been removed, and that we could see the effect. I shall never forget the nervousness with which I entered the rotunda. If the columns were wrong, nothing could ever be done about it. But they were not wrong; and they stand there now and seem perfect for this purpose" (see fig. 32).[20]

Authorized by the trustees, Finley told the architects that the two long halls extending east and west off the Rotunda would accommodate large sculpture, with the paintings distributed in rooms opening off the sculpture halls and around the two garden courts—essentially the arrangement that exists today. Finley then made, with his wife's assistance, a rough sketch of a floor plan for the paintings galleries, "with rooms of varying sizes, placing the doors in such a way that one could see through them a painting or a piece of sculpture, not another door or a series of doors as in so many other galleries." Eggers and his architects turned these sketches into finished architectural plans and renderings to present to the trustees for approval.[21] As John Walker later wrote, "Both Finleys loved architectural plans, and Margey might have been a distinguished architect. Much of the beauty of the building is due to their discriminating taste."[22]

Finley had reservations about the architect's design for the marble floors of the Rotunda and the flanking sculpture halls, finding them too "busy." He called on Irwin Laughlin, an old Pittsburgh friend of Andrew Mellon's, at his beautiful Washington home, Meridian House, where Laughlin "climbed a ladder in his library, got down some books on design of French garden parterres; and worked out with me on the floor designs that can now be seen in the rotunda and the two sculpture halls."[23] The Rotunda ensemble was stunning and to this day never fails to impress visitors with its elegant simplicity.

Finley also consulted Laughlin on painting the walls of the Gallery's English, French, and American rooms and borrowed both colors and French painting techniques from Meridian House. Finley's journal from 1930 indicates that he was already making detailed observations of the interiors at the National Gallery in London and other museums in Europe. He did not hesitate to use these in designing the interiors of the National Gallery of Art in Washington. Before Andrew Mellon's death, Finley had discussed with him the decoration of the galleries on the main floor:

> I suggested that the rooms give some indication of the place and period that had produced the works of art but that they should not be old period rooms. I recommended painted plaster for the walls and travertine stone for the doorways and trim of the rooms in which Italian paintings were shown up to the period of Titian and Tintoretto; after that, damask covered walls with travertine trim. For Rembrandt and other Dutch paintings, I suggested oak panelling, with French, English or American overdoors and cornices. Mr. Mellon was delighted with these suggestions. I warned that they would prove expensive. "I don't care how expensive they are," said Mr. Mellon, "if they don't look expensive." That remark was typical of Mr. Mellon's innate good taste.[24]

33. East Garden Court, National Gallery of Art. Finley convinced
the architect to include the two garden courts, one at either end
of the building, and he selected the plantings and the lead statues
for the fountains "to relieve their severity."

Finley's discussions with Mellon were "of the greatest help when the
architects tried to gild the lily." But characteristically, Finley took care to
credit Eggers and his associates with much of the success of the interior
of the building. At the same time, he had David Bruce's help recruiting
the prominent architect William Adams Delano to review the details of
the interior design. Delano was in Pope's league as a classical architect,
and he took great care going over such fine points as the ornaments over
doors, the fleur-de-lis motifs on grilles, and the sizes of moldings and
chair rails.[25]

Finley and Eggers had a major confrontation on the question of
sculptural embellishments for the exterior pediments. Eggers continued

to press for this decoration as an essential part of Pope's design, but Finley felt strongly about maintaining the simplicity of plain pediments. The matter came to a head in June 1939 when Eggers wrote directly to the trustees to argue his views on the matter. Finley responded with a memorandum to the trustees in which he cited his and John Walker's views, backed up by those of Ferdinand Lammot Belin, Kenneth Clark, William Adams Delano, and Major Gilmore D. Clarke, chairman of the U.S. Commission of Fine Arts. He concluded, "I feel, therefore, that no mistake would be made in overruling Mr. Eggers' views in this matter and that, in fact, it would be a very great mistake to allow him to decorate the pediments as he suggests."[26] The trustees backed Finley, and no sculpture was added to the pediments or any other element on the exterior of the building.

Another Finley stamp on the interior design concerned the two garden courts at each end of the main floor (fig. 33). He had to convince John Russell Pope to include them.[27] They were adapted from the Frick Collection in New York, and Finley immersed himself in the details of their design and in selecting the kinds of plants that would survive in that light. He wanted small fountains as the centerpiece of each court but could not find suitable statuary until 1939, when the resourceful Irwin Laughlin found two beautiful old statues at the French pavilion at the New York World's Fair. These were seventeenth-century French works by Pierre Legros and Jean-Baptiste Tubi, originally commissioned by Louis XIV for the fountains at Versailles, depicting cherubs playing with a swan and a lyre; the works were cast in lead, which had acquired a soft patina that made them look like stone. Finley, Walker, and Shepard saw them in New York and liked them very much. Shepard visited Paris later that summer and tried to bargain with the dealer who owned the pair, but the man adamantly refused to lower his price of $50,000, which the Gallery representatives thought was too high. Although disappointed, Finley did not give up. A New York dealer became involved in the negotiations, and after the outbreak of the war in Europe in September 1939, the French antiquarian began to retreat from his lofty price, no doubt realizing that the works' return to France grew increasingly difficult. Holding the upper hand, Finley then offered $25,000 and did not budge. Finally, in December 1939

34. The National Gallery's first team, 1951: John Walker, Harry McBride, David Finley, Magill James, and Huntington Cairns

the Gallery struck a deal to buy the sculptures for $27,500, plus a five percent commission for the New York dealer.

Assembling a Professional Staff

For Finley's first senior staff appointment he hired Harry McBride as the Gallery's administrator. Beginning on 1 August 1938, McBride, a former foreign service officer, assumed responsibility for the buildings, personnel, and "innumerable other things" such as printing and publications. As an old government hand, McBride knew how to navigate the civil service list when the time came to build the staff.[28]

Next came John Walker. Although appointed chief curator in August 1938, he had a prior commitment that kept him from reporting for duty in Washington until the end of the year. Originally from Pittsburgh, where he had been a friend of Paul Mellon's, he studied fine arts at Harvard, graduating summa cum laude in 1930.[29] He went to Italy for the next eight years, first to study with Bernard Berenson at I Tatti, where they became almost like father and son, and then to serve three years later as professor of fine arts at the American Academy in Rome.

As it happened, Walker and Finley had corresponded in 1931, when Walker had written from Italy to get a list and photographs of works in the Mellon collection. Hearing of plans to establish the National Gallery, Walker contacted his old friend Paul Mellon about the possibility of working for the new museum. He met Paul in Zurich in 1938 and quite to his surprise was offered the senior curatorial position.

Only thirty-two at the time, Walker, like Finley and all of the trustees except Duncan Phillips, had no museum experience. What he did have was a comprehensive knowledge of Italian Renaissance art as well as great self-confidence and savoir faire. And like Finley, he had married a cultivated and well-connected woman of high intelligence, Lady Margaret Drummond, daughter of the British ambassador to Italy. Walker later wrote: "A wife in any career is important—in a museum career she is vital. Perhaps this is truer in America than in Europe. In the United States museums are still growing rapidly, and this growth is dependent on gifts. These involve social relations. The director of a large institution must know how to entertain with a certain sophistication and charm. If his wife is inexperienced in these matters, though he may have scholarly ability, skill as an administrator, remarkable connoisseurship, the result can be, as I have seen with many of my colleagues, disastrous."[30] In Margaret Finley and Margaret Walker, the National Gallery was fortunate indeed. What the young National Gallery lacked in experience, it more than made up for in the charm, tact, and social graces of its senior executives, its trustees, and their wives. But certainly Finley, and to some extent Walker, also had an iron hand inside his velvet glove.

In another key executive appointment, Magill James became assistant director in 1940 (fig. 34). James did have museum experience, as director of the Peale Museum in Baltimore. He was also a good friend of David Bruce's and had served with him in France, both in the army and on the boulevards of Paris in the early 1920s. Finley credited "Mac" James with humanizing the Gallery through his knowledge of museums and their personnel.[31]

A fifth member soon joined Finley's first team when Huntington Cairns, formerly of the Treasury Department, succeeded Donald Shepard as the secretary-treasurer and general counsel in 1943. An able lawyer and a scholar of the visual arts and literature, Cairns had "one of the most distinguished minds ever to come to the Gallery."[32]

The Kress Collection

Just as important as completing the building, clearly the National Gallery's most critical needs included the acquisition of more art—more paintings, more sculpture, and lots of both. The Mellon collection was of superb quality but of modest size, and the marble edifice under construction extended the length of three city blocks. Mellon had intended that his gift serve as a nucleus to attract other major collections to the National Gallery and had insisted that the museum not bear his name so that others would be more willing to contribute works of art. He had spoken to Joseph Widener of Lynnewood Hall near Philadelphia about giving his fine and wide-ranging collection to the National Gallery, but Widener had been noncommittal. Now, with the death of Andrew Mellon, who could prevail upon Widener and his peers to cast their lot with the National Gallery of Art? Nowhere was the trustees' faith in Finley more richly repaid than in his virtuoso persuasion of other collectors.

Finley's first coup was convincing Samuel H. Kress of New York to donate his impressive art collection to the National Gallery of Art. Like Mellon, Kress had come from Pennsylvania, but from humbler origins. Born in 1863 and named after an uncle killed at Gettysburg, he acquired a high school education and taught school for seven years, earning $25 per month. On this meager salary he managed to save enough to open a small stationery shop, then followed F. W. Woolworth's marketing scheme in building a national chain of five-and-ten stores. He made a sizable fortune but never married, and during travels to Europe in the 1920s he began to buy a large number of Italian paintings and sculpture, which he installed in his two-story penthouse on Fifth Avenue in New York. Under the influence of the Florentine collector and dealer Count Contini-Bonacossi, he sought to assemble a collection representative of every artist of the Italian Renaissance. A quarry of this magnitude eventually came to the attention of Joseph Duveen, who began to sell Kress more Italian masterpieces in 1936. By 1937 Kress was also consulting Bernard Berenson and had decided to build his own art museum on Fifth Avenue. Finley had met Kress once, on a transatlantic crossing in 1936, but Kress in his modesty hardly mentioned his art collection. Although Finley had subsequently tried to see the collection, Kress was either sick or out of town each time, and they had never gotten together.

Then in early 1938 help came from an unexpected source. One of the secrets of Finley's success, in a highly competitive profession, was his remarkable ability to enlist colleagues from established art museums in the cause of the National Gallery of Art. When curators from the Corcoran Gallery of Art and the Smithsonian Institution traveled to New York together in January 1938 to see the Kress collection and found it dazzling, Jeremiah O'Connor of the Corcoran actually wrote to Kress urging him to give his collection to the embryonic National Gallery. Kress replied that he was interested in talking with Finley, who paid what he called a "goodwill visit" to the Kress penthouse in New York soon after being named director. Realizing immediately that the scope and quality of the Kress collection would make it an ideal complement to the Mellon collection, he wasted no time:

> I arrived at Mr. Kress' apartment at 1020 Fifth Avenue at three o'clock on April 22, 1938. We looked at his paintings and talked all afternoon. He asked me to stay on to dinner, which I did; and when I finally left in time to take the midnight train back to Washington Mr. Kress had decided to give his collection to the National Gallery. "And I will give it to you," he said, "in time for the opening of the Gallery." "Also," he said, "as I can obtain other works of art, I will exchange them for some of those I am giving you now." He had, for instance, six paintings by Sano di Pietro. Later he and, afterwards, his brother Rush Kress exchanged five of these paintings for others which were needed to fill out the collection.[33]

How could Finley have accomplished this feat in the course of a few hours? Kress had perhaps never met an American other than Berenson who could speak so knowledgeably and sympathetically about Italian painting and sculpture. Finley, too, from his long association with Andrew Mellon, may have had unique insights into the perspective of wealthy businessmen who collect art. Finally, Finley had his own charm and "inimitable powers of persuasion," as John Walker expressed it. Walker noted that "the directorship of a museum requires less knowledge of art . . . than knowledge of how to deal with human beings,"[34] and a prime example of Finley's skill was his success in persuading Kress to join forces with the National Gallery.

Samuel Kress was as good as his word and by June 1939 had given his entire collection to the National Gallery of Art. But the gift did not proceed as smoothly as Finley made it seem in his memoir on the founding of the Gallery. When he reported the news of this tremendous gift to the trustees, they did not share his euphoria. They had to be convinced that Kress's collection met the high standard of Andrew Mellon's. Indeed, their concerns had some validity, for Mellon had carefully selected only masterpieces, whereas Kress had undertaken to cover the entire development of Italian art, from the early fourteenth century through the Renaissance. Kress was offering "one of the most complete collections of Italian paintings and sculpture ever assembled by one man,"[35] and he had acquired many superb paintings, but some works did not in fact match the quality exemplified by Mellon's choices. Moreover, the Kress holdings were vast—hundreds of paintings and sculptures; thus in scale alone they threatened to overwhelm the Mellon collection of just 125 paintings and eighteen sculptures. Finally, the Mellon trustees may have felt, at least subconsciously, that Samuel Kress was, after all, no Andrew Mellon. Kress, however, stipulated that the Gallery could not simply cherry-pick from his collection: it could take either all or nothing. Kress may have been standing on pride as well, insisting that his fortune and collection could hold their own beside Mellon's. It required all of Finley's considerable skill and diplomacy to bridge this wide gulf.

Finley, as was his custom throughout his career, called on outside experts. In the summer of 1938 he and Margaret went to Europe and visited Bernard Berenson at his famous villa, I Tatti, just east of Florence. Finley had had a letter of introduction to Berenson from Duveen in 1931 but did not actually meet him at that time. Seven years later, as director of America's National Gallery of Art, he needed no introduction, and he and Margaret spent several happy days with Berenson. At last the keen student of Italian art met the renowned scholar, and an immediate spark connected Berenson, the seventy-one-year-old sage, and Finley, the forty-eight-year-old head of what Berenson had once condescendingly called "the Mellon show."[36] Finley wrote to "B. B." after he had returned to Washington, saying, "I feel as if I have found the friend I have been looking for all my life."[37] Both men had wide-ranging interests besides art—history, literature, religion, the classics, current events—and found that conversation never lagged. If Finley had not already abandoned his early admiration for Mussolini, he would certainly have been set right by Berenson, an outspoken opponent of that "arch-gangster."[38] Finley was charmed by Nicky Mariano, Berenson's constant companion by that time; and Berenson, ever the ladies' man, paid court to Margaret Finley. The Finleys were at I Tatti over a new moon, when their host introduced them to some mysterious ritual he observed on that occasion, and ever afterward the new moon brought Berenson to their minds.[39]

The Finleys invited Berenson to visit them in Washington and Virginia, and though he promised to do so, it turned out that he never crossed the Atlantic again. Yet he did take a special interest in the National Gallery in Washington. Living near Florence since 1891, he had not set foot in the United States since 1921, but he zealously guarded his American citizenship and seemed pleased that America would finally have a national art museum.[40] He also knew the Mellon collection well by reputation[41] and expressed joy that his protégé "Johnnie" Walker had accepted the position of chief curator. The news that Samuel Kress had promised his great collection of Italian art to the Gallery must have proved a topic of lively discussion between Finley and Berenson, who had received his first visit from Kress the year before and felt an instant rapport.[42] It is not known how much Finley told Berenson about his dilemma involving the Kress collection, but Finley soon brought John Walker into the discussions. Walker's appointment as chief curator had been effective 1 August 1938, but he was still under contract to the American Academy in Rome. So he spent some time in Washington that summer working on the building plans with Finley but returned to Italy in the fall. He did not come back to the United States until December, when Finley sent a cable asking Walker to meet him in New York to see the Kress collection.

When Walker went up to I Tatti to say good-bye to Berenson, he found his mentor studying photographs of the entire Kress collection, which Samuel Kress had just sent him to get his opinions. As Walker relates, "We looked at the photographs together and chuckled over some of the attributions of the Contini experts. My recollection is that there were almost a thousand prints, and on the back of each was written the opinions of the six scholars Contini was paying. Never in my life have I worked as hard as I did those few days I stayed at I Tatti. I memorized the attribution given by each expert to every painting and sculpture. Before I left for America, I was letter-perfect."[43]

Finley met Walker when he arrived in New York just after Christmas 1938 and took him to meet Kress and see his collection. Kress was duly impressed at Walker's amazing knowledge of his works of art. Finley and Walker then came up with a list of 375 paintings and sixteen sculptures they wanted for the National Gallery. At a later meeting Kress agreed to this list, and Finley almost apologized: "We are taking *all* the paintings in your apartment. It is going to be very bare and I feel rather badly about it." "Don't worry," Kress responded, "I shall get along all right, and I am glad to know my paintings will be enjoyed by so many people."[44] Walker added that Finley whispered to him as they left that Kress "had the look of a man who had just married off his daughters but was still somewhat doubtful about his new sons-in-law." Although the trustees of the National Gallery still had concerns about accepting the Kress collection, Finley resolved the problem by persuading Kress to allow lesser works to be separately displayed as a "study collection," and Walker, with some hesitations, assured the trustees that the collection met Mellon's stipulations.[45] At last they had an agreement, and the Gallery made a public announcement of the gift of the Kress collection to the National Gallery of Art in June 1939.

Eventually the Kress Collection at the National Gallery came to include such masterpieces as Giotto's *Madonna and Child* (plate 11), Giorgione's *Adoration of the Shepherds* (plate 12), Duccio's *Calling of the Apostles Peter and Andrew,* Domenico Veneziano's *Saint John in the Desert,* and Fra Angelico and Fra Filippo Lippi's *Adoration of the Magi* (plate 13) as well as paintings by Giovanni Bellini, Correggio, Carlo Crivelli, Gentile da Fabriano, Domenico Ghirlandaio, Lorenzo Lotto,

PLATE II   Giotto, *Madonna and Child*, probably 1320–1330.
National Gallery of Art, Samuel H. Kress Collection, 1939.1.256

PLATE 12 Giorgione, *The Adoration of the Shepherds*, 1505/1510, oil on panel. National Gallery of Art, Samuel H. Kress Collection, 1939.1.289

PLATE 13   Fra Angelico and Fra Filippo Lippi, *The Adoration of the Magi*, c. 1445.
National Gallery of Art, Samuel H. Kress Collection,
1952.2.2

35. Rush H. Kress before a portrait of his elder brother
Samuel H. Kress, c. 1950s

Andrea Mantegna, Simone Martini, Masolino, Perugino, Andrea del Sarto, Sassetta, Luca Signorelli, Raphael, Giovanni Battista Tiepolo, Tintoretto, Titian, and many others, some rarely seen in this country.

Now the "Mellon Gallery," as many people called it in its early years, had truly become a national gallery. But Samuel Kress had just hit his stride. Kress felt that Mellon had received preferential treatment from Duveen, from Knoedler & Co., and from other top dealers. With Mellon no longer competing, he purchased many priceless works of art, and he continued to donate them to the National Gallery. By the time of the Gallery's opening in 1941, Kress had been elected a trustee and had augmented Mellon's collection by 386 paintings and twenty-four sculptures, all Italian. When he told Finley in 1942 that he wanted to add to his collection at the Gallery but could find no suitable Italian paintings because of the war, Finley told him that the Gallery needed nothing more than French pictures of the seventeenth and eighteenth centuries and that an important collection of such paintings had just come on the market. Kress bought the collection and filled two rooms at the Gallery with the works of Jean Siméon Chardin, Nicolas Poussin, François Boucher, Jean-Honoré Fragonard, and other French painters.

Sadly, Samuel Kress suffered a stroke in 1946 and was bedridden until his death in 1955. But Finley and Walker continued to visit him regularly with updates on the National Gallery's progress, and "his eyes would brighten as we mentioned his paintings and the pleasure they gave to visitors."[46] After Samuel Kress fell ill, his younger brother

❧ PLATE 14   El Greco, *Laocoön*, c. 1610/1614.
National Gallery of Art, Samuel H. Kress Collection,
1946.18.1

Rush stepped in (fig. 35), leading the Kress Foundation to further major acquisitions in the French, German, Dutch, Flemish, Spanish, and Italian schools of painting (see plate 14) as well as important sculptures. John Walker called Rush H. Kress "a much greater collector, who raised the Samuel H. Kress Collection to its present eminence, or I might even say pre-eminence, for in quality and number of works of art it is difficult to find its equal among donations to any American museum."[47] As these additional works of art came to the National Gallery, they replaced earlier Kress gifts, which found homes in twenty regional art museums as well as colleges and universities across the country.

By the time David Finley retired as director in 1956, the Kress collection had become the full and equal partner to that of Andrew Mellon, in terms of both quantity and quality, and Finley reflected, "I think one is justified in saying that never before in the history of the world have such imagination and generosity been shown in bringing great art to the people of an entire country, continental in extent."[48] But all this might never have happened at all if Finley had not paid his historic visit to Kress at his New York apartment that day in April 1938. John Walker, who had a good deal to do with the Kress collection himself, sums it up best: "[Finley] had arrived at three in the afternoon; he left at ten in the evening. During those seven hours, with his inimitable powers of persuasion, he induced Samuel Kress to give up his plan for a private museum, for which property was already under option and architectural drawings prepared, and to send his works of art instead to the National Gallery. Had David Finley not arrived when he did, the Kress Collection would have remained on Fifth Avenue in its own building."[49]

The Widener Collection

Obtaining the Widener collection proved even more challenging for Finley and the National Gallery. Whereas Kress had come late to collecting, not having begun until the 1920s, the Widener collection had started to take shape some fifty years earlier when Peter A. B. Widener, a Philadelphia streetcar mogul, had purchased European art for his estate, Lynnewood Hall, in Elkins Park just north of the city. After his death in 1915, his son Joseph E. Widener (fig. 36) continued collecting with distinction. The Wideners owned *Feast of the Gods* by Giovanni Bellini

36. *Joseph E. Widener*, portrait by Oswald Birley, 1928. National Gallery of Art

and Titian (plate 15), among the finest Renaissance paintings in America, and no fewer than fourteen Rembrandts and two Vermeers, including *Woman Holding a Balance* (plate 16), as well as J. M. W. Turner's *Keelmen Heaving in Coals by Moonlight* (plate 17) and works by Raphael, El Greco, and Bellotto.

Andrew Mellon had spoken with Joseph Widener about donating his collection to the nascent National Gallery of Art, but their conversations had been inconclusive, even though Widener's father had once conceived a plan for a national gallery and had actually looked at possible sites on the Mall in Washington. Finley and David Bruce had made an expedition to Lynnewood Hall to see the Widener collection with its curator in early 1937, but apparently Widener was then in Florida, where he had a home in Palm Beach and horse-racing interests

PLATE 15   Giovanni Bellini and Titian, *Feast of the Gods*, 1514/1529.
National Gallery of Art, Widener Collection, 1942.9.1

PLATE 16   Johannes Vermeer, *Woman Holding a Balance*, c. 1664.
National Gallery of Art, Widener Collection, 1942.9.97

PLATE 17   J. M. W. Turner, *Keelmen Heaving in Coals by Moonlight*, 1835.
National Gallery of Art, Widener Collection, 1942.9.86

at Hialeah. Finley had expected Widener to stop in Washington during the spring of 1937 to continue discussions with Mellon, but he had not done so.[50] Now, following Andrew Mellon's death and with the Kress gift well on its way, Finley turned his attention again to the Widener collection.

Finley contacted Joseph Widener through Lord Duveen, asking for an appointment to come and see him with Paul Mellon. Widener responded by inviting Finley and Mellon to lunch at Lynnewood Hall on 12 December 1938. Widener "was a collector in the old style, so courteous as to be practically indistinguishable from his butler."[51] But few could outdo David Finley in courtesy, and more than half a century later Paul Mellon recalled being impressed by Finley's "charm and tact" on this occasion.[52] Evidently, so was Widener, who gave serious consideration to the idea of donating the collection to the National Gallery but felt concerned about his porcelains, tapestries, and decorative arts. Finley urged the trustees to accept these objects as well, placing them in special rooms on the ground floor, apart from the paintings and sculpture.

The trustees agreed, and Finley returned to Lynnewood Hall with the architect Otto Eggers to discuss with Widener just how to display his treasures. Widener still hesitated, so Finley asked Eggers to prepare color renderings of the rooms intended to house the collection, "showing the rooms with travertine walls, black marble floors, and vitrines with mirrors set into the walls, each vitrine to contain a group of the Widener porcelains just as they were arranged at Lynnewood Hall. . . . In three days Mr. Eggers had his color renderings ready; we returned to Lynnewood Hall; and as Mr. Widener looked at the drawings his eyes filled with tears. 'If you will do this for my porcelains,' he said, 'you can have everything else and I will ask no questions.'"[53]

In fact, Joseph Widener did have at least one more question. After meeting with Finley at the Gallery to approve final design details, he telephoned the next day and said, "I have been thinking about things since I left you, and I have changed my mind." Finley feared the worst, but Widener only said, "I thought those cornices ought to be a little deeper—say, six inches." Finley quickly responded, no doubt breathing a sigh of relief, "You couldn't be more right. Would you like them to be twelve inches deeper?"[54] At last, in May 1939, Joseph Widener wrote a letter to the trustees agreeing to leave his collection to the National Gallery in his will.[55] Paul Mellon wrote in his memoirs, "My father had discussed with old Mr. Widener his plans for a National Gallery, but it was only through David Finley's diplomacy, from the time of his first visit to Joseph Widener at Lynnewood Hall, in 1937, that the collection came to Washington."[56]

The Philadelphia Museum of Art and its lawyers did not sit quietly and watch this happen, however. It was known that Peter A. B. Widener's will allowed his son to give the collection "to any museum now or hereafter established in the City of Philadelphia, City of Washington, or City of New York." And Fiske Kimball, a respected art historian and director of the Philadelphia Museum of Art, had fully expected that the collection would stay in the Wideners' hometown, with his institution as the obvious beneficiary. Faced with the imminent exodus of the Widener collection to Washington, the board of the Philadelphia Museum went to the state legislature in Harrisburg, which in June 1939 passed an act exempting cultural institutions in Pennsylvania from the five percent state tax on the value of charitable bequests. The museum's lawyers doubtless knew that Peter Widener's will prohibited his estate from bearing any part of a tax that might be imposed on the gift of the collection.

Finley now had a major problem: there was no way of knowing what value might be assigned to the collection and thus what tax would be owed;[57] but the state of Pennsylvania refused to estimate the value of the collection until the National Gallery agreed to pay the tax, whatever it turned out to be.[58] The Wideners had paid $836,000 for a single Raphael, *The Small Cowper Madonna*,[59] and the Gallery's records indicated that the Wideners had paid roughly $25 million for the entire collection.[60] At that value, the tax would have been $1.25 million, and Finley felt certain the Mellon Trust would not pay the tax on another collection. But now the battle shifted to the legislative arena, where Finley was in his element. Failing to persuade the Pennsylvania legislature to exempt the federal government from payment of the gift tax, Finley approached the U.S. Congress, where he had the home-field advantage. He first went to some of his former colleagues at the

Treasury Department to line up support for a bill by which the federal government would pay the tax to the state of Pennsylvania. Then he obtained sponsors in both the Senate and the House of Representatives, who introduced companion bills on 25 August 1942, with the blessings of the Roosevelt administration. The Pennsylvania congressional delegation put up a stiff fight. They had significant power in the House, where they boasted some thirty members, for the Keystone State's population then ranked second only to New York's. The world had changed a lot since the young David Finley had helped his father, a U.S. congressman, shepherd legislation through Congress, but Congress had not changed that much, and Finley still knew how to play the game. When the votes were counted, the Pennsylvania delegation had lost, though the amount of the tax to be paid to Pennsylvania was not yet known—one of the few times Congress had ever signed a blank check. The legislation passed, the President signed it, and the Widener collection came to the National Gallery.

Once again, Finley's timing was superb. The National Gallery announced the Widener gift in August 1942, Joseph Widener saw his collection installed at the Gallery in the spring of 1943, and he died in October of that year. Ultimately, the tax totaled only $308,000—less than was feared, owing to lower valuations given at the end of the Depression and the beginning of the Second World War. Finley later made peace with Fiske Kimball and the Pennsylvania Museum of Art. He liked Philadelphia, where he had many friends and had lived and worked from 1915 to 1918, better than any city except Washington:

> But all of that did not affect my feeling of responsibility to get the National Gallery the greatest paintings I could find, regardless of where they were or how difficult it might be to acquire them. I always remembered the advice given me early in my career as a museum director by the director of a museum in Europe. "Sometimes," he said, "the going will be very rough. You will wish you had never become a museum director. But don't let that bother you. Only one thing is important. When the smoke clears away, *be sure you have the pictures.*" And that I never forgot.[61]

37. Paul Mellon and his wife Mary with Mr. and Mrs. Donald Shepard at opening of the National Gallery of Art, March 1941

A Grand Opening

By late 1940, with the building at last finished and the Mellon and Kress collections installed in their designated galleries, the National Gallery of Art prepared to open its doors. Although the Widener rooms were ready as well, Joseph Widener decided not to transfer his art from Lynnewood Hall until it could all be installed at once. In failing health, he also decided not to come up from Florida for the official opening of the National Gallery on 17 March 1941. He did, however, send a spectacular array of blooming acacia plants to adorn the museum for the occasion.

And what an occasion! For *the* event of the season in Washington, men wore black tie or military dress uniform, and women wore evening gowns (fig. 37). Anyone with connections secured an invitation, and if they could not finagle one, they simply dressed up and crashed the party. More than nine thousand people packed the building, including President and Mrs. Roosevelt, the Supreme Court, the Congress, the diplomatic corps, and trustees and directors of art museums from Boston to Los Angeles. Chief Justice Charles Evans Hughes, Paul Mellon, and Samuel Kress led the Gallery's trustees on the dais. Finley drafted Paul Mellon's speech, as he had those of Mellon's father for so many years, formally presenting the National Gallery and the Mellon art collection to President Roosevelt and the American people. Although Andrew Mellon had not lived to see the National Gallery become a reality, his spirit infused the proceedings, invoked both in his son's words and in the President's as well. As Roosevelt put it: "the giver of the building has matched the richness of his gift with the modesty of his spirit, stipulating that the Gallery shall not be known by his name, but the nation's. And those other collectors of paintings and sculpture who have already joined, or who propose to join, their works of art to Mr. Mellon's have felt the same desire to establish, not a memorial to themselves, but a monument to the art they love and the country to which they belong."[62]

For David Finley the evening unfolded almost exactly as he had planned it. The glory went to Andrew Mellon and to Samuel Kress—as well as to Franklin Roosevelt, whose administration had actually delayed the Gallery's opening for three years while prosecuting Mellon for alleged tax fraud. Finley orchestrated every detail of the opening ceremonies, but his name and face remained in the background, just as he preferred it. The only unplanned bit of excitement involved Finley's niece, Lillian Brown, who fainted during the President's speech while standing in the front row of the crowd under the heat of the photographers' floodlights and was carried off on a stretcher.[63]

As the exhilaration of the opening faded, Finley returned to the unglamorous, everyday job of making the new institution work smoothly. With war looming in Europe and the Far East, the National Gallery soon receded from public attention. Indeed, within six months both Paul Mellon and David Bruce were on active duty with the

38. David Finley giving Elizabeth, the Queen Mother, a tour of the National Gallery of Art, 1954

U.S. Army. Bruce retained his position as nominal president of the trustees, but vice president Lammot Belin took his place as de facto head of the board.[64]

Meanwhile, Finley had to fend off a series of challenges from a member of his inner circle. Donald Shepard, his former law partner and the Mellon family lawyer, had stepped down as a trustee in 1939 to become secretary-treasurer and general counsel to the National Gallery. In May 1941 he wrote a "Memorandum to Mr. Finley," pointing out that he, as secretary and a member of the committee on public relations, had not been consulted before an article and photographs that appeared in *Harper's Bazaar* were "released." Finley responded three days later with a "Memorandum to Mr. Shepard," explaining that the magazine's staff had written the article, not the Gallery.[65] A month later Shepard, in his capacity as treasurer, questioned the expenditure of $1.00 each for a shipment of chrysanthemums that Gallery administrator Harry McBride had ordered for the garden courts. Finley replied in a tactful memorandum that not only was the price extremely reasonable but the treasurer had no business taking issue with a purchase for which funds were available.[66]

In November 1941 Shepard upped the ante in a dispute over the valuation of donated works of art. The Gallery's auditors had recommended that all art be placed on the books at "fair market value" as of the date of the gift; thus Shepard requested that Finley send a letter to all donors asking them to assign a monetary value to their gifts. Finley did not think it necessary to have this information at all. The

Metropolitan Museum of Art, for example, carried its art on the books at only nominal value.[67] In any case, he feared that such an approach could offend donors—as it would have Andrew Mellon and Samuel Kress. He also argued the impossibility of establishing a value for objects one had inherited and the likelihood that asking for this information would have a chilling effect on future gifts. But Shepard persisted, and Finley referred the matter to David Bruce, as president of the trustees—with some reluctance as Bruce was then in active military service. Bruce surprised Finley by siding with Shepard and the auditors, noting that, unlike private museums such as the Metropolitan, the National Gallery was "a governmental agency created by the Congress and responsible to it and the public for its possessions." He directed Finley to cooperate with the treasurer's office and obtain fair market value either from donors or "from the best possible sources," such as "comparable known values for similar works of art [or the] advice of dealers."[68]

This contest continued to simmer, with Shepard complaining to Bruce of what he considered lax handling of funds by Finley and others under his supervision. And once again Bruce backed Shepard. This was too much for Finley, and in a memorandum to Bruce on 13 December 1941 he vigorously contested Shepard's assertion and pointed out that on four occasions during the year he had advanced his personal funds for Gallery activities for which the treasurer had not provided funds, "so that I can only construe your memorandum as a censure of both Mr. McBride and myself, which I would regret to have on record if we have not knowingly done anything to merit it." Concerning the valuation of art objects, in the last paragraph of the same memorandum Finley yielded to the extent of agreeing to "try to obtain this information verbally" but continuing to believe that "it would be the very greatest mistake to write letters requesting such valuations from the donors."[69] Fortunately, Bruce happened to be in Washington at this time between tours of OSS duty in London. Meeting with Finley in person, Bruce accepted the director's compromise and followed up with a letter that was unusual for that time in the use of their first names but was clearly a vote of confidence in Finley:

39. Television personality Arlene Francis interviews David Finley at the
National Gallery of Art, 1955

Dear David:

I am in receipt of your memorandum of December 13th, 1941,
which I am returning herewith for your files since we have now
discussed this matter. I think the procedure outlined in the last
paragraph is very satisfactory.

Very sincerely yours,

David[70]

By early 1942 Finley and Shepard had apparently patched up their
differences, though a year later Shepard resigned from the Gallery and
returned to private law practice and the management of Ailsa Mellon
Bruce's Avalon Foundation. Finley proposed Shepard for membership in the Metropolitan Club and later won his cooperation on Avalon
grants in support of historic preservation. Their correspondence in the

1950s reflects that they had left behind their quarrels of 1941, whatever the cause.

The tidal wave of the Second World War that swept over Washington in December 1941 submerged Finley's feat of completing the magnificent National Gallery building on the Mall, securing the Kress collection to complement Mellon's, and receiving a similar commitment from Widener. With the war over, Finley's work at the National Gallery began to achieve public acclaim and high-profile visitors (fig. 38). In June 1946 he received an honorary doctor of fine arts degree from Yale, and in June 1950 the University of South Carolina gave him an honorary doctor of literature.[71] The press also began to take notice of his accomplishments (fig. 39). In 1948 an article in the *Saturday Evening Post* captured the essence of what he had achieved.

The Millionaires' Best Friend

Andy Mellon picked the right director for the National Gallery of Art in David Finley. Little David, the rich man's pal, has quintupled the original Mellon contribution into one of the greatest collections of masterpieces in the world.

David Edward Finley, of Washington, D.C., has a very high opinion of American millionaires. He knows many of them and has almost invariably found them to be individuals of wide culture, extraordinary good taste and the most unbounded generosity. The things that millionaires do when Finley is around are well-nigh incredible. They sign away vast slices of their fortunes, empty their homes and apartments and strip the very pictures from their walls to give away. Sometimes, when they don't have what Finley wants, they go out and buy it, just for the pleasure of handing it over to him.

At least that's the way Finley explains it. His professional brethren tell a different story. They claim it is no coincidence that the most important art gifts of recent years have practically all gone to the institution of which Finley is the No. 1 promoter and head. They argue, in fact, that Finley is the most astute salesman-in-reverse that has ever appeared on the American art scene. "In this day of a dying plutocracy," one of them said recently, "the chief task of a museum director is making sweet music to people who have pictures to give away. David is the consummate performer in our line."[72]

Not all professional colleagues immediately welcomed David Finley and the National Gallery with open arms. The Gallery was very much a newcomer among established American art museums like the Metropolitan in New York, the Philadelphia Museum of Art, the Museum of Fine Art in Boston, and the Art Institute of Chicago. And springing suddenly to life in the nation's capital with a generous endowment from Andrew Mellon, annual appropriations from the federal government, and world-famous art collections, the Gallery sparked acute pangs of jealousy in more than one museum director. In addition, its director had only a law degree and none of the educational or professional credentials of many of his brethren. But David Finley soon won acceptance among his peers, not only for his innate administrative skills and professional courtesies but for what he achieved in elevating the visibility and prestige of American art museums.[73] Elected president of the American Association of Museums in 1945, he served in that position until 1949.

David Finley would have been content to remain as director of the National Gallery indefinitely, but when he became sixty-five in 1955, the board of trustees began to plan for his retirement. In a fascinating turn of events, a conflict arose as to his successor, with Paul Mellon, Rush Kress, and others favoring John Walker, who had been close to Finley for many years, and Chester Dale, then president of the board, backing Huntington Cairns and bluntly threatening to pull his collection from the National Gallery unless he got his way. Cairns made matters worse, presuming to *tell* Finley that he was about to succeed him, which aroused Finley's anger. It took two heavyweight lawyers—John Foster Dulles, then secretary of state and an ex-officio trustee, and his former partner, Stoddard Stevens—to persuade Dale to lower the flag and agree to accept Walker.[74] Although not eager to retire, Finley was very happy that it was John Walker who succeeded him.[75]

Finley had led the National Gallery of Art as director for over eighteen years, retiring on 1 July 1956. Realizing the dream of his mentor

Andrew Mellon, he set the Gallery on its course and brought together the team that took it to the next stage in its development. Although he achieved further distinctions in an illustrious career—as founding chairman of the National Trust for Historic Preservation, as a founder of the National Portrait Gallery, as chairman of the U.S. Commission of Fine Arts, among other roles—his early work in bringing the National Gallery into existence ranks in many ways as his most significant and most visible contribution to the cultural life of the nation and of the capital city.[76] His friend Joseph Alsop, the Washington-based writer and columnist, joined brother Stewart Alsop to sum up this phase of Finley's life in the *Washington Post* of 18 March 1956:

Kindness of David Edward Finley
By Joseph and Stewart Alsop

The National Gallery of Art is only incidentally located on Constitution Ave.; it is not local but national, as its name implies. The true address of this vast pink marble treasure house is really not Washington, D.C., but simply the United States of America.

These fairly obvious facts are worth pointing out at the moment because David Edward Finley is now retiring from the National Gallery directorship. The Almighty made the Yellowstone and the Grand Canyon. The Capitol, the White House, and our other man-made landscape features are owed to scores of hands and minds. But David Finley, the real creator of the National Gallery, has added a new and major feature to the American landscape almost single-handed.

There is a good deal of confusion on this point, no doubt. The National Gallery is often called the Mellon Gallery; and it is certainly true that Andrew W. Mellon generously spent something like $50 million buying pictures for and endowing and building the great gallery. But where Mellon gave money, Finley gave himself, which is rather more important in the long run.

On first acquaintance, to be sure, you would not suppose that David Finley is the sort of man who could matter more, all by himself, than $50 million. He is a short, slender fellow of decidedly avian appearance, with the almost exhaustingly good manners of an old-fashioned South Carolinian. He never speaks an unkind word or does an unkind thing. He is an enthusiastic gardener, but you feel he is even polite to the weeds as he uproots them. He goes to church, sits on the vestry, and is loyal to old friends.

But David Finley's beautiful manners and mild appearance mask a steely determination and a happy ruthlessness that would not be entirely out of place at the Kremlin. He has never wanted much, rather luckily, for himself. But when Finley wants something for the National Gallery, iron men are twisted into knots; strong men blanch and stand aside; and obstinate men do not know what hit them. . . .

Mellon it was who first conceived the notion of giving an art gallery to the Nation. But it was Finley, very certainly, who decided that the gallery must be fit to stand comparison with the Louvre and the Prado, the National Gallery in London, the Hermitage in Moscow [*sic*], and Pitti in Florence. And it was Finley who made the great scheme for a national treasure house into the dominating interest of Mellon's later years.

The Alsops exaggerated in giving more credit for the National Gallery to David Finley than to Andrew Mellon. Neither could have done it alone, and neither could have done it without the other. But together they achieved a miracle.

1. Finley, *Standard of Excellence,* 57.

2. Joseph Duveen to David Finley, 1 September 1937. Duveen Records, microfilm, Metropolitan Museum of Art, New York, reel 344.

3. Finley to Duveen, 15 September 1937. Duveen Records, reel 344.

4. Finley, *Standard of Excellence,* 53.

5. Paul Mellon finally brought these grievances to his father in November 1936, armed with a carefully drafted memorandum. Much to his surprise, and pleasure, he found the older man quite sympathetic, and they had the only real heart-to-heart, head-to-head talk of their lives. See Paul Mellon, *Reflections in a Silver Spoon,* 147–156.

6. Mellon, *Reflections in a Silver Spoon,* 298.

7. Mellon, *Reflections in a Silver Spoon,* 157–171.

8. Mellon, *Reflections in a Silver Spoon,* 153.

9. Around this time Bruce began to write histories and dabble in finance, and he was elected to the Virginia state legislature in Richmond. Lankford, *Last American Aristocrat,* 98–104.

10. Finley, *Standard of Excellence,* 61. David Bruce (1898–1977) was in London by July 1940 to work with British relief agencies as the special delegate of the American Red Cross and remained there during the Battle of Britain. He joined the forerunner of the OSS at its founding in July 1941 and returned to London with the rank of colonel to serve as right-hand man to OSS director William Donovan. He spent most of the war with the OSS in London, except for one foray to France in August 1944, when he and Ernest Hemingway personally "liberated" the bar at the Ritz Hotel in Paris when Allied units entered the city (see Lankford, *Last American Aristocrat,* 110–162). After he and Ailsa were divorced in 1945, Bruce remarried and went on to serve six successive Presidents: as Truman's Ambassador to France (1949–1952), Eisenhower's to West Germany (1957–1959), Kennedy's and Johnson's to Great Britain (1961–1969), Nixon's minister to China (1973–1974), and Ford's ambassador to NATO (1974–1976). No single person since John and John Quincy Adams has served this nation in more important diplomatic posts. Bruce died on 5 December 1977, soon after David Finley, and is buried at Oak Hill Cemetery in Georgetown, close to David and Margaret Finley.

11. *New York Times,* editorial, 24 February 1938.

12. Duncan Phillips moved to Washington in 1918 and opened a small gallery in his mother's home in 1921, specializing in nineteenth-century French paintings.

13. Mellon, *Reflections in a Silver Spoon,* 154.

14. David Finley's telegram to his mother, March 1938. Finley Papers, NGA Archives.

15. Finley memorandum, "Progress on plans for the construction of the National Gallery of Art," 28 October 1937. Finley Papers, NGA Archives, box 27. The original building designed by John Russell Pope is now known as the West Building, since I. M. Pei's striking East Building opened in 1978.

16. Finley, *Standard of Excellence*, 56–57.

17. After Pope's death his two principal associates, Otto R. Eggers and Daniel Paul Higgins, carried on his practice, first as "Office of John Russell Pope" and by late 1938 as "Eggers and Higgins," with offices at 542 Fifth Avenue, New York. Eggers assumed primary responsibility for completing Pope's design for the National Gallery of Art.

18. David Finley to David Bruce, 4 August 1939: "John [Walker] and I spent yesterday in Baltimore and lunched with Magill James. The Jacobs Wing horrified John as it did me, and we are determined to be more vigilant than ever with Mr. Eggers to make sure he does not perpetrate something similar on our building." Finley Papers, Library of Congress, box 27.

19. The *Mercury* was attributed by Duveen to Giovanni Bologna, and later by John Walker to Adrian de Vries; the National Gallery now gives the work the attribution "after Giovanni Bologna." NGA Web site, www.nga.gov, consulted in 2005.

20. Finley, *Standard of Excellence*, 60.

21. Finley, *Standard of Excellence*, 62.

22. Walker, *Self-Portrait with Donors*, 37. The Finleys' ward Joan Beauregard Williams recalls her adoptive parents poring over these plans and blueprints at their Georgetown home for hours, night after night. The library was taken over with five card tables on which David and Margaret worked together. Interview conducted by Anne G. Ritchie, 1 March 1991, transcript, pp. 3–4. NGA Archives, box 8-10. Mrs. Williams also remembers visiting the Gallery when construction was almost completed but before the paintings were installed; she and the teenaged son of Magill James would push each other around the marble halls and the Rotunda in wheelchairs.

23. Finley, *Standard of Excellence*, 60–61. Irwin Laughlin (1870–1955), like Duncan Phillips a grandson of one of the founders of Jones & Laughlin Steel Co., became a career diplomat who in 1919 retired to Meridian House, his stately residence in Washington, D.C., designed by John Russell Pope. At Mellon's urging, Herbert Hoover had appointed him U.S. ambassador to Spain (see Andrew W. Mellon's pocket diary, 1929. NGA Archives). Laughlin was very knowledgeable about architecture and decoration from his years in the foreign service.

24. Finley, *Standard of Excellence*, 61.

25. John Walker and Charles Seymour Jr., "Memorandum Regarding Mr. William Delano's Impressions and Advice," 15 December 1939. Finley Papers, Library of Congress, box 27.

26. David Finley, memorandum to the trustees of the National Gallery, 30 June 1939. Finley Papers, NGA Archives, box 27.

27. Kenneth Clark, obituary for David Finley, *The Times* [London], 19 February 1977, 16: "Against Pope's wishes, he made the central rooms of the Gallery into covered gardens, and refused to hang them with pictures."

28. Finley, *Standard of Excellence*, 70.

29. John Walker (1906–1995) was stricken with polio at age thirteen and went to New York with his mother for two years to recuperate, spending hours in his wheelchair at

the Metropolitan Museum of Art. He decided at an early age that he wanted to be an art historian.

30. Walker, *Self-Portrait with Donors*, 34.

31. Finley, *Standard of Excellence*, 71.

32. Kopper, *Gift to the Nation*, 251.

33. Finley, *Standard of Excellence*, 78.

34. Walker, *Self-Portrait with Donors*, 139, 293.

35. Finley, *Standard of Excellence*, 79.

36. Ernest Samuels, *Bernard Berenson: The Making of a Legend* (Cambridge, MA, 1987), 426.

37. David Finley to Bernard Berenson, September 1938. Berenson Library, Villa I Tatti.

38. Samuels, *Berenson*, 423.

39. Finley to Berenson, September 1938. Berenson Library, Villa I Tatti.

40. Having emigrated from Lithuania to the United States as a child, Berenson risked forfeiting his citizenship by his continuous absence from America, but he enlisted the help of friends in high places to prevent that from happening.

41. In 1931, for example, with Duveen trying to horn in on the sale of the Hermitage treasures, Berenson had advised him on its best pictures, most of which went to Mellon through Knoedler's. Duveen's failure, the greatest of his career, also meant lowered expectations for Berenson (Samuels, *Berenson*, 389).

42. Samuels, *Berenson*, 437. Berenson found Kress "to be the easiest of rich men to deal with." Their friendship grew over the years, and the Kress Foundation actually financed Berenson's final publications in the 1950s.

43. Walker, *Self-Portrait with Donors*, 137.

44. Finley, *Standard of Excellence*, 79–81.

45. Walker, *Self-Portrait with Donors*, 139–140.

46. Finley, *Standard of Excellence*, 85.

47. Walker, *Self-Portrait with Donors*, 140.

48. Finley, *Standard of Excellence*, 91.

49. Walker, *National Gallery of Art*, 38.

50. Finley, *Standard of Excellence*, 93–98.

51. Clark, *Another Part of the Wood*, 243.

52. Mellon, *Reflections in a Silver Spoon*, 300.

53. Finley, *Standard of Excellence*, 101.

54. Finley, *Standard of Excellence*, 65.

55. Joseph E. Widener to A. W. Mellon Educational and Charitable Trust, 29 May 1939. Finley Papers, Library of Congress, box 31.

56. Mellon, *Reflections in a Silver Spoon*, 300.

57. Finley, *Standard of Excellence*, 100.

58. Walker, *National Gallery of Art*, 34.

59. Samuels, *Berenson*, 101.

60. Walker, *Self-Portrait with Donors*, xv.

61. Finley, *Standard of Excellence*, 106.

62. Mellon, *Reflections in a Silver Spoon*, 300.

63. As a fourteen-year-old, Joan Beauregard was "mortified," but Lillian soon recovered, and Joan did not mind missing the speeches. In 1991 Joan Beauregard Williams was one of the few surviving witnesses to the opening of the National Gallery and certainly the youngest. Williams oral history interview by Ritchie, 33–34.

64. Ferdinand Lammot Belin (1881–1961) had a career as a foreign service officer, then served as U.S. ambassador to Poland in 1932–1933. He and his family lived at Evermay, an historic house with gardens in Georgetown. He was elected a trustee of the National Gallery in 1939 and served as vice president until after the Second World War.

65. Some social jealousy may have provoked this protest, for the photographs, taken by an editor for *Harper's Bazaar* the day after the Gallery's opening, showed Mrs. David Finley, Mrs. John Walker, and Mrs. Magill James but did not include Mrs. Donald Shepard.

66. Exchange of memoranda between David Finley and Donald Shepard, May–June 1942. Finley Papers, NGA Archives, box 19.

67. The National Gallery currently assigns no value to its art collections: "In conformity with accounting procedures generally followed by art museums, the value of art has been excluded from the statement of financial position. The Gallery's collections are maintained for public exhibition, education and research in furtherance of public service, rather than for financial gain." See the National Gallery of Art's 2004 Annual Report, 43, 47.

68. Bruce to Finley, memorandum, 28 November 1941. Finley Papers, Library of Congress.

69. Finley to Bruce, memorandum, 13 December 1941.

70. Finley to Bruce, memorandum, 13 December 1941.

71. It seems somehow fitting that Yale, the university that was his first choice as a youth but which he turned down under pressure from his father, forty years later honored his talents even before his own alma mater did. The citation began "Abandoning a legal and diplomatic career in 1939 [*sic*], Mr. Finley has since devoted himself to the more highly colored and more hazardous profession of persuading famous collectors to give their pictures to the nation. His skill in this regard he learned from Mr. Mellon. Together, they have shown the American people that the truly fine art is that of giving to others the blessings that one has himself enjoyed." Citation, David Edward Finley, D.F.A., Yale University commencement, June 1946. Finley Papers, NGA Archives, box 36-18.

72. Roger Butterfield, "The Millionaires' Best Friend," *Saturday Evening Post*, 8 March 1948, 30. Despite its flamboyant title and tongue-in-cheek style, this piece was well written by a respected author and historian. He clearly conducted an extensive interview with Finley, who provided important details not available elsewhere.

73. Interview with J. Carter Brown, conducted by the author, National Gallery of Art, 12 July 1999.

74. Mellon, *Reflections in a Silver Spoon*, 306–310.

75. Finley, *Standard of Excellence*, 171; interview, Joan Beauregard Williams.

76. In 1957 the Theodore Roosevelt Memorial Association awarded its Distinguished Service Medal to David E. Finley for his work as director of the National Gallery of Art. The medal was first awarded in 1923 and has gone to national leaders in many fields, including Justice Oliver Wendell Holmes (1924), General John J. Pershing (1928), Helen Keller (1936), George Washington Carver (1939), General George C. Marshall (1945), John Foster Dulles (1952), Robert Frost (1954), and Laurance S. Rockefeller (1963).

40. David Finley and John Walker (second and fourth from left) oversee
the return of the National Gallery paintings from their wartime sanctuary
at Biltmore House, Asheville, North Carolina, in 1944

7

Wartime

1941–1945

ON ST. PATRICK'S DAY 1941, as President Franklin D. Roosevelt accepted the Mellons' gift of the National Gallery of Art in Washington on behalf of the American people, the storm of war had already broken over much of Europe. The Germans by then occupied Prague, Warsaw, Amsterdam, the Hague, Brussels, Ghent, Bruges, and Paris, while London's fate still hung in the balance. Great Britain grimly withstood the German Blitz, with the help of Canada and the rest of the British Empire and with the first trickle of what became a torrent of American munitions. Although most U.S. citizens clung to the hope that the country could stay out of the war, Roosevelt knew that America's fortunes aligned closely with those of Europe, particularly Great Britain, and that it was a question of when, not if, we would join the battle. He clearly signaled as much in his speech at the opening of the National Gallery:

> To accept this work on behalf of the people of this democratic nation is to assert the belief of the people of this nation in a human spirit which is now everywhere endangered and which, in many countries where it first found form and meaning, has

been rooted out and broken and destroyed . . . to assert the purpose of the people of America that the freedom of the human spirit and human mind which has produced the world's great art and all its science shall not be utterly destroyed. . . . The dedication of this Gallery to a living past, and to a greater and more richly living future, is the measure of the earnestness of our intention that the freedom of the human spirit shall go on.[1]

Three months later Paul Mellon enlisted in the U.S. Cavalry. That same month, June 1941, Hitler opened the bloodiest chapter of the war by invading Russia along a two-thousand-mile front, from the Arctic to the Black Sea. Within another three months David Bruce had joined the OSS in London. Then on 7 December 1941, a Japanese carrier strike force surprised Pearl Harbor, and the United States not only was plunged into war in the Pacific but soon faced Nazi Germany and Fascist Italy as well. No one who lived through the Second World War will ever forget it. It was the deadliest, costliest, and most widespread war in human history, and its echoes still reverberate around the globe six decades after it ended.[2] America rebounded from its early defeats at Pearl Harbor and in the Philippines to become the dominant military, political, and economic world power in less than four years. But it was not without cost: 363,000 combat deaths and many more wounded.

The war was brought home to the Finleys and Eustises earlier than most Americans, when some of Margaret's English cousins fled the London Blitz in 1940 for the safety of the Virginia countryside, where they stayed as guests at Little Oatlands for eighteen months before returning to England. Then in October 1940, when the first young Americans were drafted into the army, Margaret Finley's only brother, Morton Corcoran Eustis, enlisted as a private in an army reserve unit in New York. As a bachelor of thirty-five, somewhat overweight, with poor eyesight, Morton Eustis seemed an unlikely soldier. Like his sisters, he had led a sheltered life, growing up on Lafayette Square and at Oatlands. A graduate of Groton and of Harvard, he lived in New York, where he wrote for *Theater Arts* magazine and authored two books on the theater. He had traveled widely in Europe, spoke fluent French, and had spent several years in France, a country he loved. Even when his age and bad vision denied him an officer's commission, Eustis served gamely in the ranks.

The war also brought forth in David and Margaret Finley leadership qualities that each exercised on a national level. Margaret emerged as a prominent volunteer for the American Red Cross, a full-time job she continued long after the war. David, as director of the National Gallery of Art, continued to preserve and build its art collections while mobilizing the new museum to do its part in the war effort. And as the sponsor and de facto head of the Roberts Commission, he played a crucial role in helping to save the monuments and artworks of Europe.

The National Gallery in the War

In hindsight, the likelihood of an enemy attack on Washington seems remote, but David Finley took no chances with the paintings and sculptures entrusted to him by Andrew Mellon and Samuel Kress. Well before the assault on Pearl Harbor, Finley had approached the owners of the great Vanderbilt mansion, Biltmore, near Asheville, North Carolina, and asked that the National Gallery be allowed to move some of its most important works of art to that remote yet secure location, presumably out of harm's way. Finley knew Biltmore from his friendship with Cornelia Vanderbilt in Washington twenty years earlier; he had attended her wedding there in 1924. The Vanderbilt family quickly agreed to make its country estate available as a wartime refuge if needed. Finley took chief curator John Walker and Gallery administrator Harry McBride to Biltmore to make the necessary preparations to store works in a large vacant room there. Thus when Pearl Harbor was attacked, the National Gallery was ready. Three weeks later, on New Year's Day 1942, Finley moved the Gallery's treasures by train to Asheville and by moving vans to Biltmore, where they stayed for the duration of the war, attended by a senior member of the Gallery staff and several guards (see fig. 40). To fill the blank spaces on the National Gallery's walls, Finley arranged temporary loans of paintings, such as those from the Louvre that had been on tour of South America when the war broke out.

Meanwhile, a near panic had seized much of the country after Pearl Harbor. Considering the dramatic ocean crossing by the Japanese (a nation lightly regarded by most Americans before the war) and the devastation of the U.S. Pacific Fleet in Hawaii, citizens feared a bolder attack.[3] What if bombs fell on mainland American cities? Just before Christmas of 1941 David Finley, John Walker, and Magill James of the National Gallery met in New York with directors of the Metropolitan Museum of Art, the Museum of Modern Art, the Frick Collection, and other major art museums from Minneapolis and Boston to Ottawa to consider their responses to this possibility. Many people expected that museums would be emptied, their contents moved to sanctuaries, and their buildings closed indefinitely.[4] Instead, museum directors insisted that not only would their institutions remain open but they would do everything they could to support the war effort by trying to boost both civilian and military morale. A motion drafted by Finley and adopted by the group began: "It is the feeling of the Association of Museums that no general evacuation from museums should take place; that museums as sources of education and entertainment owe an even greater duty to the public in time of war than under ordinary conditions; that they should, therefore, continue their usual activities and even increase them so far as practical."[5] That certainly became the policy of the National Gallery, whose director felt a particular obligation to reach out to the thousands of men and women in uniform who crowded the nation's capital during wartime. He made it a point to promote the Gallery as "a pleasant place to come—warm in winter and cool in summer, with a good cafeteria and, incidentally, interesting pictures."[6]

At the same time, Finley knew that most people can look at paintings for only an hour or two and then must have some rest or other diversion. He wanted to offer more than art to the military rank and file. When a friend suggested free Sunday evening concerts, as presented at the National Gallery in London, Finley went to Chester Dale of New York and persuaded him to fund twelve concerts as an experiment, with musicians from Washington's National Symphony Orchestra. The East Garden Court, with its palms and fountains, had more appeal than the lecture hall downstairs, even if the acoustics posed various challenges. And the concerts there met with immediate acclaim and became a permanent fixture at the Gallery—still free to this day.

One result of the wartime concerts was progress for democracy. Even though Washington in the early 1940s still largely practiced the color code of the South, Finley quietly opened the Gallery's cafeteria to all, and it was one of the few decent restaurants in town to serve people of all races.[7] But another unwritten color bar remained. When the National Gallery concerts began to draw attention, Congressman Adam Clayton Powell of Harlem wrote to recommend several black performers to Richard Bales, whom Finley had hired to direct the National Gallery music program in 1943.[8] Sensing trouble, Bales went to Finley and told him that he wanted to engage black musicians. Finley agreed. The first was the soprano Madame Lillian Evanti—a Washington native, despite her stage name—who performed without incident at a Sunday evening concert on 12 May 1946. The pianist Hazel Harrison and tenor Roland Hayes each appeared in National Gallery concerts during Finley's tenure, soon followed by Natalie Hinderas, Shirley Verrett, Frances Walker, and others.[9]

Late on Sunday afternoons during the war, David and Margaret Finley along with assistant director Magill James and his wife Bruce would walk through the galleries to round up thirty soldiers, sailors, Waves, and Wacs and serve them supper in the staff and the director's dining rooms. After a cheerful party they would all go to the garden court to hear the concert. The Finleys and Jameses paid for the food on these occasions out of their own funds and the contributions of friends.[10]

The National Gallery also converted the oak-paneled Founders' Room into a lounge where service personnel could relax, write letters, and meet friends, old and new. Thousands signed the visitors' register during the war. The opening of the World War II Memorial in the summer of 2004 provided an occasion to display this moving record of individual sentiments. One entry declares: "Only in a free country of free people can such beauty be conceived in the human soul. Who would not gladly give his life to preserve it! Cpl. R. L. Lindamond, Roanoke, Va., Sept. 2, 1942." Another comment on the same page is more down-to-earth: "Not G.I.! PFC Wm. F. Caldwell, Fort McClellan, Ala., Sept. 4, 1942."[11]

American patriotism rose to a high pitch during the Second World War. One anonymous visitor to the National Gallery of Art, clearly not a young serviceman but a person of some experience, wrote to David Bruce in July 1942 deploring the scarcity of American paintings in America's National Gallery. Referring to the servicemen thronging the building, the writer complained:

> It is regrettable that your institution has not seen fit to afford them the cultural inspiration of the American scene for which they are fighting, nor traced the development of that culture through the American primitives, the Hudson River school, the works of Remington, Homer, the Innesses or any of the beloved artists of America's past; nor any yet of the vital artists of America's present. Though neither an artist nor an art connoisseur, I have visited most of the great galleries of Europe. I did not there find a slavish obeisance before alien cultures, but rather an affirmation of the culture by which people lived.[12]

Finley responded somewhat defensively, reminding Bruce that the Gallery had a number of noteworthy American paintings and was seeking to acquire more examples, especially by Winslow Homer, Albert Pinkham Ryder, and Thomas Eakins. But in truth the many European and even British holdings outshone the few American paintings. Perhaps spurred by this bolt from the blue, Finley and Walker went to work to address the lack. Two grand canvases by John Singleton Copley came to the Gallery in 1942 as gifts of Mrs. Gordon Dexter of Boston, the widow of a descendant of the artist. Two famous paintings by James McNeill Whistler arrived in 1943, including *Symphony in White, No. 1: The White Girl* (plate 18), gifts from the Whittemore family of Connecticut, one of whom had personally known Whistler and Mary Cassatt.[13] And when Homer's *Breezing Up* appeared on the market, Finley persuaded William Larimer Mellon, Andrew Mellon's nephew, to buy it for the National Gallery (plate 19). Thus, by the end of the war, the National Gallery had begun to lay the foundation for its superb collection of American paintings. Other splendid works soon followed, such as *The Biglin Brothers*

Racing by Thomas Eakins (plate 20), *The Skater* by Gilbert Stuart, and several portraits by John Singer Sargent.

Undoubtedly the most significant development in the growth of the collection at the National Gallery during the war years related to Chester Dale (fig. 41), a Wall Street prodigy who had once been a welterweight boxer. Beginning in the 1920s Dale and his wife Maud, herself an artist and very knowledgeable about art, assembled an impressive collection of French and American paintings. Whereas Mellon, Kress, and Widener had purchased almost exclusively through established dealers, Dale bought a minority interest in a Paris dealership, which gave him an inside track on new offerings and prices, with spectacular results. As John Walker later said of him, "Chester Dale taught me a great deal. His knowledge of the history of art might be minimal, but his knowledge of the world of art was prodigious. He knew what was going on behind the scenes, and he was familiar with all the tricks of the trade. He operated his own Central Intelligence Agency, which gathered information from dealers in New York, London and Paris."[14]

Finley had first met Chester Dale through Stephen Pichetto, conservator for the National Gallery as well as for Samuel Kress and the Dales. In the autumn of 1940 Finley and Walker visited Chester and Maud Dale at their townhouse on Seventy-ninth Street in New York to see their collection. Finley turned on his formidable charm, but for once was not immediately successful. Dale, a redhead and legendary for his mercurial temperament, had dallied with several top-ranked museums over the years as possible destinations for his collection. He did agree to lend twenty-two early American paintings for the opening of the National Gallery. But it was not until well after Finley retired as director in 1956—in fact, not until after Dale's death in 1962—that the National Gallery assumed ownership of the paintings that had been on loan.

The American paintings that came to the Gallery from Chester Dale in 1963 included several works by Childe Hassam and George Bellows. An earlier gift from Dale actually comprised three paintings by Bellows, an artist with whom the donor had much in common, as both had been semiprofessional athletes in their youth and shared an interest in boxing.

❦ PLATE 18 James McNeill Whistler, *Symphony in White, No. 1:*
The White Girl, 1862. National Gallery of Art,
Harris Whittemore Collection, 1943.6.2

PLATE 19 Winslow Homer, *Breezing Up (A Fair Wind)*, 1873–1876.
National Gallery of Art, Gift of the W. L. and May T. Mellon
Foundation, 1943.13.1

PLATE 20   Thomas Eakins, *The Biglin Brothers Racing*, 1872.
National Gallery of Art, Gift of Mr. and Mrs. Cornelius
Vanderbilt Whitney, 1953.7.1

PLATE 21 George Bellows, *Both Members of This Club*, 1909.
National Gallery of Art, Chester Dale Collection, 1944.13.1

PLATE 22   Edouard Manet, *The Old Musician*, 1862.
National Gallery of Art, Chester Dale Collection, 1963.10.162

41. *Chester Dale*, portrait by Diego Rivera, 1945. National Gallery of Art

In 1944 Dale gave the National Gallery one of Bellows's most famous canvases, *Both Members of This Club* (plate 21), a powerful work from his series on prizefighters, along with portraits Bellows had painted of Dale and his wife in the years just before the artist died in 1925 at age forty-three.

The glory of the Dale collection, however, was its nineteenth- and twentieth-century French paintings, among them Edouard Manet's *Old Musician* (plate 22) and iconic works by Georges Braque, Mary Cassatt, Paul Cézanne, Camille Corot, Edgar Degas, Paul Gauguin, Henri Matisse, Amedeo Modigliani, Claude Monet, Pablo Picasso, Auguste Renoir, Henri de Toulouse-Lautrec, and many others. The first

42. David Finley with Chester Dale and John Walker, 1959

twenty-five paintings arrived at the National Gallery, on loan, in 1941.
More came in 1943, 1951, and 1952. Some of these had been removed
from the Art Institute of Chicago and the Philadelphia Museum of Art
after Dale jilted those ardent suitors. But despite Finley's and Walker's
best efforts, the Chester Dale collection remained only on loan to the
National Gallery until his death (fig. 42). This caused acute anxiety
in both directors, because Dale had demonstrated his readiness to
withdraw a collection from a major museum even after leaving it on
loan for eight or nine years, and because the director of the Louvre
had told Dale that his was the finest such collection in private hands.
John Walker discussed his anxiousness at length in his memoirs.[15] But
Finley, ever the diplomat, merely observed, "Chester Dale was a strong
character, and life around him was never dull. He shared our love for
the National Gallery and contributed greatly toward making it what
it is today."[16]

43. *Lessing J. Rosenwald*, portrait by Gardner Cox, 1955. National Gallery of Art

The Rosenwald Collection

Another major art collection came to the National Gallery of Art during the war years, not only vastly increasing the number of works available for visitors to enjoy but opening up a whole new division within the museum. Lessing Rosenwald had one of the greatest private collections of prints and drawings in the world, and David Finley is the one who persuaded him to give these holdings to the National Gallery. As Finley modestly put it, "The war brought many headaches to the National Gallery. But it also brought many blessings, one being Lessing J. Rosenwald."[17]

Lessing Rosenwald (fig. 43), like Mellon, Kress, and Widener, was a Pennsylvanian, though by adoption. His father, Julius Rosenwald, had risen to the top of Sears, Roebuck & Co. in Chicago and had transformed the organization into a mail-order and retailing powerhouse. Lessing moved from Chicago to Philadelphia in 1920 to oversee Sears' new East Coast plant, and when his father retired from business in 1924

to devote more time to philanthropic interests, he allowed a colleague to step ahead of him and assume the presidency of the company. But at his father's death in 1932, Lessing became chairman of Sears.[18] Although the retailing giant continued to have its headquarters in Chicago, Rosenwald remained in Philadelphia, from where he led it through the Depression.

Starting in the 1920s, Rosenwald began to buy rare prints and drawings as well as illustrated books dating from the Middle Ages on.[19] At first this was a hobby while he pursued a demanding business career. But from the beginning he had both a passion for collecting and a voracious desire to learn everything possible about his fields of interest. He pored over sales catalogues, eagerly researched his subject, and always sought to improve the quality of his collection, often replacing one print with a finer impression. He bought not only unique objects but groups of related works, such as a remarkable collection of prints and drawings by William Blake sold by the heirs of one of Blake's pupils, and a series of eighty-nine prints by Martin Schöngauer. Thus Rosenwald's collection had depth as well as breadth. It contained superb drawings by a wide range of artists, the best available examples of each kind of print—including woodcuts, etchings, engravings, and lithographs—as well as illustrated books and illuminated manuscripts. He housed these treasures in a private, fireproof library and print room, constructed in a wing of his home, Alverthorpe, in Jenkintown, near Philadelphia. He retired from Sears in 1939 but never stopped cultivating his collection.

A philanthropist and public-spirited citizen like his father, Lessing Rosenwald moved to Washington, D.C., in 1941 to help support the war effort through the War Production Board. Once in the capital, he began to make regular visits to the National Gallery shortly after it opened, and he lent selections from his collection to the Gallery for exhibition and study. Finley quickly saw the opportunity to expand the Gallery's collections into this field and soon began to discuss with Rosenwald a permanent donation. His first gift of 6,500 prints and drawings came to the Gallery in March 1943 and went on display immediately. Ultimately, the Rosenwald Collection at the National Gallery totaled more than 22,000 prints and drawings. These include outstanding etchings by Rembrandt and by Anthony van Dyck, engravings by Andrea Mantegna, and nearly all of Albrecht Dürer's important engravings and woodcuts (see plate 23), in addition to works by Pablo Picasso, Henri Matisse, and Edvard Munch. While Rosenwald gave his prints and drawings to the National Gallery, his rare books went to the Library of Congress at his death. He made very few restrictions as part of these gifts and even explicitly stated that both institutions could sell works from their Rosenwald collections if works of equal or superior quality became available. It was Rosenwald's strongly held belief that "a work of art that is never seen is little better off than one that has never been created."[20]

The terms of Rosenwald's gift to the National Gallery provided that the collection would remain at Alverthorpe during his lifetime, but an unusually close relationship developed between the donor and the Gallery. The National Gallery put Rosenwald's curator on its own payroll, and she not only brought selections of works from Jenkintown to Washington for regular exhibition but also advised Rosenwald on prints that became available for purchase. During the nearly forty years of his retirement he continued to enhance his collection, and he spent considerable time in his Alverthorpe Gallery, where he personally hosted visiting scholars and students. In 1976, a year before Finley's death and three years before his own, he had an edition of 250 copies of his memoirs privately printed at the Stinehour Press in Vermont. In *Recollections of a Collector* he had these words for David Finley:

> I gave long and careful thought as to what I should do with
> my collection when the proper time came to dispose of it.
> I had no desire to sell it and wanted it kept as a unit inso-
> far as I could. Finally I decided to give the drawings and
> prints to the National Gallery of Art and the books to the
> Library of Congress. This was partially owing to the efforts
> of Mr. David Finley, the first director of the National Gal-
> lery. He is a small, quiet man and very gracious in his manner.
> In the parlance of the marketplace you would say he was a
> great soft-sell artist.
>
> I do not believe that sufficient credit has ever been given
> to David Finley for what he accomplished. He was a close

friend and personal adviser to Mr. Andrew Mellon, and it was owing to his intense effort and his good judgment that the National Gallery building is as beautiful as it is and the contents as magnificent as they are. He had a fine eye for beauty and exercised it in behalf of the National Gallery. I have never regretted that I turned over this portion of my collection to that institution.[21]

Lessing Rosenwald said it well. With the Rosenwald gift in March 1943, only two years after the opening of the new museum and not quite six years after Andrew Mellon's death, David Finley not only had completed the splendid building that his mentor had begun but was filling it with art worthy of the great nation it represented. Even before Andrew Mellon died, Finley had played a major role in Mellon's final purchases of works of art for the museum and in securing the legislation to establish the National Gallery of Art's organization and funding as well as the land on which the building would stand. He had been intimately involved in the design of the building even before both Mellon and John Russell Pope died while the foundations of the building were just being laid. Finley then worked tirelessly to bring Mellon's vision to reality, insisting on the highest quality in design and construction, then deftly persuading other collectors to donate their priceless works of art to the nation's new art museum. With Mellon's nucleus of masterpieces joined by the Kress, Widener, Rosenwald, and—soon—Dale gifts, David Finley had built the National Gallery of Art into a world-class art museum, just as Andrew Mellon had hoped, in a stunningly short period of time. And much of this he did in the midst of a world war.

The Price of Victory

Many Americans were called upon to make sacrifices during the war, whether large or small. David and Margaret Finley made their share of both. Margaret spent the entire war in public service. She had become a volunteer with the District of Columbia chapter of the American Red Cross in 1939. When America went to war—with her only brother in the army and her English cousins still at Little Oatlands—she went to work full-time but unpaid at the national headquarters of the Red Cross, on Seventeenth Street near the Corcoran Gallery, dressed in

44. President Harry S. Truman with Margaret Eustis Finley wearing her Red Cross uniform, 1951

tailored uniforms (fig. 44). There she joined many prominent women such as Mrs. Arthur Vandenberg, wife of the Republican Senate leader. But this was no light social activity. She gave it all her professional energy and myriad talents, making a significant contribution to the war effort on the home front.[22]

The victory in Europe also came at the cost of personal tragedy to the Finley and Eustis families. David Finley had always been particularly close to his sister Frances, who was just eighteen months his junior. They had shared a desk at elementary school in York, and he had helped introduce her to Washington society before the First World War. He was mildly alarmed when in 1916 she married a widower twenty-one years her senior whom the family did not know. But she and J. Dexter Brown of Anderson, South Carolina, had a happy marriage and six children, all of whom were fond of their "Uncle Edward." Lillian Brown had come up to Washington from college for the opening of the National Gallery and had fainted in memorable fashion during FDR's speech. Her older brothers had military training at the Citadel and soon went on active duty. Young Dexter Brown rose to command a company of the First Armored Division and saw action in North Africa and Italy. He distinguished himself by earning two Silver Stars, the Bronze Star, and two Purple Hearts. On 25 June 1944 Captain Joseph Dexter Brown Jr. was killed in action near Florence, Italy, at the age of twenty-two.[23]

On 12 April 1944 Margaret Finley's first cousin Colonel Thomas Hitchcock Jr. was killed when the experimental fighter plane he was flight-testing crashed in England. Hitchcock had been an aviator in the First World War while he was under the age of eighteen, when he had shot down more than one German plane, was himself shot down behind German lines, and later escaped from a POW camp and made his way back to Allied lines. After the war Hitchcock had become a world-class polo player. As one newsman put it, "Tommy Hitchcock was to polo what Babe Ruth was to baseball."[24] Then at the outbreak of the Second World War he received a commission in

45. Lieutenant Morton Corcoran Eustis, Second Armored Division, U.S. Army, c. 1944

the U.S. Army Air Force at the age of forty-one. Although too old for combat operations, he served as a test pilot. Margaret's brother, Morton Eustis, had dined with him in London shortly before Hitchcock was killed.

But the cruelest blow was the death of Margaret Finley's only brother, First Lieutenant Morton Corcoran Eustis (fig. 45), who was killed while leading an assault at Domfront, France, on 12 August. After basic training and maneuvers in the States for over a year as an enlisted man, he had transferred to the Army Air Corps in March 1942 and was commissioned a second lieutenant in July. By Christmas 1942 he served in Cairo as an intelligence officer at air force headquarters, but the action had shifted far to the west, where U.S. units engaged tough German units in Tunisia and Algeria. Spurning his desk job, Lieutenant Eustis requested a transfer to Algeria in April 1943 and, after two months at a replacement depot, managed to talk himself into a combat

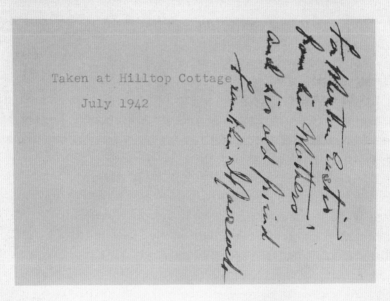

Taken at Hilltop Cottage

July 1942

46. Inscribed photograph from President Roosevelt given to Morton
Eustis on the eve of his departure overseas, October 1942, and found
in the pocket of his uniform after he was killed in action in Normandy,
13 August 1944

assignment as a platoon leader with the 82nd Reconnaissance Battalion of the U.S. Second Armored Division—a "killer unit," according to *Stars and Stripes*.[25]

Throughout his army service, Morton kept up a steady correspondence with his mother and sisters, his brother-in-law David Finley, and his friends at *Theater Arts* magazine, describing his experiences in vivid detail. He wrote most often to his mother, playing down any real danger to himself. But he was more candid in other letters, acknowledging that he was "in an extremely precarious branch of the Service. I believe only about 50% of a similar group in Tunisia survived. . . . But even if the worst should happen, I still wouldn't be sorry that I took the stand that I did about leaving Cairo."[26] His letters show a rare zeal for action in the field and an eagerness to take an aggressive personal part in what he saw as a crusade against Nazi brutality. At the same time, his intelligence and humor shine through.

Morton Eustis finally saw action in the Allied invasion of Sicily on 11 July 1943. The Second Armored Division landed near Gela on the southeast coast as part of General Patton's Seventh Army. Within twelve days they swept across the mountainous spine of the island to Palermo on the northwest coast. Eustis, who commanded two platoons of heavily armed jeeps, was awarded a Silver Star on 20 August 1943 for gallantry in action.[27] His unit soon received orders to ship out, first to Wiltshire, England, where it underwent strenuous training from November 1943 until May 1944 for the invasion everyone on both sides of the Channel knew lay ahead.[28] Three days after D-Day the Second Armored Division landed in Normandy and immediately engaged determined German units.

Morton's last letters reflect the intensity of the fighting and the Allies' difficulty in breaking out of their extended beachhead. At the same time, he continued to insist, at least to his mother, that the newspapers blew the situation out of proportion, and he reiterated his hatred of the Germans and his thirst for personal vengeance. On 22 July he wrote, "Actually, I am enjoying myself here, though I'd be happier if we were seeing more action." On 3 August he reported "another of those damn decorations—the Bronze Star this time." But the following week he wrote with prophetic candor to a friend, "I shouldn't mind, however, if the whole affair wound up before many more weeks are passed, as your luck can hold out just so long in this type of game, and sooner or later someone's aim is going to be good, especially when you're sitting out most of the time in the point vehicle."[29]

Three days later, on 12 August, shortly after the breakout at Saint-Lô, his division attacked a German battalion entrenched in the town of Domfront, with Lieutenant Eustis manning a 50-caliber machine gun on the open turret of a medium tank as he led the assault. His tank took a direct hit from a German antitank rocket, and Eustis was killed instantly. The army awarded him a posthumous Oak Leaf Cluster to his Silver Star. The citation read in part, "Lieutenant Eustis's courage and habitual contempt for the enemy was largely responsible for the success of his Platoon."[30] In eleven weeks of combat he had won three medals for heroism—two Silver Stars and one Bronze Star.

Margaret Finley had the unhappy burden of telling her mother that her only son would not be coming home. The seventy-year-old Edith Eustis received the same tragic news that more than 300,000 other American mothers did during the war. Among numerous condolences was a note from a lifelong family friend, Lieutenant Colonel Henry Cabot Lodge, who had left his Senate seat to take a commission in the U.S. Army (the first senator to do so since the Civil War).[31] She also received a letter from Morton Eustis's close friend and comrade-in-arms Lieutenant Frank Jordan of Pulaski, Virginia,[32] enclosing a photograph of President Roosevelt, personally inscribed, that was found in the pocket of Morton's uniform blouse (fig. 46).

At the end of the war Edith Eustis published a collection of Morton's war letters, edited by David Finley, who also wrote a foreword. These letters vividly bring to life the character, warmth, humor, and the remarkable courage of an exceptional man, the last male in the Eustis line. In her dedication Edith Eustis wrote: "May 8, 1945. The war in Europe is over. And he did not live to see liberated Paris again. But I like to think that, in a small way, small because he was only one among countless thousands, he contributed to that victory which is being celebrated today."[33] The publication, privately printed, gave David Finley an opportunity to pay personal tribute to a gallant man who brought home the terrible cost of a war. The closing words in Finley's foreword quote Pericles' oration for those who died for Athens centuries earlier, which begins:

> In a moment of time, at the climax of their lives, they were rapt away from a world filled, for their dying eyes, not with terror but with glory. . . . So they gave their bodies for the common weal and received, each for his own memory, praise that grows not old, and with it the grandest of all sepulchres, not that in which their mortal bones are laid, but a home in the minds of men, where their glory remains fresh to stir to speech or action as the occasion comes by.[34]

1. Finley, *Standard of Excellence*, 104.

2. In Martin Gilbert, *The Second World War* (London, 1989), 747, the British historian reckoned the total of civilian and military deaths from the war at over 48 million souls.

3. As a precaution against the possibility of espionage, the entire Japanese-American population of the West Coast, native and foreign-born citizens alike, were interned in utter disregard of their constitutional rights and moved hundreds and thousands of miles away to mountain and desert prison camps. Cities and towns on the Pacific and Atlantic coasts took precautions against aerial bombing, and even small towns in the Midwest appointed air-raid wardens on a block-by-block basis. The author, then a fifth grader in Winnetka, Illinois, recalls his father, a veteran of the First World War, earnestly performing this duty.

4. Nicholas, *Rape of Europa*, 205.

5. Association of Museum Directors, minutes of meeting, "Problems of Protection and Defense," 20 and 21 December 1941, p. 136. National Gallery of Art Library.

6. Finley, *Standard of Excellence*, 151.

7. Kopper, *Gift to the Nation*, 166.

8. As background, there was the highly publicized incident in 1939 when the Daughters of the American Revolution had blocked contralto Marian Anderson from singing at Constitution Hall because of her race. Eleanor Roosevelt resigned from the DAR in protest, and the National Park Service arranged a concert for Anderson on the steps of the Lincoln Memorial, setting the stage for Martin Luther King to speak there decades later.

9. Interview with Richard Bales, conducted by Alfred C. Viebranz, 11 January 1989, oral history transcript, p. 59. NGA Archives. E-mail from Stephen Ackert, head of the music department, National Gallery of Art, 11 February 2005.

10. Finley, *Standard of Excellence*, 152.

11. NGA Archives.

12. Letter from "Visitor" to David Bruce, 18 July 1943. Finley Papers, Library of Congress, box 20.

13. Finley, *Standard of Excellence*, 133.

14. Walker, *Self-Portrait with Donors*, 175–176.

15. Walker, *Self-Portrait with Donors*, 171–174.

16. Finley, *Standard of Excellence*, 114.

17. Finley, *Standard of Excellence*, 115.

18. Lessing Julius Rosenwald (1891–1979) was very much his father's son, following in his footsteps as a businessman, philanthropist, and public servant. Julius Rosenwald (1862–1932) began as a small manufacturer of men's clothing who joined Sears, Roebuck & Co. in 1895 as a partner and became president of the company when Richard Sears resigned in 1908. He was credited with the management philosophy of

"satisfaction guaranteed or your money back." See www.searsarchives.com, consulted on 11 February 2005.

19. Information on Lessing Rosenwald's life and collections is found in Finley's *Standard of Excellence*, 115–119; Kopper's *Gift to the Nation*, 205–215; the National Gallery's Web site, www.nga.gov; and Lessing J. Rosenwald, *Recollections of a Collector* (Jenkintown, PA, 1976). In addition to collecting art and rare books, Rosenwald was known for a wide range of philanthropic and civic endeavors. In December 1945, as president of the American Council for Judaism, he met with President Truman and submitted a proposal for a United Nations declaration that "Palestine shall not be a Moslem, Christian or a Jewish state but shall be a country in which people of all faiths can play their full and equal part, sharing fully the rights and responsibilities of citizenship." See www.trumanlibrary.org, consulted on 11 February 2005.

20. Rosenwald, *Recollections of a Collector*, 12.

21. Rosenwald, *Recollections of a Collector*, 60.

22. The Red Cross archives indicate that Margaret Finley provided leadership to the District of Columbia chapter for more than thirty-five years, serving as vice chairman, as a member of the executive committee from 1941 to 1977, and as chairman of volunteer services for several years. She was also the first woman to lead the blood donor recruitment committee. Letter from Jean Waldman, R.N., volunteer nurse historian, American Red Cross, Washington, D.C., to the author, 26 October 2004.

23. When he died, his sister Lillian enlisted in the Waves and served until the end of the war.

24. Edward T. Folliard, *Washington Post*, 20 April 1944, front page.

25. *Stars and Stripes*, 28 December 1944, reprinted in *War Letters of Morton Eustis*, edited by David E. Finley and privately printed by Edith Morton Eustis (Washington, D.C., 1945), 246.

26. Letter to Margaret E. Finley, 31 May 1943, *War Letters of Morton Eustis*, 120.

27. The citation reads, in part:

> On July 22, 1943, near S. Ciperello, Sicily, Lieutenant Eustis was given the mission as the point for the advance guard for the advance on Palermo. Because of the rate of speed at which the column was traveling and the mountainous terrain, the only possible way to determine the location of the enemy was by drawing enemy fire. When enemy fire was encountered and the column was held up, Lieutenant Eustis dismounted and advanced on foot through heavy small arms and artillery fire to locate the enemy gun positions. Lieutenant Eustis's coolness and courage under fire coupled with his aggressiveness and disregard of his own safety in fulfilling the mission given him reflect great credit upon himself and the Armed Forces.

Typically, when writing to his mother about receiving the medal, he downplayed the citation as containing "a good deal of bunk" and offering "a highly colored version of what actually occurred." *War Letters of Morton Eustis*, 167–168, 238.

28. During this time he got leave to visit London, where he met his friends Alfred Lunt and Lynn Fontaine, the distinguished Broadway actors, for cocktails and dinner at the Savoy Hotel, saw various family and friends in high places, including his cousin "Tommy" Hitchcock and Sir Archibald Sinclair at the Air Ministry. The Lunts told him that they had met General Patton, who said he had known Morton's father, Captain William Eustis, very well in the First World War and "admired him immensely." Letter to Edith Morton Eustis, 11 April 1944, *War Letters of Morton Eustis*, 197.

29. Letter to Mrs. John Parkinson, 10 August 1944, *War Letters of Morton Eustis*, 231.

30. *War Letters of Morton Eustis*, 239.

31. Lodge wrote to Mrs. Eustis and Margaret Finley:

> I am so terribly shocked by the news about Morton and my heart is so full of love and sympathy for you both—to an extent that I cannot describe. The pang I feel is so unutterably sharp that I can imagine how you both must feel. My recollections of Morton go back to his early childhood—to when you both lived in Lafayette Square. But I shall always think of him as a soldier—in the highest sense of the word—a man courageous, unselfish, and patriotic, a man to bear discomforts cheerfully, to lead other men over obstacles, to meet life with his sense of humor and his sense of proportion intact. He had the qualities I most admire in people (he was like both of you in that regard!) and I often thought of him, particularly recently when it appeared that maybe I might see him. He was always in my mind and I often thought of our reunion in Washington when the War was over. . . .
>
> I feel that my life has suddenly become a lot more drab. I enjoyed Morton's company so much, his talk and his laugh. I wish I could be with you both now to tell you how dreadfully I feel and how much I sympathize. May your pride in his life be a real comfort to you—as it should be and as he would want it to be—and may God give you strength.
>
> Ever faithfully and affectionately,
> Cabot

V-Mail Letter from "Lt. Col. H. C. Lodge, Jr.," Sixth Army Group, 17 September 1944. Finley Papers, NGA Archives, RG 28, box 9. Henry Cabot Lodge Jr. (1902–1985), grandson of the famous senator of that name, was elected to the U.S. Senate from Massachusetts in 1936. He left the Senate in 1944 to join the U.S. Army and saw active service in Europe and the Mediterranean. In 1952 he lost his Senate race to John F. Kennedy but served as ambassador to the U.N. from 1953 to 1960. As Nixon's vice presidential running mate in 1960, he again lost to Kennedy. He later accepted various high diplomatic posts from Presidents Kennedy, Johnson, Nixon, and Ford.

32. In his will Morton Eustis left his friend $5,000 toward the purchase of a law library for which Jordan, a recent law graduate, had been saving. Another bequest to Jordan was for "4 cases of high-class Scotch whiskey." *War Letters of Morton Eustis*, 247. Lamentably, Frank Jordan never enjoyed these gifts, as he too was killed in action two months later.

33. The dedication continues:

> With much to live for, with talents which had not yet fully reached their prime, there was that in him which, until the war, had never quite found expression. He was searching for something which did not come his way, something which demanded more of him than life had hitherto offered, and strangely enough, the calamity of a world war threw the opportunity he had sought in his path. . . . And again, I like to think that he was supremely happy, not because he did not enjoy life, but because of that unfulfilled desire to give all of himself to a cause he believed in. E. M. E.

Mrs. Eustis also erected a memorial in the shape of a cross, designed by Bancel La Farge, near the spot in Domfront where her son was killed, on ground deeded to her and maintained by her until her death in 1964.

34. *War Letters of Morton Eustis*, vi.

47. Navy Lieutenant George L. Stout (center), a Monuments officer, supervises the recovery of priceless works of art from a mine at Alt Aussee, Austria, July 1945

8

Mr. Finley's Roberts Commission
1942–1946

AS THE GERMAN BLITZKRIEG SWEPT relentlessly over the great European centers of art and architecture in 1940, curators and historians across the Continent were galvanized into action to protect their priceless cultural treasures from destruction and systematic looting.[1] Well before the strike on Pearl Harbor, American art scholars and museum leaders had also expressed their concerns. Indeed, soon after Paris fell to the Germans in June 1940, several members of the Harvard University faculty with special expertise in the preservation of works of art had established the American Defense Harvard Group to address the problem. Prominent in this endeavor were philosopher Ralph Barton Perry; professor of fine arts and co-director of the Fogg Art Museum, Paul J. Sachs; and professor of archaeology George Chase.[2] A younger member was George L. Stout of the Fogg, a recognized authority in paintings conservation, who published a technical studies journal.[3] Another committee formed in New York at about the same time under the auspices of the American Council of Learned Societies and its chairman, William Bell Dinsmoor, a Columbia University professor and scholar of Greek architecture. This group had access to the free advice of more than a hundred distinguished art historians, archaeologists, and other experts; it also had funding from the Rockefeller Foundation that enabled it to retain a small professional staff. The team operated out of the Frick Art Reference Library, adjacent to the Frick Collection at Fifth Avenue and Seventy-first Street, which remained closed to the public for a year during the war to facilitate the committee's work.

In 1942, once the shock of America's entry into the war had subsided and art museums in the United States had taken steps to protect their own collections, museum directors increasingly focused their attention on the vulnerability of art and cultural properties in Europe amid the maelstrom of war. Soon it was clear that the Allies would have to storm Hitler's "Fortress Europa" and that countless works of art would be in peril. At this point, in November 1942, William Dinsmoor and the director of the Metropolitan Museum of Art, Francis H. Taylor, met with David Finley at the National Gallery of Art. Together they wrote to the chief justice of the Supreme Court, Harlan Fiske Stone—who was also, ex officio, chairman of the board of trustees of the National Gallery—proposing that the federal government establish a commission for the protection of Europe's threatened art and historic monuments.

David Finley had a close relationship with Chief Justice Stone, who had succeeded to that position in July 1941. They had first met in the 1920s when Stone and his wife came to dinner at Andrew Mellon's apartment on Massachusetts Avenue and admired Mellon's paintings.[4] Stone took a keen interest in the National Gallery. With construction complete but works of art not yet installed, he and Mrs. Stone received a guided tour from Finley in late 1940, and the justice pronounced himself "delighted" with the building. As the Gallery's chairman, Stone had expressed a desire to see the Widener collection, and when Joseph Widener invited the chief justice and his wife to lunch, along with David Finley, at Lynnewood Hall in June 1942, Stone voiced enthusiasm about securing the collection for the National Gallery: "Then he added, with the chuckle which all his friends knew so well, 'I wish we could get his collection of Château Margaux also!'"[5] The chief justice enjoyed that particular bordeaux, and Finley made sure to serve it at his table during the lunch he and Margaret hosted before the opening of the

Widener collection at the Gallery in December 1942. Stone had earned his Château Margaux, for in August 1942, when Congress was considering legislation to authorize the federal payment of a five percent tax to the state of Pennsylvania on the Widener gift to the National Gallery, the chief justice took the rare step of writing Congress to support the bill.

Despite the academic and intellectual heft of Dinsmoor and Taylor and their colleagues in New York and Cambridge, none of them had a clue about how to get their case before the United States government in the midst of the war. Taylor had drafted a memorandum to the President, full of lofty references to the Turkish destruction of the Parthenon and Napoleon's looting of his conquered subjects. But it was vague on specific recommendations, except to suggest that he himself be dispatched to Spain and London to discuss protections with museum and government officials "and that if necessary we visit Sweden and Russia to learn what we can of the problem from sources of information there."[6] It was Finley who took Taylor's and Dinsmoor's concept and worked it into a concrete proposal that he presented to Chief Justice Stone. Finley outlined the formation of two committees: one an official commission, which he hoped Stone himself would chair, with an executive secretary located in Washington; and the second to consist of experts such as the New York and Harvard brain trusts.

Stone endorsed the proposal and sent it on to President Roosevelt on 8 December 1942, together with a memorandum describing the makeup of such a commission, also drafted by Finley. The President responded to the chief justice on 28 December 1942, saying that he had forwarded the plan to the appropriate government agencies for detailed study: "In the meanwhile may I express to you my appreciation of the initiative which the National Gallery of Art has taken in formulating this interesting proposal with whose objectives I am confident there will be almost unanimous agreement."[7] With some elation, Finley wrote to Taylor on 1 January 1943, giving him the encouraging news and closing, "I feel sure there will be some action soon."[8] But after almost two months without a word from the White House, Finley drafted a letter for the chief justice to send to Mrs. Henry Morgenthau, wife of the secretary of the treasury, dated 26 February 1943, asking if she had heard her husband or Mrs. Roosevelt speak of this matter.[9] Whether Stone actually sent this plea is not clear.

Meanwhile, also in February, Ralph Perry of the Harvard group wrote to the Army School of Military Government at Charlottesville, Virginia, and in March he received a return request for information on the protection of monuments in the combat areas. In addition, on 22 March Paul Sachs wrote to Finley, a longtime friend, that he was leading the technical effort for the Harvard group and preparing a handbook for army use.[10] George Stout, Sachs's conservator at the Fogg, provided vital force for this venture.

Finally, on 24 April 1943, four and a half months after first receiving Finley's proposal for a dual commission charged with protecting the artistic heritage of Europe, Roosevelt wrote back to Chief Justice Stone: "while this undertaking does not appear to promise any military advantage, the Joint Chiefs of Staff are in agreement as to its eventual desirability and will, when and if the committee is appointed, direct the American commanders concerned to give the committee every practicable assistance that does not interfere with their military operations." The President also said that the U.S. embassies in London and Moscow were approaching the British and Soviet governments to inquire whether each would be prepared to appoint similar national committees. He ended, "I shall keep you informed of any further developments."[11]

Although hardly the resounding approval Roosevelt had predicted, this was a start. But when another two months passed without results, Finley went into action on another front. Besides the chief justice, another ex-officio trustee of the National Gallery is the secretary of state. During most of the war that post was filled by Cordell Hull, a courtly Tennessean who had spent several terms in Congress, including ten years along with Finley's father, the longtime congressman from South Carolina.[12] The younger Finley got through to Hull and, using his finely honed ghostwriting skills, drafted a letter from the secretary to the President, recommending the establishment of a high-level commission to help protect cultural properties in Europe on the fields of battle. The letter spelled out the composition and duties of the commission in some detail and suggested that it collaborate with the School of Military Government in Charlottesville, already in the process of training personnel to advise the army "as to the location of, and the care to be given to, the various artistic and historic objects in occupied territories." The secretary closed by assuring Roosevelt that "if this proposal meets with your approval" he would be glad to implement it, adding that he had consulted with the secretary of war, Henry Stimson, who was "in accord with these suggestions."[13] Finley had known Stimson as secretary of state in the Hoover administration and had worked with him then on sundry matters, including the London conference on the German financial crisis in July 1931. So he had covered all his bases. Cordell Hull signed the letter on 21 June 1943, and Finley got it onto the President's desk and approved within forty-eight hours.[14] It took another two months before Hull had written to all of the prospective members and obtained their consent to participate, then he publicly announced the appointment of the commission on 20 August 1943.

By this time, the men trained at the School of Military Government in Charlottesville as Monuments, Fine Arts, and Archives (MFAA) officers—or simply Monuments officers—had a daunting task but no resources at their disposal, and their modest rank precluded any real influence on the higher command. Their colleagues in military government "regarded the inclusion of cultural protection in a military operation with a certain amount of humorous scorn."[15] The first Monuments officer, Captain Mason Hammond, had previously taught classics as a Harvard professor and had worked with John Walker in Rome. While part of Air Force Intelligence, he was sent to Algiers on 7 June 1943 and assigned to the headquarters of the Allied Military Government of Occupied Territories.[16] Learning of an imminent Allied attack on Sicily, he produced a short history of the island and a list of its most important cultural sites, which the British military governor would not distribute for "reasons of security." The invasion of Sicily began on 10 July, and when Hammond finally got there three weeks later, he was gratified to note that the ancient Greek temples at Agrigento had been spared.[17] By 17 August 1943 the Allies had conquered all of Sicily.

Of those to whom Cordell Hull had written on 16 July, inviting them to join the artistic and historic monuments commission that President Roosevelt had approved, all except Chief Justice Stone accepted.

Finley had written to Stone at his summer home in Franconia, New Hampshire, on 19 July, already laying plans to hold an organizational meeting as soon as the group received formal appointments. But Stone replied three days later, saying that he had thought the matter over and concluded that he could not accept the assignment "without sacrifice of the best interests of the Court in one of the most critical periods of its history." He told Finley that he had recommended him to Hull as having "executive ability" and "personal acquaintance which would enable you to do the job."[18] But Finley wanted a bigger name to head the commission and telephoned Stone in late July, most likely to ask permission to approach associate justice Owen J. Roberts, who had spent thirteen years on the high court, ranking second in seniority to Stone, was widely respected, and had recently gained notice as the chairman of a committee investigating the disaster at Pearl Harbor.[19]

With Stone's concurrence, Finley telephoned Justice Roberts at his farm in Chester County, Pennsylvania. Finley reported to Stone that he and Roberts had had a long conversation and that Roberts "was very much interested in the projected work of our Commission and said he would be glad to serve as Chairman, if desired, 'provided we would keep him out of trouble.' I hope his appointment comes through shortly, so that the commission can be organized. I feel that time is pressing, for events in Europe are moving very rapidly, and if our Commission is to be of any use at all it should go into action soon."[20] He was not disappointed. Two weeks later Finley received a handwritten note from Justice Roberts, advising him that the State Department had asked "whether I would serve as chairman of the committee, and, by letter mailed yesterday morning, I replied in the affirmative."[21]

Finally, Secretary of State Hull could announce the formation of the American Commission for the Protection and Salvage of Artistic and Historic Monuments in War Areas,[22] better known as "the Roberts Commission" after its chairman. David E. Finley was named vice chairman. Other members included Herbert H. Lehman, an ex-governor of New York and then head of the United Nations Relief and Rehabilitation Administration; Archibald MacLeish, librarian of Congress; Professor William Bell Dinsmoor of Columbia, representing the American Council of Learned Societies; Francis H. Taylor, director of the Metropolitan Museum in New York; and Paul J. Sachs, co-director of the Fogg Art Museum at Harvard.[23]

Successes and Failures

With formal appointments made, Roberts and Finley wasted no time in convening the first meeting of the art and monuments commission. Members gathered on 25 August in the boardroom of the National Gallery of Art. Justice Roberts presided and took an active role in the discussions, but Finley had prepared the agenda and the primary motions adopted at the meeting. Most of the energy and ideas came from Paul Sachs, Archibald MacLeish, and Finley. Huntington Cairns functioned as secretary-treasurer, and John Walker as special advisor. The National Gallery provided office space and administrative assistance to support a small staff hired by the commission.

The Roberts Commission moved quickly to clarify its status with respect to the private groups at Harvard and at the American Council of Learned Societies in New York, both of whom had representatives on the commission. Because the commission would operate on a bare-bones budget of $19,000 during its first year, with only three or four full-time staff, it needed all the help it could get from the others. But it could and did act as the nerve center connecting various branches of the federal government and the private sector.

The Sachs and Dinsmoor teams at Harvard and Columbia had already done valuable work in preparing maps to identify the principal monuments in areas likely to come under attack in Italy. They had compiled detailed lists of historic buildings, art objects, and archives to be protected; city-by-city maps showing their exact locations; and field manuals later put to good use by air crews and ground forces in the combat areas. This vital effort continued throughout the fighting in Italy, France, and the Low Countries and finally into the heart of Germany itself. In late 1944 the U.S. Air Force helped to produce these maps by flying aerial reconnaissance missions over seventy-nine Italian cities and having MMFA officers mark the sites of monuments requiring protection.[24]

The Harvard group under Dr. Sachs had also undertaken to identify men with specialized knowledge of the fine arts, archaeology, and architectural history who were already in the armed services or who could be newly recruited as Monuments officers. Most recommendations went to the School of Military Government in Charlottesville. In the course of the war more than two hundred men served in this capacity, many with great distinction, but it took a long while to integrate them into the military machinery. By August 1943 Finley reported that only eleven MFAA officers operated in the field, none of them ranked higher than major and most as captains or lower, all the way down to private. They needed more weight to convey their message to the Supreme Allied Command.[25]

Another key task addressed at the first meeting of the Roberts Commission involved establishment of clear lines of communication with the War, State, and Treasury Departments and the Office of War Information. Again Finley's extensive experience with Washington's modus operandi proved essential. He was able to pinpoint specific individuals who could make things happen in the maze of the wartime bureaucracy, both military and civilian. And he could go to see these people personally, as was often necessary, to make sure that work proceeded. The army announced that its Civil Affairs Division would assume the role of liaison between the commission and both the combat units and the military government. It also reported that General George C. Marshall cabled General Dwight D. Eisenhower that, "by direction of the President, special instructions should be issued to commanders of tactical units to take all possible steps to preserve archives and cultural treasures."[26]

The Roberts Commission created several subcommittees, with Finley heading three that dealt with the "definition of cultural value and property," "art instruction in military government schools," and "administration." Paul Sachs led the committee on "personnel" and took joint responsibility with Dr. Dinsmoor for that on the "collection of maps, information, and description of art objects." By November 1943 Finley had recruited several eminent experts—including Professor Sumner McK. Crosby of Yale, Professor Rufus Morey of Princeton, and the director of the Art Institute of Chicago, Daniel C. Rich—to lecture at military training schools across the country, such as the universities of Chicago, Harvard, Michigan, Northwestern, Pittsburgh,

Stanford, Virginia, Wisconsin, and Yale. These scholars coordinated their lectures and slide presentations through Finley to ensure uniformity; basically, they were offering a crash course in the history of European art and architecture.

With Justice Roberts fully engaged in court business, Finley in effect ran the Roberts Commission. Its most pressing need was to gain the attention and cooperation of the top military brass, like General Eisenhower, concerning the urgency of protecting cultural monuments. Although Eisenhower felt sympathetic, he had massive amphibious invasions to plan and execute, prickly allies like Generals Bernard Law Montgomery and Charles de Gaulle to handle, and a tough enemy to overcome. Thus he had little time to give to Monuments matters.

Indeed, it is remarkable that civilians pushing for cultural protections won as much cooperation from the American military as they did. When several of Finley's colleagues wrote their counterparts in London in early 1943 to ask if any official protection committee were contemplated in Great Britain, Kenneth Clark responded incredulously, "I find it hard to believe that any machinery could be set up which would carry out the suggestions contained in your petition; e.g., even supposing it were possible for an archaeologist to accompany each invading force, I cannot help feeling that he would have great difficulty in restraining a commanding officer from shelling an important military objective simply because it contained some fine historical monuments."[27] At the initial meeting of the Roberts Commission in August 1943, Chairman Roberts noted that the U.S. State Department had told the British that the Americans had established their commission and proposed an arrangement by which the two governments might cooperate, but the British had not yet appointed a similar committee. When various members suggested encouraging British colleagues in this effort, Justice Roberts closed the discussion by saying, "We should wait and not embarrass our Government." And on that note the first meeting of the Roberts Commission adjourned.[28]

Monuments officers attached to the forces in Europe eventually accomplished the fieldwork promoted by the Roberts Commission and its private counterparts, but it took many months for the army to get them into action in significant numbers. During the operations in Sicily,

Captain Mason Hammond was the sole Monuments officer on the entire island, and for over two months the Roberts Commission had received no information about what had happened there. Starting in September 1943, Finley engaged in a spirited correspondence with the assistant secretary of war John J. McCloy, insisting that MFAA officers be assigned to forward units and that more tactical assistance be given to them. When he asked pointedly if the maps already forwarded had in fact reached the air crews, he received a positive response. Finley had quickly sized up Jack McCloy as the man most likely to succeed in getting the army and air force to cooperate with the Roberts Commission, and it proved a wise choice.[29] As part of secretary of war Henry Stimson's inner circle, McCloy took an increasingly influential role at the Pentagon throughout the conflict.[30] Even if Finley did not always get his way, at least he had McCloy's ear, which in Washington is half the battle.

Still, Paul Sachs voiced dire concerns about the continuing lack of technical experts in combat areas to provide emergency aid to save, for example, fragile frescoes in roofless churches. By late 1943 Sachs and Finley began a campaign to have George Stout of the Fogg Art Museum, then a navy lieutenant stationed in Maryland dealing with airplane paint, reassigned to lead the technical work of art conservation in the field. Finley wrote a long letter to McCloy on this subject, dated 28 October, to which McCloy responded, "We are asking General Eisenhower his views on dispatching to Italy additional officers and enlisted men as recommended in your letter." But he added that "The repair of paintings, statuary and historic monuments is regarded as a civilian problem."[31] Paul Sachs was alarmed and urged Finley to convey to McCloy in the strongest terms the necessity of sending George Stout to Europe as a Monuments officer. He argued that otherwise all aspects of their work would be "put in jeopardy."[32] Finley went to see McCloy, but it was not until the spring of 1944 that Stout was sent to England in preparation for the assault on Europe. In the late stages of the war and in the chaos of the early peace in Germany, Stout would more than justify Paul Sachs's confidence in him and Finley's appeals to McCloy (see fig. 47).

By the end of 1943 the Roberts Commission and its partners began to have an impact. On 29 December 1943 General Eisenhower issued a pivotal letter sanctioning the protection of historic monuments and clarifying the role of the MFAA. Referring to operations in Italy, he said:

> Today we are fighting in a country which has contributed a
> great deal to our cultural inheritance, a country rich in monu-
> ments which by their creation helped and now in their old
> age illustrate the growth of the civilization which is ours.
> We are bound to respect those monuments so far as the war
> allows. . . . It is the responsibility of higher commanders to
> determine through Allied Military Government the location
> of historical monuments whether they be immediately ahead
> of our front lines or in areas occupied by us. This informa-
> tion passed to lower echelons through normal channels places
> the responsibility on all Commanders of complying with the
> spirit of this letter.[33]

Yet within weeks the noble thoughts expressed by Eisenhower came up against the harsh realities of war. After the Allies had landed at Salerno and Anzio and captured the lower third of the boot of Italy, the Germans under Field Marshall Albert Kesselring organized a strong defensive line in the mountains south of Rome. Bad weather turned the roads to mud, and the Allies became bogged down and frustrated near Montecassino. On a mountaintop overlooking the town, the ancient Abbey of Montecassino, founded by Saint Benedict in 529, had been rebuilt in the fourteenth century and housed the cell and tomb of the saint. This, in addition to its towering mass and spectacular setting, made it one of the most revered religious and historic sites in Italy. But because of its strategic location, commanding a view of the entire valley below, the Allied troops believed that the Germans held the abbey as an observation post and anchor of its defensive line. After much public debate in both Great Britain and the United States, as well as sharp divisions within the Allied command, the British general Sir Harold Alexander finally gave the order for aerial and artillery bombardment in February 1944, which soon reduced the abbey to rubble (fig. 48).

It turned out that the Germans had not been using the abbey before the barrage and had expressly forbidden their troops to enter it. But with

48. A Monuments officer from the U.S. and his British counterpart in the rubble of Montecassino, Italy, 1944. Signal Corps photograph

the structure now in ruins, they quickly moved into the natural defenses provided by its massive remains and kept the Allies at bay for more than three months before being outflanked and retreating from the area in mid-May 1944. In addition to complete destruction of the building, it cost the Allies more than four thousand lives to take Montecassino.[34] Though the abbey was to be meticulously reconstructed after the war, that could not be known at the time, and the controversy over its much-publicized devastation made the Allied forces in Italy more cautious in dealing with historic sites for the rest of the war. It also tempered Allied actions in the long-awaited invasion of France.

After Montecassino, most major historic monuments in Italy escaped with surprisingly little damage, although the Germans demol-ished all the bridges across the Arno in Florence—sparing only the

Ponte Vecchio, at Hitler's express command. They also appropriated countless paintings and sculptures, some for safekeeping and others for the private collections of avid art collectors such as Adolf Hitler and Hermann Goering.

On the other hand, the Allied forces did not merit a perfect record. American leaders tried to cooperate with the aims of the Roberts Commission, but the British lagged behind. At the 8 October 1943 meeting of the commission Finley reported: "I saw Mr. Richard Law, Minister of State to the Foreign Office, one of my friends at the British Embassy, who is interested in this. I took him the press release of the appointment of our Commission. He had never heard of it. I told him there was a communication sent over last spring, and we have been waiting to see if they were going to appoint a similar commission. I told him to give the thing a jog when he returned home."[35] The British finally established their own committee in early 1944 with Lord Macmillan as chairman. Other members included Sir Kenneth Clark of the National Gallery; Sir Frederic Kenyon, master of Trinity College, Cambridge; Eric Maclagan of the Victoria & Albert Museum; and Vincent Massey, the Canadian high commissioner in London.

Yet as Massey, an old friend of Finley's from his days as Canadian minister in Washington, wrote in July 1944, the Macmillan Commission made slow progress, due in part to the caution of its chairman, but also to the attitude of the military brass toward what was regarded as civilian interference. Massey closed, "I don't mind telling you very privately that our committee at present is making rather heavy weather and our course is rather confused. To have something like your 'chart of the voyage' would be very helpful indeed to those of us who are trying (if I may labour the metaphor) to steer our way out of the present fog."[36] Finley replied, giving Massey what direction and encouragement he could, but admitted, "We are able to do so little in the face of the appalling destruction going on in all theatres of war, that we can none of us avoid feeling discouraged. We must be realistic about the war and never obstruct its progress, but we have great responsibilities and must remember that later, much—perhaps too much—will be required of us when the danger of war has passed and we realize the enormous loss of cultural material which the world has sustained."[37]

In addition to relentlessly pressing for the deployment of more Monuments men with the combat forces, the Roberts Commission made a concerted effort in early 1944 to have an officer of suitable rank attached to the headquarters of the Supreme Allied Command who could act as a liaison between the commission and the army in the field. At the commission meeting of 3 February 1944, Chairman Roberts announced that the War Department had approved this suggestion. He then introduced Brigadier General Henry C. Newton, who made a favorable impression on the group. A veteran of the First World War and a California architect in civilian life, Newton was then a reserve officer with an armored division training in Texas. He had been highly recommended by the American Institute of Architects, and the combination of his military rank and professional credentials won over the commission members, who eagerly appointed him to their senior field position. Unfortunately, Newton came with some baggage. Reprimanded by his commanding officer for failing to have "an Engineer company in the right place at the right time" during training exercises,[38] he accepted a voluntary reduction in rank to that of colonel. Pending charges against him were dismissed, and in April he appeared again before the Roberts Commission with eagles on his shoulders instead of stars, eager to turn over a new leaf in Europe.

Colonel Newton arrived in England on 6 May 1944, but his usefulness had already been undermined by Finley's attempt to persuade the War Department to have Newton function as the liaison with British and other European commissions. General John H. Hilldring of the Civil Affairs Division wrote back that the War Department could not authorize this. Meanwhile, Newton antagonized the British as well as some of the American brass in London who were trying very hard to get along with their British colleagues. In response, they snubbed and excluded him, even to the extent of speaking French to one another in his presence, a language he did not understand. Finally, Hilldring forbade Newton from reporting directly to the Roberts Commission on anything but personal matters, requiring that all official communications go through him, with "appropriate extracts from your reports."[39] Furthermore, Hilldring recommended that the Roberts Commission appoint a civilian to represent them in London. When Francis Taylor managed to get to London and then to Paris in the summer of 1944, however, his well-meaning but impulsive actions made the situation worse, to the point that "the Allied High Command and the Monuments men in the field had begun to regard the Roberts Commission less as an ally and more as a badly informed and interfering adversary."[40]

Finley eventually redeemed the situation when he recruited John Nicholas Brown of Providence, Rhode Island, to serve as liaison. Scion of the family that had founded Brown University, this erudite philanthropist and art historian had been involved with the restoration of the Hagia Sofia in Istanbul before the war and was quite at home in any company, civilian or military, American, British, or European.[41] Technically a civilian, Brown received the simulated title "lieutenant colonel," which gave him enough clout to deal with his British counterparts as well as with Eisenhower's staff. But he did not arrive in London until March 1945.

Tragedy and Triumph

Despite these blunders behind the lines, the Monuments men on the ground performed well in northwestern Europe after D-Day. George Stout finally reached Normandy in early July, where he found considerable damage to churches and monuments in towns such as Caen, Saint-Lô, and Vire. But the maps and lists of historic and cultural properties provided though the Roberts Commission had reached the air crews and forward army units and had averted greater destruction.

On 26 May 1944, just before the D-Day landings in Normandy on 6 June, Eisenhower issued an order to his commanders, to be followed by similar orders for the Low Countries, confirming the "basic policy of the Supreme Commander to take all measures, consistent with military necessity, to avoid damage to all structures, objects, or documents of cultural, artistic, archaeological, or historic value."[42] MFAA officers went ashore in Normandy within a week of D-Day and worked in close collaboration with the frontline troops as they broke out across France and Belgium to reduce the incidence of careless damage.[43]

Although many incomparable structures suffered serious harm in the course of the war, including Rouen Cathedral and dozens of churches and monuments in Normandy, the Roberts Commission

49. Frankfurt, Germany, showing the cathedral and surrounding area at the close of the war, 1945. Signal Corps photograph

could take justifiable pride in the record of the Allied forces, especially the Americans. Even in Germany, target of most Allied bombing in Europe, the work of the commission helped prevent more significant losses. An aerial photograph of Frankfurt at the end of the war, for example, shows the almost total devastation surrounding the cathedral, sparing the cathedral itself (fig. 49). Its tower and spire looked miraculously intact, and although bombs destroyed the outer roof of the nave and transepts, almost all of the walls still stood.[44]

Once inside Germany, American units began to find caches of artworks that had been removed from churches and art museums all over Germany for safekeeping as well as massive hoards of loot from the occupied countries. Between April and July 1944 the Nazis confiscated 138 boxcars of art from the Louvre and other French art museums and stored them in remote castles or in deep mines within Germany.[45] The Twelfth U.S. Army group alone found 396 such stashes in April 1945.[46]

George Stout and a handful of fellow Monuments officers—while still hampered by military bureaucracy, the lack of transportation, and restrictions on their movements—labored frantically to meet the demand for their services as forward units began to grasp the magnitude of the problem. Through contacts with art professionals in France and Germany, Monuments officers such as James Rorimer, former curator of the Cloisters in New York, and Walker Hancock, a well-known sculptor, learned the locations of more than a hundred caches of stolen art from French and German collections, which Hancock pinpointed on operations maps used by the frontline commanders. On Easter Sunday in April 1945, Stout and Hancock reached a mine at Siegen and found hundreds of paintings and sculptures from European museums as well as the relics of Charlemagne and other treasures from Aachen Cathedral.

Thus in the last weeks of fighting in Germany the mission of the Monuments officers shifted from protection to salvage, as mandated by the Roberts Commission. During the chaos just before and after the Germans surrendered on 7 May 1945, MFAA officers accomplished prodigious feats in saving countless artworks found in thousands of caches all over the American zone of occupation.[47] Working alone or in two-man teams, the Monuments officers raced to identify and take custody of these troves, sometimes under fire.[48] Only one example is recounted here, for both its inherent drama and its repercussions for David Finley and the National Gallery of Art.

With the efficiency of a people who maintained and sometimes even increased their production of aircraft, submarines, and munitions despite the carpet bombing of their factories and shipyards, the Germans also achieved the seemingly impossible in securing the contents of their art museums and ancient churches, right up to the very end of the war. Hitler refused to permit the evacuation of the Berlin collections until 8 March 1945, when the Soviets were only fifty miles away. Then, over the next three weeks, with the Red Army approaching the

50. Generals Eisenhower, Bradley, and Patton inspect art treasures in a mine at Merkers, Germany, 6 April 1945

suburbs, the Germans managed to load thousands of paintings and sculptures from the city's museums onto trucks and trains and transport them westward to safe haven in deep and dry salt mines near Merkers in central Germany. The Germans correctly guessed that this would lie within the area of American occupation, and to reach it they made their way through Allied bombing of the railroads and highways, the masses of their own retreating troops, and the swarming Allied armored patrols. The last shipment reached the mines on 30 March, two days before Hitler descended into his bunker below the Reich Chancellery for the last time.[49]

When units of General George Patton's Third Army reached Merkers on 6 April, they learned that the potash mines at the Kaiseroda site contained a fabulous treasure in gold bullion, constituting a large part of Germany's gold reserves. Patton sent an entire tank battalion to secure the mine, only to discover that the main storage tunnels, up to half a mile underground, also contained thousands of works of art. So astounding was the discovery that Generals Eisenhower, Bradley, and Patton toured the mine together (fig. 50) and later joked over dinner about the good old days "when a soldier kept his loot."[50] When Monuments officers Navy Lieutenant George Stout and Captain Robert K. Posey finally received permission to inspect the art and consult the German custodian, they learned that the hoard included the most important objects from Berlin museums, including the Kaiser Friedrich. Because of the haste in which this staggering collection had been crammed into the mine tunnels, often uncrated, and because of its incalculable value, they ordered the immediate evacuation of the art along with the gold ingots.

Stout performed Herculean tasks in getting the artworks out of the mine at Merkers and packing them for transport. His diary laconically noted, "Worked out materials needed for normal packing of load. No chance of getting them."[51] But the next day he found a thousand sheepskin coats captured from the enemy, which he pressed into service. Later he improvised with old mattresses as packing and cushioning material. A labor crew, eventually numbering seventy-five enlisted men and five officers, worked around the clock, and by 15 April the first convoy held more than three thousand crates and cases. Finally Stout drafted a work crew of German POWs to finish packing and loading 393 uncrated paintings. On 17 April 1945 thirty ten-ton army trucks, each with two guards aboard and escorted by motorized infantry, antiaircraft vehicles, and even air cover (though the Luftwaffe had ceased to exist as an effective fighting force), transported the gold and the most valuable art to Frankfurt. There it was unloaded with great difficulty by 105 POWs "in poor health" and stored temporarily in bank vaults.

As more caches of this kind came to light in the American zone during the spring and summer of 1945, Stout and his fellow Monuments officers continued, working alongside German and Austrian curators who had volunteered assistance, to secure and inventory more than a thousand depositories of artworks from German museums and those looted from German-occupied Europe. The U.S. Army transported these objects to nine collecting points in the American zone.

In late June and early July 1945 the indefatigable Lieutenant Stout oversaw another enormous recovery operation, this time from a deep salt mine at Alt Aussee, near Lauffen in the Salzburg region of Austria, containing a vast store of paintings, statuary, and altarpieces stolen from France and the Low Countries. Although the Germans had surrendered in early May, relations between the Americans and the Soviets had already started to deteriorate, and Stalin demanded that the American forces vacate the areas designated at Yalta for Soviet occupation by 1 July. David Finley convinced the War Department to include looted art among the materials requiring evacuation from the future Soviet zone. Alt Aussee lay in this transitional area, and the Americans under Stout toiled feverishly to save its treasures from the hands of the Soviets, who regarded all works of art as legitimate spoils of war, which they were shipping east to the U.S.S.R. by the trainload under the supervision of art specialists.[52] By 24 June, Stout and his men clocked in twenty-hour days, working from 4:00 a.m. to midnight under nightmarish conditions: lacking telephones, fighting floods, and waiting for recycled packing materials to be returned from the collection point in Munich, 150 miles away. Incredibly, the military still balked at giving Stout the transport, workforce, and packing materials he needed.

Fortunately, Stalin missed his 1 July deadline because of the failure of the Allied-Soviet negotiators to settle the boundary details, and by 14 July 1945 Stout and his fellow Monuments officers had succeeded in transferring eighty truckloads of carefully packed artworks from Alt Aussee to Munich, including 1,441 crates of paintings, 1,850 uncrated pictures, and eleven large sculptures. On 23 July the Red Army closed the roads out of Alt Aussee, and the Iron Curtain rang down. On 29 July an exhausted George Stout flew to London on orders to return to the States after thirteen months of nonstop action.[53]

Reparations Prove Finley's Mettle

The American forces returned looted artworks rescued from Alt Aussee and elsewhere in Germany and Austria to the original owners west of the Rhine as soon as conditions permitted. But thornier problems arose over the proper disposition of the rich collections from the German museums, particularly those that had fallen under Soviet occupation in East Germany and East Berlin.

Certain prominent American officials complicated the situation with their well-publicized calls for punitive reparations from Germany. The secretary of the treasury Henry Morgenthau, for example, had proposed a plan in 1944 to reduce postwar Germany to an agricultural state by dismantling all of its industrial production. Roosevelt actually considered such a plan, and only the blunt intervention of his secretary of war Henry Stimson dissuaded him.[54] But at the Yalta Conference in February 1945 Roosevelt had agreed with Stalin, over Churchill's opposition, that Germany should once again pay reparations. And in June 1945 Sumner Crosby, representing the Roberts Commission in Europe, reported with grave concern that the President's special assistant on reparations, Edwin Pauley, along with the American military governor, General Lucius D. Clay, and Colonel Bernstein of the Treasury Department, "favor the use of works of art as a basis of reparations." John Nicholas Brown wrote Clay a long memorandum warning of the dangers of such a policy.[55]

From 15 July to 2 August 1945 the victorious Allies met at Potsdam outside of Berlin not only to determine the fate of Germany, and the rest of Europe, but to secure Soviet assistance in the unfinished war with Japan. Harry S. Truman, who had become President at the death of FDR on 12 April, now met with Stalin for the first time.[56] In the midst of the conference Clement Atlee replaced Churchill as prime minister of Great Britain. Also during the conference Truman approved the dropping of the nuclear bomb on Japan. In all essential ways, Truman looked Stalin squarely in the eye at Potsdam, and neither blinked. Stalin agreed to join the war against Japan but would not give an inch on any issue related to Europe. Truman received the news of Hiroshima while crossing the Atlantic on his way home. Eight days later Japan surrendered, and the war ended.[57]

One of the issues settled at Potsdam concerned reparations. The Americans and British concurred in awarding the Soviets the majority of the $20 billion in reparations claimed at Yalta, because they had suffered most in the war. At a meeting in Moscow earlier in July the three sides had failed to reach an agreement as to the exact form the reparations would take, other than that it would be in property, not gold, as had caused such bitterness after the First World War. Although some controversy stirred within the American delegation over what to include in the reparations pool, the British had made sure art was not on the table at Potsdam.[58]

President Truman did approve a paper at Potsdam prepared by General Clay's staff on the restitution of enormous quantities of art for which the U.S. Army found itself the reluctant custodian. With the art divided into three categories, the first two groups comprised art from the countries Germany had overrun; these works, both publicly and privately owned, would be repatriated as soon as possible. The third group, "Class C," consisted of "works of art placed in the U.S. Zone by Germany for safekeeping which are bona fide property of the German

51. David Finley reflects on a painting from the Kaiser Friedrich
Museum, Berlin, before its return to Germany from the National
Gallery of Art in 1949. Left to right: John Walker, Harry McBride,
Keith Merrill, Finley, and Lamont Moore

nation." Believing that he lacked the staff expertise and appropriate
facilities to safeguard these irreplaceable objects in the American
zone of occupation, General Clay recommended "that the works of
art in Class 'C' be removed to the US as rapidly as arrangements can
be effected and distributed among the museums in the US properly
equipped to handle these works of art."[59] A public announcement
accompanying their exhibition in the United States—addressed to the
German people as well—would set the terms: "that these works of
art will be held in trusteeship for return to the German nation when
it has re-earned its right to be considered as a nation." Even worse,
some American civilians involved in reparations went further, arguing
that the "eventual disposition" of these works should be "subject to
future Allied decision"—and so advised the British and Soviet foreign
ministers.[60]

No Monuments officer had been consulted, and their senior spokesman in Berlin, John Nicholas Brown, fired off an angry protest to General Clay. He believed that in fact facilities and personnel in the American zone could provide sufficient protection for the German art and that transporting it across the ocean posed as great a danger as leaving it in Germany. More important, he contended that removing Germany's artworks "under the questionable legal fiction of 'trusteeship' seems to the writer, and to his associates in the MFAA Branch, not only immoral but hypocritical." He suggested that the finest works from the German collections travel to the United States and other nations as part of a number of loan exhibitions, as long as the German museums underwent repairs, and not "as taken by some quasi-legal act of war." Brown came away from a final meeting with Clay reassured that President Truman had confirmed a promise to return these artworks to Germany at a future time.[61]

Controversy flared again, however, when secretary of state James F. Byrnes hedged, saying that the United States should set a "high standard of conduct" and return the art "except for such levies as may be made upon them to replace looted or artistic or cultural property which has been destroyed or irreparably damaged."[62] The British and Soviet governments had already protested the Americans' removal of the art, with the Russians surely aware that the most precious masterpieces from the Kaiser Friedrich Museum and other institutions within their zone of occupation now rested in American hands.

Monuments officers in Europe, such as Mason Hammond, generally expressed dismay at what looked at best like a clumsy military-political snafu and at worst like a blatant seizure of priceless works of art for the United States. Strong differences of opinion divided the Roberts Commission itself, with Professor Dinsmoor and Francis Taylor eagerly approving of the plan to bring the German art to America. John Walker reported at a meeting of the commission on 25 September 1945, having visited Germany in July, that in view of the confusion there, "the policy of a wise custodian would be to bring at least part of this irreplaceable treasure to the safest haven available, and that would seem to me, at the present time, to be the United States."[63] But the commission's secretary, Charles Sawyer, predicted that "the physical presence of these objects in the country would lead to strong pressure to retain at least some of them under some pretext or another."⁶⁴

This hot potato landed squarely in David Finley's lap when a high official in the War Department, whom he did not identify but who was likely assistant secretary John McCloy, asked if the National Gallery would accept temporary custody of 202 paintings from the Kaiser Friedrich Museum. Keenly attuned to the sensitivity of this mission, Finley immediately telephoned the chairman of the Gallery's board of trustees, Chief Justice Harlan Stone, at his summer home in New Hampshire and asked to come and see him about an urgent and confidential Gallery matter. He arrived the next morning and went over the situation with Stone, who responded, "If the government asks us to take care of these paintings, we must do it. It is a duty which we could not escape if we wanted to, and certainly we do not want to."⁶⁵

With doubts resolved by the chief justice, the National Gallery forged ahead with a plan to offer temporary care for the paintings from Germany. The Gallery administrator Harry McBride, then an army colonel, traveled to the collecting point at Wiesbaden in November to begin packing the Kaiser Friedrich works for shipment. But he met with a hostile reception among the MFAA officers, who had no prior knowledge of the government's intent and were offended by McBride's manner and suggestions of their incompetence. A group of twenty-five officers signed an extraordinary letter of protest, now known as the Wiesbaden Manifesto. This document forthrightly challenged orders from superior officers, but with questionable judgment likened the removal of the art to the war crimes trials just starting at Nuremberg. It concluded:

> We wish to state that from our own knowledge, no historical
> grievance will rankle so long, or be the cause of so much
> justified bitterness, as the removal, for any reason, of a part
> of the heritage of any nation, even if that heritage may be
> interpreted as a prize of war. And though this removal may
> be done with every intention of altruism, we are none the
> less convinced that it is our duty, individually and collectively,
> to protest against it, and that though our obligations are to
> the nation to which we owe allegiance, there are yet further

obligations to common justice, decency, and the establishment of the power of right, not expediency or might, among civilized nations.[66]

Needless to say, this heated rhetoric soon reached the press, much to the dismay of both Finley and Stone. The chief justice felt particularly outraged, as both he and President Truman had publicly stated that the United States was bringing these masterworks to America solely for their safekeeping and that they would be returned to Germany once order there was restored. He saw the manifesto as an attack on his and the President's integrity as well as on the honor of the U.S. government. Finley quoted Stone as asking angrily, "Have these men taken leave of their senses?"[67]

With the counsel of not only John Walker and a German exile employed by the National Gallery but the MFAA officers at the Wiesbaden collecting point as well, McBride made the final selection of 202 pictures, all but two from the Kaiser Friedrich collection. Packed in individual waterproof cases, the works received both army and navy escort on a special train to Le Havre and an army troop transport (where they occupied the entire officers' dining room) to New York, thence by motor convoy to the National Gallery of Art, where they reached air-conditioned storage.

The pot kept boiling, however, as some members of the press continued to question the motives of the government, and by extension the National Gallery. Then in May 1946 a large group of art colleagues, led by the directors of the Whitney and Frick museums in New York, sent a strongly worded petition to President Truman challenging the distinction between the current situation and the "'protective custody' of the Nazis."[68] Although Finley mourned when Harlan Stone died suddenly on 22 April 1946, at least the chief justice was spared this latest blast. But the critics had finally crossed the line, and numerous voices, including the *Washington Post* and a prominent U.S. congresswoman, Frances Bolton, rose to defend the actions of the government and the National Gallery.

With this, protests seemed to dissipate, and the German-owned paintings remained undisturbed in their private vaults until early 1948, when General Clay decided it would be safe to return them to the

American zone of Germany. By this time the Iron Curtain was firmly in place from the Baltic to the Adriatic, and Clay no longer bothered about Soviet claims to the "202" for East Berlin. But members of Congress and others had been pressing for the opportunity for the American people to see these paintings before their repatriation. So the army, which had asked a great deal of Finley three years earlier, now requested one more favor: it wanted him to organize a public exhibition of the paintings at the National Gallery, with a smaller selection to travel to twelve other American museums before the works returned to Germany. First, the organizers exempted fifty-two pictures on panel, considered most likely to suffer damage from further travel, and carefully sent them back to Germany.

Virtually without notice the National Gallery had to scramble to put together this once-in-a-lifetime presentation of 150 master paintings from Germany. An unprecedented total of 964,970 visitors thronged the galleries in just over a month, between 17 March and 25 April 1948—an average of more than 23,500 people a day.[69] To complicate the director's life, celebrities like Henry Ford, John D. Rockefeller Jr., Lady Astor, and the Duke and Duchess of Windsor asked for private viewings before or after hours to avoid the crowds. David Finley, eternally obliging, of course escorted these special guests himself.

Then, honoring the War Department's request, the Gallery sent a select exhibition on a tour of museums in a dozen American cities, attended by special curators and a military guard at all times. Finally in April 1949, four years after their rescue from the salt mine at Merkers, the last paintings sailed from New York under naval escort, having been viewed by some ten million Americans (fig. 51). The canvases reached Wiesbaden on 4 May in excellent condition. As John Walker remarked, "Never before in history have such efforts been made to care for works of art belonging to an enemy country."[70] Finley himself closed this unique chapter in art history by noting with a touch of pride and perhaps gentle reproach to those who had questioned his motives, "Not a single work of art was expropriated by the American government, not even those acquired by Hitler and Goering under conditions far from admirable."[71] The work of the Roberts Commission was terminated in mid-1946 when responsibility for the art of war-torn Europe was transferred to the State Department, which dealt with the chaos and disruptions of the war for decades to come.

Roberts's Rules

The Roberts Commission never had more than two hundred men in the field, and far fewer than that most of the time, while it worked with perhaps an equal number of civilians, both men and women, at home. Those few did not save every historic church or monument in Europe from destruction, or every piece of art from loss or looting—some of it inflicted by their fellow Americans. But they did prevent far worse damage during a consuming war, and they avoided utter chaos during a nervous peace. The wonder was not how much was lost, but how much was saved.

Most of all, the Roberts Commission gave the world a model for how a civilized country can act to protect the common heritage of mankind even in the white-hot heat of modern warfare. It is an example to ponder in a later age when, with all our advances in science and technology and all our peacekeeping efforts, important parts of the world's cultural heritage are still very much at risk.[72] Finley and his colleagues had the wisdom and the courage to speak truth to power, and power listened. It is a lesson that should not be forgotten.

NOTES

1. The author would like to acknowledge his debt to several primary sources for this discussion. The late Dr. Ernest A. Connally of Alexandria, Virginia, in 1998 first called his attention to the work of the Roberts Commission and generously gave permission to quote from his unpublished manuscript entitled "Wartime" (personal papers). In addition to the Report of the Roberts Commission (1946), the commission's records at the National Archives at College Park, Maryland, and the George Stout Papers at the Archives of American Art at the Smithsonian Institution, the author consulted Nicholas, *Rape of Europa*, which offers a comprehensive and fascinating account.

2. Connally, "Wartime," 10–11.

3. George L. Stout (1897–1980) was head of conservation at the Fogg from 1933 to 1947. After the war he became director of the Worcester Art Museum (1947–1954) and then of the Isabella Stewart Gardner Museum (1955–1970).

4. Harlan Fiske Stone (1872–1946), who graduated from Amherst College and Columbia Law School, was dean of the latter when appointed attorney general by his college

classmate Calvin Coolidge in 1924. Coolidge named him to the Supreme Court in 1925, and Franklin Roosevelt made him chief justice in 1941.

5. David Finley, notes to Alpheus Thomas Mason (Stone's biographer), January 1952. Finley Papers, NGA Archives, box 19-21. Finley also quoted Justice Stone concerning their tour of the building: "Mrs. Stone and I had been very worried about it, for we knew that Mr. Mellon had provided adequate funds to do whatever was necessary. We were afraid that, with so much money available, the building would be overdone and the background and installation would be too elaborate for the works of art. We were almost afraid to come and see it, and now we could not be happier or filled with admiration for the building in every respect."

6. Francis Taylor, memorandum, 24 November 1942. National Archives, RG 239, M1944, roll 59.

7. FDR to Harlan Stone, 28 December 1942. National Archives, RG 239, box 51.

8. David Finley to Francis Taylor, 1 January 1943. National Archives, RG 239, M1944, roll 59.

9. Letter drafted by Finley for Chief Justice Stone to send Mrs. Henry Morgenthau, dated 26 February 1943. National Archives, RG 239, M1944, roll 59.

10. Paul Sachs to David Finley, 22 March 1943. National Archives, RG 239, M1944, roll 59.

11. FDR to Stone, 24 April 1943. National Archives, RG 239, box 51.

12. Cordell Hull (1871–1955), a Tennessee lawyer and Democratic politician, served in the House of Representatives (1907–1931) and the Senate (1931–1933), then became FDR's secretary of state (1933–1944); he won the Nobel Peace Prize in 1945, recognizing his role as a "father of the United Nations."

13. Cordell Hull to FDR, 21 June 1943. National Archives, RG 239, box 51.

14. Finley, *Standard of Excellence*, 158–159; Nicholas, *Rape of Europa*, 222.

15. Quoted in Nicholas, *Rape of Europa*, 222.

16. Report of the Roberts Commission, 30 June 1946, 47. National Archives, RG 239, box 51.

17. Nicholas, *Rape of Europa*, 224.

18. Harlan Stone to David Finley, 22 July 1943. National Archives, RG 239, M1944, roll 59.

19. Owen Josephus Roberts (1875–1955) was the only Philadelphia lawyer ever to serve on the U.S. Supreme Court. Appointed by President Coolidge as special counsel in the eight Teapot Dome cases of 1924 to 1930, he argued against Frank Hogan (later Andrew Mellon's defense lawyer in the tax trial), who then called Roberts "the toughest proposition I ever went up against in my thirty years of practice." See M. R. Werner and John Starr, *Teapot Dome* (New York, 1957), 221. Appointed to the Supreme Court by President Hoover in 1930, Roberts spent fifteen years on the high court before resigning in 1945 to return to Philadelphia as dean of the University of Pennsylvania Law School. In 1943 Stone and Roberts were the only Supreme Court justices not appointed by FDR, Stone having been named by Coolidge.

20. Finley to Stone, 3 August 1943. National Archives, RG 239, M1944, roll 59.

21. Owen J. Roberts to David Finley, 16 August 1943. National Archives, RG 239, M1944, roll 59.

22. In April 1944 after the U.S. Navy requested information on cultural sites in the Far East, the focus of the commission officially expanded from "Europe" to "War Areas."

23. Alfred E. Smith, a former governor of New York who ran against Hoover for President in 1928, also agreed to join the commission but does not appear to have attended any meetings. When Smith died in October 1944, Francis Cardinal Spellman of New York replaced him on the commission.

24. Report of the Roberts Commission, 69.

25. Minutes of the Roberts Commission, 20 August 1943, 10. National Archives, RG 239, M1944, roll 59.

26. Minutes of the Roberts Commission, 20 August 1943, 11.

27. Kenneth Clark to W. G. Constable, 25 February 1943; quoted in Nicholas, *Rape of Europa*, 214.

28. Minutes of the Roberts Commission, 25 August 1943, 18.

29. By 1943 the air force, which had previously been the U.S. Army Air Force, had attained semi-independent status as the U.S. Air Force but was overseen by the War Department until the end of hostilities.

30. John McCloy (1896–1989) had risen from humble roots and graduated from Amherst College and Harvard Law School before joining the Cravath law firm in New York. He made his fame there as counsel to Bethlehem Steel in a lengthy lawsuit arising from the 1916 explosion of a munitions plant in which, after ten years of litigation, he proved that German agents were responsible. In September 1940, with another war against the Germans brewing, he accepted Stimson's call to come to Washington as assistant secretary of war. As one of the architects of victory in the Second World War, for which he won a Distinguished Service Medal, he went on to serve as U.S. high commissioner in West Germany, president of the World Bank, chairman of Chase Bank, and chairman of the Council on Foreign Relations. See Godfrey Hodgson, *The Colonel: The Life and Wars of Henry Stimson, 1867–1950* (New York, 1990), 243–244, 248, 359.

31. John McCloy to David Finley (undated), probably November 1943. National Archives, RG 239, box 51.

32. Sachs to Finley, telegram, 18 November 1943. National Archives, RG 239, box 17.

33. Connally, "Wartime," 8.

34. B. H. Liddell Hart, *History of the Second World War* (London, 1973), 554, 559.

35. Minutes of the Roberts Commission, 8 October 1943, 6.

36. Vincent Massey to David Finley, 6 July 1944. National Archives, RG 239, box 51. Massey (1887–1967) served as Canada's first minister to the United States (1926–1930) and as Canadian high commissioner in London (1935–1946). He became the first Canadian to serve as governor-general of Canada (1952–1959). His younger brother, Raymond Massey, was a Hollywood and Broadway actor.

37. Finley to Massey, 21 July 1944. National Archives, RG 239, box 51.

38. Nicholas, *Rape of Europa*, 275–276.

39. Nicholas, *Rape of Europa*, 277–279.

40. Nicholas, *Rape of Europa*, 281.

41. John Nicholas Brown (1900–1979) was the father of J. Carter Brown (1934–2002), who later followed David Finley as director of the National Gallery of Art and chairman of the U.S. Commission of Fine Arts.

42. Connally, "Wartime," 26.

43. Connally, "Wartime," 28.

44. Report of the Roberts Commission, 215, fig. 47. See also Connally, "Wartime," 30: "The city of Aachen in Germany was very nearly destroyed in the war, yet the Cathedral, the oldest portion of which was constructed in 792–804 for Charlemagne, survived with relatively light damage. Aachen Cathedral was entered on the World Heritage List in 1978. Also, it is certainly no accident that the historic and culturally important city of Kyoto was spared the intensive bombing of Japan that brought the war in the Pacific to a close." In fact, Henry Stimson vetoed a 1945 Army plan to drop the first atomic bomb on Kyoto. See Hodgson, *Stimson*, 323–324, 335.

45. Nicholas, *Rape of Europa*, 135.

46. Connally, "Wartime," 28.

47. The saga of the discovery, protection, and recovery of thousands of masterpieces hidden in the mines, castles, and vaults throughout the American zone of operations in Germany is told in breathtaking detail in Nicholas, *Rape of Europa*, to which the reader seeking the full story is earnestly referred.

48. Nicholas, *Rape of Europa*, 332. One officer, Captain Walter Hutchhausen, was mistakenly killed by American troops in April 1945 when he pressed too far and too fast into a combat area in response to a call from a forward unit.

49. Nicholas, *Rape of Europa*, 311.

50. Quoted in Nicholas, *Rape of Europa*, 333.

51. This paragraph is based on George L. Stout's diary, 13–17 April 1945. Archives of American Art, Smithsonian Institution, George L. Stout Papers, reel 1378.

52. Nicholas, *Rape of Europa*, 361–367.

53. On 6 August, the day the first atomic bomb was dropped on Hiroshima, Stout sailed on the *Queen Elizabeth*. By the time he reached Washington on 16 August, the Japanese had surrendered, and the next day the Pentagon assigned him to the Tokyo staff of General Douglas MacArthur. After a month's leave at his home in Cambridge, Massachusetts, Stout attended a Roberts Commission meeting in Philadelphia. Then in October he arrived in Japan with the rank of lieutenant commander and served there as a Monuments officer until mid-1946. Stout was honorably released from active duty with a Bronze Star "for meritorious service in connection with military operations during 17 December 1944 to May 1945" and five campaign stars. Official Records, Department of the Navy, Bureau of Naval Personnel; Stout diary, 29 July 1945.

54. Stimson thought that a just peace and a strong European economy offered the best hope for European recovery, avoiding the resentments caused by the Versailles treaty that had driven Germany into the hands of the Nazis. See Hodgson, *Stimson*, 264–265.

55. Nicholas, *Rape of Europa*, 370.

56. David McCullough, *Truman* (New York, 1992), 406.

57. Truman later said that he had known since Potsdam that the police state of Communist Russia was no different from the police state of Nazi Germany. See McCullough, *Truman*, 549.

58. Nicholas, *Rape of Europa*, 384.

59. Report of the Roberts Commission, 148.

60. Nicholas, *Rape of Europa*, 385–386.

61. Nicholas, *Rape of Europa*, 387.

62. Nicholas, *Rape of Europa*, 388. Byrnes was the South Carolina congressman who eulogized David E. Finley Sr. on the floor of the House of Representatives in February 1917. See chap. 1, n. 23.

63. Nicholas, *Rape of Europa*, 391.

64. Nicholas, *Rape of Europa*, 388–389.

65. Finley, *Standard of Excellence*, 162; and Nicholas, *Rape of Europa*, 388–389.

66. Nicholas, *Rape of Europa*, 394–395.

67. Finley, *Standard of Excellence*, 162.

68. Nicholas, *Rape of Europa*, 400.

69. Kopper, *Gift to the Nation*, 233.

70. Finley, *Standard of Excellence*, 163–164.

71. Finley, *Standard of Excellence*, 161. The reference to Hitler may recall a bit ruefully the famous Vermeer, *The Artist in His Studio*, which Mellon and Finley had repeatedly tried to buy from 1928 to 1934 without success (see chap. 3, n. 50). Hitler "bought" it for a ridiculously low price from the owners in Vienna in 1940. Monuments officers salvaged it at the end of the war and returned it to Vienna just before selecting the 202 paintings that came to the National Gallery for safekeeping.

72. The *New York Times*, on 14 February 2005, quoted a professor of archaeology at Columbia University as saying that the looting of antiquities in Iraq has increased under the American-led occupation and that tens of thousands of antiquities, some dating back five thousand years, "have just gone completely missing in the past two years. It's a cultural disaster of massive proportions." The article mentioned a special FBI "arts crime team" that is working on the link between the underground traffic in looted Iraqi antiquities and the funding of terrorism. It quoted a former senior cultural advisor to the Coalition Provisional Authority in Iraq who estimated that hundreds of thousands of significant cultural artifacts have been taken in the past two years, possibly as many as 400,000 to 600,000, valued at $10 to $20 million a year. He also pointed to recent efforts by Iraq, which "cut the looting back dramatically."

52. Hampton Mansion, Towson, Maryland. Hampton National Historic Site

9

A Congressional Charter for Historic Preservation

1944–1949

DAVID FINLEY EMERGED FROM HIS WARTIME experiences with national prestige. He had dealt personally and effectively with those in the highest echelons of the government—the President, the chief justice and the senior associate justice of the Supreme Court, and officials at the War and State Departments—as well as the leaders of the country's arts and intellectual communities. He had played a major role in one of America's noblest efforts, protecting the historic monuments and the artistic and architectural masterworks of Europe in the midst of a world war. Now he would turn his talents to combating a three-pronged threat to his own nation's cultural heritage. These threats were not as dramatic as aerial bombing and high-explosive shellfire, but they were no less real. Among them were suburban home building fueled by the end of the war, new highways to abet America's love affair with the automobile, and changes in lifestyle that did not support the grand old houses of the wealthy. Finley's work at the National Gallery of Art soon led him to the next major challenge of his career: namely, the creation of a new organization of private citizens nationwide who believed that the country's historic and architectural inheritance should be preserved—and then did something about it.

Finding a Portrait and Saving a Landmark

To begin at the beginning, when the National Gallery opened, it owned only modest examples of work by the nineteenth-century American portraitist Thomas Sully, such as a bust-length portrait of Andrew Jackson.[1] But assistant director Magill James told Finley of an elegant full-length portrait by Sully at Hampton near Baltimore, the home of his friend John Ridgely. Finley wrote to Ridgely on 16 May 1944, inquiring into the possibility of borrowing "your beautiful portrait of *Miss Eliza Ridgely* by Thomas Sully" for the Gallery. Ridgely replied that he would gladly lend the portrait for a limited time but that he also had an interest in selling it to the National Gallery. Finley wrote back that he would like to bring John Walker, his chief curator, to Hampton the following week. He wrote Ridgely again on 1 June to thank him for the hospitality he had shown them on 31 May: "I enjoyed enormously seeing Hampton and all the beautiful things which have been assembled there by so many generations of your family. Together with its gardens, it forms an authentic American document such as one seldom sees anywhere. I hope it can be maintained as it is now. I enjoyed, too, seeing the beautiful Sully portrait of Miss Eliza Ridgely. It is a fine example of Sully's best work and one which I would love to see some day in the National Gallery. Perhaps something can be worked out, and I hope we can talk about it further."[2] Finley wasted no time and apparently took the matter of *Lady with a Harp: Eliza Ridgely* to the National Gallery's acquisitions committee on 16 June 1944 (plate 24). He needed to find a donor, however, and the painting was not actually purchased until October 1945, as the gift of his friend Maude Monell Vetlesen.[3]

The Ridgelys ranked among the leading families of early Maryland, and in addition to Hampton and its tobacco plantation and iron foundry, they had extensive landholdings and business interests as well as other residences in Baltimore and elsewhere. Hampton had served as the family seat since its construction by the wealthy shipowner and iron manufacturer Charles Ridgely over a period of seven years between 1783 and 1790. One of the largest and grandest homes in the early

PLATE 24 Thomas Sully, *Lady with a Harp: Eliza Ridgely*, 1818.
National Gallery of Art, Gift of Maude Monell Vetlesen, 1945.9.1

republic (175 feet long), it closely followed the Georgian style of the colonial era.[4] After Charles Ridgley's death, the property passed to his nephew Charles Carnan Ridgely, who was governor of Maryland from 1815 to 1819.

The youthful Eliza Ridgely, a member of the following generation, posed for her portrait by Thomas Sully in 1818. Her father, the wealthy Baltimore merchant Nicholas Ridgely, paid $500 for this work, painted by one of the leading American portraitists of his day. Although Sully depicted many of the most prominent politicians, clergymen, and military heroes of his time, his reputation rests primarily on his romanticized, graceful likenesses of fashionable women, of which Eliza's portrait is a fine example. In 1828 Eliza married her cousin John Ridgely, the son of Governor Ridgely, and moved to Hampton, where they spent the rest of their lives. Her life-size portrait probably moved in with them and graced the walls of the mansion for well over a century.

During that century, and particularly after the abolition of slavery, which supported the estate's operations, the fortunes of Hampton and the Ridgely family gradually declined. Eliza's great-grandson, John Ridgely Jr., inherited Hampton and in 1929 began building and selling houses on the surrounding lands. By the time David Finley visited in 1944, the fate of Hampton itself stood in question.[5] Though it had suffered from deferred maintenance, the residence struck Finley as "so appealing in its beauty and dignity, and practically unchanged in the midst of its rolling acres, after more than a hundred and sixty years" (see fig. 52).[6] But Ridgely told him that the family might be forced to sell the superb Georgian mansion and its grounds to a developer because they could no longer afford to maintain the property and pay real estate taxes on it at suburban Baltimore rates. As soon as Finley had found a donor to buy Eliza's portrait for the National Gallery in 1945, he began to search for a way to preserve her home at Hampton.

At about this time Finley had also grown concerned about the future of Oak Hill, the retirement home of President James Monroe, just south of Oatlands in Loudoun County, Virginia. Oak Hill's owner, Frank Littleton, had told Finley in the summer of 1945 that he would have to sell the property and thought that some type of association might maintain it as an educational museum. Finley could not see then how to put together an organization to save a large country estate. But when he learned that Hampton was also threatened with a change of ownership and an uncertain destiny, he went to work.[7]

During his years in Washington, David Finley had become an expert in the workings of Congress and the executive departments of the Treasury, Justice, State, and War. Now he turned his attention to the Interior Department, which administered the government's work in the field of historic monuments. He started by meeting with Arthur E. Demaray, associate director of the National Park Service, and his assistant Ronald Lee: "and [I] found that their admiration for Hampton fully equaled mine for *Lady with a Harp*."[8] Finley had known Demaray since 1936, when the latter represented the Park Service in the complex negotiations surrounding the construction of the National Gallery of Art on the Mall. Demaray served on the National Capital Park and Planning Commission as well, working closely with the U.S. Commission of Fine Arts while Finley was a member.[9]

The National Park Service had authority under the Historic Sites Act of 1935 to acquire and preserve historically significant properties, and it owned and administered several. But in discussing Hampton, Finley found that the Park Service did not usually act without specific congressional approval and funding. And Hampton, though grand and venerable, did not rise to the same status as Independence Hall or the American Civil War battlefields. But Finley approached Fiske Kimball, his former rival for the Widener collection at the Philadelphia Museum of Art, who was on the advisory board of the National Park Service. He invited Kimball to give a lecture at the National Gallery, then he and Margaret entertained Kimball and his wife at their Georgetown home. Within a week Kimball advised Finley that Hampton had a place on the confidential list of houses declared "eligible" under the Historic Sites Act. But Park Service officials made it clear they could do nothing without the funds to acquire the property.

Finley must also have talked with Kimball about Oak Hill, because at the same meeting of the advisory board on 11 December 1945 that addressed Hampton, Kimball went on record to say that he believed Oak Hill represented Monroe's most important years and that it exemplified Monroe's mature taste in architecture. The advisory board declared Oak Hill to be "nationally significant," but the Park Service could go no further in trying to save it.[10] Director Newton Drury instead suggested "that a trust similar to the National Trust in England was needed to take care of places like Hampton."[11]

Finley persuaded John Ridgely to offer the house at Hampton and fifteen surrounding acres for $40,000, a modest figure even for that time. He then contacted Ailsa Mellon Bruce, whose share of the Mellon fortune had evolved into the Avalon Foundation, and proposed that her foundation donate the funds to buy Hampton and make it a gift to the federal government. Finley dined in New York with Ailsa, now divorced from David Bruce. Ailsa responded positively, but Finley had to convince Donald Shepard, his old law partner, former colleague at the National Gallery, and now chief advisor to the Avalon Foundation. Finley had crossed swords with Shepard at the Gallery, and the latter, still standing vigilant over the Mellon funds, replied stiffly that Ailsa wished to give the matter more thought. He added, gratuitously, "You appreciate, of course, that both Ailsa and her foundation have many more requests for most worthy charitable and educational projects, and each request must be weighed in relation to funds available for charitable purposes."[12] But Finley persisted and could write Ridgely in December 1945: "I am hopeful that I may find a donor who will buy and give 'Hampton' to the Nation as an historic house museum. I know it would be very acceptable and my only problem is to find someone who can present the house free of encumbrances. I have some encouragement about this and am just writing to let you know I have the matter very much in mind since our conversation."[13]

By early 1946 Finley succeeded in winning over Shepard, and Mrs. Bruce's Avalon Foundation would ultimately contribute $162,500 for the purchase and preservation of Hampton, with its grounds and furniture, also providing for its repair and maintenance. But the bureaucratic machinations within the Department of the Interior proved more difficult, time consuming, and frustrating. Finley had the staunch support of Kimball, who called Hampton "one of the great post-Revolutionary Houses in the United States" and said, "I know of no other 18th century house of equal importance which is apt to be given to the nation in any near future."[14] Many in the Park Service, however, saw Hampton as a white elephant that would require a large appropriation for its proper rehabilitation. Drury, the director, questioned the acquisition and doubted the Bureau of the Budget would approve the purchase. And in truth, despite Finley's and Kimball's enthusiasm, the venerable old house at Hampton did need a lot of work.

In January 1946 Ronald F. Lee returned to the Park Service as chief historian following three years in England with the U.S. Air

Force, where he had seen firsthand the efforts of the British National Trust to restore and maintain many stately homes similar to Hampton for the public's benefit.[15] Finley took Lee and Shepard to Hampton to meet John Ridgely, and Lee became convinced that the estate should be saved. At this point he began working diligently to have the Park Service assume responsibility.

In November 1946 Lee, Finley, and Shepard went back to Hampton and prevailed upon John Ridgely to sign an option to sell Hampton at a figure "substantially below market value." In January 1947 Shepard formally advised the secretary of the interior that the Avalon Foundation was prepared to donate $90,000 for Hampton—including $43,000 for the house and fifteen acres of land, $15,000 for some of the Ridgely furniture, and $25,000 for necessary repairs. But Shepard carefully added that the commitment did not include any promise of funds for Hampton's maintenance beyond 1948. The Department of the Interior and the Park Service, while expressing their gratitude to the foundation, carefully avoided committing the federal government to the upkeep of Hampton.

The resourceful Lee then brought a nonprofit group into the discussions. The Society for the Preservation of Maryland Antiquities, founded in 1931 and based in Baltimore, agreed to take over the operation and maintenance of Hampton, following protracted negotiations. This broke the logjam, and on 27 April 1947 the Avalon Foundation presented its check for $90,000 to the secretary of the interior. President Truman signed a cooperating agreement with the Maryland preservation society on 6 October 1947, and the secretary of the interior designated Hampton a National Historic Site on 22 June 1948. The society operated the site until 1979, when the Park Service assumed direct management of Hampton, which it maintains to this day.

Soon after acquiring Hampton, the National Park Service began a program of extensive repairs under the supervision of Charles E. Peterson, a preservation architect, vice chairman of the Committee on Preservation of Historic Buildings of the American Institute of Architects, and a pioneer of historic preservation in the United States.[16] The Avalon Foundation soon gave an additional $58,000, part of which funded the installation of a new water distribution system, and Hampton opened to the public as a National Historic Site on 2 May 1949. Not quite a year later, on 30 April 1950, Maryland governor William P. Lane joined David Finley along with National Park Service director Newton Drury and Society for the Preservation of Maryland Antiquities president Robert Garrett in formal dedication ceremonies.[17]

Creating a National Organization

Thus Hampton was saved. But far more important, the joint efforts of David Finley, the National Park Service, and the Avalon Foundation led to the creation of a private national organization to lead the historic preservation movement in this country. Hampton brought several facts into sharp focus for Finley and others: first, America could no longer expect a few wealthy families to look after its historic places; second, new postwar forces such as rampant suburban development (now known as "urban sprawl"), if left unchecked, would seriously threaten the nation's landmarks; third, the federal government did not have the ability to take the lead in wide-scale preservation efforts; and fourth, America had no private group on a national scale, such as Great Britain's National Trust, to care for the country's cultural heritage. In discussions with Arthur Demaray, Newton Drury, and Ronald Lee, Finley learned that "the Park Service felt that there was a great need for a non-governmental organization, composed of persons who would be in a position to focus attention on the preservation of buildings of architectural and historic importance in this country and to supplement the work the government was doing in this field."[18]

Historic preservation had by this time perhaps reached adolescence as an instrument of public policy in this country. A few private groups like the Mount Vernon Ladies' Association and the Thomas Jefferson Memorial Foundation at Monticello had succeeded in preserving important historic sites, owing to the perseverance, often over daunting obstacles, of dedicated individuals.[19] The federal government had begun to protect Civil War battlefields in 1890 and had passed the Antiquities Act of 1906, which authorized Presidents to set aside historic structures on federal land as national monuments. Creation of the National Park Service under the Department of the Interior in 1916 provided for custody of twenty-one national monuments in addition to fourteen national parks. By 1946 the Park Service maintained many properties of great national significance, such as Independence Hall and Franklin D. Roosevelt's home at Hyde Park, New York, but it struggled to meet an ever-increasing mandate for protection of natural, scenic, and recreational areas as well as historic sites.[20]

Some regional preservation groups existed, notably the very successful Society for the Preservation of New England Antiquities under the leadership of William Sumner Appleton, along with a scattering of local groups, mainly in the Northeast. Starting in 1926, the Rockefeller family had given major support to the restoration of Colonial Williamsburg. Then beginning in the 1930s, a few cities—including New Orleans, Annapolis, and Charleston, South Carolina—adopted protection ordinances for local landmarks. But America lacked a broad-based private national organization that could mobilize citizens across the country and function as a nerve center for the exchange of information and techniques among various groups and individual preservationists. Even more, Finley saw the need for an entity that could move swiftly to acquire threatened historic properties such as Hampton when the National Park Service or other government bodies could not act, or act quickly enough.

The idea was not new. Individuals had discussed this since 1901, when the English artist Charles R. Ashbee came to the United States with the intention of forming an American branch of the British National Trust. But he found people's interests narrowly focused on local landmarks, too diffuse to support a national organization. Charles Hosmer, the foremost chronicler of the American preservation movement, points to periodic attempts before 1946, both within and outside of the National Park Service, to establish a national preservation organization, none of which came to anything.[21]

Then in early 1946 David Finley and Ronald Lee crossed paths at Hampton. Lee's recent service with the U.S. Air Force in Great Britain during the Second World War gave him an appreciation for the work of the National Trust there. Founded in 1895, it had acquired and restored many historic properties and conserved open spaces, and Lee pondered how the United States could replicate British successes.[22] His experience with Hampton brought the issues into sharp relief. Finley had a lifelong interest in historic buildings, cultivated since youth. Journal entries from a 1915 visit to Bethel Church in York County and from a 1919 trip to Boston, Salem, and Concord reveal not only an early fascination with historic places but keen sensitivity to their architecture and cultural significance. Visits to Great Britain and Europe in the 1920s and 1930s refined his taste and sharpened his critical faculties. His year in London as special assistant to Andrew Mellon, who was U.S. ambassador to the Court of St. James's in 1932–1933, took him to many stately homes and must have given him some exposure to the British National Trust. His work with the Roberts Commission during the war had sensitized him to issues relating to the preservation of historic monuments. And his experience with Hampton and Oak Hill impressed on him the very real dangers to historic American buildings posed by economic and social forces released by the end of the war. Now, as director of the National Gallery of Art, vice chairman of the Roberts Commission, and a presidentially appointed member of the U.S. Commission of Fine Arts, he decided to lend the weight of his experience to the cause of historic preservation.

On 26 October 1946 Lee gave a talk to the American Association for State and Local History in Washington, D.C., entitled "The Effect of Postwar Conditions on the Preservation of Historic Sites and Buildings." He cited examples of the impending danger to historic places around the nation and "recommended a three-point action program, which included a planned campaign to arouse public consciousness of the mounting need for historic preservation; active participation in preservation efforts by national, state, and local governments and organizations on all levels; and lastly, 'a special national conference . . . to discuss problems of conserving historic sites and buildings in the United States.'"[23] Two days later Lee had dinner with George A. McAneny, president of the American Scenic and Historic Preservation Society, which concentrated its efforts on sites in the state of New York. McAneny himself had long urged the federal government to put under protection the old Custom House in Philadelphia and both Federal Hall and Castle Clinton in New York City. McAneny and Lee discussed the possibility of mobilizing new and broader interest in historic preservation among kindred groups.

When McAneny visited the Park Service in Washington the next month, Lee suggested that they call on David Finley at the National Gallery to discuss convening a meeting to explore these ideas. They were joined by Christopher Crittenden, founder of the American Association for State and Local History and head of the North Carolina history and archives division. As a result of these discussions, Finley invited six other prominent individuals to a "pre-organization meeting" in the boardroom of the National Gallery on 5 February 1947. In addition to Finley, Lee, McAneny, and Crittenden, those participating included:

> Horace M. Albright, president, American Planning & Civic Association; former director of the National Park Service (1929–1933), who had established its history division in 1931. He was then a businessman in New York.
>
> James R. Edmunds, president, American Institute of Architects.
>
> Guy Stanton Ford, executive secretary and former president, American Historical Association.
>
> Dr. Waldo G. Leland, chairman, advisory board on National Parks, Historic Sites, Buildings, and Monuments.
>
> Judge Edwin O. Lewis, chairman, Philadelphia National Shrines Park Commission. He had helped foster the national interest in preservation legislation that resulted in the Historic Sites Act of 1935.
>
> John Walker, chief curator, National Gallery of Art.

David Finley presided over the meeting, and Ronald Lee recorded the proceedings. This informal group agreed to form "a national organization or council for the preservation of historic sites, buildings, and monuments" composed of representatives from interested government agencies and private associations as well as individual members. They scheduled a larger organizational meeting for April at the National Gallery. Lee later acknowledged "the vital importance of Mr. Finley" in this process, saying that "as director of the National Gallery of Art, Mr. Finley was an extremely important figure in the cultural affairs

53. Founding delegates to the organizational meeting of the National Council for Historic Sites and Buildings, at the National Gallery of Art, 15 April 1947. David Finley is fourth from left; George A. McAneny, eleventh from left (hand on vest); U. S. Grant III, back row behind McAneny; Ronald F. Lee, front row to right of McAneny; Charles E. Peterson, ninth from right

in the national capital and in the nation. His personal interest and the background and prestige which the National Gallery of Art gave to the initiation of the National Trust made a critical difference both in its character and in its prospects for ultimate success."[24]

The gathering at the Gallery on 15 April 1947 (fig. 53) comprised thirty-seven men and four women from thirty national, regional, state, and local groups between Massachusetts and California as well as the Smithsonian Institution and other museums and universities, plus the archivist of the United States, the librarian of Congress, and six representatives of the National Park Service: Newton Drury, Arthur Demaray, Ronald Lee, Charles Peterson, Francis S. Ronalds of the Morristown National Historical Park (New Jersey), and Verne Chatelain, Lee's predecessor as chief historian. Other notable delegates included Fiske

Kimball of the Philadelphia Museum of Art, Kenneth Chorley of Colonial Williamsburg, and Major General (Retired) U.S. Grant III, chairman of the National Capital Park and Planning Commission.

As host, David Finley welcomed his colleagues and made a few preliminary remarks about the evolution of the historic preservation movement in the United States. George McAneny, a veteran of many years in the field, spoke eloquently on the fractured state of the preservation movement and the decline of federal leadership as evidenced by the War Department's efforts to dispose of historic forts. He ended by proposing that the assembled group establish a National Trust on the British model, to receive donations of both historic properties and cash. Representatives of the architectural, archaeological, planning, and engineering professions pledged their support. Ronald Lee argued that the critical need was a "strengthening of historical preservation efforts at every level of government and organization, national, state, and local."[25]

The delegates voted to found the National Council for Historic Sites and Buildings, a broad-based national membership organization whose board would in turn incorporate the National Trust for Historic Preservation in the United States along the lines of the British model. The Trust would be "concerned largely with the acquisition and operation of historic properties" and would bear fund-raising responsibility for their upkeep. The council was incorporated in the District of Columbia on 23 June 1947 as an association of "hundreds of existing local historic and protective bodies" to increase interest in historic preservation throughout the United States. Its original officers included George McAneny, chairman of the board; U.S. Grant III, president; Kenneth Chorley, vice president; and Ronald Lee, secretary.[26]

David Finley, as director of the National Gallery of Art, had the prestige and influence necessary to bring together this varied group of distinguished and visionary individuals. As a lawyer with long private and public experience in Washington, he had learned formidable negotiating skills and cultivated wide connections within the federal government. His close association with Andrew Mellon and his work at the National Gallery had given him invaluable contacts among Americans of wealth and taste who understood the importance of saving the nation's heritage. And finally, he had the persistence, the patience, and the self-effacing personality to be able to reconcile differing professional views and reach a consensus. In addition, he made available splendid facilities at the National Gallery for conferences involving Trust business. The director's office offered a gracious setting for small private meetings, and the auditorium provided ideal accommodations for large gatherings and lectures. Especially with respect to pressing for congressional action on the charter for the National Trust, Finley brought to the table skills he had honed years earlier when negotiating for federal appropriations to support the operations and maintenance of the National Gallery, and even before that in his work for the Treasury. Finley did not seek a leadership position in the new council but accepted the relatively inconspicuous post of chairman of the executive committee.

The fledgling National Council existed on paper, but it had no office, no staff, and no money. In its first month of life its officers learned an important lesson about its latent power, however. Shortly after the group's incorporation in June 1947, David Finley, in his capacity as president of the American Association of Museums, received a desperate call from citizens in Waltham, Massachusetts, who wanted to stop the town from demolishing the historic Gore Place mansion to build veterans' housing. Finley referred the matter to Ronald Lee at the Park Service, who arranged for General Grant, as president of the council, to sign a formal letter of protest to the town selectmen on 13 July 1947, noting the singular architectural and historical importance of Gore Place, which "once destroyed to meet a temporary need . . . cannot be replaced, a serious loss not only for the present generation but for posterity."[27] To their credit, the Waltham selectmen listened to the new watchdog organization and spared Gore Place. It was the first of many victories.

As Charles Hosmer observed, "This letter represented a significant breakthrough in the field of preservation because it was the first message to convey the awesome power that could come from arousing a national preservation organization."[28] On 20 October 1947 the members of the National Council met in the auditorium of the National Gallery of Art to outline their goals. George McAneny and Ronald Lee planned this first of the autumn gatherings now known as the annual preservation conferences. David Finley welcomed the participants and announced that the Avalon Foundation would soon donate Hampton to the federal government (although it took another fourteen months to consummate the deal). He invited them to visit the galleries and see Thomas Sully's portrait of Eliza Ridgely, which had set in motion the efforts to preserve Hampton. He might well have added that Eliza's face had in fact launched the National Council itself, which would soon evolve into the National Trust.

The conferees elected David Finley as chairman, U. S. Grant III as president, and Ronald Lee as secretary of the National Council. Members of the board included Mrs. Francis B. Crowninshield of Delaware; James R. Edmunds, president of the American Institute of Architects; and Kenneth Chorley. The group authorized appointment of a full-time executive officer, and on 16 August 1948 Frederick L. Rath Jr., initially on loan from the National Park Service, reported for work as executive secretary to the council in a temporary office at Ford's Theater on Tenth Street, N.W., in Washington, also courtesy of the National Park Service. Fred Rath had returned from the war to the Park Service in time to open Franklin D. Roosevelt's family home at Hyde Park to the public as a National Historic Site.[29] Ronald Lee and others at the Park Service recommended Rath's appointment to David Finley and the board of the National Council, but Rath hesitated to leave Hyde Park just as unprecedented numbers of visitors arrived following Roosevelt's death right before VE-Day. In fact, it was at the personal urging of the late President's widow, Eleanor Roosevelt, that Rath decided to cast his lot with the new National Council.

The second annual preservation conference took place at the National Gallery on 4–5 November 1948, featuring a series of addresses given by the French ambassador (on historic preservation in France), the director of the National Park Service, the chairman of the U.S. Commission of Fine Arts, and the head of the Society of American Archaeology as well as by David Finley and others. A committee on the organization of the National Trust for Historic Preservation, chaired by H. Alexander Smith Jr. of Baltimore, proposed that the National Trust be organized as soon as possible with a charter from Congress, an idea that the board of the council approved in February 1949.

In May 1949 Representative J. Hardin Peterson of Florida, chairman of the House Committee on Public Lands, introduced the Bill to Charter the National Trust for Historic Preservation into the Eighty-first Congress. J. A. Krug, secretary of the interior, enthusiastically supported the bill by letter, and on 20 June 1949 the House Committee on Public Lands approved HR 5170, which passed the House on 6 July. On 13 July the *New York Times* carried a lengthy article on its editorial page in favor of the pending bill, quoting from David Finley's remarks in the *Congressional Record:*

> The man who is speaking is David Finley, director of the National Gallery of Art, and, as he puts it, the business at hand "is preserving under glass, as it were, the finest specimens of a civilization that is not passing but changing and on which we are to graft new ways of living that, in some respects at least, will not be inferior to the old." . . .
>
> The Park Service (says Mr. Finley) has done a magnificent job no less with the historic sites than with the parks. But it has its hands pretty full. And "we must not expect the Federal Government to organize all the rescue parties and do all the work of preservation. Much of it is our own responsibility in this fortunate country of ours, where individual initiative still persists and where everyone does not expect the Government to do everything for everybody, as is the case in many countries across the seas."

But the bill languished in the Senate, and on 8 September 1949 another *Times* editorial strongly endorsed the concept of the National Trust and urged the Senate to pass the bill promptly, concluding: "These are days when, more than ever before, we need the inspiration of the past as we advance into a troubled future."

Senator Joseph C. O'Mahoney of Wyoming, chairman of the Committee on Interior and Insular Affairs, brought the bill before the Senate on 28 September, and it passed by unanimous consent on 17 October, a fact noted with approval by another editorial in the *New York Times* on 23 October. President Harry S. Truman signed the bill into law on 26 October 1949, formally establishing the National Trust for Historic

Preservation in the United States as a congressionally chartered "charitable, educational, and nonprofit corporation."[30] On 2 November the *New York Times* once again expressed its editorial approval—for the fourth time in as many months.

* * *

The stage was set for the next act in David Finley's long career. This time he was reaching out to a somewhat different segment of the public than he had addressed through his work at the National Gallery of Art. As soon as the ink was dry on Truman's signature confirming the Trust's legislative charter, Finley went to work to build its board of trustees. Based on the National Gallery's model, the ex-officio trustees of the National Trust included the attorney general of the United States and the secretary of the interior. And for good measure, he added the director of the National Gallery of Art as an ex-officio trustee, ensuring the ongoing affiliation of the two institutions he had done so much to create. In addition, his extraordinary personal and professional contacts enabled him to attract general trustees of national stature and influence.

Moreover, Finley's unique access to Andrew Mellon's two children and heirs, Ailsa Mellon Bruce and Paul Mellon, secured vital early funding, which made the dream a reality. Paul Mellon had maintained an active role at the National Gallery, both before and after his wartime military service, during Finley's tenure as director, and the two men respected one another and had a strong professional relationship. Donald D. Shepard, Finley's former law partner, served not only as a trustee of the National Gallery of Art but as a trustee of the Avalon Foundation, through which Mrs. Bruce made her philanthropic contributions. And Finley had a warm rapport with Ailsa Mellon Bruce herself. Thus David Finley brought not only his innate qualities of leadership and integrity to the establishment of the National Trust but also his prestige and professional influence, his courtesy and sterling reputation among colleagues, and his social graces and remarkable personal connections, not the least of which were with Andrew Mellon's two children. Their early support would prove critical to the success of David Finley's National Trust.

1. This portrait of Andrew Jackson, dating from 1845, had been owned for almost ninety years by the Blair-Lee family of Washington and Maryland, kin of Finley's cousin Violet Blair Janin, and was purchased by Andrew Mellon in 1934. National Gallery of Art Web site, www.nga.gov, consulted in February 2005.

2. David Finley to John Ridgely, 1 June 1944. Finley Papers, NGA Archives, RG 7, box 17, Gifts: Ridgely, Mr. and Mrs. John.

3. Maude Monell Vetlesen later bought another fine Sully portrait, *Captain Charles Stewart*, for the National Gallery.

4. A full account of the construction of Hampton and its early history is told in Charles E. Peterson, *Notes on Hampton Mansion*, ed. Sally Sims Stokes, National Trust for Historic Preservation Library Collection of the University of Maryland (College Park, MD, 1970; 2nd ed., 2000).

5. Lynne Dakin Hastings, *Hampton National Historic Site*, Historic Hampton, Inc. (Towson, MD, 1986).

6. Finley, *Standard of Excellence*, 137.

7. Charles B. Hosmer Jr., *Preservation Comes of Age: From Williamsburg to the National Trust, 1926–1949* (Charlottesville, VA, 1981), 2:814.

8. Finley, *Standard of Excellence*, 138.

9. Ronald Lee to Charles Peterson, 14 April 1970, in Peterson, *Notes on Hampton*, 132, app. E.

10. As it happened, Oak Hill, with its gardens and extensive grounds, managed to survive without outside assistance and remains in private hands, owned by a family with the taste and means to preserve its historic character while continuing to use it as a residence.

11. Hosmer, *Preservation Comes of Age*, 2:815–816.

12. Donald Shepard to David Finley, 7 December 1945. Finley Papers, Library of Congress, box 5.

13. Finley to Ridgely, 17 December 1945.

14. Hosmer, *Preservation Comes of Age*, 2:798–799.

15. Ronald F. Lee (1905–1972), a native of Minnesota and a graduate of its university, joined the National Park Service in 1933 and became its second chief historian in 1938, a position he held until 1951, except for the war years, when he served in the U.S. Air Force. He then became chief of the Park Service's interpretation division and regional director in Philadelphia. After retiring from the Park Service, he wrote histories of the national park system, the national military parks, and the Antiquities Act. See the National Park Service Web site, www.cr.nps.gov. Charles Peterson, in a letter to the author, 31 August 1999, said of Lee, "He was a deep one and deserves a biography of his own."

16. Charles E. Peterson (1905–2004), also a native of Minnesota, began his career with the National Park Service in the 1920s. In the 1930s he initiated the Historic American Buildings Survey, where many preservation architects got their start. In the

1940s he moved to Philadelphia and became a prime mover in the campaign to restore the Society Hill section of the city. In 1962 he started a private practice devoted to architectural history, restoration, and planning, which he maintained until his death in 2004 at the age of ninety-eight. A charter member of the National Council on Historic Sites, Peterson received the Crowninshield Award from the National Trust for Historic Preservation in 1966 for outstanding lifetime achievement. Peterson read a draft of the author's 1999 profile of David Finley and in his letter of 31 August 1999 pronounced it "a competent picture of an outstanding American."

17. The Hampton story is told in detail in Charles B. Hosmer's epic history, *Preservation Comes of Age*, 2:795 et seq.

18. David E. Finley, *History of the National Trust for Historic Preservation, 1947–1963* (Washington, D.C., 1965), 1.

19. Charles B. Hosmer Jr., *Presence of the Past: A History of the Preservation Movement in the United States before Williamsburg* (New York, 1965).

20. Barry Mackintosh, "The National Park Service: A Brief History" (1999), National Park Service Web site, www.cr.nps.gov, consulted in March 2005.

21. Hosmer, *Preservation Comes of Age*, 2:810–813. Charles B. Hosmer Jr. (1932–1993) was a graduate of Principia College in Elsah, Illinois, with an M.A. and a Ph.D. from Columbia University. He returned to Principia in 1961 to become a professor of history. Over the next thirty years he researched and wrote a comprehensive history of the historic preservation movement in the United States, which he chronicled in great detail in the three volumes cited here, ending with the founding of the National Trust for Historic Preservation in 1949. He also took detailed oral histories from dozens of people active in preservation up to the mid-1980s and was apparently planning to continue his chronicle before death intervened. His collected papers are held in the National Trust Library at the University of Maryland.

22. For a brief but interesting history of the British National Trust, see David Cannadine, "Conservation: The National Trust and the National Heritage," in *In Churchill's Shadow: Confronting the Past in Modern Britain* (Oxford, 2003), 224–243.

23. Lee to Peterson, *Notes on Hampton*, 132, app. E.

24. Hosmer, *Preservation Comes of Age*, 2:820.

25. Hosmer, *Preservation Comes of Age*, 2:825.

26. Hosmer, *Preservation Comes of Age*, 2:822–825.

27. Hosmer, *Preservation Comes of Age*, 2:826.

28. Hosmer, *Preservation Comes of Age*, 2:826.

29. Frederick L. Rath Jr. (1913–2001) was educated as an historian at Dartmouth and Harvard, had worked for the National Park Service before the war, then served as an American Field Service ambulance driver with the British Eighth Army in North Africa, and later with the U.S. Army in Europe.

30. Public Law 408, 81st Cong. Title 16, U.S. Code, sec. 468 (63 Stat. 927). For the legislative history, see *Congressional Record*, pp. 7783, 7933, 8951–8952, 13388, 14748, 14963, 15100, and 15102; House Report 855; Senate Report 1100, 81st Cong., 1st sess.

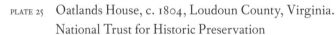

PLATE 25 Oatlands House, c. 1804, Loudoun County, Virginia.
National Trust for Historic Preservation

10

Mr. Finley's National Trust for Historic Preservation
1950–1962

DAVID FINLEY BECAME CHAIRMAN of the new National Trust for Historic Preservation at the age of sixty and led it until he was seventy-two. For those dozen years he also served as chairman of the U.S. Commission of Fine Arts, and for half of them he continued as director of the National Gallery of Art. And just for good measure, he led the founding of the National Portrait Gallery and the White House Historical Association at the same time. The weight and range of his responsibilities brought out the best in him, but it also challenged him in myriad ways. Known as a cautious man, Finley generally led by quiet persuasion rather than public confrontation, and the National Trust under his leadership followed suit. But charting a course through some of its early battles required courage and stamina as well.

An Auspicious Start

The American Institute of Architects hosted the organizational meeting of the National Trust at its headquarters in the Octagon House in Washington on 1 May 1950. With David Finley elected chairman of the board and Frederick Rath appointed director of the Trust, the newly chartered corporation began with strong and capable leaders. Finley announced the receipt of essential start-up funds for the general operating needs of the Trust in the form of grants totaling $50,000 from the Avalon and Old Dominion Foundations established by Ailsa Mellon Bruce and Paul Mellon. By 15 May 1950 the National Trust and the National Council had moved their offices to the Octagon, courtesy of the American Institute of Architects.[1]

The legislative charter provided for three ex-officio trustees—the attorney general of the United States, the secretary of the interior, and the director of the National Gallery of Art—with general trustees to be elected by the membership of the Trust. The National Council named the first general trustees, starting with individuals who served on the board of the council itself, which comprised many professionals and veterans of groups critical to the success of the national preservation movement: U. S. Grant III served as president of the new board, Ronald Lee as recording secretary, and George McAneny, Alexander Smith, and Horace Albright as continuing members. Yet Finley believed that to attract wide public attention and support, the National Trust also had to recruit trustees with high national visibility.

Finley's unique connections brought the new organization instant credibility, with the addition of such trustees as Herbert Hoover, George C. Marshall, Robert Woods Bliss, Winthrop W. Aldrich, and John Nicholas Brown. He had several regrets as well. He had invited Ailsa Mellon Bruce and Paul Mellon to serve as trustees, but neither accepted. He had also hoped to tap the well-known Rockefeller interest in preservation as exemplified at Colonial Williamsburg, but John D. Rockefeller III also declined.[2] Still, those who accepted positions of leadership created a stellar first board of trustees. Hoover was then the only living ex-President of the United States, and his association with Finley dated from 1928, when Finley's mentor Andrew Mellon had anointed him as the Republican candidate at the party's convention in Kansas City; Hoover knew Finley well and held him in high regard.[3] General Marshall, the wartime army chief of staff, secretary of state under Truman, and author of the Marshall Plan, which brought Europe back from the brink of economic and political collapse after the war, was then president of the American Red Cross, where Margaret Finley served as a prominent volunteer. The Marshalls made their home in Leesburg, Virginia, near Oatlands, where they traveled in the same social circles as the Finleys. Robert Woods Bliss was a wealthy diplomat and art collector, whose pre-Columbian art was then housed at the National Gallery under Finley's auspices before moving to Dumbarton Oaks, the Bliss estate in Georgetown. Winthrop W. Aldrich, the brother-in-law of John D. Rockefeller Jr., was president and chairman of the board of Chase National Bank and was soon to become Eisenhower's ambassador to the Court of St. James's. John Nicholas Brown of Providence, a highly cultivated man whose family had founded Brown University, served as a Monuments officer on General Eisenhower's staff in Europe during the war and knew Finley through the Roberts Commission.

A singular asset to the board, Louise du Pont Crowninshield, combined an illustrious name and family connections with a passion for and long practical experience in preserving important American houses.[4] She had been saving historic houses on her own initiative for many years when David Finley consulted her about the preservation of Hampton and invited her to join the National Trust's board of trustees, on which she served as vice chairman from 1953 to 1958. Her early membership drives recruited some one hundred organizational and five hundred individual members for the Trust. She was a shining example among generations of public-spirited American women supporting the preservation movement.[5] When her health began to fail, David Finley arranged for the 1957 annual preservation conference to be held at Swampscott, Massachusetts, near her home, so that members could pay their respects. She responded by inviting all 450 participants to lunch at her home. A few months before her death in July 1958, the executive committee of the National Trust established the Louise du Pont Crowninshield Award, which pleased her tremendously. The earliest and still the most prestigious honor conferred by the Trust, it recognizes "superlative achievement" in the field of historic preservation. The first Crowninshield Award, made in October 1960 at the annual preservation conference in Pittsburgh, went to the Mount Vernon Ladies' Association. And as David Finley then said of

Louise du Pont Crowninshield, "Her wise counsel and generous dedication to historic preservation in all its aspects, as well as her unswerving insistence upon the highest standards of scholarship, will be recalled whenever the National Trust presents this and future awards bearing her name."[6]

Thus by May 1950 the National Trust was finally up and running, with David Finley's hand having guided each stage in its creation. In his *History of the National Trust* Finley modestly points to many people responsible for the founding of the Trust. Although clearly Finley could not have accomplished everything alone, none of the other early players had the experience in public and private affairs in Washington, the wide-ranging contacts with people of influence dating back to his years with Mellon, and the personal diplomacy and tact necessary to create this kind of private organization—with a congressional charter, a board of trustees composed of government officials and private citizens of national stature, and a mandate to do for America's cultural heritage what had never been done before. As one of his successors at the National Gallery later remarked, "If anybody ever knew how things get done in Washington, it was David Finley."[7]

Thanks to Finley's extraordinary access to seats of power in Washington, and his "inimitable powers of persuasion," Supreme Court Justice Felix Frankfurter spoke at the inaugural dinner for the National Trust during its joint annual meeting with the National Council in October 1950. Frankfurter stood among the pillars of the court, a witty and cultivated man as well as a highly respected legal scholar, and it was a coup for the young National Trust to have him address the gathering. General U. S. Grant III acted as the master of ceremonies for the black-tie event, with the Brazilian ambassador to the United States and a preservation leader from Newport, Rhode Island, giving preliminary remarks. Following a warm introduction by Grant, Frankfurter began his address on a light note:

> Let me allay a curiosity of yours that must be very prominently
> on your minds: What am I doing here? [Laughter] As is true
> of many mysteries, it has a very simple explanation. I'm here
> tonight because David Finley told me to be here tonight.

[Laughter] Why did he select me to be here tonight? Because he thought that the most venerable member of the Supreme Court was a fit symbol at a gathering that is concerned with the past. [Laughter] But he took no chances. He comes from South Carolina, but he might as well be a canny Vermonter. He took no chances because he asked me to come but he also told me what to say. [Laughter] He told me what to say, but you must not charge him with my inadequacy as a medium of transmission.

Frankfurter went on to give a learned dissertation on the preservation of British country houses compared to conditions in this country, then ended with these inspiring words: "Tradition is not a barren pride in dead glory; tradition is something that provides refreshment for the spirit. It is something that gives us deep assurance and a sense of destiny and a determination to hold on fast to the great things that have been done through valor and imagination by those who have gone before us."[8]

Turning Vision into Reality

Director Fred Rath had his work cut out for him (fig. 54). Funding from the Avalon and Old Dominion Foundations ensured solvency for the first year or two of the National Trust's operation, but it came at a price. Donald Shepard, the ever-vigilant watchdog of the Mellon coffers, insisted that the Trust hire a former Internal Revenue Service lawyer, Henry H. Surface, as administrator, to oversee its legal affairs, fund-raising, and other support functions. Surface later performed certain duties at Woodlawn Plantation. But true to his Shakespearean-sounding name, he proved a mixed blessing at best. Fred Rath found him a constant complainer who absorbed up to forty percent of his time, with little to show for it. Finley, however, told Rath that he needed to keep Surface on staff to ensure continued Mellon support. Once the Mellon grants had been awarded, Finley himself took an increasingly active role in the business of the National Council and the National Trust.[9]

A second addition to the staff in October 1950 made a strong and lasting contribution to the Trust under David Finley. Helen Duprey Bullock came highly recommended by Charles Peterson, one of the

54. Frederick L. Rath Jr., first director of the National Trust for Historic Preservation

earliest to support the idea of the Trust, who promised that she would be more valuable than an entire library of books. Employed as an historian at Colonial Williamsburg and Monticello for many years and then at the Library of Congress, Bullock brought her vast store of knowledge and far-flung contacts to the Trust. Resourceful, enterprising, and dedicated, she became the backbone of the outreach and educational programs for the Trust. She edited all of the Trust publications, guided the increasingly influential *Preservation Magazine,* and created *Preservation News.* She also oversaw the publication of a wide array of both scholarly and popular books on topics of interest to preservationists, leading to the establishment of the Preservation Press.[10]

The final member of the early staff of the National Trust came aboard in 1951, when Hardinge Scholle, a former director of the Museum of the City of New York, joined the organization as a part-time unpaid consultant. An older man of independent means and a friend of Louise Crowninshield's, Scholle gave the Trust "a social presence that [it] needed desperately. . . . He loved to take ladies out to lunch and go to their teas. He was an old friend of the Robert Woods Blisses."[11]

Financial Challenges

In the early 1950s, with the National Trust organized, provisionally funded, and at least minimally staffed, David Finley—still very busy as director of the National Gallery of Art and chairman of the Fine Arts Commission—focused primarily on the traditional role for a board chairman: fund-raising and board development. In December 1950 he wrote to his fellow trustee General George C. Marshall, asking him to follow up on a fund-raising request the Trust had made to the Ford Foundation. Marshall, who had been recalled by President Truman as secretary of defense after the outbreak of the Korean War, replied on 21 December:

> I must be very frank in telling you that there might be a possibility of my overdoing myself in requests for funds. Incidentally, two days before I left Red Cross I wrote a long letter to [the Ford Foundation] asking that consideration be given to the blood program of the Red Cross, which has greatly accelerated its program in recent months. I don't think it would be advisable for me to make a second request in the space of just a few weeks, and am sure you will understand my very obvious reasons for not acquiescing to your request. Sorry.
>
> Faithfully yours,
> G. C. Marshall

Finley, perhaps a bit abashed at having troubled Marshall with this concern at a time when the Korean War was going badly, wrote back to say that he understood completely and added, "I, myself, make it a rule never to go to the same well twice."[12] The exception to that rule for Finley was the Mellons' well.

In the first of a long series of fund-raising disappointments that plagued Finley's tenure as chairman of the National Trust, Ford Foundation officials decided that the Trust's request lay "outside the scope of their programs." In fact, only the Mellons, Ailsa and Paul, supported the Trust in any substantial way through their foundations during its first fifteen years. Membership grew steadily, but at five dollars per year, dues did not produce much revenue. Finley—determined that the Trust become self-supporting—told the membership at the 1954 annual conference in Chicago: "I have been brought up all my life, and especially during my years at the Treasury, with a horror of deficits; and, so long as I have any responsibility for the operation of the Trust, I shall make sure that we make no commitments for which funds are not available."[13]

Finley's early success in persuading wealthy patrons to donate their art collections to the National Gallery, gifts valued in the tens of millions of dollars, may have led him to expect affluent Americans to contribute financial support for the National Trust. He had no problem taking priceless paintings from the walls of the Kress and Widener homes, but asking for money did not seem quite polite. Yet the chartering legislation made it clear that no federal funds would go to the National Trust, conceived as a vehicle for raising private monies to augment the government's preservation efforts.[14] It was only in 1966, well after Finley's tenure, that the National Historic Preservation Act made the Trust eligible for federal funding. But as long as he served as chairman, Finley continued to believe that Americans would support the Trust's cause, both in membership and with financial donations, once they understood the preservation story.

The dynamics of philanthropy in art, however, differed significantly from those in historic preservation. The National Trust learned this the hard way in acquiring historic house museums, its most visible activity during the Finley years. The Trust accepted ownership of five historic properties under David Finley's leadership—Woodlawn Plantation, Casa Amesti, Decatur House, Shadows-on-the-Teche, and the Woodrow Wilson House—and was hotly pursuing Lyndhurst. Each house had a rich historic and cultural significance, and each came to the Trust by outright donation or was bequeathed by its previous owners. But in each case the gifts came either with no endowment or with funds inadequate to generate revenues to cover the costs of restoration, maintenance, and operation as a house museum.

In accepting these historic sites, Finley and the trustees clearly believed that their intrinsic value to the American people would inspire generous financial contributions (either to the individual properties or to the National Trust itself) to cover their revenue shortfall. But experience proved the contrary, and the trustees began to enforce more strictly the policy that gifts of historic houses be accompanied by sufficient endowment. At the same time, stewardship of these properties, as Finley pointed out in his annual reports as chairman, showed the importance of historic preservation and gave the Trust local, regional, and even national visibility and credibility.

The membership of the National Trust grew steadily but slowly, reaching a total of 3,250 individuals and 415 organizations by the time Finley retired as chairman in 1962.[15] With financial support also slow to develop, had it not been for the very generous additional gifts from the Mellon foundations in 1957 of combined grants of $2.5 million to endow National Trust headquarters and staff, proudly announced by Finley at that year's annual preservation conference, it is quite probable that the Trust would not have survived the 1950s.[16] Finley quoted Paul Mellon's words in making the grant: "We believe that the heritage program developed by the National Trust will not only aid the actual preservation of notable buildings of historic and architectural worth, but will bring an awareness of the nation's past achievements to a wide public today."[17]

Deeds and Dreams

On the very first page of a log kept by Fred Rath when he started as director of the National Council in 1948, he recorded that Armistead B. Rood had called him about Woodlawn Plantation. Woodlawn dated from 1799, when George Washington had given two thousand acres of land at Mount Vernon as a wedding present to his nephew, Lawrence Lewis, who married Martha Washington's step-granddaughter, Nelly Custis. The Lewises had built a handsome brick house at Woodlawn early in the nineteenth century (see plate 26), where they entertained members of the extended Washington family as well as the Marquis de Lafayette when he returned in triumph to America in 1824. They kept alive the gracious traditions of life at Mount Vernon until well into the nineteenth century. But in 1948, under threat of development as the campus for a religious order, Woodlawn needed rescue.

In response, Armistead Rood and George M. Morris, two lawyers in Washington, D.C., formed the Woodlawn Foundation. Rood was a

PLATE 26　Woodlawn Plantation, c. 1800–1804, Mount Vernon, Virginia.
National Trust for Historic Preservation

visionary but not terribly practical. He contacted Fred Rath before the National Council had fully established itself, then made a lunch date with Rath the next month and failed to show up. A month later Rath recorded having "dinner and long talk with Armistead Rood about Woodlawn."[18] At this stage the Woodlawn Foundation could not succeed on its own, and in January 1951 it asked the National Trust to take a long-term lease on the plantation. David Finley then turned again to the Mellon family. Paul Mellon's Old Dominion Foundation gave the Trust a $200,000 grant earmarked for Woodlawn, which enabled the Trust to take responsibility for its first historic property. Soon after this Ailsa Mellon Bruce's Avalon Foundation made a grant that paid off the Woodlawn mortgage and enabled the Trust to restore the house and grounds "to something approximating their condition during the lifetime of Nelly Custis Lewis and her husband."[19]

The National Trust opened Woodlawn to the public with appropriate ceremonies in May 1952, including speeches by the British ambassador and a regent from the Mount Vernon Ladies' Association. In 1957 the National Trust acquired outright title to Woodlawn. As David Finley observed, its history "made it imperative that Woodlawn be preserved as an historic house."[20] But its proximity to Washington—a half-hour drive from Trust headquarters—surely contributed to its attractiveness. The Trust had received inquiries from owners of other historic homes farther afield, thus it needed to learn how to manage such properties, and Woodlawn could serve as a pilot program close at hand.[21]

Back in 1948, at Finley's prompting, the National Council had considered the purchase of Oak Hill, near Oatlands in Virginia, with a grant from the Avalon Foundation. Nothing had come of that when the owner's price remained too high even for the Mellon funds. In July 1951 the Trust received an unsolicited letter from William Weeks Hall in the small town of New Iberia, Louisiana, saying that he had willed the National Trust his historic house, with the romantic name Shadows-on-the-Teche. Acceptance of this gift came several years later and involved Finley personally. In February 1952 Finley advised Rath that the Decatur House in Washington might come to the National Trust as the gift of Mrs. Truxton Beale, which it soon did (plate 27).[22] Then in April 1952

PLATE 27   Decatur House, 1818, Lafayette Square, Washington, D.C.
National Trust for Historic Preservation

Finley sent Rath to Pittsburgh to confer with Helen Clay Frick about her deeding Clayton, the family home, to the National Trust, with a $500,000 endowment. Serious discussions with Miss Frick and her lawyers took place over the next several years, but in the end Clayton did not come to the Trust for reasons that remain unclear.

Fred Rath's Travails

Questions about the chain of command posed a vexing challenge for Fred Rath—as well as for David Finley. In September 1951 General U. S. Grant III, president of the National Council, moved his office from George Washington University to 712 Jackson Place, soon to be the site of the Trust's headquarters as well.[23] Grant took a very active interest in Trust business and had time to devote to the details, which Finley did not at that point. Rath liked Grant and initially appreciated his strong executive hand. But "the General" was accustomed to running things, and he tried to take over management of both the National Council and the National Trust. In addition, Grant micromanaged the staff, reviewing every decision and every letter, which earned him the resentment of all. Compounding these difficulties, Grant installed his overbearing secretary, Mrs. Collier, as office manager and bookkeeper.

After the National Trust staff moved to Jackson Place in February 1952, the tensions soon came to a boil, and Rath recorded in May that he, Henry Surface, and Hardinge Scholle conferred at length on the Grant problem, "then wound up in DEF's [Finley's] office for 1½ hours of down-to-earth talk about our present plight. Basically, it is that USG [Grant] has dealt with us too heavily & his well-meant efforts have only disorganized us. He and Mrs. Collier (an ill-fitting influence) have finally taxed the patience of everyone to the breaking point. DEF promised to step in strongly. I was limp after weeks & weeks of emotional conflict."[24] Finley did step in and quietly confronted Grant, but the general did not relinquish power easily, and the executive committee of the trustees debated the matter of his authority for three months before backing Finley. The upshot was Grant's stormy resignation from all leadership positions in August 1952, although he remained a trustee, at least nominally, until 1964. Rath noted that Finley felt "terribly upset by it all."[25]

55. Lieutenant Colonel Helen Hamilton Woods, Women's Army Corps, c. 1944. Woods joined the board of the National Trust for Historic Preservation in 1953.

Strains between Rath and Finley had deeper roots, however. Although Finley continued to assist with fund-raising efforts and arranged for Bess Truman to host 250 members of the National Trust for tea at the White House during the annual meeting on 14 November 1952, Rath needed more help and guidance than Finley could provide while still serving as director of the National Gallery and chairman of the Commission of Fine Arts. In addition, the dual membership and overlapping functions of the Trust and the National Council had grown confusing, even to David Finley and his colleagues.[26] Thus the boards of the two organizations approved a merger in 1952, which became effective with the agreement of both memberships at the annual preservation conference in Newport, Rhode Island, in October 1953. Henceforth the National Trust assumed all functions of the council, as ratified by a 1953 amendment to the Trust's congressional charter.[27]

Of greater import, however, Finley and Rath had different visions of what the Trust should do and how to do it. Finley's primary interest lay in preserving historic houses, and to accomplish this, he instinctively allied himself with the people who owned such properties or had friends who did, including Louise du Pont Crowninshield and Robert Woods Bliss. His long and close association with the Mellons and the Eustises had given him a top-down view of the potential for historic preservation, and he believed that if people of means became involved others would follow. Rath had more interest in the populist aspects of the movement. He wanted to cultivate working relationships with professionals like Charles Peterson, Ronald Lee, and other former colleagues at the National Park Service, as well as with local histori-cal societies and preservation groups around the country. He enlisted Louise Crowninshield on the strategic level and Helen Bullock on the nuts and bolts of building a national preservation movement from the ground up.[28]

In the end the National Trust followed both visions and served both constituencies, but not without conflict. The introduction of a new trustee, Helen Hamilton Woods, cast these differences in sharp relief. Mrs. Woods had been a friend of David Finley's since he served under her late husband, Colonel Arthur Woods, in 1919 and 1920. Finley had maintained a warm friendship with Colonel and Mrs. Woods—as well as her mother and grandmother—after he returned to Washington, D.C., and joined a private law practice. Arthur Woods had died in 1942, and Helen Woods had risen to second in command of the Women's Army Corps in the Second World War, with the rank of lieutenant colonel (fig. 55). With her executive ability, her connections both as a member of the Morgan and Hamilton families and as a friend of the Rockefellers, plus her involvement in the Woodlawn Foundation, she seemed an ideal board member for the National Trust. Experience proved otherwise.

In January 1953, when Winthrop Aldrich became U.S. ambassador to the Court of St. James's and resigned as a trustee of the National Trust, Helen Woods took his place on the board. As chairman of a trustee committee on Woodlawn between December 1953 and 1957, she wielded increasing influence over the affairs of the National Trust, to the growing discomfort of Fred Rath. Though intelligent and capable, she could be abrasive to those whom she considered her inferiors, either socially or professionally. One of the trustees described her in Rath's hearing as "a typical Morgan."

Helen Woods and her brother Alexander "Sandy" Hamilton met with Rath in April 1953 to discuss the preservation of the Hamilton Grange in New York, home of their illustrious ancestor Alexander Hamilton. The Trust had several other properties under consideration at this time—including Casa Amesti in California, Decatur House and Woodrow Wilson House in Washington, and Clayton in Pittsburgh. In December 1954 Gladys Vanderbilt, Countess Szechenyi, offered the

🎋 PLATE 28 Interior view of Casa Amesti, c. 1831–1846,
Monterey, California. National Trust for Historic
Preservation

Trust her magnificent house in Newport, the Breakers; but without an endowment, the gift could not be accepted. During these early years Fred Rath and Helen Woods did not see eye to eye on the crucial question of the Trust's acquiring new properties (Woods's elitist approach was closer to Finley's). The two seem to have first crossed swords in December 1953, when Woods presented a report on Woodlawn that essentially proposed decentralized administration of the National Trust properties, guided by special trustee committees. Rath expressed his reservations, and from that point on their relationship went steadily downhill.

Rath had his faults as an administrator; he confided in his logs that he was too lenient with the staff and was "no fundraiser." But he was unfailingly courteous. Helen Woods, on the other hand, could be rude and unyielding. And it was not just Fred Rath who bore the brunt of her autocratic behavior. She battled openly with some of her fellow trustees as well. David Finley tried to smooth over these differences but was unwilling or unable to bring Woods under control.

Richard Howland Succeeds Fred Rath

In February 1955 Helen Woods married W. Randolph Burgess, deputy secretary of the treasury, and Rath dared to hope that "the Little Colonel's interest in us will be deflected."[29] Instead, Helen Woods Burgess became, if anything, more involved and more authoritarian. She pushed for approval of one of her pet projects, Casa Amesti in Monterey, California, the home of Frances Adler Elkins, a noted interior decorator. Built between 1831 and 1846 by Don José Amesti, first mayor of Monterey under the Mexican regime, the adobe house was a fine example of California's colonial-style architecture. Elkins bought it in 1918 and decorated it with fine antiques (plate 28). Her brother, the architect David Adler of Chicago, oversaw the installation of plumbing and electricity while maintaining the integrity of the house, and he designed formal gardens in back. Though there was no question of the historic and architectural distinction of Casa Amesti, the donors had provided no endowment. Thus Helen Burgess proposed, and the trustees approved, that the National Trust accept ownership of Casa Amesti, then enter into a long-term lease with a private men's club in Monterey, which agreed to maintain the property under the supervision of a committee of National Trust board members and to open it to the public on weekends. This was far from a perfect solution, but it seemed the best the young Trust could do at the time.[30]

Meanwhile, Helen Burgess continued to find fault with Fred Rath, despite his stalwart defense by David Finley. Rath felt equally unhappy with Burgess's increasing influence on the board as well as what he saw as the Trust's movement toward the elitism she represented. In early 1956 she and another trustee, Alexander Smith of Baltimore, recommended that Finley invite Professor Richard Howland of Johns Hopkins to do an analysis of the Trust and its programs. When Finley told Rath, they "tangled but good."[31] A few days later Finley informed Rath that the executive committee of the board had decided to create the new position of president of the National Trust and to offer the job to Howland. They wanted Rath to stay on as director under Howland and do what he did best—outreach to the preservation network across the country. But Rath concluded that Burgess had won control of the board, and he resigned on the spot.[32]

Finley clearly felt torn between his allegiances. He recognized Rath's many skills and hard work but also valued the energy and analytical talents of Helen Burgess, whom he had known for thirty-seven years. Deeply pained by Rath's resignation, he tried hard to persuade him to stay. He sent Richard Howland to talk with Rath, but the meeting only confirmed Rath's decision. Although Rath held no personal animosity toward Howland, he believed that Helen Burgess had put her own man in place, perhaps over Finley's better judgment, and he had no desire to continue with the Trust under what seemed her de facto control. Finley's negotiating skills had failed him, as they rarely did.

Richard Howland had impressive scholarly credentials and a wide social network in the Baltimore-Washington area.[33] Rath himself knew Howland and agreed that he had considerable charm, but he also knew that he had little background in the field of historic preservation. Yet the elitists among the trustees, led by Helen Burgess, thought highly of Howland and felt he could relate better to people like them than Fred Rath could. Rath's resignation prompted a strong protest from several members of the board, led by Louise Crowninshield. Rath heard, probably from Ronald Lee, that Finley had borne the brunt of this storm on behalf of the executive committee, while "Burgess was shrewdly silent," and that Finley had agreed that the executive committee would no longer make major policy decisions without consulting the rest of the board.[34] On Fred Rath's last day as director at the end of May 1956, David Finley came to see him with a silver bowl and a board resolution expressing appreciation for his service to the National Council and the National Trust. Rath, seeing that Finley was "genuinely distressed," responded: "We parted friends."[35]

Fred Rath had guided the infant National Council and National Trust for almost eight years. His hard work, his programmatic vision, and his wide contacts with preservation professionals at the National Park Service and elsewhere laid a solid foundation for the growth of the National Trust in the years to come. Rath and Finley did remain friends, and Rath enjoyed a cordial relationship with the Trust for the rest of his life.[36] Ironically, Helen Burgess relinquished much of her influence at the National Trust the following year, when she moved to Paris with her husband as he took up his duties as ambassador to NATO. Although she remained a trustee until 1968, well after Finley's retirement from the board, she played a much less active role in its business, even after returning from Europe in 1961.

Richard Howland's charm, scholarship, and social skills won many friends for the National Trust, which continued to make modest gains in membership. In early 1953 Finley had heard from Fred Rath about the prospect of acquiring Shadows-on-the-Teche in New Iberia, Louisiana (plate 29), but it was during Howland's four-year tenure that the Trust accepted stewardship of the property. This romantic plantation home on the Bayou Teche, built between 1832 and 1834, was owned and occupied at the time by William Weeks Hall, a direct descendant of the family that built the house. Hall had devoted much of his life to preserving the Shadows and providing for its survival after his death. Rath found the property intriguing and the owner delightful, but he explained the Trust's requirement for an endowment fund. Hall then stinted himself to pull together $170,000 entirely from his own savings—not an enormous sum to endow an historic house, but not inconsiderable in the 1950s.

In October 1958 Finley reported during the annual meeting in New Orleans that Hall had died that June, happy in the knowledge that the National Trust had agreed to assume responsibility for the Shadows. Finley himself had visited the site and described it in glowing terms: "The house which had been in the possession of his family since it was built in the 1830's, is one of the finest examples of Louisiana plantation architecture, with its double portico and gardens of live oaks and gray moss bordering on the Bayou Teche." Hall may have sensed that Finley felt a connection with his own Southern roots, for he made a habit of calling Finley at home, "sometimes in the middle of the night, to reassure himself that the Trust would accept the property on his death."[37] The trustees did accept Shadows-on-the-Teche, still the only example of nineteenth-century plantation architecture from the Deep South among the National Trust's historic holdings.

Robert Garvey Takes Charge

For all Richard Howland's education and sociability, the trustees had several concerns, including financial problems created by the autonomy of the Trust's various properties and fund-raising shortfalls. By late 1959 they decided that the Trust needed an executive who combined knowledge of preservation with practical business experience. Robert R. Garvey, then executive director of Old Salem, North Carolina, with a track record of getting "a big chunk of money out of the legislature every year," came highly recommended by trustee Christopher Crittenden.[38] After meetings with Finley and the search committee, Garvey accepted the job as executive director and chief executive officer of the National Trust.[39] The trustees invited Howland to stay on in the position of research director, at the same salary he had received as president, but now it was his turn to resign. And once again, the decision stirred controversy. Helen Burgess wrote a commiserating letter to Howland from Athens, Greece, saying "DEF never seems to understand such things," and U. S. Grant III wrote to Finley, expressing his "deep regret at an irreparable loss" to the Trust.[40]

But like Fred Rath, Richard Howland continued to consider David Finley a friend. Two years later, on the occasion of Finley's retirement as chairman of the National Trust, Howland wrote to him: "I shall always feel grateful to you, and devoted, for your wise leadership of the National Trust and the guidance and direction that you so generously gave me during my four years with the Trust. The high ideals and goals that the Trust has always had are in large measure due to you, and the maintenance of these ideals has been because of your perseverance and selfless devotion."[41]

Finley and the board adjusted to Howland's departure. And the growth of the Trust under Robert Garvey between 1960 and 1967 confirmed the wisdom of their selection. Garvey cleaned up the long-inactive membership rolls and reorganized the staff so that each function would report to a specific trustee committee. He then sat down with Finley to restructure the board accordingly. By the fall of 1962, after fifteen years of operation, the Trust comprised five departments: education, information, finance, membership and public relations, and properties.[42]

With its headquarters in better working order, the National Trust turned its attention to new opportunities. In late 1961, at the death of Edith Bolling Wilson, the Trust took ownership of Woodrow Wilson House in Washington (plate 30). Finley had championed President Wilson ever since meeting him in 1913, and he had come to know Edith Wilson well.[43] She had zealously protected her husband after his stroke in 1919 and had continued to watch over his legacy following his death in 1924. Indeed, she had maintained the house almost exactly as it had been the day he died. His eight-thousand-book library and framed photographs of world leaders with whom he met during his triumphant trip to Europe and the Paris Peace Conference in 1919 gave a palpable sense of his presence. She had even kept his clothes and personal effects just as he had left them, preserving a vivid memorial to the only President who has ever retired to Washington, D.C.

Edith Wilson had told Finley in 1954 of her desire to leave the house to the National Trust, and Finley sent Fred Rath, Henry Surface, and several members of the Trust's board to meet her at the house in March 1954, when she made clear to them her intentions.[44] The trustees promptly accepted her gift, and she signed a deed of transfer in August 1954 that allowed her to retain a life interest and possession of the property until her death. That October, at the annual preservation

❧ PLATE 30   Woodrow Wilson House, 1915, Washington, D.C.
National Trust for Historic Preservation

conference in Chicago, Finley could announce both the gift itself and "a generous endowment for the operation of the house," which he expected to be "increased in time by friends and admirers of the late President Wilson."[45] Edith Wilson died on 29 December 1961, and soon after that the National Trust opened Woodrow Wilson House to the public. It remains to this day the only presidential house museum in Washington.

A classic example of David Finley's approach to legal controversy occurred near the end of his chairmanship. Lyndhurst, an 1838 Gothic revival masterpiece by architect Alexander Jackson Davis on sixty-seven acres along the Hudson River at Tarrytown, New York (plate 31), was bought in 1880 by the railroad baron and financial speculator Jay Gould. The controversial Gould commuted by yacht from Wall Street to Lyndhurst, where he raised his six children. After his death in 1892 the estate remained in his family and since 1938 had been owned by his youngest daughter, Anna, duchess of Talleyrand-Perigord, who spent much of her time in France.[46] The duchess had executed a will in 1959 bequeathing Lyndhurst to the National Trust.[47] But in November 1961, just six days before she died in France, she signed a codicil revoking her gift to the Trust and bequeathing Lyndhurst to her children. Finley had known the duchess and suspected that the codicil had been obtained under duress and thus should be invalid, but efforts to secure redress in France through legal counsel came to nothing. Thanks to Finley's fore-sight, however, the attorney general of the United States served as an ex-officio trustee of the Trust by its congressional charter. Representing the attorney general on the Trust's board since 1952, Patricia Collins, a Justice Department lawyer, recalled a board meeting at Decatur House in 1962, when Finley asked her if the federal government could pro-tect the Trust's interests concerning Lyndhurst. At the suggestion of a Justice Department superior, Collins sent a one-page memorandum to Attorney General Robert F. Kennedy, who asked just one question: "Can we win?" When she replied that she thought they could, Ken-nedy initialed his approval of federal action on behalf of the National Trust.[48] With the U.S. attorney in Manhattan representing the Trust in court against the Talleyrand heirs, the scales of justice soon swung into balance, and in 1964 the parties reached a settlement under which

※ PLATE 31   Lyndhurst, 1838, Tarrytown, New York.
National Trust for Historic Preservation

the heirs released their claims to Lyndhurst, which became the sixth National Trust historic property the following year.

Except for the Lyndhurst matter, the National Trust never went to court to advocate for preservation during David Finley's tenure. One reason was the lack of a substantial body of preservation case law at that time. Another was the absence of litigation experience among Trust personnel. In fact, shortly after Fred Rath resigned in 1956, Henry Surface also departed, leaving the Trust without any legal expertise on the staff. At this point the Trust engaged the eminent Washington law firm of Covington & Burling to provide legal counsel, and partner Edward Burling Jr. of Georgetown assumed responsibility for the Trust's affairs.[49] But the National Trust did not take a primary role in any litigated case until 1968, which seems curious in view of its later activism.

The minutes of the last board meeting at which Finley presided, 4 October 1962, contain this enigmatic passage: "Mr. Garvey further stated that there had been a request for a resolution supporting the preservation of Pennsylvania Station. The Board discussed Pennsylvania Station and the status of the efforts to preserve this building. *Motion:* by Mr. [Robert C.] Baker that the Board take no action regarding a resolution supporting the preservation of Pennsylvania Station; seconded and passed." Ordinary citizens as well as preservationists and architects, in New York and elsewhere, lodged outraged protests at the demolition of Pennsylvania Station, a beaux-arts masterpiece by McKim, Meade & White dating from 1910. Given the importance of the building and the heated opposition to its destruction, the Trust's failure to vote for even a resolution in support of its preservation is hard to explain. But the board then consisted largely of wealthy individuals with business backgrounds, few of them committed preservationists, and Robert Garvey later described Finley at that time as "terribly cautious."[50] Finley certainly knew how to fight when necessary. That he passed up this battle shows, perhaps, that he was ready to pass on the torch to other hands. In any event, Finley's style was to persuade, not to confront.

The National Trust during the Finley regime had responded to the changing needs of the preservation movement. Although protecting great old historic houses was still important, the Trust's mission had broadened significantly. In his annual reports to the membership at the fall meetings of 1956 and 1960, Finley pointed with alarm to the federal government's efforts in Washington to demolish the Old Patent Office Building to make room for a parking lot—despite the vigorous protests of the National Trust, the Fine Arts Commission, and the American Institute of Architects—as well as its ominous plans to erect huge new buildings flanking historic Lafayette Square.[51]

In Finley's annual report to the Trust's membership meeting in New Orleans in 1958 he noted:

> But lately another problem has arisen with which even the Park Service has been unable to cope. I refer to the destruction of both scenic and historic areas that may result as a by-product of the new federal highway program. Under the provisions of the Federal Highway Act of 1956, more than 41,000 miles of new highways are to be built and paid for largely with federal funds. The Bureau of Public Roads of the Department of Commerce [forerunner of the Department of Transportation] has placed the routing of these highways in the hands of state highway officials. . . . This means that the decision is made at the state level by highway engineers who, in their zeal to take the shortest line between two points and to save money, appear to be irresistibly drawn to the use of public parks as sites for freeways, or else go through a city, regardless of damage to historic and aesthetic values . . . which once destroyed can never be replaced.[52]

Two years later at the annual meeting in Pittsburgh he expanded on this theme, adding: "Urban renewal programs, carried out with the bulldozer approach, are sweeping away vast areas in all parts of the country." To counter these new threats, Finley said that the National Trust was "leading a vital movement to seek protection for historic areas or even single buildings. The Trust needs a larger membership to increase our sphere of influence and to stop needless destruction."[53] He noted that one of the Trust's most important functions was to act as a national clearinghouse in the field of historic preservation legislation by collecting and distributing statutes and ordinances "having among their objectives the safe-guarding of architectural and historic monuments or the preservation of certain areas within our historic cities and villages."[54]

Chairman Emeritus

By the early 1960s David Finley was beginning to feel his age and realized he needed to step down as chairman of the National Trust.[55] But he had to find someone to take his place, and none of the current trustees fit the bill. Thus Finley went out in search of his successor, and Gordon Gray was just the man. Gray's family controlled considerable wealth through its ownership of newspapers as well as television and radio stations in Winston-Salem, North Carolina. He himself had won election to the state senate, had served as an army captain in the Second World War before becoming assistant secretary of the army in the Truman administration, and then became president of the University of North Carolina. David Finley thought he could lead the National Trust, though he was not even a member at the time. Finley called on him, invited him to become a member, and asked him to join the board. Within a year Gray was chairing the finance committee and ready to accept the chairmanship. As he later told his fellow Carolinian Bob Garvey, he had never done anything in preservation before, but "if David Finley wants me to do it, I'll do it."[56] It was an inspired choice.

At the annual preservation conference in San Francisco, 5 October 1962, David Finley told the membership: "This is the last report I shall make to you as chairman of your Board of Trustees. And I must say that I have enjoyed making it, as I always do on these occasions. But I believe strongly in the wisdom of rotation in office; and so I advised our Nominating Committee several months ago, as regards the chairmanship of the Board, that I would not run, if nominated, and would not serve, if elected. That, I believe, is the correct formula to be used when one is quite definite about such matters."[57] Thus David Finley retired as chairman of the board of the National Trust on 5 October 1962 and was elected chairman emeritus. Gordon Gray succeeded him as chairman and served in that capacity from 1962 to 1973, with great success.

Finley continued to play an active role in Trust affairs as chairman emeritus, faithfully attending board meetings and annual preservation conferences until his death fourteen years later. In October 1963 he arranged a White House reception for 1,100 delegates to the annual preservation conference, when President John F. Kennedy made an appearance and spoke to the group on the South Lawn—the only occasion when an incumbent U.S. President has ever addressed the National Trust.[58] Also in 1963 Finley wrote his *History of the National Trust for Historic Preservation, 1947–1963.* In dry, succinct prose he told the story of the Trust's founding and development, focusing on the acquisitions of Woodlawn, Decatur House, Casa Amesti, Woodrow Wilson House, and Shadows-on-the-Teche—clearly the part of the Trust's work closest to his heart. Finley printed only a thousand copies, at his own expense, many of which he sent with personal inscriptions to friends and colleagues, including former Presidents Truman and Eisenhower and Mrs. Kennedy. The book remains a unique source of documentary information on the early history of the National Trust.

David and Margaret Finley continued to live in Georgetown and at Little Oatlands, next to the Oatlands mansion, then still the residence of Edith Morton Eustis. When Mrs. Eustis died in 1964 at the age of ninety, her two daughters, Margaret Eustis Finley and Anne Eustis Emmet, inherited Oatlands (see plate 25) and its three hundred acres of grounds. Margaret Finley, joined by her husband and her sister Anne, donated Oatlands to the National Trust in December 1965, in consideration of the Trust agreeing "to preserve and administer for the public 'Oatlands' in a proper manner in accordance with the tradition and history of 'Oatlands.'" In 1973 the Finleys and Mrs. Emmet also granted the Virginia Outdoors Foundation an easement over Little Oatlands and the adjacent Emmet property for conservation and preservation purposes. Oatlands opened to the public in 1966 as the National Trust's ninth historic house museum. The Finleys personally selected the membership of the Oatlands Property Council, including its first chairman, B. Powell Harrison of Leesburg, and they served on its council very actively until their deaths in 1977.

Even after their deaths the Finleys made one more gift to the National Trust, willing their late nineteenth-century townhouse at 3318 O Street in Georgetown to the Trust (fig. 56), directing that it be sold and the proceeds added to the Oatlands endowment. The Trust placed a preservation easement on the property, then sold it subject to

56. The Finleys' Georgetown home for more than forty years, at
3318 O Street, N.W. They willed the property to the National Trust
to sell, with the proceeds to be added to the Oatlands endowment.
The Trust holds a preservation easement protecting the property.

that easement. Oatlands received the benefit of the sale, but the National
Trust holds the easement in perpetuity, ensuring the physical integrity
of the house that was home to David and Margaret Eustis Finley for
four decades.

The National Trust for Historic Preservation has grown into a very
different organization than the one David Finley started and led for
fifteen years. But his name lives on, memorialized in an inscription in
the entrance rotunda of the National Trust headquarters at 1785 Massachusetts Avenue, and the "standard of excellence" he absorbed from
Andrew Mellon in that same building continues to guide the Trust in its
service to the nation.

NOTES

1. Built in 1799–1801 as Washington's grandest residence after the White House, the Octagon served as President James Madison's home after the White House was burned during the War of 1812. Restored by the American Institute of Architects around 1900 and used as its headquarters until the group built an adjacent office building in the 1960s, the Octagon still houses the nation's oldest museum devoted to architectural history.

2. The Rockefellers may have felt they were well represented by Winthrop Aldrich as well as Kenneth Chorley, president of Colonial Williamsburg from 1935 to 1958. Chorley played an active role in the National Council from the start, and then in the National Trust. In 1957 David Finley appointed him a member of the first committee for the Crowninshield Award.

3. Once, when Finley had sent Hoover materials for approval, Hoover responded on 21 May 1956: "Dear David: Anything you do is necessarily right. Yours faithfully, Herbert Hoover." Finley Papers, Library of Congress, box 38.

4. Louise Crowninshield was the sister of Henry Francis du Pont, the well-known antiquarian and collector of early American antiques, who founded the Winterthur Museum at his home near Wilmington, Delaware. Henry du Pont, fittingly, received the second annual Crowninshield Award in 1961.

5. Michael Ainslie, president of the National Trust from 1980 to 1984, at a panel of former chief executive officers, 20 May 1996, described women as the "heart and soul" of the preservation movement and likened the typical female activist to "a Mack truck disguised as a powder puff." Videotape, records of the National Trust for Historic Preservation.

6. *Annual Report of the Chairman*, 21 October 1960, 9. National Trust Library, University of Maryland.

7. J. Carter Brown, remarks at Oatlands, 14 May 1977, transcript, p. 8. Oatlands Archives.

8. Felix Frankfurter, remarks to annual meeting of the National Council, 19 October 1950, transcript, pp. 147–148. National Archives. Frankfurter taught law at Harvard from 1914 to 1939, when Franklin Roosevelt named him to the Supreme Court, on which he served for twenty-three years.

9. The initial source of information on the Rath years came from the author's interviews with Fred Rath in 1998–1999. Much greater detail is contained in the handwritten logs that Rath kept on his desk calendar between 31 August 1948 and 31 May 1956, the entire period of his service with the National Council and the National Trust. At his death in 2001 Rath left these, among voluminous other papers, to the National Trust Library at the University of Maryland, where they are archived in the Papers of Frederick L. Rath Jr., series IV, boxes 1 and 2. Anyone seeking to understand those years should start with these logs.

10. Helen Bullock retired in 1973 as senior editor and historian, after twenty-three years with the National Trust. In 1978 she became the first former staff member of the Trust to receive the Crowninshield Award. She died in a Washington nursing home in 1995 at age ninety-one.

11. Interview with Frederick L. Rath Jr., conducted by Charles J. Hosmer, 19 October 1982, transcript. National Trust Library, University of Maryland.

12. David Finley to George C. Marshall, 27 December 1950. Finley Papers, Library of Congress, box 37.

13. *Annual Report of the Chairman*, 29 October 1954, 3.

14. "The Committee recommends . . . that the Trust seek no direct Governmental financial assistance, support or contribution whatever." *Report of the Committee on Organization of the National Trust*, 4 November 1948: "The National Trust would be supported entirely by voluntary contributions. The bill does not authorize or contemplate the appropriation of any Federal funds." House Report 855; Senate Report 1100, 81st Cong., 1st sess. (1949).

15. Slow as it was, this growth compares very favorably with the British National Trust, which at the end of its first twenty-five years of existence (1895–1920) had just 713 members, with annual subscriptions of £532. See Cannadine, *In Churchill's Shadow*, 228.

16. The Old Dominion Foundation, established by Paul Mellon, and the Avalon Foundation, established by Ailsa Mellon Bruce, each contributed $1.25 million. In June 1953 Paul Mellon told David Finley that he was interested in the preservation of Waterford, an historic village in Loudoun County, Virginia, and Finley arranged for Fred Rath to have "a long talk" with Mellon. See the Rath logs, 19 and 23 June 1953.

17. *Annual Report of the Chairman*, 11 October 1957, 13.

18. The following day he had lunch at the Metropolitan Club with Rood and George Morris, "the atomic energizer of the Woodlawn matter." Rath logs, 31 August, 16 September, and 7 October 1948. A few months later "Morris resigned at Woodlawn," for unexplained reasons. Rath logs, 22 April 1949. Woodlawn's Web site in 2005, www.woodlawn1805.org, shows a photograph with the caption "George Morris, President of the Woodlawn Public Foundation, and U.S. Attorney General Tom Clark, officially accepted the key to Woodlawn from Governor of Virginia, William W. Tuck," probably from early 1949.

19. Finley, *History of the National Trust*, 7.

20. Finley, *History of the National Trust*, 7.

21. In 1951, while negotiations over Woodlawn continued, Fred Rath met with the proprietor of Cypress Gardens in Florida to discuss the possibility of its becoming a National Trust property (Rath logs, 14 March 1951), but nothing came of this.

22. Also in February 1952 Rath heard from a doctor at the Mayo Clinic who wanted to establish a memorial to Dr. Walter Reed at a house in a suburb of Havana and to found a Cuban National Trust to maintain it. Rath flew to Havana in April 1952 to meet with Maria Teresa Rojas about preserving her home, Quinta San José, which she had offered to the National Trust, as well as Dr. Reed's Camp Lazear, where he made his famous yellow fever discovery. Nothing came of either proposal.

23. In 1951 and 1952 the National Council and the National Trust moved their offices from the Octagon to 712 Jackson Place on the west side of Lafayette Square near the

Decatur House, courtesy of the A. W. Mellon Educational and Charitable Trust, which had occupied the historic townhouse since the early 1930s.

24. Rath logs, 20 May 1952.

25. Rath logs, 1 October 1952.

26. *Annual Report of the Chairman*, 1954, 2.

27. Public Law 160, 83rd Cong., 1st sess. (67 Stat. 228).

28. He focused the Trust's early efforts on developing criteria for evaluating historic sites, acting as a clearinghouse for information on historic preservation nationwide, and offering state and local preservation groups a technical services kit and training courses, the first of them held in Cooperstown, New York, in 1955. Fred Rath, "A Talk to the National Trust Staff Conference," 21 February 1989. Papers of Frederick L. Rath Jr., National Trust Library, University of Maryland.

29. Rath logs, 22 February 1955.

30. This arrangement worked reasonably well for almost fifty years, with the Old Capital Club taking good care of the property. Starting in the 1970s, however, the Trust became uncomfortable with the all-male composition of the club, and in 2000 the Trust deeded the property to the Casa Amesti Foundation, retaining preservation easements over the house and grounds.

31. Rath logs, 9 April 1956.

32. Rath logs, 13 April 1956. Ann Rath wrote that Fred Rath was also very disappointed that David Finley had not responded to a memorandum he had written in March 1956 addressing the National Trust's programmatic, organizational, and financial needs. She said that Rath wrote a friend in 1959: "Dick Howland's appointment as president was the occasion not the cause for his resignation." Letter from Ann Rath to the author, 18 May 1999.

33. Richard Hubbell Howland (b. 1910) got his B.A. from Brown University in 1931 and his M.A. from Harvard in 1933. He did archaeological work in Greece from 1933 to 1938, taught art and architecture at Wellesley from 1938 to 1941, and served with the OSS in pictorial records during the Second World War. He earned his Ph.D. in classical archaeology from Johns Hopkins in 1946, then served as chairman of its art history department until 1956.

34. Rath logs, 22 May 1956.

35. Rath logs, 31 May 1956.

36. Fred Rath moved to Cooperstown, New York, to become vice director of the New York State Historical Association. He kept in touch with the National Trust and in 1989 received the Crowninshield Award, which must have given him special satisfaction, as Louise Crowninshield had risen to his defense in 1956. As late as May 1996 Rath appeared in Washington on a panel of former chief executive officers of the Trust to share his reminiscences of the organization's early days.

37. *Annual Report of the Chairman*, 31 October 1958, 13.

38. Christopher Crittenden headed the North Carolina department of history and archives. Interview with Robert R. Garvey Jr., conducted by Charles J. Hosmer, 1980, transcript, p. 7. National Trust Library, University of Maryland.

39. Robert Robey Garvey Jr. (1921–1997), a North Carolinian, studied at Davidson College and at the College of William & Mary, then served as a Marine Corps pilot in the southwestern Pacific during the Second World War with the rank of major. Afterward he went into business in Winston-Salem for ten years before becoming executive director of Old Salem, Inc. He left the Trust in 1967 to become the first executive director of the federal Advisory Council on Historic Preservation, where he stayed until his retirement in 1986. He received the Crowninshield Award in 1991.

40. Helen Burgess to Richard Howland, 6 March 1960; U.S. Grant III to David Finley, 13 May 1960. Richard Howland Papers, National Trust Library, University of Maryland.

41. Richard Howland to David Finley, 22 October 1962. Howland became head curator of the department of civil history of the Smithsonian Institution. As of December 2004 he was retired and living in Washington.

42. With the addition of departments of law and public policy as well as development, this basic structure still existed at the time of the Trust's fiftieth anniversary in 1999. But in 1962 William J. Murtagh led education; Helen Bullock, information; Robert Garvey, finance as well as membership and public relations; and Robert G. Stewart, properties. Murtagh had served as assistant to the president under Richard Howland; he was also the first keeper of the National Register of Historic Places at the National Park Service and has taught and written extensively on the subject of preservation. Murtagh received the Crowninshield Award in 1980. Bullock later became vice president for publications. Stewart became a curator at the National Portrait Gallery.

43. David and Margaret Finley also became close friends of President Wilson's physician and his wife, Rear Admiral and Mrs. Cary Grayson. In fact, the first time David Finley mentions Margaret in his journal in December 1922, they went to dinner at the Graysons' home. Dr. Grayson had worked hand in glove with Mrs. Wilson to shield the President after his stroke.

44. Rath logs, 11 March 1954.

45. *Annual Report of the Chairman*, 1954, 5.

46. William Seale, *Of Houses & Time* (New York, 1992), 147–151, 216–218.

47. According to Richard Howland, the duchess made this bequest to the National Trust on the recommendation of her New York lawyer. See the interview with Richard Howland, conducted by Charles J. Hosmer, transcript, p. 56. National Trust Library, University of Maryland.

48. Interview with Patricia Collins Butler, conducted by the author, 15 September 1999. One of the first woman lawyers at the Justice Department in the 1930s, Butler represented the attorney general on the National Trust's board until her retirement from Justice in 1973. She was then elected a trustee in her own right, serving from 1973 to 1982,

for a total of thirty years, under four chairmen. As of December 2004 she remained an active supporter of the National Trust as an emeritus trustee.

49. The National Trust did not establish the staff position of general counsel until 1981.

50. Garvey interview by Hosmer, p. 38.

51. *Annual Report of the Chairman*, 19 October 1956, 7–8; and *Annual Report of the Chairman*, 21 October 1960, 11.

52. *Annual Report of the Chairman*, 31 October 1958, 10.

53. *Annual Report of the Chairman*, 21 October 1960, 13.

54. *Annual Report of the Chairman*, 19 October 1956, 6.

55. Finley had intended to step down in 1956, but with the changes in staff leadership and other issues he felt "it would have been cowardly to quit at that moment." *Annual Report of the Chairman*, 5 October 1962, 7.

56. Garvey interview by Hosmer, p. 37.

57. Finley's detailed annual reports of the National Trust's activities, presented at each annual preservation conference, were a highlight of his chairmanship.

58. *Washington Post*, 17 October 1963.

57. Chairman Finley presides over a Fine Arts Commission that was
sharply divided on preservation versus contemporary architecture, 1962.
Left to right: Ralph Walker, William G. Perry, Peter Hurd, Michael
Rapuano, Felix de Weldon, Douglas Orr, and David Finley

11

Mr. Finley's Fine Arts Commission

1943–1963

ALTHOUGH DAVID FINLEY RETIRED as director of the National Gallery
of Art in 1956, he by no means retired from public service. Indeed, he
continued to have a profound influence on the cultural life of Washington and the nation as a whole until well into the 1960s. He remained as
chairman of the National Trust for Historic Preservation for another
six years and participated in board meetings for another fourteen. He
joined the board of trustees of the Corcoran Gallery of Art almost as
soon as he stepped down from his position at the National Gallery. And
he embarked on several high-profile projects that grew out of his interest
in preservation and his devotion to building a strong arts community.

Finley perhaps made his broadest mark on the nation's capital in
his role as chairman of the U.S. Commission of Fine Arts. Generally
known as the Fine Arts Commission, it was created by an act of Congress in 1910 and served as an independent advisory body consisting of
seven "well-qualified judges of fine arts" appointed by the President.
Originally the commission had authority only over statues, fountains,
and monuments in the public squares, streets, and parks of the District

of Columbia, but executive orders under Presidents William Howard Taft and Woodrow Wilson soon widened its role so that plans for all public buildings "which affect in any important way the appearance of the City" had to be submitted to the commission for comment and advice before final approval. In 1930 the Shipstead-Luce Act extended the advisory scope of the commission to private buildings bordering public spaces such as the Mall, the White House, the Capitol, and Rock Creek Park. In 1939 the act was amended to include Lafayette Square.[1]

First appointed to the Commission of Fine Arts by President Franklin D. Roosevelt in 1943, Finley was reappointed by Presidents Harry S. Truman, Dwight D. Eisenhower, and John F. Kennedy. From 1950 to 1963 he served as chairman, elected by his fellow commissioners. Although exercising purely advisory powers, the commission had great influence on political decision-making, private enterprise, and public opinion concerning a wide range of topics affecting design questions in the city—largely because of the stature of its members and particularly its chairmen. Members have included such respected figures as architect John Russell Pope and landscape architects Frederick Law Olmsted and Hideo Sasaki. Early chairmen included the Chicago planner and architect Daniel Burnham and the sculptor Daniel Chester French. Following in David Finley's footsteps, J. Carter Brown, the third director of the National Gallery of Art, served as chairman from 1971 until his death in 2002. The current director of the National Gallery, Earl A. Powell III, now serves as a member of the commission.

The burning issue before the Fine Arts Commission during Finley's first term involved the addition of the Truman Balcony behind the columns in the south portico of the White House. For more than forty years the White House staff had erected canvas awnings within the portico every spring to protect the first-floor Blue Room from the hot summer sun. President Truman found the awnings unsightly and especially objected to the mildew that occurred after a rain. During a speaking engagement on 4 July 1947 at the University of Virginia in Charlottesville, he noticed second-story balconies on some of the buildings there designed by Thomas Jefferson and thought that a similar feature would improve not only the appearance of the south front of the White House but the living conditions in the family quarters. The chief usher of the White House, Howell Crim, called David Finley, who suggested a conference at the White House. On 29 July 1947 Finley and two other members of the Fine Arts Commission, including Gilmore D. Clarke, then its chairman, met with Crim and another White House staffer, but not with the President.[2]

The commissioners believed the proposed balcony would compromise the integrity of the tall Ionic columns and recommended that the respected architect William Adams Delano be consulted.[3] President Truman assumed that this meant the commission had approved the concept of the balcony, subject to working out the details of the design. In fact, the commissioners felt confident that Delano, who had advised Finley on the interior design of the National Gallery, would oppose the idea and get them off the hook with the President, who had expressed his own wishes quite plainly. This strategy backfired when Delano endorsed the balcony proposal, saying that in his judgment it would not detract from the dignity of the south portico. The Commission of Fine Arts unanimously disagreed, and in November 1947 Chairman Clarke wrote the President: "The Commission still feel that a porch would seriously mar not only the south portico but as well the entire south façade ... which in itself would materially change the design of this, the most notable of American historic monuments ... and consequently they hope that, in the interest of preserving the integrity of the original design of the White House, the President will abandon the project."[4]

Harry Truman not only refused to abandon the project but shot back a hotly worded letter to Clarke: "My understanding was when the matter was discussed with you with regard to the arrangement on the south portico that when Mr. Delano made up his mind, the situation would be satisfactory to you. Now you confess that you hoped he would make up his mind in a manner you approved of and that you didn't enter into the matter at all with an open mind—that is a great statement for the Chairman of the Commission of Fine Arts to make to the President." Truman continued, "those dirty awnings are a perfect eyesore ... and they look like hell when they are on the porch."[5] Truman was furious that an advisory commission he had appointed would disagree with him publicly. Newspapers soon picked up the battle, with editorial indignation, cartoons, and jokes that branded him "Back Porch Harry" and accused him of interfering with a structure that did not belong to him and that he was thought unlikely to occupy for long.[6]

Defying all expectations, however, Truman defeated Thomas E. Dewey for President in 1948, and overriding all objections, he had his balcony built. The only thing he abandoned was most members of the Fine Arts Commission, including its chairman Gilmore Clarke, who had dared to criticize him and had made the fatal error of letting himself be quoted in the press. Truman resolved to drop Clarke from the commission when his term expired in 1949. When this intention became clear, Finley and his fellow commissioners took the unusual step of writing the President privately to urge him to reappoint Clarke, who had served with distinction as chairman since 1937. Truman wrote back, thanking Finley for his views, and saying, "I am certainly glad to have your views on that subject and to know your high opinion of Major Clarke."[7] But Harry Truman was not one to forgive and forget. He did not renew Clarke's appointment, nor did he return three of the four other members of that commission to new terms. In fact, the only member of the Clarke commission whom Truman did reappoint was David Finley, who was then elected chairman by his new colleagues in 1950 (see fig. 57).[8] This episode illustrates Finley's style of speaking truth to power, which was low key and avoided public confrontation.

Finley's Fine Arts Commission confronted several difficult and highly visible design projects during his term as chairman. Official Washington had traditionally followed a restrained style of classical architecture, much of it built in the Federal Triangle during the late 1920s and early 1930s under the auspices of Andrew Mellon's Treasury Department. But the end of the Second World War brought a surge of new development and bold adventures in modern architectural design. The commission and its chairman faced major challenges to Washington's basically conservative milieu. Prominent projects that came up for review included the avant-garde designs for a performing arts center later named after John F. Kennedy, the Watergate complex, a sports stadium later named after Robert F. Kennedy, and a radically abstract design for a memorial to Franklin Delano Roosevelt. All put Finley's legendary diplomatic skills to the test.

The Fine Arts Commission under Finley's leadership rejected designs for each of these proposals in turn, offending progressive architects, developers, patrons, and a vocal segment of the press. But the commissioners had only advisory power, so it was solely by persuasion, particularly by that master practitioner David Finley, that the commission managed to avert several drastic mistakes. The commission eventually, if reluctantly, did approve construction of the Watergate and Kennedy Center after significant design changes. RFK Stadium was built without revision—and without commission approval—a rare defeat for Finley.

Then came a proposal for a monument to Franklin Delano Roosevelt. FDR himself had tried to forestall any attempt at a grandiose memorial by telling Justice Felix Frankfurter that all he wanted was a plain block of stone the size of his Oval Office desk, with just his name and dates of birth and death, to be placed in the small plot of grass on the Pennsylvania Avenue side of the National Archives building. This was done according to his wishes and stands there still today in elegant simplicity. But in 1955 Congress in its wisdom decided that the capital city needed a more elaborate remembrance of the great man. After securing a site in West Potomac Park near the Tidal Basin and the Jefferson Memorial, the Franklin Delano Roosevelt Memorial Commission held a competition for designs in 1960. The proposed plan, chosen from among six hundred entries, called for the erection of eight immense, lopsided concrete stelae—the largest rising 165 feet—each pillar inscribed with a quotation from FDR (fig. 58). Devotees of the avant-garde raved about the breathtaking drama of the design; most Washingtonians were appalled.

When this proposal came before Finley's Fine Arts Commission in January 1962, it provoked an intensely contentious hearing.[9] The editor of *Architectural Forum* and several prominent architects praised it enthusiastically. Philip Johnson called it the "epitome of mid-century art." Others, including the president of the American Academy of Design, had equally vociferous negative opinions. After lengthy debate the commission unanimously withheld approval of the design as being too large, too tall, out of keeping with the neighboring memorials to Washington, Jefferson, and Lincoln, and "lacking in repose, an essential

58. The proposed FDR memorial rejected by David Finley's Fine Arts
Commission in 1962

element in memorial art, and the qualities of monumental permanence that are the essence of the three memorials with which it must by law conform." The commission also questioned the durability of the concrete materials specified, notwithstanding Philip Johnson's opinion to the contrary.

Supporters of the proposed FDR memorial went before Congress in anticipation that the solid Democratic majority would insist on building this dramatic monument to their fallen leader. As commission chairman, Finley testified in June 1962 before a House Appropriations subcommittee. In classic Finley style, he clearly, but graciously, criticized the design. And he just as politely, but firmly, refused to allow a congressman to put stronger words in his mouth:

> Representative Jensen, Republican of Iowa, brought up the subject of the Franklin D. Roosevelt Memorial.
> Mr. Jensen: When I looked at that thing I thought there is a number of great big tombstones that should not be indicative of the life of Franklin D. Roosevelt because he was a long ways from a dead man while he was alive. That is the first thought which came into my mind. What came into your mind when you saw it?
> Mr. Finley: They were very tall.
> Mr. Jensen: Did you mean they were tombstones?
> Mr. Finley: No. They go quite high into the skyline. I think 165 feet.[10]

Finley concluded his testimony by saying simply that because the commission had not approved this design he could not recommend an authorization of funds to approve it. In October 1962 Congress also rejected the "tombstones" design, sending it back to the FDR Memorial Commission with instructions to work with the Commission of Fine Arts to find a more acceptable design.[11] The tombstones concept did not die easily, and a post-Finley commission actually approved a version of it, with some modifications, in 1964. But by then the Roosevelt family had taken a close look at the proposal, and James Roosevelt, FDR's eldest son, telephoned the chairman during a commission meeting to say that the family opposed the stelae design and would prefer a memorial in the form of a garden area with specimens of principal American trees. When the Roosevelt family made public their opposition to the stelae project, it finally expired.[12]

Finley's Fine Arts Commission quietly tabled many other ill-conceived projects as well, including "plans for the inner-loop of the freeway system that was going to cut right across the Mall, plans for the Three Sisters bridge, and all of those encroachments on the national environment of our Capital." According to J. Carter Brown, Finley's successor as director of the National Gallery and as chairman of the Commission of Fine Arts, "these battles were spearheaded by Mr. Finley in ways that many of us will never be able to appreciate sufficiently."[13]

At the end of Finley's term as chairman of the Fine Arts Commission in 1963, he asked President Kennedy to appoint someone else to replace him as a commissioner, and Kennedy accepted his resignation with regret. His successor as chairman, William Walton, surely had in mind the Roosevelt memorial as well as Lafayette Square and other unnamed projects when he praised Finley in July 1963, saying: "The monstrosities that are not here are a monument to you." Burnham Kelley, the dean of architecture at Cornell University and another member of the commission, put it in similar terms: "Mr. Finley has a lot of un-monuments."[14]

* * *

Finley used his position as chairman of the U.S. Commission of Fine Arts to exert a positive influence on two other proposals involving the General Services Administration (GSA), both of which have had long-term benefits not only for the city of Washington but for the entire nation. In 1955 the GSA, as the federal agency with jurisdiction over government buildings, supported a proposal to tear down the Old Patent Office Building to make room for a parking lot. Finley particularly admired that building, which he thought one of the most beautiful and historic in Washington, and his successful effort to save it by securing the support of the White House led to the founding of the National Portrait Gallery, which opened on those premises in 1968 after extensive renovations. Another proposal met a quicker resolution in 1962, when the GSA planned to tear down a number of historic old houses facing Lafayette Square and to erect massive contemporary federal buildings on two sides of the square. This time Finley teamed up with a young but determined First Lady to prevent what they viewed as a desecration at the gates of the White House. We will consider each of these episodes in the following two chapters.

NOTES

1. Sue A. Kohler, *The Commission of Fine Arts: A Brief History, 1910–1995* (Washington, D.C., 1995).

2. This account of the Truman Balcony is taken largely from William Seale, *The President's House,* White House Historical Association in cooperation with the National Geographic Society (Washington, D.C., 1986), 2:1011–1016.

3. In a letter to Jacqueline Kennedy of 27 March 1963, David Finley added a postscript, explaining that the commission believed that an "eighteenth century Georgian house, such as the White House, should not have a line of columns broken by a balcony, as was done in the nineteenth century plantation houses," though he acknowledged that the line at the White House had already been broken by an awning. Copy of this letter in the Finley Papers, NGA Archives, box 12-13.

4. Gilmore D. Clarke to Harry S. Truman, 26 November 1947. Records, U.S. Commission of Fine Arts.

5. Seale, *The President's House,* 2:1014.

6. McCullough, *Truman,* 593–594. The Republicans had won control of both the House and the Senate in 1946, and it was widely predicted that Thomas E. Dewey, who had run against FDR in 1944, would trounce Truman in November 1948.

7. Harry S. Truman to David Finley, 15 February 1949. Finley Papers, Library of Congress, box 5.

8. Interview with Charles Atherton (secretary of the U.S. Commission of Fine Arts), conducted by the author, July 1999.

9. This account is based on Kohler, *Commission of Fine Arts,* 86–89.

10. *Washington Star,* 8 March 1962.

11. Kohler, *Commission of Fine Arts,* 88–89.

12. The design for the FDR memorial that was finally approved by the Fine Arts Commission under the chairmanship of J. Carter Brown has been widely praised by planners, historians, and the public alike. The memorial opened in 1997.

13. J. Carter Brown, remarks at Oatlands, 14 May 1977, transcript, p. 21. Oatlands Archives.

14. *Washington Post,* 27 July 1963.

59. David Finley, chairman of the White House Historical Association, presents the first copy of *The White House: An Historic Guide* to President and Mrs. John F. Kennedy as Melville Bell Grosvenor of the National Geographic Society looks on, 1962

12

Mrs. Kennedy and Mr. Finley

1961–1964

DAVID FINLEY'S ROLE AS CHAIRMAN of the U.S. Commission of Fine Arts led to one of the most remarkable and successful collaborations in his long career, when he joined Jacqueline Bouvier Kennedy in a mission to preserve Lafayette Square and restore the furnishings and art collections in the White House. Despite her youth, Jacqueline Kennedy knew Washington better than any new First Lady since Dolley Madison. Through her mother and stepfather, Janet and Hugh Auchincloss, she already had long and wide-ranging acquaintances in Washington and northern Virginia, and she had lived in the area since she was thirteen.[1] An accomplished horsewoman, she rode near Middleburg with friends like Paul Mellon, and she moved easily in such company even before marrying Senator John F. Kennedy of Massachusetts in September 1954. During his last three years in the Senate they made their home in a Federal-style brick townhouse on N Street in Georgetown, one block away from David and Margaret Finley.

At first the Finleys must have viewed the Kennedys with mixed emotions. John Kennedy had won his Senate seat in 1952 by defeating Henry

Cabot Lodge Jr., a lifelong friend of the Eustis family. In addition, the unsavory reputation of the family patriarch, Joseph P. Kennedy, and his views on appeasing Hitler when he served as Roosevelt's ambassador to the Court of St. James's at the outbreak of the war compared unfavorably with Andrew Mellon's conduct a few years earlier in that same post. And by that time the Finleys' political stance had moved decidedly to the right. But David Finley was too astute to let his private opinions get in the way of access to the White House, and he no doubt welcomed Jacqueline Kennedy's keen interest in the history and restoration of the White House as well as in the fine arts—so rare in political circles.

Jacqueline Kennedy combined an uncommon aesthetic sensibility with hard-headed realism. She had grown up in privileged surroundings, had gone to the best schools, and had come to embrace good taste and decorum as core values. She had traveled widely in Europe, even visiting Bernard Berenson at I Tatti, and had spent a year in Paris studying art history at the Sorbonne. She also had a broad streak of independence. She did not follow trends; she set them. But she had also known pain. She had watched her beloved father "Black Jack" Bouvier slowly destroy himself with drink and philandering. She had met good-natured ridicule, as well as a certain hostility, from the powerful Kennedy clan. And after six years of marriage, she was acutely aware of her husband's relentless womanizing and self-centeredness, along with his great gifts and matchless charm. By the time she arrived at the White House, she knew what she wanted and how to go about getting it.

Restoring the White House

Restoring the interior of the White House was one of Jacqueline Kennedy's highest priorities. The landmark mansion had suffered from neglect and clumsy redecorating, especially during the Truman and Eisenhower regimes, and the private quarters had hardly any antiques or period furnishings. One observer dismissed the decor as "Statler Hilton."[2] In response, Jacqueline Kennedy, who was determined to restore the beauty of the White House in a meaningful way, decreed, "Everything in the White House must have a reason for being there, it would be a sacrilege merely to 'redecorate' it—a word I hate. It must be restored—and that has nothing to do with decoration."[3]

Refurbishing efforts quickly consumed the official budget of $50,000, however, and Mrs. Kennedy came to realize that she needed outside help for fund-raising and for expert advice. She also realized that she needed the "cover" of well-known authorities, lest the press, public, and politicians of the opposing camp accuse the Kennedys of meddling with a national icon to suit their own preferences. The most respected authority in the field of period furnishings, Henry F. du Pont of Wilmington, Delaware, had put together a superb collection of early American antiques and had founded the Winterthur Museum. Du Pont had known David Finley from the earliest days of the National Trust for Historic Preservation, when his sister, Louise du Pont Crowninshield, had joined the board. But it was Jacqueline Kennedy who flew to du Pont's winter home at Boca Grande, Florida, and persuaded him to become the chairman of the Fine Arts Committee for the White House. His acceptance of this position was a triumph, for in addition to his prominent name, impeccable taste, and money, Henry du Pont was a staunch Republican, who gave bipartisan credibility to the enterprise.

Illustrious people who served on this committee included Mrs. Paul (Bunny) Mellon, Mrs. Charles (Jayne) Wrightsman, Charles Francis Adams (a descendant of two Presidents), John S. Loeb, John Walker, and David Finley. Skillfully tapping their personal connections as well as the combined appeal of the Kennedys and the patriotic impulses of citizens, the committee produced a stream of donations of antiques and artworks from wealthy Americans, carefully screened by the Fine Arts Committee. Bolstering these efforts, new legislation declared the public areas of the White House to be a national museum and specified that any gifts to the White House became the property of the nation and not of the current residents.

Few people in Washington knew the White House better than David Finley. He had visited it in every administration since his father took him there to meet Woodrow Wilson in 1913. He had served on the Commission of Fine Arts committee on the White House since the 1940s, participating in the infamous battle with Harry Truman over his balcony in 1947—and surviving the subsequent presidential purge of the commission. And as chairman of the commission since 1950, he

60. President Kennedy and David Finley before the Federal highboy the Finleys gave to the White House to inaugurate Mrs. Kennedy's restoration program. Polaroid photograph taken by Jacqueline Kennedy, 1961

had ready access to its occupants. He wasted no time making himself available to help Jacqueline Kennedy in her efforts to restore the White House. As soon as the Kennedys had moved in, David Finley made the first gift, a Federal highboy for the presidential living quarters, which had stood in the Finleys' home in Georgetown. Mrs. Kennedy later recorded the event by taking a Polaroid photograph of Finley and her husband in front of the highboy, which she sent to him with a fond note in the summer of 1961 (fig. 60).

The charismatic First Lady and the soft-spoken elder statesman of the arts clicked from the start. He was a seasoned veteran of battles over the nation's cultural life; she had unerring instinct and unique access to power. He was pleased to share his decades of experience and offer guidance and wise counsel. They came to have a deep mutual respect and affection, and both had an innate sense of taste and a love of Washington's architectural heritage. She always addressed him as "Mr. Finley," while he showed her the same courtesy, addressing her always as "Mrs. Kennedy." They made a great team.

Although far apart in age and background, they had acquired at least one common trait. According to one who saw Jacqueline Kennedy at close hand in those days: "She had a will of iron, with more determination than anybody I have ever met. Yet she was so soft-spoken, so deft and subtle, that she could impose her will upon people without their ever knowing it."[4] Those who knew David Finley well used almost identical words to describe his influence over people. In addition, Mrs. Kennedy was a connoisseur of powerful men, and Mr. Finley had considerable power in a field that interested her greatly.

In November 1961 the Kennedys' special counsel, Clark Clifford, established the White House Historical Association as a nonprofit corporation, with David Finley, John Walker, and himself as the incorporators. David Finley was elected the first chairman of its board, which included, ex officio, the director of the National Park Service, the chairman of the U.S. Commission of Fine Arts, the director of the National Gallery of Art, and the secretary of the Smithsonian Institution. In the following year Clark Clifford and Melville Bell Grosvenor, head of the National Geographic Society, also became members of the board.

The nominal purpose of the association was educational, but the underlying purpose was to raise funds for the White House restoration program. To this end, it entered an agreement with the National Geographic Society to publish *The White House: An Historic Guide* in 1962. Finley worked closely with Jacqueline Kennedy on the book as well as with the photographers and staff of the National Geographic. Mrs. Kennedy wrote him to express some reservations: "My only feeling about the National Geographic is that they have a slight tendency to be corny—pictures of the Kitchen & Caroline, etc.—but they are so full of goodwill I know they will see my point & to their amazement it will sell much better than if it is just another series of slick pictures of people marching into State Dinners!"[5] She was also concerned about the production schedule, worrying that the book would miss the peak of the summer tourist season. Finley wrote back to say he would work with the National Geographic on the text and pictures, assuring her "we can produce a book of which we can be proud," that the people at the National Geographic were working overtime, and the book should be ready for sale by 1 July.[6]

As it turned out, the book was ready by the end of June, when Finley and the National Geographic presented the first copies to President and Mrs. Kennedy at the White House (see fig. 59). As Finley had promised, the book made them all proud. It combined her style, his dignity, and the National Geographic's splendid color photography, and it was a phenomenal success from the start. By the fall of 1963 Finley could report to Mrs. Kennedy that the *Guide* had gone through four editions, with a total of 1.1 million copies in print, and that the association had been able to donate $137,000 of the proceeds to the White House restoration fund.[7] The *Guide* is still in print more than forty years later, and by 2004 had sold more than 4.5 million copies.[8] Subsequently, the association published other books related to the White House, such as *Presidents of the United States,* and by the early twenty-first century it had more than 8 million copies in circulation, as well as videos and other educational materials, and had raised over $20 million for the refurbishing of public areas of the White House.[9]

Saving Lafayette Square

With the restoration of the White House well under way, Jacqueline Kennedy turned her attention to its immediate surroundings. Lafayette Square, directly across Pennsylvania Avenue to the north of the White House, had originally belonged to the White House grounds, and it constituted the heart of historic Washington. It was bounded on the west by Jackson Place, with Blair House and Decatur House at either end; on the north by H Street, with Washington's oldest church, St. John's Episcopal (1815); and on the east by Madison Place, anchored by the Dolley Madison and Tayloe houses (fig. 61). These low-rise structures surrounding the square all dated from the first half of the nineteenth century, and the park enclosed by these streets had an equestrian statue of Andrew Jackson at the center, monumental statuary to the heroes of the American Revolution at the four corners, and old trees, spacious lawns, and beds of flowering plants throughout.

A few twentieth-century intrusions had appeared facing the square, some relatively unobtrusive, some not. Opposite the northwest corner of the square the white marble Chamber of Commerce building had replaced the old Corcoran mansion, and the Hay-Adams Hotel had taken the place of the stately townhouses of Henry Adams and John Hay, which once stood next door. The Belasco Theatre building, adapted to house the United Service Organizations during the war, and the beaux-arts Treasury annex occupied the middle and south end of Madison Place. But three jarring high-rises, ranging from eight to ten stories, had gone up on Jackson Place and stuck out like sore thumbs above the rooflines of the townhouses between the Blair and Decatur Houses.

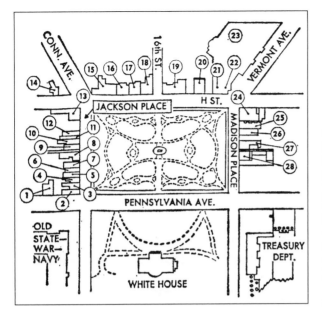

61. Schematic map of Lafayette Square, showing the location of the historic buildings that Jacqueline Kennedy and David Finley fought to preserve. (The Henry Adams House is incorrectly assigned to the owner's grandfather, John Quincy Adams.) *Washington Post*, 14 June 1960

Buildings bordering three sides of Lafayette Square are identified by the following numbers: 1. Blair House; 2. old Parker Home; 3. John McLean home; 4. old Admiral Dahlgren home; 5. old home of Maj. Henry R. Rathbone; 6. old Boardman home; 7. once the home of Mrs. James Blair (of the famous Blairs); 8. now the Brookings Institute and once the home of a Vice President and at least six Cabinet members; 9. old Parke home; 10. old home of publisher William J. Murtagh; 11. Glover home; 12. Marcy home, which was used in 1902 as temporary White House for President Theodore Roosevelt; 13. Decatur House; 14. old Bancroft home; 15. present Chamber of Commerce Building—once the home of Daniel Webster; 16. old Slidell home; 17. and 18. present Hay-Adams Hotel—once site of double home of John Quincy Adams and John Hay; 19. St. John's Church; 20. old Ashburton home, now St. John's parish house; 21. old Senator Pomeroy home; 22. old Senator Sumner home; 21. present Veterans Administration; 24. Dolley Madison House; 25. old Windom home; 26. old home of Col. Robert E. Ingersoll; 27. Benjamin Tayloe House—nicknamed "Little White House" in President McKinley's Administration; 28. present USO Center—site where Secretary of State Seward was stabbed.

Moreover, during the Eisenhower administration the government had begun to eye Lafayette Square as an ideal location for several new edifices, including a courthouse in the middle of Madison Place and an executive office building in the middle of Jackson Place. In 1958 the General Services Administration (GSA) retained two firms of Boston architects who came up with plans for large contemporary structures quite out of keeping with the existing low-rise fabric of the square, which would require demolition of a number of historic buildings, among them the old Corcoran Gallery of Art at Pennsylvania Avenue and Seventeenth Street (now the Renwick Gallery) and the Dolley Madison and Tayloe houses on Madison Place.

The Commission of Fine Arts, chaired by David Finley, was deeply divided on this issue. Finley of course opposed the destruction of the historic buildings and the further disruption of the nineteenth-century character of Lafayette Square, which he knew so well.[10] But several architects on the seven-member commission, including Ralph Walker, former head of the American Institute of Architects, felt it was time to allow contemporary designs to go forward without worrying about the past.[11] Between 1959 and 1961 the commission struggled to reconcile the clear need for more government buildings with the historic integrity of Lafayette Square, which had already been compromised to some extent.

In June 1961 the Fine Arts Commission received proposals from the GSA for two massive contemporary buildings on the west and east sides of Lafayette Square. The commissioners reached a deadlock, with Ralph Walker, architect Douglas Orr, and landscape architect Michael Rapuano voting to approve, while Finley, painter Peter Hurd, and sculptor Felix de Weldon "wanted the designs to address the scale and historic character of the nineteenth-century square." The seventh member of the commission did not participate at that time. Finley then took the modernist schemes to members of the Bureau of the Budget. As Finley could have predicted, the bureau director was dismayed by what he saw and quickly telephoned William Walton, the President's confidant.[12] On the following day David Finley met with President Kennedy and William Walton to review the plans. Kennedy was not impressed, and Finley reported to his fellow commissioners that the President "expressed the hope that the building on the west side of the square should be designed with more masonry and less glass" and "hoped the architect would design a building which would not clash with its surroundings."[13] In late July 1961 Walton traveled to Boston to convey the President's ideas to the architects, who produced several more possible designs, which Walton went over with the President at the Kennedy compound on Cape Cod over the Labor Day weekend and at Walton's home in Georgetown later in September.[14] The extent of Jacqueline Kennedy's involvement at the time is not known.

These proposals came to a head at the November 1961 meeting of the Commission of Fine Arts. The architects had modified their designs slightly in response to President Kennedy's suggestions. Although the final plan still called for two immense buildings on either side of Lafayette Square, it did preserve the Decatur and Blair Houses—some consolation for the loss of the old Corcoran Gallery and the Dolley Madison and Tayloe Houses. This time the commission voted 4–3 in favor of the plan, overriding Finley's vote as the chairman. And when the architects met with President Kennedy and William Walton in January 1962, the President reluctantly approved the modernist structures and the demolition of the historic buildings.[15]

But the President had not reckoned on the skill and determination of his wife and David Finley. That very month Janet Auchincloss had sent her daughter an idea first advanced not by an architect but by a banker. Charles Glover, an officer and director of the Riggs Bank, belonged to an offshoot of the American Civic Association called the Committee of 100 on the Federal City, which had served since 1923 as a "force of conscience," with no statutory authority, in Washington planning matters and had included such influential men as U. S. Grant III and David Finley.[16] Glover had grown up on Jackson Place, and in the summer of 1960 he had written to Finley suggesting that the new federal buildings could be set back from Jackson Place behind the existing buildings. Finley found the idea intriguing and agreed to bring it to the attention of the Commission of Fine Arts. A year later Glover sent the same idea to William Walton, who forwarded it to the Boston architects, without any results.

In December 1961 another member of the Committee of 100, the architect Grosvenor Chapman, made a sketch to illustrate how Glover's concept would look.[17] The chairman of the Committee of 100 sent Chapman's sketch directly to President Kennedy, who apparently thought the project had progressed too far to be reconsidered. But when Mrs. Kennedy saw this ingenious solution to the problem of setting back the big new buildings while preserving the small old ones, things began to happen.

In February 1962 Jacqueline Kennedy stepped into the Lafayette Square matter. Time was short, but Arthur Schlesinger recalled her saying, "The wreckers haven't started yet, and until they do, it can be saved."[18] She asked David Finley to meet her on 15 February, and on that morning the thirty-two-year-old First Lady and the seventy-one-year-old chairman of the National Trust and the Commission of Fine Arts walked together around the square, with Finley pointing out the various buildings. Her questions went right to the heart of the issue: "She asked me who decided these matters, and I said our recommendations were advisory only and that the final decision was made by the Administrator of General Services. She asked why the recommendations of the Commission of Fine Arts could not be mandatory, and I told her the Act that established the Commission provided that its powers should be advisory only, and I felt it was wiser that this should be the case."[19] On 2 March Mrs. Kennedy wrote Finley that she had discussed the plans for Lafayette Square with the President and that he wanted Finley to "ask the architects to come up with a design for the Court Building more in keeping with the 19th century architecture of the Square." She also expressed a strong desire to save Dolley Madison's house and the old Corcoran Gallery and asked for his counsel on those as well.[20]

Finley responded in writing, carefully stating that because the Commission of Fine Arts had already approved the proposals, over his dissent, he could not take any action contrary to the commission's decision, even if told to do so by the President of the United States. But he continued:

> The views of the Commission are advisory only; and if you
> and the President wish to do so, the most effective way to

proceed, it seems to me, is for the President to write or speak to Mr. Bernard Boutin, Administrator of General Services, who has the final decision as to design and also the responsibility for erecting the buildings. . . .

I am delighted that you and the President have taken so much interest in Lafayette Square, and I am sure the Administrator of General Services would try to carry out your ideas if the President asked him to do so.[21]

That was all Jacqueline Kennedy needed to know. The next day she wrote a strong letter to Bernard L. Boutin, the GSA administrator, which began:

Dear Bernie:
I am enclosing a letter from David Finley, Chairman of the Fine Arts Commission, about the proposed plans for Lafayette Square.

Because of our interest in history and preservation, it really matters a great deal to the President and to myself that this is done well; we have received so much mail on the subject.

Unfortunately, last summer, the President okayed some plans for buildings; he was in a hurry, he doesn't have time to bother himself with details like this, he trusted the advice of a friend, Bill Walton, and I really don't think it was the right advice.

In all he has to do, at least I can spare him some minor problems like this. So, I turn to you for help.

(1) —The East Side of Lafayette Square: They are now planning to put up a hideous white modern court building. All architects are innovators, and would rather do something new than in the spirit of old buildings. I think they are totally wrong in this case, as the important thing is to preserve the 19th Century feeling of Lafayette Square. So, you do as Mr. Finley suggests—write to the architects and tell them to submit you a design which is more in keeping with the 19th Century bank on the corner.

* * *

Bobby says you are the most wonderful head of GSA there ever was or ever will be. I am sure that is true, and I cannot tell you how much I am counting on you for your help in this matter. It is so discouraging, for months now these plans have gone back and forth; no one seems to know who has the final say—and before you know it, everything is ripped down and horrible things put up in their place. I simply panic at the thought of this and decided to make a last-ditch appeal. Thank you again.[22]

The letter captured Jacqueline Kennedy's forthright style, her passionate intensity, and her reliance on David Finley's advice. It skillfully invoked the President's personal interest, forcefully argued her case, even indulged in outrageous flattery. And it worked.

Within weeks Boutin had hired a new architect, John Carl Warnecke of San Francisco, an old acquaintance of JFK's who just happened to be at a White House event in March 1962 while Jacqueline Kennedy and her sister were making a well-publicized trip to India.[23] William Walton took him to meet Boutin at the GSA, where Warnecke pored over the plans and concluded that Glover's approach, which he had seen reflected in some of the Boston architects' drawings, would work, with some modifications: "The old buildings in the historic district are a symbol of the White House and a symbol of America. They should all be kept, as many as you can keep. Not just one or two on the corners. . . . Make the historic buildings be an important part of the project. Make the other buildings of secondary importance. But relate them to it. Make them work together."[24]

On 18 April 1962 Jacqueline Kennedy, just back from India, sent David Finley an enthusiastic report:

Dear Mr. Finley
I just wanted you to know you had a brainstorm in saying to contact the head of GSA about Lafayette Square.
      I didn't know who was head then—it turns out he is an old friend, Bernard Boutin. I just think you should know how extraordinary this man is—Not only is he the first head of GSA in a long time to really crack down on waste—

spending—& naughty little contracts given to everyone's pet contractor (a Republican told me this—so I don't want you to think I am applauding my husband's appointment!), but out of the morass of conflicting opinions—so many cooks in the broth—all the things that upset you & me—all the long delays & despair that our hopes for Lafayette Square would ever be realized—& we would just have to give up & let it turn into a modern square—*he has brought order & in 2 wks. will have definite plans for your approval.*

I so admire people who can use power efficiently & wisely—& cut through red tape—& I just wanted you to know what a godsend this man is—in case there are other preservation problems you may have that I don't know about—he is the man to solve them.

Hold your breath—because this is what is going to happen—all our wildest dreams come true. I dictated a long letter to him the afternoon of our trip around Lafayette Square—

1) The new court building will be 19th century in feeling—similar to bank.
2) * The Dolley Madison & Tayloe houses will be saved !!!
3) The Court of Claims will be saved—It will be I think turned into a Museum of Modern Art which people are trying to get started here—& which I said I would sponsor as I think it is wrong to identify oneself solely with art of the past—& never encourage what is happening now. So it will be used as it used to be.
4) The whole Decatur House side facades will be saved except for the 2 tall modern buildings !!! ***
Some will be used as extension of guest facilities at Blair House—the rest as offices—So Theodore Roosevelt's old house—& place where Nat. Gal. was born will be preserved—This is what delights me most—Everyone wants to raze things & build efficient new buildings—Bernard Boutin is a preservationist & also says it will be

62. Architect John Carl Warnecke reviewing plans for the preservation of
Lafayette Square with Jacqueline Kennedy and GSA administrator Bernard
Boutin, 25 September 1962

cheaper! Who else could ever have said that! None of those naughty show off architects! The gaps that are left will be filled with some 19th cent. D.C. houses that he will have moved there. So if you know any special ones you want saved—tell him.

5) On 17th St a big building will go up to provide space for Bureau of the Budget or whoever it is who wants all this space—

He has found a brilliant architect to help him whom I imagine will work with the ones already signed up under previous administration—or rather tell them what to do. It is time someone asked with authority—before they happily destroyed the most historical part of Washington—& at last we found him—

I was so excited when I heard this I just had to tell you.
Sincerely,
Jacqueline Kennedy[25]

As it turned out, Warnecke completely replaced the "naughty" Boston architects, who were formally released by GSA in July. He commissioned an historical study of the houses around Lafayette Square by a respected Washington preservationist and in September 1962 unveiled an ingenious design based on the Glover-Chapman concept (fig. 62). The two big new redbrick buildings would be set back from the Jackson and Madison Place facades, while almost all of the best old buildings, including the old Corcoran Gallery of Art, would be retained. New buildings would replace the more egregious modern intrusions on Jackson Place, replicating the character of the original townhouses between Decatur House and Blair House. The government would get the buildings it needed, and the nineteenth-century character of the square would be preserved, with the White House the dominant element.

The new proposal still had to clear one final hurdle by winning approval from the Commission of Fine Arts on 16 October 1962, where Ralph Walker and Douglas Orr mounted a last-ditch defense of the modernist approach that Mrs. Kennedy had so abhorred. Walker, seeing that the influence of the First Lady proved the critical factor, sniped in his defeat, "I just hope Jacqueline wakes up to the fact that she lives in the twentieth century."[26] But under Finley's leadership the commission approved Warnecke's plan and preserved the essence of Lafayette Square. Finley wrote Mrs. Kennedy to say he was delighted with the plans that Boutin and Warnecke had made for Lafayette Square, and that the Fine Arts Commission had approved them, "though not unanimously."[27] The battle of Lafayette Square had many heroes, notably Charles Glover, Grover Chapman, John Carl Warnecke, Bernard Boutin, William Walton, and of course President John F. Kennedy. But all their efforts would have been for naught without the iron will and dogged persistence of two deceptively gentle souls, who combined aesthetic taste and a love of history with the artful use of raw power: Jacqueline Bouvier Kennedy and David Edward Finley.[28]

This effort was one of Finley's last campaigns as chairman of the Commission of Fine Arts. After he submitted his resignation to the President in early 1963—having served on the commission for twenty years, the last twelve as chairman—Jacqueline Kennedy wrote him on 22 March to say:

> It absolutely broke my heart when the President came home the other day and told me of your adieux. . . .
>
> It is inconceivable to think of existing without you— What will I do? You have been such a marvelous and unselfish helper and your fantastic backing and loyalty are what gave me the courage to do all the things people said we were mad to attempt. . . .
>
> I could never find words to express all the gratitude and affection and indebtedness I will feel for you until my dying day. . . .
>
> One thing you can <u>NEVER</u> do is resign from the White House Historical Association! Please promise that. . . .
>
> I just wanted you to know how desperately you will be missed & if there is some secret—that is not the right word, unorthodox is better—way you can think of to still be there— please do wrack your brain and come up with it (& tell me soon!).
>
> With the greatest affection and appreciation,
> Jacqueline Kennedy[29]

After President Kennedy's assassination, his widow wrote to her old friend David Finley on 22 August 1964, enclosing a small gold box that she had commissioned for him, explaining that the President had intended to award him the Citation of Merit for his great service to his country: "It comes with my devotion—and my great sadness that we could not have all been together in the Rose Garden—his beloved garden—to see you receive the Citation of Merit from President Kennedy. So please accept this poor substitute. With love from, Jacqueline Kennedy."[30] David Finley treasured this gift. Following Finley's death in 1977, Jacqueline Kennedy Onassis, then widowed for a second time, wrote Margaret Finley a heartfelt letter of condolence (see fig. 76).[31]

Both David Finley and Jacqueline Kennedy Onassis achieved many other distinctions in their lives and careers, but their triumphs in restoring the White House and in rescuing Lafayette Square rank among their greatest legacies. And the deep affection they had for one another reveals a special bond between these very public yet very private people.

1. In 1942, two years after Jacqueline's parents divorced, her mother married Hugh Auchincloss II, heir to a Standard Oil fortune. He had two grand homes: Merrywood, on a bluff overlooking the Potomac in McLean, Virginia; and a summer "cottage," Hammersmith Farm, in Newport, Rhode Island. Jackie loved Merrywood, which remained her permanent home, even while she was away at school, until she married. For a balanced account of her life, see Sarah Bradford, *America's Queen: The Life of Jacqueline Kennedy Onassis* (New York, 2000).

2. Attributed to Joseph Alsop in Bradford, *America's Queen*, 170.

3. Arthur M. Schlesinger Jr., *A Thousand Days: John F. Kennedy in the White House* (New York, 1965), 676.

4. J. B. West, chief usher at the White House, quoted in Bradford, *America's Queen*, 174.

5. Jacqueline Kennedy to David Finley, 1 February 1962. Finley Papers, Library of Congress, box 81, White House Historical Association Correspondence, 1962–1963.

6. David Finley to Jacqueline Kennedy, 2 February 1962. Finley Papers, Library of Congress.

7. Finley to Jacqueline Kennedy, 10 October 1963.

8. *White House History*, no. 14 (winter 2004): 22.

9. White House Historical Association Web site, www.whitehousehistory.org.

10. Finley had deep roots on Lafayette Square. Since at least 1913 he had often visited his cousin Violet Blair Janin at her home on Jackson Place (around no. 5 on the map illustrated in fig. 61). His law office in the 1930s was on Jackson Place, as was his office as director of the National Gallery of Art before its building was completed. The National Trust and its forerunner had their offices on Jackson Place in the 1950s. And his wife had grown up in the old Corcoran mansion facing the square.

11. The modernist versus the contextual argument was presented in Douglas Haskell, "Saying Nothing, Going Nowhere," *Architectural Forum* 111 (August 1959): 134–137, 198.

12. Kurt Helfrich, "Modernism for Washington? The Kennedys and the Redesign of Lafayette Square," *Washington History* 8, no. 1, Historical Society of Washington, D.C. (Spring/Summer 1996): 23.

13. David Finley, memorandum for the file, 28 June 1961. Records of the Commission of Fine Arts; quoted in Helfrich, "Modernism for Washington?," 23. In addition to the records of the Commission of Fine Arts, the author has relied on this excellent article for many details.

14. Helfrich, "Modernism for Washington?," 23–24.

15. Helfrich, "Modernism for Washington?," 24.

16. Charles C. Glover Jr., of an old Washington family, had attended George Washington University Law School with Finley. He combined a long career in Washington's banking and business communities with a wide variety of public service positions.

17. Grosvenor Chapman, an architect who practiced first in New York and after 1940 in Washington, was past president of the Committee of 100 and active in numerous civic and preservation causes in Washington.

18. Schlesinger, *A Thousand Days*, 676.

19. Finley, memorandum for the file, 19 February 1962. Finley Papers, NGA Archives, box 12-13.

20. Jacqueline Kennedy to Finley, 2 March 1962. Finley Papers, NGA Archives, box 44-2.

21. Finley to Jacqueline Kennedy, 5 March 1962. Finley Papers, NGA Archives.

22. Jacqueline B. Kennedy to Bernard L. Boutin, 7 March 1962. Kennedy Library, Boston. Papers of Bernard L. Boutin, Kennedy Library. Copy in files at Commission of Fine Arts.

23. According to Warnecke's article in *White House History*, no. 13 (Summer 2003), he met JFK at Stanford in the fall of 1940. He was in Washington on other business when a mutual friend, Paul "Red" Fay, took him to the White House on 14 March 1962. At a small private dinner at the White House the following evening, Fay told Kennedy that Warnecke had become a successful architect. Four days later Kennedy called him to ask for his help on Lafayette Square.

24. Interview with John Carl Warnecke, conducted by Thomas S. Page, September 1992; quoted in Helfrich, "Modernism for Washington?," 32.

25. Jacqueline Kennedy to Finley, 18 April 1962. Finley Papers, NGA Archives, box 12-13.

26. Commission of Fine Arts minutes, 16 October 1962; quoted in Helfrich, "Modernism for Washington?," 33.

27. Finley to Jacqueline Kennedy, 19 October 1962. Finley Papers, NGA Archives.

28. After Jacqueline Kennedy Onassis's death in 1994, the National Trust placed a plaque in front of Decatur House honoring her role in saving Lafayette Square. In 1998, a few doors to the south, a stone plaque was mounted on the wall of the White House Conference Center at 726 Jackson Place, under the leadership of Charles Atherton, longtime executive secretary of the Commission of Fine Arts: "Dedicated to those whose spirit and vision helped preserve the historic architecture of Lafayette Square." It names (in alphabetical order) Grover Chapman, David Finley, Charles Glover Jr., and William Walton. The inscription includes a replica of Chapman's sketch and the note: "This sketch so impressed Jacqueline Kennedy that she became its chief advocate. The principles it evoked became the basis for the historic restoration of the Square."

29. Jacqueline Kennedy to Finley, 22 March 1963. Finley Papers, NGA Archives. Faithful to his young patron's wishes, Finley remained chairman of the White House Historical Association until his death in 1977. In fact, he chaired his last meeting of its board of directors less than a week before he died. His work for the association later brought him into contact with Lady Bird Johnson and Patricia Ryan Nixon.

30. Jacqueline Kennedy to Finley, 22 August 1964. Finley Papers, NGA Archives.

31. Photocopy in the Finley Papers, NGA Archives.

63. President Dwight D. Eisenhower and David Finley at the National
Gallery of Art, January 1956

13

Creating the National Portrait Gallery
1948–1968

LONG BEFORE DAVID FINLEY or Andrew Mellon came to Washington, others had foreseen the value of a national portrait gallery in the nation's capital. Mellon himself had hoped that some of his American portraits would be included in a national portrait gallery "if and when such a gallery should come into being,"[1] but he took no concrete steps to create one. It took David Finley to make that happen.

In the late eighteenth century the American portrait painter Charles Willson Peale created "Peale's Collection of Portraits of American Patriots."[2] Early records of the Smithsonian Institution going back almost to its founding in 1846 include references to the desirability of organizing a gallery of American portraiture.[3] The opening of the British National Portrait Gallery in 1859 prompted further discussion of an American counterpart, but without result.[4] Then in 1919 a National Art Commission, a private group of American citizens that included the then-Secretary of the Smithsonian, Charles Doolittle Walcott, came together and organized, under the auspices of the American Federation of the Arts, an exhibition of twenty portraits of American and Allied leaders from the First World War; the paintings were displayed at the Museum of Natural History in Washington, then sent on a tour of American cities. The National Gallery of Art Commission, established in 1921, made more definite plans for a national portrait gallery and began to accept donations.[5]

Meanwhile, Andrew Mellon had begun to collect early American portraits. When he moved to Washington in 1921, he had portraits of George Washington and Alexander Hamilton hanging in his bedroom at 1785 Massachusetts Avenue. In 1932–1933 Mellon purchased an oil portrait of Pocahontas by an unknown artist after an engraving that dated from 1616 (plate 32), for which David Finley acted as the straw man because Mellon had promised himself not to buy any paintings during his year in London as U.S. ambassador. David Bruce brought the Pocahontas to Mellon's attention and also let him know that a collection of American portraits assembled by Thomas Clarke was on the market. In January 1934 the A. W. Mellon Educational and Charitable Trust bought about a hundred portraits through Knoedler's from the Clarke Collection,[6] which included more than twenty paintings by Gilbert Stuart, five by Thomas Sully, two by John Singleton Copley, one by Benjamin West, and one of the Washington family by Edward Savage. Other portraits in the purchase depicted such famous Americans as John Quincy Adams, Henry Clay, Stephen Foster, Benjamin Harrison, Nathaniel Hawthorne, Andrew Jackson, John Marshall, and Franklin Pierce. Not all of these paintings had artistic merit worthy of inclusion in the National Gallery of Art, but according to Finley, Mellon also had in mind an historical collection for a portrait gallery of notable Americans.[7]

In January 1936 Mellon spoke with the secretary of the Smithsonian and "suggested that, in connection with the gallery which the Mellon Trust would erect, a portrait gallery might be provided which would include portraits, carefully selected, from those owned by the Smithsonian Institution."[8] Mellon's momentous letter to President Roosevelt of 22 December 1936 included these words: ". . . and there is, in addition, a large assemblage of American portraits from the Clarke and other collections, which would be suitable for a national portrait gallery."[9] Moreover, the congressional hearings on the National Gallery in February 1937 featured the following exchange:

Ætatis suæ 21. Aº.1616.

Matoaks als Rebecka daughter to the mighty Prince
Powhatan Emperour of Attanoughkomouck als Virginia
converted and baptized in the Christian faith, and
Wife to the Worsll Mr Tho: Rolff.

🎔 PLATE 32   Unknown artist, copy after Simon van de Passe (?),
Pocahontas, after 1616. National Portrait Gallery, Smithsonian
Institution; gift of Andrew W. Mellon, 1942, NPG.65.61

PLATE 33

🌀 PLATE 33 Henry Inman, copy after Charles Bird, *Sequoyah*, c. 1830. National Portrait Gallery, NPG.79.174. Sequoyah was a distant cousin of David Finley's on his mother's side.

PLATE 34   G. P. A. Healey, *John Caldwell Calhoun*, 1845, NPG.90.52.
Calhoun (1782–1850). National Portrait Gallery. Calhoun
was another distant cousin of David Finley's, this time through
his father.

Mr. Treadway: Did you say how many paintings there were?

Mr. Finley: There are about a hundred old masters.

Mr. Treadway: That does not include this group of portraits, I take it.

Mr. Finley: That is correct; it does not include the portraits. In addition to the 100 paintings, there is the Clarke collection. It was Mr. Mellon's intention that such portraits in the Clarke collection as are of general historic interest should be contributed to a National Portrait Gallery and that some of the others, which have artistic merit, should go into the National Gallery of Art. Anything in the Clarke collection that is good enough will be given to one of these two galleries.[10]

On Mellon's death the National Gallery of Art acquired his private collection of paintings, with the proviso that those works of mostly historical interest should go to a national portrait gallery, if such an institution became a reality within twenty-five years.[11] In August 1942 the A. W. Mellon Educational and Charitable Trust conveyed another twenty-three paintings and one engraving to the National Gallery of Art by indenture, stipulating that these works be transferred to a portrait gallery, if one were founded within twenty years. In 1947 the Mellon Trust conveyed to the National Gallery a number of additional portraits from the Clarke Collection, on the condition that they be turned over to a portrait gallery, if one were established.

After the war, with the National Gallery of Art firmly on its feet, David Finley turned his attention to founding an American portrait gallery. In 1948 he drafted a bill to create such a museum under the auspices of the National Gallery, siting it in a building designed by George Hadfield that had served as a federal courthouse at Fifth and E Streets.[12] He shopped the bill among various agencies and approached Senator Henry Cabot Lodge, an old friend of the Eustis family, and other senators as potential sponsors.[13] In 1950 he persuaded Senator Theodore F. Green of Rhode Island to introduce the bill and briefed him on the proposal by sending him materials on the National Portrait Gallery in London. Finley even drafted talking points for the senator, "which I thought might be useful to you in connection with introducing the Bill, or later at hearings before the Committee."[14] Green brought the bill to the floor on 29 August 1950 and the next year spoke about it to President Truman, who "expressed great sympathy with the plan and assured me he would help me in every way he could to bring it about."[15]

In July 1952, while in the midst of his struggle with General U.S. Grant III over the management of the National Trust, Finley wrote directly to President Truman, reviewing Senator Green's bill and ending, "I know how deeply interested you are in this subject and hope you may find it possible to approve the allocation of the Hadfield Court House for use as a National Portrait Gallery under the direction of the National Gallery of Art."[16] The following month he spoke with Truman personally about the portrait gallery when he had been asked to see the President about another matter.[17] But the General Services Administration (GSA) dashed his hopes when it advised him in October 1952 that the Hadfield Courthouse had been promised to the Selective Service for office space.

In 1953 Finley contacted the architect Otto Eggers in New York. Eggers had earlier worked very closely with Finley on the completion of the National Gallery building, and Finley now asked him to design a structure to house a national portrait gallery on the block to the east of the National Gallery, where I. M. Pei's East Building of the National Gallery now stands. Eggers did so—and estimated the cost of construction at $10 to $12 million. Finley then wrote to the trustees of the Mellon Trust proposing a donation in that amount, plus an endowment of $5 million to establish a portrait gallery along the lines of the National Gallery.[18] Nothing came of this proposal.

Late in 1953, however, through his position on the Fine Arts Commission, Finley learned that the GSA was promoting legislation to permit demolition of the Old Patent Office Building at Ninth and F Streets to make way for a parking garage. He considered this building among Washington's most beautiful and most historic. It was a Greek revival classic designed by Robert Mills and others and constructed between 1838 and 1867. Walt Whitman had nursed wounded soldiers there during the Civil War, and Lincoln's second inaugural ball had taken place in its great hall. Finley was also proud of the fact that a South Carolinian had designed it.[19]

Alarmed, Finley went to work in earnest. As chairman of the Commission of Fine Arts, he went on record with the GSA and with Congress to oppose the destruction of the Old Patent Office Building. He lined up the American Institute of Architects to protest the action as well. He worked with Leonard Carmichael, the secretary of the Smithsonian Institution, to come up with a plan for the building to accommodate both the National Portrait Gallery and the Smithsonian's National Collection of Fine Arts. The latter comprised a group of paintings then installed "sort of behind the elephant in the Museum of Natural History," as J. Carter Brown later put it, and Finley's proposition solved that problem as well.[20]

Finally, Finley pulled out all the stops. He went right to the top and managed to get his case brought to the attention of President Dwight D. Eisenhower. He most likely accomplished this through his association with Eisenhower's top aide, Sherman Adams, with whom Finley was then working on the fine arts division of the People to People program.[21] Writing with typical understatement, he later recounted: "We met with some opposition in government offices. So I took the matter to The White House, and President Eisenhower ordered that the building be saved for a National Portrait Gallery."[22] The date of Eisenhower's intervention is uncertain, but it most likely happened in the spring of 1956, after the President visited the National Gallery of Art to see an exhibition of Asian art in January (see fig. 63), for on 1 June of that year GSA announced a "government plan to preserve the old Patent Office Building and later use it as a National Portrait Gallery."[23]

In May 1957 legislation was introduced in Congress—sponsored by Representative Frank Thompson Jr. of New Jersey and by Senators Hubert Humphrey of Minnesota and Clinton Anderson of New Mexico, who was also a Smithsonian regent—to transfer the Old Patent Office Building to the Smithsonian for use as a national portrait gallery.[24] The legislation passed Congress in early 1958, and President Eisenhower signed it on 28 March 1958. But the government, once in such a hurry to tear down the grand old building for a parking lot, now delayed vacating it until it could construct a new building for the current occupant, the Civil Service Commission. It was not until 1962 that President John F. Kennedy signed into law "An Act to provide for a National Portrait

Gallery as a bureau of the Smithsonian Institution." The act provided that the portrait gallery "shall function as a free public museum for the exhibition and study of portraiture and statuary depicting men and women who have made significant contributions to the history, development, and culture of the people of the United States and of the artists who created such portraiture and statuary."[25]

With the Old Patent Office Building finally vacated, extensive interior renovation began, with Finley's Fine Arts Commission approving minor exterior modifications that maintained the historic integrity of the building. Perhaps not surprisingly, the first official accession of the new National Portrait Gallery came from David Finley himself, accepted in 1963, when he donated a group of portrait etchings by Oskar Stoessel of Franklin D. Roosevelt, Harlan F. Stone, James F. Byrnes, and William O. Douglas.[26] Also in 1963 the board of regents of the Smithsonian appointed the National Portrait Gallery Commission, chaired by Finley's old friend John Nicholas Brown of Providence, with Finley also a member of the commission. After its first meeting in September 1963 Finley gave Brown two suggestions for possible directors of the new gallery. His first candidate, Charles Nagel, then director of the City Art Museum of St. Louis, got the job and began work in early 1964.

True to form, Finley soon immersed himself in the details of establishing the new museum, from its interior design and furnishings to its organization and staffing. He also took a leading role on the acquisitions committee, participating in discussions concerning which subjects to include in the portrait gallery and helping identify potential donors.[27] For example, he put Charles Nagel in touch with a friend of his in Leesburg, Mrs. A. D. Pollock Gilmour, who owned several portraits of her ancestors, including Charles Lee, attorney general in Washington's second term, which she gave to the National Portrait Gallery in 1964.[28]

In an interesting letter from this period, Mrs. Stanley McCormick of Boston, who had once owned 1785 Massachusetts Avenue, the former home of Andrew Mellon and future home of the National Trust for Historic Preservation, wrote to David Finley: "It was wonderful to hear from you again and I was delighted with your letter. I have often regretted that my fine apartment house in Washington could not be turned into

Matoaks als Rebecka daughter to the mighty Prince
Powhatan Emperour of Attanoughskomouck als virginia
converted and baptized in the Christian faith, and
wife to the worth Mr. Joh. Rolff.
Si. Pass: sculp: Compton Holland excud:

64. Simon van de Passe, *Pocahontas*, c. 1616, engraving. National Portrait Gallery, Bequest of David E. Finley, NPG.77.43

a National Gallery, as you so helpfully suggested at one time. Unfortunately, it was the inheritance taxes that prevented it!" Mrs. McCormick went on to tell Finley that, "prompted by your suggestion," she would change her will to leave her 1908 portrait of Henry James by Jacques-Émile Blanche to the National Portrait Gallery.[29]

In early 1965 the National Portrait Gallery received its first sizable accession, which comprised thirty-four portraits from the Mellon collection at the National Gallery of Art. These included works by famous American artists such as John James Audubon, John Singleton Copley, Augustus Saint-Gaudens, Charles Willson Peale, and Rembrandt Peale as well as by more contemporary artists. The subjects spanned American history from Pocahontas to Dwight D. Eisenhower. There were ten Presidents—Washington, Monroe, Jackson, Tyler, Pierce, Buchanan, Lincoln, Benjamin Harrison, Truman, and Eisenhower—along with Henry Clay, chief justice John Marshall, and Daniel Webster; New York governor De Witt Clinton; artists such as Audubon and James McNeill Whistler; and composer Stephen Foster. Most focused on nineteenth-century or earlier Americans, but a few depicted contemporary subjects, including General George C. Marshall and the first secretary of defense, James V. Forrestal. Almost all of the older portraits came from the collection of Andrew Mellon. In 1966 Margaret Eustis Finley and her sister, Anne Eustis Emmet, donated an oil portrait of their great-grandfather, William Wilson Corcoran.[30] David Finley himself bequeathed funds to the National Portrait Gallery that were used to purchase the engraving of Pocahontas by Simon van de Passe on which the painted portrait given by Mellon was based (fig. 64).

Interior remodeling dragged on, but in late 1966 David Finley wrote General Eisenhower to give him a progress report on the National Portrait Gallery, set to "occupy the beautiful Greek revival building saved largely by your efforts." In it he briefly reviewed the events of a decade earlier.

> As you may remember a bill was introduced in Congress to demolish the building for a parking lot. The Commission of Fine Arts passed a resolution opposing this action. I took the resolution to the Administrator of General Services Administration who seemed to think the proposed parking lot was more important than the building. So I went to the White House where the bill was brought to your attention by one of your aides, with the result that you directed that the building was to be saved for a National Portrait Gallery. . . . I shall always be grateful for what you have done in this matter.[31]

Eisenhower responded from his farm near Gettysburg, beginning, "Dear Dave: I cannot tell you how pleased I am about the news you have given me about the National Portrait Gallery. I am more than happy that the project has come to fruition and that you will soon be open for business."[32]

Yet as the years went by and the National Portrait Gallery continued to take shape, Finley's health began to decline. Always small, but wiry and energetic in his younger days, he had battled a series of ailments throughout his career, much of it brought on by overwork. Now, in the late 1960s, his frame had shrunk, and he began to use a cane. His spirit was willing, and his mind as sharp as ever, but his flesh was visibly weak. Late in 1966 Charles Nagel wrote to S. Dillon Ripley, then secretary of the Smithsonian, recommending that David Finley be given an award in recognition of his many services to the Smithsonian, the Commission of Fine Arts, the National Gallery, and the National Trust: "I do not want to seem importunate, but he is an old gentleman and of late has seemed quite a bit more frail than he used to be. I realize he will probably outlast all of us, but it does seem a good moment to give such an award serious consideration."[33] Ripley agreed, and on 19 July 1967 Vice President Hubert Humphrey presented the Joseph Henry Medal to

65. Joseph Henry Medal, awarded to David Finley by the Smithsonian
Institution, 1967

David E. Finley in a ceremony held in the great hall of what is now the
Arts and Industries Building. The citation read:

> David Edward Finley, devoted friend of art in all its mani-
> festations, you have served the City of Washington and your
> country for over thirty years as an arbiter of taste, a molder of
> form, and a conservator of all that is eclectic. The regents of
> the Smithsonian delight in honoring you with the first award
> of the Henry Medal for your services to the Institution and the
> Nation [fig. 65].

As the National Portrait Gallery neared its opening, Finley made
a motion approved by the rest of the commission to seek donations of
period American furniture to place in the galleries where the pictures
would be hung. He got the ball rolling by donating a beautiful Duncan
Phyfe table and four chairs designed by Phyfe. Margaret Finley and
her sister, Anne Emmet, also donated a sideboard that had belonged to
Daniel Webster, over which his portrait was to be hung.[34]

66. Mrs. Richard M. Nixon dedicates the Old Patent Office Building as a National Historic Landmark, 3 April 1974. David Finley is second from the right, and Margaret Finley is at the left behind Mrs. Nixon.

The National Portrait Gallery finally opened to the public in 1968, twenty years after David Finley had first begun to press Congress to charter it. The story seems ironic, but also fitting. In 1944–1945 Finley's quest for an important American painting by Thomas Sully for the National Gallery of Art had led him to rescue Hampton, the historic home in which he found it, and to establish the National Trust for Historic Preservation by 1949. In 1956 it was the threat to tear down an historic building that prompted David Finley to ask the President of the United States to intervene, which led to its preservation to house the National Portrait Gallery.

By 1973 Finley's health had continued to decline, and Marvin S. Sadik, who had succeeded Charles Nagel as director of the National Portrait Gallery, tried hard to secure one final honor for David Finley: the Presidential Medal of Freedom. Sadik sent "a stack of letters" to the White House recommending Finley for the award based on his long service to the arts. In March 1973 he sent a follow-up letter to the President's assistant for domestic affairs, noting Finley's advancing age:

David is not going to live forever. He admits to 82, but we all think he lies about his age. Everybody and his brother heartily recommends this award, including the Chief Justice [Warren Burger] and Rogers Morton [secretary of the interior]. My special interest is that David almost single-handedly saved this building from becoming a parking lot. I am not sure that all the late arrivals on the preservation bandwagon realize that David Finley is one of the founders of the preservation movement in our time. In addition, he is absolutely devoted to the President and everything he is trying to do. I need hardly tell you how distressed so many people would be if David should slip away before being awarded the Medal of Freedom. I wholeheartedly urge action in the matter.[35]

Unfortunately, the recipient of this letter was John D. Ehrlichman, one of the principals in the Watergate scandal, who had more pressing action to deal with just then.[36] Four years later David Finley indeed slipped away before being awarded the Medal of Freedom.

Finley faithfully attended all of the meetings of the National Portrait Gallery Commission until his death. J. Carter Brown, as a later director of the National Gallery of Art and chairman of the Commission of Fine Arts, recalled his fascination attending some of the commission's early meetings and watching David Finley, "who in a career sense was my grandfather," at work with his own father, John Nicholas Brown.[37] He also expressed deep admiration for the man who had done so much to put Washington on the map as a major cultural center: "There were always battles to be won and he never shrank from them. They always seemed to have to do with the institutions that he loved, and if there weren't an institution already to fight a battle, he would create one."[38] In Brown's opinion, the saving of the Old Patent Office Building and its adaptation for the National Portrait Gallery (fig. 66) was Finley's "masterpiece."[39] After Finley's death in 1977 the National Portrait Gallery Commission adopted a "very beautiful" resolution in his memory, "because it was recognized by everyone around that table that without David Finley that National Portrait Gallery would simply not exist."[40]

NOTES

1. Finley, *Standard of Excellence*, 32.

2. Bob Thompson, "America's Hall of Fame: A National Portrait Gallery and the Culture of Celebrity," *Washington Post Magazine*, 13 June 1999, 16, quoting Margaret Christman, historian at the National Portrait Gallery, Smithsonian Institution. Ms. Christman has graciously reviewed a draft of this chapter and provided important details and factual support for David Finley's vital role in founding the Portrait Gallery.

3. Leonard Carmichael (then secretary of the Smithsonian Institution) to David Finley, 2 December 1954. Finley Papers, Library of Congress, box 35.

4. Thompson, "America's Hall of Fame," 16.

5. Carmichael to Finley; "Guide to Smithsonian Archives," 1996, 222.

6. National Gallery of Art Web site, www.nga.gov, consulted on 12 December 2004. Thomas Benedict Clarke, a New York manufacturer of collars and cuffs, made a fortune and retired from business at age forty-two to pursue his interest in collecting art. Starting in the early 1900s, he began to collect portraits by or of famous Americans and considered establishing a national portrait gallery, but at his death in 1931 his will directed that his collection be sold.

7. David Finley to the trustees of the A. W. Mellon Trust, 22 December 1953. Finley Papers, Library of Congress, box 35; and Finley, *Standard of Excellence*, 32.

8. Confidential minutes of an interview with Andrew Mellon, 8 January 1936. Smithsonian Archives, RG 426, box 5.

9. Finley, *Standard of Excellence*, 48.

10. Hearings, Committee on the Library, House of Representatives, 75th Cong., 1st sess., 17 February 1937.

11. Finley, *Standard of Excellence*, 32; J. Carter Brown, remarks at Oatlands, 14 May 1977, transcript, p. 22. Oatlands Archives.

12. In *Standard of Excellence*, 56–57, Finley recalled spending hours in front of the courthouse with John Russell Pope, considering the building as a model for the National Gallery of Art.

13. David Finley to Huntington Cairns, 31 March 1948. Finley Papers, Library of Congress, box 35.

14. David Finley to Senator Theodore F. Green, 6 July 1950. Finley Papers, Library of Congress, box 35.

15. Green to Finley, 15 June 1951. Finley Papers, Library of Congress, box 35.

16. David Finley to President Harry S. Truman, 14 July 1952. Finley Papers, Library of Congress, box 35.

17. Finley to Green, 22 August 1952.

18. Finley to the Mellon Trust, 22 December 1953.

19. Robert Mills (1781–1855), born in Charleston, was one of the first professional American-born architects. His best-known works are the Washington Monument and the Treasury Building. Mills designed the first wing of the Old Patent Office Building before his death, but Finley always gave his fellow Carolinian credit for the whole building, the rest of which followed Mills's original design.

20. Carter Brown, remarks at Oatlands, 22.

21. The People to People program was a favorite project of President Eisenhower's to combat the spread of communism by encouraging Americans to work directly with citizens overseas in areas of common interest. Sherman Adams, who had general oversight of the program as Eisenhower's domestic policy advisor, was a former governor of New Hampshire and bore the title "Assistant to the President," equivalent to today's chief of staff.

22. Finley, *Standard of Excellence*, 33.

23. "Legislative History of Transfer of Patent Office Bldg. To the Smithsonian Institution" (1960). Smithsonian Archives, RG 426, box 18. David Finley had developed a close working relationship with President Eisenhower, and in 1954 Eisenhower sent Finley a note of condolence on the death of his mother, "with warm regard." Later that year Eisenhower thanked Finley "for your helpfulness in furnishing pictures for my office" and lent Finley a book called *The Secret Formulas and Techniques of the Masters* by Jacques Maroger. Finley sent Eisenhower a book for his grandchildren, *Signs and Symbols in Christian Art*, following the President's tour of an exhibition at the National Gallery. Letters from Eisenhower to Finley, 9 May and 19 June 1954, 31 January 1956, Finley Papers, box 8, NGA Archives.

24. Legislative History (1960), Smithsonian Archives, RU 426, box 18.

25. Public Law 87-443, 87th Cong., S. 1057, 27 April 1962.

26. Carmichael to Finley, 18 March 1963. Finley Papers, Library of Congress, box 34.

27. Charles Nagel to Finley, 28 January and 23 February 1966; and Wilmarth Sheldon (Lefty) Lewis to Finley, 1 February 1966. Finley Papers, Library of Congress, box 35.

28. Mrs. A.D. Pollock Gilmour to David Finley, 10 September 1964. Finley Papers, Library of Congress, box 34. She attributed the portrait to Gilbert Stuart, but it is now in the National Portrait Gallery, attributed to Cephas Thompson, c. 1810–1811.

29. Kathleen Dexter McCormick to David Finley, 1 December 1964. Finley Papers, Library of Congress, box 34. This bequest came to the National Portrait Gallery in 1968.

30. The Corcoran portrait was painted in 1884 by George P.A. Healey. It remains as part of the collection of the National Portrait Gallery.

31. David Finley to Dwight D. Eisenhower, 8 November 1966. Finley Papers, Library of Congress, box 35.

32. Eisenhower to Finley, 14 November 1966.

33. Charles Nagel to S. Dillon Ripley, 15 December 1966. Smithsonian Archives, RG 426, box 18.

34. David Finley to Mrs. Francis Lenygon, 12 December 1967. Finley Papers, Library of Congress, box 36. Daniel Webster was a close friend of William Wilson Corcoran's and had rented Corcoran House for many years. The sideboard may date from that period.

35. Marvin S. Sadik to John D. Ehrlichman, 2 March 1973. Smithsonian Archives, RG 426, box 36. The Finleys attended Nixon's inaugural ball in 1969 and in 1970 went to a state dinner the Nixons hosted at the White House for Andrew Wyeth and his wife. Both David and Margaret were stalwart supporters of Richard Nixon during the Watergate scandal, believing right up to his resignation in 1974 that the President was entitled to the benefit of the doubt. Interview, Joan Beauregard Williams.

36. Within a month Ehrlichman himself was gone, and Sadik's recommendation became one more casualty of Watergate.

37. Carter Brown, remarks at Oatlands, 23.

38. Carter Brown, remarks at Oatlands, 8.

39. Interview with J. Carter Brown, conducted by the author, 12 July 1999.

40. Carter Brown, remarks at Oatlands, 23–24.

67. Margaret and David Finley in the gazebo at their garden at
Little Oatlands, 1962

14

The Man Within

1890–1977

NO ACCOUNT OF THE FACTS OF David Finley's life and career, no matter how complete, can do full justice to the measure of the man. Always a private person, much of his substance was known only to himself and to Margaret, though his family and close friends had glimpses of the man within and gained a rich sense of his character and values. From his youth in York, South Carolina, until his death in Georgetown, he took care of his family, his friends, friends of friends, acquaintances—even total strangers.[1] Anyone who needed assistance, whether they asked for it or not, got help from David Finley. Within him was a broad vein of generosity that never gave out.

As a young man, spending a few months in York in 1915 before he left for Philadelphia, Finley organized a night school with his friend Bedford Moore for workers at a local cotton mill, many of them illiterate. Appalled to learn that "one fifth of the white population" of York County could not read or write,[2] Finley and Moore set up three classrooms in a vacant cottage belonging to one of the local mills and began to teach some seventy of the workers the rudiments of reading and arithmetic. David's sister Frances and two church volunteers taught the women, while David and Bedford and two friends taught the men. Kerosene lamps provided lighting, and the Finley family contributed fifty books for a library.[3] Finley was encouraged by the response of the students, most of whom were eager to learn, even at the end of twelve-hour workdays. But conditions were far from ideal. As Finley noted in his journal, "I shall always associate the smell of kerosene oil & unpainted walls with night school. Frances was unkind enough to suggest dirt, long undisturbed, as the offending element; and it probably is, though we have labored long and hard to make it presentable."[4] How long their "University," as his father called it, continued after Finley left for Philadelphia is not known. But it had at least one lasting result: the marriage in 1916 of his sister Elizabeth to Bedford Moore.

After his father died in 1917 at the age of fifty-five, David Finley assumed responsibility for his younger siblings. When his youngest sister, Margaret, graduated from Winthrop College in 1920, he had a dress made for her by a French woman in New York "at a cost which nearly equaled the expense of a year at Winthrop."[5] In the 1920s he found time to help his brothers get into good schools and colleges and get started in their careers, even while he often worked overtime for the Treasury Department. He put them up in his home for months at a time when they were in Washington for work or study.[6] David Finley always kept in close touch with his South Carolina family. His mother lived to the age of ninety-two, making her home in York with her son Gist and his wife but spending a few weeks with each of her eight children every year, even into her old age. When Bessie Gist Finley died in 1954, all of the children gathered for her funeral, the first time they had been together since their youth (fig. 68).[7]

Meanwhile, in 1935, just four years after David Finley and Margaret Morton Eustis were married, the Finleys took into their hearts and home two orphaned daughters of friends and raised them as their own. Renée and Joan Beauregard, ages nine and eight, were the children of Pierre G. T. "Gustave" Beauregard II, a lawyer from New Orleans who was the grandson of the famed Confederate general. David Finley and Gustave Beauregard had met during the First World War, becoming close friends, and Finley served as an usher at Beauregard's wedding

68. David Finley with his siblings in 1954. Front: David, Frances, Margaret,
Elizabeth and John; rear: Robert, Gist, and States

to Mildred Green, who was by coincidence related to Margaret Eustis through a distant connection.[8] The ceremony took place in Washington on 28 November 1922, and Finley recorded in his journal going to a supper for the wedding party two nights before, when they "drank the bride's health in a silver cup filled with the last of 14 quarts of whiskey given by an admirer to Gen. Beauregard in 1868, to be drunk at the wedding of his oldest grandson."[9]

The Beauregards then moved to New York, where David Finley often visited them. Between 1924 and 1928 they had one son and three daughters.[10] But Gustave contracted tuberculosis in 1929 and died in 1931. And when Mildred died of tuberculosis four years later, their son and youngest daughter went to live with cousins in Tennessee, and the two middle girls, Renée and Joan, came to the Finleys' weekend home, Little Oatlands, ostensibly for the summer; then in September the girls were told that they would be staying permanently. They became wards of the Finleys but were never legally adopted, because David Finley

69. Richard and Joan Beauregard Williams at a National Gallery reception with Jane and Bedford Moore III, the latter David Finley's nephew, 1956

felt they should retain the distinguished Beauregard name. The girls were brought up properly, with governesses and private schools, and Joan remained particularly close to her "Uncle David" and "Muzzy" throughout their lives.[11]

Finley held Renée and Joan to the same high standards he expected of himself. He abhorred self-promotion and encouraged modest behavior, cautioning the girls against boasting, even in their youthful excitement. He resisted any pressure to bend rules in their favor, enforcing a strict but loving code of conduct. When Joan graduated from Bryn Mawr College, for instance, having minored in art history, she interviewed with Harry McBride, the administrator of the National Gallery, and was thrilled when he offered her a job. But Finley quickly vetoed the idea, calling it "nepotism" and insisting that none of his relatives be allowed to work at the Gallery while he was director, no matter how lowly the position.[12] In 1950 Joan Beauregard married Richard P. Williams, a young lawyer, Yale graduate, and Marine Corps veteran (fig. 69). They made their home in northwest Washington and raised three sons—David Finley, Richard P. Jr., and Ian—visiting Little Oatlands often. The Finleys formed a strong bond with their growing grandsons.[13]

In their prime David and Margaret Finley enjoyed a stimulating professional, intellectual, and social life in the city. Socially, David maintained memberships at the Metropolitan, the Alibi, and the Chevy Chase Clubs in Washington and the Century Club in New York. He and Margaret (always known to her friends as "Margie") gave elegant small dinner parties at home in Georgetown. Guests would arrive in black tie and dinner dress at 8:00 p.m. sharp, to be greeted at the door by their hosts and introduced to other guests over cocktails. Seated for dinner, which was served promptly at 8:30, those gathered could bask in the Finleys' warm hospitality, restrained charm, and attentive conversation. These intimate occasions not only nurtured important professional connections but also encouraged intelligent discourse, a cordial exchange of ideas, and friendships in the best tradition of old-school Washington.[14]

At a dinner for Lady Nancy Astor, who was visiting the Finleys in 1956, the guest list included Senator and Mrs. J. William Fulbright, Governor and Mrs. Sherman Adams (he was Eisenhower's principal aide), Mr. and Mrs. David K. E. Bruce, Mr. and Mrs. Allen Dulles (he was head of the CIA), and Joseph Alsop.[15] Another frequent British visitor was Sir Kenneth Clark, later Lord Clark of Saltwood. Finley first came to know Clark as the director of the National Gallery in London in the 1930s, and their friendship blossomed after the war. In 1949 Finley sponsored Clark's son Alan on a working visit to the United States, and during the next twenty-five years, when Clark was an increasingly popular lecturer and television personality in America, he and his wife, Jane, stayed with the Finleys in Georgetown on several occasions, often for more than a week at a time. As with all distinguished visitors, Finley arranged the visits with great care. For instance, in 1951

70. The Finleys in Hollywood in 1947, with Douglas Fairbanks Jr. and his wife, Mary Lee, whom Margaret had befriended during the war

he introduced Clark to Secretary of State and Mrs. Dean Acheson, Walter Lippman, Mrs. Truxton Beale, Duncan Phillips, Mrs. Arthur Woods, and Joseph Alsop.[16]

At home Finley seldom talked about his work at the National Gallery, but his professional life inevitably overlapped with his private life to some degree. He was often called upon to welcome important visitors, for instance, and told his family one Saturday that he had to give a tour to a special guest, later admitting that the woman was charming. When asked her name, he said it was "a Miss Bergman from Hollywood." Margaret and Joan were both "crushed" not to meet Ingrid Bergman, then at the height of her fame. But the Finleys did become good friends with Mr. and Mrs. Douglas Fairbanks Jr. when Fairbanks was stationed in Washington with the navy and his wife volunteered at the Red Cross, where she met Margaret Finley. After the war the couples exchanged visits in Georgetown and Hollywood (fig. 70).[17]

71. The Andrew Mellon Memorial Fountain, 1952, planned and realized by David Finley, designed by Otto Eggers

And the Finleys entertained many illustrious people from the art world in their home, including Andrew Mellon, John Russell Pope, Chester Dale, Rush Kress, and Andrew Wyeth. Ailsa Mellon Bruce would stay with the Finleys in Georgetown and at Little Oatlands.

In 1952, fifteen years after Andrew Mellon's death and more than ten years after the opening of Mellon's "gift to the nation," David Finley created a memorial to him—this one with Mellon's name on it. He arranged for a graceful fountain to be built at the apex of the Federal Triangle on Constitution Avenue across from the National Gallery, personally raising the funds and overseeing the design by Otto Eggers. In season, water flows over the lip of a large, circular black marble basin in an unbroken veil, an enduring tribute to both Mellon and Finley—marked by beauty, dignity, and repose, and notably avoiding ostentation (fig. 71).

Those who knew David Finley best used similar words to describe his formidable influence on people, a combination of personal grace and resolve. Joseph Alsop published a newspaper column in 1956 that tried to convey the unique quality of his friend's appeal: "David Finley's beautiful manners and mild appearance mask a steely determination and a happy ruthlessness that would not be entirely out of place in the Kremlin." Lord Kenneth Clark wrote an obituary of David Finley that also invoked his disarming impact: "He was the most modest and inconspicuous of men, small, quiet, courteous, and as thin as a piece of paper; but he had a will of iron and a matchless skill in overcoming bureaucratic and political obstruction." And J. Carter Brown in May 1977 observed: "There was a marvelous combination in David Finley in which at one and the same time he had the softness of velvet gloves but one of the most iron and determined wills underneath them, and this I think was the secret of his immense achievement."[18] Yet Finley's closest friends and relatives also mention his wit, his warmth, and his genuine interest in people of all stations in life—not just the rich and powerful. He undoubtedly had an elitist approach in terms of going to the top to solicit support for his many causes. But he extended himself to meet those at every level.[19]

The Finleys were also content to keep their own company. They felt most at home in the northern Virginia countryside, sheltered by the grand old oaks and walnut trees of Little Oatlands, near Leesburg. Margaret's mother, Edith Eustis, had overseen the restoration of the splendid formal gardens on the adjoining grounds of the Oatlands mansion, and Margaret and David Finley were happiest working in their lovely garden at Little Oatlands (fig. 72). It covered two acres, bordered by stone walls in a classic Italian design. Boxwood allées led to fountains and figural statues, two of which Margaret had herself sculpted in her youth. A small gazebo in the west wall of the garden (see fig. 67) had a beautiful view of the surrounding valley and provided a delightful spot where they often relaxed with a drink at the end of the day. Next to the garden in 1952 they added a swimming pool, walled in fieldstone, where David Finley occasionally swam laps in a stately breaststroke. A guest cottage on the property provided hospitality for grown children, grandchildren, and other visitors. Anne Eustis Emmet, Margaret's sister, lived

72. A replica of the *Mercury* from the Rotunda of National Gallery
of Art in the garden at Little Oatlands

down the hill from Little Oatlands in a remodeled historic house called
the Hamlet and also maintained a house in Georgetown. The two sisters
remained close and jointly donated Oatlands House and its gardens
to the National Trust in 1965 after inheriting the property from their
mother.[20]

David Finley was a lifelong churchgoer, active in both city and
country parishes. He spent much of thirty years (1946 until his death) as
a member of the Cathedral Chapter of the Washington National Cathedral and a vital participant in the building committee and was president
of the National Cathedral Association for three years (1956–1959). He
then referred to the cathedral as "the most important building operation
I know of."[21] In addition, Finley was elected to the vestries of both the
historic St. John's Episcopal Church on Lafayette Square, where the

Finleys attended services during the winter, and the Church of Our Saviour near Oatlands, which they attended in summer and on holidays. He took pleasure in the fact that he was the junior warden of the Oatlands church at the same time his gardener was the senior warden.[22] And he put his faith into practice. A colleague at the National Gallery and at church for thirty years said of him, "He was Christian. He believed in doing the right thing."[23]

For many years the Eustis and Finley families had sustained their small country church with both financial contributions and leadership. When attendance at the Oatlands church declined in the mid-1960s to the point where some in the Episcopal hierarchy thought it should be closed, it was David Finley who persuaded the dean of the Episcopal Virginia Theological Seminary to recruit an energetic young seminarian, Elijah B. White III, to lead regular Sunday morning services there. Within two years attendance increased sufficiently to revitalize the church. White left for missionary service in the Fiji Islands, where he was ordained to the priesthood and served for several years before returning to Virginia in 1971. When a subsequent rector of Our Saviour announced his retirement in late 1976, David Finley again rendered "the most sagacious and farsighted service" at a vestry meeting held in his study at Little Oatlands on New Year's Day of 1977. As the group considered possible candidates to replace the departing rector, "Mr. Finley did not mince words. 'There's no need to drag this out,' he told them. 'We all know we need to get Lige White back here.'"[24] The Reverend Elijah B. White III returned to Our Saviour in time for Easter 1977. Although David Finley was no longer there to greet him, Finley's wisdom and generosity live on in the still-flourishing parish of the Church of Our Saviour, where Elijah White is still the rector.

Anita Graf (Mrs. Elijah B.) White, now chair of the Oatlands board of directors, served as parish treasurer at Our Saviour and attended that meeting of the vestry at Little Oatlands. She later recalled that David Finley's frame had shrunk by then but that every Sunday he was at Little Oatlands he still attended morning services at the country church, bundled up in a heavy overcoat and leaning on Margaret's arm. Margaret had always been a few inches taller than he, but the

73. David Finley with President Lyndon B. Johnson at the White House, c. 1968

difference became more marked in their final years, even as his mind remained as clear and decisive as ever. True to their principles, the Finleys attended official events in Washington under all administrations, right up to the last years of their lives (figs. 73 and 74), and he chaired a meeting of the White House Historical Association within a week of his death.

David Finley was in good spirits when the Finleys helped celebrate Joan Beauregard Williams's fiftieth birthday on 27 January 1977. But two days later he took to his bed and had difficulty breathing. Margaret and Joan had an oxygen tank brought to the house in Georgetown as well as nursing care around the clock. But within thirty-six hours it was all over. Early in the morning of 1 February 1977 David Edward Finley died quietly in his sleep. The little man with the big heart who had overcome delicate health all his life had lived for eighty-six years, four months, and nineteen days.

The author and columnist Joseph Alsop may have captured him best when he wrote to Margaret Finley after David's death:

74. Active to the end, David and Margaret Finley greet Secretary
Henry Kissinger and Clement Conger at the State Department in
1976, the year before their deaths.

Dear Margie:

If you asked me who was the kindest, sweetest, and most gentle
person I'd ever known, I should have to say "David."

What was so amazing, however, was that with this extreme
kindness & sweetness he contained a strength of perfect iron
where the service of our country was concerned. If you asked
me who, of all our friends, had left the finest personal monument, I should have to say "David"—for it's to him, more I
think than those who gave the money or anything else, that we
have the wonderful gift of our great national art museum. "Si
monumentum requiris, circumspice" [If you would seek the
man's monument, look around] is written on Wren's tomb in
the crypt of St. Paul's. They should have a memorial plaque to
David with the same legend, for it <u>is</u> his monument.

But it was only one item in a long list of self-service to his country & his community—all performed with total dedication, with no thought of personal advantage, in short, with no idea in mind except the public good.

I shall miss him always. So I send you all my loving sympathy.

All love,

Joe [25]

Without David, Margaret was lost. As Jacqueline Kennedy wrote in her note of condolence, "Your loss is so deep—you spent so many years together" (fig. 76). And as the years went by, they had grown ever closer. Just four months after he died, on the day before their forty-sixth wedding anniversary, Margaret died also. Their graves in Georgetown's Oak Hill Cemetery are marked by simple stones engraved with a cross above their names and the years of their births and deaths. At their request, their stones are of Tennessee marble, like the West Building of the National Gallery. [26]

In his will, in addition to providing for Margaret, Renée, Joan, and the Williams family, David Finley left bequests to each of his siblings or their surviving spouses, to fifteen nieces and nephews, to his gardener, a maid, and two former secretaries. He left specific works of art and heirlooms to the Museum of Fine Arts, Columbia, South Carolina; the Corcoran Gallery of Art; and the Robert E. Lee Memorial Foundation, Stratford Hall, Virginia. He made cash bequests in varying amounts to St. John's Church, Lafayette Square, the Church of Our Saviour at Oatlands, Washington National Cathedral, the National Gallery of Art, the National Portrait Gallery, the Corcoran Gallery of Art, and the National Trust for Historic Preservation in the United States. [27] He made gifts of real estate to the National Gallery, to the National Trust, and to the American Red Cross. In the case of his gifts to the National Trust, he stipulated that the proceeds were to be added to the Oatlands endowment. Finally, he left the Library of Congress all his papers pertaining to the National Gallery, the Fine Arts Commission, and the National Trust as well as all other papers "as may be of interest to said Library." [28]

David Finley had lived a long and rich life. He had been given many gifts, and he made the most of them. In the words of his citation from Yale in 1946, he had shown that "the truly fine art is that of giving to others the blessings that one has himself enjoyed."[29] Following his death Finley's fellow trustees at the National Trust resolved to name the rotunda of the new headquarters building in his memory. At the Washington National Cathedral, set just inside the southwest portal, is a stone tablet with an inscription in memory of both David and Margaret Finley (fig. 75). On the other side of the portal a stone bench has an intricately embroidered needlework cushion with three medallions: the National Gallery's West Building on the left, the fountain in the Little Oatlands garden in the center, and Oatlands mansion on the right.[30] At the entrance to the New Executive Office Building on Jackson Place, Lafayette Square, another stone tablet records David Finley's support for Jacqueline Kennedy's efforts to preserve the square. And in the Church of Our Saviour, twin bronze plaques detail both David and Margaret Finley's many services in Washington and at Oatlands.

But David Finley's true memorials are the painting galleries, sculpture halls, garden courts, and the grand Rotunda of the National Gallery of Art; the avenues, squares, buildings, and vistas of monumental Washington; and the thousands of historic structures in communities across America that have been preserved, restored, and adapted for public benefit with the help of the National Trust. None of these bear his name, but together they attest to the life's work of a man who had so much to do with defining the cultural maturity of his country.

"If you would see the man's monument, look around."

75. Finley memorial tablet, Washington National Cathedral

THE VIKING PRESS INC · PUBLISHERS

625 MADISON AVENUE · NEW YORK · N Y · 10022

Cable: Vikpress Telephone: *(212) PL 5-4330*

Dear Mrs Finley

I was so terribly sad to hear that Mr Finley was gone from a world which he brought so much light to.

Please accept my deepest sympathy. Your loss is so deep— you spent so many years together.

I will never forget Mr Finleys generosity of spirit. There can be few

76. Letter of condolence from Jacqueline Kennedy Onassis to Margaret Finley, February 1977

THE VIKING PRESS INC · PUBLISHERS
625 MADISON AVENUE · NEW YORK · N Y · 10022
Cable: Vikpress   *Telephone: (212) PL 5-4330*

who were like him. I will never forget the morning after Jack's Inauguration — He so kindly came to see me — there I was propped up in bed. I knew none of one's hopes for restoring the White House could work without his approval. He gave it so generously, so gaily, with such warmth. And then, sent over that beautiful highboy, the very first gift to the White House. I would have

3

THE VIKING PRESS INC · PUBLISHERS
625 MADISON AVENUE · NEW YORK · N Y · 10022
Cable: Vikpress   Telephone: (212) PL 5-4330

loved him whichever way I had known him. He had such warmth, was so kind to young people.

I hope it may be some consolation to you to know, from so many people, how much he was loved and how much he will be missed —

Most Sincerely

Jacqueline Kennedy Onassis

1. When Finley had risen to a visible post at the Treasury in the early 1930s, he helped a struggling South Carolina architect whom he had never met get a job designing a post office. Correspondence wih Charles C. Wilson, Columbia, South Carolina, August and September 1931. Finley Papers, Library of Congress, box 79.

2. "They are typical of York County in respect to being poorly educated." Finley journal, 31 March 1915. The classes met two nights a week, from 7:00 to 9:00, using rough benches with long boards twelve inches wide to serve as desks.

3. Finley had lobbied the South Carolina legislature to fund a traveling library that would serve farm families and mill workers in smaller towns, but his bill was stalled. The lawmakers "debated passing a child labor law, raising the minimum age limit from 12 to 14 years, but in their usual spineless fashion they merely talked about it. Nothing was done." Finley journal, 21 March 1915.

4. Finley journal, 11 April 1915.

5. Finley journal, 12 June 1920. Margaret Adams Finley was the salutatorian of her class at Winthrop College in Rock Hill, South Carolina.

6. For example, he arranged for his youngest brother, John Campbell, to attend the Episcopal High School in Alexandria and got him an appointment to Annapolis. John Campbell left the Naval Academy for some reason after one year but graduated from the University of North Carolina at Chapel Hill.

7. Elizabeth Moore lived in Columbia, South Carolina, where she and her husband were active in community affairs, including the founding of the Columbia Museum of Art in 1950, with assistance from her oldest brother, "Edward." Gist Finley earned his law degree at Georgetown University in Washington and returned to York, where he had an active law practice and was the solicitor of the Sixth Judicial District of South Carolina for many years. A bluff sportsman, he enjoyed calling his older brother "Lord Alger," for his union with the Eustis family and friends in high places. Bob was an accountant and banker in North Carolina; States an engineer with a power company in Tennessee; Margaret Collins a schoolteacher in Spartansburg, South Carolina; and John an executive with Alcoa (a Mellon enterprise) in Seattle.

8. Both were cousins of Arthur Hellen, a Washington lawyer and an usher at David and Margaret's wedding. Mildred's grandfather was Charles Green of Savannah, Georgia, who hosted General Sherman after he had taken the city just before Christmas 1864. According to the family, Green, a leading citizen of the city, feared that Sherman would burn Savannah, as he had Atlanta. So Green went to see Sherman and invited him to stay at his home. Sherman accepted Green's hospitality for a month, and Savannah was spared. Related by Joan Beauregard Williams to the author, December 2004.

9. Finley journal, 7 December 1922.

10. Pierre G. T. Beauregard III in 1924; Renée in 1925; Joan Douglass Toutant in 1927; and Susanne in 1928.

11. The girls were always awed by Margaret's mother, the majestically tall Mrs. Eustis, whom they called "Gran."

12. Joan Beauregard Williams interview by Ritchie, 17.

13. Margaret saw that Little Oatlands went to Joan and Richard Williams at her death, and the Williams family continues to provide leadership for Oatlands in the Finley tradition into the twenty-first century. The Williams family, particularly Joan, has also taken a strong interest in this biography of David Finley. In a series of meetings and interviews, formal and informal, at Little Oatlands and elsewhere, between 1998 and 2005, Joan Williams has provided numerous details of her life with David and Margaret Finley. David Finley Williams and Richard P. Williams Jr. have offered valuable suggestions and encouragement and reviewed early manuscript drafts. Then in 2001 Mrs. Williams found an old box in a bookcase at Little Oatlands that contained David Finley's journals from 1913 through 1928, which had somehow been overlooked when the bulk of his personal papers were donated to the National Gallery Archives in the early 1980s. These proved to be a bonanza of new material and provided the inspiration for a full biography of David Finley.

14. Ann Rath recalled that when she and her husband, Fred Rath, the first director of the National Trust, were dinner guests in the Finley home in the 1950s, David Finley went out of his way to be sure they were introduced to everyone and paired with appropriate partners during cocktails and dinner. He, not Margaret, was the social organizer.

15. Nancy Langhorne, Viscountess Astor (1879–1964), was born in Virginia, married first Robert Gould Shaw II of Boston and later Lord Waldorf Astor. She was the first woman elected to parliament and served for twenty-five years in the House of Commons, where she often exchanged barbs with Winston Churchill. Blunt and outspoken, she attracted wide publicity on both sides of the ocean. The Finleys had come to know Lady Astor during their stay in London in 1932–1933 and had visited the Astors at their country house at Cliveden, on the Thames in Buckinghamshire.

16. During a later visit from Clark in 1970, the Finleys' dinner guests included the Russell Trains, the Dillon Ripleys, the James Biddles (president of the National Trust), Joseph Alsop, J. Carter Brown, and the Richard Williamses. Finley Papers, NGA Archives, box 4.

17. During one visit in Georgetown, a female servant was apparently so excited by the presence of the dashing Fairbanks at a dinner party that she spilled gravy on him.

18. See Joseph Alsop, *Washington Post*, 18 March 1956, and Alsop's letter to Margaret Finley (see note 25). See also Lord Kenneth Clark's obituary of David Finley in the *Times* [London], 19 February 1977, 16; and J. Carter Brown's remarks at Oatlands, 14 May 1977, transcript, p. 5. Oatlands Archives. B. Powell Harrison, of Leesburg, Virginia, longtime preservation activist and for many years chairman of the Oatlands property council, described Finley in similar terms: "He had stamina and guts. He loved a good fight and always won, even though nobody knew he was fighting. Small and insignificant-looking at first sight, he could get people to do what he wanted without their ever knowing they were being maneuvered." Interview by the author in May 1998.

19. In 2004 Thomas McGill, a longtime National Gallery employee, who began working there when David Finley was still director, recalled that Finley made it a point to walk through the entire Gallery building on Christmas Eve, to shake hands with every single employee, from the maintenance men and guards on up, and to wish each of them a Merry Christmas. Interview by the author, October 2004. McGill began as a guard at the National Gallery in January 1955 after service in the Marine Corps. He later transferred to the National Gallery library, where he has acquired an unequaled reputation for being able to track down rare books from libraries all over the world. In January 2005 he celebrated the completion of fifty years of work for the Gallery, its longest-serving employee.

20. David Finley kept a close eye on Oatlands until his death. He personally selected its first property council of prominent local people and attended every meeting; although he sat on the sidelines and seldom said a word, when he did speak, it was worth listening. Anne Eustis Emmet and her children remained strong supporters of Oatlands along with the Finley and Williams families.

21. David Finley to Dean Francis B. Sayre of the Washington National Cathedral, 14 September 1957. Cathedral Archives.

22. The Rev. John C. Harper, former rector of St. John's Episcopal Church, Lafayette Square, interview by the author, July 1999. The Rev. Elijah B. White III, rector of the Church of Our Saviour, added that at times the roles were reversed, with David Finley serving as senior warden and the Little Oatlands gardener, Clarence Sutphen, as junior warden. Interview by the author, December 2004.

23. Kopper, *Gift to the Nation*, 161.

24. Augusta Adams, *The Church of Our Saviour, Oatlands, Virginia* (Hamilton, VA, 2001), 53–54.

25. Joseph Alsop to Margaret Finley, February 1977. Personal papers, Joan Beauregard Williams.

26. Williams interview by Ritchie, 51.

27. At the National Gallery the Finley bequests were used to fund the ongoing David E. Finley Fellowships at the Center for Advanced Study in the Visual Arts and to purchase two major paintings: Hans Mielich's *Member of the Fröschl Family*, c. 1539/1540 (1984.66.1), and Eastman Johnson's *Brown Family*, 1869 (1978.72.1).

28. Will executed 19 December 1975; admitted to probate in the Superior Court of the District of Columbia, 24 March 1977.

29. Citation, David Edward Finley, D.F.A., Yale University, June 1946. Finley Papers, NGA Archives, box 36-18.

30. These memorials were made possible by donations to the Cathedral Chapter from the Finleys' many friends, colleagues, and admirers.

Epilogue

SOME THIRTY YEARS AFTER David Finley's death, the Washington that he knew so well and did so much to beautify has become the undisputed capital of the world. Democratic and Republican administrations come and go, as they did throughout his life, but despite increasingly bitter partisanship on many issues, both parties continue to support the institutions he built.

In 1978, the year after David Finley died, the National Gallery of Art dedicated its new East Building, brilliantly designed by I. M. Pei, who was personally selected for that job by Paul Mellon, in much the same way Andrew Mellon had selected John Russell Pope for what is now called the West Building four decades earlier. J. Carter Brown succeeded John Walker as director in 1969 (fig. 77), and he served in much the same capacity that David Finley had for the senior Mellon in 1936. But there was a major difference. Both Paul Mellon and I. M. Pei lived to see their dream become a reality, whereas Andrew Mellon and John Russell Pope both died in the early stages of the construction of their project, before many critical design issues had been resolved. It fell to David Finley to carry on their mission.

77. The first three directors of the National Gallery of Art in 1969—
David Finley flanked by J. Carter Brown (left) and John Walker
(right)—at Walker's retirement. They led the National Gallery for a
total of fifty-five years, succeeded by the fourth and current director,
Earl A. Powell III.

David Finley's death marked the end of the beginning of the
National Gallery of Art. The Gallery remains preeminent in Washington and stands alongside the world's greatest art museums. Although no
one from the Mellon family now sits on its board of trustees, the basic
structure David Finley established endures. Finley, and for that matter
Andrew Mellon, would feel very comfortable there, at least in the West
Building. But the opening of the East Building ushered in a new age,
and the efforts of David E. Finley have sometimes been forgotten. Yet
in the main reading room of the National Gallery Library in the East
Building, two bronze busts stand silent guard at opposite sides of the
room. One is of Andrew W. Mellon, the other of David E. Finley.[1]

The National Trust for Historic Preservation, from its headquarters
in the building where Andrew Mellon lived and where he and Finley

studied his masterpieces, leads a robust historic preservation movement in all fifty states and in more than 2,500 cities and towns across the nation. It still protects great houses like Lyndhurst, Oatlands, and James Madison's Montpelier,[2] but it looks more and more to every kind of building and historic property that defines our past and our greatness as a nation, from Touro Synagogue in Newport, Rhode Island, to naval installations at Pearl Harbor, Hawaii.

The National Trust continues to work closely with the government, as David Finley envisioned, but now sometimes challenges it on matters of principle. Of the nearly 200 court cases brought by the National Trust to date, many have been against the government. Many of its trustees still have wealth and power, but many others represent the grassroots of the preservation movement. The scope of the buildings and districts protected as well as the people and methods involved have grown more diverse since Finley's day. But the basic values of pride in our country and in its history, architecture, and culture are basically the same as when David Finley went to the Hampton mansion to see Thomas Sully's *Lady with a Harp* in 1944, saw the threats to such properties, and went on to create a national organization to address the problem.

The U.S. Commission of Fine Arts remains an active player in the cultural and political life of Washington, though perhaps not as much as in Finley's day. Recently the commission approved the massive World War II Monument on the Mall between the Washington Monument and the Lincoln Memorial. One cannot help but think that David Finley would somehow have found a better resolution to this controversial issue.

The Washington National Cathedral was finally finished in 1990 and stands proudly atop Washington's highest hill as a physical as well as a spiritual and cultural landmark. The National Portrait Gallery in the Old Patent Office Building is undergoing a major restoration, scheduled to reopen on 4 July 2006, and will anchor the revitalization of the old business district of Washington. The houses in which David Finley and his family lived in Georgetown, at Little Oatlands, and at the Oatlands mansion remain very much as they were when the Finleys and the Eustises were in residence. Thanks to preservation and conservation easements, they should remain so, even in the face of relentless development pressures.

The old-fashioned manners and mores that David Finley exemplified are vanishing from Washington and the nation at large. Much as he would rue many aspects of this, he would probably applaud broadening the economic, cultural, and political opportunities for his fellow Americans. Finley applied some of his favorite lines from the Greek classics to the lives of Andrew Mellon and Morton Eustis. But they apply equally well to him: "For the whole earth is the sepulchre of famous men; and their story is not graven only on stone over their native earth, but lives on far away without visible symbol, woven in the stuff of other men's lives."[3]

* * *

David Finley explained to Jacqueline Kennedy when he resigned as chairman of the Commission of Fine Arts: "I should get my papers in order, especially those about the formation and growth of the National Gallery, and write down some of the things which should be recorded."[4] Finley sent an early draft of his *Standard of Excellence: Andrew W. Mellon Founds the National Gallery of Art* to David Bruce in 1969 for review and received an encouraging note in return. Writing to thank Bruce, he made a typically modest protest: "I did not like to inject myself so much into my account of the founding of the National Gallery, but it was impossible to avoid it."[5]

The Smithsonian's publication of Finley's memoir, though modest in size and lacking a single photograph of Finley except one solemn studio portrait on the back of the original dust jacket, was handsomely printed and bound and contains a number of excellent black-and-white photographs of the Gallery as well as several works in its collections. The illustrations were presumably chosen by David Finley, and the present publication reproduces a number of them in color. Indeed, this biography of David Finley is enlightened by Finley's memoir of Mellon in many ways and could scarcely have been written without it. Though Finley was in his eighty-second year when he finished writing it, its crisp style and lively pace suggest a man in his prime. It is only regrettable, at least to a Finley biographer, that the author did not "inject" himself just a bit more into the story. But then, it would not have been Finley's, a man who avoided self-promotion in any form. Perhaps he would forgive a stranger for trying to correct the record.

"Let another man praise thee, and not thine own mouth; a stranger, and not thine own lips" (Proverbs 27:2).

NOTES

1. The bust of Mellon was created by the American sculptor Jo Davidson in 1927; the one of Finley by the Italian sculptor Fausta Vittoria Mengarini in 1930.

2. In 1984 the National Trust accepted stewardship of Montpelier, near Orange, Virginia. With a major grant from the Estate of Paul Mellon, Montpelier is now being carefully restored to the period of James Madison, who lived there all his life (1751–1836). The restoration will also honor the legacy of the William du Pont family, who tended Montpelier from 1901 to 1984.

3. Extract from the funeral oration of Pericles at Athens, in Thucydides, *History of the Peloponnesian War*, Jowett translation, vol. 12.

4. David Finley to Jacqueline Kennedy, 27 March 1963. Finley Papers, NGA Archives. Indeed, he did complete his *History of the National Trust for Historic Preservation* in 1963, which was privately published in 1965, and then went on to write *A Standard of Excellence: Andrew W. Mellon Founds the National Gallery of Art in Washington*, completed in 1971 and published by the Smithsonian Institution Press in 1973.

To the end of his life David Finley maintained an office in downtown Washington, on H Street overlooking Decatur House and staffed by Susan Bennett, his faithful and efficient National Gallery secretary. It was there that he completed his two books. Finley published the first book at his own expense and sent inscribed copies to many friends and colleagues. When David Bruce, then in London as ambassador to the Court of St. James's, received his *History of the National Trust*, he wrote to thank Finley and to say he hoped Finley would write a history of the National Gallery as well. Finley kept in touch with Miss Bennett after her retirement to Richmond, Virginia, and kept her informed of the activities of several successors and of the events of his own life. Finley Papers, NGA Archives, RG 28, box 2-6.

5. David Finley to David Bruce, 14 May 1969. Finley Papers, NGA Archives, RG 28, box 12.

Acknowledgments

THIS BOOK COULD NOT HAVE BEEN done without the help of two of the principal institutions that David Finley built: the National Trust for Historic Preservation and the National Gallery of Art. And it seems particularly fitting that the Estate of Paul Mellon played a key role, continuing a great partnership that began eighty years ago between David Finley and the Mellon family. Ted Terry and Beverly Carter, the Mellon executors, took a keen interest in this project and have provided steady support.

At the Trust, Tom Mayes, a Carolina gentleman like Finley, read the entire manuscript and made many improvements; his legal help was also invaluable, as was Paul Edmondson's. Dick Moe and David Brown gave encouragement from the start. Bob Benn, Frank Sanchis, Peter Brink, Byrd Wood, and Margaret Welch all lent a hand, as did David Boyce and his staff at Oatlands.

This publication would have stalled but for Judy Metro, editor in chief at the National Gallery, whose patient guidance made the dream a reality. The ever-gracious staff at the Gallery Archives, including

Maygene Daniels, Anne Ritchie, Tara Wellington, and especially Michele Willens, went well beyond the call of duty. Earl A. Powell III, Carol Kelley, Lamia Doumato, John Hand, David Alan Brown, Elizabeth Cropper, Therese O'Malley, and Tom Magill also helped in vital ways.

Charles Atherton and Sue Kohler at the U.S. Commission of Fine Arts set me on the right path many times. At the National Portrait Gallery, Margaret Christman read part of the manuscript and made several corrections, while Lisanne Garrett was unfailingly helpful. Neil Horstman and William Bushong of the White House Historical Association provided an elusive identification. A dozen libraries and their staffs were always responsive, but I would particularly like to thank the manuscript division of the Library of Congress, the Caroliniana Library at Columbia, South Carolina, and Fiorella Superbi of the Berenson Library at I Tatti.

The Richard Williams family, and especially Joan Beauregard Williams, brought David Finley alive for me. Their encouragement and financial support for my short profile of Finley in 1999 laid the foundation for this work; Joan's discovery of the Finley journals two years later was the tipping point that led me to undertake a full biography. David Finley's niece Elizabeth Brown Wakefield and nephew Jack Brown provided many essential details and filled out the portrait of the family. Others who had known Finley added a great deal, notably J. Carter Brown, Fred and Ann Rath, Powell Harrison, Patricia Collins Butler, Rev. John Harper, Rev. Elijah B. and Anita Graf White, Richard Howland, and Frank Gilbert.

I should make special mention of Phil Kopper of Preservation Press, who took an early interest, pointed out avenues of research, and offered editorial advice on part of the manuscript. Many others lent active support: Sally Sims Stokes and Jenny Levine of the University of Maryland libraries; Ernest Connally and Charles Peterson; and Terry Brust Morton and Bill Murtaugh, National Trust staffers from the Finley era; and our prompt and efficient research assistant, Jonathan Powell.

Marquand Books provided professional editorial, design, and production services of the highest order, under the insightful leadership of Ed Marquand. I would like to thank here Andrea Thomas,

Linda McDougall, Marie Weiler, Marissa Meyer, and Larissa Berry as well as Zach Hooker, Lydia Jenson, Gretchen Miller, Kate Miss, Marta Vinnedge, Carrie Wicks, and freelancers Paula Brisco and Laura Iwasaki.

And finally we come to two ladies whose skill and dedication were well nigh miraculous. Our virtuoso researcher Mary Pixley cheerfully delved into the mountains of Finley papers and related materials at the National Gallery Archives, the Library of Congress, and the Smithsonian/National Portrait Gallery archives in Washington; the National Archives at College Park, Maryland; and the Duveen Records at the Getty Research Institute, on microfilm at the Metropolitan Museum of Art in New York. She then organized and labeled everything so meticulously that even I could keep it all straight, and made numerous sapient suggestions.

I have often thought that authors must exaggerate their debts to their editors. Now I know better. Tam Curry Bryfogle brought her many years of editorial experience at the National Gallery and elsewhere to bear on my prolix and disorganized manuscript and crafted it into a cogent book, with enormous skill, untiring labor, and unfailing kindness. I shall never forget her enthusiasm, her generosity, and her sheer hard work.

And the last word must go to my wife Tess, who good-heartedly welcomed David Finley into our home and bore my frequent absences, both physical and mental, with a smile or at least a shrug. I hope she finds the effort to have been worthwhile.

D. A. D.
September 2005

Selected Bibliography

A Note on Sources

David E. Finley left a clearly marked paper trail. Beginning with his service at the Treasury Department in 1922, he kept extensive files of correspondence, memoranda, and a variety of official documents. At the National Gallery of Art his notebooks on the Andrew W. Mellon Collection laid the foundation for the Gallery's curatorial records, and his correspondence with trustees, collectors, and others provides a detailed account of the Gallery's first two decades. The early history of the National Trust is also well documented, not only in Finley's files but also in the Trust's archives at the National Archives at College Park, Maryland, and at the National Trust Library at the University of Maryland, College Park. Finley's service on the U.S. Commission of Fine Arts is documented in the commission's files at the National Building Museum in Washington. After his official retirement from most of his positions, he kept an office in downtown Washington and a secretary to maintain his files, including his correspondence with Jacqueline Kennedy.

After Finley's death in 1977 his son-in-law and executor, Richard P. Williams, oversaw the transfer of his official papers to the Library of Congress, in accordance with his will, where they are preserved in the manuscript division as the Papers of David E. Finley, running to thirty-six linear feet in eighty-seven file boxes and five scrapbooks.

David Finley also kept voluminous personal records, journals, and correspondence with his extended family and network of friends and colleagues in this country and abroad as well as photographs and other memorabilia. After the National Gallery Archives was established, the Williams family in February 1978 donated an extensive collection of David Finley's personal papers, photographs, home movies, and scrapbooks to the Gallery Archives. They are maintained there as the David Finley Papers, Record Group 28, with a volume of twenty-nine cubic feet in sixty-five file boxes, plus more than a dozen rolls of film, some of which have been transferred to videotape.

In addition, Finley kept a series of private journals intermittently between 1913 and 1930. Most of these were found at Little Oatlands by Joan Beauregard Williams in 2001 and were deposited in the National Gallery Archives in 2002. They cover a wide range of matters relating to his family, his social and professional life, and his travels in the United States and Europe. Finley was always on close guard in public, and these private journal entries provide a fascinating counterpoint to his official life.

The National Archives at College Park, Maryland, has extensive materials on the work of the Roberts Commission during the Second World War as well as the archives of the National Trust for Historic Preservation. The National Portrait Gallery, the U.S. Commission of Fine Arts, the White House Historical Association, and the National Cathedral, all of Washington, D.C., have materials relating to Finley's work with each of them.

The South Caroliniana Library at the University of South Carolina in Columbia has two important collections relating to Finley: the papers of his father, David E. Finley Sr., and of his aunt, Margaret Adams Gist. Winthrop University in Rock Hill, South Carolina, has the papers of Finley's brother William Gist Finley. The courthouses in York, South Carolina, and Gastonia, North Carolina, have land and probate records pertaining to the Finley and Gist families, as do the archives of

Bethel Presbyterian Church in Clover, South Carolina. The DAR Library in Washington has published genealogies of the Gist family.

Additional material has been obtained from the Library of Congress, the Alderman Library at the University of Virginia in Charlottesville, the public libraries of York and Rock Hill, South Carolina, and the Berenson Library at the Harvard Center for Renaissance Studies at I Tatti, Settignano, Italy, which has a file of Finley's letters to Bernard Berenson between 1938 and 1959.

The Archives of American Art at the Smithsonian Institution contain the George Stout Papers, including his wartime journals, on microfilm.

Finally, the Duveen Records, Getty Research Institute, on microfilm at the Metropolitan Museum of Art in New York, yielded extensive details of the dealings of that firm, and particularly of Joseph Duveen, with both Andrew W. Mellon and David E. Finley, from 1918 to 1939.

Interviews

Charles H. Atherton, Washington, D.C.
J. Carter Brown, Washington, D.C.
John F. (Jack) Brown, Columbia, South Carolina
Patricia Collins Butler, La Jolla, California
Ernest A. Connally, Arlington, Virginia
Frank B. Gilbert, Washington, D.C.
Rev. John C. Harper, Washington, D.C.
B. Powell Harrison, Leesburg, Virginia
Terry B. Morton, Chevy Chase, Maryland
William J. Murtagh, Rockport, Maine
Charles E. Peterson, Philadelphia, Pennsylvania
Ann Richardson Rath, Cooperstown, New York
Frederick J. Rath Jr., Cooperstown, New York
Elizabeth Brown Wakefield, Anderson, South Carolina
Anita Graf White, Oatlands, Virginia
Rev. Elijah B. White III, Oatlands, Virginia
David Finley Williams, Esq., Chevy Chase, Maryland
Joan Beauregard Williams, Little Oatlands, Virginia
Richard P. Williams, Esq., Little Oatlands, Virginia
Richard P. Williams Jr., AIA, Washington, D.C.

Unpublished Sources

Bethel Presbyterian Church records, Clover, South Carolina

J. Carter Brown, remarks at Oatlands, 14 May 1977. Oatlands Archives

Ernest A. Connally, "Wartime," private collection, Arlington, Virginia

Homer Stillé Cummings diaries, University of Virginia

Duveen Brothers Records, The Getty Research Institute, Los Angeles, on microfilm, Metropolitan Museum of Art, New York

Warner Eustis, "The Eustis Family in the United States from 1657 to 1968," Newton, Massachusetts, 1968, 1970

David E. Finley journals, 1913–1929, property of Joan Beauregard Williams, Little Oatlands, Virginia. On deposit at the National Gallery of Art (NGA), Gallery Archives

David E. Finley Papers, Library of Congress, manuscript division, Washington, DC

David E. Finley Papers, NGA Archives, Washington, DC

David Edward Finley [Sr.] Papers, South Caroliniana Library, Columbia

Gaston County land records, Gastonia, North Carolina

Margaret Adams Gist Papers, South Caroliniana Library, Columbia

Burton J. Hendrick, "Andrew William Mellon, 1855–1937: A Biography," Estate of Paul Mellon

Andrew W. Mellon diaries from 1927, 1928, and 1929, NGA Archives

National Cathedral Archives, Washington, DC

National Council of Historic Sites, minutes of meetings, National Archives, College Park, Maryland

National Trust for Historic Preservation, minutes of meetings of board of trustees, Washington, DC

National Trust Library, University of Maryland, College Park: Charles B. Hosmer Papers; Richard H. Howland Papers; Frederick J. Rath Jr. Papers; and transcripts of oral history interviews with Robert R. Garvey Jr., Frederick J. Rath Jr., and Richard Howland, conducted by Charles B. Hosmer

U.S. Commission of Fine Arts Archives, Washington, DC

York County, South Carolina, land and probate records

Published Sources

Adams, Augusta. *The Church of Our Saviour, Oatlands, Virginia*. Hamilton, VA, 2001.

Auchincloss, Louis. *Woodrow Wilson*. New York, 2000.

Bailey, Kenneth P. *Christopher Gist*. Hamden, CT, 1976.

Behrman, S. N. *Duveen*. New York, 1952. [A widely available paperback version, subtitled *The Story of the Most Spectacular Art Dealer of All Time* and including an introduction by Glenn Lowry, published in New York, 2000, has different pagination.]

Berenson, Bernard. *The Italian Painters of the Renaissance*. Greenwich, CT, 1952.

Blum, John Morton. *From the Morgenthau Diaries*. Boston, 1959.

Boskovits, Miklós, and David Alan Brown with Robert Echols. *Italian Paintings of the Fifteenth Century*. Systematic Catalogue of the Collections, National Gallery of Art. Washington, DC, 2003.

Bradford, Sarah. *America's Queen: The Life of Jacqueline Kennedy Onassis*. New York, 2000.

Brown, David Alan. *Raphael and America*. National Gallery of Art, Washington, DC, 1983.

Burnham, David. *A Law Unto Itself: Power, Politics, and the IRS*. New York, 1989.

Butterfield, Roger. "The Millionaires' Best Friend." *Saturday Evening Post*, 8 March 1948.

Cannadine, David. *In Churchill's Shadow: Confronting the Past in Modern Britain*. Oxford, 2003.

Cisco, Walter Brian. *States Rights Gist: A South Carolina General of the Civil War*. Shippensburg, PA, 1991.

Clark, Kenneth. *Another Part of the Wood: A Self-Portrait*. London, 1974.

Cohen, Lester. *Frank Hogan Remembered*. Washington, DC, 1985.

Daniels, Jonathan. *Washington Quadrille: The Dance beside the Documents*. New York, 1968.

Dorsey, Jean Muir, and Maxwell Jay Dorsey. *Christopher Gist of Maryland and Some of His Descendants, 1679–1957*. Chicago, 1957.

Eustis, Morton Corcoran. *War Letters of Morton Eustis*. Edited by David E. Finley. Privately printed by Edith Morton Eustis. Washington, DC, 1945.

Ferrell, Robert H. *The Presidency of Calvin Coolidge*. Lawrence, KS, 1998.

Finley, David E[dward]. *Annual Report of the Chairman, Board of Trustees, National Trust for Historic Preservation*. Washington, DC, 1954 through 1962.

———. *History of the National Trust for Historic Preservation, 1947–1963*. Privately printed. Washington, DC, 1965.

———. *A Standard of Excellence: Andrew W. Mellon Founds the National Gallery of Art at Washington*. Washington, DC, 1973.

Fitzgerald, Rory. *God's Frontiersmen: The Scots-Irish in Colonial America*. London, 1989.

Freeman, Douglas Southall, *George Washington* (1948). Abridgment by Richard Harwell. New York, 1995.

Gee, Wilson. *The Gist Family of South Carolina and Its Maryland Antecedents*. Charlottesville, VA, 1934.

Gilbert, Martin. *The Second World War*. London, 1989.

Haskell, Douglas. "Saying Nothing, Going Nowhere." *Architectural Forum* 111 (August 1959).

Hastings, Lynne Dakin. *Hampton National Historic Site*. Historic Hampton, Inc. Towson, MD, 1986.

Helfrich, Kurt. "Modernism for Washington? The Kennedys and the Redesign of Lafayette Square." *Washington History* 8, no. 1. Historical Society of Washington, DC (Spring/Summer 1996).

Hodgson, Godfrey. *The Colonel: The Life and Wars of Henry Stimson, 1867–1950*. New York, 1990.

Hoover, Herbert. *The Great Depression*. New York, 1952.

———. *Memoirs: The Cabinet and the Presidency, 1920–1933*. New York, 1952.

Hosmer, Charles B., Jr. *Presence of the Past: A History of the Preservation Movement in the United States before Williamsburg*. New York, 1965.

———. *Preservation Comes of Age: From Williamsburg to the National Trust, 1926–1949*. Vol. 2. Charlottesville, VA, 1981.

Irey, Elmer Lincoln. *The Tax Dodgers*. West Albany, NY, 1948.

Jackson, Robert H. *That Man: An Insider's Portrait of Franklin D. Roosevelt*. Edited by John Q. Barrett. New York, 2003.

Kohler, Sue A. *The Commission of Fine Arts: A Brief History, 1910–1995*. Washington, DC, 1995.

Kopper, Philip. *America's National Gallery of Art: A Gift to the Nation*. New York, 1991.

Koskoff, David E. *The Mellons: The Chronicle of America's Richest Family*. New York, 1978.

Lankford, Nelson D. *The Last American Aristocrat: The Biography of Ambassador David K. E. Bruce*. Boston, 1996.

Lash, Joseph P. *Eleanor and Franklin*. New York, 1971.

Liddell Hart, B. H., *History of the Second World War*, London, 1973.

Life and Times at the South Carolina College: 1805–1905, exh. cat., McKissick Museum, University of South Carolina. Columbia, SC, 2003.

Love, Philip H. *Andrew W. Mellon, The Man and His Work*. Baltimore, 1929.

McCullough, David. *Truman*. New York, 1992.

McPherson, James M. *Battle Cry of Freedom*. New York, 1988.

Mellon, Andrew W. *Taxation: The People's Business*. New York, 1924.

Mellon, Paul. *Reflections in a Silver Spoon*. New York, 1992.

Mellon, Thomas. *Thomas Mellon and His Times*, 2nd ed. Pittsburgh, 1885.

Nicholas, Lynn H. *The Rape of Europa*. New York, 1994.

Okrent, Daniel. *Great Fortune: The Epic of Rockefeller Center*. New York, 2003.

Peterson, Charles E. *Notes on Hampton Mansion*. Edited by Sally Sims Stokes. National Trust for Historic Preservation Library Collection of the University of Maryland. College Park, MD, 1970; 2nd ed., 2000.

Plaut, James S. "Hitler's Capital," *Atlantic Monthly* (October 1946).

Samuels, Ernest. *Bernhard Berenson: The Making of a Legend*. Cambridge, MA, 1987.

Schlesinger, Arthur M., Jr. *A Thousand Days: John F. Kennedy in the White House*. New York, 1965.

Schreiner, Samuel A., Jr. *Henry Clay Frick: The Gospel of Greed*. New York, 1995.

Seale, William. *The President's House*. White House Historical Association in cooperation with the National Geographic Society. Washington, DC, 1986.

Secrest, Meryle. *Duveen: A Life in Art*. New York, 2004.

Simpson, Colin. *Artful Partners: Bernard Berenson and Joseph Duveen*. New York, 1986.

Sobel, Robert. *Coolidge: An American Enigma*. Washington, DC, 1998.

Thompson, Bob. "America's Hall of Fame: A National Portrait Gallery and the Culture of Celebrity." *Washington Post Magazine*, 13 June 1999.

Trelease, Allen W. *White Terror: The Ku Klux Klan Conspiracy and Southern Reconstruction*. Baton Rouge, LA, 1971.

Walker, John. *National Gallery of Art, Washington*. Rev. ed. New York, 1984.

———. *Self-Portrait with Donors*. Boston, 1974.

Ward, Geoffrey C. *A First-Class Temperament, The Emergence of Franklin Roosevelt*. New York, 1989.

Wharton, Edith, *A Backward Glance*, New York, 1934.

White, William Allen. *A Puritan in Babylon*. New York, 1938.

Whitehill, Walter Muir. "The Right of Cities to Be Beautiful." In *With Heritage So Rich*. New York, 1966.

Wilson, Howard McKnight. *The Tinkling Spring, Headwater of Freedom: A Study of the Church and Her People*. Fisherville, VA, 1954.

Index

Illustrations are indicated by page numbers in italics.

Photographic Credits

Pages 13, 15, 355, photographs by the author; 268, photograph by Ron Blunt for the Decatur House Collection; jacket, frontispiece, pages 82, 93, 95, 349, photographs by Lee Ewing ©; 262, photograph by Harris & Ewing, courtesy of Ann Rath; 306, Polaroid photograph by Jacqueline Kennedy; 140, photograph by Irving Penn, courtesy of Condé Nast; 286, photograph by Thomas M. Slade.

The National Gallery of Art, Gallery Archives, provided photographic materials for pages 5, 14, 17, 18, 30, 40, 45, 54, 58, 66–67 (courtesy *Time* magazine), 89 (courtesy *The New York Times*), 90, 94, 99, 102, 110, 128, 138, 140, 162, 164, 174, 188, 194–196, 226, 248, 306, 309, 322, 334 (courtesy Smithsonian Institution Archives), 335, 344, 346, 347, 351, 352, 356–358, 364, 368. The National Gallery of Art, division of imaging and visual services, provided color transparencies and black-and-white photographs for pages 50, 69–72, 74, 106, 115–119, 147–149, 151, 153–156, 182–187, 189–190, 239.

In addition, the Hampton National Historic Site provided the photograph on page 236; the John F. Kennedy Library, Boston, 302 and 316; the Samuel H. Kress Foundation, 150; the Library of Congress, page 6, fig. 1; the Estate of Paul Mellon, 53 and 106; the National Archives, 204, 216, 220, and 222; the National Portrait Gallery, 325–327, 332 and 362; the National Trust for Historic Preservation, viii, 97, 256, 266, 268, 270, 272, 276, 279, 281, 286, and 372; © The Saul Steinberg Foundation/Artists Rights Society (ARS), 56; Jerry L. Thompson, 36; the U.S. Commission of Fine Arts, 292 and 298; © *Washington Post*, courtesy the D.C. Public Library, 76, 160 and 340; Elizabeth Brown Wakefield, page 6, fig. 2 and page 343; Joan Beauregard Williams, 194; and the Colonial Williamsburg Foundation, 42.